Fodor's

NATIONAL PARKS AND SEASHORES
OF THE
EAST

Fodor's Travel Publications, Inc.
New York • Toronto • London • Sydney • Auckland

First Edition

ISBN 0–679–02632–0

Fodor's National Parks and Seashores of the East

Editors: Christopher Billy, Andrew Collins

Contributors: Steven Amsterdam, Susan Bain, Robert Blake, Hannah Borgeson, Karen Cure, Fionn Davenport, Edie Jarolim, Lisa Kremer, Andrea Lehman, Kristin McGowan, Linda K. Schmidt, Mary Ellen Schultz, Craig Seligman

Creative Director: Fabrizio La Rocca

Cartographer: Eureka Cartography

Cover Photographs: Peter Guttman

Design: Tigist Getachew

Special Sales

Fodor's Travel Publications are available at special discounts for bulk purchases for sales promotions or premiums. Special editions, including personalized covers, excerpts of existing guides, and corporate imprints, can be created in large quantities for special needs. For more information, contact your local bookseller or write to Special Markets, Fodor's Travel Publications, Inc., 201 East 50th Street, New York, NY 10022. Inquiries from Canada should be directed to your local Canadian bookseller or sent to Random House of Canada, Ltd., Marketing Department, 1265 Aerowood Drive, Mississauga, Ontario L4W 1B9. Inquiries from the United Kingdom should be sent to Fodor's Travel Publications, 20 Vauxhall Bridge Road, London, England SW1V 2SA.

MANUFACTURED IN THE UNITED STATES OF AMERICA

10 9 8 7 6 5 4 3 2 1

CONTENTS

ACKNOWLEDGMENTS

We would like to thank all those who helped to ensure the accuracy of this book. Special thanks go to the following people, who, unless stated otherwise, are all employees of the U.S. National Park Service.

Acadia: Deb Wade, Judith Steeves, Alice Long. **Adirondack:** Ken Brown, Edmund Lynch, Karen Brooks, Tony Goodwin, Willie Janeway, Maurice Kenny, Beth Bullock (all of Adirondack State Park Interpretive Center). **Allegheny:** Janeal Hedman, Wanda Mata. **Assateague:** Chris Seymour. **Big Cypress:** Elizabeth Dupree. **Biscayne:** Rob Shanks. **Blue Ridge:** Phil Noblitt. **Cape Cod:** Frank Ackerman. **Cape Hatteras:** Robert Woody. **Cape Lookout:** Laurie Heupel. **Catoctin:** Sally Griffin. **Chincoteague:** Larry Points. **Cumberland:** Rolland Swain, Linda King (Coastal Georgia Historical Society), Mary Jo Ferguson, Carol Dumas, Carol Knapp (Georgia residents). **Delaware Water Gap:** Randy W. Turner. **Everglades:** Alan Scott. **Fire Island:** Steven Czarniecki, Quentin Goodson, Maria Wagenbrenner. **Great Smoky:** Nancy Gray. **Green Mountain:** Ann Mates. **Gulf Islands:** Mary D. Jones. **Hot Springs:** Earl Adams. **Isle Royale:** Terry Lindsay. **Mammoth Cave:** Phyllis Brandon. **Natchez Trace:** Dale L. Smith. **Okefenokee:** Gracie Gooch, Pete Griffin (Stephen Foster State Park), Jimmy Walker (Okefenokee Swamp Park), Linda Lee (Waycross Chamber of Commerce). **Ouachita:** Cheryl Chatham. **Shenandoah:** Barb Stewart, Judy Watkins (Virginia Department of Economic Development). **Voyageurs:** Bill Gardiner. **White Mountains:** Alexis Jackson.

While every care has been taken to ensure the accuracy of the information in this guide, the passage of time will always bring change, and consequently, the publisher cannot accept responsibility for errors that may occur.

All prices and opening times quoted here are based on information supplied to us at press time. Hours and admission fees may change, however, and the prudent traveler will avoid inconvenience by calling ahead.

Fodor's want to hear about your travel experiences, both pleasant and unpleasant. When a campground, hotel, or restaurant fails to live up to its billing, let us know and we will investigate the complaint and revise our entries where the facts warrant it.

Send your letters to the editors of Fodor's Travel Publications, 201 East 50th Street, New York, NY 10022.

Every year millions of people pack up their outdoor gear and head for the U.S. national parks and seashores. They come from many backgrounds in search of many things, but they are all eager to take in the landscapes for which the parks are famous—the wide-open spaces, sky-skimming mountains, wilderness beaches, and coral reefs. But, although these travelers are familiar with the natural beauty preserved in our national parks and seashores, many don't fully understand what a national park is and why it has been set aside as such. Malinee Crapsey, a park ranger at Sequoia and Kings Canyon National Parks, explains:

"National parks are *internationally* significant. They are one of this country's greatest contributions to global culture. They preserve for everyone not only areas of great scenic beauty, but also areas whose scientific values are both known and not yet discovered. They hold a tremendous genetic resource and offer outstanding outdoor laboratories for researchers.

"In general, Americans are aware that laws protect our national parks, but they do not realize that long-term protection involves preserving the *processes* that create the landscape so that it will still be a natural environment when future generations venture here. That is why it is so important that visitors not pick flowers, feed bears, or expect the environment to be otherwise manipulated for their comfort. Not only are the individual plants and animals affected, so are the processes of growth and life that are supposed to proceed unimpeded.

"For these reasons we encourage altruistic behaviors in visitors. Their enjoyment is extremely important, but of equal importance is the enjoyment of future generations. Rules and regulations are designed to support both ends; without the public's cooperation, neither can be fully achieved."

As you visit the parks and seashores, please keep in mind that these lands will not thrive without your care, will not last without your support.

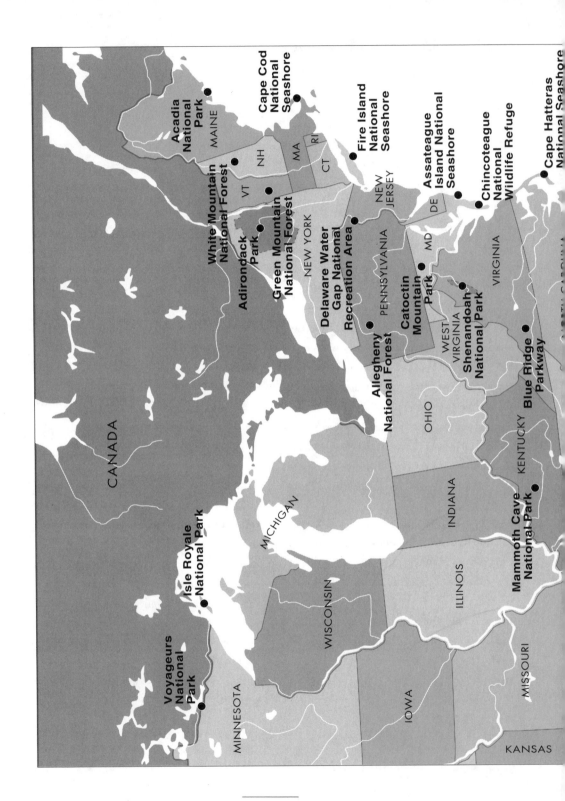

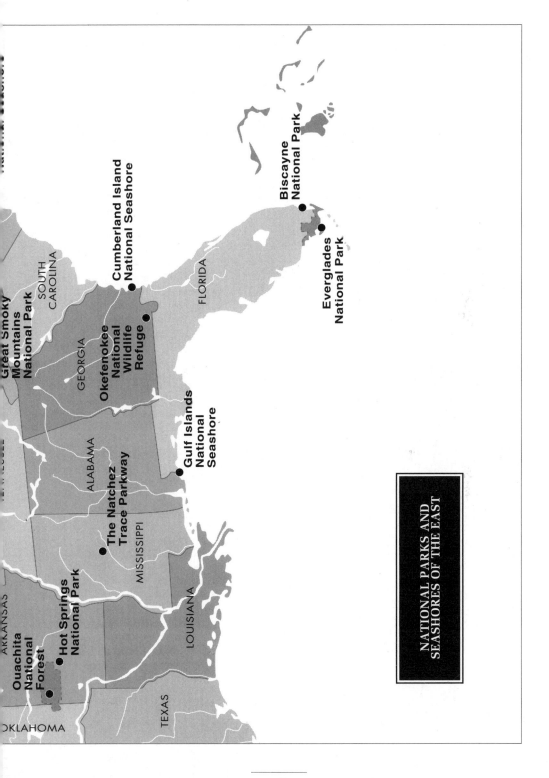

NATIONAL PARKS AND
SEASHORES OF THE EAST

Essential Information

VISITOR INFORMATION For general information on the U.S. national park system, contact the Office of Public Inquiries, National Park Service, Box 37127, Washington, DC 20013, tel. 202/208–4747. For information on the Canadian park system, contact the Canadian Parks Service, Western Regional Office, Room 520, 220 4th Ave. S.E., Box 2989, Station M, Calgary, Alberta T2P 3H8, tel. 403/292–4440. For detailed information on the individual parks (weather, special events, campsite availability), contact each park directly (*see* individual park chapters). In addition, the following regional offices of the U.S. National Park Service provide general information on parks in their areas.

Mid-Atlantic region: National Park Service, 143 S. 3rd St., Philadelphia, PA 19106, tel. 215/597–7013.

Midwest region: National Park Service, 1709 Jackson St., Omaha, NE 68102, tel. 402/221–3431.

National Capital region: National Park Service, 1100 Ohio Dr. SW, Washington, DC 20242, tel. 202/619–7005.

North Atlantic region: National Park Service, 15 State St., Boston, MA 02109, tel. 617/223–5001.

Southeast region: National Park Service, 75 Spring St. SW, Atlanta, GA 30303, tel. 404/331–5185.

When you arrive at a park, stop by one of the visitor's centers and pick up a free map and literature. Some visitor's centers have exhibits, slide presentations, and brief films that will help you understand the area.

SPECIAL TOURS One way to visit the national parks is to go with an environmental tour group. A variety of associations offer naturalist-led tours that may include hiking, biking, camping, and/or canoeing. Some offer special educational programs, seminars, workshops, and field trips. These tours can be rugged and ambitious or relaxed and luxurious. Here's a sampling of what you'll find.

Backroads Bicycle Touring (1516 5th St., Suite Q333, Berkeley, CA 94710-1740, tel. 415/527–1555 or 800/245–3874) runs cycling/camping tours to several of the eastern national parks, including Acadia, Blue Ridge Parkway, Cape Hatteras, and Natchez Trace.

Earthwatch (680 Mount Auburn St., Watertown, MA 02272, tel. 617/926–8000) recruits volunteers to serve in their Earthcorps as short-term assistants to scientists on research expeditions, some of which are conducted in or near national parks. You may wind up counting and photographing wildlife populations in the Shenandoah Valley; or documenting dolphin pods and behavior from boats off the eastern coast of Florida.

National Wildlife Federation (1400 16th St. NW, Washington, DC 20036, tel. 703/790–4363 or 800/432–6564) runs a series of week-long seminars in the national parks that include nature hikes, classes, and workshops.

The **Sierra Club** (730 Polk St., San Francisco, CA 94109, tel. 415/776–2211) will take you backpacking and put you to work. The group runs trips in which participants work to help preserve the environment in several of the national parks.

Wild Horizons Expeditions (West Fork Rd., Darby, MT 59829, tel. 406/821–3747), a guide and outfitter that is licensed by the National Park Service, offers customized wilderness trips every year within various national parks.

WHEN TO GO Summer is without question the busiest time of the year to visit most of the national parks, so be prepared to deal with full parking lots and traffic jams. If you must travel during summer, go early or late in the season to avoid the mid-season peak. Be aware, however, that in tropical parks sum-

mer's heat and insects keep the crowds away. Spring and fall are good times of the year to visit most of the eastern parks. During winter, some parks close certain roads because of heavy snowfall. Others have just as much going on in winter as they do in summer: In Voyageurs, for example, winter is prime time for snowmobiling, ice fishing, and cross-country skiing.

Keep in mind that even in summer the weather can vary—especially in the mountainous parks. Temperatures can rise into the 90s during the day and drop into the teens or lower at night. Also, the climate often changes with elevation. Within a matter of minutes, a blue sky and brilliant sunshine can erupt into an extravaganza of hail and lightning. The key to enjoying your time in the parks is always to have warm clothing and rain gear handy, no matter how promising the day.

OPENING AND CLOSING TIMES The buildings within national parks, including visitor's centers, are generally open daily from 9 to 5, but these times do vary from park to park and season to season. Most park buildings are open every day of the year except Christmas. Natural areas of the parks are usually open 24 hours a day, 365 days a year, but fees are generally collected only during peak seasons and hours. If the fee station is closed you may enter the park free, but consider making a donation to help maintain the park.

CAR RENTALS Renting a car to drive to and around the national parks is easy, provided you are over 21 (25 in some states) and have a valid driver's license and a major credit card. Rates vary from state to state as well as from company to company and season to season. Generally, the smaller the car, the lower the rate, but ask about temporary rental promotions, which can mean substantial savings. Be aware that over-the-phone quotes do not include the collision damage waiver (CDW), personal accident insurance, or tax. To save money, check with your insurance agent to see whether your personal coverage includes rental cars, and find out if your credit card company insures car rentals that are charged to your card. The CDW covers travel in all U.S. states but not necessarily in Mexico and Canada. If you plan to cross borders, ask the agency if you will be covered. If you want to leave the car at a location different from the one where you picked it up, you will most likely have to pay an additional drop-off charge, which can be a couple of hundred dollars, depending on your route. Always ask in advance.

Many companies charge a flat daily or weekly rate with unlimited mileage; others charge by the mile over a certain number of miles. The rates for a subcompact vehicle with unlimited mileage start at about $30 or $35 a day and about $195 a week.

Once you find the best rate, make a reservation over the phone. If you're picking the car up at an airport, have your arrival time handy when you call. Record the reservation number, the name of the agent to whom you spoke, and the time and date of your call. Be sure to verify that the company will honor your credit card.

Among the major national car-rental firms are: **Alamo** (tel. 800/327–9633), **Avis** (tel. 800/331–1212), **Budget** (tel. 800/527–0700), **Dollar** (tel. 800/421–6868), **Hertz** (tel. 800/654–3131), and **National** (tel. 800/227–7368).

RV RENTALS The same rules for renting a car apply when you rent an RV: You must be over 21 (25 in some states) and have a valid driver's license and a credit card. No special license or driving skills are required. In fact, driving an RV is much like driving a car, thanks to automatic transmissions and power brakes. The difficult part is handling a vehicle of that size (a motor home can be anywhere from 20 to 34 feet long), especially getting in and out of parking spaces and backing up. Many veteran RVers avoid having to go in reverse as much as possible. Most rental agencies provide a brief (30-minute to one-hour) familiarization course in which drivers can get acquainted with the operation of the RV. All the technical equipment—the propane system for heating and cooking, the water tanks, the waste-disposal system, and

the generator—is fully explained when you arrive at the rental office. Once you're on your way, stay in the slow lane, and go easy when braking and accelerating. Try to avoid driving at night.

You must reserve far in advance if you plan to rent an RV in summer. Also, prices are at their highest during these months.

Depending on the size of the vehicle you rent, you will be charged $75 to $150 a day during high season. That may include unlimited mileage, or it may include a set number of free miles, and you will have to pay more for each additional mile. Most RVs use regular, unleaded gasoline, and it can be expensive: The gas tanks usually hold 40 to 79 gallons, but RVs only get 8 to 9 miles to the gallon. Add to that the campground fees—roughly $15 to $20 per night—and an RV vacation may not be as inexpensive as you had hoped.

First-time motor-home renters should get a copy of "Rental Ventures," a $5 guide published annually by the **Recreation Vehicle Rental Association** (tel. 703/591–7130 or 800/336–0355). It includes information on campgrounds, safety, and the types of motor homes available and their features and accessories. Another RV-vacation planner is available free by calling **Go Camping America** (tel. 800/477–8669). It includes information on RV campgrounds and events.

To locate a rental agency, look under "Recreation Vehicles—Renting and Leasing" in the yellow pages for the dealer nearest you. You can also order a directory of RV-rental agencies called *Who's Who in RV Rentals,* published by the **Recreation Vehicle Dealers Association** (tel. 703/591–7130 or 800/336–0355). It costs $7.50, including first-class delivery. One nationwide RV-rental firm is **Cruise America** (tel. 800/327–7778).

DRIVING Before setting out on any driving trip, it's important to make sure your vehicle is in top condition. It is best to have a complete tune-up before setting out; at the very least, you should make the following checks:

See that all lights are working, including brake lights, backup lights, and emergency lights; make sure tires are in good shape (including the spare); check the oil; check the engine coolant; fill the windshield-washer bottle, and make sure the blades are in good condition; and make sure brakes are in good condition, too.

For emergencies, take along flares or reflector triangles, jumper cables, an empty gas can, a fire extinguisher, a flashlight, a plastic tarp, blankets, and coins for phone calls. If you're traveling in winter, be sure to have a collapsible shovel, an ice scraper, traction mats, sand, and antifreeze. Chains are a good idea.

Many roads in eastern national parks are narrow and winding. Some have restrictions on large vehicles. If you are driving a large RV or pulling a trailer, be sure to call the park in advance of your trip to find out about road restrictions.

COSTS Almost all the national parks have an entrance fee, ranging from $3 to $10 per vehicle and good for seven consecutive days. Senior travelers, travelers with disabilities, and frequent park goers can take advantage of the **Federal Recreation Passport Program,** which includes a number of passes that waive entrance fees for the cardholder and an accompanying carload of passengers.

For travelers 62 years and older, the **Golden Age Passport** is good for life, and available at national parks upon arrival. The passport costs $10, a one-time fee. You must have proof of your age and U.S. citizenship or permanent residency status; a driver's license or birth certificate is fine. In addition to free admission to the parks, the pass gives the holder a 50% discount on park facilities and services (excluding those run by private concessionaires).

The **Golden Access Passport** is free and available to those with permanent disabilities. The passport can be obtained at a park entrance with proper proof of a disability; it is good for life. Holders of this pass also receive a 50% discount on all park facilities and services

(excluding those run by private concessionaires).

The **Golden Eagle Pass** costs $25 and entitles the cardholder and an accompanying party to free admission to all parks for the calendar year. It is neither refundable nor transferable and does not cover additional park fees such as those for camping and parking. The Golden Eagle Pass can be purchased in person or by mail, by sending $25 to any of the National Park Service headquarters or regional offices (*see* Visitor Information, *above*).

For those planning to visit one specific park repeatedly, a **Park Pass** is available for $10 or $15, depending on the park. It gives the pass holder and accompanying party free admission to that park for the calendar year (January 1 through December 31). The pass can be purchased in person or by mail from the specific national park at which it will be honored. It is neither transferable nor refundable.

In addition to entry fees, most of the national parks charge fees at their drive-in campgrounds. These fees range from $5 a night for tenters to $12 a night for RVs.

The U.S. Fish and Wildlife Service's **Duck Stamp** pass is also honored for entry to national parks.

PETS Generally, pets are allowed only in developed areas of the national parks, including drive-in campgrounds and picnic areas, but they must be kept on a leash at all times. With the exception of guide dogs, pets are not allowed inside buildings, on most trails, on beaches, or in the backcountry. They also may be prohibited in areas controlled by concessionaires. Some of the parks have kennels, which charge about $6 a day, but before you decide to bring a pet to a national park, call to find out about specific restrictions.

FURTHER READING Many of the national parks have bookstores, which sell field guides, maps, and other publications on the history, geology, plants, and wildlife of their specific area.

Three bibles for identifying plant and animal life are part of the Peterson Field Guide Series: *Eastern Birds (East of the Rockies), Wildflowers of Northeastern and North Central North America,* and the classic *Wildflowers.* The Audubon Society Field Guide Series (Knopf) puts out *Familiar Birds: North American East; Familiar Trees of North America: Eastern Region;* and *Familiar Wildflowers of North America: Eastern Region.* Two other good sources of information are *Wild Plants of America: A Select Guide for the Naturalist and Traveler* (John Wiley & Sons), by Richard M. Smith; and *The Traveling Birder* (Doubleday), by Clive Goodwin.

The most detailed topographical maps of the national parks are those published by the **United States Geological Survey (U.S.G.S.)** (Box 25286, Denver Federal Center, Denver, CO 80225, tel. 303/236–7477). Printed on plastic, U.S.G.S. maps are waterproof and tearproof—ideal for hiking trips. **Trails Illustrated** (Box 3610, Evergreen, CO 80439-3425, tel. 303/670–3457) also offers a line of topographical maps printed on plastic.

The **National Parks and Conservation Association** (tel. 900/PARK–KIT, ext. 89) sells National Park Vacation Kits, focusing on several eastern parks; the kits include a 60-minute audiotape, a fact book, a topographical map, a National Park Service handbook, trail guides, and campground information. Each kit costs $39.95.

VISITING THE PARKS

STAYING HEALTHY AND SAFE The three leading causes of death in the parks are, in order, motor-vehicle accidents, drownings, and falls. Accidents often occur when drivers take their eyes off the road to look at wildlife and scenery. Experienced swimmers are often the people who drown; they don't understand that cold water and swift currents make swimming in parks far more difficult (and treacherous) than swimming in pools. People fall off cliffs when they get too close to the unstable edge, and rock climbers fall when they use frayed or weathered ropes. It is important that you make it a point to learn the rules when visiting the parks. Pay attention to signs warning of potential dangers, stay on the trails, and, when in doubt, don't do it. Chances are you will have a safe and fulfilling park experience. Following, however, are a number of problems you should know how to deal with.

Foot Care. If you're planning to do a lot of hiking, by all means do not start your trip with a new pair of shoes or boots: Break them in before you leave home. Wear boots that have good ankle support. Once you're out and about in the wilderness, it's important to always watch your step. Sprains can happen easily, especially on loose rocks and slippery paths.

Sun Protection. Take great care in protecting yourself from the sun—even when it's cloudy out or there's snow on the ground. Keep in mind that at higher altitudes, where the air is thinner, you will burn more easily, and that sun reflected off the snow, off sand, and off water can be especially strong. Apply sunscreen liberally before you go out, and wear a visored cap or sunglasses. Many scientists fear that overexposure to UV rays may cause increased rates of skin cancer and cataracts.

If you are exposed to extreme heat for a prolonged period, you run the risk of heat stroke (also known as sunstroke), a serious medical condition. It begins quite suddenly with a headache, dizziness, and fatigue, but can quickly lead to convulsions and unconsciousness or even to death. If someone in your party develops any of the symptoms, have one person go for emergency help; meanwhile, move the victim to a shady place, wrap her in wet clothing or bedding, and try to cool her down with water or ice.

Lyme Disease. When walking in woods, brush, or through fields in areas where Lyme disease has been found, wear tick repellent and long pants tucked into socks. When you undress, search carefully for deer ticks, which are not much bigger than the period at the end of this sentence. If you should find one attached to the skin, remove it with rubbing alcohol and tweezers. Watch the area for several weeks. If you spot a rash or develop flulike symptoms, see your physician immediately. Lyme disease can be treated with antibiotics if caught early enough.

Snake Bites. Snakes will do everything to avoid you, but in the event you have a run-in and are bitten, it's necessary to act quickly. If it's a harmless snake, ordinary first aid for puncture wounds should be given. If it is poisonous, the victim should remain as still as possible, so as not to spread the venom through the body. He or she should lie down, keeping the wound area below the rest of the body, and another person should seek medical help immediately.

Animal Bites. Some animals, especially rodents, carry dangerous diseases. If you are bitten by a wild animal, it's important to see a doctor as soon as you possibly can. Many animal bites require a tetanus shot and, if the animal is rabid, a rabies shot.

Frostbite. Caused by exposure to extreme cold for a prolonged period of time, frostbite is marked by the numbing of ears, nose, fingers, or toes. A sure sign that you aren't simply cold is when the skin turns white or grayish yellow. The victim should be taken into a warm place as soon as possible, and wet clothing in the affected area should be removed. The area should then be immersed in warm—not hot—water or wrapped in a warm blanket. When the area begins to thaw, the victim should exercise it, to stimulate blood circulation. If bleeding or other complications develop, it's important to get to a doctor as soon as possible.

Hypothermia. It does not have to be below freezing for you to get hypothermia: If you're not dressed warmly enough for the outdoor temperature, you're at risk. A person with hypothermia will at first feel chilly and tired and will then suddenly begin shivering uncontrollably and acting irrationally. The minute these signs are spotted, get the victim to shelter of some kind and wrap him in warm blankets or a sleeping bag. If the sleeping bag is cold, another member of the party should warm it up by getting into it first; it may even be wise for that person to remain in the sleeping bag with the victim. If practical, it's best for both people to be unclothed, but if clothing remains on, it must be dry.

Plant Poisons. If you touch poison ivy, poison oak, or poison sumac, wash the affected area immediately with soap and water and then with rubbing alcohol. Later, apply Calamine lotion to relieve itching.

Safe Water for Drinking. It is best to carry bottled water for day trips, and drinking water is available at many campgrounds. But if you're hiking into the backcountry you may not be able to carry enough water, so you will have to purify spring or stream water for drinking. Do this no matter how crystal clear the water looks: You can't see *Giardia,* but these tiny organisms can turn your stomach inside out. The easiest way to purify water is to add a water-purification tablet to it. These come in packages with directions. The most widely used brand is Potable Aqua, which is made by Wisconsin Pharmacal and sells for about $5.50 for 50 tablets (good for 50 quarts of water). You can also purify water by filtering it through a water-purification pump available at camping equipment stores. Boiling water is the least favorite method since it takes time and uses fuel, but, if it is the only method available to you, use it; bring the water to a boil for at least 15 minutes.

First Aid. Packing a complete first-aid kit is essential for all trips in the great outdoors. Be sure to have a first-aid manual, any necessary prescriptions for allergies or preexisting diseases or disorders, aspirin, adhesive bandages, butterfly bandages, sterile gauze pads (2″ x 2″ and 4″ x 4″), 1″-wide adhesive tape, an elastic bandage, antibiotic ointment, antiseptic cream, antihistamines, razor blades, tweezers, a needle, scissors, insect repellent, Calamine lotion, and sunscreen.

MEDICAL EMERGENCIES The best way to deal with medical emergencies is to avoid them. Never hike alone in the national parks—especially not into the backcountry. Ideally, you should hike with at least two other people. That way, if one person is injured, a companion can stay with the injured person while the other goes to get help. Fortunately, in the national parks, rangers and other hikers are usually close by—especially during July and August. If you find yourself in an emergency situation, you can call 911 from telephone booths at visitor's centers and other locations throughout the parks. Some of the parks have their own emergency numbers, as well.

If you break a leg or arm on the trail, it is best to keep the broken area as still as possible and elevated, while someone goes for help. If help is far away, make a splint from a branch, and strap it on with a bandanna or article of clothing.

For information on specific health and safety hazards, *see* Staying Healthy and Safe, *above.*

PROTECTING THE ENVIRONMENT More than ever, our national parks are being discovered and rediscovered by travelers who want to spend their vacations appreciating nature, watching wildlife, and taking adventure trips. But as the number of visitors to the parks increases, so does stress on wildlife and plant life. Tourism can drum up concern for the environment, but it can also cause great physical damage to parks. Many of the trails and roadways in our national parks are overused and abused.

In national parks that include barrier islands, you should walk on marked pedestrian dune crossovers and paths, not on the dunes themselves. Continual climbing of a dune system will cause erosion and weaken the protection of the natural primary dune system. Also refrain from picking dune grasses because they preserve the dunes.

Take great care as you explore the parks. Have respect for the animals you encounter: Never sneak up on them, don't disturb nests and other habitats, don't touch animals or try to remove them from their habitat for the sake of a photograph, don't stand between animal parents and their young, and never surround an animal or group of animals. You can also help to protect endangered species by reporting any sightings. (For more information on endangered species in the national parks, write: Chief, Wildlife and Vegetation Division, National Park Service, Box 37127, Washington, DC 20013.)

Respect the environment. Do not leave garbage on the trails or in campgrounds. If you hike into the backcountry, carry your trash out with you. Bury human waste at least 100 feet from any trail, campsite, or backcountry water source. Some parks and many environmental organizations are starting to advocate packing out even human waste. Do not wash dishes or clothing in lakes and streams. If you must use soap, make sure it is biodegradable, and carry water in clean containers 100 feet away from its source before using it for cleaning. A free brochure titled "Leave No Trace" supplies more information on protecting the environment; to obtain a copy, call 800/332–4100.

Many of the national parks are threatened by serious problems, including air pollution, acid rain, wildlife poaching, understaffing of rangers, and encroaching development. These problems are being addressed by the National Park Service, but you can play a role by donating time or money. The National Park Service's Volunteers in the Parks program welcomes volunteers to do anything from paperwork to lecturing on environmental issues. To participate, you must apply to the park where you would like to work.

To make financial contributions to the parks, contact the **National Park Service,** Budget Division, Box 37127, Washington, DC 20013; or the **National Parks Preservation Fund,** 1101 17th Street NW, Washington, DC 20036. The latter is a nonprofit organization that supports the park service with supplementary assistance programs.

FIRE PRECAUTIONS When it comes to fire, never take a chance. Keep the following pointers in mind. Don't build fires when you're alone. Build small fires. Always build campfires in a safe place (away from tinder of any kind). Use a fireplace or fire grate if one is available. Clear the ground around the fireplace so that wind cannot blow sparks into dry leaves or grass. Throw used matches into the fire. Never leave a fire unattended. Always have a pot of water or sand next to a campfire or stove. When finished, be sure the fire is out cold (meaning you can touch it with your bare hands). Never cook in your tent or a poorly ventilated space.

CANOEING Safe canoeing requires common sense and advance planning before the trip. If you're going on a river outing, it's a good idea to obtain information about your route ahead of time and speak to those well acquainted with the river who have recently paddled it. You should learn how to read moving water and, if possible, get a map of the route to study. The course chosen should take into consideration the experience and skills of each member on the trip.

Scout out ahead of time any potential obstacles and problems, such as high water, cold water, rapids, logjams, boulders, and low dams; either line or portage the craft past most obstacles. You should also know what side of the river the nearest road is on in case of emergency. Novices are advised to receive paddling instruction beforehand and to take their first trip with a local paddling club who will choose a safe course that recognizes a beginner's limitations. Actually, even more experienced paddlers may enjoy going on a trip with a local outfitter or paddling club if they're unfamiliar with the territory.

It's important to keep in mind that rivers change, presenting different challenges depending on precipitation and the time of year. To help characterize a river's potential, a class system has been established: A Class I river, for example, is as calm as pond water; a Class V river churns with rapids that can summon the mayhem of a washing machine gone haywire. Bear in mind that conditions vary dramatically according to season and weather; a river that earns a Class V rating during the spring runoff may be an impassible trickle by late summer. The rating system gives you an approximation of what sort of thrills or hazards to expect. Anything above a Class II river is probably unsuitable for small children.

Paddlers should be good swimmers and wear PFDs (personal flotation devices) that are Coast Guard approved. As many participants as possible should know CPR, and you should bring along a first-aid kit and extra paddles. You should also be acquainted with safety procedures in case of tipovers. It's wise to bring a change of clothing in a waterproof duffel bag that is tied down in case the canoe overturns. Paddlers should run a course in groups of at least three canoes, and a canoe should never get out of sight of the boat in front of it. Of course, you should travel during daylight hours in good weather. If you're paddling on a large body of water, such as a lake, you need to stay close to shore; avoid canoeing if there's a strong wind.

For safety tips on canoeing, get a copy of *Canoeing/Kayaking,* prepared by the American Red Cross (150 Amsterdam Ave., New York NY 10023; $9, plus $2.30 shipping and handling).

HIKING Three things should be taken into consideration when choosing hiking trails suitable to your physical condition and the amount of weight you plan to carry: (1) How long is the trail? (2) How steep is it and how quickly does the elevation increase? (3) How acclimated are you to the altitude at the start and finish?

One of the most common problems for hikers is altitude sickness, which results when a hiker ascends to heights over 8,500 feet without being properly acclimated. The symptoms include headache, nausea, vomiting, shortness of breath, weakness, and sleep disturbance. If any of these occur, it's important to retreat to a lower altitude. If you have a history of heart or circulatory problems, talk to your doctor before planning a visit to areas at high altitudes.

CAMPING Most automobile campsites in the national parks are offered on a first-come, first-served basis. If you are traveling during the peak summer months, be sure to arrive as early in the day as possible or make reservations at a nearby public campground. At some campgrounds in some parks (Acadia, Assateague Island, Cape Hatteras, Great Smoky Mountains, and Shenandoah) you can make camping reservations prior to your visit through Mistix (tel. 800/365–2267).

Tips on Camp Cooking. How fancy your food preparation can be will depend on whether you are traveling on foot or by car and how long your trip is. If you're traveling with a group, take time to coordinate in advance who should pack what. Some staples that travel well: cheese (for summer backpacking, take hard cheeses that don't have to be refrigerated), dry milk, seeds and nuts, dried fruits, powdered eggs, pasta, bagels, rice, flour, baking soda, popcorn, instant soups, instant drinks, honey, cooking oil, lentils, split peas, oatmeal and other cereals, coffee, tea, and freeze-dried foods.

If you're traveling on foot, it is best to carry food in a large drawstring sack inside your pack. Be sure to bring a long, strong cord so you can hang your food out of reach of animals at night. Tie a rock to one end of the cord and the sack to the other and throw it up over a branch, about 10 feet off the ground. If you're traveling in summer and have food that should be kept cool, once you arrive in your camp, put the food in a waterproof container and submerge it in a stream. This is especially effective at high altitudes, because the water usually remains icy cold even during the hottest months. Although this is a good way to keep food cold, it is not a good way to keep it safe from bears and raccoons.

When packing for camping trips, be sure to include the following supplies: a stove and a supply of fuel, matches in a waterproof case or a lighter, a cookset, pot holders, spoons, forks, knives, cups, plates, a water bottle, a can opener, a cooking spoon, a spatula, salt, pepper, sugar, aluminum foil, plastic wrap, trash bags, a scouring pad, a sponge, and a lantern (optional).

SAMPLE RECIPES Cooking outdoors can be something of a challenge when you consider the shortage of pots and pans, the weather conditions, and, usually, the limited ingredients. Your best bet is to stick with familiar or very easy recipes. A lot of campers prepare dishes ahead of time, such as cold pasta salads, hearty soups, chili, ratatouille, and fried chicken. One excellent method of preparing food is to use aluminum foil to wrap the ingredients and then place the bundle on hot coals to steam cook the food. Salt, pepper, and other spices can make an otherwise bland meal tasty. Potatoes cook well in foil, although they are heavy to carry, and you can steam corn on the cob directly on your campfire without removing the husks.

Here are two easy camp-dinner dishes:

Baked Fish in Foil. *Ingredients:* fresh-caught fish (perch, trout), salt, pepper, butter. *Preparation:* Clean the fish completely. Sprinkle with salt and pepper. Add a dollop of butter. Wrap fish individually and tightly in aluminum foil, so steam cannot escape. Place the package on red-hot wood (not in flames) and turn it a couple of times. When cooked (at least 20 minutes), the foil is your plate.

Couscous with Steamed Vegetables. *Ingredients:* couscous, butter, water, broccoli, carrots, snow peas (or any vegetables that steam well). *Preparation:* Prepare couscous according to instructions on box (takes about five minutes). While cooking, steam vegetables. Spread vegetables on couscous.

HIKING AND CAMPING EQUIPMENT Before you pack, do yourself a big favor and write a checklist, using the following list as a starting point:

Clothing and footwear (warm weather): cotton T-shirt, shorts, cotton or cotton-blend long pants, long-sleeved cotton shirt, swimsuit, lightweight long-sleeved wool shirt or sweater, cotton briefs, insulated underwear (for cold nights), inner socks, two pairs wool socks, rain gear (hooded parka and pants), visored cap or rain hat, hiking boots, sneakers.

Clothing and footwear (cold weather): cotton T-shirt, lightweight long-sleeved wool shirt, wool pants, cotton briefs, insulated underwear, inner socks, two pairs wool socks, insulated vest or wool sweater, down or polyester-insulated parka, rain gear (hooded parka and pants), wool cap, wool or insulated gloves or mittens, insulated hiking boots, sneakers. Down bootees are a comforting nicety.

Personal gear: belt, bandanna, eyeglasses, sunglasses, toothbrush, toothpaste, soap and other toiletries, toilet paper, lip balm, sunscreen, insect repellent, first-aid kit (*see* Staying Healthy and Safe, *above*), watch, compass, maps, multipurpose pocketknife, small flashlight, extra batteries, binoculars, water bottle, field guide.

Equipment: tent, ground cloth, sleeping bag, sleeping pad, backpack, day pack or fanny pack for day trips.

DINING The restaurants you are most apt to find in or near the national parks are casual places serving everything from pizza, sandwiches, and burgers to pasta, steak, and fish. America's move toward healthy diets has certainly affected restaurants throughout the East, with salad bars and low-cholesterol entrées found in every state. Your craving for Chinese, Italian, or other ethnic cuisines can often be satisfied in larger cities outside the parks (although you may have to drive several miles to get there). Fast-food chains are present near some parks.

Within the parks themselves there are plenty of picnic areas complete with tables and fire grates.

Prices for meals (per person, excluding drinks and taxes) at restaurants listed in this book are as follows: **Expensive,** over $25; **Moderate,** $10 to $25; **Inexpensive,** under $10.

LODGING In addition to campgrounds in and near the national parks, you can choose from a range of accommodations, from chain hotels and motels with modern appliances to rough and rugged wilderness camps with kerosene lamps instead of electricity. Cabins with housekeeping facilities are one of the most popular types of lodging. There are also small, family-owned bed-and-breakfasts and grand old established hotels.

If you're traveling during the high season—roughly between Memorial Day and Labor Day—it's advisable to make reservations three or four months in advance. At some of the most desirable hostelries, guests are known to make reservations for the next summer as they check out.

Also, bear in mind that prices are higher in summer. In fact, they sometimes drop as much as 25% when the season comes to a close.

Prices for lodgings (for two people in a double room) listed in this book are as follows: **Expensive,** over $70; **Moderate,** $40 to $70; **Inexpensive,** under $40.

CREDIT CARDS The following credit-card abbreviations are used throughout this guide: AE, American Express; D, Discover; DC, Diners Club; MC, MasterCard; V, Visa.

GETTING MONEY Carry credit cards, traveler's checks, and some cash when visiting the national parks. Many hotels and restaurants take all major bank traveler's checks, and major credit cards—American Express, MasterCard, Visa—are honored at car-rental agencies, most hotels, and some restaurants.

If you need cash quickly, you will probably have to drive into the nearest town or city to find an automated teller machine (ATM). Cirrus and Plus cards are widely accepted. Before you leave home, check with your credit-card company or bank to find out where there is an ATM near your destination that will accept your card. Also ask what the fee is for obtaining cash from a machine (it varies from bank to bank).

TRAVELING WITH CHILDREN **Packing.** When traveling into the national parks with children, it's important to be as self-sufficient as possible. Bring diapers, formula, and any special foods your child may require. Consider packing airtight fresh milk cartons, which don't need refrigeration, or powdered milk and distilled water. Be sure your first-aid kit is complete: You can't expect to easily run to the pharmacy to have prescriptions filled. And always carry your pediatrician's phone number.

If you're planning to rent a car, take along your child's own safety seat. Chances are, you will spend a lot of time in the car, whether getting to and from the national parks or traveling within them. You might also have your children pack their own "car bags" (preferably kiddie knapsacks), with crayons, coloring books, and toys to play with en route. Older kids may want to take along books and tape players with cassettes and extra batteries. For snacking along the way, stock up on finger foods (raisins, cereal, anything not sticky) and juice boxes (with straws).

Getting There. If you're flying with children to one of the national parks, keep these pointers in mind when making your travel arrangements: (1) Don't go with the most economical flight; look for the quickest, easiest way to reach your destination. (2) If getting on a direct flight means shifting your vacation a day or two, do it. (3) For in-flight meals, order a child's meal ahead of time. (4) Request bulkhead seats for more space.

Park Activities. As a family you will find many trails to follow, lakes to swim in, routes to bicycle on, and all sorts of animals and birds and geologic wonders to look at. In addition, some parks offer guided horseback rides, campfire programs, and ranger-led naturalist walks that are geared to children. Some of them have special child-care programs in which parents leave their children for the day.

To help your child get the most out of the trip, you might want to encourage him or her to keep a travel log. Start little ones off with a large sketchbook, so they can draw what they see. Encourage older children to take pictures with a point-and-shoot camera so that they can make their own photo albums.

Never let children play unattended, particularly near streams or lakes.

Staying Overnight. When setting up camp, it's important that all children have their own jobs or duties. Before arriving at your campsite, determine who will do what. For example, one child may be responsible for helping put up the tent; another may be expected to unload the kitchen gear. That way, when you arrive after a long day of driving and the kids are cranky, everyone will have to get busy with his own chore.

Most of the motels, hotels, and lodges near the national parks are child-friendly; in fact, they cater predominantly to families. Try to stay where guest rooms have kitchenettes or refrigerators (for milk and snacks) and the dining room has a children's menu. If you have a small child, request a room on the first floor. Terraces and balconies are potential hazards, and it can be tiresome carrying your child and paraphernalia up and down stairs.

To find out more about traveling with children, contact the following agencies:

Rascals in Paradise (650 5th St., Suite 505, San Francisco, CA 94107, tel. 415/978–9800 or 800/872–7225), a full-service travel agency, prides itself on taking care of all the details of traveling with children, everything from getting bumper pads for cribs to arranging for distilled water for breast-feeding moms.

Family Travel Times is a newsletter published 10 times a year by Travel with Your Children (TWYCH, 45 W. 18th St., 7th floor, New York, NY 10011, tel. 212/206–0688). A one-year subscription costs $55.

HINTS FOR TRAVELERS WITH DISABILITIES The parks are meticulously accommodating to the traveler with a disability. Visitor's centers provide information in braille, large print, and tape-recorded formats. In some visitor's centers and park museums, free wheelchairs are available; and ramps are strategically placed throughout the parks. The **Golden Access Passport** entitles those with permanent disabilities to free access to all U.S. national parks (*see* Costs *in* Planning Your Trip, *above*).

A handful of nonprofit organizations take mixed-ability groups on guided adventure trips to some of the parks. These include **America Outdoors** (Box 1348, Knoxville, TN 37901, tel. 615/524–4814), **Outward Bound** (309 Walker Ave. S, Wayzata, MN 55391, tel. 800/243–8520), **People and Places** (3909 Genesee St., Cheektowaga, NY 14225, tel. 716/631–8223), and **Shake-A-Leg** (Box 1002, Newport, RI 02840, tel. 401/782–6280).

The following organizations provide travel advice and services for the traveler with a disability:

The **Information Center for Individuals with Disabilities** (Fort Point Pl., 1st floor, 27–43 Wormwood St., Boston, MA 02210, tel. 617/727–5540) provides a list of travel agents who specialize in tours for people with disabilities.

Moss Rehabilitation Hospital Travel Information Service (1200 W. Tabor Rd., Philadelphia, PA 19141-3009, tel. 215/456–9600, TDD 215/456–9602) provides travel information by phone (free of charge) for those with disabilities.

HINTS FOR OLDER TRAVELERS If you have any special dietary or medicinal needs, be sure to carry your own supplies when visiting the national parks. The **Golden Age Passport** entitles those over 62 to free admission to all U.S. national parks (*see* Costs *in* Planning Your Trip, *above*).

The **American Association of Retired Persons** (601 E St. NW, Washington, DC 20049, tel. 202/434–2277) offers several cost-cutting programs for the older traveler, including discounts on hotels, airfares, car and RV rentals, and sightseeing attractions. AARP membership is open to those 50 and over; annual dues are $8 per person or couple.

Mature Outlook (6001 N. Clark St., Chicago, IL 60660, tel. 800/336–6330), a travel club for people over 50, offers hotel and motel discounts and a bimonthly newsletter. Annual membership is $9.95 (covers a single person or a couple).

National Council of Senior Citizens (1331 F St. NW, Washington, DC 20004, tel. 202/347–8800) is a nonprofit group that offers members a multitude of travel discounts. Annual membership is $12 per person or per couple.

Acadia National Park
Maine
By Sarah Scott

ach year millions of people travel down the coast of Maine (in Maine one travels "down" the coast in an easterly direction), following the winding seaside routes in search of ocean views and traditional fishing villages. For many, Acadia National Park is their ultimate destination. Located about two-thirds of the way down the coast on Mount Desert Island, which is connected to the mainland by a short causeway, Acadia boasts some of the most spectacular and varied scenery on the Eastern Seaboard, with a rugged coastline of surf-pounded granite and an interior graced by sculpted mountains, quiet ponds, and lush deciduous forests.

In 1604, the French explorer Samuel de Champlain saw the peaks of Acadia rising out of the sea and named the island L'Isles des Monts-Déserts, the Island of Barren Mountains. Today, the island is anything but deserted: It's one of America's most visited national parks. Each year 4 million travelers come here to walk, hike, bike, paddle, and drive amid extraordinary and diverse natural beauty. Comprising just over 40,000 acres, Acadia is small but dramatic. Mt. Cadillac, at 1,530 feet the highest point of land on the Eastern Seaboard, dominates the park, which is surrounded by ocean and dozens of satellite islands.

Acadia is open and used year-round, but is most popular in the summer. That's when tourists descend upon the island, as much for the sights of tony Bar Harbor, where you'll find most of the accommodations, restaurants, and shops, as for the park. Although there's been talk of instituting a shuttle-bus system in Acadia to relieve the summer traffic, cars remain the primary mode of park transportation. Many attractions lie along the 20-mile Park Loop Road, which encircles a significant section of the park. There are, however, plenty of opportunities to leave the car behind and explore Acadia on foot, for example on hiking trails or the well-maintained network of gravel carriage roads that meanders through the park.

With its steep cliffs and rocky shoreline, Acadia is rugged—a stone fortress buffeted by the sea. But it's also a land of graceful stone bridges, horse-drawn carriages, and the elegant Jordan Pond Tea House. This sense of gentility stems no doubt from Mount Desert Island's long history as a summer resort for society families—Rockefellers, Vanderbilts, and Morgans among them—dating back to the late 1800s. In fact, Acadia National Park was established by a group of concerned summer residents who purchased much of the island and donated the land to the federal government; the process was finalized in 1919. The extensive carriage road system is the legacy of John D. Rockefeller, Jr., who wanted to ensure that automobiles could never overrun the park's interior.

ESSENTIAL INFORMATION

VISITOR INFORMATION Contact the **National Park Service** (Acadia National Park, Box 177, Bar Harbor 04609, tel. 207/288–3338). Maps and information are available from May to October at the main visitor's center (Rte. 3, Hulls Cove, just before entrance to Park Loop Rd.) and from May to October 15 at the much smaller visitor's center on Thompson Island (just before you drive onto Mount Desert Island). Hulls Cove is open summer, daily 8–6; spring and fall, daily 8–4:30. The Thompson Island center is open July and August, daily 10–8; spring and fall, daily 10–6. Run jointly with the **Bar Harbor Chamber of Commerce,** the latter provides additional information on accommodations. When these seasonal centers are closed, the park headquarters on Route 233 maintains an information center (open daily 8–4:30).

For information on lodging and dining outside the park, and other local tourist facilities, contact the **Bar Harbor Chamber of Commerce** (Box 158, Bar Harbor 04609, tel. 207/288–5103) and the **Southwest Harbor Chamber of Commerce** (Main St., Rte. 102, in old clapboard building on left as you drive south, tel. 207/244–9264).

There is no backcountry camping in Acadia (*see* Camping, *below*).

FEES Some areas require no entrance fee, but to get onto the Park Loop Road the fee, which is good for seven days, is $5 per vehicle and $3 per pedestrian or cyclist. A $15 annual Acadia park pass entitles the bearer to road admission for one calendar year.

PUBLICATIONS In addition to the park's free newspaper, *Acadia Beaver Log,* numerous publications, maps, and guidebooks are available from both the **Eastern National Park and Monument Association** (Acadia National Park, Box 177, Bar Harbor 04609) and from the park's main visitor's center in Hulls Cove (*see* Visitor Information, *above*).

Some great books are *Mount Desert and Acadia National Park,* by Sargent F. Collier, an informal but thorough history of the park; *A Walk in the Park,* by T. A. St. Germain, Jr., with maps and text on what may be the most popular activities in Acadia; *A Pocket Guide to the Carriage Roads of Acadia National Park,* by Diana F. Abrell, a small booklet with maps and information on the carriage roads; *Activity Guide to Acadia National Park,* by Carol Peterson and Meg Scheid, geared toward teachers and parents; and *Native Birds of Mount Desert Island and Acadia National Park,* by Ralph H. Long.

GEOLOGY AND TERRAIN Most of Acadia is on Mount Desert Island, the third-largest island off the coast of the continental United States. Bisected by Somes Sound, a dramatic fjord carved out by a glacier that melted 10,000–12,000 years ago, the island has two "lobes." The park extends over both of them, but the most popular sights—Sand Beach, Mt. Cadillac, and the Park Loop Road—are on the eastern lobe. Additional sections are on Isle au Haut, a much smaller, heavily forested island in Penobscot Bay, about 12 miles southwest of Mount Desert (as the crow flies); Schoodic Peninsula, farther down east on the mainland; and tiny Baker Island, reached by boat from Mount Desert Island.

Mount Desert began to form about 500 million years ago when ancient rivers deposited sediments on the ocean floor, forming the first bedrock. Its current appearance is the result of the last glacier, which advanced and retreated several times over New England: the seventeen glacially rounded mountains; such water basins as Eagle Lake and Echo Lake, which were carved out by the glacier; and huge boulders on the sides of Cadillac and South Bubble Mountains, which the glacier transported over long distances and deposited randomly. Although most of Acadia's shoreline is rugged pink granite, the sea has shifted tons of sand and crushed shell into one location to create the curving Sand Beach on the island's eastern side.

■ **FLORA AND FAUNA** Acadia is heavily forested, with a mix of deciduous and coniferous trees including alder, sugar maple, northern white cedar, aspen, and red and white pine. On the windswept, rocky mountaintops, shrubs such as highbush blueberry, mountain holly, and creeping juniper thrive. In the low-lying marshes, many of which were created when beavers flooded areas of land, you'll find such common plant species as water lilies and cattails. You can identify a wide range of flora at the **Wild Gardens of Acadia at Sieur de Monts Spring**, where more than 400 plants are labeled and displayed (*see* Exploring, *below*).

Marine mammals commonly spotted in Acadia's waters include harbor seals, porpoises, and finback and minke whales, with the occasional appearance of humpback and right whales. Several companies offer whale-watching excursions off Mount Desert Island (*see* Other Activities *in* Exploring, *below*). On shore, the most commonly seen animals are the white-tailed deer and snowshoe hare, although coyotes, weasels, beavers, and several species of rodents, turtles, snakes, and salamanders are also abundant. Dozens of species of birds inhabit the park, too, from great blue herons and hawks to herring gulls and common eiders. Acadia sponsors a Peregrine Reintroduction Program, aimed at bringing back the peregrine falcon, a species nearly extinct in the eastern United States by the mid-1960s. In 1993 a pair of peregrines raised four chicks on the cliffs of Champlain Mountain in Acadia, and trails in this area may be closed off in early spring if mating or nesting behavior is suspected.

■ **WHEN TO GO** Acadia is lovely during any of New England's distinctly different seasons. Although summer is by far the most popular, it's by no means the only time to enjoy the park. From mid-May to late fall, Bar Harbor is swarming with tourists; expect higher lodging prices. On the other hand, summer is the best time to take advantage of shopping in, dining out on, and touring Mount Desert Island; the town of Bar Harbor virtually shuts down in winter. Because the park is also heavily trafficked in summer, you might try the fall foliage season or winter to avoid crowds. Opportunities to cross-country ski, snowshoe, and snowmobile are plentiful, and camping is free from October 15 to May 15 at Blackwoods Campground. Though some roads are left unplowed in winter (but remain open to skiers and snowmobilers), almost all of the park is accessible by one means or another.

Because of its island setting, Acadia is both cooler in summer and more moderate in winter than is the mainland. Average summer temperatures are in the mid-60s, although windless summer days can drive the thermometer into the 90s. Rain and fog are frequent at this time: After the Pacific Northwest, the Maine coast receives more annual precipitation than any other U.S. climate; be prepared for sudden weather changes. Fall temperatures drop into the 40s and 50s and rainfall increases slightly. Winter temperatures fall into the 20s, with an average monthly snowfall of 12 to 17 inches. Spring rolls in around late April, delivering highs in the 50s. Several trails, particularly those at higher elevations, are covered with ice and snow until this time.

■ **SEASONAL EVENTS** **July:** Bar Harbor's **Downeast Dulcimer and Folk Harp Festival** (tel. 207/288–5103), which usually takes place over three days in mid-July, puts on concerts and workshops. **July–August:** For several weeks during these two months, the **Arcady Music Festival** (Arcady Music Society, Box 1265, Southwest Harbor 04679) brings excellent weekly classical music performances to the Bar Harbor area. The **Bar Harbor Music Festival** (off-season, tel. 212/222–1026; in summer, 207/288–5744) presents ten classical and jazz concerts, most of them held at a local church, but one is always held in the amphitheater at Blackwoods Campground. **October:** The annual **Bar Harbor Scottish Performing Arts Weekend** (tel. 207/288–5103) has workshops and concerts at a local church.

WHAT TO PACK Pack a warm sweater and windbreaker to fend off stiff ocean breezes, even when taking short strolls. Appropriate hiking and walking footwear is a must, especially for clambering over the rocky shore. Running shoes are fine for walking on the carriage roads, but hiking boots are better for any of the park's trails, many of which require steep climbs. It's always wise to bring sunscreen and a water bottle. In winter, waterproof footwear, warm headgear, mittens, and layers of warm clothing are essential.

GENERAL STORES The major grocery store in Bar Harbor is **Shop 'n Save** (86 Cottage St., tel. 207/288–3621), which is open summer, Monday–Saturday 7 AM–9 PM, Sunday 9–6, and fall–spring, Monday–Saturday 8–7, Sunday noon–5. For gourmet- and health-food supplies, try the **Alternative Natural Foods Market** (99 Main St., tel. 207/288–5271), which features exotic coffees and high-end groceries and is open summer, daily 7:30 AM–11 PM, and fall–spring, daily 7:30–6. On the western side of the island, try **Southwest Food Mart** (Rte. 102, Southwest Harbor, tel. 207/244–5601), which is open summer, daily 8–8, and fall–spring, daily 8–6; or **Sawyer's Market** (Main St., Southwest Harbor, tel. 207/244–3315), a small family-run store with high-quality foods, open summer, daily 5:30 AM–8 PM, and fall–spring, daily 5:30 AM–6:30 PM.

ATMS In Bar Harbor, try the **Bar Harbor Banking and Trust Company** (82 Main St.) or the **First National Bank of Bar Harbor** (102 Main St.). **Bar Harbor Banking and Trust** also has offices and an ATM on Main Street in Southwest Harbor.

ARRIVING AND DEPARTING Most visitors arrive by car, which is by far the easiest way to travel here.

By Plane. The **Bar Harbor/Hancock County Airport** (Rte. 3, Trenton, tel. 207/667–7432) is serviced by Colgan Air, which flies to and from Bangor and Portland. Rental cars are available at the airport from Avis, Budget, and Hertz.

By Car and RV. Most visitors arrive from the south, from which there are two main routes to the park. After taking I–95 north to Bangor (47 miles from the park), cut east on U.S. 395, then take Route 1A to Ellsworth, the largest mainland city near the park. From Ellsworth, follow Route 3 to Mount Desert Island. A more scenic route is to get off I–95 in Brunswick, 115 miles southwest of Ellsworth, and follow coastal U.S. 1 to its junction with Route 3.

By Train. There is no train service to this part of Maine.

By Bus. **Greyhound Lines** (tel. 800/231–2222) runs daily in the summer from Bangor to Bar Harbor. **Down East Transportation** (tel. 207/667–5796) has bus service between Ellsworth and several locations on Mount Desert Island.

EXPLORING

Acadia is best visited by car, even though there's an annoying surplus of them at times. With dozens of sights scattered along park roads, you'll be happy to find that parking is provided at most locations. To see the best parts of the park, though, you may want to abandon the car for a bike or a pair of hiking boots.

The sections of the park linked by the Park Loop Road get very crowded, but they are among the most spectacular sections of Acadia and should not be missed. You can easily spend one to three days exploring the sights just along this 20-mile paved road, which

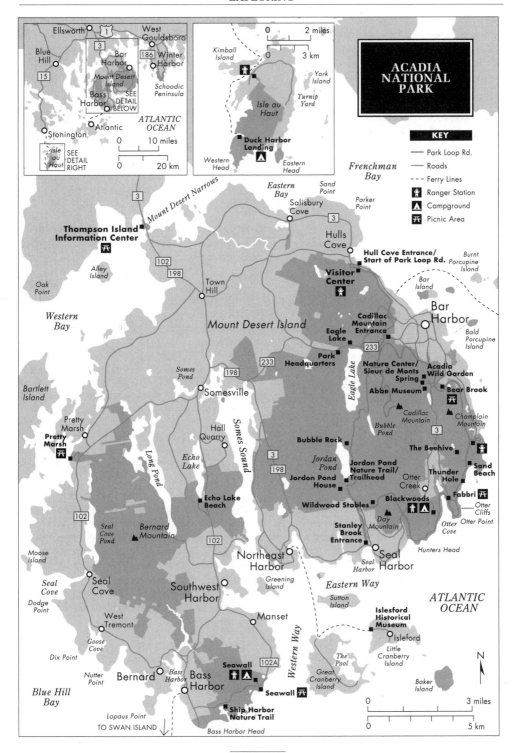

ACADIA
NATIONAL
PARK

KEY
— Park Loop Rd.
— Roads
- - - Ferry Lines
Ranger Station
Campground
Picnic Area

begins near the visitor's center on Route 3. It's two-way for a few miles until it crosses Route 233 and becomes one-way for a large section of the loop. The road winds past the entrance to the Wild Gardens of Acadia at Sieur de Monts Spring, where a nature center is open mid-June–mid-September, daily 9–5, and visitors can walk through the gardens for free or pay 25¢ for an interpretive brochure. Admission to the nature center is free. The road then follows the shoreline, providing excellent views of Frenchman Bay, and finally reaches a cluster of attractions, including Sand Beach, Thunder Hole, and the Otter Cliffs, which drop precipitously into the sea. The road eventually loops back up, away from the shore, and becomes two-way again, cutting through the wooded, mountainous interior of Acadia. Attractions along this span include the Jordan Pond House (*see* The Best in One Day, *below*) and the Bubbles, where a huge boulder perches atop a high cliff on South Bubble Mountain. Just before the end of the loop, a side road branches off the Park Loop Road and climbs 3.5 miles to the summit of 1,530-foot Cadillac Mountain, from which the view of Acadia and the surrounding seas is unmatched.

You can drive the Park Loop Road in a day, but the perfect trip requires at least a day of exploring by car plus several more days for the relatively uncrowded interior. You can rent a bicycle in Bar Harbor (*see* Biking *in* Other Activities, *below*) and bring it into the park for an extended ride on the park roads or carriage roads. Hiking (*see* Nature Trails and Short Walks *and* Longer Hikes, *below*) is another great way to experience the park, and the options are limitless: from climbing to the summit of Cadillac to exploring the less-trafficked western side of the island.

If you have three or four days in Acadia, try getting off the beaten path and visiting parts of the park that aren't on Mount Desert Island. One of the most beautiful is Isle au Haut (meaning "High Island"), an island accessible by boat from the fishing village of Stonington on Deer Isle. It requires some backtracking from Mount Desert to get to Stonington, so this excursion is best saved for the end of your

trip to Acadia. Remote and heavily wooded, Isle au Haut is magical; few hikers cross paths on its 18 miles of trails. Although a small year-round community exists on Isle au Haut, there is no auto ferry to the island, and space on the mail boat is limited. Tickets are sold on a first-come, first-served basis, though access is rarely denied. For information on Isle au Haut and for camping reservations, contact the **National Park Service** (*see* Visitor Information *in* Essential Information, *above*); for boat schedules, call **Isle au Haut Ferry Company** (tel. 207/367–5193, $18 round-trip).

Other sections of the park include Baker Island, a small, undeveloped island off Mount Desert to which park staff lead excursions (*see* Guided Tours, *below*); and Schoodic Peninsula, a bold, granite peninsula famous for the impressive surf that pounds its shore. Reach Schoodic by taking U.S. 1 north from Ellsworth to West Gouldsboro, then taking Route 186 to Winter Harbor and following signs to the park.

THE BEST IN ONE DAY Stop first at the Hulls Cove Visitor's Center to see a short orientation video and obtain maps and brochures about the park; then begin your drive on the Park Loop Road. To truly appreciate the coast between Sand Beach and Otter Cliffs, leave your car at the beach parking lot and walk down **Ocean Trail**, a flat 1.8-mile trail that parallels the Park Road. For a short but rigorous hike, try the trail that begins just across the road from Sand Beach and makes a 1-mile loop over the **Beehive**, a 520-foot outcropping of granite that offers a wonderful view of Sand Beach and the ocean. If you're afraid of heights and climbing, however, pick another hike; this one entails several steep climbs that require the use of iron rungs for foot- and handholds.

After spending the morning exploring this magnificent stretch of Acadia's coastline, continue to the **Jordan Pond House** (*see* Dining, *below*), famous for its view of the Bubbles. Teatime here is a century-old tradition; stop in for some popovers with strawberry jam and homemade ice cream. Or opt instead to walk the nearby self-guided **Jordan Pond Nature Trail** (*see* Nature Trails and Short Walks, *below*) or explore some carriage roads, many of which intersect near Jordan Pond. **Wildwood Stables,** down the road from the Jordan Pond House, has daily horse-drawn carriage rides in the summer (*see* Horseback Riding *in* Other Activities, *below*).

Finish your day by driving up the **Mount Cadillac Road,** 7 miles round-trip. On the summit is a large parking lot, gift shop, and interpretive plaques explaining various aspects of Cadillac and its history. More important, you can savor the magnificent view of islands and sea beneath the setting sun.

ORIENTATION PROGRAMS A 15-minute orientation video is shown every half hour at the visitor's center in Hulls Cove. With astounding footage of Acadia's scenery, the video includes the natural and human history of Mount Desert Island and acquaints you with things to do in the park, and emphasizes Acadia's dual nature—extremely trafficked in spots, but ripe with the opportunity for solitude in others.

GUIDED TOURS Rangers lead a variety of tours; ask at the visitor's center (tel. 207/288–3338) or obtain a copy of *Acadia Beaver Log* for times and themes. Some terrific land tours are "Mr. Rockefeller's Bridges Walk," a 1.5-mile walk over carriage roads and stone bridges, which takes about 2¹/₂ hours; and "At the Summit," a one-hour program atop Cadillac Mountain during which participants study the glaciation that shaped the park, and discuss Acadia's natural and cultural history. Both tours are free.

Park naturalists also interpret trips aboard several commercial boats; make reservations with the private companies that own them. The "Baker Island Cruise" is a 4¹/₂-hour excursion that departs from Northeast Harbor (tel. 207/276–3717; $13 adults, $8 children). The "Islesford Historical Cruise" takes visitors on a 2³/₄-hour trip to the village of Islesford on Little Cranberry Island, which is just off Mount Desert Island but is not part of Acadia (tel. 207/276–5352; admission $10 adults, $8 children). The park operates a

small historical museum here; admission to the museum is free.

A few private companies operate summer tours inside the park. **Oli's Trolley** (tel. 207/288–9899) runs 2¹/₂-hour narrated trolleybus tours on the Park Loop Road and to the summit of Cadillac Mountain. **National Park Tours** (tel. 207/288–3327) does narrated bus tours along the Park Loop Road and to some of the area's mansions. For information on the wealth of boat cruises around the island, contact the **Bar Harbor Chamber of Commerce** or the **Southwest Harbor Chamber of Commerce** (*see* Visitor Information *in* Essential Information, *above*). The **Frenchman Bay Company** operates nearly two dozen sightseeing trips daily, including two-hour cruises of the bay on a topsail schooner (tel. 207/288–3322, $16.75 adults, $10.75 children under 11). The company is next to the town pier in Bar Harbor. **Acadian Whale Watcher** (60 West St., tel. 207/288–9794) offers four-hour whale-watching trips ($29 adults, $19 children).

SCENIC DRIVES AND VIEWS The 20-mile **Park Loop Road** can be driven in about an hour without stops, but who would want to drive the whole stretch without pulling over to admire the views? You can spend at least a day exploring the sights along this road. The trip to the top of **Mt. Cadillac** is a must, with the most spectacular views in the early morning or late afternoon. Traffic on the Park Loop Road is heaviest between 10 AM and 2 PM.

Another excellent scenic loop is on the western half of Mount Desert Island. Take **Route 233** off the Park Loop Road, and head west past the park headquarters and Eagle Lake. This road connects with **Route 198** and eventually **Route 102,** making a 40-mile loop around the western lobe of the island. The scenery here is less dramatic than on the eastern lobe, but there are several points of interest on Route 102 and Route 102A, which makes an additional loop along the shore. Some of these stretches are inside the park boundaries, but most of the road winds through residential areas. In addition to passing through the small towns of Somesville,

Seal Cove, Bass Harbor, and Southwest Harbor, you can stop to enjoy the views at the Pretty Marsh Picnic Area, Seawall Campground and Picnic Area, the Ship Harbor Nature Trail, and the Bass Harbor Head lighthouse, all of which are easily explored on foot from parking areas. Echo Lake on Route 102, which has a beach area and lifeguard, provides some of the best swimming in the park.

For dramatic views of Somes Sound, take **Sargent Drive** from Route 3/198, near Northeast Harbor. This narrow, 5-mile road follows the eastern shore of the sound. No buses or RVs are allowed.

HISTORIC BUILDINGS AND SITES Though no historic buildings here are open to the public, two museums provide glimpses into Acadia's history. The privately run **Robert Abbé Museum,** just off the Park Loop Road, maintains a collection of Native American antiquities and has special exhibits on the culture of Maine's Native Americans. *Tel. 207/288–3519. Admission: $2 adults, 50¢ children. Open July–Aug., daily 9–5; slightly shorter hours May, June, Sept., Oct.*

The **Islesford Historical Museum,** on Little Cranberry Island, has exhibits on island and maritime history. Take the mailboat to the island or one of the park-service tours (*see* Guided Tours, *above*). *Tel. 207/288–3338. Admission free. Open July–Aug., daily; check at visitor's center for hours.*

NATURE TRAILS AND SHORT WALKS There are two self-guided nature trails in the park. The **Jordan Pond Nature Trail** begins and ends near the Jordan Pond House, making a smooth 1-mile loop along the shore and through nearby fields and wooded areas. Interpretive pamphlets provide information on natural and park history at selected points along the loop, which takes about 45 minutes to complete. The **Ship Harbor Nature Trail,** a 1.3-mile loop, covers slightly hillier ground; it begins off Route 102A on the island's western lobe, not far from the Seawall Campground. This trail cuts through the woods to the shore and follows a section of pink granite shoreline along an inlet filled with striking

deep-green water. Pamphlets are also available for this trail, which takes close to an hour to hike.

Another short hike is the 1.2-mile round-trip **Bubble Rock Trail,** accessible from the Park Loop Road at the north end of Jordan Pond. The trail climbs over steep grades and level areas to the top of South Bubble Mountain, where the famous Bubble Rock perches on the edge of a cliff. The view below of Jordan Pond is outstanding. A slightly longer trail in this same area is the Jordan Pond Shore Path, a moderately strenuous, 3.3-mile loop that essentially follows the pond's shoreline.

LONGER HIKES Acadia is better known for short hikes than for long ones, simply because the lay of the land is not conducive to extensive hikes or backcountry expeditions. By combining several shorter trails, however, one can hike for miles in Acadia.

One of the longest trails is the strenuous **Cadillac Mountain South Ridge Trail,** which begins just south of the entrance to Blackwoods Campground. The 7.4-mile trail heads north and climbs steadily through the woods, eventually cutting above the treeline to the summit of Cadillac. This isn't a loop, so prepare for a long day of hiking unless you have a car waiting for you at the summit parking area.

A more moderate route to the top of Cadillac is the 4.4-mile **North Ridge Trail,** which includes some steep grades and level stretches through woods and over rocky areas. The trail begins at the North Ridge Cadillac Parking Area, on the Park Loop Road just after it becomes one-way; this, too, is not a loop.

OTHER ACTIVITIES Biking. Acadia is a wonderful place to cycle, with routes as varied as the bikers who come here. If you choose to ride on the paved park roads—especially the Park Loop Road—it's best to do so either in the early morning or early evening, when the traffic is lighter. The hilly Park Loop Road is a little treacherous, thanks to the steady flow of auto traffic, but the scenery is marvelous. In general, however, park rangers recommend leaving the paved roads and exploring the carriage road system. The bike routes on these bumpy and rocky gravel roads are almost limitless, but you need a mountain bike for most of them (two loops are maintained for narrow-tire bikes). Some carriage roads are relatively level, requiring only ordinary athletic prowess. Others wind up and around the smaller mountains in Acadia and can be quite rigorous. The park's staff will help you select an appropriate route.

A good place to take off for a variety of carriage-road bike routes is from the visitor center in Hulls Cove; the trail system begins at the far end of the parking lot. From here, bikers can ride a short distance to link up with the 3.3-mile **Witch Hole Pond Loop,** which is surfaced with fine gravel and maintained especially for bicycles. A **carriage road** connects with this loop and leads south to a 5.8-mile loop around **Eagle Lake.** The carriage-road system connects the park's northernmost and southernmost parts, so ambitious riders can begin at the visitor center and work their way south, past Eagle Lake and Jordan Pond, all the way to Route 3 in Seal Harbor.

Bikes can be rented in Bar Harbor from **Bar Harbor Bicycle Shop** (141 Cottage St., tel. 207/288–3886), **Acadia Outfitters** (106 Cottage St., tel. 207/288–8118), and **Acadia Bike and Canoe** (48 Cottage St., tel. 207/288–9605). Average rates are $15 for a full-day rental, $10 for half a day.

Bird-Watching. Acadia attracts more than 300 species of sea, shore, and land birds. Ship Harbor Nature Trail, the Wonderland Trail near Bass Harbor on the western part of the island, Otter Point near Otter Cliffs, and Sieur de Monts Spring are known for prime bird-watching, or you can take a cruise with a park naturalist. In winter, several species of sea ducks can be spotted off Acadia's shores, including common eiders, buffleheads, red-breasted mergansers, and white-winged scoters. Peak birding is from late May through September, when birdsong fills the woods of Acadia. The **Audubon Society** (tel. 207/288–2829) operates a birding hot line that is updated weekly.

Boating. The many lakes and ponds of Mount Desert Island are ideal for canoeing, and the waters around Acadia are filled with yachts and tour boats—as well as working fishing and lobster boats—throughout the summer. Although the park maintains several boat-launching facilities, boats are not rented inside the park. Two options among many in the area are **National Park Canoe Rentals** (137 Cottage St., Bar Harbor, tel. 207/288–0342; end of Long Pond, Mount Desert, tel. 207/244–5854) and **Acadia Bike and Canoe** (48 Cottage St., Bar Harbor, 207/288–9605). The average price of a full-day rental is $20.

Options for plying the waters around Mount Desert Island range from taking a schooner or whale-watching cruise (*see* Guided Tours, *above*) to trying your hand at sea kayaking, an increasingly popular sport in Maine. The waters here are known for their dangerous currents, however, so hook up with a tour company if you lack experience. **Coastal Kayaking Tours** (Bar Harbor, tel. 207/288–9605) operates half-day, full-day, and overnight outings and also rents kayaks.

Fishing. Freshwater fishing in Acadia rates from fair to poor, but that shouldn't discourage anyone from canoeing around one of Mount Desert's ponds in search of landlocked salmon, lake trout, brook trout, or smallmouth bass. People do ice fish in Acadia as well.

Horseback Riding. You'll have to bring your own horse; there are no rentals in the park. However, **Wildwood Stables** (tel. 207/276–3622), near Jordan Pond, offers a variety of horse-drawn carriage rides on the carriage roads from June 15 to Columbus Day. Wildwood leads three one-hour rides daily ($10.50 per person) with 10 people in a carriage, plus a two-hour evening ride to the summit of Day Mountain ($13.50 per person).

Rock Climbing. Acadia's granite makes for some excellent rock climbing. Popular locations are on the Bubbles, the south face of Mt. Champlain (the Precipice), and Otter Cliffs—where climbers negotiate routes high above the pounding surf. Unfortunately, the best book on climbing routes in Acadia is out of print, but a desk copy is kept at the visitor's center, and climbers are welcome to take notes from it. The park does not provide any guide services or gear. Permits are not required.

Skiing. Cross-country skiing on Acadia's carriage roads is a magical experience. Although the park makes no tracks and maintains no trails, local volunteers often make tracks to ensure that skiers make the most of each snowfall, which can be a disappointingly rare occurrence. Ski rentals are available at **Cadillac Mountain Sports** (26 Cottage St., Bar Harbor, tel. 207/288–4532).

Snowmobiling. In winter, the entire Park Loop Road is left unplowed and open to snowmobilers. A short stretch of carriage road along the eastern shore of Eagle Lake is also open, but carriage roads are otherwise off-limits. The speed limit is 35 miles per hour, towing people on skis or sleds is prohibited, and adult supervision of drivers under the age of 14 is required.

Snowshoeing. You can snowshoe anywhere in the park, but the carriage roads and unplowed roads are recommended over the steeper hiking trails or the Cadillac Mountain Summit Road, which gets icy. For rentals, try **Cadillac Mountain Sports** (*see above*).

Swimming. The best swimming in Acadia is at Echo Lake, on the western part of the island, where there is a large beach, changing rooms, and a lifeguard. There is also a lifeguard at Sand Beach, which is a spectacular spot with a good surf—but the water is, quite frankly, freezing. Swimming is not allowed in the other lakes and ponds of Acadia because they are sources of drinking water for surrounding communities. The one exception is the north end of Long Pond.

CHILDREN'S ACTIVITIES Two of the park's naturalist-led programs, "Nature's Way" and "The Island's Edge," are geared toward children ages five to twelve; reservations are required for both programs (tel. 207/288–5262). Acadia also sponsors a Junior Ranger program. By following the activities outlined in a booklet (available for $1.50) and attending two naturalist programs, participants earn a Junior Ranger badge.

EVENING ACTIVITIES The park service offers evening programs in the amphitheaters at the Blackwoods and Seawall campgrounds. The one-hour programs cover such topics as Acadia's geology, the carriage roads, shore ecology, and park history. Check the *Acadia Beaver Log* or call Visitor Information (tel. 207/288–3338) for a schedule. Park rangers also offer an astronomy program.

DINING

If you love seafood, you'll be in heaven on Mount Desert Island, whether in a down-home sandwich shop or elegant restaurant. If you don't like seafood you're sure to find something to suit your palate among the dozens of restaurants in Southwest Harbor and Bar Harbor, the latter being home to most of the island's dining establishments. Most restaurants are closed from November through Memorial Day.

INSIDE THE PARK **Jordan Pond House.** This park landmark has been serving delicious food since the 1870s. The original structure burned in the late 1970s, and the new, gray-shingled house overlooking Jordan Pond is quite contemporary, with high, angular ceilings, massive windows, and a large stone center-chimney fireplace. Although both lunch and dinner are served here in season, the restaurant is best known for its afternoon tea, a long-standing tradition at which popovers, strawberry jam, and homemade ice cream are served. Otherwise the menu is basic and unexciting, with such items as filet mignon, baked haddock, and seafood pasta. *Park Loop Rd., tel. 207/276–3316. Reservations advised. Dress: casual but neat. AE, D, MC, V. Closed mid-Oct.–mid-May. Moderate–Expensive.*

NEAR THE PARK **George's.** In a restored 1850s farmhouse a block off Main Street, George's offers some of the most inventive dining in town and is considered the best by most locals. Decorated in terra-cotta and shades of peach with tapestries and art adorning the walls, the restaurant has several dining rooms and seating on the quiet outdoor terrace overlooking the garden. George recommends the lobster strudel, prepared with white sauce, cheese, and fresh herbs. Other specialties include tofu tempura, a nightly lamb special, and honey-rum breast of duck with mango sauce. The fixed-price menu is a popular option. *7 Stephens La., Bar Harbor, tel. 207/288–4505. Reservations advised. Dress: casual but neat. AE, D, DC, MC, V. No lunch. Closed Nov.–mid-May. Expensive.*

The Opera House. This restaurant-*cum*-listening room is the choice among local opera lovers—the decor is a real conversation piece; it's not appropriate, however, for families with small children. The walls of the dimly lit dining room are covered with photos and illustrations of opera stars, and opera sets the tone of every meal. The menu is long and elaborate, featuring such dishes as chateaubriand Ponselle, tenderloin of beef stuffed with lobster tails and served with a creamy crabmeat sauce; and Cornish game hen stuffed with Minnesota wild rice. *27 Cottage St., Bar Harbor, tel. 207/288–3509. Reservations not accepted. Dress: casual. AE, D, MC, V. No lunch. Closed Mon. and mid-Oct.–mid-May. Expensive.*

The Reading Room. Both guests and nonguests frequent the large, oceanfront dining room at the Bar Harbor Inn (*see* Lodging, *below*). With crystal chandeliers, a grand piano, and conspicuous flower arrangements, the elegant Reading Room offers great harbor views. Breakfast and dinner, as well as a buffet Sunday brunch, are served inside; lunch is outside on Gatsby's Terrace under bright yellow umbrellas. For dinner try lobster pie, grilled jumbo shrimp with spicy peanut sauce, or one of the mouth-watering grills and roasts—perhaps grilled boneless breast of chicken with fresh mango sauce or seared boneless loin of lamb with asparagus and pine nuts. *Bar Harbor Inn, adjacent to municipal pier, tel. 207/288–3351. Reservations advised. Dress: casual but neat. Jacket advised for dinner. AE, D, DC, MC, V. Closed Nov.–mid-Apr. Expensive.*

The Claremont. Southwest Harbor's finest restaurant is at the Claremont Hotel (*see* Lodging, *below*), where you'll dine to wonderful views of Somes Sound, if in a slightly worn dining room. The menu changes weekly; prime rib on Fridays and roast beef with Yorkshire pudding on Saturdays are house traditions. Other dinner specialties include Maine shrimp cakes—sautéed and served on watercress with scallion-citrus mayonnaise, or glazed rack of pork au poivre. *Claremont Rd., Southwest Harbor, tel. 207/244–5036. Reservations advised. Jacket and tie required at dinner. No credit cards. No lunch. Closed mid-Sept.–mid-June. Moderate–Expensive.*

Galyn's Galley. This cavernous, two-story restaurant, across from Agamont Park, has a bar upstairs and a few tables streetside. The dining room has wooden floors and paneling, a brick fireplace, and stained-glass panels; cheerfulness is favored over character. Seafood sandwiches and salads are the main fare at lunch; dinner specials include Frenchman Bay stew—a spicy bouillabaisse; daily specials of haddock, scrod, sole, halibut, and swordfish; and combinations of lobster and filet mignon, sautéed in butter and sherry. It's one of the few local restaurants open year-round. *17 Main St., Bar Harbor, tel. 207/288–9076. Reservations advised. Dress: casual. AE, MC, V. Moderate.*

Parkside Restaurant. Set in downtown Bar Harbor, the Parkside is on a busy corner across from the village green. White trellises, white wicker furniture, and hanging plants create a light, airy mood. The restaurant is lively—and noisy, its terrace packed with bons vivants sipping frosty drinks and dining on fresh shellfish marinara with lobster, shrimp, mussels, crab, and scallops or veal scaloppine served on wilted spinach with wild mushrooms. *2 Mount Desert St., Bar Harbor, tel. 207/288–3700. Reservations accepted. Dress: casual but neat. AE, D, MC, V. Closed mid-Oct.–mid-May. Moderate.*

Village Green Café. A combination bakery-deli-restaurant, the Village Green Café is in the heart of downtown and is a convenient—

if rather noisy—place to grab breakfast, lunch, or dinner. The restaurant has a small bar and about ten tables with linoleum benches. Specialties include Bah Habah Bob's 5 oz. Burgers (Bar Harbor with a Maine accent); seafood pasta with lobster, shrimp, and fresh mushrooms; and fried seafood baskets, pizzas, sandwiches, and lobster specials. *150 Main St., Bar Harbor, tel. 207/288–9450. No reservations. Dress: casual. No credit cards. Closed Nov.–Mar. Inexpensive–Moderate.*

Epi's Pizza and Subs. Fancy it ain't, but this is Bar Harbor's hometown pizza joint and the food is good. Just order at the cash register, find a table, and wait for your food. The restaurant is neat, with tile walls, wall mirrors, and red-and-black tables and lamps. A couple of video games in the back keep kids happy. Aside from pizza, you can get "grinders" (submarine sandwiches), calzones, and salads. *8 Cottage St., Bar Harbor, tel. 207/288–5853. Reservations not necessary. Dress: casual. No credit cards. Closed Jan. Inexpensive.*

PICNIC SPOTS Almost any site in Acadia has picnicking potential, from Sand Beach to the summit of Cadillac. The park operates five official picnic areas with tables and grills: Pretty Marsh and Seawall on the western part of the island; Bear Brook, Thompson Island, and Fabbri on the eastern part. Each offers its own brand of scenery, from the tidal mudflats at Thompson Island to the exposed rocky beach at Seawall. The Thompson Island Picnic Area is just after the bridge to Mount Desert, and supplies can be picked up in Ellsworth or Trenton—a small town on Route 3. For the Bear Brook and Fabbri picnic areas, both along the Park Loop Road, one should shop in Bar Harbor. Seawall, on Route 102A across from the Seawall Campground, is close to Southwest Harbor's grocery store, and supplies for Pretty Marsh, on the westernmost part of Mount Desert, are sold at the small grocery store in Somesville.

LODGING

You'll have dozens of choices including motels, beachside cottages, small family-run bed-and-breakfasts, inns, and resort hotels. Many of the best accommodations are in and around Bar Harbor or Southwest Harbor; others are scattered around the island, on back roads, and on Route 3 between Ellsworth and Mount Desert. If you're arriving during the peak season of July 1 to Labor Day, when rates are at their highest, reserve a room at least a couple of weeks ahead. Many accommodations close in winter. If you do arrive without reservations and need help finding a place, try any of three Bar Harbor Chamber of Commerce offices: the **Thompson Island Information Center** (tel. 207/288–9702, open daily 10–5), the **Bluenose Ferry Terminal** (Rte. 3, tel. 207/288–3393, open daily 9 AM–11 PM), and the **main office** (93 Cottage St., tel. 207/288–5103, open weekdays 8–4).

Breakwater 1904. The Breakwater is the crème de la crème—the best place to experience Bar Harbor's Gilded Age. The 1904 Tudor oceanfront mansion, on a quiet side street, was rescued from deterioration and lavishly restored in 1992. The current owners overlooked no detail, from the hundreds of tiny, leaded-pane windows to the needlepoint rugs and specially commissioned billiard table. Public areas include the living room, parlor, dining room, billiard room, and a second-floor sitting room opening onto a veranda. The decor of the six guest rooms, each about 500 square feet, lives up to expectations, with plush rugs, canopy beds, chaise longues, and huge walk-in closets. Four of the six rooms have direct ocean views. Bar Harbor is a short stroll away on the Shore Path, which runs right by the breakwater. *45 Hancock St., Bar Harbor 04609, tel. 207/288–2313, fax 207/288–2377. 6 rooms with bath. Facilities: dining room (full breakfast included in room rate), billiards. AE, MC, V. Closed Jan. 2–Mar. Expensive.*

Claremont Hotel. Built in 1884, the Claremont is the oldest summer hotel on Mount Desert Island. Its setting, atop a hill overlooking Somes Sound, and the graceful four-story hotel itself definitely evoke the charm of an earlier era, as do the quiet grounds with a private dock and a croquet court. The hotel feels a little damp and rickety, and the public areas are decorated with an undistinguished jumble of wicker and upholstered furniture, and marine paintings. The rooms, accessible off long corridors, are done in bright floral or pastel bedspreads and wallpaper; beds are four-poster, brass, or wicker. Some rooms have claw-foot tubs; about half have ocean views. There are also twelve modern house-keeping cottages and six large rooms in two outlying guest houses. One of these, the Phillips House, is a short walk from the main hotel and has a cozy public area with a huge stone fireplace, walls of bookcases, and a grand piano. *Claremont Rd., Box 137, Southwest Harbor 04679, tel. 207/244–5036, fax 207/244–3512. 43 rooms. Facilities: dining room, boathouse for lunch and cocktails, tennis, croquet, rowboats and bicycles for rent, moorings. No credit cards. Closed mid-Oct.–mid-May. Expensive.*

Atlantic Oakes by-the-Sea. A large resort hotel and conference center, Atlantic Oakes is on Route 3 adjacent to the Nova Scotia ferry terminal. It's a short walk to town, but most guests drive there. Atlantic Oakes comprises the Willows, a restored 1913 summer home; a large main building added in 1991; and several outlying motel-style buildings dating from the mid-'70s. The best rooms are in the Willows, also referred to as the mansion, a white clapboard building with eight rooms recently redecorated with floral wallpaper, reproduction furniture, ceiling fans, and private decks overlooking Frenchman Bay. The incongruous newer building, whose public areas recall those of an airport terminal, has rooms with floor-to-ceiling windows, private balconies, and dark-wood furniture, with brass fixtures. The hallways and stairwells in this building are unpleasant and institutional. Rooms in the outlying buildings are rather stuffy, with rugs and furnishings that have seen better days. *Rte. 3, Bar Harbor 04609, tel. 207/288–5801 or 800/336–2463; in ME, 800/696–2463; fax 207/288–5801. 150 rooms with bath. Facilities: breakfast in common area, nightly lobster bakes, indoor and outdoor pools, whirlpool, lighted tennis court. DC, MC, V. Moderate–Expensive.*

Bar Harbor Inn. An inn since the 1950s and a yacht club before that, the inn sits directly on lovely Bar Harbor. The shingled main building houses the Reading Room restaurant (*see* Dining, *above*), has a large lobby with fireplace and wing chairs, and offers rooms with either ocean or poolside views. These are the smaller of the inn's accommodations. The Oceanfront Lodge, a separate dwelling built in 1985, has larger rooms with private balconies and ocean views. Decorated with floral prints, these are more up-to-date, with oversize beds and ceiling fans. *Newport Dr., Bar Harbor 04609, tel. 207/288–3351 or 800/248–3351, fax 207/288–5296. 130 rooms with bath. Facilities: restaurant, lounge, breakfast area (Continental breakfast included in room rate), room service until 10 PM, outdoor pool, Jacuzzi. AE, D, DC, MC, V. Moderate–Expensive.*

Briarfield Inn. This 1887 house in downtown Bar Harbor was refurbished using columned bookcases, moldings, diamond-pane and beveled-glass windows, and antique furniture salvaged from old churches and other buildings. Each room is individually decorated with Victoriana, crocheted bedspreads, canopy beds, mosquito-net canopies, and the owner's collectibles. In the front hall, upstairs hallways, and the parlor, shelves and cupboards house dozens of china teacups, figurines, and objets d'art. A side porch is home to one of the world's few elephant museums, with its impressive collection of carvings, statues, and figurines. The Briarfield is, in a word or two, quirky but comfortable. *60 Cottage St., Bar Harbor 04609, tel. 207/288–5297 or 800/228–6660. 12 rooms with bath. No phone in rooms. AE, MC, V. Closed Dec.–Mar. Moderate–Expensive.*

Park Entrance Oceanfront Motel. As its name suggests, this motel is opposite the Route 3 entrance to the park, about 2.5 miles from downtown. The large, oceanfront complex comprises three long buildings facing out over a huge lawn and the ocean. The rooms, many of which have sliding glass doors leading out to the lawn or a small balcony, are decorated with basic motel materials: fake wood paneling, hanging prints, and unexciting upholstered furniture. Although the rooms are nothing special, the recreational facilities make this a great place for families. *Rte. 3, RR 1, Box 180B, Bar Harbor 04609, tel. 207/288–9703 or 800/288–9703, fax 207/288–9703. 58 rooms with bath. Facilities: outdoor pool, hot tub, picnic area with grills, horseshoe pits, volleyball, private pier, croquet, kitchenettes available. MC, V. Closed Nov.– Apr. 29. Moderate–Expensive.*

The Black Friar Inn. The Black Friar is a funky little B&B on a side street in Bar Harbor. Built in 1905 and restored in 1980, the house has plenty of colorful decorative touches, such as the orange and terra-cotta trim and the painted columns near the front door, the several stained-glass panels, and a green-glass lamp shaped like a bunch of grapes. The rooms are small—three are garrets—and are decorated individually, some with handmade lace bedspreads and pillowcases, wooden bedsteads with mirrors in the headboards, and antique chairs and stools with needlepoint cushions. The bathrooms echo the Victorian decor, some with claw-foot bathtubs, large old porcelain washbowls, and dark-wood floors and paneling. The Black Friar may feel a little cramped, but the warm ambience created by furnishings, mantels, and other woodwork salvaged from Mount Desert Island summer cottages makes up for it. The pub is especially pleasing with its paneled walls, red-leather benches, fireplace, and wall paintings of monks. *10 Summer St., Bar Harbor 04609, tel. 207/288–5091. 6 rooms, some with bath in hall. No phone or TV in rooms. Facilities: pub for guests only, breakfast included in room rate. MC, V. Closed Nov.–May 1. Moderate.*

Harbor View Motel and Cottages. Harbor View is in downtown Southwest Harbor and has a variety of rooms, including seven cottages, two groups of older rooms, and a new building that houses the office and nine new rooms. The rooms in the new section are the best, with pine wainscoting and sliding glass doors onto private decks overlooking the har-

bor. Some of these are actually two rooms, a bedroom and a sitting room separated by an archway of glass panels. The top-floor efficiency apartment has a large modern kitchen, a whirlpool tub, a private bedroom, and a large living room with peaked ceilings and huge, geometrically shaped windows overlooking the water. The older rooms, part of the original motel, are cramped, and although some have been renovated in the last five years, others are rather shabby, with gaudy curtains, old shower stalls, and little room to maneuver. *Main St. and Lawler La., Box 701, Southwest Harbor 04679, tel. 207/244–5031. 28 rooms with bath. Continental breakfast included in room rate in July and Aug. No phone in rooms. D, MC, V. Closed Nov.–May. Moderate.*

Inn at Southwest. This large Victorian in downtown Southwest Harbor has served as an inn for more than 100 years. The 1884 structure has been completely renovated in the last six years. Downstairs public areas, which include a parlor and a small breakfast nook, are carefully decorated in the Victorian style with burgundy wallpaper, hanging glass lamps, old photographs, and antiques. The rooms, some of which have harbor views, are equally well done, with handmade quilts— some of them down-filled—standing mirrors, and such old-fashioned touches as an antique dollhouse, a teddy bear, or a top hat. A wraparound porch is used frequently by guests for reading or eating breakfast. *Main St. (Rte. 102), Box 593, Southwest Harbor 04679, tel. 207/244–3835. 9 rooms with bath. Facilities: full breakfast and afternoon snack included in room rate. No phone or TV in rooms. AE, MC, V. Closed Dec.–Mar. Moderate.*

Acadia Hotel. Located just across from the village green, this small hotel is not the island's most peaceful spot. Though quite appealing on the outside, with natural-wood clapboards, green shutters, and a new wraparound porch, it is unremarkable inside— with only a small desk area downstairs and ten rooms on the first and second floors. Renovations of the hallways are under way, however, and a lounge area is planned. Rooms, which are furnished individually but not especially creatively, offer the basics: vinyl-covered chairs, patterned bedspreads, and simple furniture. The management is extremely friendly. This hotel is best if you're planning a short stay and wish to spend plenty of time downtown. *20 Mount Desert St., Bar Harbor 04609, tel. 207/288–5721. 10 rooms. Facilities: free use of pool at next-door YMCA. No phone in rooms. AE, D, MC, V. Closed Oct. 15–May 15. Inexpensive.*

Rose Eden Cottages. Of the many lower-end motels and cottages on Route 3, this is one of the best. The neat little white cottages sport bright red doors and shutters and window boxes filled with geraniums. The oldest cottages are about thirty years old but have been recently upgraded with new showers and kitchens, and all are pleasantly decorated with colorful spreads, white-ruffle curtains, and either bright wallpaper or white walls with stenciling. The newer cottages, set farther back from the highway, are larger and have knotty-pine walls and floors and wicker furniture. About 7 miles from Bar Harbor, Rose Eden Cottages is an economical and pleasant option—away from the downtown hubbub and a .5-mile walk to a public sand beach. *Rte. 3, RFD 1, Box 1850, Bar Harbor 04609, tel. 207/288–3038. 10 cottages. Facilities: picnic area with grills, pay phone (no phone in rooms). MC, V. Closed mid-Oct.– May 1. Inexpensive.*

CAMPING

INSIDE THE PARK There are two park campgrounds on Mount Desert Island and a much smaller campground on Isle au Haut. In summer, both Blackwoods and Seawall have rest rooms with cold running water but no showers. Both campgrounds can accommodate RVs up to 35 feet long. Each has a dump station but no utility hookups.

Blackwoods Campground is off Route 3, 5 miles south of Bar Harbor, and is the only park campground open year-round. The sites are all located in a heavily wooded area, but a footpath leads down to the rocky shore not far away. Facilities from mid-October to mid-May are limited to picnic tables, fire rings, pit toilets, and a hand pump for water. *Tel. 207/288–3338. 220 tent sites, 50 RV sites, 30 sites for vans and pop-ups, and 5 accessible sites. June 15–Sept. 15: Reservations (Mistix, Box 85705, San Diego, CA 92138, tel. 800/365–2267, TDD 800/274–7275) are required and must be made no earlier than 8 weeks ahead; sites cost $13 nightly. Mid-May– mid-June and mid-Sept.–mid-Oct.: reservations on first-come, first-served basis; sites cost $11 nightly. Mid-Oct.–mid-May: first-come, first-served; sites free.*

Seawall Campground on Route 102A, 4 miles south of Southwest Harbor, across the street from the oceanfront Seawall Picnic Area, is first-come, first-served from late May until late September, and is closed the rest of the year. The walk-in sites provide more privacy than the other wooded sites, although all are attractive. Arrive here as early in the morning as possible; campsites are in high demand. Station hours are 8:30–8. *Tel. 207/288–3338. 65 tent sites, 104 walk-in tent sites, 45 RV sites, and 1 accessible site. Drive-up sites cost $11; walk-in sites are $8 nightly.*

On remote Isle au Haut, campers may stay in one of five lean-tos at **Duck Harbor Campground,** near the water, which has picnic tables, fire rings, a hand pump for drinking water, and a pit toilet. Reserve in person at the park headquarters or, beginning April 1, through the mail (Acadia National Park, Isle au Haut Reservations, Box 177, Bar Harbor 04609). Applications sent before April 1 or called in by telephone are not accepted.

NEAR THE PARK On Route 102A in Bass Harbor, just .5 mile from the Bass Harbor lighthouse, is Bass Harbor Campground, a quiet spot with 90 tent sites and 40 RV sites. Some sites are wooded, and amenities include a Laundromat, playground, heated in-ground pool, and tent and camper rentals. No dogs are allowed. The cost of sites is based on two adults (no extra charge for children) and is $16 for a tent site and $20 for a site with hookups. *Box 122, Bass Harbor 04653, tel. 207/244–5857. Open June 15–Sept. Reservations advised July and Aug.*

On Route 3 in Trenton, about 10 miles northwest of Bar Harbor in the direction of Ellsworth, **Narrows Too Camping Resort,** on the water, has 19 tent sites in a field and 120 RV sites, some with ocean views. Facilities include a heated pool, minigolf, Laundromat, showers, car rentals, hookups, a dumping station, and a shuttle-bus service into Bar Harbor. *RR 1, Box 193B, Trenton 04605, tel. 207/667–4300. $18 for 4-person tent in-season; $24.50 for basic hookup; $35 for oceanfront hookup. Reservations advised at least 1 month in advance for peak season. Open Memorial Day–Columbus Day.*

Adirondack State Park

New York

By Neal Burdick

dirondack State Park is almost too big, and too complicated, to grasp. Consider first its size. At 6.1 million acres, it's the largest U.S. park outside Alaska, occupying the greater interior of the northern third of New York State. Covering more land than any three national parks combined, it's roughly the size of Massachusetts—you could fit New Jersey in it and have room left over for Rhode Island. It takes in all or parts of 12 counties, two area codes, and more than 200 zip codes.

Consider also its location. It's within a day's drive of every Eastern Seaboard city between Washington, D.C., and Boston; a few hours from Montréal; and a few more from Detroit. Yet some of the most remote patches of wilderness east of the Rockies are here.

Finally, consider its diverse attributes. Most people associate the park with the Adirondack Mountains, but these peaks make up only a fraction of the landscape. The Adiron-dacks are at once a wilderness park and a popular resort. Tumbling rivers, secluded ponds, and the rugged shoreline of Lake Champlain, "the sixth Great Lake," are full of opportunities for fishing and boating. You'll find cross-country ski trails, crafts fairs and horse shows, scenic roads, tranquil communities, plant life rarely seen south of the tundra, and the rink where the U.S. hockey team toppled the Soviets in the 1980 Winter Olympics.

The Adirondack Park, although a state park—the only one in this book—clearly merits inclusion. However, it differs in several important ways from most public lands. Only about 47% of the park is public property; the rest is private—owned by individuals, corporations, clubs, or municipalities; you can't set foot in these sections without the owner's approval. Lake George's motel-pocked main drag is just as much a part of the park as Saddleback Mountain's soaring pines. There are no user fees and no "entrances," other than occasional road signs demarking boundaries. Park services are relatively limited. There are just two official visitor's centers, and they're both in the middle of the park, more or less.

A glance at the park's topsy-turvy history sheds dim light on some of these conundrums. Sidestepped by the westward migration, the Adirondack region was not carefully explored until the mid-1800s. Pike's Peak, Colorado, was tackled before climbers reached the Adirondacks' highest peak, Mt. Marcy. And the source of the Nile was discovered before the source of the Hudson River—again, the peak of Mt. Marcy. Once people settled the region, the sacking of its dense forests transformed New York into the nation's leading lumber state. White pines were turned into ship's masts, spruce into paper pulp, and hardwoods into either furniture or charcoal—necessary to the success of the region's secondary enterprise, iron mining.

It was predicted that the resulting deforestation would wreak havoc upon the Erie Canal, New York's commercial lifeline, whose water level depended heavily upon the Adirondack watershed. In 1885, state business leaders and solons, on the advice of America's pioneer conservationists, instituted one of the country's first measures of enlightened conservation. The legislature established the Adirondack Forest Preserve, declared it state-owned, and disallowed the removal of trees. The purpose was clear: Protect the state's business interests.

Resentful lumberers scoffed at the preserve law, inspiring the legislature to create a second layer of protection in 1892, called the Adirondack Park. The original forest preserve and much of the private land around it fell within this new designation. With loggers still disregarding these measures, however, an amendment was added to the state constitution in 1894, declaring the state-owned forest preserve portions of the park "forever wild" and rendering it unconstitutional to take down a tree on preserve lands. Subsequent alteration, such as construction of the highway to the top of Whiteface Mountain, has required state voter approval. No other wilderness area in the world enjoys such protection.

The park has grown to its present size through additions over the years. Since 1971, development on private land has been controlled by the Adirondack Park Agency.

Park and forest preserve—the distinction is important. The park comprises all land within the lopsided circular boundary called "the Blue Line." The forest preserve is the state-owned public land within the park, spread out among dozens of individual fragments. It is identified by small, usually yellow signs marked with the words FOREST PRESERVE along with that area's use classification: "Canoe Area," "Wild Forest," or "Wilderness."

ESSENTIAL INFORMATION

VISITOR INFORMATION For information on the park, contact either of two state-operated **Visitor Interpretive Centers:** the main one, near Paul Smiths (12 mi north of Saranac Lake on Rte. 30, Box 3000, Paul Smiths 12970, tel. 518/327–3000), and its smaller subsidiary in Newcomb, on Blue Ridge Road, 25 miles west of Exit 29 on I–87 (Box 101, Newcomb 12852, tel. 518/582–2000). Each center is staffed by paid naturalists and volunteers and has handouts, an orientation film, lectures and displays, and interactive computers that print out information on hiking, motels, restaurants, and more. They're open May–September 1, daily 9–7; October–April, daily 9–5.

The **New York State Department of Environmental Conservation** (DEC, 50 Wolf Rd., Albany 12233, tel. 518/474–2121) and its regional offices and public campgrounds, which exist throughout the region, distribute camping permits and information on backcountry use. Backcountry campers staying three or more days need permits; there are no other restrictions beyond those outlined in DEC brochures.

The **Adirondack Mountain Club** (ADK, RR 3, Box 3055, Lake George 12845, tel. 518/668–

4447), a nonprofit outing and education organization, runs an information center at its headquarters just inside the park. It's at Exit 21 on I–87, near Lake George, and open mid-June–mid-October, weekdays 8:30–5; late October–early June, weekdays 8:30–4:30. ADK also operates the **High Peaks Information Center** (end of Loj Rd., off Rte. 73, 9 mi south of Lake Placid, tel. 518/523–3441) at the principal trailhead in the heart of the High Peaks. The center is open daily 8–7, sometimes a bit later on weekends. It provides information on current weather and trail conditions and sells guidebooks, maps, and camping supplies.

For information on local attractions, lodgings, and restaurants, contact the many **chambers of commerce** throughout the North Country. The biggest ones are in Lake George (Rte. 9 S, tel. 518/668–5755), Lake Placid (Olympic Center, Main St., tel. 518/523–2445), Saranac Lake (30 Main St., tel. 518/891–1990), Tupper Lake (60 Park St., tel. 518/359–3328), and Old Forge (Main St., 315/866–7820).

FEES There are no backcountry camping or entrance fees. DEC campground rates are $9–$15 nightly, or $3–$5 for day use (*see* Camping, *below*).

PUBLICATIONS By far the superior comprehensive guide to the park is the 473-page *The Adirondack Book: A Complete Guide* by Elizabeth Folwell, published in 1992 by Berkshire House Publishers (Box 297, Stockbridge, MA 01262, tel. 518/298–3636) as part of its Great Destinations series. The **Adirondack North Country Association** (183 Broadway, Saranac Lake, NY 12983, tel. 518/891–6200) publishes the best road map of the park. **Plinth, Quoin & Associates** (Keene, NY 12942, tel. 518/576–9861) has a series of highly detailed maps, some for specialized purposes such as canoeing. For natural history, try the *Adirondack Wildguide,* by Michael DiNunzio, published by the Adirondack Conservancy (Box 65, Keene Valley, NY 12943, tel. 518/576–2082) and the Adirondack Council.

The **Adirondack Mountain Club** (*see* Visitor Information, *above*) publishes several guidebooks on specific park activities: seven on hiking, two on canoeing, one on rock climbing, one on winter use, and two "samplers"—*Day Hikes for All Seasons* and *Backpacking Trips*. U.S. Geological Survey topographical maps, showing trails and shelters (called "lean-tos" in the Adirondacks), accompany each of the hiking guides. The ADK also publishes *Adirondac,* which comes out six times per year as a magazine and four as a newsletter. Another fine magazine is the bimonthly full-color *Adirondack Life* (Box 97, Jay, NY 12942, tel. 518/946–2191).

GEOLOGY AND TERRAIN The Adirondack region is the only mountainous area in the eastern United States not part of the Appalachians. Instead, it's a southern appendage of the vast Canadian Shield, a base of firm granite underlying much of central Canada. Unlike the Appalachians, which are a series of long ridges, the Adirondack region is a tilted dome, with its highest elevations in the mountains of the east-central portion (imagine the dome of the U.S. Capitol canted so that its peak is well off center toward the east-northeast). Exposed rock in the Adirondacks is among the oldest in the world, having been dated at about 1.1 billion years old—nearly twice the age of the Appalachians. The landscape you see today throughout the park was shaped by several periods of heavy glaciation, the most recent just 10,000 years ago.

Most of the highest peaks occupy the east-central part of the park. On the far east, the range drops rather precipitously into Lake Champlain. The highest point, Mt. Marcy, at 5,344 feet, is only 25 miles west of Lake Champlain, which is a mere 95 feet above sea level. Within a short radius of Mt. Marcy are all 42 of the high peaks: those mountains whose elevation exceeds 4,000 feet. The highest of these, all within a few miles of Lake Placid, are rugged and rocky, with sharp profiles. The lower ones are more rounded, with forested summits. Many of the latter are officially trail-less, although unmarked "herd paths" often lead to the summits.

To the south, west, and north, the dome slopes more gradually away, characterized by gently rolling upland forests and wetlands. Elevation averages 1,000 to 2,000 feet, with the odd peak exceeding 3,000 feet. Here is the true wilderness of the park: miles of rarely traversed forest, broken frequently by ponds, streams, and bogs. It can feel as though you're in the Yukon, when in fact you're never more than 30 miles from civilization.

FLORA AND FAUNA The park's astounding variety of animal life ranges from "Champ," a cousin of the Loch Ness Monster, who may or may not live in Lake Champlain and was the subject of a 1992 *Unsolved Mysteries* episode, to moose and timber rattlesnakes. Plant life includes enormous, ancient white pines and hardy mosses and lichens clinging tenaciously to the rocks of high summits.

The Adirondacks straddle an unmarked, indistinct boundary between North America's temperate-zone forests and its northern, or boreal, habitat. The temperate forests are characterized by pines, ashes, and oaks, the boreal forests by birches, maples, spruces, and firs. These regions mingle throughout the Adirondacks, creating a vast arboretum and an especially colorful display of fall foliage.

All but a tiny fraction of the park was once heavily logged, so most of the forests are at least second-growth, and few of the trees are older than 100 years. Some antediluvian specimens do stand, but if the loggers didn't get to them you can imagine how inaccessible they are.

A hike to one of the higher peaks, or a drive to the top of Whiteface, will take you through diverse vegetation zones. As you gain altitude, you'll see smaller trees until, on the rocky, windswept summits, their presence is almost nonexistent. Generally, a gain of 1,000 feet in elevation is comparable to traveling 300 miles north; therefore, on the highest summits you're in a subarctic ecosystem.

While the existence of a true timberline in the Adirondacks is endlessly debated, these highest summits encompass a treeless world marked by such rare plants as Lapland diapensia. On the summits, you're likely to run into volunteers who will urge you to stick to the trails so as not to damage these delicate residents.

Much Adirondack wildlife is typical of that in eastern woodlands: Chipmunks raid picnic grounds, and black bears (harmless unless famished or cornered) hang around campsites. The significant whitetail-deer population presents a concern to drivers, especially in the evening.

Among species not found farther south are two that for many visitors define the Adirondack wilderness experience: the moose and the loon. Moose, having been wiped out by hunters 125 years ago, are reintroducing themselves as herds farther north outgrow their ranges. The loon, with its haunting cry and aura of mystery, is a common if reclusive denizen of backcountry ponds.

The bald eagle has also been reintroduced. These magnificent creatures, while not numerous, are sometimes seen perched in tall trees along lakeshores or soaring on thermal currents above cliffs.

The Adirondacks, long known for sport fishing, have lately felt the effects of overharvesting and acid rain. You can still catch trophy-size fish in a few places; however, you'll never get anyone to tell you where these places are.

WHEN TO GO Ten of the 13 major U.S. storm tracks pass over the Adirondacks, so the weather has a way of making itself known. Lousy spells are tough to predict, but they seldom last long. The first frost traditionally hits around Labor Day, the last around Memorial Day. The all-time coldest temperature in New York State (-52°F) has been measured in the park; semiofficial lows of -60°F have been reported. On the other end of the scale, the temperature has never officially reached 100°F in the region.

Though it is a park for all seasons, most visitors come in summer, the only season when many tourist attractions are open. Summer temperatures range from 80°F daily highs to 55°F nightly lows; humidity is sometimes a problem. Lake George and Lake Placid bear the brunt of summer's gridlock; they're especially crowded in July and August. The visitor's centers can steer you away from overcrowded destinations.

By Labor Day the crowds thin, but the weather remains hospitable, with daytime highs in the 60s. Foliage is as bright as any in New England, usually peaking during the last week in September. After that the thermometer plummets, usually to below freezing at night.

Winter sees great fluctuation in temperature. Highs are about 20°F, and lows of 0°F are common—although cold spells with highs below 0°F and lows of -40°F alternate with rare thaws that may see daytime highs in the mid-40s. This is the season for winter sports: The deepest snows in the east make for excellent downhill and cross-country skiing and snowmobiling.

Few people other than anglers come in the spring, partly because there isn't one. Snow, or its effects, can last through May—later in the high country. Summer then kicks in a few weeks later. Locals refer to the time in between as "mud season."

These generalizations about the weather apply to the lowland areas of the park. High peaks often see severe winter conditions from September through June.

SEASONAL EVENTS Lake Placid, with its world-class winter sports facilities, hosts sporting events throughout the year—you can even watch ski jumping on the Fourth of July. Other activities include freestyle-skiing championships, bobsled races, the best college hockey in the country, and figure-skating and ice-dancing competitions. Call 800/462–6236 for schedules.

Late January–early February: Winter festivals in many communities feature snow sculpture contests, broomball games, snowmobile or cross-country ski races, and a parade. The most famous is in Saranac Lake, where you can enter a giant ice castle, one of the few still built with ice actually cut from a nearby lake (tel. 518/891–1990). **First week-**

end in May: The **Hudson River Whitewater Derby** at North Creek (tel. 518/207–2612) brings some of the world's best canoeists and kayakers to test the rampaging spring runoff. **Mid-July:** Lake Placid's "I Love New York" Horse Show (tel. 518/523–1655) draws top U.S. show jumpers; next door, ski jumpers and freestyle skiers practice on artificial snow off the 70-meter and 90-meter Olympic ski jumps. **Late July: Woodsmen's Days** in Tupper Lake celebrate the region's logging heritage with competitions in ax-throwing, chainsaw sculpture, log rolling, and more. **Early August:** Westport's **Essex County Fair** (tel. 518/434–1214) is a classic of its kind. It's small enough to be accessible, and the setting—in a gingerbread-Victorian town on one of Lake Champlain's scenic little bays—is calendar-like. **Early October:** The event billed as the **World's Largest Garage Sale** (tel. 518/623–2161) takes place in Warrensburg, in the southeastern corner of the park. One caveat: The traffic it generates would overflow the world's largest garage.

WHAT TO PACK If you're going to stay in motels and go to amusement parks, you needn't haul along anything other than the usual vacation garb. The one exception might be warm jackets and sweaters; evenings and rainy days can be quite cool, even in midsummer. High-country hikers should prepare year-round for a sudden deterioration of weather by packing a warm sweater and hat, foul-weather gear, first-aid equipment, fire starters, flashlights, and good maps. If camping overnight, bring a water filter or purification pills; *Giardia* contamination, which causes the dreaded "beaver fever," is common up here. Do not drink water directly from streams or lakes, even in the backcountry. Illness, sometimes severe, and death can result.

ARRIVING AND DEPARTING You'll need a car once you get here, so you might as well arrive in one. Train, bus, and plane service is available into or near the park, but car rentals inside the park are few and far between.

By Plane. Adirondack Airport, near Saranac Lake, Tupper Lake, and Lake Placid, has flights to and from Albany on **Commutair** (tel. 800/428–4322), a puddle-jumper subsidiary of USAir Express. At press time, there are three round-trip flights on weekdays, one on Sunday, none on Saturday. Daily except Saturday, you can rent a car at the airport (Hertz, tel. 518/891–4075).

Peripheral cities with major airports and a full range of car rentals are Albany and Syracuse, New York, and Burlington, Vermont. Commuter service is also offered to Watertown International Airport (tel. 315/639–6247) and Plattsburgh's Clinton County Airport (tel. 518/565–4795).

By Car. Principal highway access is on I–87, also called the Northway. The main link between New York City and Montréal, it runs between the mountains and Lake Champlain, along the eastern edge of the park, for 90 scenic miles. Other main routes are, from the Midwest or Boston, I–90; from northern New England, I–89 to the Lake Champlain ferry crossings in Grand Isle, Burlington, and Charlotte, Vermont; from Ontario and the northern Midwest, Highway 401 in Ontario to the St. Lawrence River toll-bridge crossings in Alexandria Bay, Ogdensburg, and Massena, New York; from points of New York State, I–88 and I–81.

New York City is about four to five hours from the park boundary and about six or seven hours from Lake Placid. From I–87, take Exit 21 for Lake George, Exit 23 for Warrensburg, Exit 29 for the Newcomb Visitor Interpretive Center, or Exit 30 for Lake Placid and Saranac Lake.

Other times to Lake Placid from major cities are: Montréal, two hours (plus possible border delays); Buffalo, six hours; Boston, six hours; Philadelphia, eight hours; Detroit, 10 hours; Washington, D.C., 11 hours.

Main roads in the park are mostly two-lane and in good to excellent condition. Aside from the occasional hamlet or log truck chugging along in front of you, it's possible to cruise along at 55 miles per hour with little trouble. Principal north–south roads are Routes 9N, 22, and 9, all in the eastern corridor and listed in order of their scenic appeal and historic interest, and Route 30, which splits the park in two from Amsterdam to Malone. The wild western part of the park has no major north–south roads. Main east–west roads are Route 28, which arcs from Warrensburg up to Blue Mountain Lake and back down to Utica; Route 8, which zigzags from Lake George to Utica; and Route 3, which runs from Plattsburgh to Watertown via Saranac Lake, Tupper Lake, and Cranberry Lake.

By Train. Amtrak (tel. 800/872–7245) operates one train daily through the eastern part of the park. Like I–87, *The Adirondack* connects New York (Penn Station) and Montréal. This route, at times carved out of sheer cliffs plunging into Lake Champlain, is one of the most scenic train rides in America. It's best to disembark in Westport; you can arrange ahead for a shuttle to Lake Placid or nearby towns through Lake Placid Sightseeing (tel. 518/523–4431). The New York City–Westport fare is $60 one-way. Amtrak also serves nearby Albany, Utica, and Syracuse several times daily with its Empire (New York State) service, and with Toronto–New York City, Chicago–New York City, and Chicago–Boston trains. Car rentals in all three cities are available from **Hertz** (tel. 800/654–3131) and **Avis** (tel. 800/331–1212). Gore Mountain and Whiteface ski areas offer complete packages from several northeastern cities (tel. 800/333–3454).

By Bus. Adirondack Trailways (tel. 212/947–5300) runs daily between New York City and the Adirondacks. This local service stops virtually everywhere, including Lake George, Keene Valley, Lake Placid, and Saranac Lake. There's also weekends-only service to Tupper Lake and summer-only runs along Lake George to Ticonderoga. **Greyhound** (tel. 518/434–8095) has service from Albany to Montréal, with stops in Glens Falls and Plattsburgh, the park's southern and northern gateway cities, respectively. **CHAMP Express** (tel. 518/523–4431) connects Lake Placid and the Plattsburgh Greyhound station.

EXPLORING

It's impossible to explore the entire park in a short period—it's bigger than Vermont, remember. Acadia National Park has a loop road that orients you to its wonders in a few minutes; even if such a road existed in the Adirondacks, it would take about 10 hours, nonstop, to circumnavigate it. Your best bet is to pick a small part of the park and get to know it. It may be the High Peaks around Lake Placid, or the resort and dude ranch country of Lake George, or the wilderness lakes and ponds of the northwest backcountry; but familiarizing yourself with small sections at a time will be more satisfying than trying to comprehend the whole in one bite. Getting to know the Adirondacks thoroughly could involve several days in museums if your interest is in human history, or several days on the trails and canoe routes if you wish to understand the natural history.

THE BEST IN ONE DAY It'll be a very long day, but if it's all you have, enter the park heading from I–87, taking Exit 30 to Lake Placid via Routes 9 and 73. Between here and Lake Placid you'll navigate a couple of dramatic deep passes (called "notches" in the Adirondacks), drive through the picturesque hamlets of Keene and Keene Valley, and view such high peaks as Whiteface (4,867 feet), Algonquin (5,114 feet), and Marcy (5,344 feet). In Lake Placid, do some window-shopping and have lunch at the Artist's Cafe (*see* Dining, *below*).

From Lake Placid take Route 86 through Saranac Lake to Paul Smiths then turn right onto Route 30 for the visitor's center. After a brief orientation stop here, take Route 30 south through Tupper Lake, Long Lake, and Indian Lake. This is the core of the Adirondacks, where logging and hunting are more common pursuits than retailing and skiing. You'll also be in the wettest part of the park, where ponds and lakes pop up around almost every turn.

In Indian Lake, take Route 28, which gradually descends along the banks of the upper Hudson River, past signs advertising whitewater rafting and rustic-furniture making.

You'll reach I–87 at Warrensburg, about 45 miles south of where you exited I–87 earlier in the day. Drive this tour in late June; you'll need all the daylight you can get.

ORIENTATION PROGRAMS The **Visitor Interpretive Centers** and the **Adirondack Mountain Club** (*see* Visitor Information *in* Essential Information, *above*) conduct educational programs year-round, appropriate to each season. Topics range from animal-track identification to minimum-impact camping, from park history to beginning snowshoeing. The **Adirondack Museum** (tel. 518/352–7311) and the **Adirondack Center Museum** (tel. 518/873–6466) also have seasonal lectures and demonstrations (*see* Historic Buildings and Sites, *below*).

GUIDED TOURS **North Country Tours** (Box 210, Lake George 12845, tel. 800/743–6278) offers one- to four-day bus tours, popular especially with senior citizens. **Lake Placid Sightseeing** (Hilton Plaza, Lake Placid 12946, tel. 518/523–4431) provides bus and van tours of historic and sports sites around Lake Placid. The cost is $18 adults, $17 senior citizens, and $14 children.

If you plan on roughing it, the following services can provide guides. For fishing, try **Jones Outfitters** (37 Main St., Lake Placid 12946, tel. 518/523–3468). For wilderness hiking, try **Middle Earth Expeditions** (Cascade Rd., Lake Placid 12946, tel. 518/523–9572) and **Tahawus Guide Service and Backcountry Outfitters** (Rte. 86, Ray Brook 12977, tel. 518/891–4334). For white-water rafting, try **Hudson River Rafting Co.** (Cunningham's Ski Barn, Lake Placid 12946, tel. 800/888–7238). A directory of licensed guides, most of whom work in the Adirondacks, is available from the **New York State Outdoor Guides Association** (Box 916, Saranac Lake 12983, no tel.).

SCENIC DRIVES AND VIEWS The best views of mountains are along **Route 73** from Exit 30 off I–87 to Lake Placid; **Route 86** from Jay—which has a classic covered bridge—past Whiteface Mountain to Lake Placid, Saranac Lake, and Paul Smiths; **Route 9N** from Eliza-

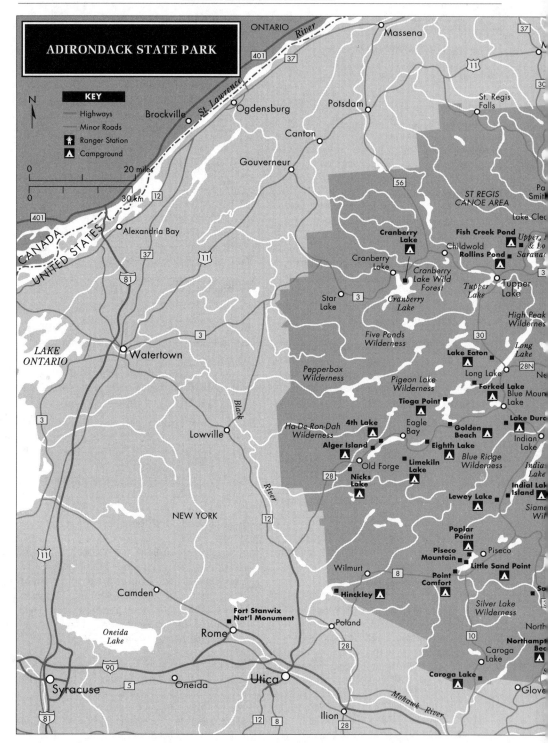

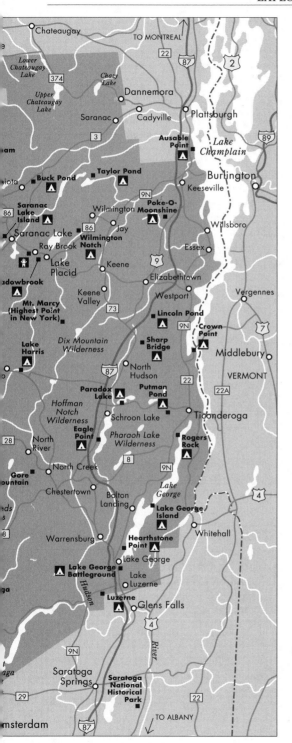

bethtown to Keene; and **Route 28N** from Long Lake to Newcomb.

The best views *from* mountains are along the **Prospect Mountain Veterans Memorial Highway** (open May–Oct., $5 per car), which allows commanding views of Lake George; and along **Whiteface Mountain Veterans Memorial Highway** (open May–Oct., $4 adults, $3 students, senior citizens, and children), which runs to within a few yards of the fifth-highest Adirondack peak. Here you'll have a 360° view of the park, the Champlain and St. Lawrence valleys, Vermont, and even Montréal, Canada.

The best lake drives are **Route 9N,** from Lake George to Ft. Ticonderoga, from which you'll see the length of Lake George; **Route 22** from Ticonderoga to Willsboro, from which you'll see Lake Champlain and its valley, as well as several historic towns; **Route 374** from Chateaugay to Plattsburgh, from which you'll see the Chateaugay lakes, Chazy Lake, and Lake Champlain, as well as long-distance panoramas of the Adirondack peaks and Vermont's Green Mountains; **Route 3** to **Route 30** to **Route 28,** past Saranac, Tupper, Long, Blue Mountain, and Indian lakes; and **Route 28** from Blue Mountain Lake to Old Forge to see the Eckford and Fulton chains.

You'll see pastoral river valleys and villages from **Route 9N** and **Route 73,** between Keeseville and Keene Valley. **Route 3,** from Tupper Lake to the western edge of the park; **Route 56,** from Sevey's Corner on Route 3 to the park's northern boundary; **Route 30,** just about anywhere; and **Stillwater and Big Moose roads,** from Eagle Bay to the park's western boundary near Lowville, all offer miles and miles of dense woods. About half of the latter trip is on unpaved road, but a ride on these roads gives the truest sense of Adirondack wilderness.

HISTORIC BUILDINGS AND SITES Preserved homes of many prominent early Adirondack citizens are open to the public, often under the auspices of local historical societies.

Ft. Ticonderoga, on Route 22 in the southeastern quadrant of the park, is beautifully restored to its Revolutionary War grandeur. It's the site of one of America's legendary moments, when Ethan Allen and his Green Mountain Boys took the fort from the British, without a shot, "in the name of the Great Jehovah and the Continental Congress." Other nearby fort remnants, near Lake George and on Crown Point, recall the 17th and 18th centuries, when the Champlain–Hudson corridor was North America's principal battleground, a legacy recounted in James Fenimore Cooper's *The Last of the Mohicans.* *Rte. 22, Ft. Ticonderoga, tel. 518/585–2821. Admission: $7 adults, $5 children 10–13, under 10 free. Open early May–mid-Oct., daily 9–5.*

John Brown's Farm, near Lake Placid, is where the famous abolitionist's "body lies a-molderin' in his grave." He and his associates tried unsuccessfully to establish a community of freed slaves here in the 1850s. The grounds are open year-round, the buildings from May through October, free of charge. *John Brown Rd., south of town off Rte. 73, across from horse-show grounds, tel. 518/523–3900.*

In Saranac Lake, stop by the **Robert Louis Stevenson Cottage,** where the famed British novelist wrote much of *The Master of Ballantrae.* In search of respite from tuberculosis, he wound up enduring the unusually harsh winter of 1887–88. *Stevenson Lake, off Pine St., tel. 518/891–1990. Donation: $1 adults, 50¢ children under 12. Open July–Sept. 15, Tues.–Sun. 9:30–noon and 1–4:30.*

The Gilded Age saw construction of so-called "Great Camps" in the Adirondacks. These were actually multibuilding retreats constructed by some of the giants of industry and commerce of that era. Several survive, and one, **Sagamore,** is open for tours. It was owned by the Vanderbilts for 50 years. *Off Rte. 28 at Raquette Lake, near center of park, tel. 315/354–5311. Admission: $6 adults, $3 children 5–12. Open July 4–Labor Day, twice daily for tours; Labor Day–Columbus Day, weekends.*

The **Adirondack Museum,** a magnificent 22-building complex, is by far the best such facility in the park. It contains a top-notch art gallery, one of the largest collections of freshwater boats in America, dioramas and exhibits on the human and natural story, photo archives, and several period structures. Lectures and demonstrations are given, too. *Blue Mountain Lake, tel. 518/352–7311. Admission: $10 adults, $7 children 7–16, under 7 free; maximum $26 per family. Open Memorial Day–Oct. 15, daily 9:30–5:30.*

Exhibits of logging, conservation, pioneer living and related aspects of the region's history, as well as lectures on these subjects, are also presented at the **Adirondack Center Museum.** Its 19th-century formal garden offers a pleasant change of pace. *Main St. (U.S. 9), Elizabethtown, tel. 518/873–6466. Admission: $3.50 adults, $2.50 senior citizens, $1.50 students. Open Mid-May–mid-Oct., Mon.–Sat. 9–5, Sun. 1–5.*

At the **Six Nations Museum,** Native American founder and curator Ray Fadden discusses native cultures and gives tours of his personal collection of artifacts. Fadden, who also conducts lectures and gives demonstrations, is part and parcel of the museum. *Buck Pond Campsite Rd., Onchiota, tel. 518/891–0769. Admission: $2 adults, $1 children under 16. Open July–Aug., daily 10–6; Memorial Day–June and Sept. by appointment only.*

NATURE TRAILS AND SHORT WALKS There are literally hundreds of these throughout the Adirondacks. Each visitor's center has a network of signed trails that can be hiked, skied, or snowshoed in 30 minutes to three hours. Trails radiating from the **Adirondack Mountain Club's Heart Lake trailhead/High Peaks Information Center** (*see* Visitor Information *in* Essential Information, *above*) offer a range of distances and difficulties.

The 5-mile round-trip **Hurricane Mountain Trail** offers some of the best summit views for the least effort. Begin on Route 9N between Keene and Elizabethtown, 3.6 miles east of its split from Route 73. The panorama incorporates dozens of other mountain views, the Champlain Valley, and Vermont. Blueberries are free for the picking in August.

Another easy climb is the 2-mile round-trip **Bald Mountain Trail,** which takes you through deciduous and then spruce-fir forest to an open summit with great views of nearby lakes and distant mountains. Begin on Rondaxe Road, .2 mile off Route 28, 4.5 miles north of the tourist information center in Old Forge.

The **Cathedral Pines Trail,** on Route 28 near the state's Eighth Lake Public Campsite, near Raquette Lake, though only .1 mile long, is an enchanting walk through soaring old-growth white pines, the likes of which are rarely seen in the East.

The **Charles Lathrop Pack Demonstration Forest Nature Trail,** on U.S. 9, just north of its junction with Route 28, loops for about 1.5 miles through mixed forest past a wide variety of flora.

The 1.5-mile **Warren County Parks and Recreation Nature Trail** passes 29 marked points of ecological interest along the Hudson River. Pick up a pamphlet, which explains what you're seeing along the trail, at the trailhead on River Road, 2.5 miles north of Route 9 at Warrensburg's center.

To take the two most dramatic river-related hikes you must pay admission, since they're operated as tourist attractions by private companies. At **Ausable Chasm,** after passing through the souvenir-stocked entrance building, you can walk a .75-mile trail down into the spectacular gorge known for its fascinating rock formations, which were gouged out by the Great Ausable River. At the end of the trail you climb into a boat piloted by an experienced and knowledgeable guide for an exciting .75-mile ride down the churning river; boats depart whenever enough people arrive to fill them, which usually is every few minutes. The last leg of the adventure is a bus ride back to the starting point. *U.S. 9, 2 mi north of Keeseville, tel. 518/834-7454. Admission: $11.95 adults, $9.95 senior citizens, $7.50 children. Open Memorial Day–mid-Oct. daily 9–4.*

The trek through **High Falls Gorge** is a self-guided, half-mile, round-trip walk on bridges and paths past three waterfalls plunging 700 feet into a rock-strewn gorge; it should take about 45 minutes. *Route 86 between Wilmington and Lake Placid. Admission: $4.95 adults, $3.95 senior citizens, $2 children 12–17, $1.50 children 4–11. Open Memorial Day–Columbus Day.*

LONGER HIKES The hundreds of miles of Adirondack trails are carefully maintained by the state DEC. The visitor's centers have excellent information on longer hikes, as do several useful books (*see* Publications *in* Essential Information, *above*). Touch-screen computers at the visitor's centers can recommend hikes of varying duration. If you plan to venture into the high country, check forecasts before you set out. Life-threatening weather occurs year-round, and there can be snow on the summits in the High Peaks in any month.

An easy 7-mile round-trip on the **Phelps Trail** proceeds through the Johns Brook Valley to **Johns Brook Lodge** (no tel., but tel. 518/523–3441 for information), a rustic hut run by the Adirondack Mountain Club. Begin this hike at the Garden, a parking area 2 miles off Route 73 in Keene Valley; follow the signs for the trail to Mt. Marcy. The trail undulates through pleasant, mixed, mature forest, crossing several small brooks before hugging the shore of Johns Brook for the last half-mile to the lodge.

The strenuous 16-mile round-trip **Tongue Mountain Trail** will afford you splendid views of Lake George, considered by many the most beautiful lake in America, thanks to its steep forested shores, the many islands that dot its surface, and the mountains that ring it. Begin at the Clay Meadow trailhead on Route 9N, 13 miles north of Lake George village. There is a less demanding hike that departs from the same trailhead and hugs Lake George's Northwest Bay shoreline for 5.5 miles.

Mt. Marcy is the highest and most popular peak in the park; consequently, its trails are the most trampled. There are better, less crowded trails, but if you must climb Marcy, the easiest of three routes begins at the Adirondack Mountain Club's High Peaks Information Center at the end of Loj Road, off Route 73, east of Lake Placid. The round-trip is 15 miles.

You'll have a better time climbing the second-highest peak, **Algonquin,** whose trail branches off from Mt. Marcy's. It's just 8 miles up and back, but it's much steeper. From the summit you'll have spectacular views of many of the Adirondacks' highest peaks to the east, of Lake Placid far below, and across the vast forest-and-pond country rolling away to the west and northwest. On top you'll be in an arctic ecosystem dominated by rare and fragile plant life; observe it closely, but do not stray from the marked trail.

Among less demanding climbs with great views are **Ampersand Mountain,** a 5.5-mile round-trip from Route 3, 8 miles west of Saranac Lake; **St. Regis Mountain,** a 5-mile round-trip from just near the Paul Smiths Visitor Interpretive Center; and **Pharaoh Mountain,** a 6-mile round-trip from the Crane Pond trailhead 6.5 miles east of Schroon Lake, Exit 27 off I–87.

If you're a serious long-distance hiker, try tackling the **Northville–Placid Trail,** a 132-mile footpath that bisects the park north–south. "End-to-enders" usually take 10 to 15 days, camping in lean-tos. You can hike segments of this relatively level trail, which crosses three major roads: Route 8 near Piseco, Route 30 near Blue Mountain Lake, and Route 28N near Long Lake. The **Adirondack Mountain Club** (*see* Visitor Information *in* Essential Information, *above*) has a guidebook devoted exclusively to this trail.

OTHER ACTIVITIES **Biking.** Though designated wilderness areas are off-limits to mountain bikes, more than 1,000 miles of old logging roads and abandoned railroad beds lure cyclists. The park's main roads are also excellent for bicycling, with wide shoulders and relatively little traffic. **High Peaks Cyclery/Adirondack Bicycle Tours** (13 Saranac Ave., Lake Placid, tel. 518/523–2752) rents bikes and arranges guided and self-guided tours; **Sundog Ski & Sport** (90 Main St., Lake Placid, tel. 518/523–2752) offers guided

mountain-bike tours. The **Adirondack Mountain Club** (tel. 518/668–4447) and the **Adirondack North Country Association** (tel. 518/891–6200) sell a list of mountain-bike trails on the park's state lands.

Boating. Larger lakes (George, Placid, Long, Cranberry, and the Fulton chain) have marinas and liveries that rent canoes and motorboats. Try **Ward's Marina** (Rte. 9N, Hague, tel. 518/543–8888) for Lake George; **Captain Marney's Boat Rentals** (3 Victor Herbert Dr., Lake Placid, tel. 518/523–9746) for Lake Placid; and **St. Regis Canoe Outfitters** (Floodwood Rd., Lake Clear, tel. 518/891–1838) for St. Regis Lake. Sailing is popular on Lake Champlain, which has the advantages of a large water surface and plenty of wind. Iceboating enthusiasts convene on Lake George. Canoeists favor the network of ponds in the St. Regis Canoe Area, which is off limits to motorized vessels; the Bog River southwest of Tupper Lake; and the Raquette River between Tupper Lake and Long Lake (actually a widening of the river).

Bobsledding and Luging. If you really want to get your blood flowing, try North America's only public bobsled-and-luge runs, built at the Mt. Van Hoevenberg complex (*see* Snowshoeing and Cross-Country Skiing, *below*) for the 1980 Winter Olympics. Here, when conditions are right, you can go down the serpentine bobsled runs with a professional driver ($25 per person per ride; Tues.–Sun. 2–4). You're mostly on your own when you do a luge run, the closest thing to supersonic sledding ($15 per person; weekends 2–4). Definitely not for the timid.

Downhill Skiing. The biggest area is **Whiteface** (tel. 800/462–6236)—of Olympics fame—near Lake Placid; **Gore Mountain** (tel. 518/251–2411), near North Creek, has a gondola and is popular with families. Smaller local areas include **Big Tupper** (tel. 518/359–7902), just outside Tupper Lake, and **McCauley Mountain** (tel. 315/369–3225), near Old Forge. All areas have snowmaking capability.

Fishing. Famous trout streams include the East and West branches of the Ausable River, reachable from Routes 9N and 86, respectively; the Boquet River, south of Elizabethtown off U.S. 9; the South and Middle branches of the Saranac River, accessible from Route 3; the Little Salmon, Salmon, Little Trout, and Trout rivers in Franklin County; and the Chateaugay River off Route 374. Tupper Lake and the Saranac Lakes are noted for northern pike and bass, and the rivers that run into Lake Champlain see fall-spawning runs of landlocked Atlantic salmon. Lake Colby, Upper Saranac Lake, and Lake Clear, all in the Saranac Lake vicinity, also yield creels of salmon, as does Lake George.

There are plenty of fishing guides in the Adirondacks; just look in the Yellow Pages of any local telephone directory. In the High Peaks area, Jones Outfitters (37 Main St., Lake Placid, tel. 518/523–3468) can supply guides. One of them, Bob Hudak (tel. 518/523–3577), also works independently, taking parties of up to three people on single- and multiple-day trips on rivers in the northeastern quadrant of the park. In Saranac Lake, Brian McDonnell (McDonnell's Adirondack Challenges, tel. 518/891–1176) goes after brook trout, lake trout, and bass on canoe trips lasting anywhere from a day to a month, on backcountry ponds within an hour of Saranac Lake. Working with 15 other guides, he keeps the guide-to-client ratio at 1:3. Francis Betters (Rte. 86, Wilmington, tel. 518/946–2605) will introduce you not only to good fishing in the High Peaks but to good tall tales. The Warren County Department of Tourism (tel. 518/761–6366) can supply a list of guides in the Lake George area. Sportfishing Charters (tel. 518/793–7396) operates guided five-hour trips on Lake George from April through November.

The DEC has several fishing hot lines that provide up-to-date information on conditions. Call 518/891–5413 for the Lake Placid region, 518/623–3682 for Lake George, or 315/782–2663 for the western part of the park.

Horseback Riding. In the High Peaks area, **Wilson's Livery Stable** (at the Bark Eater Inn,

Keene, tel. 518/576–2221) has guided trail rides, tours, and lessons year-round. The hub of equestrianism in the park, however, is Warren County. Head west out of Lake George toward Lake Luzerne on Route 9N and you'll pass dude ranches, rodeos, and stables enough to make you think you're in Wyoming, including Ridin Hy Ranch Resort (Sherman Lake, Warrensburg, tel. 518/494–2742) and 1000 Acres Ranch Resort (Rte. 418, Stony Creek, tel. 518/696–2444).

Rafting. The upper Hudson River, famed for the volume of logs it once carried out of the mountains, is better known today for the number of rafters it floats downstream each spring and summer. Several outfitters in the North River–North Creek area along Route 28 offer guided trips. Try **Whitewater Challengers** (tel. 800/443–7238), **Wildwaters Outdoor Center** (tel. 518/494–7478), and **Hudson River Rafting Co.** (tel. 518/251–3215). The latter also runs trips on streams on the periphery of the park, such as the Black River, near Watertown.

Rock Climbing. The High Peaks region is a mecca among climbers in the East; such names as Wallface, Pok-o-Moonshine, and Chapel Pond are legendary. The **Adirondack Mountain Club** (tel. 518/523–3441) sponsors climbing workshops at Adirondack Loj, a rustic lodge named by a 19th-century advocate of phonetic spelling. For guided expeditions, try **Adirondack Rock and River Guide Service** (Keene, tel. 518/576–2041) and **Alpine Adventures** (Keene, tel. 518/576–9881).

Snowmobiling. Old Forge, in the southwestern quadrant of the park, and Cranberry and Star lakes, in the northwest, are hubs of snowmobiling. Old Forge is known especially for its miles of marked trails and heavy snowfall. The **Old Forge Tourist Information Center** (tel. 315/369–6983) and **Cranberry Lake/Star Lake Chamber of Commerce** (tel. 315/848–2900) have information on rentals and guided tours.

Snowshoeing and Cross-Country Skiing. Most Adirondack hiking trails, except those in the High Peaks, are great for novice snowshoers and cross-country skiers. The **Paul**

Smiths Visitor Interpretive Center trails are ideal for cross-country skiing; there's also a trail designated for snowshoeing at the Newcomb center. The trail network at the **Adirondak Loj** (tel. 518/523–3441) is the best way to check out the High Peaks backcountry; parking is $6 per day and rentals, trail information, and instruction are available.

You don't have to be an expert to tackle the trails the 1980 Olympians used at **Mt. Van Hoevenberg** (Rte. 73 east of Lake Placid, tel. 518/523–4436); the center is open daily 9–4 in season, and tickets are $9 adults, $8 senior citizens and children 5–12 ($6 to all after 1:30). Nearby on Route 73 is the **Cascade Ski Touring Center** (tel. 518/523–9605), with a network of trails for those with less than first-class ability; equipment can be rented at the lodge. The 24-mile **Jackrabbit Trail,** maintained by the Adirondack Ski Touring Council (tel. 518/523–1365), connects Keene, Lake Placid, and Saranac Lake; named for "Jackrabbit" Johanson, a pioneer of recreational Nordic skiing, it challenges those with experience and endurance but has several spurs to roads that put it within the ability of intermediate skiers.

Outside the Lake Placid area, there are two outstanding cross-country ski centers: **Garnet Hill Lodge** (Thirteenth Lake Rd., North River, tel. 518/251–2821), with 37 miles of groomed trails, and **Lapland Lake** (RD 2, Box 2053, Northville, tel. 518/863–4974), with 27 miles of groomed trails.

CHILDREN'S PROGRAMS Other than programs at the visitor's interpretive centers covering such topics as wildflower and animal-track identification, there is little in the park specifically geared toward kids. The Adirondacks are, however, home to several examples of that childhood nirvana: the theme park. At **Santa's Workshop** (tel. 518/946–2211), just before the Whiteface Memorial Highway tollbooth near Wilmington, you'll be entertained by Santa and the reindeer; there are also rides, shows, and "workshops," where you can watch local craftspeople at work. Lake George's **Great Escape Fun Park** (tel. 518/792–3500) is New York State's largest theme park, with live shows, water rides, roller coasters, and all the rest. These diversions are open from Memorial Day to early fall.

EVENING ACTIVITIES The performing and visual arts thrive in the Adirondacks, especially in summer. **Pendragon Theater** (148 River St., Saranac Lake, tel. 518/891–1854) stages contemporary drama. The **Lake Placid Center for the Arts** (tel. 518/523–2512) presents theater, music, dance, film, and art exhibits. Both are open year-round. The **Lake Placid Sinfonietta** (tel. 518/523–2051), a small professional orchestra, performs in July and August, often in a bandshell overlooking Mirror Lake. The **Adirondack Lakes Center for the Arts** (tel. 518/352–7715) in Blue Mountain Lake presents crafts workshops, classical-music concerts, folk festivals, and plays.

DINING

There are literally hundreds of options, from fast-food outlets (the ubiquitous golden arches loom over nine Adirondack towns) and coffee shops to sophisticated restaurants presided over by Continental chefs, and ethnic eateries—Chinese, Mexican, Greek. And we won't even attempt to discuss all the options near the park. The following suggestions hardly even scratch the surface; you can learn more from chambers of commerce and tourist offices, and by keeping your eyes and ears open in the various communities.

CENTRAL ADIRONDACKS **Big Moose Inn.** You find a lot of Adirondack flavor at this chef-owned, off-the-beaten-track restaurant and cocktail lounge overlooking the lake. A fireplace warms things up when the weather's chilly, and tables are set up outside when it's fine. Homemade breads, soups, and desserts, as well as prime rib, veal, and lamb dishes are the draws. Specialties include Australian cold-water lobster tails and rack of lamb, marinated in herbs, Dijon mustard, and garlic. The restaurant also serves pasta and vegetarian dishes. Wines are vintage, and the daily specials are a good buy. *5 mi from Rte. 28, Eagle Bay, tel. 315/357–2042. Reservations* advised. Dress: casual but neat. AE, MC, V. Closed Apr. and weekdays Nov.–Christmas. Expensive.

Eckerson's. Long lines testify to the popularity of this roadside restaurant. Like many structures in the Adirondacks, the building has little to distinguish it, but the evident pleasure of people enjoying good food, made and served without frills, is unmistakable. Try the Angus-beef prime rib, New York strip steak, and filet mignon. *Rte. 28, Eagle Bay, tel. 315/357–4641. Reservations not accepted. Dress: casual. MC, V. Closed Easter week; Tues. in June and Sept.; Nov.; and sporadically during off-season, especially when there is no snow. Moderate.*

Old Mill Restaurant. The huge mill wheel that dominates the front of this restaurant on Old Forge's main street recalls the building's original function. No one seems to mind the dark, somewhat gloomy interior, especially once the substantial, thoroughly American food arrives: steaks; seafood simply prepared; chicken breast stuffed with Swiss cheese, spinach, vermouth, and garlic; and home-baked bread. In summer, dining is outdoors and very relaxed. *Rte. 28, Old Forge, tel. 315/369–3662. Dress: casual. MC, V. Closed Apr., Nov. Moderate.*

Van Auken's Inn. In this inn, in a restored historic building fronted by large white columns and two levels of porches, the dining room recalls the region's lumbering days with its 19th-century decorated tin ceilings, hardwood floors, and walls punctuated by oil paintings. The Taylor family, which owns the inn, is dedicated to good food, and the menu ranges from steak au poivre and roast duck in raspberry sweet-and-sour sauce to roast pork tenderloin in raspberry-pepper sauce. *Off Rte. 28, Old Forge, tel. 315/369–3033. Reservations advised. Dress: casual. MC, V. Closed Apr. and sporadically first 2 wks Nov. Moderate.*

Cobblestone. An Adirondack ambience prevails in this family-run restaurant. The restaurant has two dining rooms: One is big, airy, and carpeted, with dark blue walls and floral patterns; the other has paneled walls and wood rafters. The service is generally good, and the menu includes everything from chicken wings and pizza to broiled steak and seafood. *Rte. 30, Long Lake, tel. 518/624–6331. Reservations not accepted. Dress: casual. AE, D, DC, MC, V. No lunch mid-Oct.–May. Inexpensive.*

LAKE GEORGE AREA **The Algonquin.** Guests of this restaurant, a local favorite for more than 30 years, arrive by boat as often as by car. The paneled Pub Room downstairs, which has heavy wood beams overhead and a slate floor under foot, offers burgers, sandwiches, and other light fare. Topside, the dining room, has pastel-color walls and elegant windows and is the perfect setting for meals based on excellent beef and seafood dishes, such as filet mignon Danish style (done with blue cheese and Bermuda-onion sauce) and Greek shrimp (with a sauce of fresh tomatoes, scallions, feta cheese, and sherry). The front tables in both rooms offer splendid views of the lake; weather permitting, there's dining and entertainment outdoors on the decks. *Lake Shore Dr., Bolton Landing, tel. 518/644–9442. Reservations required for Topside. Dress: casual but neat. AE, D, DC, MC, V. Closed weekdays Dec.–Apr. and mid-Oct.–early Dec. Expensive.*

Mario's. Many local food lovers call this the best Italian restaurant between Albany and Montréal. Outside, it's a sizable, white-clapboard building of no particular distinction; inside, it's a stucco-wall Italian villa full of red velvet, archways, and imitation Renaissance statues and paintings—with all of the appropriate aromas. Try the veal ossobuco, veal scaloppine Marsala, or shrimp scampi alla Mario, served in garlic wine over rice or fresh pasta. *469 Canada St., Lake George, tel. 518/668–2665. Reservations advised Sun. and holidays. Dress: casual. AE, DC, MC, V. Closed Nov. Moderate.*

LAKE PLACID AREA **Charcoal Pit.** The main dining room of this chef-owned restaurant has a fireplace, hanging plants, high ceilings, walls full of paintings, and big windows on two sides. The veal and seafood are particularly well done, and the menu draws on Italian, Greek, and French culinary traditions. You might order veal Marsala, or Greek shrimp *efrosini* (sautéed in olive oil and garlic, finished with *plaki* sauce, feta cheese, and Greek olives), or *coquilles St. Jacques à la Parisienne* (sea scallops sautéed in butter and garlic and finished with white wine and heavy cream). Also worth trying is the beef: The restaurant serves a variety of cuts, from a 6-ounce filet mignon to a 12-ounce New York–cut boneless sirloin steak. *Rte. 86 near Cold Brook Plaza, Lake Placid, tel. 518/523–3050. Reservations advised. AE, D, DC, MC, V. Closed Apr., Nov.–mid-Dec. Expensive.*

Alpine Cellar. Traditional German fare stars in this large restaurant on the lower level of a modest motel; the view of Whiteface Mountain from its high windows is the main draw, however. It's fun to have cocktails—or, better still, big steins of beer—in the lounge, on a small balcony overlooking the dining area. Try the sauerbraten, the various schnitzel dishes, or the cheese fondue. *Rte. 86, Wilmington Rd., Lake Placid, tel. 518/523–2180. Reservations advised. Dress: casual but neat. AE, MC, V. No lunch. Closed late Oct.–Christmas. Moderate.*

Great Adirondack Steak and Seafood. This restaurant is at once sophisticated and rustic, with its wood paneling and scattering of antiques and collectibles; the view of Mirror Lake and the mountains behind it is spectacular. The menu is basically American, but ethnic dishes such as jerk chicken add interest. The lively bar is in its own small room, away from the dining area. *Main St., Lake Placid, tel. 518/523–1629. Reservations not accepted. Dress: casual but neat. AE, DC, MC, V. Moderate.*

Artist's Cafe. This popular spot on Lake Placid's Main Street has an enclosed lakeside deck and a cozy dining room and bar. Paintings by local artists, all for sale, hang on the walls. At lunch there are hearty soups, quiches, and imaginative sandwiches; at dinner you can order steak (try the 16-ounce T-bone or the filet mignon) or standard fare with a distinctive twist, such as shrimp scampi served over fresh pasta. *Main St., Lake*

Placid, tel. 518/523–9493. Reservations not necessary. Dress: casual. AE, DC, MC, V. Inexpensive.

Casa del Sol. Travelers who know the Southwest will be surprised to find this bright, funky Mexican outpost so far east; the tiny bar is mobbed on Friday night during the off-season and daily in summer. Although the kitchen exercises restraint with the spice bottle, the food is unquestionably authentic. Try the *mole poblano* (boneless chicken breast served with rice and beans and doused with mole sauce, here made with peanut butter, raisins, and chili powder) or the haddock prepared Veracruz style, with tomatoes and olives and served with rice and salad. *Rte. 86, Lake Flower Ave., Saranac Lake, tel. 518/891–0977. Reservations not accepted. No credit cards. Inexpensive.*

LODGING

Chain motels rub elbows with swank resorts in the Lake George and Lake Placid regions (you can find about 325 places to stay within a half hour of Lake George), and elsewhere there's an abundance of locally owned motels, cabin colonies, bed-and-breakfasts, and, yes, a few dude ranches. There are even a couple of pet motels. B&Bs are your best bets for economy, especially during peak travel periods (which include ski season in the Lake Placid region). A great many lodgings, even around Lake Placid, are not open year-round. *The Adirondack Book: A Complete Guide* (*see* Publications *in* Essential Information, *above*) provides more information.

CENTRAL ADIRONDACKS **Copperfield Inn.** The cathedral ceilings and tall, slender columns in the lobby reflect the elegance of this hotel, which was built in 1990. The guest rooms combine European style and American practicality—you can take a telephone call while relaxing in a marble bath. It is a short walk from the Hudson River, where there's fishing, canoeing, and rafting, and is not far from golfing and antiques shopping. The hotel provides a free shuttle service to nearby Gore Mountain, where there is downhill and cross-country skiing. *224 Main St., North*

Creek 12853, tel. 518/251–2500 or 800/424–9910, fax 518/251–4143. 25 rooms. Facilities: restaurant, grill, cocktail lounge, tennis, pool, gym, power boats; VCR in all rooms. AE, D, DC, MC, V. Expensive.

Dun Roamin Cabins. Although this cottage complex may look from the outside like a relic of the '30s, knotty-pine paneling, carpeting, and up-to-date furnishings create an entirely different effect inside. The cabins, especially those with a fireplace, are cozy and welcoming. This property is on one of the region's snowmobiling networks, and public hiking and cross-country ski trails are next door. Ice fishing is another option. In summer there's boating—the resort moors its craft at a nearby marina. Rte. 9, Box 535, Schroon Lake 12870, tel. 518/532–7277. 9 rooms (3 cabins with fireplace and 6 cottages, 2 with full kitchen and 4 with efficiency kitchen). Facilities: outdoor pool, canoes, lawn games, grills, picnic tables. D, MC, V. Moderate.

Garnet Hill Lodge. In winter, guests come here for the skiing, which is not surprising, because in 1992 Snow Country Magazine voted this hotel's cross-country ski trails among the best in the country. The main lodge, built in 1936, is a large log cabin whose big common room is dominated by a striking fireplace made from stone quarried nearby. Except for one vintage summer cottage, outlying buildings and the lodge are decorated in knotty-pine paneling (frequently seen in area hotels). The kitchen, one of the best in the region, serves American cuisine and a magnificent Saturday-night buffet that includes fresh poached Atlantic salmon, roast beef, turkey, and a house favorite, onion pie. Dining is also available on the porch, which has a wonderful view of Thirteenth Lake and the Adirondack Mountains. In summer you can take a boat or canoe out on the lake or go for long hikes in the surrounding woods, among other activities. Thirteenth Lake Rd., North River 12856, tel. 518/251–2821 or 518/251–2444, fax 518/251–3089. 25 rooms, 20 cottages. Facilities: restaurant; 2 tennis courts; mountain-bike, boat, and canoe rental. No credit cards. Moderate.

Blue Spruce Motel. Tall spruces stand guard over this compact motel near the village center. Guest rooms are standard but have an unusual sparkle design in the ceiling. Some are connected, and one is an efficiency. The motel is next door to one of the best restaurants in Old Forge, the Old Mill (see Dining, above). There's plenty of parking for snowmobile and boat trailers. Main St., Box 604, Old Forge 13420, tel. 315/369–3817. 13 rooms. Facilities: heated outdoor pool. AE, MC, V. Inexpensive.

LAKE GEORGE AREA **Canoe Island Lodge.** Complete with its own private island and 48-acre mountain, this elegant 14-acre complex along 30-mile-long Lake George is a private retreat that has been carefully preserved. The main lodge, last refurbished in the 1960s, has oak paneling, a large fireplace, a scattering of handmade braided rugs, and comfortable sofas, which give it an Early American look. Rooms are in log cabins and cottages (all with carpets, modern bath, and TV). If you feel like a little privacy, head for the island facing the complex; it's .75 mile, or five minutes, by hotel shuttle. You can water ski or take a cruise along the lake in the hotel's 40-person cruise boat. The restaurant serves American fare, and box lunches are provided. Guests may bring their own boats. Lake Shore Dr., Box 144, Diamond Point 12824, tel. 518/668–5592, fax 518/668–2012. 65 rooms. Facilities: restaurant, cocktail lounge, 3 tennis courts, canoes, kayaks, lake-cruise boat. No credit cards. Closed mid-Oct.–mid-May. Expensive.

Colonial Manor Inn. The trim, well-tended look of the buildings and a convenient location make the Colonial Manor appealing. It has cottages and motel units, and children under 12 stay free. The pool faces the street, but lawns, trees, and a playground are at the rear. Canada St., Box 528, Lake George 12845, tel. 518/668–4884. 35 rooms, 20 cottages. Facilities: pool, playground. AE, D, DC, MC, V. Moderate.

Briar Dell Motel. The pleasant motel rooms and cabins of this property, one of the smaller resorts on the steep shoreline of Lake George, are all along the lakeside. A motel with a private beach, boats, and dockage and at such a modest price is unusual so close to Lake George village. *Shore Dr., RR 2, Box 2372, Lake George 12845, tel. 518/668–4819. 22 rooms. Facilities: private beach with rowboats, picnic area. MC, V. Closed mid-Oct.– Memorial Day. Inexpensive.*

Travelodge. The front units of this inn have one of the area's premier views—north down the length of Lake George. Rear units view the outdoor pool, playground, picnic area, and Prospect Mountain. Breakfast is served in the coffee shop, which also has a view. *Rte. 9, Lake George 12845, tel. 518/668–2507. 102 rooms. Facilities: coffee shop, outdoor pool, playground, picnic area. AE, D, DC, V. Closed mid-Oct.–mid-Apr. Inexpensive.*

OLYMPIC REGION **The Point.** Once the home of William Avery Rockefeller, this elegantly rustic inn is the most exclusive retreat in the Adirondacks and feels like a sophisticated private home; guests are required to dress for dinner. All but two rooms have their own bath, and most have stone fireplaces. The beds are made in traditional Adirondack style from polished yellow pine. The inn is a member of Relais et Châteaux. *Star Rte., Upper Saranac Lake 12983, tel. 518/891–5674. 11 rooms. Facilities: dining room; lounge; open bar; game room; swimming, sailing, cross-country skiing on premises. AE. Very Expensive.*

Hotel Saranac. From the outside this is an imposing six-story redbrick hotel, but once you step inside, you find yourself in an ornate palazzo-style main lobby complete with high ceilings, pillars, and paintings on the walls. The upstairs decor is even more sumptuous: The second-floor Grand Hall is an exact replica of the Grand Salon of the Davanzati Palace in Florence, Italy. The hotel is operated as a training ground for Paul Smiths College's hotel-management students, but occasional goofs by neophytes in the hospitality business are more than made up for by their warmth and enthusiasm. The pleasant dining room is one of Saranac Lake's social centers; it serves three meals daily, prepared by the aspiring chefs of the Culinary College. A lighter menu of munchies and salads is available in the Boathouse Lounge, where the decorative theme is the Adirondack guide boat, a traditional wood craft that is broader in the beam than normal canoes. Although the hotel has no sporting facilities on its grounds, its location in downtown Saranac Lake is convenient; you'll find hiking trails on Mt. Baker, only five blocks away; swimming, sunbathing, and fishing on the lake, only .75 mile from the hotel; and skiing a short drive by car. *110 Main St., Saranac Lake 12983, tel. 518/891–2200, fax 518/891–5664. 92 rooms. Facilities: restaurant, bar. AE, D, DC, MC, V. Moderate.*

Schulte's Motor Inn. Alpine-style stucco-and-wood buildings with peaked roofs and balconies make this compact motel attractive. Country fabrics, bright colors, and modern appointments carry the cheerful theme indoors. *Cascade Rd., Rte. 73, Lake Placid 12946, tel. 518/523–3532. 30 rooms, 15 cottages. Facilities: restaurant, lounge, picnic area, playground, outdoor pool. AE, MC, V. Inexpensive.*

CAMPING

There are private campgrounds throughout the Adirondacks. The New York State Department of Environmental Conservation (DEC) operates 41 public campgrounds about the park. These are the most reliable. Some of these are at historic sites; some are on islands in the larger lakes, such as Lake George and Indian Lake. Most are open from around Memorial Day through Labor Day, some longer to accommodate hunters and leaf-peepers. Most also have a table and grill at each site, a beach, running water, and adequate lavatories, but not all offer showers, and none offers hookups, which can, however, be found at most of the private campgrounds. Reservations at DEC campgrounds can be made by calling 800/456–CAMP, but except at the busiest ones it's often easy to get a spot without prearrangement. The following are some of the best. The **Lake George Islands** campground (tel. 518/656–9426, 518/644–9696, or 518/499–1288), in the Lake George area, consists of 398 waterfront sites on 50 islands, each area with fireplaces, picnic tables, and pit toilets; the sites are accessible only by boat. **Rogers Rock** (tel. 518/585–6746), on the shore of Lake George, has 314 sites with flush toilets and showers, as well as fireplaces, picnic tables, a beach, a boat launch, and lots of French and Indian War history.

Cranberry Lake (tel. 315/848–2315), in the western part of the park, has 172 sites, with picnic tables, fire grates, flush toilets, showers, and a beach; there's also a disposal station. The campground is the site of the trailhead for Bear Mountain, a 1.5-mile hike with great views.

Wilmington Notch (tel. 518/946–7172), near Lake Placid, has 54 sites with showers and picnic tables; it's the site of a dramatic waterfall and gorge on the West Branch of the Ausable River and is near Whiteface and the other High Peaks. **Fish Creek Pond** (tel.

518/891–4560), with 355 sites, has a recreation program, boat rentals, a boat launch, and a beach with a bathhouse, in addition to showers and picnic tables. The adjacent 290-site **Rollins Pond** (tel. 518/891–3239), near the St. Regis Canoe Area, the Paul Smiths Visitor Interpretive Center, and several favorite hiking areas, has showers, boat rentals, and a boat launch; although somewhat less developed, it can become an RV megalopolis, complete with gridlock, in summer. **Meacham Lake** (tel. 518/483–5116) has 62 sites, showers, and a recreation program; it is rarely crowded and offers some beautiful wooded campsites and one of the largest sandy beaches in the park.

The DEC also maintains primitive campsites (usually with no facilities, other than a privy, and some not even that) along major canoe routes such as Bog River/Lake Lila and the St. Regis Canoe Area. Local forest rangers, listed in phone books, are the best source of information about these sites.

Allegheny National Forest
Pennsylvania

By Carolyn Price

Mention Pennsylvania, and the horse-and-buggy charm of Lancaster County or the stone bank barns of an Andrew Wyeth painting come to mind. It would probably come as a revelation to the state's residents that in their northwest—an area traditionally evoking images of oil refineries, felled timber, and breweries—lies an area of woodland romance. Allegheny National Forest comprises more than half a million acres, most of them forested, with the largest tract of old-growth timber in the East. The terrain is gouged by three river corridors: the Allegheny, the Clarion, and the Tionesta. The 25-mile-long Allegheny Reservoir, on the upper Allegheny, presents a gleaming waterscape of 7,634 acres with almost 100 miles of shoreline. A hunter's delight? An angler's dream? You bet. But Allegheny National Forest is also becoming a family camper's haven.

The forest's privileged location (half the nation's population lives within a day's drive of its boundaries) draws visitors with its year-round sports opportunities and its vast parcel of woods and waterways. Summer visitors fish, hike, swim, canoe, camp, ride, bike, and bird-watch; autumn devotees drive through the brilliant foliage of black cherry and red oak; winter travelers tour by snowmobile and cross-country skis. The cool, dark hardwood forests (packed with black cherry, maple, oak, ash, beech, and hemlock) contain more than 200 miles of pedestrian trails, more than 90 of maintained all-terrain vehicle (ATV) trails, and more than 300 of trails open to snowmobiles. Crisscrossing the alternately flat and rolling plateau are some 500 miles of stream, much of it generously stocked with brown trout and northern pike.

The forest service, the game commission, and the private sector (more than 90% of energy mineral rights are privately owned) have collaborated to manage, protect, and judiciously develop this four-county area. Recreational facilities offer day- and overnight trippers a myriad of outdoor pastimes; the resources include four beaches, six boat launches, seventeen developed campgrounds, three overlooks, and nine picnicking areas. There are campgrounds and fishing trails accessible to the disabled. The shoreline of the Allegheny Reservoir has remained protected and pristine, and 10,000 acres of designated federal wilderness make it possible for backpackers who bristle at the thought of "developed" recreation to attain true seclusion.

ESSENTIAL INFORMATION

VISITOR INFORMATION Contact the **Supervisor's Office** of the Allegheny National Forest (222 Liberty St., Box 847, Warren 16365, tel. 814/723–5150, TTY 814/726–2710). Four ranger's stations are located on forest grounds: **Bradford Ranger District** (Kinzua Heights Star Rte., Bradford 16701, tel. 814/362–4613); **Marienville Ranger District** (Rte. 66, Marienville 16239, tel. 814/927–6628); **Ridgway Ranger District** (Box 28A, Ridgway 15853, tel. 814/776–6172); and **Sheffield Ranger Station** (U.S. 6, Sheffield 16347, tel. 814/968–3232). Backcountry camping opportunities are ample and require neither a permit nor a fee.

FEES There are no entrance fees. The only fees charged are at developed campgrounds ($6–$15 a night) and at four day-use areas ($3 per car or $1 per pedestrian or cyclist).

PUBLICATIONS First and foremost, shell out $3 for the administrative map of the Allegheny National Forest published by the Forest Service, your principal resource when planning driving or hiking excursions. It indicates campsites, trails, boat launches, picnic areas, and every recreational facility available within the forest's boundaries. Topographical maps are available from the Supervisor's Office for $3. You can order both maps by mail from the Supervisor's Office (see Visitor Information, above); each map costs $3.18, including tax and postage.

In addition, free brochures with information on camping, canoeing, hiking, hunting, fishing, trail biking, cross-country skiing, snow-mobiling, and off-road vehicle use are available from forest headquarters and ranger's stations (see Visitor Information, above).

The Supervisor's Office on Liberty Street in Warren carries a number of interesting publications on the forest's cultural and natural history and recreational opportunities. The *Allegheny National Forest Hiking Guide,* by Bruce Sundquist, Carolyn Weilacher Yartz, and Jack Richardson (Sierra Club, $7.50), is indispensable for hikers. *Allegheny River: Watershed of the Nation*, by Jim Schafer and Mike Sajna (Pennsylvania State University, $45), is a lushly photographed coffee-table book. For those interested in Native American culture, *The Death and Rebirth of the Seneca*, by Anthony F. C. Wallace (Vintage, $10.95), chronicles the history of the Seneca nation. You can order these books from the Supervisor's Office (see Visitor Information, above).

GEOLOGY AND TERRAIN The Allegheny Forest includes two basic types of terrain. The Allegheny Plateau is flat, with heavily forested areas packed with hardwoods. It is distinguished from the Allegheny chain by the general absence of steep slopes and by high, rolling terrain rather than dramatic ridges and deep valleys. The surface is gashed by fish-filled streams and waterways. The second type of terrain comprises the river corridors of the Allegheny, Tionesta, and Clarion, rugged canyons populated predominantly by oak-type trees. The Kinzua Dam, built as a flood dam on the Allegheny in 1965, created the 25-mile-long Allegheny Reservoir.

The more challenging sections of the forest, from a hiker's point of view, are in the west; the best snowfall is in the north; and the highest elevations are in the east. There are plenty of roads but also sizable wilderness areas; Hickory Creek Wilderness alone occupies 9,000 acres.

Evidence of the terrain's economic importance is reflected in the forest's many roads, wells, and razed timber. Abundant oil, gas, and lumber have created livelihoods for residents for years. More than 200 new wells are drilled annually, and in one recent year local industry harvested 60 million feet of black cherry, maple, ash, and oak.

FLORA AND FAUNA With the deer population, which browses on tree seedlings, acorns, and shrubs, at a historic high, at least half of the forest's understory has been dramatically affected. What you'll see on the forest floor is what the deer have left behind, mostly lush green fern or striped maple. Whitetails evidently turn up their nose at New York fern and hay-scented fern, which remain the forest's most common ground vegetation. You may also run into little clearings with apple trees planted by turn-of-the-century homesteaders. These trees provide excellent nutrition to many resident species, including bears and deer.

From late May through July, you're sure to notice the showy mountain laurel blossoms, which typically bloom in open hardwood forests. Pennsylvania's shade-tolerant state flower flourishes happily in this region. Drive through the Bradford Ranger District in late May and early June for some of the best views.

The list of mammals is long (49 species have been reported), but the white-tailed deer seems to pose the greatest concern in terms of management. As evidence that the land cannot support their huge numbers, you can note the adult's small size and poor antler development. Both the Forest Service and the Pennsylvania Game Commission are working to lower the population.

While black bears now inhabit the forest in substantial numbers, they are shy and secretive; they frequent recreation areas only when they get wind of garbage cans full of campers' leftovers. If you've heard reports of bears foraging at campgrounds and would like to observe from a safe distance, try either Twin Lakes or Kiasutha Recreation Areas. The Forest Service is proud of how successfully they have managed bears here. Fifty years ago the numbers were in the single-digit range; now close to 300 are bagged annually, and the population estimate is around 1,000.

Beavers are multiplying and may be observed in the low gradient streams around Buzzard Swamp. As long as pelt prices are low, they continue to flourish in areas like Sugar Run and Willow Bay as well as the Branch Salmon Creek in the Marienville district. Appropriately enough, Beaver Meadows Campground near Marienville also reports quite a few spottings.

Wild turkeys are quite common and sought after during hunting season. Serious birders should head for Buzzard Swamp, just south of Marienville, where a series of impoundments creates an ideal habitat for a variety of waterfowl. There are two bald eagle nests: on Allegheny Reservoir and just south of Tionesta on a ridge overlooking the Allegheny River. The best time to view either one is in the spring before the leaves appear on trees. Warblers—including scarlet tanagers, morning warblers, and black-throated blue and black-throated green warblers—are common, especially during their spring migration. Migrating raptors glide through in the fall months. Make sure to pick up trail brochures at forest headquarters; they profile various species and tell you where a particular animal lives or browses.

One of the nicest things about camping at Allegheny National Forest is the relative absence of pests and poisonous vegetation. A few rattlesnakes have been spotted, but their numbers are low. Poison ivy, long associated with drier climates, is not happy in these damp, shaded woodland areas.

WHEN TO GO The busiest season lasts from late June to September, when nights have warmed up enough for overnight campers, and daylong hikes through lush wilderness can be topped off with a fishing stop or a dip in the reservoir. But the other seasons have their assets, too. Fall foliage is spectacular, even if you merely tour along forest roads by car. Winter visitors in '92–'93 were rewarded with 78 inches of snowfall; cross-country skiing and snowmobiling conditions were exceptionally good. If you don't mind the cold spring nights (they extend well into June), camping can be wonderful then simply because there aren't many people around.

SEASONAL EVENTS Last weekend of January: Chapman State Park, a 20-minute drive from Warren, sponsors a **Winter Carnival** with sleigh rides, ice skating, toboggan races, and other winter sports. **Third weekend in June:** The **Forest Fest** invites visitors to enjoy the forest's developed campgrounds for free. The all-out promotional effort includes naturalist-led tours, boat rides, evening programs, children's entertainment, crafts displays, and dozens of recreational activities. **Fourth of July:** Come to the **Independence Day Festival** in Warren for fireworks, an arts-and-crafts show, and a midday parade. **Third weekend in August:** Learn about the tribal history of northwestern Pennsylvania—and take in a parade, food, and crafts—at the **Native American Festival** in Tionesta. **September:** The **Pennsylvania State Championship Fishing Tournament** in Tidoute, the nation's oldest tournament, has been attracting anglers for over 30 years.

WHAT TO PACK Pack a metal container suitable for boiling water or, at least, bring a water purifier, especially if you're doing backcountry touring away from developed campgrounds equipped with potable water pumps. Consult the salesperson at the place of purchase: You need a purifier with a screen fine enough to filter out *Giardia lamblia,* a parasitic flagellate protozoan that can cause intestinal disorders.

Up until late June or early July, nights remain cool, so pack long underwear if you're an overnight visitor. The forest lies on a storm pathway from the Midwest to the Northeast, so bring rain gear no matter what the season. Water-repellent boots are especially important even when showers abate, since heavy dew accumulates year-round and makes for wet vegetation.

Finally, consider a small backpacking stove and waterproof matches if you're camping overnight. With all the rainfall, firewood— while ubiquitous—gets wet, and you may need a backup system for dinner preparations.

GENERAL STORES If you're approaching from the east via Route 59, stop at **Costa's True Value Hardware** (323 Water St., Smethport 16749, tel. 814/887–5542; open daily) for fishing and hunting supplies. **Love's Canoe Rental and Sales** (3 Main St., Ridgway 15853, tel. 814/776–6285; open daily), right on the southeastern edge of the forest in Elk County, carries camping equipment, mountain bikes, and all the hunting, fishing, and cross-country ski gear you'll need. **Allegheny Outdoors** (N. Fraley St., Kane 16735, tel. 814/837–7261; closed Sun.) sells supplies and arranges cabin rentals in Allegheny National Forest. **Allegheny Outfitters** (Box 691, Warren 16365, tel. 814/723–1203; call ahead for hours) carries camping equipment and arranges boat trips on the eponymous river.

ATMS In **Ridgway** (in Elk County on the southeastern edge of the forest), there are automated teller machines at Integra Bank (301 Main St., tel. 814/776–6141) and Marine Bank (Court and Center Sts., tel. 814/776–6147). If you're staying nearer the northern reaches of the forest, try the 24-hour ATM at the Integra Bank in **Warren** (315 2nd Ave., tel. 814/723–5300).

ARRIVING AND DEPARTING The easiest—and usual—way to arrive is by car. Allegheny National Forest lies no more than a few hours from Buffalo (100 miles); Erie, Pennsylvania (60 miles); and Pittsburgh (140 miles). If you hail from New York City or Washington, D.C., you're still within a day's drive.

By Plane. Bradford Regional Airport (tel. 814/368–5928) is served by USAir (tel. 800/428–4322). You can rent cars from the National or Hertz branch on its premises. Bradford lies near the northeast corner of the forest in McKean County; a short 10- to 15-minute drive will deposit you within forest boundaries.

By Car and RV. Approaching from the south, whether from Pittsburgh, Philadelphia, or Washington, D.C., you can make use of I–80, then jog north via U.S. 219, Route 36, or Route 66. If you're departing from the New York or New Jersey area you might opt for the slower

U.S. 6, a scenic byway that winds through the northern Alleghenies, and enter the forest via Kane in McKean County.

By Train. The nearest passenger train station is in Erie, about 60 miles northwest of the forest. Call Amtrak (tel. 800/872–7245) for schedule and fare information.

By Bus. There aren't any bus stations nearby, but Greyhound (tel. 800/231–2222) does drop off and pick up passengers in Bradford, the northern gateway to the Forest region.

EXPLORING

Most visitors drive the roadways to view fall foliage or springtime's flowering mountain laurel. With its many roads, the forest offers easy access to almost any location outside of designated wilderness. To view wildlife or observe vegetation more closely, however, you'll do better on foot or in a boat.

THE BEST IN ONE DAY Don't miss the **Tionesta Scenic Area,** a 6-mile drive from Ludlow (located on U.S. 6). What you'll see is a 2,000-acre virgin forest packed with centuries-old hemlock and beech—the largest tract of old-growth timber in the East. If you've never seen what a twister can do to woodlands, walk to the overlook to view the destruction that a single tornado wrought in the spring of 1985 (*see* Nature Trails and Short Walks, *below*). Summer visitors who want to boat or swim gravitate to the **Allegheny Reservoir,** but the pristine beauty of its 96-mile shoreline warrants a trip any season of the year (*see* Scenic Drives and Views, *below*). Birders should head toward **Buzzards Swamp** to observe waterfowl in a wetlands environment.

ORIENTATION PROGRAMS There are no orientation programs here, but all the information about camping or recreational facilities that you'll need is available at the ranger's stations (*see* Visitor Information *in* Essential Information, *above*).

GUIDED TOURS The Forest Service doesn't offer any formal guided tours. **Allegheny Outdoors Guide Service** (137 W. Corydon St., Bradford 16701, tel. 814/368–8608) offers good hiking, hunting, and fishing trips, with prices beginning at $75 for a half-day excursion.

SCENIC DRIVES AND VIEWS One of the prettiest byways in the country, **U.S. 6,** travels through Allegheny National Forest for 29 paved miles. You can hook up to this route, also known as the "Grand Army of the Republic" highway right outside of Warren in the northwest portion of the forest, and then move southeast to Sheffield, where the road doglegs east to Kane and then jogs northeast outside the forest limits.

No one should leave before driving by the **Allegheny Reservoir.** The following route, beginning and ending in Warren, will take you on a loop around and across. Starting in Warren, travel east on the scenic U.S. 6, then hop onto Route 59 heading east (the entryway is just outside the Warren town limits). Follow 59 to Kinzua Dam; Route 59 will intersect with Route 321: Take this road north to Route 346 and turn left. Over the state border in New York, Route 346 turns into Route 280; stay on 280 until you reach Route 17. Head west on 17, but take your first exit, which occurs immediately after you cross the reservoir, and travel back to Warren via Route 394 and Scandia Road.

NATURE TRAILS AND SHORT WALKS There are more than 200 miles of pedestrian trails in Allegheny National Forest, 84 of which belong to the North Country National Scenic Trail (NCNST), which runs all the way from Upstate New York to the Dakotas. Most of the trails are heavily wooded, with species like black cherry, pine, oak, hickory, beech, and hemlock shading a bright green understory of dense fern cover. You'll see deer along most of the trails. In 1991, the Pennsylvania Game Commission estimated whitetails' density at 21 to 30 per square mile—so numerous that you may tire of spotting them.

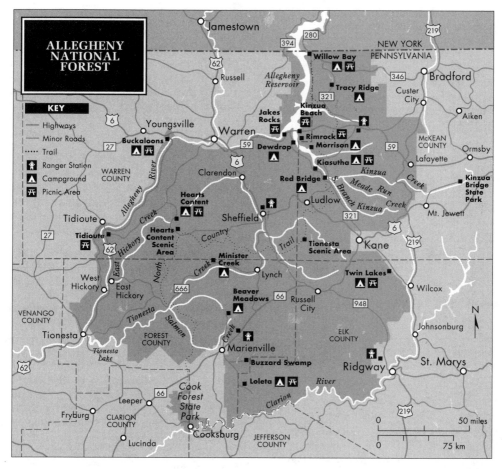

ALLEGHENY NATIONAL FOREST

KEY

--- Highways
–– Minor Roads
···· Trail
👫 Ranger Station
🅰 Campground
🌲 Picnic Area

Safety Tips. Some trails are used by hunters in the late spring and fall, so hikers should wear fluorescent or brightly colored clothing during these seasons. The pump water in the developed campgrounds and recreation areas is potable, but campers who obtain water from streams should boil or purify collected supplies.

The **Hearts Content Scenic Interpretive Trail** is a 1.25-mile loop in the Sheffield Ranger District. It crosses the west branch of the Tionesta Creek at two points on its circuit. Start at the trailhead in the picnic area of the Hearts Content Recreation Area. You will travel through a dense hardwood forest of beech, hemlock, white pine, and black cherry (one of the most valuable harvests in Allegh-

eny). This is wilderness area, all of it either purchased by or given to the federal government in the early 20th century, and some of its trees have been around for more than four centuries. Small mammals (rabbits, chipmunks, raccoons) inhabit the area, but deer aren't as numerous in an old-growth forest like this one, with limited browse, as they are in the rest of Allegheny.

Also in the Sheffield Ranger District, but east of Route 948, lies the **Tionesta Scenic Area Interpretive Trail.** Really two loops that share some common ground, these self-guided tours are marked with diamond-shaped blazes on tree trunks and venture through virgin forests of 400-year-old hemlock, 300-year-old beech, black cherry, and sugar maple. For the most part you'll be walking a plateau, but the course includes some sharp descents into stream-filled valleys. The longer (1.5-mile) foot trail requires only a leisurely, hour-long jaunt. The shorter (.5-mile) trail doesn't take more than 20 minutes. It begins and ends at the same points as the longer trail (look for signs on Forest Road 133E to find the trailhead), but it follows a north fork shortly after the first bridge crossing and cuts back quickly to the end of its course. The longer path continues farther west, to converge with a section of the North Country National Scenic Trail, before it swings back to the same terminus. You'll find dramatic evidence here (especially apparent from the observation deck near the parking area) of the tornado that in the spring of 1985 razed one-third of the trees growing in the 2,000-acre Tionesta Scenic Area.

LONGER HIKES Minister Creek Trail, a 6.6-mile stretch traveling north to intersect with the North Country National Scenic Trail before circling back to the original trailhead, takes off from the Minister Creek Campground in Forest County. Right after crossing the Warren County border, the trail forks and becomes a loop encompassing various branches of Minister Creek, where fishing for native brookies is popular. Ascents onto shale plateaus, descents into valleys, and rocky overlooks characterize the terrain. Look for the new off-white markers that have replaced the blue tree blazes.

The 11.1-mile loop of the **Hickory Creek Trail** starts at the Hearts Content Recreation Area and travels west into rolling, forested backcountry, then dips south and east as it returns, traversing several creeks and streams as it runs roughly parallel to the more southerly Middle Hickory Creek. The northern half of the loop winds through woodlands of black cherry, hemlock, oak, and beech in which sunlight and noise are so excluded that an otherworldly atmosphere prevails. The more exposed forests of the southern division have less even terrain than the northern half. The trail markers are weather-worn patches of yellow paint on the trees. No motors or mechanized traffic are allowed here; visitors

can hike, fish, or photograph in quiet seclusion.

The **Morrison Trail** in the Bradford Ranger District consists of two contiguous loops that share a 1.3-mile segment and together provide 15 miles of backpacking pleasure. The western portion of this trail runs along the eastern brow of Kinzua Creek near the Allegheny Reservoir. Because of frequent steep grades, hiking this trail is challenging, and the Forest Service strongly advises that you use a buddy system. You'll be rewarded with fine views of the reservoir, waterfalls, and flowering meadows in springtime. Wildlife sightings are frequent: grouse, turkey, black bear, and—you guessed it—whitetail deer.

Also in the Bradford Ranger District is the **Johnnycake/Tracy Ridge Trail**—two contiguous loops, the larger looking on the map like a round-bottomed basket about to wobble over onto its side. If you hike the larger loop (you must hike part of the smaller one to reach it), you'll cover 10.3 miles of terrain much like the Morrison Trail's (*see above*), so be prepared for a workout. You'll also incorporate about 5 miles of the North Country National Scenic Trail as you travel along the eastern rim of the Allegheny Reservoir. The smaller loop, which lies to the east and includes an interpretive trail on its southern leg, encircles Tracy Ridge Campground, which sits at a 2,245-foot elevation. Follow the off-white markers.

The big daddy of them all, the North Country National Scenic Trail, chalks up some 84 miles within the forest's boundaries. Many of the above trails converge with or lead to branches of the NCNST. Request the national forest's pamphlet and map (*see* Publications *in* Essential Information, *above*), and you can choose from 10 sections of its course, from 2-mile to 13-mile stretches. Horseback riding is not permitted on this trail.

OTHER ACTIVITIES ATVs. Trail bikes and all-terrain vehicles can make full use of the 98 miles of ATV trails now in place at Allegheny National Forest. The season begins the Friday before Memorial Day weekend and lasts until September 20. You must have an ATV registration from either Pennsylvania or your home state; if, however, your home state doesn't have a reciprocity agreement with Pennsylvania, you must obtain a Pennsylvania registration from the state's Department of Environmental Resources (Snowmobile/ATV Unit, Box 1467, Harrisburg 17120, tel. 717/783–9227). The speed limit is 25 miles per hour, but drivers should stay below 15 miles per hour on most trails, since these vehicles don't have great traction on gravel. Contact forest headquarters (*see* Visitor Information *in* Essential Information, *above*), which will send you a stack of brochures, including maps that cover each ATV trail in the forest.

Biking. Mountain biking is particularly fine in the fall, when arching corridors of brilliant foliage light up the roadways. The numerous Forest Service roads, whether gravel or dirt, are perfect surfaces for mountain-bike touring. Love's Canoe Rental in Ridgway (*see* General Stores *in* Essential Information, *above*) carries many different models.

Bird-Watching. *See* Flora and Fauna *in* Essential Information, *above*.

Boating. Power boating is permitted on the Allegheny and Tionesta reservoirs; there are no limits on motor size. The forest manages 6,700 acres of shoreline, and there are five launch sites on the Allegheny Reservoir alone. Motorboats, rowboats, canoes, and pontoon boats can be rented at the 300-slip Kinzua–Wolf Run Marina (tel. 814/726–1650), 4 miles east of Kinzua Dam on Route 59. You can purchase bait, tackle, and lunch-type fare here as well.

Canoeing. The going is mostly easy on the Allegheny, Tionesta, and Clarion rivers (except for a few rapids on the Clarion) and on the Allegheny and Tionesta reservoirs. The 60-mile course of the Clarion is recommended for intermediate canoers before mid-May, when water levels begin to drop and less experienced paddlers can dip in. All these waterways are rich with scenic stopping points; you'll have no trouble finding a place to camp overnight, fish, or view wildlife. Many developed canoe-in campsites are

available, and there are canoe liveries in Warren, Kane, Tionesta, West Hickory, Ridgway, Cooksburg, and Clarington. A marina at the south end of the Allegheny Reservoir also rents canoes. Contact the Supervisor's Office (*see* Visitor Information *in* Essential Information, *above*) for a brochure that shows canoe launches and ranger's stations and gives brief descriptions of boat campgrounds. Call the Western Pennsylvania Conservancy (tel. 412/288–2777) for maps of the Allegheny River.

Cross-Country Skiing. Conditions are less predictable here than in other parts of the Northeast, so call ahead. If you don't own your own skis and poles, there are plenty of rental shops in the area, among them Love's Canoe Rental (*see* General Stores *in* Essential Information, *above*).

Fishing. Anglers on the Tionesta Creek, the Allegheny River, and the Allegheny Reservoir find muskies, walleye, smallmouth bass, and—in record numbers—brown trout and northern pike. If you're in the reservoir area (accessible from Warren via Route 59), try Sugar and Hodge Run bays. Bring your boat or rent one; launches are plentiful around the perimeter of the 25-mile-long reservoir. Many streams on the Allegheny River are stocked with trout; the opening day for their harvest is in April. If you venture south of Kinzua Dam all the way to Tionesta, you'll discover walleye in abundance. A disabled-accessible fishing trail encircles Twin Lake in the Ridgway district. A **fishing hot line** (tel. 814/726–0164) will keep you abreast of current conditions on the Allegheny reservoir and south of it along the river's course. A fishing license ($12 and up) can be acquired at various sporting goods outlets.

Horseback Riding. Bring your own horses and camp if you wish, but be apprised that the North Country National Scenic Trail is closed to horses. Otherwise, you have more than 1,000 miles of Forest Service road and more than 600 miles of OGM (oil, gas, and minerals) roads to choose from. The **Flying "W" Ranch** (Rte. 666, Star Rte. 2, Box 150, Tionesta 16353, tel. 814/463–7663) in Forest

County east of Tionesta is a top-notch operation with a stable of some 50 horses. The ranch also has guides who lead trail rides through the forest.

Hunting. Hunting of small game, big game, waterfowl, and the ever-present whitetail is very, very big here. Black bear, turkey, grouse, pheasant, snowshoe hare, squirrel, woodchuck, and quail are among the prizes in Elk, Forest, McKean, and Warren counties. The various seasons generally begin around early October and end during the early spring. Request the "Hunting the Alleghenies" pamphlet from the forest headquarters, and you'll receive information on the best areas for each species along with a detailed map. A hunting license can be obtained from various sporting goods stores; at time of purchase, proof of having passed a hunting education course is required. For a complete list of seasons, regulations, and permit costs, contact the **Pennsylvania Game Commission** (2001 Elmerton Ave., Harrisburg 17110, tel. 717/787–4250 or 800/533–6764).

Snowmobiling. More than 325 miles of trail are open to snowmobilers. Many are segments of roadway that don't get plowed in the winter months (December 20–April 1). Another 100 miles are groomed, and one part of these maintained stretches is dubbed the Allegheny Snowmobile Loop, which, while loosely fitting loop status, does contain three breaks. Make sure to get the Forest Service's activities map. Available by December each year, it provides an annually updated model of the trail system for snowmobilers.

Swimming. The sandy shoreline of Kinzua Beach is perfect. A $2 day-use fee gives visitors access to shower facilities and some 100 picnic sites. You'll find a large, grassy beach and picnic area at Kiasutha Recreation Area, 10 miles northwest of Kane. Twin Lakes Recreation Area, 8 miles southeast of Kane, has day-use swimming areas on both grassy and sandy shoreline.

CHILDREN'S PROGRAMS No specific children's programs are scheduled by the Forest Service, but this is decidedly a family vacation spot, and young ones will find plenty to

do sportswise. Several of the developed campgrounds have playgrounds, and many private operations just outside forest boundaries cater to the young set. Contact the local **chambers of commerce** for information on game parks and pony rides: **Warren** (tel. 814/723–3050), **Kane** (tel. 814/837–6565), **Bradford Area** (tel. 814/368–7115), and **Smethport** (tel. 814/887–5648).

One private enterprise stands out. The **Knox, Kane, Kinzua Railroad Train Excursion** (Box 422, Marienville, PA 16239, tel. 814/927–6621) is a steam-and-diesel locomotive that chugs through 100 miles of the Allegheny National Forest. It's the only train that travels over the Kinzua Railroad bridge, originally built in 1882 and now listed on the National Register of Historic Places.

EVENING ACTIVITIES During the summer, three developed campgrounds—Kiasutha, Loleta, and Twin Lakes—offer Saturday evening lectures on a fairly regular basis. Forest Service or game commission employees speak or present slides on such topics as wildflowers and resident animal life under a big tarp or pavilion.

DINING

Everything's casual. Elegance may be minimal, but you can count on fresh, inexpensive, and frequently homemade fare that includes some of the nation's best pies and down-home victuals. The only food concession on forest grounds is the Kinzua–Wolf Run Marina's little snack bar (sandwiches and ice cream), so bring a picnic lunch if you're an all-day visitor or else try out one of the nearby family restaurants. Don't worry about reservations at any of the following, except perhaps for dinner at the Jefferson House.

NEAR THE NATIONAL FOREST **Bucktail Inn.** Ever seen 6-inch-tall meringues on fresh banana cream or lemon pies? A glass-doored refrigerator in the casual lunchroom allows a close look at these wonders as well as at the delectable apple, blueberry, and cherry confections baked on the premises each morning. The other dining areas vary in sophistication, but all have Tiffany-style lamps and wood paneling, and all are housed in a modest brick structure in the heart of Marienville. The bill for a light lunch with a pastry dessert won't exceed $10. *S. Forest St., Marienville, tel. 814/927–8820. MC, V. Open Tues.–Sun. 8 AM– 9 PM. Moderate.*

Jefferson House Restaurant and Pub. This stately, 102-year-old mansion, refurbished with a warm burgundy-and-huntergreen color scheme, is listed on the National Register of Historic Places. In addition to moderately priced bed-and-breakfast accommodations, it houses a pub and restaurant where you can feast on steaks, chops, baby back ribs, and seafood, plus homemade soups and sandwiches. The pub specializes in imported beers and English draft ale. You can order a deli lunch for $6 or less; dinners run $7–$20. *119 Market St., Warren, tel. 814/723– 2268. Reservations advised for dinner. MC, V. Closed Sun.–Mon. Moderate.*

John Williams European Pastry Shop. It's good, it's cheap, and it's right across the street from forest headquarters in Warren. Townspeople here for a sandwich or a salad or a hot-plate special with a pastry dessert fill the wooden booths along the side walls, which are loaded with local artisan Minor Kaltenbach's litho prints. *211 Liberty St., Warren, tel. 814/726–7884. AE, D, MC, V. Open weekdays 7 AM–8 PM, weekends 8–3. Inexpensive.*

Pennsy Restaurant. You may have to wait five minutes longer for your soup here, but that's because it's not from yesterday's pot. Everything is homemade, and nothing is baked, roasted, boiled, or braised the day before. The Pennsy serves breakfast and lunch only, but it makes up for lost time with celebrated breads, pies, sweet rolls, sausages, and Sunday specials like meat loaf, Cornish hen, and goulash. A rock-bottom $4–$5 will buy you a hearty portion. *157 N. Broad St., Rte. 219, Ridgway, tel. 814/772–9935. No credit cards. Open Mon. 6–11, Tues.–Fri. 6– 1:30, Sat. 6–1, Sun. 7–1:30. Inexpensive.*

PICNIC SPOTS Consult the administrative map (*see* Publications *in* Essential Information, *above*) for exact locations of all the for-est's picnic areas. Some of the most scenic ones are on or near the Allegheny Reservoir just off Route 59.

LODGING

The little towns and cities on the forest's edge are the kind that still take pennies in parking meters. (In Ridgway, a dime will buy you an hour's reprieve.) You're not going to find stainless steel high-rises or luxury resorts. Warren, home of the forest headquarters and renowned for its tree-lined streets and Victorian homes, has a Holiday Inn and Super 8 Motel, but most of the options operate on a smaller scale and with modest appointments or lodgelike facilities.

NEAR THE NATIONAL FOREST North Fork **Lodge Vacation Resort and Bed & Breakfast.** The stones of this self-contained lodge were quarried straight out of the North Fork stream traversing the grounds. Some 9,000 acres encircle the 1924 structure, and every seasonal sport imaginable in rolling woodlands is available to patrons: trapping and skeet shooting, fishing, snowmobiling, downhill and cross-country skiing, hiking, ice skating, volleyball, and horseback riding fill the calendar year to brimming. The resort is ideal for families or large groups, but be advised that accommodations in the main lodge and two auxiliary houses are primarily dormitory style. North Fork lies about 10 miles outside St. Mary's in Elk County, with the national forest less than a half hour's drive to the west. *797 West Creek Rd., St. Mary's 15857, tel. 814/834–4194, fax 814/834–4192. Accommodations for 26 people max. Facilities: dining room, guided hunting, downhill-ski tow rope, trap- and skeet-shooting range, meeting rooms, golf driving range, 2 lakes. No credit cards. Moderate.*

Old Charm Bed & Breakfast. The first B&B in St. Mary's is in the former home of the Straub family, founders of Straub Brewery. It was built in 1917 and did not open its doors to travelers until 1993. Each of the six units offers a private bath and a collection of antique furnishings. Business travelers enjoy the benefit of a conference room and fax machine. A full breakfast is included in the rate. The national forest is less than 30 minutes away. *444 Brusselles St., St. Mary's 15857, tel. 814/834–9429, fax 814/834– 9274. 6 units with bath. AE, MC, V. Moderate.*

Super 8 Motel. This economical option is so close to the national forest that guests can smell the black cherry bark. A mere 10 miles from Kinzua Dam, it offers standard but clean accommodations and friendly service. The three-story structure houses 56 units with carpeting, light wood furnishings, and framed prints of local wildlife. You'll be within walking distance of some of Warren's family restaurants, but take advantage of the free Continental breakfast spread downstairs in the lobby area. *204 Struthers St., Warren 16365, tel. 814/723–8881 (fax same) or 800/800–8000. 56 units. Facilities: 24-hour desk, disabled-accessible units, nonsmoking rooms. AE, D, MC, V. Inexpensive.*

CAMPING

For the most part, the policy on campsites is first-come, first-served. However, a limited number of developed sites—specified in a list available from the Supervisor's Office (*see* Visitor Information *in* Essential Information, *above*)—can now be reserved in the summer (tel. 800/280–2267). Camping is permitted year-round, but after the summer season (Memorial Day weekend–Labor Day weekend) some recreation areas close completely and others shut down certain facilities. Flush toilets and showers, for instance, are turned off in the winter. Daily charges are $6–$18 for individual sites, $30 for group sites.

Allegheny National Forest provides 17 developed campgrounds with a total of 740 sites. The recreation area with the largest capacity, Tracy Ridge, furnishes 120 campsites; the smallest, Minister Creek, supplies 6. Eleven other campgrounds are on the Allegheny Reservoir. Six of these are "primitive type"—accessible only by boat or hiking trail. They provide pit toilets, rock ring fireplaces, and wells with pumps on them; no fee is charged. Of the remaining five, four are shoreline sites

with gravel pull-in areas for trailers, and one is on the Allegheny plateau.

Most developed campgrounds are in sheltered, shady areas surrounded by hardwoods or conifers. You may be able to see or hear your neighbors during the summer months, when camping activity is at its peak, but the woods between individual sites afford some privacy. A campground "host" lives on the premises and can answer questions about recreational facilities or nearby trails. Campgrounds vary in sophistication and range of facilities. Generally, you can count on the bare minimum of a picnic table, a fire ring, and a parking space large enough for one vehicle, plus latrines (vault toilets) and drinking water from a hand pump within easy walking distance. Campgrounds in some recreation areas provide tent pads for each site and a trail dump station. The Dewdrop Recreation Area even has flush toilets, pressurized water fountains, and hot showers, as well as a playground and a concrete boat launch. Group sites are available for $25–$30 per day at Buckaloons, Loleta, Tracy Ridge, and Twin Lakes recreation areas. Contact the Supervisor's Office for the "Recreation Areas Facilities and Schedules" brochure, which gives a rundown of recreation areas and their accommodations.

In this dense forest you're obviously not going to have to worry about **firewood.** All you need to do is gather dead debris from the ground. However, the supply gives out if the weather doesn't hold, and it rains with some frequency. So accumulate what you need for the length of your stay when you arrive, or come with your own supply.

Backcountry camping is permitted anywhere except the following restricted areas: around the Allegheny Reservoir or within 1,500 feet of the timberline (in other words, it's legal only at developed shoreline campgrounds); within 1,500 feet of Allegheny Reservoir Scenic Drive and the roads that lead into Jakes Rocks and Rimrock Overlook areas; within 1,500 feet of Kinzua Creek—that is, on either side of the creek—all the way from Red Bridge campground to Mead Run.

RVs. Electricity, sewage, and water hookups are not generally available, though Buckaloons and Twin Lakes recreation areas do provide some sites equipped with electricity.

There are trailer dump stations at Buckaloons, Dewdrop, Kiasutha, Red Bridge, Tracy Ridge, Twin Lakes, and Willow Bay recreation areas.

Assateague Island National Seashore and Chincoteague National Wildlife Refuge
Maryland, Virginia
By Carolyn Price

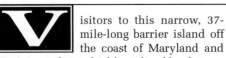isitors to this narrow, 37-mile-long barrier island off the coast of Maryland and Virginia confront a highly stylized landscape: low, flat stretches of beach, forest, and marsh with a weathered palette of sand- and sun-bleached hues. Shore areas, buffeted by salt spray and the ocean's force, bear the whites, silvers, and fawns of beach and berm, of dune, of parched golden beach grass. In the forest, colors turn to evergreen, fragrances to resin: Loblolly pines shoot high over a tangled understory of greenbrier, fern, and flowering serviceberry. And the marsh, with its cordgrasses and mudflats—is as silent and enigmatic to the uninitiated as its hidden biotic activity is frantic and nonstop.

The camouflage conceals surprises. Estuarine action goes on beneath swampy wraps. Shorebirds nest on eggs the color of seashells. Bashful species forage after sunset. But there are bold displays of life, too: shaggy feral horses scrounging for cordgrass; loons issu-

ing their sharp, territorial tremolos; and, on summer nights, thousands of the protozoa known as *Noctiluca scintillans* studding the ocean with microscopic fireworks.

It's also a place of year-round human activity, from the summer cyclists and bikinied "june bugs" (the locals' term for summering students) to the winter hunters and anglers. Almost 2.3 million visitors arrived in 1992 to camp, canoe, swim, hunt, fish, surf, birdwatch, walk the beach, and observe the celebrated wild horses that populate the island. This could have become another Ocean City—a swaggering strip of neon and entertainment—but the residents of neighboring townships voted construction out and preservation in. As a result, the Assateague Island National Seashore, established in 1965, and the Chincoteague National Wildlife Refuge, established in 1943, share (along with Assateague State Park, not covered in this book) the nearly 40,000 acres of the island and its surrounding waters. The national seashore, on the northern end of the island in Maryland, is maintained for recreational use by the National Park Service; the refuge, to the south, manages and protects wildlife on the Virginia shore under management of the U.S. Fish and Wildlife Service.

ESSENTIAL INFORMATION

VISITOR INFORMATION Contact the **Assateague Island National Seashore** (Rte. 611, 7206 National Seashore La., Berlin, MD 21811, tel. 410/641–3030 or 410/641–1441) for information on camping, fees, and recreational activities on the northern, or Maryland, portion of the island. The **Chincoteague National Wildlife Refuge** (Box 62, Chincoteague, VA 23336, tel. 804/336–6122), south of the seashore boundaries across the state line in Virginia, has its own set of rules and regulations.

Three visitor's centers are at your disposal: the Barrier Island Visitor Center in Maryland and the Chincoteague Refuge Visitor Center and Toms Cove Visitor Center in Virginia. All offer free brochures and sell a host of publications, and you can get cheerfully dispensed information at each site from a refuge naturalist or park ranger.

No camping of any kind is permitted in Virginia on the refuge. Backcountry camping is free at Assateague Island National Seashore in Maryland, but the use of an overnight site and parking requires a permit. The MISTIX reservation system, which administers regular campsites in the high season, does not cover backcountry sites. The leader of each backcountry camping party must obtain permits in person at the campground registration office, off Bayberry Drive, by midafternoon on the day of arrival. Your chances of nailing a regular site on a summer weekend are 50-50; it's easier before Memorial Day and after Labor Day.

FEES **Entrance Fees.** Every vehicle entering the national seashore grounds is charged $4; upon payment you receive a paper pass, good for seven days, that should be displayed prominently on your dashboard. Pedestrians and cyclists pay $2 per person.

Pedestrians and cyclists are admitted free to Chincoteague National Wildlife Refuge; drivers pay $4 per carload.

Frequent visitors to the national seashore can purchase a $10 annual entrance pass. The refuge's equivalent comes in the form of a Duck Stamp, which can be obtained for $15 at most post offices, some sporting goods stores, and at the refuge itself. You may also obtain the federal Duck Stamp through the mail, by sending $15.50 (which includes postage and handling) to the U.S. Postal Service, Philatelic Sales Division, Washington, D.C. 20265.

The Maryland and Virginia portions of the island honor three of the authorized entrance passes: the annual Golden Eagle Passport ($25), the lifetime Golden Age Passport (available to those 62 years or older for a one-time fee of $10), and the lifetime Golden Access Passport.

Recreation Use Fees. Overnight campers on the Maryland end pay $10 a night for a site May 15–September 30, when reservations can be made in advance. During the rest of the year, sites cost $8 but are doled out on a first-come, first-served basis. The Group Campsite, available to legitimately established groups only, must be reserved in advance at a charge of $18 a night for each of five sites available. (*See* Camping, *below,* for information on the reservation system.) Camping of any kind is prohibited on the wildlife refuge, but the grounds are open for day visitors year-round.

ORV (Off-road vehicle) owners must fill out an application for a permit and submit $40 in payment by mail or in person. The permit is valid for one year, from February 1.

PUBLICATIONS The 127-page *Assateague Island Handbook* ($6.95) is your best bet for an overview of Assateague's natural history and terrain. Produced by the National Park Service, the book features color photographs of plant and animal life and eight pages devoted to the highly publicized wild horses.

Pick up a copy of *The Life of Assateague,* a handy 5-by-7-inch paperback by Bill Perry, for a guide to the three short nature trails, each devoted to different ecosystems, on the island's northern end. There are black-and-white photographs and pen-and-ink renderings of sundry flora and fauna.

Dr. Stephen P. Leatherman's *Barrier Island Handbook* is a valuable study of island environments and their evolution; it also analyzes the effect of human and vehicular traffic on islands like Assateague.

At the top of the list for ornithologists are *A Field Guide to the Birds of Eastern and Central North America* by Roger Tory Peterson and *The Birder's Handbook* by Paul R. Ehrlich, David S. Dobkin, and Darryl Wheye. The latter, at almost 800 pages, isn't for carrying around in the field, but it's one of the best resources on bird biology and behavior. Peterson's classic text, on the other hand, is a general, portable, user-friendly accompaniment for walks and is especially useful for its field identification tips.

Birdlife at Chincoteague and the Virginia Barrier Islands by Brooke Meanley, a biologist who specialized in ornithology and spent many years in the Chesapeake Bay region, is a 100-odd-page paperback with black-and-white photographs. It gives a nice overview of bird populations on the North American barrier islands, from Assateague in the north to the southerly Fishermans Island.

Misty of Chincoteague by Marguerite Henry practically put Chincoteague and its wild horses on the map. It remains a children's classic and is very good reading. If your child prefers the factual, try the Center for Marine Conservation's wonderful 113-page paperback *The Ocean Book;* it's full of experiments, crossword puzzles, riddles, and educational activities for all ages.

Finally, take advantage of the multitude of free brochures available at every visitor's center. They cover all areas of interest and activity on the island; from the resident populations of mammals and birds to opportunities for shelling, shellfishing, hunting, and camping. A color map of the island and basic rundown of seasonal sports, also free, will be mailed to you on request.

GEOLOGY AND TERRAIN Assateague Island is about 6,000 years old. Evidence of its makeup points definitively to the Appalachian Mountains, eroded fragments of which traveled down the Delaware River valley and settled on the continental shelf. Assateague started out as a peninsula of Delaware. Through the action of winds and waves, the island grew longer and longer, like a slightly decurved Pinocchio's nose composed of sand. These sands shift constantly, and regular visitors will note a decidedly different shoreline from one season to the next. During this century alone, the southern tip has extended more than 2 miles, and the northern reaches have sidled hundreds of feet westward.

FLORA AND FAUNA Wild horses are among the largest animals at Assateague; they're certainly the most publicized. Stalwart creatures with thick skin and stout silhouettes, they consume a salty diet of cord and beach grass, which makes for a plump profile as well as a shorter life than domesticated species. They arrived with 17th-century English settlers, for whom they were a food source. Today the island supports about 150 of them; they wander the wilderness areas or linger, in very small numbers, near roads or camping sites. *Please do not interact with these creatures.* Eleven have been killed by cars in the past five years after discovering how easy it is to get food from humans on roadways. Appealing as they may seem, the horses will bite and kick; children, especially, should keep their distance. An overlook spanning Black Duck Marsh on the Woodland Trail at the refuge is a good place to view grazing bands of two to ten.

Other frequently sighted mammals include the white-tailed deer and the smaller, exotic sika elk; the latter, with a dark stripe down its back and white spots on its sides, was imported from Asia in the early 20th century.

The maritime forest surrounding the Woodland Trail on the Virginia end is a good place to observe both species; for sika, in particular, try the Lighthouse Trail within the shrub habitat areas.

Many of the other land mammals are elusive. The opossum, brown bat, meadow jumping mouse, raccoon, and red fox are all nocturnal. The Delmarva fox squirrel, an endangered species carefully managed and monitored by the refuge, does most of its stuff in the early morning and late afternoon. The river otter, though shy, may be seen in the bay or in impoundments during the day if you keep your distance. Educational exhibits along the Woodland Trail edify walkers on wildlife.

With Assateague Island's position on the Atlantic flyway, its proximity to miles of open sea, and its rich food supply in the form of grasses, bulrushes, and aquatic creatures, both migratory and resident bird populations prosper. Even Christmas Counts on Chincoteague usually document over 150 species. Nesting colonies of willets, oystercatchers, laughing gulls, herons, egrets, terns, and ibises abound; warblers, clapper rails, and black ducks breed consistently; and large concentrations of migratory birds winter along the coastal strands. Due to the endangered status of the piping plover—a little, sand-colored shorebird—the seashore and the refuge often seal off parts of the island, including the entire southern hook, during nesting season.

As for flora, the beach, forest, and marsh each nourish distinctive forms. The dune area, though markedly devoid of vegetation, does support some hearty, low-lying plants with powerful root systems (*Hudsonia*, American beach grass). Loblolly pine, a species not found north of the Delmarva Peninsula, dominates the island's landscape but contorts into gnarled roots and branches seaside, where sand and wind wreak havoc on its growth. In the woodland areas, however, it climbs to heights of 80 to 100 feet.

The salt marshes and meadows are filled with salt marsh cordgrass (which the horses eat in great quantity), seashore salt grass, and salt meadow cordgrass. Wetlands also sustain a rich supply of three-square rush, a crucial nourishment for the migratory waterfowl that winter here. Aster, rose pink, bayberry, wax myrtle, and many common ferns light up the otherwise uniform hues of the field and forest.

A word on the pests that show up around late May and don't retreat until autumn. Mosquitoes are the most pesky. The greenhead, or American horsefly, lands but gives its victim three or four seconds before it bites, so at least you have a chance of swatting it. The very persistent stable fly is gray and looks like the common housefly but bites when it lands. This one has a penchant for ankles. The only other annoyance—but a serious one—is the tick that causes Lyme. Stay on trails to avoid it; it also helps to wear long trousers and long sleeves.

WHEN TO GO Assateague Island is a year-round destination. The best weather is in late spring and fall, but winds can be unpredictable during these seasons, and nighttime temperatures drop. In May, the average temperature is almost 70°F, but the water temperature is still only in the high 50s. The crowds (and insects) arrive in the summer, when you can count on ocean temperatures climbing to the mid-70s. Stick some industrial-strength insect repellent in your beach bag.

If you're a birder, come during the migratory waterfowl season between September and December. In September, both air and water temperatures are usually in the 70s, and biting insects have dwindled. December averages 40° temperatures, but unpredictable winds and precipitation make long underwear essential. Those who like solitude and pristine surroundings may prefer the winter, despite occasional storms.

Campsites are usually full from mid-June to Labor Day. In the spring and fall, weekends are heavily trafficked as well.

SEASONAL EVENTS **Easter weekend:** The **Chincoteague Easter Decoy Festival** celebrates the talents of about 150 local artists who exhibit their works and submit them for viewing and sales. **Last Wednesday and Thursday in July:** After two weeks of food and fireworks at the Chincoteague Volunteer Firemen's Carnival, visitors watch the herds of wild horses cross the Assateague Channel and mount the shores of Chincoteague Island during the **Firemen's Annual Pony Swim and Auction,** a tradition dating from 1925. **Columbus Day weekend:** Oysters come in many guises—raw, steamed, fried, or frittered—at the annual **Oyster Festival** in Chincoteague. **Thanksgiving week:** Come to the **Waterfowl Open House** and you'll get a crack at observation points on the refuge's northern end that are not open the rest of the year. Refuge representatives present guided walks and lectures on wildlife. **Christmas week:** Participants in the annual **Christmas Count,** sponsored by the National Audubon Society, document the populations of birds sighted within a 15-mile area of Chincoteague.

PETS The best advice is not to bring them. No pets of any kind are allowed on the refuge, even if kept in your car the whole time. Dogs are allowed, on leashes no longer than 6 feet only, on much of the national seashore. But hot beach sand can be hard on paws, and sand-loaded winds may sting the eyes of even hardy breeds.

WHAT TO PACK Between mid-May and September, bring insect repellent. You may need long trousers and long sleeves in marshy areas. Bring a windbreaker and rain gear no matter what the season. You don't necessarily need hiking boots (trails are easy and beach-face doesn't require them); but if you're going out in marshy areas, consider packing high-top waterproof footwear. If you're doing any shellfishing, bring wading shoes—rangers warn that thongs aren't suitable. Since only one food concession operates on the island—and offers little more than hot dogs and sodas—pack a lunch if you're a day-tripper.

GENERAL STORES The **Assateague Market** (7643 Stephen Decatur Hwy., tel. 410/641–3377; open Mar.–Oct., weekdays 7–7, weekends 7 AM–10 PM) carries everything from subs and beer to firewood and beach rafts. Canoe

rentals are available as well. **Bucks Place** (corner of Rtes. 376 and 611, tel. 410/641–4177; open Apr.–Oct., weekdays 7 AM–9 PM, weekends 7 AM–11 PM) offers an array of camping supplies—propane stoves, steamers, sleeping bags, crab traps, bait, and tackle—and the staff cheerfully dispenses information on local campsites and the area's restaurants. You can also bring in your film for developing.

Since there are no food concessions on the Virginia end within the refuge, you might want to pick up a lunch on your way in: Try **J&B Cold Cuts** (3571 Main St., Chincoteague, tel. 804/336–5500) or **Steve's Mini Market** (Maddox Blvd., Chincoteague, tel. 804/336–1958).

ATMS On the Virginia end, go to the Marine Bank (6395 Maddox Blvd., tel. 804/336–6539) in Chincoteague; it's only about 2 miles from the entrance to the refuge. At the Maryland end you'll have to shoot north for Ocean City; Coastal Highway, the main drag of this resort town, has unlimited choices.

ARRIVING AND DEPARTING Traveling between the entrance to the national seashore in Maryland and the entrance to the wildlife refuge in Virginia, a distance of approximately 57 miles, requires about 1¹⁄₂ hours on the road. The Maryland entrance is 259 miles from New York City and 135 miles from Baltimore; the Virginia entrance is 166 miles from Washington, D.C., and 177 miles from Philadelphia. The best way to get here is by car; any other transportation involves a combination of modes that will run you ragged or broke.

By Plane. The nearest airport is in Salisbury, Maryland, 30 to 45 minutes from the national seashore entrance and about an hour to the front gates of the refuge. **USAir** (tel. 800/428–4322) is the only major carrier that services this small airport. (Book on an advance-reservation special or you'll pay a fortune for your fare.) You can rent a car at the airport from **Avis** (tel. 800/331–1212), **Hertz** (tel. 800/654–3131), or **National** (tel. 800/328–4567); there is no municipal bus service, and a cab ride to either park entrance will run you $50–$60. By car from Salisbury, take the billboard-infested Route 50 for the most direct approach to the national seashore entrance, or follow Route 12 to the Virginia coast.

By Car and RV. The national seashore begins about 10 miles south of Ocean City, Maryland, on Route 611. It takes about three hours to drive here from either Washington or Baltimore. Use the Chesapeake Bay Bridge; then make your way east on Route 50, or take the more scenic passage across the Delmarva Peninsula via Routes 404 and 113. From Wilmington, you can come directly down Route 13 through Dover to Route 113 South (though you might have fewer traffic headaches by jogging a bit west to the lovely Route 213, then picking up either Route 50 or Route 404). The latter option takes quite a bit longer, but the eastern shore of the Chesapeake Bay through Kent County is blessed with the coastal plain and long stretches of farmland that have made the area famous.

By Train. While not recommended, it's possible to travel by Amtrak (tel. 800/872–7245) to Wilmington, then walk over to the **Hertz** offices across from the station and rent a car for the rest of your journey.

By Bus. The closest terminal is in Ocean City, Maryland, 10 miles north of Assateague Island. Two buses run there daily from Wilmington, at 2:45 PM and 6:45 PM ($26.75 one way). You'll need to rent a car or hire a taxi for the last leg of the trip.

EXPLORING

The two entrances to the seashore boundaries are about 1¹/₂ hours apart, so decide where you're going to station yourself for the day rather than shuttling back and forth. Then get out and walk or ride a bike. These forms of transport allow you to absorb the setting much more fully than if you're huddled in a car or a tour bus. It's easy to park at the major trailheads, and since changing facilities and rest rooms are ample near the major parking areas, there's no need to return to your car.

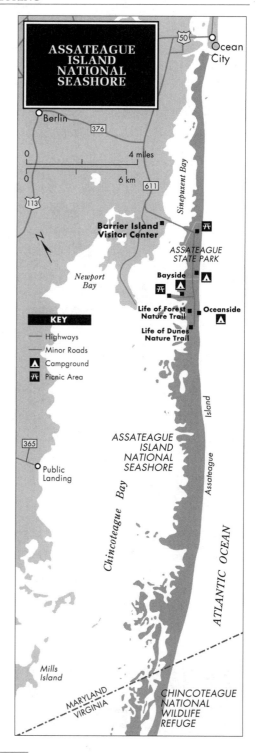

ASSATEAGUE ISLAND NATIONAL SEASHORE

KEY

— Highways
— Minor Roads
▲ Campground
🏕 Picnic Area

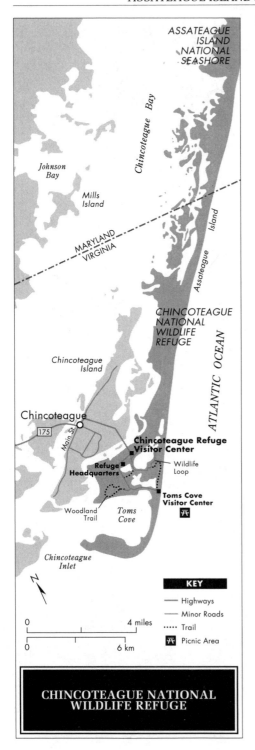

ASSATEAGUE
ISLAND
NATIONAL
SEASHORE

Chincoteague Bay

Johnson
Bay

Mills
Island

Assateague Island

MARYLAND
VIRGINIA

CHINCOTEAGUE
NATIONAL
WILDLIFE
REFUGE

ATLANTIC OCEAN

Chincoteague
Island

Chincoteague
175
Main St.

Chincoteague Refuge
Visitor Center

Refuge
Headquarters

Wildlife
Loop

Toms Cove
Visitor Center

Woodland
Trail

Toms
Cove

Chincoteague
Inlet

N

0   4 miles
0   6 km

KEY
— Highways
— Minor Roads
····· Trail
🅰 Picnic Area

**CHINCOTEAGUE NATIONAL
WILDLIFE REFUGE**

THE BEST IN ONE DAY Again, get out of the car and use your feet. Try the trails recommended under Nature Trails and Short Walks *(see below)* if you want to combine exploring wildlife areas or various island ecosystems with sunbathing or beach activities. *See* the walk outlined in Longer Hikes, *below,* for a more vigorous trek.

If the northern portion of the island isn't closed off during the piping plover's nesting season, you can walk that beachface to see the more pristine segments of the shore. If you're partial to bay (as opposed to surf) activities, the bayside day-use area on the Maryland end offers a beautiful, unobstructed view of Chincoteague Bay, where you can windsurf for 20 miles to the south, as well as a wonderful picnic spot with tables and one of the best locations for clamming in the summer.

ORIENTATION PROGRAMS Stop for information at the Barrier Island Visitor Center on the Maryland end, or at the refuge center if you enter via the southern portion. A seasonal schedule of events, including interpreter-led walks, videos, demonstrations, and children's activities, should help you plan the day's itinerary. The walks vary from 45 minutes to 2 hours and are an excellent introduction to the seashore. Educational videos play hourly at the refuge visitor's center. On the Virginia end, an amphitheater operated by the National Park Service and an auditorium run by the Fish and Wildlife Service feature programs with subjects that change with the season.

GUIDED TOURS Ranger-led tours, lectures, and nature walks are free and are announced on bulletin boards at the Barrier Island Visitor's Center in Maryland and both the Chincoteague Refuge Visitor Center and the Toms Cove Visitor Center in Virginia.

A private operation, **Wildlife Tours** is the only concessionaire within the seashore boundaries; they maintain a booth at the Fish and Wildlife Refuge Visitor's Center. For information, call the visitor's center (tel. 804/336–5593) or the Refuge Motor Inn (tel. 804/336–5511). A 1½-hour safari tour takes you on a bus trip through the heart of the refuge (Apr. 1–Nov. 15; $5 adults, $2.50 children under 12). Book in person, a day in advance if you can. An evening cruise (Memorial Day–Oct.; $8 adults, $4 children) takes passengers through the Assateague channel.

SCENIC DRIVES AND VIEWS The Wildlife Loop in the refuge is open to vehicular traffic daily 3 PM–dusk. Ocean lovers need only seek out the coastline for 30 or so miles of amusement. The best view of Chincoteague Bay is probably on the northern end at the bayside day-use area. For opportunities to view wildlife, *see* Flora and Fauna *in* Essential Information, *above,* and Nature Trails and Short Walks and Longer Hikes, *below.*

NATURE TRAILS AND SHORT WALKS All the trails on the island are relatively short; only the refuge's Wildlife Loop (*see below*) exceeds 3 miles. The trails cover flat terrain, paths are well maintained, and trailheads are clearly marked. Walkers and cyclists should stay on them so as not to trample the sand-trapping vegetation that stabilizes dunes or to disturb habitats crucial to the survival of wildlife. Moreover, you're far more likely to pick up disease-carrying ticks off the trail.

Assateague. Three nature trails on the Maryland end of the island—none more than .5 mile long—wander through three different ecosystems. Their trailheads are all within easy walking distance of both the oceanside and bayside campgrounds; the Life of the Dunes and Life of the Forest trails start right off Bayberry Drive, and the Life of the Marsh loop begins about .25 mile northwest of the intersection of Bayberry and Bayside drives. Pick up the booklet *The Life of Assateague* (*see* Publications *in* Essential Information, *above*) on your way into the park, and follow its commentary on local vegetation and animal life as you amble along the flat, sandy pathways. The text's numbered format corresponds to strategically posted signs.

Chincoteague. The refuge passes out free maps of the grounds, indicating the locations of trails and nature walks, at both visitor's centers. The **Woodland Trail** (1.6 miles) is a short, paved loop appropriate for pedestrians and cyclists as well as wheelchairs. The maritime forest is on view here, and visitors can look forward to sighting migrating songbirds, possibly the endangered Delmarva squirrel, and both the native white-tailed deer and the sika elk. Freestanding exhibits dot the trail. While a chance to view the horses isn't guaranteed, interested visitors should stop at the overlook for vistas that include this animal's grazing compartments.

The **Black Duck Trail** is less than .5 mile long and really serves as a connector between the Woodland Trail and the Wildlife Loop, with no trailhead as such. It's for foot, bike, and wheelchair traffic only. The paved path is an interface between two managed impoundments where ducks, geese, swans, and various shorebirds gather.

The little **Lighthouse Trail** is only .25 mile long but includes a boardwalk over natural terrain and sandy traverses that are appropriate for foot traffic only. This route should not be attempted by the disabled, as there is some steep grade up the side of old sand dunes. You'll be covering unique barrier island habitats—shrub, forest, and dune. The lighthouse still operates under the auspices of the Coast Guard.

Swan's Cove Trail is partly paved, partly graveled. The trailhead starts at the Toms Cove Visitor's Center parking lot, and passage is permitted to pedestrians and bicyclists only—no mopeds allowed. The 1.25-mile trail parallels the shoreline (though you don't see the Atlantic because the sand dune is high), then bends westward to hook up neatly with the longer Wildlife Loop. Wading birds are commonly sighted here.

The **Wildlife Loop** is a 3.2-mile ellipse, open all day to pedestrians and bicyclists; from 3 PM until dusk, vehicular traffic is also permitted. Begin your walk at the parking lot adjacent to the Chincoteague Refuge Visitor's Center, or use one of the smaller trails—Black Duck or Swan's Cove—as a warm-up before heading directly into the loop. The Wildlife Loop crosses over coves, traverses loblolly forests, and borders grass-filled marsh.

LONGER HIKES The beach is where strong walkers can get a workout. Even at low tide, the sand is soft, and walkers end up nearly doubling their actual walking distance because their foot muscles flex an extra 20° to 30° in order to traverse the malleable surface. If you're not in great shape, watch out for shinsplints. Or walk backward if you're not too self-conscious. According to park rangers, it minimizes the damage to unpracticed muscle groups.

For a longer walk through numerous ecosystems, habitats, and terrains, park in the lot north of the Toms Cove Visitor's Center. Take Swan's Cove Trail to its terminus, then turn right onto the Wildlife Loop and continue over Snow Goose Pool until you hit an intersection. If you were to turn left here, you'd still be on the loop; but by turning right (bicycles are not permitted beyond this point) you can walk parallel to the shoreline past the first dune crossing (closed to all traffic, including pedestrian) to the second dune crossing. Take this crossing, which is marked D DIKE, all the way to the sea, and walk back to your car via the beach; you can go barefoot from here, if it's warm enough, and pick up shells along the way. You'll have covered about 7 miles, but it will feel like more due to the beachface. Strong walkers can do the distance easily in an afternoon.

OTHER ACTIVITIES **Back-Road Driving.** Four-wheel-drive vehicles have been scooting up and down the beachface on the island's eastern rim for decades. The 12-mile stretch open to off-road vehicles (ORVs) on the Maryland end fills up by 9:30 each weekend morning between Memorial Day and Labor Day.

ORV drivers should call the seashore or refuge and request an application for an ORV permit and the brochure entitled "Off-Road Vehicles." Permits cost $40 a year and may be obtained through the mail or in person on either end of the island. The brochure includes a clear graphic of both the Virginia and Maryland ORV zones, which run north and south along the beachface, and indicates the locations of air pumps, emergency telephones, and dune crossings. Trucks must stay on the ocean side of the post areas and adhere to the existing track, for the sake both of the environment and transmissions. The speed limit of 25 miles per hour is strictly enforced. All the rules and regulations regarding ORV use (including vehicular size and equipment requirements) are specified in the brochure.

The Maryland seashore controls ORV traffic by imposing a limit of 145 vehicles; the Virginia end takes only 48 at a time. Bad news for privacy-seekers: Trucks lined up on the shore in the summer may not sit more than 3 or 4 yards apart from each other. During the piping plover's nesting season (March 15–August 31), the Refuge Hook is closed to all traffic, and the number of ORVs allowed drops to 18. In the event that plovers nest in a four-wheel-drive area in Maryland, the park then seals off the area and .5 mile to the south and north.

Biking. The beachface is strictly off-limits; on the Maryland end, use the 3-mile paved path marked for bicycles along Bayberry Drive; in Virginia, peddle around the Wildlife Loop, the Woodland Trail, or Swan's Cove Trail. All are flat, well-maintained routes that present no serious aerobic challenge, and surfaces are paved or sandy with strewn gravel. The Wildlife Loop is best before 3 PM, when the road opens to vehicular traffic.

Go to the south end of the island for rentals. (You won't need anything fancy.) **T&T Riding Rentals** (Maddox Blvd., Chincoteague, tel. 804/336–6330; open daily 6 AM–9 PM) rents cycles of all types and speeds. A standard one-speed is $2 an hour, $10 a day. **Piney Island Country Store** (Maddox Blvd., Chincoteague, tel. 804/336–6212) will tack on a child carrier for 50¢ more per hour or $1 extra daily.

Bird-Watching. Almost 300 species have been spotted on Assateague Island. While one hears sad tales of endangerment with ever-increasing frequency, the good news on the Maryland seashore is that both the osprey and brown pelican appear to be healing from their DDT-inflicted troubles. A brochure available on both ends of the island gives a rundown of the predominantly migratory bird population and tells you when each species is most likely to be sighted. Bring a field guide and binoculars; the serious birder should pack a spotting sight. Check the bulletin boards at the visitor's centers for upcoming ranger-led bird walks.

Boating. If you launch from the national seashore, boat motors must not exceed 7.5 horsepower. Canoers launch into Chincoteague Bay from Old Ferry Landing, within a mile of the campgrounds, and venture south to choose from four bayside canoe-in camping sites (off-limits to motorboats). Each site is marked by a sign showing a silhouette of two boaters in a canoe. The closest is 2 miles away, the farthest 13. The sites are open year-round but are most welcoming in the spring and fall; summer mosquitoes drive even the island's horses away. The only permissible landing point in Virginia is at the southernmost tip of the island, called Fishing Point. Canoe rentals are available at **Assateague Market** (Rte. 611, tel. 410/641–3377), a mile north of the national seashore, at $30 a day (plus a credit-card deposit of $200). At **Rainy Day Canoes** (Rte. 589, Racetrack Rd., Berlin, MD, tel. 410/641–5029), you can get one for $20 a day and a $50 deposit. **Barnacle Bill's** (568 S. Main St., Chincoteague, VA, tel. 804/336–5188) carries bait, tackle, ice, and maps as well as boats for rent.

At the Chincoteague National Wildlife Refuge, boats are allowed to land only at Fishing Point on the Hook (September 1–March 14).

Fishing. People do fish in the bay (by boat only) on the Maryland end around the first three buoys, but conditions aren't great. At the refuge, fishing and crabbing are permitted in Toms Cove, Swan's Cove adjacent to Beach Road, and a few other seasonally assigned areas.

Surf Fishing. Anglers flock here for flounder, croaker, spot, kingfish, weakfish, black drum, red drum, striped bass, bluefish, northern puffer, and shark. You can fish 24 hours a day if you want, but the rule specifies that all members of your party must be participating. Late spring and fall are the optimum seasons,

but in summer there are regularly scheduled demonstrations by park experts. The Toms Cove Visitor's Center at the Chincoteague National Wildlife Refuge is an official weigh station.

Shellfishing. Several succulent bivalves— quahog clams, oysters, ribbed mussels—and the blue crab populate the waters around the island. Oyster season is September 15–March 15 only; clams must measure an inch in width to be kept; crabs of less than 5 inches from point to point must be thrown back, and no crab fishing is permitted from January through March. More than one collapsible crab pot qualifies you as a commercial fisherman, which requires a license. Ask for the blue "Shellfishing in Maryland" brochure at the Barrier Island Visitor Center: It specifies maximum catches for the day and provides a map showing the best sites for each species. Shellfishing is also allowed on the refuge at Toms Cove.

Horseback Riding. *Maryland:* Riding is allowed on the national seashore October 9– May 14; in the summer and early fall, mosquitoes and flies plague humans and horses alike. If you are traveling with a group that includes five or more horses *or* you intend to stay overnight, you need a permit from the Office of the Superintendent before you arrive. The Horse Group Site, on the ocean side, accommodates no more than 12 units (any combination of motor homes, horse trailers, and tents with vehicles), no more than 25 people, and no more than 25 horses; the overnight charge for the entire site is $25.

Hunting. Before you come, contact the Assateague Island National Seashore and request the "Hunting Plan" literature on all aspects of regulations, fees, and traditions. Hunters must pay the normal entrance fee and obtain an ORV permit ($40). Individual registration at the Sinepuxent Ranger Station, where campers register for campsites, is mandatory when entering and leaving the hunting zone.

Sika season runs from mid-September through January. Foxhunting is permitted during daylight hours November 15–December 31. White-tailed deer may not be hunted. Huntable waterfowl include Canada geese, snow geese, brant, and nine genera of duck. Each bird has its own season, the earliest starting in mid-October and the latest wrapping up by mid-February. The mourning dove, king and clapper rails, Virginia and sora rails, woodcock, common snipe, and common moorhens and purple gallinules go up for grabs at various times from September to mid-January.

The Chincoteague National Wildlife Refuge allows sika hunting for population-management purposes; there are no limits on the number you may bag. Archery enthusiasts pay $10 apiece and must acquire a permit by mail; they must also pass a bow-hunter education test. Gun hunters, determined by public drawing, are charged $15 each.

Shelling. At the national seashore you'll find everything from spiraling whelks and tough little periwinkles to the smooth, concentric sculpture of the surf clam. You may take out no more than one gallon of shells per beach visit. Thirty-odd bivalves and gastropods comprise a park checklist available at the ranger station.

Surfing. Daredevils venture out in wet suits weeks before most mortals would consider dipping their toes. Each year designated areas are set aside for surfing; swimming and other beach activities are prohibited there. Ask at the visitor's center when you arrive.

Swimming. Between Memorial Day and Labor Day, the North Beach in Maryland and the Toms Cove area of the refuge offer life-guarded stretches of beach. At Assateague there is a bathhouse next to the day-use parking lot where you can shower and change; toilets and potable water are also available. On the Virginia end, two bathhouses with similar facilities sit right off the beach at Toms Cove.

Windsurfing. The bay is ideal when the wind is up. Launch from the bayside day-use area on the Maryland end, and you'll have 20 miles to play in.

CHILDREN'S PROGRAMS **Assateague.** The Barrier Island Visitor Center houses a 220-gallon aquarium, a 110-gallon touch tank populated by harmless marine creatures, and a beachcomber room with hands-on museum displays. Aquarium feedings are held regularly with a young audience in mind. Check the weekly schedule posted at the center for talks or walks that children would enjoy. Many of the park brochures are written in simple prose that will stimulate a child's curiosity. There is also a typed sheet for children, the "Visitor's Center Explorer."

Chincoteague. During the summer, the refuge center offers two programs specifically for children. "Kids and Critters" (Thurs. and Sat. at 2) engages four- to six-year-olds; "Junior Refuge Manager" sessions (Mon. and Sat. at 2) are for seven- to ten-year-olds.

EVENING ACTIVITIES Evening programs vary with the season. An amphitheater and auditorium on the Virginia end offer nighttime lectures and illustrated programs. The Barrier Island Visitor's Center in the north schedules weekend evening talks throughout the year. During the summer, the Toms Cove Visitor's Center hosts ranger-led programs nightly at 8:30. Outdoor campfire programs are held Sunday, Wednesday, and Friday evenings; indoor slide shows every Monday, Thursday, and Saturday.

DINING

Fresh seafood and shellfish are the draw here—crab cakes, fresh flounder, softshell crabs, and Chincoteague oysters. Plenty of fast-food eateries and deli markets operate in Chincoteague (there's a McDonald's immediately outside the refuge entrance). For something more substantial (but where casual dress is still appropriate), consider the following establishments.

INSIDE THE PARK Only one small concession operates on the island, on the Maryland end, on state park grounds east of the state park entrance. Apart from cheeseburgers and ice cream the menu is limited. It's a good idea to pack your own lunch.

Captain's Galley II. This spruced-up waterfront property on the commercial fishing harbor in West Ocean City has a large seating capacity, and boats are granted free docking privileges for the evening. Fresh seafood, including crab cakes made with Maryland back-fin crabmeat, is the byword. Entrées run $10–$20. *12817 Harbor Rd., West Ocean City, MD, tel. 410/213–2525. Reservations only for parties of 12 or more. AE, D, MC, V. Moderate.*

The Steamer Restaurant. The menus may be greasy and the exterior weathered, but the seafood is fresh, you can eat inside or out, and you get an aromatic view of the harbor. All fried dishes are given the noncholesterol oil treatment. A pound of snow crab clusters can be had for as little as $7, and broiled scallops run about $11; but big steamer combos will take you up toward $20. There's carryout all summer. Tropical cocktails, Irish coffee, and a small wine list will satisfy imbibers. Take Route 611 from the Assateague Island National Seashore and turn right at the Sunoco station onto Sunset Avenue; the Steamer is one block down on your right. *Golf Course Rd. and Sunset Ave., West Ocean City, MD, tel. 410/213–2263. Reservations not required. AE, MC, V. Inexpensive– Moderate.*

Bill's Seafood Restaurant. Decoys sit atop the window valances, and wooden booths line the walls. Come as early as 5 AM: French toast and sausage will set you back only $3. Dinners feature native seafood—crab cakes, stuffed jumbo flounder, popcorn shrimp— but chicken and steaks are also available, and liquor is served. *4037 Main St., Chincoteague, VA, tel. 804/336–5831. Reservations not required. D, DC, MC, V. Closed Wed. Moderate.*

The Village Restaurant. White tablecloths, candles, and pink napkins dress up this second-story dining room and lounge. Fried Chincoteague oysters and softshell crabs top a menu interspersed with nonmarine selections like stuffed veal and baby beef liver. You'll find a longer wine list here than elsewhere. Homemade desserts are baked daily.

6576 Maddox Blvd., Chincoteague, VA, tel. 804/336–5120. Reservations advised. Dress: casual but neat. AE, D, DC, MC, V. Moderate.

Maria's Family Restaurant. Maria's is divided into three spaces: a family-style dining room with a big brick fireplace, a quick-stop shop with carryout menu for pizza and subs, and a recreation room with pinball machines and piped-in rock. The menu ranges from Italian (manicotti, veal parmigiana) to Eastern Shore (chowder, seafood platters); service is very pleasant. *6506 Maddox Blvd., Chincoteague, VA, tel. 804/336–5040. Reservations not required. No credit cards. Inexpensive.*

PICNIC SPOTS The Maryland end has two designated picnic areas, one on the ocean and one bayside; there is a third near the Toms Cove Visitor's Center on the Virginia end. These are exposed day-use sites, furnished with picnic tables and grills only, and no overhead coverings. If you're on the northern end and want to see the water, pick the bayside site; the sand dunes off the ocean site obstruct all views of the sea.

LODGING

Outside of campsites, there are no accommodations at the national seashore or the refuge. You can always stay in Ocean City, Maryland, but unless you're into Las Vegas kitsch or miniature golf, we suggest the more appealing Berlin, Maryland, and Chincoteague, Virginia. Do consider a bed-and-breakfast: Rooms aren't always cheap, but the owner/manager's lowdown on local shops and watering holes adds to the value. Book well ahead for the smaller establishments. The fewer the units, the more likely they are to be full.

Chanceford Hall. The spruce little town of Snow Hill sits inland on the Pocomoke River, about halfway between the entrances to the national seashore and the wildlife refuge. This bed-and-breakfast was constructed in three stages, beginning with the Georgian front section in 1759. Some 230 years later it was restored and turned into a showplace. The Federal-style mantels, in cool Williamsburg greens and blues, match the moldings, and there are merino-wool mattress pads and down comforters on the lace-canopy beds. The house has seven working fireplaces and reproduction furniture crafted by the owner himself. *209 W. Federal St., Snow Hill, MD 21863, tel. 410/632–2231. 4 double rooms with bath, 1 suite. Facilities: pool, bicycles. No credit cards. Expensive.*

The Atlantic Hotel. The historic district in Berlin, Maryland (7 miles from the entrance to the national seashore), got a boost when a group of local investors renovated and opened the town's Victorian centerpiece, the Atlantic Hotel, built in 1895. The guest rooms line a wide central corridor and are decorated with Oriental and floral-patterned rugs, tasseled draperies, and Tiffany-style lamps, as well as antique double beds. The Victorian arrangements extend to the piano bar and pricey restaurant downstairs, where you may leisurely partake of the Continental breakfast included in your room rate. There's a two-night minimum during the summer. *2 N. Main St., Berlin, MD 21811, tel. 410/641–3589. 16 double rooms with bath. Facilities: restaurant, piano bar. MC, V. Moderate–Expensive.*

NEAR CHINCOTEAGUE NATIONAL WILDLIFE REFUGE

Watson House Bed & Breakfast. Turn left on Main Street after you cross the bridge into the town of Chincoteague, and look to your right at the corner of Main and Poplar: You can't miss this big white Victorian. Each room, appointed with modest country furnishings, potted plants, and wicker, has a private bath, air-conditioning, and a ceiling fan. A lavish breakfast is included in the rate, along with afternoon tea. *4240 Main St., Chincoteague, VA 23336, tel. 804/336–1564. 6 rooms with bath. Facilities: off-street parking; complimentary bicycles, beach chairs. MC, V. Expensive.*

Refuge Motor Inn. Within spitting distance of the refuge, this two-story motel is equipped with modern amenities (sauna, Jacuzzi, indoor pool, exercise room) and also acts as a

kind of commercial headquarters for the refuge. The decorations are innocuous, with ducks and Canada geese on the wallpaper borders and shower curtains. The heaters rattle a bit. You can rent a bike at the front desk to pedal up to the refuge. *7058 Maddox Blvd., Box 378, Chincoteague, VA 23336, tel. 804/336–5511 or 800/544–8469. 234 rooms. Facilities: sauna, whirlpool, exercise room, indoor pool, gift shop, laundry, playground, minirefrigerators, sundeck, picnic tables, outdoor grills. D, DC, MC, V. Moderate.*

Beach Road Motel. This is a small, single-story, family-operated motel five minutes from the refuge, in downtown Chincoteague near restaurants and night spots. The standard rooms are moderately priced in summer but drop to as low as $37 after Labor Day. The more modern units utilize an earthtone decor and were recently remodeled with small refrigerators, cable TV, and small dining tables and chairs. *6151 Maddox Blvd., Chincoteague, VA 23336, tel. 804/336–6562. 23 rooms. Facilities: pool, grills, picnic tables. D, MC, V. Inexpensive–Moderate.*

Mariner Motel. The blue-carpeted rooms of this simple two-story structure are equipped with cable TV and air-conditioning, but the most appealing features are two adjoining restaurants, a pool, and a playground. It's about a mile from the refuge entrance. *6273 Maddox Blvd., Chincoteague, VA 23336, tel. 804/336–6565 or 800/221–7490, ext. 12. 92 rooms. Facilities: laundry, conference room. AE, D, MC, V. Inexpensive–Moderate.*

CAMPING

Campsites at the national seashore are available all year but fill up almost every day from mid-June to Labor Day and weekends through spring and fall. All sites operate on a first-come, first-served basis October 1–May 14; the rest of the year sites can be reserved up to eight weeks in advance, in person (no later than the day before your arrival), by mail (*see* Visitor Information *in* Essential Information, *above*), or by phone (tel. 619/452–8787 or 800/365–2267, TDD 800/274–7275). Credit cards (D, MC, V) are accepted, as is payment by check received at least 10 days before you arrive. Campers may use sites for up to seven days May–September, and for no more than 30 days for the entire calendar year. Drinking water, chemical toilets, cold showers, and sanitary dumps are all available.

The national seashore offers oceanside and bayside sites. The 104 oceanside sites are open year-round and feature both drive-in types for RV and tent camping and walk-in sites for tents only. Each individual site includes a picnic table and upright grill (no ground fires are permitted); bring your own firewood or a propane stove for cooking. The sites are all exposed and vulnerable to strong winds, which are common.

The 48 bayside sites are open spring through fall, with drive-in pads suitable for tents, trailers, and RVs. None are shaded. There are no electrical or water hookups. Fire ring grills (no other fires allowed) are provided. Again, bring your own firewood.

The oceanside group campground, open year-round, occupies five sites developed for tents only. Each site accommodates a minimum of 12 and a maximum of 25 persons. Reservations are required. Make them up to 12 weeks in advance; seven days is the maximum visit. Your particular spot won't be assigned until you arrive. Groups must be legitimate, so don't round up all your first cousins and call yourself an "organization." Ground fires are prohibited.

Backcountry Campsites. These are available on both ocean and bay sides. You'll need a parking permit, and a (free) backcountry camping permit must be obtained the day you arrive (*see* Visitor Information *in* Essential Information, *above*). Transportation of campers and their equipment by motor vehicle or motorized boat to any backcountry camp is

strictly prohibited. The two **oceanside sites,** open year-round, are hike-in only; the nearest is 4 miles from parking. The signs on the beach are hard to see, especially in foggy or rainy weather. Chemical toilets and picnic tables are provided, but drinking water is not. There are emergency telephones at dune crossings 7 and 12. The four **bayside sites** are open year-round, but biting insects make the summer uncomfortable. All four are tent-only, hike-in or canoe-in. There's a seven-day limit here, too. (Assateague State Park, next door, has hot showers, and remains popular for that reason. It also costs more. Call 410/641–2120 for more information.)

While no camping is allowed on the refuge, there are lots of private campgrounds in Chincoteague. Call or write the Chincoteague Chamber of Commerce (Box 258, Chincoteague, VA 23336, tel. 804/336–6161).

Tent Camping. Tent campers should bring 18-inch-long stakes: Sandy soil and occasional strong winds render little pegs useless. Lock up your food supplies in car trunks at night. The wild horses can tear off the tops of Styrofoam coolers, rip through tents, and create a general tornado effect at your campsite. Don't leave leftovers on picnic tables, either. If you've gotten so grungy you can't stand it any longer, there's a self-service laundry at 4037 Main St. in Chincoteague, across from Bill's Seafood Restaurant.

RVs. The maximum length allowed for a camper/motor home is 36 feet. Most vehicles have a 48-hour storage area for both freshwater and sewage treatment, and they'll do fine here. There's a water-fillup station that can fill storage tanks, and a dump station as well; so visitors in RVs can flush systems out before going home. No electric, sewer, or water hookups are available.

Biscayne National Park
Florida
By Herb Hiller

Pristine, magical—Florida the way it once was exists in the imagination nowhere more freshly than in Biscayne National Park. You can see Miami's towers from many of the park's 44 islands, yet the park itself is virtually undeveloped, and large enough for escaping everything that Miami has become. Here, preserved on 181,500 mostly watery acres, is the northernmost reach of what for many Americans remains paradise: the Florida Keys and tropical Atlantic coral reefs.

Biscayne was established in its present form in 1980. One of the newest parks in the national system, it marks a turning point for the state—from runaway development to the preservation of the one-of-a-kind realms that, from its earliest promotional history a little more than a century ago, have made Florida a favorite vacationland. The park is largely underwater, and its islands remain unbridged—conditions that have always attracted adventurers. These days, to be sure,

the adventure is on the milder side, the sort that appeals to snorkelers and divers, hikers, campers, and anglers.

In 1992 Hurricane Andrew slapped the park with winds of 150 miles per hour that mowed down the jungle canopy and sheared the park's coastal mangroves. Surging seas tumbled deepwater corals at the edge of the Gulf Stream. Park headquarters and the visitor's center were badly damaged. These facilities have been reestablished, and a new visitor's center should be completed in 1995. Not yet restored are some of the park's offshore amenities, so that camping on Boca Chita Key has been curtailed and the former interpretive center on Elliott Key is being used as a ranger station.

But Hurricane Andrew's damage was nothing compared to the ruin that loomed only 30 years ago. Pressed by developers eager to promote the next Miami Beach, the county government had incorporated the bay realm as the municipality of Islandia; there were plans to link these northernmost keys by a 20-mile causeway from the foot of Key Biscayne to the head of Key Largo.

Instead, history blinked. As alarm grew that the beauty of the upper keys and the surrounding waters might be lost forever, one of south Florida's folk heroes, then-Congressman Dante B. Fascell, arranged for the purchase of the islands and the bay portion by the federal government. In 1968 most of the present-day park was designated as Biscayne National Monument. Six years later the boundary was adjusted to connect with the northern boundary of John Pennekamp Coral Reef State Park. In 1980 Congress upgraded Biscayne's status to national park.

Today Biscayne attracts a half-million visitors a year. They come mainly during the cooler months, especially January through April, when mosquitoes are less active. A concessionaire at the Convoy Point park headquarters provides boat service to the reefs for divers, snorkelers, and glass-bottom viewers, but only rare service to the islands. The side-by-side mainland cities of Homestead and Florida City provide anything else that visitors might need, including sailboats and powerboats. Boating the shallow waters of the bay can be risky, and getting pulled off the bottom is costly. Biscayne is for people who know what they're doing—and whose idea of a good time is somewhat more demanding than plopping down at a resort.

ESSENTIAL INFORMATION

VISITOR INFORMATION Contact **Biscayne National Park** (Box 1369, Homestead 33090–1369, tel. 305/247-PARK, fax 305/242-9601). Backcountry permits are not required for the campgrounds on Elliott Key or Boca Chita Key. Permits are only required for camping outside of the official campground on Elliott Key; they are free and are available at the Convoy Point park headquarters.

FEES No fees are charged for admission, for access to the islands, or for berthing boats at the Elliott Key docks. However, the park con-

cessionaire charges for trips to the coral reefs and, when the service is provided, to Elliott Key (*see* Guided Tours, Boating, *and* Diving and Snorkeling *in* Exploring, *below*).

PUBLICATIONS Literature beyond the official park brochure is limited. *Biscayne: The Story Behind the Scenery* by L. Wayne Landrum, the park's former chief ranger, provides beautiful pictures and adequate descriptions of the principal zones of interest; but it overlooks the story of how the park was saved for the public. It costs $5.95. Free (though with advertising) is *Everglades & Biscayne National Parks,* published by American Park Network (22 Battery St., San Francisco, CA 94111, tel. 415/788–2228). This booklet contains more practical information (such as advice on taking pictures), but it's slanted toward Everglades. Neither publication contains information about the impact of Hurricane Andrew. Both are available at the park.

GEOLOGY AND TERRAIN The park occupies the southern portion of Biscayne Bay, below Miami and north of the bridged Florida Keys. Its area combines four distinct zones of water and land formed during the Ice Age, going back some 100,000 years. From shore to sea, the four zones include mangrove forest along the coast; Biscayne Bay, a shallow nursery for marine life; the undeveloped upper Florida keys; and the coral reefs. The park is 95% below water and ranges from 4 feet above sea level to 10 fathoms, or 60 feet, below.

The setting was formed as glaciers alternately advanced, absorbing water, and retreated, releasing water, thereby gently cradling the formation of life in the shallows. Freshwater released by the glacier in its last retreat combined with the lagoon contained by the outer reefs along the edge of the Gulf Stream, creating the brackish basin that remains today.

During interglacial periods, when the climate was warmer and the sea level higher, a chain of patch reefs grew in the shallow sea. These reefs were formed by the interaction of corals and algae in a process only slightly different from today. Corals and algae both extracted chemicals from the sea, which they converted to calcium carbonate and which over centuries became compacted into limestone. (Erosion of this limestone became the primary source of south Florida's beaches.) Then, as seawater was reabsorbed by advancing glaciers, lowering the level of the sea, the limestone formations emerged above the surface, attracted plant life, and became what we know as the Florida Keys.

Reef building continues today, though the process is microscopic. Branching corals add about 3 inches a year, while a hard coral may take 50 years to reach the size of a basketball. The corals are actually colonies of tiny, soft-bodied polyps that catch drifting plankton from outstretched tentacles. They use the calcium to build skeletons, which form the shapes so attractive to snorkelers and divers. The clustered corals form reefs, attracting a huge and diverse population; sea life lodges in every hole and crack.

The reef-building process is as geographically limited as it is slow, because the corals tolerate only the narrowest range of conditions. Seawater must be just the right temperature and depth, clean, and bright. Conditions at Biscayne remain salubrious, though the reefs are ever threatened by pollution from the mainland, the grounding of ships, and fisherfolk and recreational divers who drop anchor on them and otherwise harm them by touch—or, worse—by taking.

FLORA AND FAUNA Biscayne's corals range from the soft, flagellant fans, plumes, and whips found chiefly in the shallower patch reefs to the hard brain corals, elkhorn, and staghorn forms that can withstand the heavier wave action and depths along the ocean's edge. But some of the forms that predominate on each set of reefs are also found on the other.

More than 200 species of fish inhabit the reefs, from flamboyant angelfish, wrasses, and neon gobies to ordinary moray eels. Some, like the grunts, dart about in schools of thousands, swimming with balletlike precision. Sharp-beaked parrot fish can be seen—even heard—munching on coral, from which they extract algae and coral polyps. (They're the only creatures allowed to molest the corals.)

This marine life depends heavily on the park's plant life, particularly the red mangroves that line the mainland shore of the bay and the islands. These hardy trees have roots that arch low above the shallow waters. The roots filter out pollutants from the shore, while providing a safe habitat for microscopic sea life and young shrimp and fish, which feed here before venturing into the fish-eat-fish reefs and depths beyond.

Most of the islands are covered with dense tropical forests formed from seeds borne here on the north-flowing winds and currents of the Caribbean. These hardwood forests, called hammocks, include such species as the buttonwood, gumbo-limbo, Jamaican dogwood, lignum vitae, mahogany, pigeon plum, poisonwood, red and black mangrove, strangler fig, torchwood, and wild lime. The forest on Boca Chita Key is different—mainly casuarina (or Australian) pine, a nonnative tree introduced around 1900 as a windbreak for erosion control. Plans call for removing these trees because they tend to crowd out native species.

Walking along trails through the keys, you are likely to see other natives such as zebra butterflies, the rare Schaus swallowtail butterfly, and golden orb spiders. Raccoons, rabbits, and various rodents live here (they are not to be fed); deer, no longer. Bird life includes brown pelicans, white ibis, blue herons, snowy egrets, and other wading birds, as well as bald eagles, ospreys, and peregrine falcons.

HUMAN HISTORY The Tequesta, the first known inhabitants of the area, seem to have collected the abundant seafood, fashioned their canoes from trees of the hammocks, and crafted implements from shells.

The Spanish nominally controlled these islands for 300 years beginning in the early 16th century. Before Florida's acquisition by the United States in 1821, the islands had become hideouts for pirates who raided merchant ships in the offshore straits. Among the last of these was Black Caesar, a 6½-foot-tall African who intercepted slave ships. He set the slaves free on uninhabited islands on both sides of the straits. The name Caesar Creek (between Adams Key and Old Rhodes Key) bears witness to his exploits—as may a yet-undiscovered 24 tons of silver said to have been buried just before the U.S. Navy captured him in 1822.

Wreckers followed pirates. Ostensibly, they salvaged cargo and crew from ships that ran aground on the offshore reefs. But many ships were lured to their doom by venal wreckers who flashed false navigational lights that brought ships onto the very reefs they sought to avoid. Records verify 499 wrecks between 1848 and 1858 alone, with a combined loss valued at $16.3 million. The situation changed after the government began building aids to navigation; by 1900, wrecking was no longer profitable.

Later inhabitants grew pineapples, limes, tomatoes, and yams, smuggled liquor during Prohibition, and carved out playtime hide-aways for the wealthy. Mark Honeywell, of the company best known for its heating system controls, owned Boca Chita Key from 1937 to 1945. His most notable legacy, a 65-foot decorative tower, was built as a light-house but was never approved by the Coast Guard.

Adams Key was the site of the Cocolobo Club, where rich and famous visitors included Presidents Harding, Roosevelt, Johnson, and Nixon. Elliott Key, the park's largest island, was once the site of Camp Recovery, a county detox center for alcoholics.

One of the most colorful chapters of the pre–national park era will end in 1999, when state-issued leases expire on the remaining homes in Stiltsville, just below Key Biscayne. The park plans to renew none of them. Starting in the early '30s, the rustic houses here were built on pilings. At one time 14 occupied the tidal flats. Most of them have been lost to hurricane and fire; only six remain.

The Ragged Keys, just north of Boca Chita Key, are still privately owned.

WHEN TO GO The park is open year-round. Mosquitoes, however, are a problem during south Florida's long summer. Most of the region's 65 or so inches of rain falls during this time of year, typically in brief but drenching afternoon showers. Hurricanes, too, are a summer and fall phenomenon. Thus, it's best to visit between November and April. Temperatures during the winter months drop to the 60s and low 70s (in extreme cases, the low 40s) at night and rise to the 80s and 90s (occasionally the high 90s) by day. Humidity is especially high in summer.

SEASONAL EVENTS Two annual events upset the park's usual tranquillity. The controversial two-day public **"sport season" for lobster** (before the commercial lobstering season begins) usually takes place at the end of July. Many groups have called for the discontinuation of this event, since it can't be policed either for limits or for the protection of the reefs. The **Columbus Day Regatta** brings thousands of boats onto the bay—for debauchery as much as for sport.

WHAT TO PACK Biscayne is a water park, so you'll want swimsuits, T-shirts, shorts, hardy footwear, and maybe jeans and a long-sleeve shirt and hat if you burn easily. (Here, most people do. The summer sun is especially hot.) Binoculars are a useful idea, as is a backpack if you plan to hike much of the 7-mile trail on Elliott Key. None of the islands provides food facilities, and only Elliott Key has potable water. Snorkelers and divers will want to bring their gear or rent what they need from the park's concessionaire, the Biscayne National Underwater Park Company (tel. 305/247–2400). There is nothing to dress up for in the park.

GENERAL STORES The nearest food source is Cole's Bait and Tackle Shop (Homestead Bayfront Park, tel. 305/245–2273, open daily 7–7), just across the canal from Biscayne National Park and less than a mile by car. The shop stocks sandwiches that can be microwaved, soft drinks, and beer. The nearest supermarkets and convenience stores are in Homestead, 9 miles west. The concessionaire at Biscayne National Park sells candy bars.

ATMS Sites in Homestead, 9 miles west of the park, include Barnett Bank (850 Homestead Blvd./U.S. 1, tel. 305/825–3376); Coconut Grove Bank (777 N. Krome Ave., tel. 305/245–6666); and First National Bank of Homestead (1550 N. Krome Ave. and 1750 N.E. 8th St., tel. 305/247–5541).

ARRIVING AND DEPARTING The only ways into Biscayne National Park are by car, charter bus, and bicycle. The park is an uninteresting place to hike to. The entry is 9 miles east of Homestead and 9 miles south and east of Exit 6 (Tallahassee Rd.) of the Florida Turnpike.

By Plane. The nearest airport is Miami International. Several car rental agencies have desks in the airport, and another dozen or so have offices immediately south of the airport on LeJeune Road.

By Car. The drive is about an hour from the airport. Take LeJeune Road south from the airport to Route 836, and head west to the Florida Turnpike; get on and head south to Exit 6. Two toll stations on the turnpike require 25¢ and 50¢ (more for RVs.)

By Train. The nearest Amtrak station is in Hialeah. Dade County Bus L will take you from there to the Metrorail at Northside station; from there you can take the elevated train to Allapattah station and then the J bus to the airport, where you can rent a car. The trip can take an hour. Fare is $1.25 plus 25¢ for the transfer to the Metrorail and another 25¢ to the second bus.

By Bus. There is no convenient bus service to Biscayne National Park.

EXPLORING

Biscayne is a great place if you like getting wet, but otherwise you're going to find the park ornery. It lacks recreational features outside of a little beach accessible only by your own boat. The nearest accommodations are 9 miles to the west—they're commercial all the way. There are no restaurants and no bucolic cycling trails; the park concessionaire is unenthusiastic about providing anything but

dive trips. With a boat you can explore, laze on the water, camp on the beach, and head down to the Florida Keys. Without your own boat, Biscayne is for snorkeling and diving.

Incidentally, Boca Chita Key, which has an enclosed harbor but no slips, a picnic area, rest rooms, and the ornamental lighthouse, is closed until at least the winter of 1995–96, by which time hurricane damage ought to have been repaired.

THE BEST IN ONE DAY Most visitors come to snorkel or dive; few have their own boats. It's best, therefore, to schedule a trip with the park concessionaire (tel. 305/247–2400, daily 8–6) and spend the better part of the day in the water. With your own boat, you can dive as well as visit Elliott Key to hike the trails. Be sure to apply mosquito repellent, as well as sunscreen, regardless of time of year.

ORIENTATION PROGRAMS A continuous eight-minute slide show presents an overview of the park (pre-hurricane) at the visitor's center. A 13-minute educational video that focuses on the bay and the ecosystems can be seen on request. Displays are limited, offering less information than the official park brochure, though visitors can poke around a few "please touch" exhibits of conch and tortoise shells and pieces of coral. The Adams Key Environmental Center probably won't reopen before 1995, though environmental education programs will resume before that time on Elliott Key. There are no special programs for children (except school groups), nor does the park conduct evening activities.

GUIDED TOURS Biscayne National Underwater Park Company (Box 1270, Homestead 33030, tel. 305/247–2400), the park's authorized concessionaire, operates daily 8–6 from an office adjacent to the visitor's center. The company runs two 53-foot boats year-round for glass-bottom sightseeing on the reefs. Though schedules vary depending on weather and demand, trips generally depart daily at 10 AM and last about three hours; the cost is $16.50 ($8.50 for children 12 and younger, free for infants under 1). Advance reservations are required. Go/no-go decisions

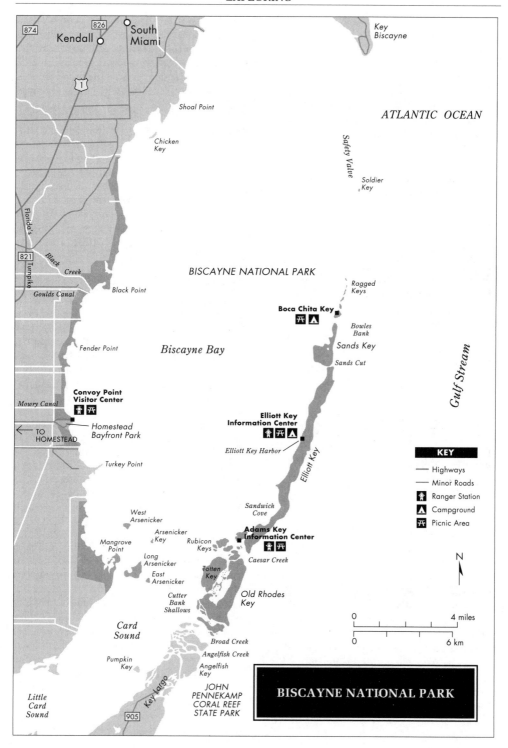

BISCAYNE NATIONAL PARK

are made two hours before scheduled departure times. It's a good idea to call.

TRAILS AND HIKES The best land exploring is on Elliott Key, which has free slips for 64 boats and offers campsites, picnic shelters, rest rooms with freshwater showers, drinking fountains, and a swimming area with marker buoys north of the harbor. Elliott is the largest of the keys (more than 7 miles long), with a trail running nearly its whole length and a shorter loop trail, with a boardwalk, of slightly more than a mile from bay to ocean and around. The 7-mile trail, by the way, is known as the "Spite Highway." When the government announced its intention to acquire the keys for park use, quashing the developers' dream of an offshore resort, the owners of the island began bulldozing the land to preclude public use. They quit under pressure—but not before destroying many inland areas of ecological and scenic importance. The "highway," which was once 120 feet wide, has been steadily filling back in from both sides; it will eventually become a more scenic, more canopied trail.

Unfortunately, the concessionaire typically runs trips to Elliott Key only when bad weather (heavy winds, rain, low visibility) makes snorkeling and diving impractical—which is hardly a time you'll enjoy hiking, either. Ask the concessionaire why he schedules no trips to the key, and he'll tell you, "It's full of mosquitoes and the trees are all busted." Park personnel say that when the concession is put up for bids (the date is still uncertain), they will require regular trips to Elliott Key.

OTHER ACTIVITIES **Bird-Watching.** The park is a bird sanctuary. You can expect to see flocks of brown pelicans patrolling the bay suddenly rise, then plunge beak first, to capture their prey in their baggy pouches. White ibis probe exposed mudflats for small fish and crustaceans. Large colonies of little blue herons, snowy egrets, and other wading birds nest seasonally in the protected refuge of the Arsenicker Keys, where visitors are not allowed ashore.

More rarely seen are several endangered species, including the American peregrine falcon, which migrates through the park; the bald eagle, which can sometimes be seen in coastal or inland areas; and the wood stork, a large white wading bird with black head and black wing linings.

Boating. Canoes can be rented from the park concessionaire (*see* Guided Tours, *above*) at $10 for two hours, $17.50 for four, for one or two people; it's another $3 per extra person. The nearest source for powerboat rentals was Marine Management in nearby Princeton, but they were wiped out by Hurricane Andrew and it's uncertain whether they will reopen. The closest source is now **Gilbert's Holiday Island,** 45 minutes south (107900 Overseas Hwy., Key Largo, tel. 305/451–1133, fax 305/451–1435), where rentals run $175–$250 per day, or $200 per night for houseboats. The nearest sailboat rentals are in Miami at **Easy Sailing** (3360 Pan American Dr., Dinner Key Marina, Coconut Grove, tel. 305/858–4001). Prices range from $18 an hour ($105 a day) for a 19-footer up to $200 a day for a 37-footer; a captain will cost you another $50 per half-day.

There is no channel into Elliott Key harbor. The harbor entrance can fall below 3 feet at low tides. University Dock, 2 miles to the north, contains a marked anchorage area, dock, and sandy beach. There are no other facilities here. Note that water-skiers are required to stay out of the anchorage area and at least 100 feet away from other boats and docks.

Diving and Snorkeling. Pick your reef, anchor at least 300 feet from any other anchored boat, drop your hook in a sand patch and not on the corals (the lightest bottom in the clear water is sand), fly your dive flag whether you're diving or snorkeling, slip on your gear, and you're overboard. Beginning divers will want to explore any of the nearly 100 patch reefs 2 to 3 miles east of Old Rhodes and Elliott keys. (Among the most popular are Dome, Elkhorn, Schooner, and Star Coral reefs.) An easy boat ride from Caesar Creek, all stand in less than 6 feet of water, and all are triangulated for easy-to-find navigation in a free booklet available at the park. The outer reefs attract a wider variety of sea life, including the larger snapper and grouper and the migratory game fish that range through the Gulf Stream. Barracuda and sharks are everywhere, but neither is likely to trouble you if you're not spearfishing.

The park concessionaire (*see* Guided Tours, *above*) operates two sightseeing boats for snorkeling and dive trips in the afternoon. You'll need a reservation. Schedules vary with weather and demand; departure time is generally daily at 1:30, and trips usually last four hours. Snorkelers pay $24.50 per person, regardless of age, including mask, fins, snorkel, and vest. Divers pay $34.50, with equipment rental extra for those who haven't brought their own. In-the-water trips generally give snorkelers and divers two hours on the reef. Since go/no-go decisions are made two hours before scheduled departure times, it's a good idea to call ahead.

Fishing. On the flats look for bonefish, permit, and tarpon, available year-round, as are the bottom fish found around the reefs: snapper, grouper, grunt. Deepwater catches can include billfish, bluefish, mackerel, and sailfish, all migratory and typically found in winter; and dolphin, typically summer—though billfish and sailfish often show up in summer, too. Dolphin can range from schoolies up to 60–70 pounds. Deepwater fish tend to be found wherever the bait fish—the flying fish and the ballyhoo—are. Boating conditions vary widely in the Gulf Stream. Sometimes a 30-footer can't get out, but sometimes you can take a canoe out. Everything depends on how the wind is blowing. Your best bet is to bring up the Weather Channel on your radio or TV for sea and wind conditions for the coming day. The National Oceanic and Atmospheric Administration (NOAA) gives additional information on marine VHF radio.

Swimming. The only designated swimming area is just north of the harbor on Elliott Key. There's open ocean swimming with surf, depending on winds, on the east side of Elliott

Key. Neither the northern nor the eastern site has lifeguards.

DINING

No food is available inside the park. There are **picnic areas** on Elliott Key, Adams Key, and Boca Chita Key (the latter two, however, are currently closed for repairs).

NEAR THE PARK Your best bets for nearby dining are Florida City and Homestead, both 9 miles west of the park. The following restaurants tend toward the affordable rather than the showy.

Chez Jean Claude. This 60-seat restaurant in a '30s Mediterranean-style house, on the main street just north of downtown, specializes in the Alsatian and French regional cooking of its owner-chef. The decor features French art prints, white table covers, and fresh flowers in each of three intimate rooms. Specialties include roast duck, homemade linguine, beef burgundy, and aged steaks. It's as good as you get near the park. To get here from the park (about 15 minutes), drive west on Southwest 328th Street to Krome Avenue; turn right to the restaurant. *1235 N. Krome Ave., Homestead, tel. 305/248–4671. Reservations advised. Dress: casual but neat. AE, MC, V. Dinner only. Closed Mon. Moderate–Expensive.*

Mutineer Restaurant. This roadside restaurant with its indoor-outdoor fish- and duck-pond went up back in 1980, when Florida City, pre–Hurricane Andrew, was barely on the map. The large split-level dining rooms have etched-glass sea-scene dividers, striped velvet chairs, pirate art, stained glass, and a few portholes, but there's no excess. The Wharf Lounge is equally imaginative, with a magnified aquarium and nautical antiques (a crow's nest with a real stuffed crow). The menu features 18 seafood entrées and another half-dozen daily seafood specials, as well as game, ribs, and steaks. There's live music Thursday–Saturday evening. *11 S.E. 1st Ave., Florida City, tel. 305/245–3377. Reservations accepted. Dress: casual but neat. AE, D, DC, MC, V. Moderate.*

Richard Accursio's Capri Restaurant and **King Richard's Room.** The best of the Italians in the park vicinity, dating from 1958, is in a one-story roadside structure, dark but not swank, with captain's chairs and banquettes. The service is friendly and fast. Specialties include pizza with light crunchy crust and ample toppings; mild, meaty conch chowder; mussels in garlic cream or marinara sauce; Caesar salad; yellowtail snapper française; and Key lime pie with plenty of real Key lime juice. *935 N. Krome Ave., Florida City, tel. 305/247–1542. Reservations advised. Dress: casual. AE, D, MC, V. Closed Sun. except Mother's Day. Moderate.*

Angie's Place. The breakfasts and lunches at this 90-seat homespun-tropical roadside restaurant are local, fresh, and cooked to order. In the morning you might get corned beef hash and eggs, Angie's Italian sandwich (fried egg, melted cheese, and Italian ham on an English muffin), or a special of an egg, a pancake, and a strip of bacon or sausage. Lunch favorites include the Italian salad, the Italian sub, and the "crabby crabber" (crab legs, fresh spinach, and Monterey Jack grilled on rye). The restaurant is the last place on U.S. 1 just before the road narrows on its way to the Keys. *404 S.E. 1st Ave. on U.S.1, Florida City, tel. 305/245–8939. No reservations. Dress: casual. No credit cards. No dinner. Inexpensive.*

El Toro Taco. The Hernandez family makes the best Mexican food you can find: salt-free tortillas and nacho chips with Texas corn that they cook and sometimes grind themselves. The cilantro-dominated salsa is mild; if you like more fire, you can mix in minced jalapeño peppers. Specialties include chili *rellenos* (green peppers stuffed with chunks of ground beef and topped with three kinds of cheese) and chicken fajitas (marinated in Worcestershire sauce and served with tortillas and salsa). Bring your own beer and wine. *1 S. Krome Ave., Homestead, tel. 305/245–8182. No reservations. Dress: casual. No credit cards. Inexpensive.*

Potlikker's. This Southern country-style restaurant takes its name from the broth left over from the boiling of greens. Live plants hang from open rafters in the lofty pine-lined dining room. Among the specialties are lemon-pepper chicken breast with lemon sauce, fresh-carved roast turkey with homemade dressing, and at least 11 vegetables served with lunch and dinner entrées. Try the 4-inch-tall frozen Key lime pie; it tastes great if you dawdle while it thaws. *591 Washington Ave., Homestead, tel. 305/248–0835. No reservations. Dress: casual. AE, MC, V. Inexpensive.*

Tiffany's. This charming tearoom-restaurant is part of a complex of specialty shops in a house designed to resemble a pioneer Miami homestead. For breakfast try the Banana Split, a double-decker Belgian waffle layered with strawberries, bananas, and yogurt and topped with chopped nuts. Featured lunch dishes include crabmeat au gratin, asparagus supreme (rolled in ham with hollandaise sauce), and Caesar salad with chicken or seafood. Save room for the strawberry whipped-cream cake or the harvest pie (filled with apples, cranberries, walnuts, and raisins and topped with caramel). *22 N.E. 15th St., Homestead, tel. 305/246–0022. Reservations accepted. AE, MC, V. Breakfast and lunch only; brunch Sun. Inexpensive.*

LODGING

NEAR THE PARK There is no lodging within the park; you'll have to stay in Homestead or Florida City. It's all motels since Hurricane Andrew blew away Grandma Newton's, the only bed-and-breakfast. Everything is in the moderate range ($50–$100), though you can find single rooms and occasionally doubles for less with AAA or AARP discounts in the off-season. It pays to ask.

Days Inn. A two-story motel just at the end of the Florida Turnpike. The rooms are stylish, with floral bedcovers and armoires for the TV and for hanging clothes (every other inn in the area has open racks for hanging). It's almost on par with the Hampton Inn *(see below)*; vacationers who want quiet and comfort will pick one or the other. *51 S. Homestead Blvd. (U.S. 1), Homestead 33030, tel.*

305/245–1260, fax 305/247–0939. 110 rooms. Facilities: outdoor pool, restaurant, bar, no-smoking rooms, coin laundry. AE, D, DC, MC, V. Moderate.

Hampton Inn. This two-story motel is the best in the area. Lying just off the highway, it has clean rooms and friendly policies: free Continental breakfast, free local calls, and the Disney Channel at no extra charge. All rooms are color-coordinated and carpeted, with at least two upholstered chairs, twin reading lamps, and a desk and chair. The bathrooms have tub-showers. 124 E. Palm Dr., Florida City 33034, tel. 305/247–8833 or 800/426–7866. 102 rooms. Facilities: outdoor pool, no-smoking rooms. AE, D, DC, MC, V. Moderate.

Holiday Inn Express. After Hurricane Andrew this Holiday Inn was downgraded to the new Express standard, which means no restaurant. Yet, unlike other Expresses, it has kept its outdoor pool and "Banana Bar" and is a pleasant place. The rooms are done in tropical florals and rattan furniture; all have digital clock radios, and some have king-size beds. Continental breakfast is included in the room rate. 990 N. Homestead Blvd., Homestead 33030, tel. and fax 305/247–7020. 130 rooms. Facilities: outdoor pool and pool bar, no-smoking rooms, coin laundry. AE, D, DC, MC, V. Moderate.

Hurricane Andrew Motor Inn. The chief advantage of this plain, two-story, gray-and-white motel is that it's right next to the very efficiently operated visitor's information center on U.S. 1. People pick it mostly for that reason and typically stay one night on the way to or from the Keys. The rooms, done in pickled wood paneling with blue carpet, are nothing special, except for their strong smell of disinfectant. 100 U.S. 1, Florida City 33034, tel. 305/247–3200 or 800/521–6004. 160 rooms. Facilities: heated pool. AE, DC, MC, V. Moderate.

Super 8 Motel. This one-story gray motel is a bit more upscale than the Hurricane Andrew Motor Inn (see above)—better fabrics, carpet with a bit of texture. It should also have a pool before the end of 1993. 1202 N. Krome Ave.,

Florida City 33034, tel. 305/245–0311, fax 305/247–9136. 52 rooms. Facilities: coin laundry, no-smoking rooms. AE, D, DC, MC, V. Moderate.

A-1 Motel. This one-story, U-shaped motel stands directly across from the Pioneer Museum, a modest historical attraction. The rooms are clean, if basic, and done in brown and tan. Some have fridges, for which there's no extra charge. The place is utterly commercial, with a lot of paved parking space inside the U, and a pool, too. It's your best bet for cheap doubles (as low as $40) in the summer. 815 N. Krome Ave., Florida City 33034, tel. and fax 305/248–2741. 45 rooms. Facilities: pool, no-smoking rooms, coin laundry. AE, D, MC, V. Inexpensive–Moderate.

CAMPING

The only place at present where you may camp within the park is at Elliott Key in the vicinity of the little harbor. There is no charge for tent sites, which are available on a first-come, first-served basis. But of course you must have your own transportation. Freshwater showers are available, as is potable water.

There are several campsites in and near Homestead. Three of the best are:

Goldcoaster Mobile Home & RV Park. This luxurious park with 547 sites, a 45-minute drive from Biscayne National Park, is less than 10 minutes from the entrance to Everglades National Park, southwest of Homestead. It offers full hookups but no pull-throughs. The site widths are 45x80; the surface is grass. There is no liquid propane gas. The facilities include a recreation center (rebuilt in 1993 following Hurricane Andrew), heated pool and Jacuzzi, and coin laundry. 34850 S.W. 187th Ave., Homestead 33034, tel. 305/248–5462, fax 305/248–5467. MC, V.

Miami South KOA. This park has more than 300 sod and gravel RV and trailer sites in varied sizes that will accommodate any camping vehicle. They offer full hookups and pull-throughs. Facilities include a recreational hall, heated pool and hot tub, coin laundry, and liquid propane gas. There are also two air-conditioned cabins (but without cooking facilities). The site lies about 4 miles north of Homestead in the mango- and avocado-growing district. *20675 S.W. 162nd Ave., Miami 33187, tel. 305/233–5300. Inquire about credit cards.*

The Southern Comfort RV Resort. Completely renovated after Hurricane Andrew, this campground offers 350 RV sites with full hookups, a pool, a barbecue area with a bar, a recreation pavilion, and liquid propane gas. It's 6 miles from the Everglades National Park entrance off U.S. 1, and 7 miles from Biscayne National Park. *345 E. Palm Dr., Florida City 33034, tel. 305/248–6909, fax 305/242–1345. MC, V.*

The Blue Ridge Parkway
North Carolina, Virginia
By Paul Calhoun

his 470-mile-long scenic corridor traverses the spine of the southern Appalachian Mountains from Shenandoah National Park, in Virginia, to Great Smoky Mountains National Park on the North Carolina–Tennessee border. It shares much in common with the parks at its northern and southern limits—notably the motor-vehicle access to hiking, camping, and picnicking opportunities; cultural and historical attractions; and modern lodgings nestled in some of the most striking mountain scenery in the East.

At the heart of the parkway is the road itself, a 469-mile ribbon of two-lane blacktop that winds through rural, mountainous backcountry that would otherwise be nearly inaccessible. Created as the first rural national parkway, today the roadway still encourages relaxing driving; there are endless through-the-window sightseeing opportunities and well-placed, paved overlooks where you can safely stop for a lingering look at grandeur.

Stopping on the roadway's shoulder is legal if not encouraged, but motorists should choose their spots with an eye for safety and minimizing damage to the grassy border. Be prepared for the quick stops of fellow travelers and roaming wildlife. Although the speed limit is 45 miles per hour in most places (35 miles per hour in some stretches), the twists and turns and alluring views drop the average speed closer to 30 miles per hour. Relax and enjoy the scenery; take an alternate route if you're in a hurry.

Born in 1933 as a Great Depression–era public works effort, the parkway was begun in 1935 and finished in 1987. The aim was to link Shenandoah and Great Smoky Mountains national parks, and to fight the area's dire unemployment. In addition to achieving its short-term goals, the parkway provided unexpected long-term benefits; today it attracts more than 21 million visitors and generates $1.3 billion of revenue per year for North Carolina and Virginia.

Attracting travelers to the Blue Ridge are the elevated views of the wooded mountains and valleys that typify the Southern Highlands: modest peaks cloaked in a lush, leafy canopy of oak, hickory, and maple, with an occasional evergreen highlight of hemlock, spruce, or fir. With the exception of North Carolina's 6,684-foot Mt. Mitchell, the highest mountain east of the Mississippi, only a few Blue Ridge summits peak above 4,000 feet. Enveloping this expanse is the bluish haze that allegedly gave the Blue Ridge its name. Originally a product of moisture given off by the forest, today's haze is frequently infiltrated by airborne pollution that occasionally restricts views and has damaged some of the high-elevation foliage.

The parkway attracts a steady but uncrowded flow of weekday visitors from April through September; highest visitation is on summer weekends and during October's peak fall foliage, which usually occurs the second or third week of the month. In particularly popular areas, such as Virginia's Mabry Mill (Milepost 176.1), the traffic can sometimes resemble a big-city traffic jam; such instances typically occur in October; otherwise, they are few and far between. Few travel the road in winter, and sections are frequently closed due to ice and snow. The protected domain bordering the parkway has an average width of only 1,450 feet. Despite the relative narrowness of the corridor, many places offer short walks and even a few extended hikes. The feeling of wilderness is more illusion than reality, but the typical walker on the average trail will never feel near the bustle of civilization. If you seek roadside access to stunning views and modest outdoor jaunts, all within easy access of several towns and even a few major cities, the Blue Ridge Parkway is the perfect national park.

ESSENTIAL INFORMATION

VISITOR INFORMATION For information on the parkway, including advice on camping and on-parkway dining, lodging, and sightseeing opportunities, contact the Executive Director, **Blue Ridge Parkway Association** (Box 453, Asheville, NC 28802, tel. 704/627–

3419), or the Chief Ranger's Office (200 BBT Bldg., 1 Pack Sq., Asheville, NC 28801, tel. 704/298–0398 for 24-hour recorded information or 704/271–4779 for the office; open daily 9–5).

Visitor centers at Humpback Rocks, Peaks of Otter, Museum of North Carolina Minerals, and Craggy Gardens are open May through October.

For information on accommodations, restaurants, and local sights, contact the **North Carolina Division of Travel and Tourism** (430 N. Salisbury St., Raleigh, NC 27611, tel. 919/733–4171) or the **Virginia Division of Tourism** (1021 E. Cary St., Richmond, VA 23219, tel. 804/786–4484 or 800/932–5827).

Note: Mileposts—small gray concrete markers with black mileage indicators—are numbered from north to south on the parkway. Most parkway literature (and this chapter) refers to locations in terms of miles (mi) from the parkway's northern junction with the Skyline Drive, at the U.S. 250 crossover at Rockfish Gap on Afton Mountain. Mile 216.9 is the Virginia–North Carolina state line.

The only two backcountry camping areas on the parkway are North Carolina's Doughton Park (Milepost 238.5) and Rock Castle Gorge in Virginia's Rocky Knob area (Milepost 169.0). You'll need a backcountry permit, which you can get free from park headquarters and district ranger's offices.

FEES There are no fees on the parkway.

PUBLICATIONS *The Blue Ridge Parkway Directory,* a full-color, 38-page, magazine-size annual guide is available free from the Blue Ridge Parkway Association (*see* Visitor Information, *above*). The guide gives an overview of parkway history and regulations, as well as lodging, dining, camping, and shopping opportunities and visitor attractions both along the roadway and convenient to it. It also has some hard-to-read maps and some coverage of the adjoining Shenandoah and Great Smoky Mountains national parks. You can get a nifty, full-color, pocket-size strip map, "Blue Ridge Parkway," from park headquarters or at visitor's centers and district ranger's offices. They also give out the "Blue Ridge Parkway Bloom Calendar," a pamphlet telling where and when to spot the myriad varieties of wildflowers blooming on the parkway. *Parkway Milepost,* a parkway newspaper published by Friends of the Blue Ridge Parkway (2301 Hendersonville Rd., Box 341, Arden, NC 28704, tel. 704/687–8722 or 800/228–7275) is available free at parkway visitor's centers; it provides seasonal news about parkway events and attractions, natural history, and regulations.

One of the best books on the parkway, especially if you're looking to stop and stretch your legs a little, is *Walking the Blue Ridge: A Guide to the Trails of the Blue Ridge Parkway,* by Leonard M. Adkins, who has actually walked each of these trails with a measuring wheel to ensure accuracy.

GEOLOGY AND TERRAIN The southern Appalachian Mountains are ancient by any standard; some rocks are an estimated 1.2 billion years old. Over the aeons the mountains were uplifted and shifted by changes in the earth's crust, then weathered and worn into their present configuration during the past 100 to 200 million years. The southern Appalachians have only a handful of peaks reminiscent of the towering, rock-studded mountains of the West; most of that lofty presence eroded long ago and now makes up the soil of the coastal plains of the Atlantic Ocean and Gulf of Mexico. Exceptions occur, such as Sharp Top, at Peaks of Otter (Milepost 86.0), which has an unusually sharp peak of aged, coarsely crystalline rock, and Flat Rock (Milepost 308.3), a quartzite outcrop that provides a stunning vantage point overlooking North Carolina's Grandfather Mountain and the Linville Valley.

Most of the roadway follows the backbone of the Blue Ridge, providing lofty views of surrounding lowlands and distant mountain peaks; the southern 114 miles wind through North Carolina's Black Mountains, Craggies, Pisgahs, and Balsams before ending in the Great Smokies. To the east of the parkway is the fertile, gently contoured terrain of the Piedmont section of Virginia and North Carolina. To the west are the rugged mountains that form the western rampart of the southern Appalachians; in Virginia, from Waynesboro to Roanoke, the southern section of the famed Shenandoah Valley lies between the southern Appalachians and the Piedmonts.

FLORA AND FAUNA Having been softened and worn down by the elements and the ages, the mountains provide fertile footing for a wide variety of vegetation. Particularly famous is the parkway's display of fall foliage and, thanks to strict rules against collecting, the spring and summer proliferation of wildflowers.

Except for the dark green spruce and fir blanketing the high elevations of the Black Mountains and the Mt. Mitchell area (Milepost 340–355), most of the parkway foliage is typical of the deciduous oak-hickory blend common to the region. Interspersed throughout are dogwood, sourwood, tulip poplar, black gum, sassafras, red maple, hemlock, and Virginia and white pine.

Bursting forth in June, flame azalea and catawba rhododendron are the splashy stars of the parkway's wildflowers; more furtive blooms can be spotted throughout the season. The wetland-dwelling skunk cabbage appears in February, and the colorful bull thistle is common along the roadside and in lowland pastures from June to the first killing frost. In between, some 110 other species are notable enough to be included in the "Blue Ridge Parkway Bloom Calendar" (*see* Publications, *above*).

Although wild animals abound along the parkway, they tend to be harder to spot and more wary of human approach than in the adjoining Shenandoah and Great Smoky Mountains national parks.

The Virginia white-tailed deer is a common roadside grazer in the parks; it is a rare sight along the parkway, its place taken by the woodchuck, known colloquially as the groundhog. Likewise, the black bear is a reclusive parkway denizen. Joining the woodchuck as common daytime sightings, especially along nature trails, are squirrels and chipmunks. At night you might see foxes, raccoons, opossums, and skunks; bobcats are fairly common after-dark travelers, but sÑeing one is a once-in-a-lifetime treat.

More than 100 species of birds appear along the parkway during the spring migration, and more than 200 additional species visit year-round (*see* Other Activities *in* Exploring, *below*). During the fall raptor migration, several birds-of-prey species glide southward along the mountain ridgeline, a seasonal event that attracts an ever-increasing number of birders. The parkway's two poisonous snakes, the timber rattler and copperhead, are rare; there is also a wide variety of nonpoisonous snakes, lizards, frogs, and salamanders.

WHEN TO GO The parkway is most crowded on summer weekends and during October's fall-foliage season (usually during the second and third weeks of the month). Because of unpredictable weather and limited options for accommodations, winter is the parkway's quietest season; unexpected cold fronts and snowfalls can strike from October to April. Spring can arrive from March through May, varying with elevation and late-winter weather patterns. Although it is farther north, Virginia usually experiences warm weather before North Carolina because of the latter's higher elevations. Summer temperatures are usually 10° to 15° cooler than in the nearby lowlands, ranging from the 40s to 90s.

SEASONAL EVENTS Summer, Sunday evenings: Roanoke Mountain Campground (Mill Mountain Spur Rd., 1 mi from parkway at Milepost 120.0, tel. 703/982–6490) hosts miniconcerts and demonstrations of traditional Southern Highlands music; they're generally held at 7 PM. July: Linville Falls Music Festival celebrates traditional mountain music and dance at the Linville Falls Campground (Milepost 316.4). Late August: Brinegar Day (tel. 919/372–4744 or 919/372–8568) at Brinegar Cabin (Milepost 238.5) in historic Doughton Park features a crafts festival. October, weekends: Fall harvest activities (tel. 703/952–2947) at Mabry Mill

(Milepost 176.1) include crafts demonstrations, apple butter– and sorghum molasses–making, and old-time music.

WHAT TO PACK Year-round, bring sunscreen, sunglasses, a hat or cap, rain gear, and comfortable walking shoes. Long-sleeve shirts and light jackets are often needed, even in July and August. Most of the parkway is relatively pest free, but pack insect repellent to ward off ticks and the few chiggers, mosquitoes, or gnats you might encounter. It's a good idea to bring your own drinks and snacks; concessions are far apart and offer a limited assortment. You might also bring a couple of aerosol tire-inflator cans, should you have a flat you don't want to change on the spot.

GENERAL STORES Development along the parkway is kept minimal to contribute to its wilderness appeal. Stores are plentiful in nearby towns and cities, but on-parkway general stores are many miles apart. The camp store at **Peaks of Otter** (Milepost 86.0, tel. 703/586–1614; no credit cards) sells snacks and camping supplies and is open late April–late May, weekdays 9:30–6, weekends 9–6:30; early June–late October, daily 9–7. **Doughton Park** (Milepost 241.4, tel. 919/372–4744) has a combination gift shop, variety store, and service station open early May–late October, daily 8–6. **Crabtree Meadows** (Milepost 339.5, tel. 704/675–4236) has similar facilities but a better selection of goods than the Doughton Park store; it's open early May–late October, daily 9–6. **Pisgah Inn**'s full-service camp store (Milepost 408.6, tel. 704/235–8228) has a service station and Laundromat and is open early April–late May and late October–late November, daily 8–4:30; late May–late October, daily 8–8.

Other than full-service restaurants (*see* Dining, *below*), several other parkway food-and-rest stops carry limited general-store supplies: **Whetstone Ridge** (Milepost 29.0, tel. 703/377–6397) has a restaurant and gift-crafts shop open May, September, and October, weekdays 9–5, an hour later on weekends; June–late August, weekdays 8:30–6, an hour later on weekends. **Otter Creek**

(Milepost 60.8, tel. 804/299–5862) has a restaurant and gift-crafts shop open April, May, and Labor Day–November, daily 9–7; June–Labor Day, daily 8–8. **Mabry Mill** (Milepost 176.1, tel. 703/952–2947) has similar facilities open May, September, and October, daily 8–6; open June–late August, daily 8–7. **Northwest Trading Post** (Milepost 258.8, tel. 919/982–2543), the largest gift-crafts shop on the parkway, also sells snacks; it's open mid-April–late October, daily 9–5:30.

There are just four gas stations along the 469-mile route: In addition to Doughton Park, Crabtree Meadows, and Pisgah Inn (*see above*), you can get gas at **Peaks of Otter** (Milepost 86.0, tel. 703/586–1233; open late Apr.–late May and Sept., weekdays 9–5:30, weekends 8–7; June–late Aug. and Oct., weekdays 8–7, weekends 8–8); in an emergency, ask for gas at the Peaks of Otter Lodge desk (tel. 703/586–1081, open 24 hours).

ATMS There are no ATMs on the parkway; there are several in towns and cities near the parkway. In Virginia, try the **First Union National Bank** (Towers Mall, Roanoke, tel. 703/563–7534): Take U.S. 220/I–581 north toward Roanoke; take the Colonial Avenue/Wonju Street exit; turn right at the stoplight, then left into Towers Mall. In North Carolina, try the Biltmore branch of **First Union National Bank** (1 Angle St., Asheville, tel. 704/251–7251): Take I–40 west and follow the signs to the Biltmore House/Estate; the bank is across from the Biltmore entrance.

ARRIVING AND DEPARTING There is no rail or air service to the parkway itself, but several communities near the parkway are accessible by air, rail, or bus.

By Plane. Charlottesville–Albemarle Airport (201 Bowen Loop, Charlottesville, VA, tel. 804/973–8341), 8 miles north of Charlottesville on U.S. 29, is closest to the parkway's northern access and is served by **American Eagle** (tel. 800/433–7300), **Comair/Delta** (tel. 800/354–9822), **United Express** (tel. 800/241–6522), and **USAir Express** (tel. 800/428–4322). You can rent a car at the airport from **Avis** (804/973–6000), **Budget** (804/973–5751), and **Hertz** (804/973–8349).

There is no public transportation to the parkway; taxi service (**Yellow Cab,** tel. 804/295–4131) to the closest parkway lodging, Peaks of Otter (Milepost 86.0) costs about $150, one way.

By Car and RV. The parkway is accessible to any motor vehicle, although the steep climb may challenge larger RVs. From Charlottesville, take I–64 west to Exit 99 to the parkway's northern entrance at Rockfish Gap; driving time is approximately 30 minutes.

By Train. Charlottesville, Virginia, has the closest train station (600 E. Water St.); it's served by **Amtrak** (tel. 800/872–7245). There is no public transportation from the station to the parkway. Cab fare (**Yellow Cab,** tel. 804/295–4131) to the car-rental agencies at the airport (*see* By Plane, *above*) is about $20.

By Bus. Greyhound Lines (tel. 800/231–2222) serves Charlottesville (310 W. Main St.), Roanoke (26 Salem Ave.) in Virginia, and cities that are convenient to sections of the parkway farther south. Once there, however, you'll need to rent a car to reach the parkway.

EXPLORING

The parkway's major appeal is to motor tourists, although it offers enough hiking, camping, and bicycling opportunities that appeal to your more active side. Cyclists must follow certain rules (*see* Other Activities, *below*).

THE BEST IN ONE DAY Stop to enjoy the most inviting overlooks, take a couple of walks, visit one or two of the more popular attractions, and you've gotten about as much out of the parkway as one day will allow. Seeing the best of the entire roadway calls for at least two days, and preferably three or more.

Must-see stops in the Virginia section of the parkway are the historical exhibits and hiking opportunities at Humpback Rocks (Milepost 5.8), Peaks of Otter (Milepost 86.0), Rocky Knob (Milepost 169.0), and Mabry Mill (Milepost 176.1). Worth the detour, if you have the time, are the view from the foot of Roanoke's towering Mill Mountain Star (on the spur road that intersects the parkway at

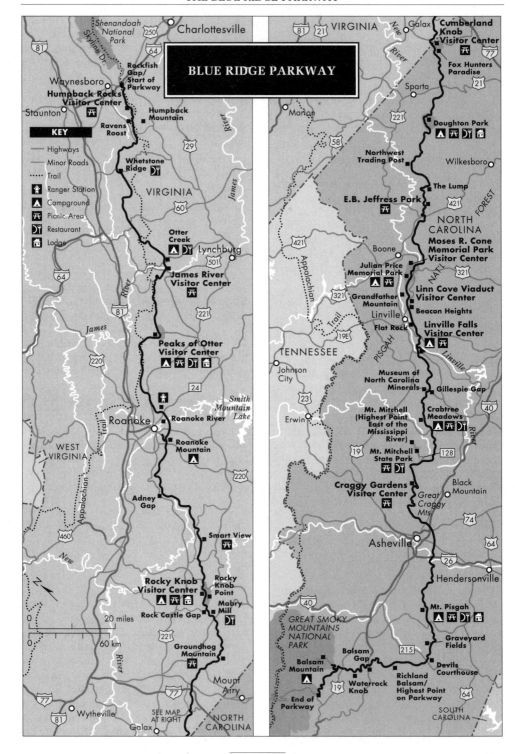

BLUE RIDGE PARKWAY

KEY

- Highways
- Minor Roads
- Trail
- Ranger Station
- Campground
- Picnic Area
- Restaurant
- Lodge

Shenandoah National Park
Skyline Dr.
Charlottesville
VIRGINIA
Galax
Cumberland Knob Visitor Center
Rockfish Gap/Start of Parkway
Fox Hunters Paradise
Waynesboro
Humpback Rocks Visitor Center
Staunton
Ravens Roost
Humpback Mountain
Sparta
Marion
Doughton Park
Whetstone Ridge
VIRGINIA
Northwest Trading Post
Wilkesboro
The Lump
E.B. Jeffress Park
NORTH CAROLINA
Otter Creek
Lynchburg
Boone
Moses R. Cone Memorial Park Visitor Center
James River Visitor Center
Julian Price Memorial Park
Linn Cove Viaduct Visitor Center
Grandfather Mountain
Beacon Heights
Linville
Flat Rock
Linville Falls Visitor Center
TENNESSEE
Peaks of Otter Visitor Center
Johnson City
Museum of North Carolina Minerals
Gillespie Gap
Mt. Mitchell (Highest Point East of the Mississippi River)
Crabtree Meadows
Erwin
Mt. Mitchell State Park
Smith Mountain Lake
Roanoke River
Roanoke
WEST VIRGINIA
Roanoke Mountain
Craggy Gardens Visitor Center
Great Craggy Mts.
Black Mountain
Appalachian Trail
Adney Gap
Asheville
Hendersonville
Smart View
Rocky Knob Visitor Center
Rocky Knob Point
Mt. Pisgah
Mabry Mill
Rock Castle Gap
GREAT SMOKY MOUNTAINS NATIONAL PARK
Graveyard Fields
Groundhog Mountain
Balsam Gap
Devils Courthouse
Balsam Mountain
Waterrock Knob
Richland Balsam/Highest Point on Parkway
Mount Airy
SEE MAP AT RIGHT
End of Parkway
SOUTH CAROLINA
Wytheville
NORTH CAROLINA
Galax

0   20 miles
0   60 km

Milepost 124.5) and the expansive picnic area and walking opportunities at Smart View (Milepost 154.5) and Ground Hog Mountain (Milepost 189.0).

In North Carolina, be sure to see Doughton Park (Milepost 241.1), Linville Falls (Milepost 316.4), Crabtree Meadows (Milepost 339.5), Craggy Gardens (Milepost 364.6), Mt. Pisgah (Milepost 408), and Waterrock Knob (Milepost 451.2)—all of which have wondrous walking, picnicking, and sightseeing opportunities. Also well worth the stop is Linn Cove Viaduct (Milepost 305.0), the inventive, structurally elegant bridge that enables the parkway to continue uninterrupted.

ORIENTATION PROGRAMS There are no visitor's center slide shows or introductory movies along the parkway; there are informative seasonal programs conducted at campground and visitor's center amphitheaters from May through October. To find the topic, time, and locations of upcoming programs, read the *Parkway Milepost* (*see* Publications *in* Essential Information, *above*) or look for the blue sheets on bulletin boards at visitor's centers, district ranger's offices, picnic areas, and campgrounds.

GUIDED TOURS There are no commercial guided tours on the parkway; there are numerous high-quality, very informative, ranger-led walks and programs. Typical presentations include nature lore, storytelling, and night prowls. Attendance averages 10 to 30; although some activities, such as mountain music, often have an audience approaching 150. Consult the *Parkway Milepost* (*see above*) for advice.

From April through October, bus trips are available from the Peaks of Otter camp store (Milepost 86.0, tel. 703/586–1614) to a parking area 500 yards from the summit of **Sharp Top.** The cost is $2.50 per person, round-trip; $1.50 per person, one way—choose the latter if you enjoy the thought of walking down but don't want to tackle the strenuous, 1.5-mile hike up the famous peak. The 500 yards from the bus stop to the peak are moderately challenging, but if you're used to walking uphill you shouldn't have a problem.

SCENIC DRIVES AND VIEWS The parkway is a scenic drive from end to end, with 469 miles of outstanding scenery and eye-catching views at nearly every turn. The following lists include some of the most popular roadside vantage points.

Virginia. Ravens Roost (Milepost 10.7): This spot allows a bird's-eye view of the Shenandoah Valley, Torry Mountain, and other Allegheny peaks to the west. **Otter Lake** (Milepost 63.1): This small lake has a densely wooded shoreline and an especially scenic area near the dam. **Peaks of Otter** (Milepost 86.0): The sparkling waters of modest-size Abbott Lake rest in the shadow of towering Sharp Top, one of the parkway's oft-visited attractions. **Roanoke River Gorge** (Milepost 114.9): View the wooded river canyon from the 165-foot-high parkway bridge, or pull over and take the 10-minute walk to a pedestrian overlook. **Smart View** (Milepost 154.5): The small pond and open meadows on a mountaintop plateau allow a typical glimpse of Virginia farm country. **Rocky Knob area** (Milepost 167.0–174.0): This is a famed 10-mile stretch of varied scenic views, from 3,572-foot Rocky Knob Point to the wild and rugged Castle Rock Gorge.

North Carolina. Fox Hunters Paradise (Milepost 218.6): This elevated vantage point is where hunters once listened to the hounds chasing their quarry in the valley below. **Doughton Park area** (Milepost 238.5–244.7): At this open expanse of bluegrass downs, you can view an isolated mountain homestead. **The Lump** (Milepost 264.4): Take in the towering view of the Carolina foothills to the east. **Moses H. Cone Memorial Park** (Milepost 292.7): This historic 3,600-acre estate has miles of scenery, picnicking, hiking, camping, and fishing. **Julian Price Memorial Park** (Milepost 295.0): Adjoining Cone Memorial Park, here are an additional 4,200 acres of scenery and outdoor activities. **Linn Cove Viaduct Information Center** (Milepost 304.4): View the 1,243-foot-long viaduct, where creative engineering enabled the parkway to span uninterrupted a section of particularly rugged terrain on the rocky slope of Grandfather Mountain. **Linville Falls Visitor**

Center (Milepost 316.3) and **Linville River Parking Area** (Milepost 316.4): Exhibits tell a story about this massive waterfall, and a short trail takes you to it. At the parking area you'll see one of the parkway's largest stone arch bridges, with three 80-foot spans. **Mt. Mitchell State Park via Route 128** (Milepost 355.8): Stop to see the highest peak in the East; you can drive nearly to the top on Route 128 for a short walk to the observation tower. **Craggy Gardens Visitor Center** (Milepost 364.4): These gardens are scenic year-round, but especially so in mid-June, when they're cloaked in purple rhododendrons. **Mt. Pisgah** (Milepost 408.6): Panoramic views are had from 5,000-foot elevations at this spot, once part of a 100,000-acre estate George W. Vanderbilt purchased in the late 1800s; it is the nucleus of Pisgah National Forest. **Richmond Balsam Overlook** (Milepost 431.4): Towering views from the highest point on the roadway.

HISTORIC BUILDINGS AND SITES **Johnson Farm** at Peaks of Otter (Milepost 85.9) is a preserved mountain farmstead, typical of communities that existed in the Blue Ridge region in the 1920s and 1930s, is reached via a moderate 2.1-mile loop trail from the Peaks of Otter Visitor Center.

Mabry Mill (Milepost 176.1), arguably the most popular single attraction on the Virginia span of the parkway, was run by E. B. Mabry from 1910 to 1935. Old-time apple butter– and sorghum molasses–making skills are exhibited during the season.

Moses H. Cone Memorial Park (Milepost 292.7) and **Cone Manor House** (Milepost 294.0): This historic estate encompasses some 3,600 scenic acres, with miles of carriage trails for horseback riding and walking, and picnicking, hiking, camping, and fishing opportunities.

Julian Price Memorial Park (Milepost 295.0), the former summer retreat of life-insurance pioneer Julian Price, adjoins Cone Memorial Park with an additional 4,200 acres of scenery and outdoor activities.

NATURE TRAILS AND SHORT WALKS Several excellent short walks are just off the parkway.

If you're a serious hiker, pick up *Walking the Blue Ridge* (*see* Publications *in* Essential Information, *above*), which gives an extensive list of where to walk and what you'll see. The trails below, however, give a nice sampling of the parkway's offerings; times and mileages are round-trip.

Otter Lake Trail (Milepost 63.1, .8 mi, 30 minutes). This is a moderate leg-stretcher around the wooded shoreline of small Otter Lake; it's very convenient to the roadway, with only occasionally tricky footing.

Abbott Lake Trail (Milepost 85.7, 1 mi, 30 minutes). From the parking lot at Peaks of Otter Lodge, this easy loop springs through an open meadow and around the lake, offering stunning views of Sharp Top.

Roanoke River Trail (Milepost 114.9, .7 mi, 25 minutes). This short but scenic trail to a pedestrian overlook allows views of a steep-sided section of the Roanoke River valley.

Rocky Knob Picnic Loop Trail (Milepost 169.0, 1.3 mi, 45 minutes). This is an easy meander around the scenic picnic area, taking you through rhododendron and hemlock forest.

Craggy Gardens (Milepost 364.6, 2 mi, 1 hour). Highlights of this moderately challenging, self-guided nature trail from the visitor's center to the picnic area are the cloaking presence of trailside rhododendron and the view from the observation platform on Craggy Flats.

Graveyard Fields Loop Trail (Milepost 418.8, 2.2 mi, 1 1/2 hours). This moderately easy loop to an area of fallen tree trunks, victim of a 1925 fire, also runs to Yellowstone Falls, where, aptly, the landscape reminds one of the Rocky Mountains.

Devil's Courthouse (Milepost 422.4, .9 mi, 45 minutes). Take this short but moderately strenuous hike through spruce and fir forest to see the "courthouse," a huge rock outcropping with a 360° view into South Carolina and Georgia, and toward the Balsams.

Waterrock Knob Trail (Milepost 451.2, 1.1 mi, 55 minutes). A short, moderately strenuous climb from the parking area through red spruce and Fraser fir to the highest trail elevation on the parkway, this climb yields a four-state view and a panoramic vista of the Great Smoky Mountains.

LONGER HIKES Although the parkway offers only limited backcountry territory, it does have access to a number of moderately strenuous hiking opportunities and a few quite challenging ones. Times and mileages are round-trip.

Starting from the Humpback Gap parking area, the **Appalachian Trail to Humpback Rocks** (Milepost 6.0, 4.3 mi, 2 hours) heads uphill and doesn't ease up until it reaches the saddle at the top of the mountain; from here it is .3 mile to the rocks and the stunning views over the valley. This relatively short hike definitely gets the blood flowing; it's not easy. The trail is poorly marked where it reaches the rocks at the top of the mountain; pay particular attention so you're able to retrace your steps to the parking area.

Sharp Top Trail at Peaks of Otter (Milepost 86.0, 3 mi, 2 hours), the most popular trail on the parkway, starts at the camp store at the base of Sharp Top and climbs to 1,400 feet. Steep in some places and moderate in others, it requires an overall strenuous effort to reach the view of the lodge, lake, and distant Blue Ridge Mountains from the rock outcroppings at the summit. There is seasonal bus access to the .5-mile loop near the peak (*see* Guided Tours, *above*); hikers are not allowed to walk on the road.

The **Rock Castle Gorge Trail** (Milepost 167.1, 10.6 mi, all day) starts innocently enough at the entrance to the Rocky Knob campground, but after you walk 3.3 miles and descend to the backcountry camping area in the gorge, you begin to understand why this pathway was given National Recreational Trail status. And you still have a 7.3-mile ascent back out of the gorge on the return trail. Your rewards for this truly rugged backcountry experience are views of thick mountain foliage and a splashing stream.

You can hike a short stretch of the **Tanawha Trail** (Milepost 305.2; 13.5 mi, all day), or you can try to do the whole run in one day—the latter option is not for the faint of heart. In its entirety, this trail—with elaborate bridges and wooden staircases—runs from the Beacon Heights parking area (Milepost 305.2) to Julian Price Memorial Park (Milepost 297.2). It is easiest hiked from south to north, and other good access points include the Stack Rock parking area (Milepost 304.8) and Linn Cove information center (Milepost 304.4). Part of the trail's appeal is its intricate engineering; its natural beauty derives from views of the southeast face of Grandfather Mountain, the falls on Stack Rock Creek, and the tunnels through lush growth of mountain laurel and rhododendron.

Other excellent nearby hiking opportunities include the **Appalachian Trail** (Box 807, Harpers Ferry, WV 25425, tel. 304/535–6331), **Mt. Mitchell State Park** (Rte. 5, Box 700, Burnsville, NC 28714; tel. 704/675–4611), and the **Shining Rock Wilderness Area** (District Ranger, U.S. Forest Service, 1001 Pisgah Hwy., Pisgah Forest, NC 28768, tel. 704/877–3265).

OTHER ACTIVITIES **Arts and Crafts.** You can buy crafts and watch demonstrations at **Parkway Craft Center** at Moses Cone Memorial Park (Milepost 294.0, tel. 704/295–7938), **Folk Art Center** (Milepost 382.0, tel. 704/298–7928), and **Northwest Trading Post** (Milepost 258.8, tel. 919/982–2543), the largest crafts shop on the parkway.

Biking. Accomplished cyclists will delight in the scenery and challenge of the parkway; inexperienced riders may be intimidated by the narrow shoulders, heavy summer weekend and October foliage traffic, and distances between food outlets and services. Climbs and descents vary from 600 feet to 6,000 feet. Mountain bikes are ideal for such steep terrain but may be used only on paved areas. During times of limited visibility—at night and in tunnels—bikes must have a white light on the front and a red light or reflector on the back. Wear gloves and a helmet. The parkway association (*see* Visitor Information *in* Essential Information, *above*) distributes a printout of major climbs and descents.

Bird-Watching. You can see more than 100 species along the parkway during the spring migration, and another 200 species annually. The fall raptor migration is a favorite attraction along the Virginia span, where these birds of prey have a major flyway along the Blue Ridge. Popular viewing spots include the Ballroom Terrace, a covered viewing platform at the **Waynesboro/Afton Mountain Holiday Inn** (Exit 99 off I–64 at the parkway's northern terminus, tel. 703/942–5201) and **Harvey's Knob** (Milepost 95.3). Although not on a flyway, North Carolina's **Waterrock Knob** (Milepost 451.2) is popular for raptor scanning.

Boating. Price Park Lake, in Julian Price Memorial Park (Milepost 297.1) has rowboat and canoe rentals (tel. 919/372–4499; open May 8–31 and Sept. 11–Oct. 31, weekends 10–6; June–Sept. 6, daily 8:30–6).

Fishing. Anglers trying their luck along the parkway must obey the rules of the state in which they are fishing; further restrictions include specially designated areas, a ban on live bait, and a parkway prohibition against fishing from a half-hour after sunset to a half-hour before sunrise. Lures in designated "special waters" are restricted to single-hook artificials only, and in some cases artificial flies only. Licenses are available at off-parkway sporting goods stores and the Peaks of Otter Lodge. Under a reciprocal agreement, Virginia and North Carolina licenses are honored in all parkway waters. Price Park Lake (*see* Boating, *above*) is stocked with trout.

Hang Gliding. Two Virginia areas are open to hang gliding: Ravens Roost (Milepost 10.0) and Roanoke Mountain (Milepost 120.3). Both are cliff-launch locations. A free special-use permit is required; apply in person at the district ranger's office .1 mile north of Route 24 (Milepost 111.0) near Roanoke and bring proof of a Hang 3 (advanced) rating.

Horseback Riding. Two popular spots are Moses Cone Memorial Park (Milepost 294.1) and an 18-mile span of trail near Roanoke

(Milepost 109.0–121.0). At the Virginia trail, you'll need your own horse; contact the district ranger's office (tel. 703/982–6490) for information. At Moses Cone Memorial Park, one- and two-hour rides are conducted from April 15 to December 1 by **Blowing Rock Stables** (tel. 704/295–7847) at a cost of $15 per person per hour. Reservations are recommended and novices are welcome; no riders under age 9 allowed.

Rock Climbing. There are no commercial outfitters on the parkway. The only designated area in Virginia is at Ravens Roost (Milepost 10.0); contact the district ranger's office (tel. 703/377–2377) for advice on how to get under way. The most popular North Carolina location is Devil's Courthouse (Milepost 421.0), near the intersection of Route 215 and the parkway. This is not a sanctioned area, and the parkway provides no information about contacts; the best hope for further details is to attempt to locate a regional climbing club.

Snowshoeing and Cross-Country Skiing. These are popular activities when weather allows, despite there being no touring centers or rental shops on the parkway. In North Carolina, head for the Heintooga Spur Road (Milepost 458.2), south of Asheville; contact the district ranger's office (tel. 704/456–9530) for conditions and advice. In Virginia, try the winter recreation area (Milepost 121.0–136.0) between U.S. 220, south of Roanoke, and U.S. 221 at Adney Gap; contact the district ranger's office (tel. 703/982–6490).

Swimming. No swimming is allowed on parkway property.

CHILDREN'S PROGRAMS Children are welcome at seasonal interpretive programs and tours (*see* Orientation Programs *and* Guided Tours, *above*), but they must be accompanied by an adult. The *Parkway Milepost* (*see* Publications *in* Essential Information, *above*) and the blue sheets on bulletin boards at visitor's centers, district ranger's offices, picnic areas, and campgrounds list scheduled activities for kids.

EVENING ACTIVITIES After-hours attractions for parkway visitors include seasonal interpretive programs and tours (*see* Orientation Programs *and* Guided Tours, *above*). The *Parkway Milepost* (*see* Publications *in* Essential Information, *above*) and the blue sheets on bulletin boards at visitor's centers, district ranger's offices, picnic areas, and campgrounds list times and locations.

DINING

You're never too far from good dining while traveling the parkway: Ethnic and gourmet specialties are found within a short drive of the parkway; two full-service restaurants and seven informal eateries are on the parkway itself. Except for a rustic cabin snack shop at Peaks of Otter and the weathered cedar of Mabry Mill, parkway dining spots are of similar design: exteriors of weathered gray, rough-sawn, board-and-batten siding with native stone walls and walks. Interiors are attractive and unpretentious, with natural wood floors and paneling, potted plants, and fabulous views through expansive sections of glass. In the north, three options are clustered within 50 miles; from Peaks of Otter (Milepost 86.0) south, it is 65 to 100 miles between restaurants. You'll find traditional Southern Highlands fare, such as ham, beef, and fish. Overall, the food and service are very good by typical national park standards. Only Peaks of Otter and the Pisgah Inn serve alcoholic beverages. Dress everywhere is casual, although a dressed-for-dinner look is appropriate at the full-service restaurants. Reservations are not accepted on the parkway.

ON THE PARKWAY **Peaks of Otter Restaurant.** This attractive, gray, board-and-batten building on a shore of small Abbott Lake has good food and trails leading up to famous Sharp Top; this is perhaps the parkway's most favorite place to eat and walk it off. The dining room, with its iron chandeliers, potted plants, and rustic wood paneling, grants dazzling views of the lake and the rocky peak of Sharp Top, which towers over it. Regional residents have been known to drive a couple of hours for a special meal here—feasting on baby back ribs, roast turkey, trout, or red snapper. Tackle the climb up Sharp Top and you can justify the feature dessert: Peaks ice

cream pie. There is also a convenient lunch counter adjacent to the dining room where you can have a full breakfast or a burger for lunch, and there's a camp store at the base of the trail where you can get snacks or ice cream. *Milepost 85.9, Blue Ridge Pkwy., VA, tel. 703/586–1081. MC, V. Inexpensive–Moderate.*

Pisgah Inn. Along with traditional Southern Highlands dishes, the Pisgah Inn's window-walled dining room serves such specialty entrées as herb-crusted, oven-baked walleye and char-grilled lamb. A stunning panoramic view of the southern Blue Ridge is featured. This is another eatery where attention to detail, fresh vegetables, and chef's specials attract travelers and regional residents alike. You can get fresh mountain trout at any meal. *Milepost 408.6; Blue Ridge Pkwy., NC, tel. 704/235–8228. MC, V. Closed late Nov.–early Apr. Inexpensive–Moderate.*

Bluffs Coffee Shop. This popular spot serves typical highlands food, including homemade desserts. *Doughton Park, Milepost 241.1, Blue Ridge Pkwy., NC, tel. 919/372–4499. Open late Apr.–early Nov., daily 7:30–7:30. Inexpensive.*

Crabtree Meadows. With a design and menu similar to Virginia's Whetstone Ridge and Otter Creek facilities (*see below*), Crabtree Meadows is great if you want a quick-but-hearty meal or you're a camper with no desire (or ability) to cook for yourself. The country menu offers a full breakfast and a lunch of ham, chicken, corn cakes, or sandwiches. *Milepost 339.5, Blue Ridge Pkwy., NC, tel. 704/675–4236. AE, DC, MC, V. No dinner. Closed Nov. 1–Apr. 30. Inexpensive.*

Mabry Mill. The buckwheat-and-corn cakes, country ham biscuits, and strawberry cobbler at this rustic restaurant are nearly as famous as the oft-photographed gristmill itself. The most popular dining spot at this cedar board-and-batten restaurant is the enclosed porch; there is also a paneled and wallpapered counter area with 12 stools. With limited seating but unlimited appeal, expect to wait during peak season. *Milepost 176.1, Blue*

Ridge Pkwy., VA, tel./fax 703/952–2947. AE, DC, MC, V. Closed Nov. 1–Apr. 30. Inexpensive.

Otter Creek. This clone of the Whetstone Ridge facility (*see below*) differs in its low-elevation setting with a view of scenic Otter Creek; it's also open later in the evening. *Milepost 60.8, Blue Ridge Pkwy., VA, tel. 804/ 299–5862. No credit cards. Inexpensive.*

Whetstone Ridge. One of the restaurant-cum-gift-shop facilities along the northern section of the parkway, Whetstone Ridge has a sandwich counter and a small dining room. Specialties include buckwheat pancakes, open-face roast beef sandwiches, fried chicken; there's also a striking view over the Shenandoah Valley. *Milepost 29.0, VA, Blue Ridge Pkwy., tel. 703/377–6397. Closed Nov.– late Apr. Inexpensive.*

NEAR THE PARKWAY **Buck Mountain Grille.** The casual, airy interior and sophisticated menu belie the Grille's 1950s-era roadhouse exterior. Very popular locally and regionally, food is prepared from scratch, including vegetarian dishes, seafood, chicken, and steaks. *5006 Franklin Rd., Roanoke (on U.S. 220 just south of Roanoke, across from the Blue Ridge Pkwy. exit at Milepost 121.4), VA, tel. 703/776–1830. Reservations accepted. AE, DC, MC, V. No lunch. Closed Mon. Moderate.*

Captain Sam's Landing. This seafood restaurant, with decor to match, is topped off with antiques, a wooden deck, and a patio. One week each month features a "shrimp feast"; chicken and steak are always on the menu. *2323 W. Main St., Waynesboro (on U.S. 250, 10 minutes from the south entrance to Skyline Dr.), VA, tel. 703/943–3416. No reservations weekends or during shrimp feast. AE, DC, MC, V. No lunch. Closed Sun. except during shrimp feast. Moderate.*

Old Mill Room. In an 1830s-era, water-powered gristmill that was moved and reassembled at the elegant Boar's Head Inn, guests dine under exposed wood beams and a huge Spanish chandelier. The menu is Continental, but the sauces and seasonings carry a distinctly French accent. Excellent choices include locally raised lamb and veal, and fresh fish. Check out the extensive wine list. *Boar's Head Inn, U.S. 250 W, Charlottesville (3 mi west of town, 30 mi east of Blue Ridge Pkwy. via U.S. 250), VA, tel. 804/296–2181. Reservations advised for dinner. AE, D, DC, MC, V. Moderate.*

Woodberry Inn. Three dining areas in this gray-stucco, brown-trim Tudor-style lodge, near a small lake, accommodate 84 guests in a setting rich in antiques and reproductions. Dining is casual, with a varied menu that includes steaks, baked and fried chicken, sautéed shrimp, and an acclaimed shrimp cocktail. *Rte. 758 E, Blue Ridge Pkwy. (.1 mi from parkway on Rte. 758/Woodberry Rd., 2 mi north of Mabry Mill at Milepost 174.0), VA, tel. 703/593–2567 or 800/763–2567. Reservations advised. AE, D, MC, V. Closed Jan. 1–late Mar.; closed weekends late Mar.–early June and early Nov.–Jan. 1. Moderate.*

PICNIC SPOTS Picnicking along the parkway is a great way to savor the scenery. The 12 developed sites, each with tables, cooking grills, drinking water, and rest rooms, are Humpback Rocks (Milepost 5.8), James River (Milepost 63.8), Peaks of Otter (Milepost 86.0), Smart View (Milepost 154.5), Rocky Knob (Milepost 169.0), Cumberland Knob (Milepost 217.5), Doughton Park (Milepost 238.5), E.B. Jeffress Park (Milepost 272.0), Linville Falls (Milepost 316.4), Crabtree Meadows (Milepost 339.5), Craggy Gardens (Milepost 364.6), and Mt. Pisgah (Milepost 408.6). Picnicking is also permitted on the grassy shoulder of the parkway and at overlooks. Note: Fires (including charcoal in grills) are allowed only in designated picnic areas. Peaks of Otter, Doughton Park, Crabtree Meadows, and Mt. Pisgah have camp stores and/or snack shops. Peaks of Otter and Smart View are particularly popular for summer and fall-foliage picnicking; Rocky Knob and Craggy Gardens are known for their vibrant spring bloom.

LODGING

There are four lodgings along the parkway and countless more nearby. Three-season, on-parkway options run the gamut from house-keeping cabins to rustic-looking but modern lodges with full-service restaurants; only Peaks of Otter Lodge (Milepost 85.9) is open year-round. Vacancies are rare in October, and almost as scarce on major holidays and summer weekends; to be safe, make your reservations as far in advance as possible. Off-parkway options include inexpensive chain motels, B&Bs, and elegant country inns.

ON THE PARKWAY **Peaks of Otter.** This gray-stained, board-and-batten complex has 59 rooms in three separate two-story motel-style units, plus three suites in the main lodge. The view across Abbott Lake to the rocky peak of Sharp Top is one of the parkway's most famous. All rooms have either patios or balconies, and all face the lake. Only the lodge suites have phones or TVs. *Milepost 85.9, Box 489, Bedford, VA 24523, tel. 703/586–1081 or 800/542–5927 in VA, fax 703/586–4420. 59 rooms with bath, 3 suites. Facilities: restaurant, lounge, snack shop, gift shop, fishing, hiking trails, gas station. MC, V. Moderate.*

Pisgah Inn. This board-and-batten mountain inn is nestled in the outstandingly scenic area that was part of the 100,000-acre estate George W. Vanderbilt purchased in the late 1800s. The property was the site of the first forestry school in the country and the nucleus of Pisgah National Forest. The 51 guest rooms are clustered in three separate two-level, motel-style units; all are recently remodeled and have TVs (but no phones) and patios or balconies with stunning views of the southern Blue Ridge. *Milepost 408.6, Box 749, Waynesville, NC 28786, tel. 704/235–8228, fax 704/648–9719. 50 rooms with bath, 1 suite; 17 are nonsmoking. Facilities: restaurant, coffee shop, crafts shop, golf privileges nearby. MC, V. Closed late Nov.–early Apr. Moderate.*

Rocky Knob. These rustic housekeeping cabins were built with concrete floors and squared logs by the Civilian Conservation Corps in the 1930s; they were sided and renovated into modern lodgings in the 1950s. Flooring is modern sheet vinyl; all utensils and linens are supplied; the cold-water-only kitchens have combination sink-stove-refrigerator units. This is a rustic setup with no TVs or phones. The cabins are in a quiet area at the head of Rock Castle Gorge and are popular with travelers wanting to economize by self-catering or to avoid the crowds at the larger lodges. *Milepost 174.1, VA, tel. 703/593–3503. 7 units share 3 baths. AE, DC, MC, V. Closed Labor Day–Memorial Day. Inexpensive.*

NEAR THE PARKWAY **Cataloochee Ranch.** This rustic, ranch-style resort has two lodges and seven cabins set on 1,000 acres adjacent to Great Smoky Mountains National Park. The view from the 5,000-foot elevation is worth the visit alone, but there are plenty of other reasons to come: horseback riding, fishing, hiking, and a relaxation center with a Jacuzzi-style tub. The buildings are of squared logs and stone; guest rooms are likewise rustic but modern, with handmade quilts. *Rte. 1, Box 500F, Maggie Valley, NC 28751 (on U.S. 19, 8 mi north of Blue Ridge Pkwy.), tel. 704/926–1401 or 800/868–1401, fax 704/926–9249. Facilities: 2 restaurants, fishing, hiking trails, horseback riding, tennis, conference room, nearby public golf and winter ski area. AE, MC, V. MAP required. Closed early Nov.–Dec. 26, Mar. 1–late Apr.; closed weekdays Jan. 3–Mar. 1. Expensive.*

Waynesboro/Afton Mountain Holiday Inn. This three-story, white-brick hotel stands at the northern tip of the Blue Ridge Parkway, where the roadway joins the Skyline Drive. The outstanding attraction is the soaring view over Rockfish Valley (36 rooms have a full view and another 36 a partial view). The covered Ballroom Terrace is a popular spot for watching the fall raptor migration. *Jct. of I–64 (Exit 99) and U.S. 250 atop Afton Mountain, Box 849, Waynesboro, VA 22980, tel. 703/942–5201 or 800/HOLIDAY, fax 703/943–8746. 118 rooms with bath. Facilities: restaurant, lounge, conference rooms, heated indoor pool, golf privileges nearby. AE, D, DC, MC, V. Moderate.*

Woodberry Inn. A luxury lakeside inn of stucco and brown, Tudor-style trim, with a main lodge building and 12 rooms in two separate multi-room buildings. Rooms feature wainscoting and handmade bedspreads; they have TVs, phones, individual climate control. Four rooms are more secluded and farther from the lake. Some have drive-to-the-door parking; others have porch views of the lake. One is disabled-accessible. *Box 908, Meadows of Dan, Rte. 758E, Blue Ridge Pkwy. (.1 mi from parkway on Rte. 758/Woodberry Rd., 2 mi north of Mabry Mill at Milepost 174), VA, 24120, tel. or fax 703/593–2567 or tel. 800/763–2567. 14 rooms with bath. Facilities: restaurant, fishing lake, hiking trails, golf and tennis nearby, antiques and art gallery. AE, D, MC, V. Moderate.*

Apple Valley Motel. This brick motel harkens to the days before interstates, but it has been renovated and is nicely maintained in a secluded setting convenient to the parkway. Despite its private surroundings, it is less than 2 miles from major shopping centers and only 5 miles from downtown Roanoke, the largest city along the parkway. *5063 Franklin Rd., Roanoke, VA 24014 (on U.S. 220, just south of the Blue Ridge Pkwy. exit at Milepost 121.4), tel. 703/989–0675. 18 rooms with bath. AE, D, DC, MC, V. Inexpensive.*

Super 8. This traditional motel, with the signature beige-stucco exterior and dark trim, sits in a modern retail district between Charlottesville and the regional airport. Carpeted guest rooms have cable TV and phones; shopping and dining are close by. *390 Greenbrier Dr., Charlottesville, VA 22901 (1 block off U.S. 29, 5 mi north of the city and 9 mi south of the Charlottesville–Albemarle Airport), tel. 804/973–0888, fax 804/973–2221. 66 rooms with bath. AE, D, DC, MC, V. Inexpensive.*

CAMPING

The parkway offers nine developed campgrounds and limited backcountry camping in two areas. The campgrounds have tent and RV sites (no water or electrical hookups); each site has its own cooking grill and picnic table. All campgrounds have rest rooms (but not showers) and RV sewage stations, seasonal ranger-led interpretive programs, and hiking opportunities. Most have telephones nearby. Campgrounds are generally open early May through late October. Winter camping is sometimes available, weather permitting; contact parkway headquarters in advance. Campers are limited to a total of 14 nonconsecutive days between June 1 and Labor Day; 30 days for the calendar year. Reservations are not accepted nor are they usually needed, though you should come early on summer holiday weekends and during October's peak fall foliage. Pets are allowed, but they must be on a leash no longer than 6 feet. Fees at all of the parkway campgrounds are $9 per site per night for up to two adults; $2 per extra adult. Children under 19 are free.

A free permit, which you have to get in advance from the parkway association (*see* Visitor Information *in* Essential Information, *above*) or regional ranger's stations, is required for backcountry camping (*see* Visitor Information *in* Essential Information, *above*).

Otter Creek. At the parkway's northernmost and lowest-elevation (800 feet) campground, the sites are laid out in two loops along Otter Creek and within a short walk of small but scenic Otter Lake. Closest to the creek and the restaurant are Loop A (RV) sites 1 and 11–25, and Loop B (tent) sites 1–17 and 41; tent sites 18–32, on the outside of Loop B, are the most secluded. *Milepost 60.9. 45 tent sites, 24 RV sites. 552 acres. A pay phone is near the restaurant.*

Peaks of Otter. Nestled in the shadow of Sharp Top and within a stone's throw of Abbott Lake, this is one of the parkway's most popular—and crowded—campgrounds. Closest to the lake are Loop A (tent or RV) sites 1–16, and Loop T (RV) sites 21–46. Most secluded are Loop A sites 19–42 and Loop B sites 1–28. *On Rte. 43, .5 mi east of Milepost 86.0. 86 tent sites, 62 RV sites. 4,150 acres. A pay phone is at the entrance station.*

Roanoke Mountain. A surprisingly secluded campground despite its close proximity to one of the most exclusive neighborhoods in

Roanoke, the largest city on the parkway. It's only a 4-mile drive from downtown Roanoke and has many cultural and historic attractions. Most sites offer privacy, especially Loop A (tent) sites 18–60 and all 30 Loop B (RV) sites. *On the Mill Mountain Spur Rd., 1 mi from Milepost 120.4. 74 tent sites, 30 RV sites. 1,142 acres. A pay phone is at the entrance station.*

Rocky Knob. This large, four-loop, exceptionally scenic campground is especially rich in scenery when mountain laurel and rhododendron bloom in May and June. Loop T offers RV camping only, Loops A, B, and C accommodate tent or RV campers. All sites are secluded; Loops C and T have a slight edge over the others in terms of scenery and privacy. *Milepost 167.1. 81 tent sites, 28 RV sites. 4,200 acres.*

Doughton Park. The largest (6,430 acres) of the parkway campgrounds, this site is laid out in two separate loops: 25 large RV/trailer sites and 110 small RV/tent sites. The large RV sites are well spaced and private, particularly sites 8–12; sites 87–96 have the most privacy of those in the small RV/tent loop. *Milepost 239.0. 110 tent sites, 25 RV sites. 6,430 acres. There is a pay phone across from the small RV/tent loop entrance.*

Julian Price Memorial Park. This rhododendron-cloaked campground offers great diversity: The Tanawha Trail runs near the five loops on the west side of the parkway; it is a short walk to Price Lake from Loop A on the east side of the parkway. For the most privacy, try either Loop B (RV/tent) sites 22–44 or Loop F (RV) sites 1–129. *Milepost 297.0. 129 tent sites, 68 RV sites. 3,900 acres. A pay phone is at the main entrance station on the west side of the parkway.*

Linville Falls. Along the spur road to the campground is a parking area with a view of a bend in the Linville River; the camping area itself is between the road and another bow in the river. From the nearby visitor's center a number of short trails (.5 to 1 mile) provide breathtaking views of the Linville Falls and gorge areas. *On the spur rd. at Milepost 316.3. 50 tent sites, 20 RV sites. 996 acres. A pay phone is at the entrance station.*

Crabtree Meadows. The smallest of all the parkway campgrounds, Crabtree Meadows has outstanding scenery and a .9-mile hike to Crabtree Falls. Trail access is from Loop A at the main entrance parking area or from between sites 9 and 11. For the most privacy, head to Loop A, sites 7–17, or Loop C, sites 44–69. *Milepost 339.5. 71 tent sites, 22 RV sites. 253 acres. A pay phone is at the camp store.*

Mt. Pisgah. The parkway's southernmost, highest-elevation (5,000 feet) campground is in the shadow of Big Bald Mountain, with spruce and fir replacing the typical oak- and hickory-dominated forest. Loop C, sites 78–102, and Loop A, sites 14–30, are most private. *Milepost 408.6, tel. 704/235-9109. 70 tent sites, 70 RV sites. 690 acres. A pay phone is at the lodge.*

Cape Cod National Seashore
Massachusetts
By Karl Luntta

From its surface we overlooked the greater part of the Cape. In short, we were traversing a desert with the view of an autumnal landscape of extraordinary brilliancy, a sort of Promised Land, on the one hand, and the ocean on the other . . . A thousand men could not have seriously interrupted it, but would have been lost in the vastness of the scenery as their footsteps in the sand.— Henry David Thoreau (1817–62), *Cape Cod*

Thoreau, the naturalist and writer, made several visits to Cape Cod between 1849 and 1857. In the florid passage above, he refers to the Wellfleet Bluffs area, now part of Cape Cod National Seashore—and while "Promised Land" may be hyperbole, much of truth remains in his description. The seashore today comprises some 40 miles and over 43,000 acres of smooth beaches, tidal flats, sand dunes, forests, and marshes along the outer arm of the Cape, much of it unsullied by human development.

Cape Cod National Seashore was established in August 1961, under the administration of President John F. Kennedy, for whom Cape Cod was home and haven. The park is unusual, the first to be established around residential and commercial areas. The seashore stretches through six towns on the Lower Cape including Chatham, Orleans, Eastham, Wellfleet, Truro, and Provincetown. (If you picture Cape Cod as an upraised arm, think of the Upper Cape as the towns near the shoulder, the Mid-Cape as the biceps, and the Lower Cape as the forearm and fist.)

The seashore figures conspicuously in Cape Cod's maritime history. An estimated 3,000 ships have met their match on the sandbars, rocks, and pounding breakers of this side of the peninsula. The first recorded wreck was the *Sparrowhawk,* a British vessel that went down near Nauset Beach in 1626. The *Whydah,* a pirate vessel, met a similar fate in 1717, taking with it millions of dollars in treasures; it's now being salvaged. So horrendous was the sailing here that Congress, in 1872, established the U.S. Life Saving Service with nine stations along the Cape. The service evolved into today's U.S. Coast Guard, which still maintains stations on several seashore beaches. Today, the bulk of Cape Cod National Seashore's acreage braces this eastern Atlantic coast, the "Outer Beach." The beaches here are the best on the Cape—some say the best on the East Coast. They are certainly the park's main attraction. Miles of lifted sand dunes and sand beaches buttress the often brawny surf of the open Atlantic. The beaches are characterized by tidal flats, coves and marshes, and rivers and rivulets, creating small microcosms of Cape Cod's environmental curiosities.

Though the ocean and beaches may be the seashore's most popular attraction, other park facilities are well worth exploring. They include 11 miles of bicycle trails and 25 miles of hiking trails (some ranger-guided, others self-guided, one equipped for the sight-impaired); two visitor's centers as well as a park headquarters; five working U.S. Coast Guard lighthouses; and preserved swamps, forests, and a cranberry bog. Surf fishing on the beaches and freshwater fishing are allowed—as is shellfishing in specified areas. Access to seashore beaches and trails is easy: paved roads are the norm. Some areas, in the Truro and Provincetown sections of the seashore, allow off-road vehicles.

Because of the odd mix of residential areas within the seashore's jurisdiction, you will encounter new as well as antique park-maintained homes and buildings. One, the ornate Captain Edward Penniman House, is open to the public. In addition, 30 park-owned sites and structures are listed in the National Historic Register. Within the boundaries, there are more than 600 residences, besides several privately owned motels, campgrounds, and concession businesses.

ESSENTIAL INFORMATION

VISITOR INFORMATION For information on the park, contact **Cape Cod National Seashore** (Park Headquarters, South Wellfleet 02663, tel. 508/349–3785, ext. 200; open weekdays 8–4:30). For information specific to their respective areas, contact the **Salt Pond Visitor's Center** (tel. 508/255–3421; open late June–Labor Day, daily 9–6; fall and spring, daily 9–4:30; Jan.–Feb., weekends 9–4:30) or **Province Lands Visitor's Center** (tel. 508/487–1256; open late June–Labor Day, daily 9–6, and fall and spring, daily 9–4:30). Beaches are closed midnight–6. Trails and beaches are open year-round, but such facilities as bathhouses and concession stands, as well as hotels and restaurants, close in winter. Beaches "officially" open mid-April or early May and close around Labor Day.

For information on accommodations, restaurants, and local sights, contact the **Cape Cod Chamber of Commerce** (Rtes. 6 and 132, Hyannis 02601, tel. 508/362–3225). For 24-hour local weather information, call 508/790–1061.

Backcountry camping is not permitted on Cape Cod National Seashore, although several private grounds operate within the park (*see* Camping, *below*).

FEES Since town-owned and other private facilities fall within park boundaries, fees for parking at town beaches vary. At national seashore–operated beaches, daily entrance fees are $3 for walk-ins and cyclists, $5 for cars. A seasonal pass costs $15. Children 16 and under enter free. Fees are collected only from late June–Labor Day, 9–5 (although beaches remain open until midnight). Pay at the entrances to beach parking lots. Trails and roads within seashore boundaries are not subject to fees.

The use of off-road vehicles requires a $45 permit fee good for the season. RVs, which are allowed overnight stays in specified areas, require a seasonal fee of $75. These fees are payable at the visitor's centers.

PUBLICATIONS Contact the park headquarters (*see* Visitor Information, *above*) for free maps, guides, trail descriptions, and regulations, which you can also pick up in person at the visitor's centers. The park headquarters also has a small library with general information on Cape Cod flora, fauna, geology, history, and the like; the books are for research purposes and are not allowed off the premises. The Salt Pond and Province Lands visitor's centers operate small bookstores selling books, maps, videos, puzzles, postcards, and other seashore paraphernalia.

Among the best publications, *Cape Cod,* by Henry David Thoreau, is a classic travel journal and passionate description, published posthumously in 1864. *The Outermost House,* by Henry Beston, is a 1928 log of the solitary year spent by the naturalist on Coast Guard Beach in a small shack, which was swept into the sea during a 1978 blizzard. *The Life Savers of Cape Cod,* by J. W. Dalton, is a 1902 account of the historic U.S. Life Saving Service, forerunner of the U.S. Coast Guard. *A Guide to Nature on Cape Cod and the Islands,* edited by Greg O'Brien, is an excellent all-around guide, with naturalist-written chapters on birds, seashores, wetlands, weather, and more. *A Guide to the Common Birds of Cape Cod* was written by Peter Trull, a senior field naturalist with the Cape Cod Museum of Natural History.

GEOLOGY AND TERRAIN Of Cape Cod National Seashore's 43,569 acres, 27,398 are owned and administered directly by the National Park Service. The rest fall into public, town, or private interests. This mix of private and public ownership gives the seashore an unusual feel; just minutes away from a briny marsh flushed by ocean tides, you'll come across a small residential section or village center. It can be a little disorienting; at times you're not sure if you're within seashore boundaries. But along the 40-mile stretch from Chatham to Provincetown, or on one of the trails operated by the park, there's no mistaking it: You're on protected land.

Cape Cod is the world's largest glacial peninsula. The whole of the Cape, including the islands of Martha's Vineyard and Nantucket, was formed by great sheets of ice, up to 2 miles thick, that descended from the north about 21,000 years ago into what is now New England. Here, in more temperate climes, and

over time, the glacier's advance was halted and it eventually receded. As the ice melted, sea levels rose—today's level is about 400 feet higher than it was during glacial times. The ice melted unevenly, gouging great chunks of the earth, which in turn fused with underwater springs to become today's bogs and freshwater ponds, called kettle ponds. At the seashore, the aptly named Salt Pond was once a freshwater kettle pond. Here the sea finally broke through and connected Salt Pond with the larger Nauset Marsh.

Rock debris, glacial till (sand and clay), and other deposits pushed south by the great sheets of ice were left behind after the glacier retreated, forming much of the terrain as we now know it. Observe, for example, the moraines—small hills formed from glacial deposits—along Cape Cod Bay and Buzzards Bay on the Upper Cape, and outwash plains— the flat or gently sloping surfaces most common in the Mid- and Lower Cape.

Throughout the seashore, you'll find small dunes covered with scrubby beach grass, forests of pitch pine and scrub oak, pungent saltwater marshes, and great boulders; all have their origins somewhere farther north. Doane Rock at the Salt Pond Visitor's Center is the largest glacially deposited rock on Cape Cod.

The wind and ocean have most profoundly— and, in cases, dramatically—rearranged the terrain of the seashore. Changing tides and the fury of storms have taken sand and shore from one place and deposited them in others. Along the Atlantic coastline, roughly 3 feet of shoreline are lost annually. The cliffs that dominate the coastline are literally falling into the sea. Erosion is starkly evident at the site of Marconi Station—which, dismantled in 1920 because of cliff erosion, has all but disappeared. Sand, however, is rapidly redeposited farther north, first as underwater sandbars, then as sandspits and sandbars that break the water's surface. Province Lands, at the very tip of the seashore, is relatively new, formed about 5,000 years ago. It continues to expand westward as sand is deposited from the south. The Province Lands area is also characterized by immense and shifting dunes, tidal flats, pitch pine and other forests, kettle ponds, and flat areas of sand grass.

FLORA AND FAUNA The flora and fauna of Cape Cod National Seashore exist only with permission from the ocean. Its tides, saltwater breezes, and storms have all affected the seashore's several interlinked habitats. This is strikingly evident in the marshy wetlands, where the sea meets freshwater. Here, in an almost laboratory environment, springs much of the plant and animal life that supports the seashore.

Whale-watching is a popular summer activity. Stellwagen Bank, a feeding ground, is to the north of the seashore's northernmost point, Race Point. The guaranteed way to see whales is through whale-watching companies operating out of Barnstable and Provincetown (*see* Guided Tours *in* Exploring, *below*). But on a clear day, in the spring and summer waters off Race Point, you might see a giant finback whale, up to 70 feet long. Also visible are minke, humpback, and pilot whales, as well as white-sided and white-beaked dolphins. From November to May, harbor seals migrate south from breeding grounds along the Maine and Canadian coast, and can be seen in groups at points along the seashore, notably Race Point, Coast Guard Beach, and Great Island.

Smaller marine life is often jostled and washed up on shore, only to scurry back or be gobbled up by a waiting tern or gull. Along the more quiescent intertidal flats (the often muddy area between the high point and low point of tides) live hermit crabs, spider crabs, snails, and several varieties of shrimp and sea worms. Whelks, including the knobbed whelk, a snail that is sometimes a foot long, are also found here. Clams, such as quahogs (pronounced *ko*-hogs), steamers, and razor clams, make their home in mudflats and sandy flats. The surf clam, a wide-bodied clam, is most common along the beach. Fiddler crabs, easily recognized by the one oversize claw, can be found in several environments, from sandy beaches to grass-covered dunes. Occasionally, a jellyfish—not really a fish but a primordial glob of membrane with nerve bundles—washes up on shore; they're more common in the warmer waters of Nantucket Sound. Among local species are seawattle jellyfish and the large Portuguese man-of-war. Most jellyfish tentacles have small, stinging organisms that either detach or emit toxins. Although the stings are not fatal, they can irritate the skin. Stear clear of them, even if they appear dead or dying on the beach.

From large seabirds to woodland and wetland birds, more than 300 species make their home for at least part of the year on Cape Cod. In the 19th century, hundreds of species were decimated by hunters; in this century, many have returned. The tern, including the common, roseate, and least tern, is found in summer. The largest tern colony in New England is at Nauset Marsh, near the Salt Pond Visitor's Center. Signs are posted in tern breeding areas; avoid disrupting them. Other summer birds include the endangered piping plover, also protected during its breeding season. Swallows, bobolinks, mockingbirds, and great blue herons are found along the shore and around Fort Hill, where views of Nauset Marsh and Nauset Beach are spectacular. Herons, along with several types of egrets, are common marshland dwellers.

In spring and summer, common birds include species of warblers, blackbirds, catbirds, flycatchers, sparrows, orioles, titmice, chickadees, tanagers, and—that quintessential symbol of spring—the robin. Seagoing birds include species of gannets and cormorants (spring–fall), and gulls (year-round). In winter, several types of freshwater and seagoing ducks, including mergansers, scaup, scoters, eiders, buffleheads, goldeneyes, and mallards, are found in seashore waters. Birds of prey, less common but equally fascinating, include hawks, ospreys, and some species of vultures.

The seashore is not brimming with large land mammals, but white-tailed deer are often seen. Opossums, rabbits, raccoons, foxes, squirrels, muskrats, and many of the usual woodland rodent suspects are seen regularly.

The coyote, once thought to be eliminated on Cape Cod, has made recent appearances.

The most dominant flora found in the seashore are forests of pitch pine and several types of oak. Pitch pine, a small, hardy—let's admit it—ugly pine tree, is one of the earliest inhabitants of the Cape, and it plays an enormous role in mitigating the erosion of the sandy soil of the Outer Cape. The most common oaks are the scrub oak, black oak, and white oak. Also widespread is the American holly, most often associated with the red winter berries popular at Christmas. Red cedar is found inland; red maple, brilliant in spring and fall, is found along the Fort Hill Trail. The Atlantic White Cedar Swamp Trail, near the Marconi Station Site, features the tree that was once abundant here but is now severely reduced due to deforestation. Beech, also once common but now virtually absent from the area, is seen on the Beech Forest Trail in Province Lands, along with black birch and eastern hemlock. Near ponds and swamp areas, you'll see tupelo, inkberry, swamp azalea, wild sarsaparilla, sweet pepperbush, and laurel. Beach grass, beach pea, and beach heather are common on windswept dunes, as are beach plum and bayberry bushes. Wildflowers grow abundantly in the marshes and ponds.

Poison ivy grows in almost every habitat. Dog ticks and deer ticks are also found in grassy areas. Deer ticks carry the spirochetal bacteria that cause Lyme disease. Insect repellents can discourage some ticks, but be sure to tuck in your trouser cuffs and shirttails. Wear light clothing so ticks can be easily spotted, and check your entire body after exploration. The height of the infectious season is May through July, but infection can occur year-round.

WHEN TO GO Cape Cod National Seashore is a year-round park with a summer busy season. Route 6, the major thoroughfare from Orleans to Provincetown, is a two-lane roadway and, from June through Labor Day, a study in gridlock. It's especially grueling on weekends and holidays, when seashore beach parking lots sometimes fill before 10 AM.

Summer temperatures on Cape Cod average 71°F–78°F from June through August; they rarely exceed 80°F or fall below 55°F. Shoreline temperatures are usually several degrees cooler, particularly in the evening. Rainfall is heaviest in summer, with an average of 3½ inches in August. The seashore's ocean waters are, at 50°F–60°F, among the coldest on the Cape; the shallow waters of Cape Cod Bay and Nantucket Sound are about 10° warmer. July through September is hurricane season, and the Cape gets its fair share of major storms.

Some consider the seashore more appealing in the spring and fall. Spring is a short season, with cool temperatures, overcast skies, and foggy mornings through late May or mid-June. Fall is pleasant, with bright foliage and mild temperatures—perfect for hikes along the marshes and beaches. The ocean is at its warmest in late August through part of October, when it is great for swimming. Fall temperature highs range from 51°F to 70°F; lows are 35°F–56°F.

Winter, because of moderating ocean breezes and the relative warmth of Gulf Stream waters, is more temperate on Cape Cod than on the mainland. Snow is common but doesn't linger. However, this is the season of nor'easters, the vicious blizzards and gale-force winds—potentially more dangerous than hurricanes—that come from the northeast.

SEASONAL EVENTS **May–July:** The **Figawi Race,** held over Memorial Day weekend since 1972, features hundreds of sailboats in a race from Hyannis to Nantucket. The **Hyannis Harborfest** (tel. 508/775–2201) is a weekend festival in early June that includes live music, jugglers, clowns, boat races, food vendors, and activities for children. The bishop of southeastern Massachusetts is the master of ceremonies during Provincetown's **Blessing of the Fleet** (tel. 508/487–3424), held on the last Sunday in June; the fleet in question is a colorful collection of fishing vessels and pleasure craft, some mighty, some modest. A few weeks later, in July, parades and street musicians and vendors crowd the streets of

Provincetown during **Carnival Week.** The **Barnstable County Fair** (Rte. 151, East Falmouth, tel. 508/563–3200), begun in 1844, is Cape Cod's biggest event. Held in late July, the six-day affair features livestock and food judging; horse, pony, and oxen pulls and shows; arts and crafts demonstrations; musical and stage entertainment; carnival rides; and some truly artery-clogging food. The traffic is horrendous, but the fair is worth the trip.

August to early September: The **Hyannis Street Festival** (tel. 508/775–2201) is a weekend of Main Street shopping, food, and fun. Merchants display sale items on the sidewalk; clowns, jugglers, and other entertainers stroll the street, and up to 20 bands perform. The **Harwich Cranberry Harvest Festival** (tel. 508/430–2811) is 10 days of festivities, including a country-western jamboree, an arts and crafts show, a parade, fireworks, pancake breakfasts, and an antique-car show.

WHAT TO PACK Take along a bathing suit and towel for lying on the beach; long-sleeved shirts and trousers for hiking; and insect repellent, a hat, and sunscreen for both activities. Also pack whatever gear you'll need for your bicycle. Cameras, camcorders, and binoculars are allowed—and there are scenes you will not want to miss. Drinking water is available at bathhouses throughout the park, but you might want to carry some for use on the trail. The only snack bar on seashore property, at Herring Cove Beach, is likely to be crowded in summer. Consider carrying lunch or snacks in with you. There are three picnic areas within the seashore.

What not to pack: The six seashore-maintained beaches have designated "protected beach" areas, which are under the surveillance of park lifeguards. Rafts, rubber tubes, and other inflatables, as well as glass containers, are not allowed on any seashore beaches. Surfboards, face masks, snorkels, and scuba gear; stoves or grills using propane, white gas, or charcoal; fires; and pets are not allowed on the protected areas of beaches. Leashed pets are allowed on all other seashore beaches. Metal detectors are prohibited anywhere within the seashore.

GENERAL STORES **Eastham Superette** (Rte. 6, between Fort Hill and the Salt Pond Visitor's Center, tel. 508/255–0530) sells a full line of groceries, supplies, and wine and liquor. It's open Monday–Saturday 7 AM–9 PM, Sunday 7:30 AM–9 PM, and remains open until 10 on busy weekends. The two **Cumberland Farms** (Rte. 6, Wellfleet, tel. 508/349–3719; Shank Painter Rd., Provincetown, tel. 508/487–9668) sell a similar line of goods (but no alcohol) and are open daily 6 AM–11 PM.

ATMS **Wellfleet:** Cape Cod 5 bank (Main St.). **Provincetown:** Seaman's Savings Bank (221 Commercial St.); A&P Supermarket (Shank Painter Rd.).

ARRIVING AND DEPARTING Seashore and town roads enter the park from points along Route 6, east from Orleans to Provincetown. Visitor's centers as well as beach and trail entrances are well marked. You'll first encounter the Salt Pond Visitor's Center; the Province Lands Visitor's Center is farther north.

By Plane. Barnstable Municipal Airport (tel. 508/775–2020) is roughly 50 miles from Provincetown and about 25 miles from the Salt Pond Visitor's Center in Eastham; the **Provincetown Municipal Airport** is within the seashore boundaries. They both have commercial flights to Boston. Barnstable Municipal is served by **Cape Air** (tel. 800/352–0714), **Delta's Business Express** (tel. 800/345–3400), **USAir** (tel. 800/428–4322), and **Northwest Airlines** (tel. 800/225–2525); Provincetown Municipal is served by **Cape Air.** You'll want a car once you're here: From Barnstable, try **Avis** (tel. 508/775–2888 or 800/831–8000) and **Budget** (tel. 508/775–3832 or 800/527–0700); from Provincetown, try **Thrifty** (tel. 508/487–9418). Call well ahead to reserve a car in summer.

By Car and RV. From the Sagamore and Bourne bridges, your entry points to Cape Cod, the drive to the Salt Pond Visitor's Center is 40–45 miles. It takes less than an hour on most days, at least another 30 minutes on busy summer days. If you come across the Sagamore, stay on Route 6. From the Bourne

Bridge take Route N to Route 6. Follow Route 6 to the visitor's center. For a more scenic jaunt, exit Route 6 after the bridge and head north to Route 6A, which follows Cape Cod Bay's shoreline. The two routes join at the Orleans rotary, about 3 miles before the Salt Pond Visitor's Center.

By Train. Amtrak (Main St., Hyannis, tel. 800/872–7245) has limited weekend summer service from Providence. Take **Town Taxi** (tel. 508/771–5555) 2 miles to the Barnstable Municipal Airport, where you can rent a car (*see* By Plane, *above*). Or try **Bargain Rent-A-Car** (about 2 mi from station, tel. 508/771–1200) or **Trek Rent-A-Car** (2 blocks from station, 233 Barnstable Rd., tel. 508/771–2459).

By Bus. Plymouth and Brockton Street Railway (tel. 508/746–0378 or 508/775–5524) provides daily service from Boston's Logan Airport to Hyannis ($13.75 one way). From Hyannis, the bus continues to Provincetown ($7.50 one way), making additional local stops. Once in the park, however, public transportation is limited (*see* Exploring, *below*).

EXPLORING

Public transportation within the seashore is limited to the shuttle buses between the Salt Pond Visitor's Center and U.S. Coast Guard Beach, or those carrying ranger-guided tours. Your exploring will have to be done by car or bicycle, or on foot—a combination of all three works best. Cars have access to beach and trail parking, as well as to several scenic roads.

Bicycles are not allowed on hiking trails, nor is hiking allowed on bicycle trails. You'll need a combination of both types of trail to cover the whole park; though it is questionable whether one needs to cover seashore to fully experience it. Probably not. It's a question of time: You can see the major sites in less than a week—the dunes at Province Lands, the trails of Great Island, the Atlantic White Cedar Swamp Trail at the Marconi Station Site, and Nauset Marsh and Coast Guard Beach at Salt Pond Visitor's Center.

Two or three days are sufficient to get a good sense of the seashore's habitats and terrain, and to stay in one of the Cape's wonderful inns.

THE BEST IN ONE DAY Start out early, especially in summer. Visit the Salt Pond Visitor's Center, gathering a few brochures and seeing *Sands of Time,* a 10-minute video shown every half hour. You can browse through a small museum with exhibits of scrimshaw, whaling history, and more; and then talk to a ranger about your day's possibilities. Plan one to two hours to hike the 1-mile Nauset Marsh Trail (*see* Nature Trails and Short Walks, *below*), which winds around Salt Pond and Nauset Marsh. There is much to stop for, particularly in summer when the marsh is in ecological splendor. Return to the visitor's center and take a short drive to Nauset Light Beach (*see* Swimming *in* Other Activities, *below*), where you can see a working lighthouse and spend some time frolicking in the ocean.

Leave the park and have lunch in Wellfleet, a picturesque town of cafés and antiques shops. For some adventure, take Route 6 to Truro (about a 20-minute drive), where you can relax at Pilgrim Heights and walk the .75-mile Pilgrim Spring Trail (*see* Nature Trails and Short Walks, *below*). This is said to be the site of the Pilgrims' first landing in New England, and where they drank their first New World water.

From here, make the 10-mile drive to Province Lands. Stop in at the visitor's center to get a feel for the local trails and beaches. Race Point (*see* Swimming *in* Other Activities, *below*), the northernmost point on Cape Cod, is prime for whale-watching in summer. If you've got your bike and a little energy remaining, ride the Province Lands Trail (*see* Biking *in* Other Activities, *below*), a 5.25-mile trail that loops in and out of the dunes and passes Great Pond.

ORIENTATION PROGRAMS The Salt Pond Visitor's Center shows rotating 10-minute orientation films daily (late June–Labor Day). They concentrate on the history and geography of the seashore and surrounding areas. Among

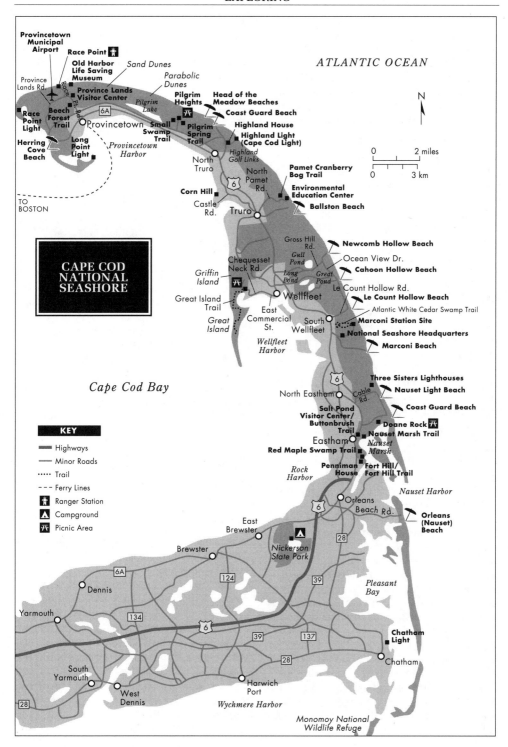

ATLANTIC OCEAN

Provincetown Municipal Airport

Race Point

Old Harbor Life Saving Museum

Sand Dunes

Parabolic Dunes

Province Lands Rd.

Province Lands Visitor Center

Pilgrim Heights

Head of the Meadow Beaches

Coast Guard Beach

Race Point Light

Beech Forest Trail

Pilgrim Lake

Small Swamp Trail

Pilgrim Spring Trail

Highland House

Highland Light (Cape Cod Light)

Herring Cove Beach

Long Point Light

Provincetown Harbor

North Truro

Highland Golf Links

Pamet Cranberry Bog Trail

Corn Hill

North Pamet Rd.

Environmental Education Center

Castle Rd.

Truro

Ballston Beach

N

0   2 miles

0   3 km

TO BOSTON

Gross Hill Rd.

Newcomb Hollow Beach

Gull Pond

Ocean View Dr.

Cahoon Hollow Beach

Griffin Island

Chequesset Neck Rd.

Long Pond

Great Pond

Le Count Hollow Rd.

Le Count Hollow Beach

Great Island Trail

Wellfleet

Atlantic White Cedar Swamp Trail

Great Island

East Commercial St.

South Wellfleet

Marconi Station Site

National Seashore Headquarters

Marconi Beach

Wellfleet Harbor

Cape Cod Bay

Three Sisters Lighthouses

Nauset Light Beach

North Eastham

Cable Rd.

Coast Guard Beach

Salt Pond Visitor Center/ Buttonbrush Trail

Doane Rock

Nauset Marsh Trail

Eastham

Nauset Marsh

Red Maple Swamp Trail

Penniman House

Fort Hill/ Fort Hill Trail

Rock Harbor

Nauset Harbor

CAPE COD NATIONAL SEASHORE

KEY

—	Highways
—	Minor Roads
.....	Trail
- - -	Ferry Lines
🏠	Ranger Station
▲	Campground
🏕	Picnic Area

Orleans

Beach Rd.

Orleans (Nauset) Beach

East Brewster

Nickerson State Park

Pleasant Bay

Brewster

Dennis

Yarmouth

Chatham Light

South Yarmouth

West Dennis

Harwich Port

Chatham

Wychmere Harbor

Monomoy National Wildlife Refuge

the titles are *Sands of Time, Voice of Cape Cod, Thoreau's Cape Cod,* and *Wooden Ships, Men of Iron.* Times are posted at the visitor's center. Slide shows and other activities also are presented at the Salt Pond amphitheater. Special programs for children are offered, too (*see* Children's Programs, *below*). Call or write ahead for the seasonal schedule.

GUIDED TOURS Most local tours are led by rangers, organized from both visitor's centers. The schedule varies, depending more upon tides than times; the meeting place is often at the site itself. It's best to write ahead for the current schedule or call on the day you wish to visit. Most tours are free, but tickets are limited. Among the tours the Fort Hill Walk, a 1.5-mile hike through the Fort Hill area of Eastham; the Pilgrim Lake Dunes Walk, a 1.5-mile walk around Pilgrim Lake and the parabolic dunes of Truro; the Tidal Flats Walk, a two-hour hike around the tidal flats of Great Island in Wellfleet (wear sneakers or boots); Cape Cod Whales, a one-hour talk about the local presence of whales; and the Nauset Marsh Canoe Trip, a 1.5-mile canoe trip through the marsh—this tour costs $5 per person. There are dozens of additional tours; most are given in spring, summer, and fall.

Several private organizations offer specialized tours: The **Massachusetts Audubon Society's Wellfleet Bay Wildlife Sanctuary** (Box 263, South Wellfleet 02663; tel. 508/349–2615) has naturalist-led natural history walks year-round throughout the seashore. Call ahead to reserve; fees vary. The **Cape Cod Museum of Natural History** (Rte. 6A, Brewster 02631; tel. 508/896–3867 or 800/479–3867) offers one or two hiking tours per month in summer. Called Eco-Treks, the naturalist-led tours focus on seashore trails; some even venture off the trails into regions of the park. The hikes are two to six hours, moderately strenuous, and cost $3.50–$7. Daylong trips cost $15–$20. The **Center for Coastal Studies** (59 Commercial St., Box 1036, Provincetown 02657; tel. 508/487–3622) is a small, nonprofit group dedicated to the study and preservation of Cape Cod's coastal environment. Most of its tours are for school groups and educational organizations,

but about a dozen tours are open to the public for a small fee in July and August. Naturalists conduct these hikes through the dunes, salt marshes, beaches, and tidal flats of Provincetown.

Art's Sand Dune Tours (tel. 508/487–1950) gives tours of the Provincetown dunes. The cost is $8 per person for the 1¼-hour trip with a four-person minimum. There's also a sunset ride costing $9 per person. Narrated whale-watching boat tours are highly recommended; they run from about late spring through mid-fall. Although they make several trips daily, reservations are advised. In Provincetown, try **Portuguese Princess Whale Watch** (tel. 508/487–2651 or, in New England, 800/442–3188), **Dolphin Fleet** (tel. 508/349–1900 or 800/826–9300), or **Ranger V** (tel. 508/487–1582 or 800/992–9333). The average cost is $15 for adults, $13 for children.

SCENIC DRIVES AND VIEWS Several dozen roads flit in and out of Cape Cod National Seashore; many are access roads to trails, beaches, and visitor's centers; others are town roads through residential centers. Scenic vistas and, in fact, the park's more compelling acreage, are best seen by bicycle or foot.

The drive eastbound along **Route 6,** which borders and intersects the park from Eastham to Provincetown, is a contrast in styles. Haphazard development vies with small-town charm, eventually unfolding at the open pitch-pine forests and dunes of the Lower Cape. On the 5-mile stretch from **Eastham to Wellfleet,** the road is congested and lined with motels, convenient but tacky gas stations, shops selling sunbathing paraphernalia, and the other usual seaside attractions. Along here you'll pass entrances to the Salt Pond Visitor's Center and the park headquarters, at the Marconi Station Site. You can also turn off for the town of **Wellfleet** and **Great Island,** seashore property that has a 4-mile hiking trail past marshes. **Ocean View Drive** in Wellfleet, between Le Counts Hollow Road and Gross Hill Road, is a scenic drive past four Wellfleet town beaches.

North of Wellfleet, Route 6 narrows a bit and the congestion abates. Here you are surrounded by large forests of pitch pine, with the ocean never much more than 2 miles to the east and the bay never more than 2 miles to the west. Along here you'll pass **Highland Light,** also called Cape Cod Light, the first lighthouse built on the Cape (*see* Historic Buildings and Sites, *below*).

Continuing on Route 6, you'll drive by **Pilgrim Lake,** a quiescent and brackish body of water abutted by immense dunes. Beyond the lake, the dunes reach the road and the resultant blown sand can be hazardous in windy weather. **Race Point Road** and **Province Lands Road** cover the Province Lands section of the seashore, and pass the great dunes. At the Province Lands Visitor's Center, climb to the observation deck and take in one of the seashore's most breathtaking views—a panoramic sweep of Provincetown, dunes, and ocean.

HISTORIC BUILDINGS AND SITES Because of the area's singular history as the site of the Pilgrims' first New World landing in 1620, the background of the towns along the seashore, particularly Truro and Provincetown, is rich and seminal. There are several historic buildings and sites on seashore property. Many more, however, are in the six towns along which the seashore lies. Check with the Cape Cod Chamber of Commerce (*see* Visitor Information *in* Essential Information, *above*) and local chambers of commerce for information on historic sites and artifacts.

The following are seashore-operated and do not charge admission:

The Second Empire **Captain Edward Penniman House** (circa 1888) is in the Fort Hill area of Eastham. Once the home of a wealthy whaling captain, it has a front gate framed by a startling whale jawbone. Tours are conducted regularly, and "open house" hours are often announced. Check the Salt Pond Visitor's Center for details.

The **Atwood-Higgins House** (circa 1675), in Wellfleet, is a classic full Cape. Tours are by reservation, and tickets and the shuttle bus are picked up from the Salt Pond Visitor's Center.

The **Marconi Wireless Station Site** is just that—a site, not a building. On the same road as the park headquarters, this is where the Italian wireless-communications pioneer Guglielmo Marconi built his extraordinary transmitting station at the turn of the century. At that time, the station used four 210-foot wooden towers, equipped with 25,000-volt transmitters, to send radio waves across the Atlantic. The first successful messages, transmitted in Morse code, traveled to England on January 18, 1903. President Theodore Roosevelt sent his "most cordial greetings and good wishes" to Edward VII. The station operated for 15 years, but with the wind and ocean eroding three feet of cliff each year, it was doomed. The station was dismantled in 1920; the original site has since fallen into the sea. At the current site, you'll see a model of the station, artifacts, and a memorial to Marconi. This spot is one of the narrowest parts of Cape Cod; from an observation platform you can see the Atlantic on one side and Blackfish Creek and Cape Cod Bay on the other.

The white **Three Sisters Lighthouses,** looking a bit like small playhouses, are on Cable Road at Nauset Light Beach. Built in 1838, they were once working lighthouses on the nearby beach. They were removed due to beach erosion and replaced by wooden structures and later by today's steel tower. Ranger-led tours are conducted through the Salt Pond Visitor's Center.

Old Harbor Life Saving Station, on Race Point Road, just beyond the Province Lands Visitor's Center, was once part of the old U.S. Life Saving Service. The building was plucked from an eroding beach in Chatham and transported here by barge in 1977. Now a museum, the station houses artifacts from the early days of 19th-century lifesaving, as well as plaques describing the history of the service and the shipwrecks along this shoreline. Hours vary, so call the Province Lands Visitor's Center for details.

Highland Light (turn off Rte. 6 onto Highland Rd. in Truro), also known as Cape Cod Light, is not under seashore protection but is worth special mention here. The oldest lighthouse on Cape Cod, this 66-foot version was built in 1857 and is now automated. The first lighthouse on this site opened in 1798, here in the Truro Highlands, one of the more treacherous stretches of beach on the East Coast. Thousands of ships—and lives—were lost offshore. The current lighthouse is in danger of falling into the sea, possibly by the turn of this century, due to erosion of the 120-foot cliff on which it stands. A small stand run by the Truro Historical Society sells Cape Cod Light souvenirs and collects signatures petitioning Congress to move the lighthouse back to a safer spot. Though the lighthouse is closed to the public, you'll find the **Highland Golf Course,** which operates as a park concession and was built in 1892, and the **Highland House Museum,** the site of an old Truro inn, now home of the historical society museum.

NATURE TRAILS AND SHORT WALKS Each of the seashore's nine walking trails has trailhead boxes with free pamphlets explaining the trail's background and its notable characteristics.

The 1.5-mile **Fort Hill Trail,** which passes through Red Maple Swamp, begins and ends at the parking lot of the Captain Edward Penniman House. Follow the signs on Route 6 in Eastham. This is a fairly easy trail with some mild slopes, fitted with log steps, and a boardwalk. The swamp is particularly vibrant in fall, when the maples turn vibrant shades of red and gold. Year-round, this is one of the seashore's premier bird-watching areas. Watch for the stilt-legged and elegant great blue heron. Allow at least an hour for the trail.

Buttonbush Trail is relatively short, about .25 mile. It is, however, unique in that it is designed for the sight-impaired. Access is from the Salt Pond Visitor's Center in Eastham; the trail has text on plaques in Braille, large-print trail markers, and a guide rope. The trail passes by Salt Pond and has some steps and a boardwalk. Also for the

sight-impaired is the "touch and feel" exhibit at the visitor's center.

Also beginning from the Salt Pond Visitor's Center, the 1-mile **Nauset Marsh Trail** is one of the seashore's most enticing. Past Salt Pond, the trail quickly comes upon Nauset Marsh, fringing its north side. Stop at the overlook and spend some time observing the marsh and the ocean beyond. The bird life here is rich and colorful, as are the odors emanating from the decaying salt grasses. On the return trip you'll pass an old farmstead. Allow at least an hour for this walk.

Start at the Marconi Station Site for the 1.25-mile **Atlantic White Cedar Swamp Trail,** a loop that entails a walk over some steep stairs, sandy areas, and a boardwalk.

The .5-mile **Cranberry Bog Trail** is short, with some log steps and a boardwalk. Take North Pamet Road in Truro to the Environmental Education Center parking lot. This is swampland, once covered by red maple, that became a working cranberry bog in the late 19th century and eventually fell into disuse. After the seashore acquired the land, it re-created the historic landscape and refurbished the bog and an old bog house. This is an interesting look at an industry that was once Cape Cod's economic bedrock.

The **Small's Swamp** and **Pilgrim Spring** trails are both accessed at Pilgrim Heights in Truro. There is a small interpretative center here. Small's Swamp Trail is .75 mile long, and Pilgrim Spring Trail is just over .25 mile. Both are loops, with moderate grades and some log steps. These trails are more historical than nature-oriented. "Small" refers to the settler, Thomas Small, who built a farm here in the 1860s. Native Americans inhabited the land before Small and artifacts of that time are displayed here along with signs explaining them. Pilgrim Spring swings by what is said to be the spot where the Pilgrims first dipped their lips upon landing.

The .5-mile **Beech Forest Trail,** off Race Point Road on the way to the Race Point Visitor's Center, is somewhat difficult because of steep steps and lots of sand. It loops around two small kettle ponds and allows a fascinating look at one of the last remnants of pre-Pilgrim forest.

LONGER HIKES The longest hikes at the seashore are along the beach itself. You could actually walk the 25-mile length of its Atlantic side, between Coast Guard Beach and Race Point. You'd want to bring water and food, though, and you'd have to complete the walk in one day. Rangers are quick to remind you that walking a mile in sand is like walking 2 miles on solid ground.

A better alternative is to walk any stretch between **Coast Guard Beach** and **Marconi Beach.** This distance is less than 5 miles one way and features views of the marsh and Nauset Light.

The 4-mile (one way) **Great Island Trail** traverses a small spit of land at the seashore's western side on Cape Cod Bay. Great Island was once an island, but the southward current of the bay shifted sand over time to connect it to the mainland. It was a whale-watching outpost and home to whalers, fishermen, and, before them, Wampanoags. To get there, follow the signs to Wellfleet center, turn left onto Commercial Street, right at the town pier onto Kendrick Road, and then left onto Chequesset Neck Road.

OTHER ACTIVITIES Biking. All public seashore roads are open to cyclists, but heavy summer traffic can make for an unpleasant— if not dangerous—ride. It's better to stick to the seashore's three trails, which cover about 11 miles. They are moderate to easy, for the most part paved, and also very crowded in summer. All trails are two-way and unforeseen obstacles, such as blown sand, can pop up unexpectedly. Go slowly, and when braking, use both rear and front brakes.

The **Nauset Trail** covers a bit more than 1.5 miles from the Salt Pond Visitor's Center, past Nauset Marsh, and on to Coast Guard Beach. Access points are at the visitor's center and at the Doane Rock picnic area. The **Head of the Meadow Trail** in Truro covers about 2 miles of easy path from the Head of the Meadow Beach parking area, past a great salt meadow

and Pilgrim Lake, and on to High Head Road. The 7.3-mile **Province Lands Trail** is quite challenging, dipping and looping through sand dunes, past kettle ponds, through the Beech Forest, and on to Race Point. Access is at the Race Point Beach parking area, the Beech Forest parking area, Province Lands Visitor's Center, and the Herring Cove Beach parking area.

For year-round rentals in Eastham and Wellfleet, try **Idle Times** (Rte. 6, Eastham, tel. 508/255–8281; Rte. 6, Wellfleet, tel. 508/349–9161). They've got 3- to 10-speed adult mountain bikes for $10 for four hours, $15 for a 24-hour period, and $60 for a week. In Provincetown, try **Tim's Bicycle Shop** (306 Commercial St., tel. 508/487–6628; open approximately May–Sept.), where 18- and 21-speed mountain bikes can be had for $6 for two hours, $17 for a 24-hour period, and $70 weekly. The 10- and 12-speed bikes cost slightly less. These shops rent children's bikes and equipment.

Bird-Watching. The place to start is the Salt Pond Visitor's Center, where you can inquire about the ranger-led tours "Birds of the Beach" and "Early Bird Walks." Nauset Marsh is a particularly popular spot for year-round bird-watching, where you'll see terns, the great blue heron, and other marsh birds. Check with the **Wellfleet Bay Wildlife Sanctuary** (*see* Guided Tours, *above*) for bird-watching activities.

Boating. You're free to bring your motorboats, canoes, and kayaks, and launch them at appropriate town-landing areas and piers. Each town enforces its own bylaws regarding boating in freshwater ponds, maximum horsepower allowed, and waterskiing regulations.

For boat rentals, try **Jack's Boat Rentals** (Gull Pond, tel. 508/349–7553; Rte. 6, tel. 508/349–2141) in Wellfleet. They rent a full line of boating toys, including pedal boats, aqua bikes, and kayaks (all $12 per hour, $45 per day); canoes ($15 per hour, $55 per day); sailboards ($15 per hour, $50 per day); and catamarans (starting at $20 per hour, $95 per day). They also offer windsurfing and sailing lessons, and rent beach chairs, umbrellas, boogie boards, and more. In Provincetown, contact **Flyer's Boat Rental** (131A Commercial St., tel. 508/487–0898; open June–late Sept.) for small motorboats (16 feet, 6–8 horsepower) for fishing or just drifting around Provincetown Harbor. The cost is $16 per hour (two-hour minimum); $80 per day. They also rent Sunfish sailboats, starting at $14 per hour, and 19-foot sailboats, starting at $20 per hour.

Fishing. A license is required for all freshwater fishing. There are, however, only a few places on seashore property accessible to fishing enthusiasts. Gull Pond, Great Pond, and Long Pond—all in Wellfleet—are the best fishing holes, where you can catch trout, bass, pickerel, perch, and bullheads. There are size and quantity limits. The **Goose Hummock Shop** (Rte. 6A, Orleans, tel. 508/255–0455) sells bait, tackle, and licenses, and provides free tide charts.

Noncommercial shellfishing areas and seasons are strictly regulated by town ordinances. Local town halls issue licenses, which often require a fee, and regulations.

Surf casting is allowed outside of protected beach areas and at town beaches. You're likely to catch bluefish, striped bass, fluke, or other sea fish. No licenses are required, but minimum legal lengths for certain fish should be observed; ask any fishing-supply shop for such requirements.

Off-Road Driving. Several miles of ATV corridors, primarily from High Head in Truro to Race Point in Provincetown, are open to ATVs. Sections close down periodically due to the nesting patterns of endangered birds, beach erosion, or inclement weather; call the **Oversand Vehicle Information Line** (tel. 508/487–3698) for status reports. You can get an ATV permit from the **Province Lands Visitor's Center** (mid-April–Nov. only); operators are required to view a short educational video. The seasonal fee for ATVs is $45.

Swimming. At Cape Cod National Seashore, life is literally (we had to say this somewhere) a beach. The six beaches—Coast Guard, Nauset Light, Marconi, Head of the Meadow, Race Point, and Herring Cove—are characterized by rugged surf, lofty cliffs, and wide expanses of sandy shore. The water is cold and the undertow strong, but you won't find better places to sunbathe and dip. Beaches have restrooms and parking, and some have showers and picnic tables. Parking lots fill up by midmorning on summer weekends. Plan your visit around traffic.

Interspersed among seashore beaches are more than a dozen town-operated beaches, most with rest rooms and some picnic tables. Parking is a challenge; fees vary from one town to another, and some do not admit nonresidents. Nauset Beach, in Orleans, at the southernmost section of the seashore, is one of the best.

CHILDREN'S PROGRAMS **Children's Hour,** at Salt Pond Visitor's Center, is for children five and older, and includes scavenger hunts and sea stories (parents must be present). A Junior Ranger Program is offered for children 8–12 at the Salt Pond center. Call ahead for schedules or to reserve space.

At the Province Lands Visitor's Center, **Sea, Surf, and Sand: A Children's Discovery** takes kids through an hour of beachside activities, including discoveries about sea creatures. The hour-long **Sharing Nature with Children** lets kids play environmental games with adults.

EVENING ACTIVITIES Salt Pond's **Evening Program,** usually held at 8, presents slides and illustrated talks at the Salt Pond amphitheater. The Province Lands center conducts a **Sunset Beach Walk,** a family activity that includes storytelling around a campfire.

DINING

Cape Cod is named for a fish, so you won't be surprised to find that seafood in all forms—from fish-and-chips to Wellfleet oysters—is fresh here and abundant. Most restaurants are on Route 6, some within seashore boundaries, others in the towns that border the park. All are privately operated. The tonier, more expensive restaurants are in town centers, particularly Provincetown; along Route 6 you'll find family-style seafood joints and fast-food eateries.

NEAR THE PARK **Chillingsworth.** The Cape's best restaurant, this elegant spot offers award-winning French and nouvelle cuisine and an outstanding wine cellar. The frequently changing dinner menu is a five-course prix fixe and features such entrées as venison with celery root purée and fried pumpkin; or sweetbreads and foie gras with wild mushrooms and ham, asparagus, and smoky sauce. *2449 Main St. (Rte. 6A), Brewster, tel. 508/896–3640. Reservations required at dinner, advised at lunch. Jacket advised at dinner. AE, DC, MC, V. Closed late-Nov.–Memorial Day; Mon. June–mid-Oct.; weekdays rest of year. Expensive.*

The Lobster Pot. As you might guess, lobster, excellent chowders, and seafood are specialties of this homey, noisy, family-owned restaurant, with views of Provincetown Harbor and MacMillan Wharf. The homemade breads and desserts are also good. It's one of the town's busiest restaurants in summer—not the place to go if you're in a hurry. *321 Commercial St., Provincetown, tel. 508/487–0842. No reservations. Dress: casual. AE, D, DC, MC, V. Closed Jan. Moderate.*

The Moors. This restaurant is decorated with ship's planks and nautical debris. Specialties are seafood and Portuguese cuisine, including soup made from *chourico* and *linguiça* (two types of spicy Portuguese sausage). And—a blessing in Provincetown—parking is available. *5 Bradford St. W, Provincetown, tel. 508/487–0840. Reservations advised. Dress: casual. AE, D, DC, MC, V. Closed Thanksgiving–Mar. Moderate.*

The Wellfleet Oyster House. Less than a mile off Route 6 near Wellfleet center, this restaurant is housed in a mid-18th-century house, overlooking a duck pond and a creek. The decor is Colonial, and the food is an eclectic blend of Continental and classic American with a seafood slant. Specialties include the mixed-seafood platter of broiled shrimp, crabmeat, scallops, and oysters in garlic butter; and mussels Isabella, steamed in wine and herb sauce. Try jumbo frogs' legs, if you're feeling adventuresome. *E. Main St., Wellfleet, tel. 508/349–2134. Reservations requested. Dress: casual. AE, D, DC, MC, V. Closed late fall–Apr. 1; weekdays Apr. 1–July 4. No lunch. Moderate.*

Land Ho! This busy, landmark Orleans restaurant is famous for its extensive lending rack of daily newspapers and the numerous business signs hung over the bar. The food is hearty and simple: Fish-and-chips, burgers, sandwiches, chowders, and soups are the staples, and they're good. *Rte. 6A, Orleans, tel. 508/255–5165. No reservations. Dress: casual. MC, V. Inexpensive–Moderate.*

Box Lunch. A local chain, Box Lunch is great for a take-out picnic lunch. The shop features the "Rollwich," sandwich ingredients rolled in a pita. Try the Jaws Rollwich, a quarter-pound of roast beef, horseradish, mayo, and onions. Other rollwiches include the standard sandwich meats, as well as lobster, egg salad, and vegetarian. Order ahead for quickest service. Breakfast—rollwiches filled with eggs, sausages, and cheese—is also served. *Briar La., Wellfleet, tel. 508/349–2178. No reservations. Dress: casual. No credit cards. Inexpensive.*

Poit's. This is a fine example of substance over style. With picnic-table seating and video games inside, and an ice-cream hut and miniature golf outside, the restaurant's style is pure kitsch and has been since its 1954 opening. But the food—fish-and-chips, fried clam plates, chowder, and lobster rolls—is unfailingly fresh and tasty. The crowds lined up outside prove it. There is no service—you place your order, and they'll give you a shout over the loudspeaker. You can't miss it: just south of the Marconi Station Site in North Eastham. *Rte. 6, North Eastham, tel. 508/255–6321. No reservations. Dress: casual. D, MC, V. Closed Sept.–Mar. Inexpensive.*

PICNIC SPOTS The four park picnic areas are the **Beech Forest Trail** in Province Lands, **Pilgrim Heights** in Truro, the **head of the Great Island Trail** in Wellfleet, and **Doane Rock** near the Salt Pond Visitor's Center. All are in shaded areas in woods, with parking, rest rooms, and grills. Many town beaches have picnic tables, as well.

Picnicking on seashore beaches is allowed, with the provision that glass is forbidden. Outside protected areas, you can cook on a white gas, propane, or coal stove or grill. Douse coal fires and remove fire remnants—do not bury the coals.

LODGING

You'll find a plethora of hotels, motels, inns, B&Bs, condos, and campgrounds in every season except winter. Reserve well ahead in summer, particularly for holiday weekends. Those accommodations open in winter reduce their rates by as much as 50%. Rates begin to rise in May, peak from Memorial Day through Labor Day, and fall off after Columbus Day. Several hotels, motels, hostels, and campgrounds operate within seashore boundaries, some on private property and several as park concessions. The seashore is long and thin—no accommodation is more than a few minutes from a beach.

NEAR THE PARK **Chatham Bars Inn.** A little farther from the seashore than some of the others, this inn embodies all that is (or should) be Cape Cod: a relaxed vacation retreat that says old, stately, and subdued. In operation for more than 80 years, the hotel comprises 26 authentic bungalows and the Main Inn, which is fronted by sweeping steps, a veranda, and a chintz-laden reception hall. Dinner (open to the public) here is formal, sophisticated, and relaxing—the view of Pleasant Bay and the Atlantic is near perfect. The drive to Salt Pond Visitor's Center is about 25 minutes. *Shore Rd., Chatham 02633, tel. 508/945–0096 or 800/527–4884, fax 508/945–5491. 152 rooms in Main Inn and 26 cottages. Facilities: 2 restaurants, beach grill, lounge, fitness room, outdoor heated pool, tennis. AE, D, DC, MC, V. Expensive.*

Sheraton Ocean Park Inn. For those who find a certain comfort in staying at a familiar chain hotel, the Sheraton in Eastham provides a restful feeling. This is a slick, efficient hotel that doesn't try to ape antiquity. The rooms are decorated in a generic, eminently forgettable hotel style; but the location—just minutes from Fort Hill and Salt Pond—is a major plus. Poolside rooms, adjacent to the tropically decorated indoor pool, are best. *Rte. 6, Eastham 02642, tel. 508/255–5000 or 800/533–3986, fax 508/240–1870. 107 rooms. Facilities: restaurant, lounge/nightclub, health spa, 2 swimming pools, whirlpool, sauna, 2 tennis courts. AE, D, DC, MC, V. Expensive.*

The Masthead. The best of several worlds converge at this informal hotel and resort, an eclectic collection of rooms, small efficiencies, and cottages in several seaside buildings. A little more than a five-minute walk from downtown Provincetown, the property sits on 450 feet of private beach. Rooms are equipped with kitchens and are decorated individually, some with antiques. *31–41 Commercial St., Provincetown 02657, tel. 508/487–0523 or 800/395–5095, fax 508/487–9251. 8 rooms (2 rooms share one bath), 6 apartments, 3 efficiencies, 4 cottages. Facilities: kitchenettes, sundeck. AE, D, DC, MC, V. Moderate–Expensive.*

Fairbanks Inn. This 1776 inn, originally a sea captain's home, consists of a main house and several outbuildings filled with canopy beds, antiques, and Oriental rugs on wide-board floors. This is a good base for exploring Provincetown. *90 Bradford St., Provincetown 02657, tel. 508/487–0386. 15 rooms, 4 with shared bath. Facilities: Continental breakfast included, rooftop sundeck. AE, D, MC, V. Moderate.*

Inn at Duck Creek. Minutes from Route 6, the seashore, and Wellfleet center, this circa-1815 inn looks out over 5 acres of rolling landscape and a duck pond. The setting is informal and authentically antique; diversely and individually decorated rooms are situated in several on-site buildings, including the old carriage house and saltworks. *Main St., Box 364, Wellfleet 02667, tel. 508/349–9333. 25 rooms, 8 with shared bath. Facilities: restaurant, tavern with entertainment. AE, MC, V. Closed mid-Oct.–mid-May. Moderate.*

Wellfleet Motel & Lodge. This unspectacular medium-size resort motel is on Route 6 between the Salt Pond Visitor's Center and the Marconi Station Site, with the Audubon Society's Wellfleet Bay Wildlife Sanctuary across the road. Rooms are clean and sparse, with king- and queen-size beds, and basic amenities. Set on 12 wooded acres abutting the seashore, it's a good value. *Rte. 6, Box 606, South Wellfleet 02663, tel. 508/349–3535 or 800/852–2900. 65 rooms. Facilities: café and restaurant, bar, indoor pool, heated outdoor pool, whirlpool, game room, gift shop. AE, DC, MC, V. Moderate.*

Provincetown Inn. Located at the extreme west end of town, this rambling seaside hotel has great charm to complement its weathered, kitschy ambience. The hotel lobby features immense and alarmingly ugly murals depicting Provincetown's history. Still, the rooms, some of which are seaside, are clean and comfortable. Surrounded by water on three sides, the inn offers Continental breakfast and packages for whale-watching and other local activities. *1 Commercial St., Provincetown 02657, tel. 508/487–9500 or 800/WHALE–VU, fax 508/487–2911. 100 rooms. Facilities: restaurant, lounge, indoor pool, sauna, gift shop, sundeck. MC, V. Inexpensive–Moderate.*

Two **American Youth Hostels** offer cheap alternative accommodations. Call ahead for reservations; they fill quickly on weekends. Both are dorm style, with kitchens, and discounts on some local shopping and attractions. **The Mid-Cape AYH-Hostel** (75 Goody Hallet Dr., Eastham 02642, tel. 508/255–2785; closed mid-Sept.–mid-May) has 50 beds in eight cabins, volleyball, barbecues, and family rooms; it's less than 3 miles from the Salt Pond Visitor's Center. **Little America AYH-Hostel** (Box 402, Truro 02666, tel. 508/349–3889; closed mid-Sept.–late June) sits on a breezy dune by the Cranberry Bog Trail on North Pamet Road in Truro—the heart of the seashore. Once a Coast Guard station, the 42-room hostel has a spectacular view of Ballston Beach and the surrounding dunes.

CAMPING

Cape Cod National Seashore does not allow tenting on park property. Self-contained vehicles (a motor home or truck with attached shell and permanently mounted holding tanks for sewage and gray water) are allowed access to certain beaches, with a park permit, for 72 consecutive hours per visit. Park permits are $75 per season, and reservations are taken, in writing, for the 4th of July and Labor Day weekends only. Otherwise, it's first come, first served for the approximately 100 vehicles allowed inside the park at any one time.

NEAR THE PARK The following take both tent and RV campers: **Atlantic Oaks Campground** (Rte. 6, Eastham 02642, tel. 508/255–1437 or 800/332–CAMP) is less than a mile north of the Salt Pond Visitor's Center. Primarily a 100-site RV camp, they take tents, too. The setting is a pine and oak forest, and you're minutes from the seashore. On the grounds are a store, laundry, playground, and bike rentals. RV hookups (including cable TV) are $29 per double; tent sites are $22. Showers are free. **Paine's Campground** (Box 201, South Wellfleet, tel. 508/349–3007 or, in eastern MA, 800/479–3017; closed mid-Sept.–mid-May) is primarily a tent site, though they have a half-dozen RV hookups. The location is excellent, about a 25-minute walk from the beach and a mile north of the Marconi station. Set in 16 acres of forest and huckleberry trees, the camp is very private and separated into family, couples, and singles sites. Sites cost $10.50 per person. RV hookups are $4 extra per site per day. Dogs (must be leashed and have rabies certification) are $3. There is a reservation fee of $5, and showers are metered. The good-natured Paines have owned this campground for more than 35 years.

Special mention goes to Nickerson State Park (Rte. 6A, East Brewster 02631, tel. 508/896–3491). Located in Brewster, this is Cape Cod's largest and most popular site. It's set on 2,000 wildlife-filled acres of white pine, hemlock, and spruce forest, dotted with opportunities for trout fishing, walking, or biking along 8 miles of paved trail; canoeing; sailing; motor-boating; and bird-watching. The park operates 418 RV and tent sites; sites go for $12 nightly, and there are no hookups available. Facilities include showers, bathrooms, picnic tables and barbecue areas, and a store. Maps and schedules of park programs are available at the park entrance. No reservations are taken, and the park does not accept credit cards.

Cape Hatteras and Cape Lookout National Seashores

North Carolina

By Susan Ladd

istory, mystery, and myth pepper these islands like sea oats. The first settlers, remembered today as the Lost Colony, landed here in 1587, only to disappear shortly thereafter without a trace. Pirates plundered ships in these waters; it was here that the notorious Blackbeard met his end, cornered near Silver Lake Harbor at Ocracoke.

Those who endured drew their living from the sea, fishing and whaling, and setting out in small boats as the ocean raged to rescue sailors whose ships had foundered on these treacherous shores. They stayed for the same reason people flock here today: for the unparalleled beauty of the ever-changing coastal landscape. In its gentler moods the ocean casts pearly shells on the wide, flat beaches and laps at the sand. In moments of fury, it lashes and churns at the dunes, gouging out channels and reshaping the shoreline. The ocean is forever resculpting these banks;

Bodie Island and Pea Island (for example) are islands no more.

Cape Hatteras and Cape Lookout offer two very different beach experiences. Cape Hatteras is an 80-mile strand of narrow islands connected to the mainland by a series of bridges and ferries, and bisected by a modern road that allows easy access to the shoreline. When the national seashore was established in 1953, the small towns along the island were permitted to remain, so accommodations, supplies, and recreational opportunities are always close at hand.

Cape Lookout, a 55-mile span of three unconnected islands, is essentially a beach wilderness—as close as you can get to experiencing the coast as the original colonists did. Because no bridge ever connected it with the mainland, it has remained undeveloped and relatively pristine. The only access is by boat, the only accommodations are tents and primitive cabins.

Rich in history and natural beauty, Cape Hatteras National Seashore draws more than 2 million visitors annually; some 300,000 make their way by ferry to the desolate shores of Cape Lookout. These visitors range from family vacationers and garden-variety sun-worshipers to bird-watchers, anglers, shell collectors, surfers, sailors, and divers. But the allure is always the same: the chance to find a quiet strip of beach all your own.

ESSENTIAL INFORMATION

VISITOR INFORMATION For information on Cape Hatteras, contact the **Cape Hatteras National Seashore** (Rte. 1, Box 675, Manteo 27954, tel. 919/473–2111). You'll find up-to-date listings of events and activities at the visitor's centers and ranger stations on Bodie, Hatteras, and Ocracoke islands. For more information on nearby towns, contact the **Dare County Tourist Bureau** (Box 399, Manteo 27954, tel. 919/473–2138) or the **Outer Banks Chamber of Commerce** (Box 1757, Kill Devil Hills 27948, tel. 919/441–8144 or 919/995–4213).

For information on Cape Lookout, contact the **Cape Lookout National Seashore** (131 Charles St., Harkers Island 28531, tel. 919/ 728–2250). The visitor's center at Harkers Island has information on the latest beach and weather conditions and ferry schedules. For further information on nearby towns, contact the **Carteret County Tourism Development Bureau** (Box 1406, Morehead City 28557, tel. 800/786-6962).

FEES There are no fees to enter the national seashores.

PUBLICATIONS The Cape Hatteras National Seashore publishes a newspaper, *In the Park,* with information on camping, ferries, programs, and more. You can pick up a copy, along with many other free park publications, at any visitor's center or ranger's station. Cape Lookout National Seashore ranger's stations and visitor's centers also have free publications on park attractions and activities.

To learn more about the forces that shape the barrier islands, read *Ribbon of Sand* by John Alexander and James Lazell (Algonquin Books). Coastal author David Stick has written some of the best volumes on the history and lore of the Outer Banks, including *The Outer Banks of North Carolina* and *Graveyard of the Atlantic* (both University of North Carolina Press). All three are sold at the visitor's centers on Bodie, Hatteras, and Ocracoke islands.

GEOLOGY AND TERRAIN The two national seashores are part of a long, thin strand of islands stretching 175 miles from the Virginia border to the tip of Cape Lookout. The islands, separated from the mainland by large shallow sounds, form a buffer between land and sea.

Two great ocean currents—the cold Labrador Current from the north, and the warm waters of the Gulf Stream from the south—converge offshore. In the dead heat of August, swimmers at Avon shiver deliciously in waters still only 72°F, while 90 miles south at Shackleford Banks, the water is a balmy 80°. The currents converge at Diamond Shoals, just off the tip of Cape Hatteras, in turbulent, treacherous seas. The churning waters and shifting sands have claimed more than 2,000 ships since sailors first began exploring these waters, thus earning the name "Graveyard of the Atlantic."

The dynamics of land and sea have slowly but inexorably moved the barrier islands south and west. You can see evidence of the westward movement in the black peat moss uncovered in areas of the beach; this is where the marsh was thousands of years ago. The southward current has shifted the inlets. As the current enters an inlet, it deposits sand at the bottom of the island to the north and carves it away from the top of the island below. Oregon Inlet, just south of Bodie Island, provides the most dramatic example. It is moving away from the Herbert C. Bonner Bridge, and only constant dredging by the Army Corps of Engineers keeps the inlet open under the bridge.

Barrier islands consist essentially of dunes, forest, and marsh. The shifting dunes are anchored by vegetation with a special ability to withstand the salt spray and unrelenting wind. The small shrubs that take hold in the shelter provided by the dunes give rise, in turn, to the maritime forest. The marsh is the place where freshwater and salt water meet, an ideal incubator for many ocean residents.

FLORA AND FAUNA Not much can survive on the wind-whipped dunes. Sea oats, whose deep roots anchor the dunes, are so crucial to the stabilization of the Outer Banks that they're protected by federal law. Pennywort and prickly cactus also grow nearby.

Birds that can be seen along the shoreline include the tiny sanderling, the orange-beaked oystercatcher, the seagull, and the brown pelican—the last formerly endangered but now a common and welcome sight. The piping plover, a small, shy gray-and-white bird that feeds at water's edge, is very much endangered. Its tiny nests on the open beach are easily destroyed by humans, storms, and predators. The authorities occasionally bar sunbathers and vehicles from parts of the beach to protect plover nesting grounds.

Ghost crabs, which venture out of their burrows to skitter along the sand, pose the gravest danger to another endangered animal that comes here to nest in the summer: the loggerhead turtle. The massive loggerheads, weighing an average of 250 pounds, drag themselves to the shores of Cape Lookout and Cape Hatteras in the spring and dig large holes in the sand, where each female deposits more than 100 leathery, golfball-size eggs. But an estimated 98% of the hatchlings die on their way to the surf, mostly picked off by seagulls and ghost crabs. Rangers and volunteers do what they can, marking nests and moving them when necessary, and even patroling the beaches at night to help the hatchlings make it to the sea.

Behind the protective barrier of the dunes, the maritime forest takes hold. Live oaks, sculpted by the wind, will grow no higher than the safety of the dune. Wax myrtle, yaupon holly, and cedar are a few of the trees you'll find at Buxton, Ocracoke, and Shackleford Banks.

In the shelter of the forest live raccoons, rats, rabbits, river otters, and snakes. One of the rarest inhabitants is the Outer Banks king snake, smaller than a regular king snake and sporting different color bands. Cape Lookout has no native species, but the early settlers introduced many animals to the islands. Other survivors include nutria (a member of the beaver family) and ring-necked pheasants.

The marsh is home to a great variety of birds. Herons and egrets pick their way delicately through the grasses, and ducks glide along the water's surface. Whistling swans, snow geese, Canada geese, and 25 species of ducks winter here; sparrows, warblers, and terns can be seen during the spring and fall migrations. The marsh also provides a nursery ground for oysters, shrimp, clams, scallops, and many species of fish, some of which grow to maturity in the calm, mineral-rich waters before entering the ocean. More than 90% of the sea creatures we commonly eat spend part of their lives in the salt marsh.

WHEN TO GO Fall is the most popular season at Cape Lookout, largely because it's the best time for fishing. Many people find the heat, humidity, and mosquitoes too much to handle in the summer.

Cape Hatteras, which draws more of a family crowd, is busiest in July and August, when school is out and recreational opportunities reach their peak. But if you're more interested in solitude than a suntan, visit in spring or fall, when the weather is milder, the beaches less crowded, and the insects not as hungry.

From March through May, temperatures reach the 60s and 70s and rainfall is lowest; wildflowers bloom in the maritime forests and birds begin nesting. Sun worshipers flock in during June, July, and August, when temperatures average 80°–84°. The beach remains pleasantly warm in September and October, with highs in the 72°–80° range.

November and December, with temperatures 56°–64°, are a good time for shelling and fishing, and you'll often have the beach to yourself. The only two months to avoid are January and February, when temperatures average 38°–53° and the winds are most intense. Many businesses close down for these two months.

June 1 to November 1 is hurricane season, but it's a good idea to check the weather radio anytime you visit the Outer Banks: Conditions can change rapidly, bringing severe storms with dangerous lightning.

SEASONAL EVENTS *Near Cape Hatteras.* **June–August: The Lost Colony,** America's longest-running outdoor drama (tel. 800/488–5012), tells the story of the colony, founded near Manteo in 1587, that vanished without a trace. (The settlers' journey to the New World is re-created year-round aboard the *Elizabeth II,* a 16th-century sailing ship at Roanoke Harbor in Manteo, tel. 919/473–1144.) **May and June:** The **Hang Gliding Spectacular** in May and the **Rogallo Kite Festival** in June are held at Jockey's Ridge in Nags Head to honor Kitty Hawk resident Frank Rogallo, who invented the flexible wing used in hang gliders today (tel. 919/441–4124). **June–August:** The history of the **U.S. Lifesaving Service** is re-created with reenactments of beach drills at the Chicamacomico Lifesaving Station in Rodanthe every Thursday. Contact the park service (tel. 919/473–2111) for more information. **December 17:** The **First Flight Commemoration,** held at the Wright Brothers Memorial in Kill Devil Hills, marks the brothers' first powered flight here in 1903 (tel. 919/266–7661).

Near Cape Lookout. **May:** The **Traditional Wooden Boat Show,** hosted by the North Carolina Maritime Museum in Beaufort, explores the enduring craft of boatbuilding in the area (tel. 919/728–7317). **June:** The **Beaufort Old Homes Tour** showcases the extensive historic district (tel. 919/728–5225). **August:** The **Strange Seafood Exhibition,** also hosted by the North Carolina Maritime Museum (tel. 919/728–7317), serves up a host of unusual sea critters. **December:** The **Core**

Sound Decoy Festival celebrates an aspect of carving that dates back seven generations in Harkers Island (tel. 919/728–3769).

WHAT TO PACK The two most important items are sunscreen and insect repellent. The sun, reflecting off the water and white sand, can produce intense and painful sunburns. Shelter is scarce in most of the isolated beach areas. A hat is a must, and a beach umbrella is a good idea if you plan to make a day of it.

The need for insect repellent cannot be overemphasized. Park rangers joke that the mosquitoes must carry glass cutters, since they even seem to get into your car. Wooded areas are worse for mosquitoes, ticks, and biting flies; the seashore for sand fleas. Deet is probably the best-known insect repellent, but a less toxic and more fragrant alternative is Avon's Skin So Soft bath oil, which seems to ward off just about everything.

On Cape Lookout National Seashore, even a day trip requires more gear than a typical day on the beach, because there are no stores, water fountains, snack bars, or concessions of any kind. Bring everything you need, including plenty of fresh water, food, and protective shoes such as sneakers. Bring a trash bag, too, so that you can carry out everything you bring in.

GENERAL STORES *At Cape Hatteras.* The **Oregon Inlet Fishing Center,** just north of the Herbert C. Bonner Bridge, stocks groceries, film, suntan lotion, clothing, beach supplies, fishing supplies, boat equipment, and more. It also has a restaurant, boat ramp, and fishing charters (tel. 919/441–6301; open late Mar.– early Nov., daily 5 AM–7 PM). The **Lee Robinson General Store,** less than a mile from the ferry dock in Hatteras Village, carries clothes, toys, groceries, and gifts in its new wood-shingled building (tel. 919/986–2381; open Apr.– Dec., daily 8 AM–9 PM) **The Community Store** on Silver Lake in Ocracoke has been a mainstay in the community since 1918. You can sit in the rockers out front or stock up on groceries, hardware, office supplies, fishing gear, camping gear, or auto parts (tel. 919/928–3321; open Mon.–Sat. 7 AM–8 PM, Sun. 8–8; winter hours vary).

Near Cape Lookout. **East'ard Variety Store,** 1 mile south of the ranger's station on Harkers Island, is the quintessential if-we-don't-have-it-you-don't-need-it store. You'll find beach supplies, groceries, commercial and recreational fishing gear, bottled propane gas, and plumbing, automotive, and mobile-home supplies and parts (tel. 919/728–7149; open Sun.–Thurs. 5:30 AM–10:30 PM, Fri.–Sat. 5:30 AM–11:30 PM).

ATMS **At Cape Hatteras.** The nearest ATM location is the Centura Bank on Route 158, 2 miles from the park entrance at Whalebone Junction in Nags Head. There is also a Centura Bank ATM in Buxton.

At Cape Lookout. The nearest ATM is at the Wachovia Bank on U.S. 70 in Beaufort, 17 miles from the ranger's station at Harkers Island.

ARRIVING AND DEPARTING You can get close to both parks on public transportation, but to actually reach either one and explore the area properly you'll need a car. When visiting **Cape Hatteras,** the most practical access is via Manteo from the west or Nags Head from the north; the southern approach requires a 2¹/₂-hour ferry ride from Cedar Island or Swan Quarter to Ocracoke. Most people visiting **Cape Lookout** will probably take the southern approach, catching the ferry from Harkers Island; to visit the park's northernmost island, you may catch a vehicle ferry from Atlantic on the mainland or a passenger ferry from Ocracoke Village in the Cape Hatteras National Seashore.

By Plane to Cape Hatteras. The closest airport is the **Dare County Regional Airport** in Manteo (tel. 919/473–2600), roughly 6 miles from Whalebone Junction; it is served by two small commuter airlines, Southeast Airlines (tel. 800/927–3296) and Outer Banks Airways (tel. 919/473–3014). You can rent a car at the airport from **B&R Car Rental** (tel. 919/473–2600). Nearby taxi services include **Ray's Taxi** (tel. 919/473–2716) and **Beach Cab** (tel. 919/441–2500). The closest major airport is **Norfolk International Airport** (tel. 804/857–3351), 90 miles to the north in Virginia. You can rent a car there from **Avis** (tel. 800/331–

1212), **Budget** (tel. 804/855–8035 or 800/527–0700), **Dollar** (tel. 804/855–1988 or 800/800–4000), **Enterprise** (tel. 804/853–7700), **Hertz** (tel. 804/857–1261 or 800/654–3131), or **Thrifty** (tel. 804/855–5900 or 800/367–2277).

By Plane to Cape Lookout. The closest airport is **Craven County Regional Airport** (tel. 919/633–1400) in New Bern, 56 miles northwest of Harkers Island. But locals warn that connections to New Bern from most major airports usually involve long layovers; they recommend flying into **New Hanover International Airport** (tel. 919/341–4125) in Wilmington, 108 miles south of Harkers Island. You can rent a car there from **Avis** (tel. 919/763–3346), **Budget** (tel. 919/762–8910), **Hertz** (919/762–1010), or **National** (tel. 919/762–0143).

By Car and RV to Cape Hatteras. From Norfolk, Virginia, take U.S. 17 south to Elizabeth City, North Carolina. Pick up U.S. 158 to Nags Head and proceed south to Whalebone Junction. Route 12 goes straight through the park. From Raleigh take U.S. 64 east 200 miles to Whalebone Junction, then pick up Route 12 south.

By Car and RV to Cape Lookout. From Raleigh take U.S. 70 east 147 miles to Morehead City; continue on U.S. 70 to Otway, then turn right on Harkers Island Road. From Wilmington take U.S. 17 north 51 miles to Jacksonville, then Route 24 east 43 miles to Morehead City; pick up U.S. 70 east to Otway, then turn right on Harkers Island Road.

By Bus to Cape Hatteras. The closest bus station is **Greyhound** (tel. 919/335–5183 or 800/531–5332) in Elizabeth City, 60 miles to the north. You can rent a car in Elizabeth City at **National** (tel. 919/335–1860 or 800/227–7368).

By Bus to Cape Lookout. The closest bus station is **Carolina Trailways** (tel. 919/726–3029) in Morehead City, 20 miles west of the park. You can rent a car at **Budget** (tel. 800/527–0700), **National** (tel. 919/726–2626 or 800/227–7368), or **Thrifty** (tel. 919/247–3030 or 800/367–2277).

By Train. Because Amtrak routes in North Carolina are limited, this is not a practical option. The train station nearest to either park is in Rocky Mount, 136 miles west of Manteo and 140 miles northwest of Harkers Island. There you can rent a car at Budget, Hertz, or National.

EXPLORING

Cape Hatteras is the more accessible of the two seashores. A two-lane highway, Route 12, cuts from one end to the other, broken only by the Herbert C. Bonner Bridge across Oregon Inlet and the modern ferry system that carries passengers and vehicles to Ocracoke Island. At periodic access ramps you can park and walk over the dunes to the beach. There are also numerous access ramps for four-wheel-drive vehicles.

The mostly undeveloped shore, fringed with sea oats, stretches more than 80 miles from end to end. You can drive all the way down and back in one day, but that doesn't leave time to linger. To really enjoy a visit, catch an early morning ferry to Ocracoke and spend the day. If you want to visit nearby historic sites, such as the Wright Brothers Memorial and Fort Raleigh, set aside another full day. But don't get so caught up in attractions that you miss the joy of a solitary walk down deserted stretches of beach.

Cape Lookout presents more challenges to the visitor, and if your priorities are comfort and ease of travel, it's probably not for you. The seashore consists of three unconnected islands—Shackleford Banks, North Core Banks, and South Core Banks—and the only way to reach them is by boat. Passenger ferries (Sand Dollar Transportation, tel. 919/728–3533, or Barrier Island Transportation, tel. 919/728–3575) run from Harkers Island to Shackleford Banks and to the southern tip of South Core Banks near the Cape Lookout Lighthouse. It's a 40-minute ride to the dock, a .25-mile walk to the lighthouse, and another 3 miles to the point.

The open beach stretches as far as your legs can take you, but to really explore the islands

you need a four-wheel-drive. Vehicle ferries run from Davis to the midpoint of South Core Banks (Alger Willis Fishing Camps, tel. 919/729-2791) and from Atlantic to the southern end of North Core Banks (Morris Marina, tel. 919/225–4261).

It's a 40-minute drive from the ferry landing on North Core Banks to the village of Portsmouth at the island's northern tip. There's an unpaved road through the interior, but you'll find smoother traveling on the beach. If you want to visit Portsmouth but don't have a four-wheel-drive, you can take a 20-minute passenger ferry from Ocracoke (Rudy Austin, tel. 919/928–4361).

Many people visit the islands by private boat, dropping anchor on the shallow sandy bottom of the sound and wading ashore. But take care if you try this: The shifting sandbars of Core Sound have put many a boat in dry dock for repairs.

THE BEST IN ONE DAY **Cape Hatteras.** There are few structures as evocative as the three lighthouses along the Cape Hatteras National Seashore. Begin at the 1872 **Bodie Island Lighthouse** near the northern end. The 150-foot tower with wide horizontal stripes is the only one on the Carolina coast that still has its original Fresnel glass lens. The candy-striped 1870 **Cape Hatteras Lighthouse,** farther south at Buxton, is, at 208 feet, the nation's tallest. Erosion has threatened the tower since 1935; the current plan is to move it inland. A recent renovation has once again made it possible for visitors to climb the 268 steps to the top (summer only). From Buxton, head south to the town of Hatteras and catch the free ferry to Ocracoke; then drive to Ocracoke Village on the south end of the island, and turn left on Lighthouse Road to reach the 1823 **Ocracoke Lighthouse.** Unlike the others, this one stands a mere 75 feet, its whitewashed sides bare of any design. The state's oldest operating lighthouse serves mostly as a guide to Silver Lake Harbor.

Cape Lookout. Catch an early ferry to the point at Cape Lookout. (Be sure to pack everything you'll need.) From the dock, walk to the lighthouse and visit with the volunteer caretakers. The old keeper's quarters is also a visitor's center, staffed from March through November. Take the path to the beach and follow it southward to the point, where the island ends. Along the dune line, look for the massive timbers of old shipwrecks that are covered and uncovered periodically by the shifting sands. Fishing and shelling here can be very good. (Each visitor may take two gallons of uninhabited shells out of the park each day.) You can continue around the point to the gun mounts—massive, partially submerged metal structures that served as submarine defenses during World War II.

GUIDED TOURS Cape Hatteras. **Kitty Hawk Aero Tours** (U.S. 158 Bypass, Kill Devil Hills, tel. 919/441–4460) provides an aerial tour of the Outer Banks from the airstrip beside the Wright Brothers Memorial for $19–$24 per person. **Dolphin Tours** (Ramada Inn, 9½ MP Beach Rd., Nags Head, tel. 919/441–2151) offers one-hour tours ($22 per person on pontoon boats) along the shoreline frequented by dolphins, rays, and sea turtles.

Cape Lookout. Capt. Stacy Harbor Tours (Atlantic Beach Causeway, Atlantic Beach, tel. 919/247–7501) cruises the inland waterways around the Beaufort and Morehead City waterfront areas. Two-hour afternoon and evening tours cost $7 ($4 children).

SCENIC DRIVES AND VIEWS A ferry is a delightful way to experience the islands and also the best means of getting from one national seashore to the other. If you want just a taste, try the free ferry from Hatteras to Ocracoke Island (tel. 919/726–6446). Cars are loaded on a first-come, first-served basis, so drive to the first open space. Ferries depart every hour in the winter, every half hour in the summer—when you may have to wait. The ride takes 40 minutes. Bird-watchers should bring binoculars to observe the many species that nest on the small sandbar islands that dot Pamlico Sound. If you want more, head to the south end of Ocracoke and catch the Cedar Island Ferry (tel. 919/928–3841 or 800/BY–FERRY; pedestrians $1, bicycles $2, cars and motorcycles $10). In the summer

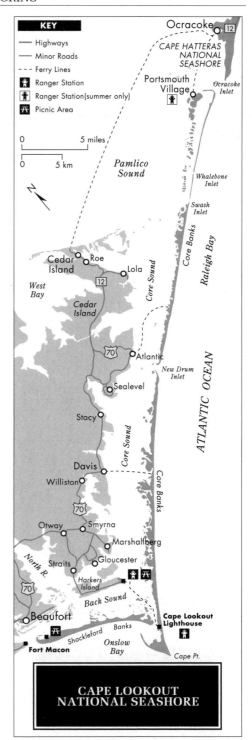

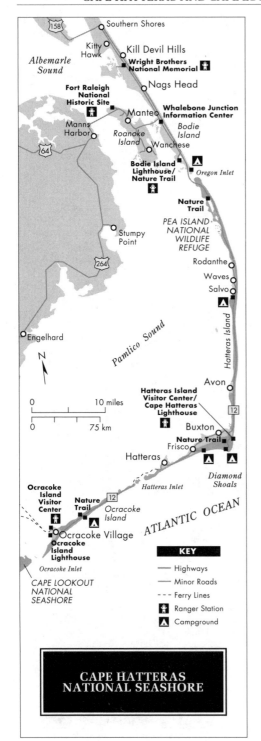

Southern Shores
Kitty Hawk
Kill Devil Hills
Wright Brothers National Memorial
Albemarle Sound
Nags Head
Fort Raleigh National Historic Site
Whalebone Junction Information Center
Manteo
Manns Harbor
Bodie Island
Roanoke Island
Wanchese
Bodie Island Lighthouse/ Nature Trail
Oregon Inlet
Nature Trail
PEA ISLAND NATIONAL WILDLIFE REFUGE
Stumpy Point
Rodanthe
Waves
Salvo
Pamlico Sound
Engelhard
N
Hatteras Island
0   10 miles
0   75 km
Avon
Hatteras Island Visitor Center/ Cape Hatteras Lighthouse
Buxton
Nature Trail
Frisco
Hatteras
Diamond Shoals
Hatteras Inlet
Ocracoke Island Visitor Center
Nature Trail
Ocracoke Island
ATLANTIC OCEAN
Ocracoke Village
Ocracoke Island Lighthouse
Ocracoke Inlet
CAPE LOOKOUT NATIONAL SEASHORE

KEY
—— Highways
—— Minor Roads
- - - Ferry Lines
Ranger Station
Campground

CAPE HATTERAS NATIONAL SEASHORE

and fall, you must reserve ahead and be at the dock 30 minutes prior to departure.

There are two views to go out of your way for at **Cape Hatteras.** One is from the **Herbert C. Bonner Bridge:** Drive slowly as you cross Oregon Inlet on this silver ribbon curving over the turbulent waters. At the crest you can see a beautiful cross-section of the barrier island, with marsh and sound on one side and the ocean and shoreline on the other. But the best view on the Outer Banks may be from the **Cape Hatteras Lighthouse.** Your knees will ache from climbing the 268 steps up to the wrought-iron balcony at the top, but you'll be able to see Diamond Shoals and the point of the island to the south. Walking around the balcony, you get a complete view of the village of Buxton, the interior of the island, and the shoreline stretching north.

Scenic drives on **Cape Lookout** require a four-wheel-drive. From the ferry docks at Davis and Atlantic, you can strike out by beach or inland path. Once past the fishing camps, there's nothing but pure deserted island. The beach here changes every day; the dark timbers of ancient shipwrecks are uncovered periodically, as are the rusted remains of autos abandoned before the beach became a national seashore. Because so few people frequent these beaches, they're a sheller's paradise, as well as a great spot for bird-watching and nature study.

HISTORIC BUILDINGS AND SITES Cape Hatteras. The bones of the schooner *Laura A. Barnes* rest amid the dunes at Coquina Beach, just off Route 12 across from the entrance to the Bodie Island Lighthouse. The ship was bound for Georgetown, South Carolina, with an empty hold and no passengers when a nor'easter stripped its masts and ran it aground some 4 miles north in 1921. The crew was rescued, but the ship was unsalvageable. It was moved here in 1973.

U.S. Lifesaving Service stations were built every 7 miles along the Outer Banks to rescue passengers and crews of ships that foundered in the fierce seas. The 1874 **Chicamacomico Lifesaving Station,** on Route 12 in Rodanthe, was one of the first. The original, one-story station was converted to a boathouse when the two-story shingled station with lookout tower was built in 1911. Both still stand, along with outbuildings and cisterns dating from 1874 to 1911. *Open May–Oct., Tues., Thurs., and Sat. 11–5.*

There's a pocket of foreign soil on Ocracoke Island. To help protect shipping lanes during World War II, Great Britain sent antisubmarine craft; one of them, the H.M.S. *Bedfordshire,* was sunk by a U-boat 40 miles off Cape Lookout. When the bodies of four sailors washed ashore on Ocracoke Island, the people of the village buried them in a small plot and deeded the land forever to England. The Union Jack flies over this small, fenced **British Cemetery** maintained by the U.S. Coast Guard at Ocracoke. To reach it, take Route 12 to Ocracoke Village and turn right on British Cemetery Road.

Cape Lookout. On the northern tip of North Core Banks, the once-thriving **Portsmouth Village** was established in 1753 to aid the commercial shipping trade. By 1860, nearly 700 people lived there. But shipping eventually moved north and the population declined; the last residents left in 1971. Today the village is a beautifully preserved ghost town. A town genealogy, old photos of its residents, and other memorabilia are on display in the Salter/Dixon house. The best way to reach Portsmouth is a 20-minute ride by ferry from Ocracoke Island; the village is a short walk from the dock. Allow at least a half-day to tour it.

NATURE TRAILS AND SHORT WALKS There are no formal trails in the Cape Lookout National Seashore, but the Cape Hatteras National Seashore offers a number of short, easy trails. The **Bodie Island Pond Trail** begins behind the Bodie Island Lighthouse. A boardwalk leads through hedges of bayberry hung with saw greenbrier to the marsh, where dense undergrowth gives way to salt-meadow cordgrass and cattails. From the observation platform at trail's end, you can see snow geese in autumn, as well as egrets and herons.

The **Bodie Island Dike Trail,** which begins at the far end of the lighthouse parking lot,

shows how human influence has changed the landscape. Dams and dikes built in the early 1900s to promote waterfowl hunting turned a section of the marsh into a freshwater pond. Artificial dunes constructed on the oceanfront in 1938 blocked salt spray and flooding, giving rise to the trees and shrubs that have overtaken the wetlands. It's a 30-minute walk to the spot where the trail meets Route 12; you can retrace your steps or walk back along the highway.

The **North Pond Interpretive Trail** at the Pea Island National Wildlife Refuge begins at a rest area a few miles south of the Herbert C. Bonner Bridge. The trail runs atop a dike between two ponds. There are several observation decks equipped with binocular viewers on the open areas around North Pond. It's an easy 15-minute walk to the end of the pond, but the dedicated birder can continue on the service road that winds 2.5 miles around the pond and ends at Route 12 about 2 miles from the rest area.

The **Buxton Woods Trail** takes visitors to one of the few remaining maritime forests on the Outer Banks. The .75-mile loop trail begins at a parking area off the road that leads to the Cape Point Campground. The terrain is surprisingly hilly, rising and falling over old dunes that once marked the beach. Thirty miles from the mainland, one is struck by the strangeness of birdsong coupled with the crashing of ocean waves.

The **Hammock Hills Nature Trail** on Ocracoke Island offers the best cross-section view of barrier island ecology. The .75-mile loop trail begins at a parking area across from the Ocracoke Campground on Route 12, within view of the dunes, and plunges into the maritime forest. Here you can see how plants adapt: Live oaks are sculpted and stunted by the salt spray; cedar will be thin and stripped on the ocean side, full and green on the protected sound side. The trail cuts through the forest to the marshland. From the observation platform here, you can see where the marsh meets the sound. The trail reenters the forest and loops back around to the parking lot.

Keep an eye peeled for fast-moving (and non-poisonous) black racer snakes.

LONGER HIKES Most of the marked trails in the national seashores are short, but in a sense the seashore is one very long walk. You can trek the entire length of the Cape Hatteras National Seashore on the **Cape Hatteras Beach Trail,** which begins at the Whalebone Junction Information Center and spans 75.8 miles of sound and seashore. Maps—which include comfort stations, campgrounds, and off-road vehicle (ORV) ramps—are available from the National Park Service at the seashore headquarters in Manteo or any of the visitor's centers.

OTHER ACTIVITIES **Back-Road Driving.** It is extremely important to follow the regulations in this fragile environment; driving on the dunes destroys the sea oats and other vegetation that hold the sand in place. Carry a shovel, tire-pressure gauge, first-aid kit, spare tire, tow rope at least 14 feet long, litter bag, fire extinguisher, flashlight, and bumper jack. Be sure to lower the pressure in all tires. Travel on the firm, wet portion of the beach located just below the high-tide mark.

At **Cape Hatteras,** there are more than 20 beach access ramps marked with jeep signs for four-wheel-drive vehicles only. Check the weather forecast and tide tables before you leave, and ask a ranger about current beach conditions. No permit is needed. At **Cape Lookout,** four-wheel-drives and all-terrain vehicles (ATVs) are the only way to travel on North and South Core banks. If you plan to keep a vehicle on either island overnight, you must get a permit ($5 per week) at the Harkers Island headquarters of the national seashore.

Biking. The beautiful drive on **Cape Hatteras** from Whalebone Junction to Ocracoke Village is becoming more and more popular with cyclists. The roads are mostly straight and flat, so they don't require advanced skills. But the heavy summer traffic on Route 12 calls for caution. Lighter traffic and cooler weather make spring and fall better seasons for cycling. By bike is also the best way to see Ocracoke Island any time of year; you can tour the quaint village and easily reach any

beach access area on the 13-mile span. Bicycling is not an option on **Cape Lookout;** there are no paved roads and mountain bikes are prohibited.

Bird-Watching. On the Cape Hatteras National Seashore **Pea Island National Wildlife Refuge** is a birder's paradise. More than 265 species visit the refuge on a regular basis, and another 50 show up sporadically. The **Bodie Island ponds** are a good place to spot migratory shorebirds, as are the salt ponds at **Cape Hatteras Point.** The dikes at Pea Island and in the maritime woods at Buxton and Ocracoke are the best vantages from which to observe land-bird migration in the fall. Cape Lookout is home to great numbers of terns and black skimmers, which nest in colonies along the beach. Endangered piping plovers also nest here, and threatened eastern brown pelicans have made a dramatic comeback in the area.

Boating and Windsurfing. The wide, shallow sounds make for excellent sailing, windsurfing, and kayaking. One soundside access area between Avon and Buxton, swept by sea breezes, is so popular with Canadian windsurfers that it now bears an official road sign: **Canadian Hole, Le Trou Canadien.** The **Albemarle and Pamlico sounds** are ideal for sailboats and kayaks, too. Rentals are available at **Kitty Hawk Sports** in Avon (tel. 919/995–5000) or Nags Head (tel. 919/441–6800), **Fox Water Sports** in Buxton (tel. 919/995–4102), or **Hatteras Island Surf Shop** in Waves (tel. 919/987–2296).

At Cape Lookout, kayaking is becoming a popular way to visit Shackleford Banks. You can rent kayaks, windsurfing equipment, and sailboats at **Island Rigs** (tel. 919/247–7787) in Atlantic Beach. Sailors and windsurfers can also rent at **The Sailing Place** (tel. 919/726-5664) on the Atlantic Beach Causeway.

Fishing. Anglers discovered these shores long before tourists. Fall and spring are the best times for surf and pier fishing; offshore fishing is best in summer, when blue marlin and other billfish are abundant.

At **Cape Hatteras,** one of the most popular spots for surf fishing is the mouth of **Oregon Inlet,** where red drum, striped bass, and large bluefish are plentiful. In summer, four-wheel-drive vehicles line this beach right up to the Bonner Bridge. Pier fishing centers around three locations: **Hatteras Island Fishing Pier** in Rodanthe (tel. 919/987–2323), **Avon Fishing Pier** (tel. 919/995-5480), and the **Frisco Pier** (tel. 919/986–2533). Daily entrance fees are $5–$6. The **Oregon Inlet Fishing Center** (tel. 919/441–6301), just north of the Bonner Bridge, offers Gulf Stream charters, inshore and inlet trolling charters, and specific charters for big bluefish.

At **Cape Lookout,** mackerel, mullet, sea trout, drum, and bluefish are among the prime quarry. Cape Lookout Point can be a good spot, as can the old gun mounts (*see* The Best in One Day, *above*), which provide a reeflike habitat for fish. Deep-sea fishing charters are available on the *Carolina Princess* (tel. 919/726–5479) at Morehead City or the *Capt. Stacy IV* (tel. 919/247–7501) on the Atlantic Beach Causeway.

Hang Gliding. Cape Hatteras is a mecca for hang gliders because of windswept Jockey's Ridge, the tallest sand dune on the East Coast, which reaches anywhere from 110 to 140 feet. **Kitty Hawk Kites** (tel. 919/441–4124), just across from the dune in Nags Head, provides rentals and instruction.

Horseback Riding. For trail rides in the maritime forest or on the beach at Cape Hatteras, contact **Buxton Stables** (tel. 919/995–4659). **Seaside Stables** (tel. 919/928–3778) offers rides on the ocean or sound at Ocracoke. **White Sand Trail Rides** (tel. 919/729–0911) offers trail rides at Cedar Island near the Cape Lookout National Seashore.

Scuba Diving. The Graveyard of the Atlantic offers some of the best wreck diving in the world, including the World War II U-85 off Cape Hatteras and the U-352 off Cape Lookout. In addition, there are tankers, liberty ships, tugboats, and artificial reef sites. Dive operators at Cape Hatteras include **Nags Head Pro Dive Center** (tel. 919/441–7594), **Hatteras Divers** (tel. 919/986–2557), and **Ocra-coke Divers** (tel. 919/928–1471). **Olympus Dive Center** (tel. 919/726–9432) in Morehead City offers dive charters near Cape Lookout.

Swimming. Obviously, the opportunities are unlimited, but ocean currents can be dangerous and unpredictable. There are few lifeguards on the beaches of the Cape Hatteras National Seashore and none along the Cape Lookout National Seashore.

CHILDREN'S PROGRAMS The Cape Hatteras National Seashore has a wide variety of programs for children, including crab catching, cast-net fishing, wildlife discovery, cross-island walks, fishing with a ranger, soundside snorkeling, and refuge bird walks. Programs are held from mid-June to Labor Day; all are free, though some are limited to small groups. Check *In the Park* (*see* Publications *in* Essential Information, *above*) for a current schedule.

The North Carolina Maritime Museum sponsors the **Cape Lookout Studies Program,** a series of natural history workshops at the former Coast Guard Station on Cape Lookout National Seashore. Workshops include dolphin biology and behavior, sea turtle conservation, and an introduction to the marine environment (tel. 919/728–7317).

DINING

The challenge when visiting the national seashores is not finding a good restaurant but narrowing the choices. Though there are technically no restaurants in either park, there are plenty to choose from close by. Fresh seafood is the primary attraction; the flounder or shrimp you eat in the evening may well have been swimming in the Atlantic that morning.

Ten years ago, most coastal seafood restaurants weren't big on variety. You could count on shrimp, oysters, scallops, and flounder, and sometimes you could get it broiled instead of fried. Today, North Carolina's coastal restaurants serve a far wider variety in a much more cosmopolitan style. Salmon, tuna, calamari (squid), and mussels are on the menu, grilled, sautéed, poached, and baked. If you don't like seafood, your choices will be more limited, but you won't go hungry.

NEAR CAPE HATTERAS **Chardo's.** This former fish house has been converted into one of the best Italian restaurants on the coast. Lace curtains, glass doors, and draped valances set the mood in the dining room, while in the dark, tiny bar, the tables are embossed with wine labels. The extensive menu includes fresh pasta, fish, veal, chicken, and grilled specialties. Salmon lovers should try the *tagliatelle al salmone*—the fish is tossed in brandy-tomato cream sauce with sun-dried tomatoes. Though the ambience is formal, folks in sport shirts are treated like royalty by the staff. *Milepost 9, U.S. 158 Bypass, Kill Devil Hills, tel. 919/441–0276. Reservations advised. AE, MC, V. Delivery service only at lunch. Expensive.*

Queen Anne's Revenge. This local favorite is tucked back into a residential section of Roanoke Island, 10 minutes from Whalebone Junction. Inside, juniper paneling, fresh flowers, and seascapes give it an airy, comfortable feel. The regular menu is extensive; favorites include the Hooker's Landing Special (a platter of fried fresh seafood) and scallops Queen Anne (sautéed with tomatoes, mushrooms, and peppers). There's usually a page of specials, too. Be sure to get "posh squash" as a side dish. *Old Wharf Rd., Wanchese, tel. 919/473–5466. No reservations. Dress: casual but neat. AE, D, MC, V. Closed Tues. Oct.– May. Expensive.*

Billy's Fish House. The old building sags on one side where the supports have settled into the sand of the harbor, and the floor has a pronounced tilt. But you get the feeling that if it ever did give way, most of the patrons would grab for one last hush puppy before they started paddling for shore. Billy May himself goes to the docks each day to hand-pick the seafood he serves, and it shows. The menu includes oysters, scallops, shrimp, flounder, and the local favorite, soft-shelled crabs. *Rte. 12, Buxton, tel. 919/995–5151. No reservations, Dress: casual. MC, V. Moderate.*

Weeping Radish Brewery and Bavarian Restaurant. From the Bavarian-style building to the rousing polka music to the waiters in lederhosen, this place exudes a festive atmosphere. German pot roast, bratwurst and sauerkraut, and warm spicy potato salad are a few of the delights—you don't come here for seafood. The beer, brewed on site, is full and rich. *U.S. 64, Manteo, tel. 919/473–1157. Reservations advised for large parties. Dress: casual. MC, V. Closed two days each week Jan.–Feb. Moderate.*

NEAR CAPE LOOKOUT **Beaufort Grocery.** This restaurant is so named because it's in a converted grocery store, tucked away on a side street. The dining room is open and breezy, with white walls, light pine paneling, and ceiling fans. The lunch menu includes gougeres (herbed pastries stuffed with a variety of meats, cheeses, and salads) and homemade tuna, chicken, and shrimp salads. At night, the white tablecloths come out; dinner entrées include grilled yellowfin tuna with marinated Chinese vegetables, and roast duck with raspberries. *117 Queen St., Beaufort, tel. 919/728–3866. Reservations advised for dinner. Dress: casual but neat. D, MC, V. Closed Jan. Moderate.*

Sanitary Fish Market and Restaurant. An institution in Morehead City for more than 50 years. It's set on the waterfront, with a huge dining room and big tables to accommodate families and groups. The extensive menu contains just about any seafood you can think of, fried or broiled, as well as grilled tuna and swordfish. Don't look for fancy sauces or exotic vegetables; the strength of this establishment is good, fresh seafood cooked simply, and lots of it. *501 Evans St., Morehead City, tel. 919/247–3111. No reservations. Dress: casual. MC, V. Moderate.*

Spouter's Inn. This dark and cozy waterfront restaurant is a good place for a romantic meal, but it also draws families and tourists. Glass doors open onto the dock to admit the seagoing crowd. The Seafood Supreme—baked grouper, crabmeat, and shrimp in cream sauce—is one dinner specialty, while the Out Island Sandwich, with shrimp, provolone, and sprouts, draws raves at lunch. Be sure to save room for the banana crepes. *218 Front*

St., Beaufort, tel. 919/728–5190. Reservations advised. Dress: casual but neat. MC, V. Closed Mon. Moderate.

PICNIC SPOTS At Cape Hatteras, one nice spot is the visitor's center at **Ocracoke Island.** The deck overlooks Silver Lake Harbor, the Coast Guard station, and the ferry docks. Another pretty spot is the **Buxton Woods Picnic Area**, where tables are set in the shelter of the trees at the edge of the maritime forest.

Any meal on Cape Lookout is a picnic. There are shade shelters just behind the dunes. Shade shelters with picnic tables are also on the point at **Shackleford Banks** and just across from the visitor's center on Harkers Island. There's also a picnic area by the keeper's quarters at the Cape Lookout lighthouse.

LODGING

You can find almost any kind of accommodation near **Cape Hatteras.** The intermittent towns all have hotels, motels, B&Bs, and rental cottages, but the widest selection is on the park's north end in Nags Head and Kill Devil Hills. Where to stay depends on your interests. For restaurants, attractions, and historic sites such as Fort Raleigh or the Wright Brothers Memorial, Nags Head and Kill Devil Hills are best. If you want to spend most of your time in the park itself, you might consider the more isolated Buxton. If you want a quaint coastal village, stay in Ocracoke.

The only accommodations within the park at **Cape Lookout** are primitive and isolated. Harkers Island, the closest point of entry, has only a handful of small hotels and few other attractions. Families will probably be happier in Beaufort or Morehead City, which offer a wider selection of accommodations and restaurants, as well as movies, shopping, and other amusements.

In both areas, make reservations at least six months in advance if you plan to visit during the summer. In the spring, fall, or winter, you can easily find a place to stay, often at half the summer rate.

CAPE HATTERAS **Nags Head Inn.** One of the newer oceanfront hotels, this plain, white, four-story structure has parking underneath. The rooms are simple but large, with a desk between the beds and a table and chairs to the side. Seaside photos and muted shades of pink and blue make for a restful atmosphere. Streetside rooms lack both an ocean view and a balcony. It's well located, dead center between the Wright Brothers Memorial and Whalebone Junction. *4701 S. Virginia Dare Trail, Nags Head 27959, tel. 919/441–0454 or 800/327–8881. 100 rooms. Facilities: heated indoor and outdoor pools, Jacuzzi, spa, cable TV. AE, D, MC, V. Closed Christmas. Expensive.*

Surf Side Motel. Just a mile from the park entrance at Whalebone Junction, the yellow stucco Surf Side comprises two high rises, the 1986 main hotel and the 1989 annex. Families like the main building, while couples gravitate to the annex, which has a honeymoon suite, private Jaccuzis, and oceanfront efficiencies. Guests stop by the cozy lobby, with its floral-print sofas and hanging plants, for morning coffee, or stretch out on the large wooden deck by the pool. The room decor varies widely, from country pine to dark Colonial furniture, and from light mauve and dusty blue to rich burgundy and navy. *MP 16 (Box 400), Nags Head 27959, tel. 919/441–2105 or 800/552–SURF. 76 rooms. Facilities: indoor and outdoor pools, cable TV, Continental breakfast. AE, D, MC, V. Expensive.*

Comfort Inn. Probably the prettiest chain hotel you'll ever see—it's patterned after the old lifesaving stations that dot the coast. The gray shingled building even has a crow's nest lookout tower with a balcony. Built in 1991, it's one of the newest hotels on Hatteras Island, and it's within walking distance of restaurants, shopping, and the beach. Continental breakfast is served in the spacious lobby, which has a TV, sofas, and rich teal draperies. The rooms are decorated in cool seaside tones. Choose a second-floor room for an ocean view. *Rte. 12 (Box 1089), Buxton 27920, tel. 919/995–6100 or 800/432–1441. 60 rooms. Facilities: outdoor pool, cable TV. AE, D, DC, MC, V. Moderate.*

Island Inn. This 1901 white frame hotel has a front porch with rocking chairs and a large wood-paneled lobby furnished with nautical relics. Like any good historic inn, it also has a resident ghost (in room 22). Many of the rooms are right out of grandmother's house: antique beds with ornate headboards, wardrobes with mirrored panels, and Victorian photographs. (The charming atmosphere far outweighs the drawbacks—dripping faucets, cracked plaster, phoneless rooms.) The best rooms are in the crow's nest of the main hotel and have spectacular views of the village. The annex, built in 1981, has less personality, but it's adjacent to the pool. *Rte. 12 (Box 9), Ocracoke 27960, tel. 919/928–4351. 35 rooms. Facilities: restaurant, heated outdoor pool, cable TV. D, MC, V. Moderate.*

CAPE LOOKOUT Long before Cape Lookout was a park, anglers were coming to cast their lines on its isolated shores, and crude cabins and shelters went up amid the dunes to house them. These cabins continue to operate under two park service concessions. Some are little more than plywood shacks, while others are stripped-down beach houses with appliances. In some cases they are wired for electricity, but you must supply the generator, as well as the food, utensils and dishes, linens—everything. The cabins are still patronized mostly by fisherfolk, but an increasing number of families are using them. They vary in size, sleeping 4 to 12 people. Summer is the slackest time; fall is usually booked a year in advance.

Alger Willis Fishing Camps (Box 234, Davis 28524, tel. 919/729–2791) serves South Core Banks. Rates: $20–$120 per cabin per night. Ferry service: $12 passenger round-trip; $60–$80 vehicle round-trip.

Morris Marina Kabin Kamps (1000 Morris Marina Rd., Atlantic 28511, tel. 919/225–4261) serves North Core Banks. Rates: $30–$120 per cabin per night. Ferry service: $12 passenger round-trip; $60–$80 vehicle round-trip.

NEAR CAPE LOOKOUT **Inlet Inn.** A modern hotel that pays homage to the past with a private courtyard garden, a widow's-walk lounge, and transient boat slips. The inn overlooks the Beaufort waterfront and Carrot Island, and Beaufort's shops and restaurants are within easy walking distance. The rooms are oversize, with white walls, ceiling fans, and light-wood furniture. Harborfront rooms have French doors that open onto private porches with rocking chairs. The third-floor rooms have large window seats that afford a distant view of Cape Lookout. *601 Front St., Beaufort 28516, tel. 919/728–3600. 35 rooms. Facilities: cable TV, Continental breakfast. AE, MC, V. Expensive.*

Beaufort Inn. It's on the Beaufort Channel, tucked away from the crowded waterfront area but not far enough away to be inconvenient. Nautical paintings, model boats, and oil lamps decorate the warm, dark-paneled breakfast room; breakfast (the specialty of the house is Katie's breakfast pie) is complimentary. The rooms are formal, with dark Colonial furniture and valances on the windows, and private balconies with rocking chairs. There's also an outdoor deck on the waterfront. Little touches make the difference here: the antique washstand on the landing, the azaleas around the parking lot, and the friendly care provided by owners Bruce and Katie Ethridge. *101 Ann St., Beaufort 28516, tel. 919/728–2600. 41 rooms. Facilities: cable TV, bicycle and boat slip rentals. AE, D, DC, MC, V. Moderate.*

Calico Jack's Inn and Marina. The shocking-blue concrete motel on the waterfront at Harkers Island isn't fancy, but it is extremely convenient: The Cape Lookout ferry leaves from this marina, so all you have to do is get up and walk to the far end of the parking lot. It's a '50s-style motel with fake wood paneling, ribbed cotton bedspreads, and furniture and carpets that show more than a little age. It is, however, clean and well tended. The recreational facilities and restaurant are across the street. *Harkers Island Rd., Harkers Island 28531, tel. 919/728–3575. 24 rooms. Facilities: restaurant, pool, 2 tennis courts. MC, V. Closed mid-Dec.–Apr. Inexpensive.*

CAMPING

The two national seashores offer two distinctly different camping styles. If you prefer a manicured campground with picnic tables, bathhouses, and proximity to civilization, Cape Hatteras is the place to head. If it's the primitive, get-away-from-it-all experience you're looking for, you'll find it on Cape Lookout.

Cape Hatteras National Seashore has four campgrounds with more than 580 sites, all of which serve tents, trailers, and motor homes. All have modern rest rooms, potable water, unheated showers, grills, and picnic tables. No utility hookups are available, but there are dump stations at Oregon Inlet, Cape Point, and Ocracoke campgrounds. Though all the campgrounds except Frisco are located on level ground, you'll still need longer tent stakes in the sandy soil.

Between May 28 and September 7, campsites cannot be rented for more than 14 days. All sites cost $11 per night. Reservations are available only for the Ocracoke Campground (tel. 800/365-CAMP). There is a fifth campground at Salvo, but it has been closed in recent years due to budget cutbacks. Camping at Cape Hatteras is permitted only at designated campgrounds.

Because of its proximity to the Oregon Inlet Fishing Center, where many charter boats go out, and the area's excellent surf fishing, the most popular campground is the **Oregon Inlet Campground.** It has 120 sites in three loops, each with its own comfort station and bathhouse. Anglers like Loop C, where there is a trail to the marina, but the most secluded is Loop A, which is closer to the dunes. *Open Apr. 16–Sept. 7.*

The **Cape Point Campground,** near the Cape Hatteras Lighthouse, is also popular with fisherfolk because of its proximity to the point. The huge, grassy compound has 202 sites, a fish-cleaning station, and a large additional parking lot with boardwalks to the beach. *Open Apr. 16–Sept. 7.*

The relatively isolated **Ocracoke Campground** is the only one that takes reservations. The 136 sites are set in a large loop parallel to the dunes. It's open April 16–September 6, but reservations are not taken until May 28.

The **Frisco Campground,** with 127 sites, is the only one that's among the dunes—and grand dunes they are, with great views of the ocean and steady breezes. *Open May 28–Sept. 7.*

Cape Lookout National Seashore offers primitive camping with no developed sites. You can pitch your tent anywhere you like as long as you don't disturb the vegetation and stay at least 100 yards from the Cape Lookout Lighthouse and Portsmouth Village. No permit is required. In the summer you'll want to find a spot among the dunes and close to the beach, where the wind will keep the heat and insects in check. Use a tent with mosquito netting and one that can withstand high winds, and use extra-long wooden or plastic tent stakes. Driftwood campfires are allowed below the high-tide line only. Be sure to bring everything you need with you, including water.

For a current list of campgrounds near Cape Lookout, contact the Carteret County Tourism Development Bureau (Box 1406, Morehead City 28557, tel. 800/786–6962.)

Catoctin Mountain Park
Maryland
By Michael Pretzer

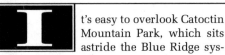

It's easy to overlook Catoctin Mountain Park, which sits astride the Blue Ridge system of the Appalachian Mountains in central Maryland. Unlike the other national parks in the region—Gettysburg National Military Park, Antietam National Battlefield, Monocacy National Battlefield, Harpers Ferry National Historical Park, and C&O Canal National Historical Park—Catoctin isn't tied to historical events or feats of engineering. No Indian wars were fought on the land; no towns or canals were built there. Civil War soldiers marched past the mountain without firing a shot.

Cunningham Falls State Park, immediately to the south, hogs the local attention. Cunningham Falls has glitzier attractions—such as the 78-foot-high cascading waterfalls for which the park is named and a 44-acre lake with two beaches where up to 500 cars' worth of swimmers and sunbathers can enjoy the outdoors.

Catoctin, on the other hand, is downright secretive about what could be its most enticing feature. On the mountain's peak, at an elevation of 1,880 feet, stands Camp David. Developed for President Franklin D. Roosevelt as a secure and secluded retreat from Washington, D.C., Camp David has been a working getaway for presidents since the 1930s. It's the site where the Camp David Accords—the Israeli-Egyptian peace pact brokered by President Jimmy Carter—was signed in 1978. But Camp David is off-limits to the public; don't think you'll see it or learn much about it from the park rangers or the volunteers at the visitor's center. Only grudgingly will they even admit that Camp David is within the confines of Catoctin.

You would do yourself a disservice, however, if you bypassed Catoctin. It's a hospitable park that inspires feelings of peace and serenity even at its most crowded, and it will give you glimpses into Maryland's history. The 30 miles of trails within its 5,770 acres offer a variety of experiences. You can sample the gentle terrain of the well-worn mountain, or you can challenge yourself to a rigorous half-day hike that includes scrambling up rocky inclines. You can opt for a self-guided trail that introduces you to bygone mountain cultures, following in the footsteps of charcoal makers and moonshiners; or you can choose a nature trail that walks you through the environment that Catoctin's white-tailed deer find so appealing.

Catoctin derives from *Kittocton*, the name of an Algonquian tribe that is believed to have lived in the foothills south of Catoctin near the Potomac River. (Catoctin Mountain Park officials say the word probably meant "land of the big mountain" or "land of the white-tailed deer.") The Monocacy River valley, to the east and the south of Catoctin Mountain, was home base for both the Algonquian and the Iroquois nations. They lived in harmony, but the Susquehannough, a tribe that had broken from the Iroquois and occupied the shores of Chesapeake Bay, continually harassed the Algonquian and Iroquois who lived near the perimeter of their territory. Eventually the Algonquian and Iroquois concentrated their encampments in the Monocacy valley; Catoctin Mountain became a neutral zone where the tribes could hunt and fish in peace, but where no tribe lived permanently.

In the 1730s white settlers began moving into the valley, and the Indians departed. The first residents of European stock were second-generation Americans and German immigrants, both lured by Lord Baltimore's offer of 200 acres of land for three years at no cost, to be followed by an annual rent of one cent an acre. By the middle of the century the first settlers had been joined by many others, including immigrants from Switzerland, Scotland, and Ireland.

Some of them took up charcoal manufacturing or logging. The charcoal makers sold to the Catoctin Iron Furnace, the remains of which can be seen off Route 806 just inside the southeast border of Cunningham Falls State Park. The loggers supplied the bark of

oak and chestnut trees, sources of tannin, to tanneries in the Monocacy River valley. Other settlers established farms, traces of which—stone fences and cellar pits, for example—can still be seen in the woods.

Conservation was unheard of in the mountains during the 1800s, and the forest and the soil became depleted. The sawmills began to close at the turn of the century. The iron furnace converted from charcoal to coal in the 1880s and closed in 1903. The chestnut blight hit in 1904. Many of the mountain residents headed for the city, primarily to Baltimore.

In 1935 the 10,000 acres that today form Catoctin and Cunningham parks were purchased by the federal government, which planned to develop the Catoctin Recreational Demonstration Area as a park and then turn it over to the state of Maryland. The plan changed, however, when Roosevelt settled on part of Catoctin as his Camp Shangri-la. (When Dwight D. Eisenhower was president, he renamed the retreat Camp David in honor of his favorite grandson.) Catoctin was indeed developed as a recreational area, but to ensure security at Camp David, the federal government retained control of the park.

During Harry S. Truman's presidency, however, Maryland began to clamor for ownership. In 1954 the federal and state governments reached a compromise: The area was divided in half. The land north of Route 77 stayed in federal hands as Catoctin Mountain Park; the land to the south of the highway went to Maryland as Cunningham Falls State Park.

Since becoming parkland, the 10,000 acres have reverted to hardwood forest. Today, the woodland is much like it was when the first European settlers arrived.

ESSENTIAL INFORMATION

VISITOR INFORMATION For detailed information about the park, contact the Superintendent, **Catoctin Mountain Park** (6602 Foxville Rd., Thurmont 21788, tel. 301/663–9388). The visitor's center is open year-round (Mon.–Thurs. 10–4:30, Fri. 10–5, weekends

8:30–5) except for federal holidays in the winter.

For information on the state park, contact the Park Manager, **Cunningham Falls State Park** (14039 Catoctin Hollow Rd., Thurmont 21788, tel. 301/271–7574). For information on the area immediately surrounding the two parks, contact the **Catoctin Mountain Tourist Council** (Cunningham Falls State Park, Thurmont 21788, tel. 301/271–3285) or the **Tourism Council of Frederick County, Inc.** (19 E. Church St., Frederick 21701, tel. 301/663–8687 or 800/999–3613). For information on the Gettysburg area north of Catoctin, contact the **Gettysburg Travel Council** (35 Carlisle St., Gettysburg, PA 17325, tel. 717/334–6274).

FEES There is no fee to enter Catoctin Mountain Park or Cunningham Falls State Park. Cunningham Falls has seasonal fees for the use of its Hunting Creek Lake (*see* Boating *and* Swimming *in* Other Activities *in* Exploring, *below*) and some of its picnic areas; both parks have fees for camping (*see* Camping, *below*).

PUBLICATIONS Maps, trail guides, and brochures are available at the visitor's center, located at the intersection of Route 77 and Park Central Road about midway between the park's eastern and western borders. The center has a limited number of brochures on other attractions in the region. It also sells books about nature and the national parks, but none is specifically or exclusively concerned with Catoctin. A less extensive selection of brochures and publications is available at the park's administrative office, along Route 77 about a mile from the park's eastern border.

You can find maps and brochures about Cunningham Falls at the state park's administrative center (across Catoctin Hollow Rd. from the Hunting Creek Lake boat launch) and at the booths at the entrances to the lake and the camping areas. The park also has a visitor's center in its Manor Area (off Rte. 15, about 2¹/₂ mi south of the intersection of Rtes. 15 and 77).

GEOLOGY AND TERRAIN The Blue Ridge system of the Appalachian Mountains once had peaks as tall as the Rockies, but glaciers (during the Ice Age, glaciers came within 100 miles of Catoctin) and the forces of wind and water eventually wore them into soft mountains. Today the peak of the aged Catoctin Mountain is 1,880 feet above sea level; the highest point that's accessible to the public is Hog Rock, at 1,671 feet. Hog Rock and similar outcroppings are primarily of Catoctin greenstone, which originated from the lava flows of 600 million years ago.

Owens Creek, a fishing brook, runs along the western and northern sides of the mountain. Big Hunting Creek, also a fishing brook, winds along its base to the south. Over the past centuries Big Hunting Creek has cut a valley, which was partially cleared to make way for Route 77. Big Hunting Creek slips back and forth across the border between the national and state parks. At Cunningham Falls it drops 78 feet in elevation over the course of 220 feet. It feeds into the man-made Hunting Creek Lake in the state park, then proceeds back into Catoctin. Both creeks flow in a southeasterly direction, ending at the Monocacy River, which flows south to the Potomac River.

FLORA AND FAUNA Catoctin Mountain Park is an eastern hardwood forest that has entered its mature, or climax, stage. Walk the trails and you'll discover sugar maple, chestnut, oak, hickory, and black birch trees. Near the creeks and in the valleys you'll see black locust, wild cherry, sassafras, yellow poplar, hemlock, ash, and white oak.

The park's stands of American chestnut trees were decimated by the blight that struck the country in the early 1900s. For a time, a small section of the park near the Chestnut Picnic Area was used for research on the blight, but today you'll see only stumps, with an occasional sapling shooting up; a cure for the blight has yet to be found.

Spring is always a colorful season here, thanks to the wildflowers that carpet the park. Along the roadsides you'll see the ox-eyed daisy, garlic mustard, yarrow, chicory, and common strawberry. In the upland woods you'll find the wood anemone, bedstraw, common fleabane, and mountain laurel. In the lowlands, look for bloodroot, sweet cicely, miterwort, and blue violets. If you're lucky, you may uncover one of the park's seldom-seen flowers—cancerroot, say, or nodding trillium. You might even be as lucky as the hiker who, in 1993, became the first person to spot the rare Maryland cuckoo flower in the park.

In recent years, mild winters and the absence of predators allowed the white-tailed deer to overpopulate the area severely; as many as 500 were estimated to be living in the park in 1992. But the harsh weather of early 1993 robbed the deer of their winter food supply, and now the herd is down to a more appropriate size, about 250. But you're still likely to see deer in the morning or evening along the roadways, trails, and creeks. In the summer look for them grazing on raspberries and wineberries; in the fall, they'll likely be nosing for acorns under the park's oaks; in the winter, you'll catch them sheltering under low-hanging limbs of evergreens.

Barred, eastern screech, and great horned owls; the broad-winged hawk; downy and pileated woodpeckers; wild turkeys; and many other birds are plentiful in Catoctin, as are a host of small mammals, such as squirrels, woodchucks, and chipmunks. Two poisonous snakes, the timber rattlesnake and the copperhead, inhabit the park, but a snakebite hasn't been reported in years.

Brook, brown, and rainbow trout spawn in Big Hunting Creek and Owens Creek, and Big Hunting Creek below the lake is stocked with rainbows. As you might expect, rainbows are the most abundant species in Big Hunting; the brook trout is the rarest of the three.

WHEN TO GO Catoctin Mountain Park is used mostly as a weekend escape for Baltimoreans and Washingtonians. Fall is without a doubt the most popular season. On a Saturday or Sunday in October, when the sugar maples and the other trees are in full glory, Catoctin's parking lots, picnic areas, and campground have been known to fill up, leaving late-arriving visitors with nothing to do but drive slowly through and out.

Spring is popular, too, but the springtime colors are more subtle, and the weather less predictable. It's been known to snow in March, and rain is always a possibility.

SEASONAL EVENTS Mid-March weekends: Cunningham Falls State Park holds its annual **maple syrup demonstration.** Events include tapping trees, boiling sap, and eating pancakes and sausages drenched with syrup, as well as storytelling and horse-drawn wagon rides. Contact the park (tel. 301/271–7574) for particulars. **Saturday evenings in summer:** Cunningham Falls sponsors a series of **concerts at Hunting Creek Lake,** featuring folk, bluegrass, country-and-western, and other forms of American music; contact the park for specifics.

WHAT TO PACK The mid-Atlantic location makes for relatively mild weather. In midsummer temperatures climb into the 80s or, occasionally, the 90s. Walking shorts and short-sleeved shirts will suffice during the day, but you may want trousers and long sleeves for the evening. The mountaintops will be windier and colder than the trailheads, so take warmer clothes with you when you hike. Snow is a possibility between November and March, with downfalls most likely in January and February. In a hard winter, a couple of feet of snow cover the ground for as long as a month. You'll need warm, layered clothing for a winter visit.

For the most part the trails range in difficulty from easy to moderate, and you're unlikely to find yourself more than an hour away from a road, supervised campground, or trailhead. Sturdy walking or hiking shoes are recommended, although many hikers wear sneakers. Even on short hikes, take along water; it's not advisable to drink from the streams, which may harbor the *Giardia lamblia* protozoan that can cause diarrhea. Pack a pair of binoculars if you plan to bird-watch or to hike in search of vistas.

GENERAL STORES The general store closest to Catoctin Mountain's campground (a little over 2 miles away) is **Moser's Market** (tel. 301/662–4751), just west of the intersection of Route 77 and Manahan Road. (It's marked "store" on the map you get at the visitor's center.) Moser's has groceries and camping supplies, including firewood, and hot and cold sandwiches (open Tues.–Sat. 6 AM–8 PM, Sun. 8–6).

Thurmont, which lies about a mile beyond Catoctin's eastern border, has two supermarkets. **Jubilee** is in Thurmont Plaza along Route 806 a few blocks north of the town's main intersection (open Mon.–Sat. 8 AM–9 PM, Sun. 9–7). The newer **Food Lion** opened in 1993 in the recently developed Orchard Village Shopping Center, at the southern edge of town. From the intersection of Route 77 and U.S. 15, travel south less than a mile to the exit for Route 806. The supermarket is just up the hill to the right (open daily 8 AM–10 PM).

There's a **camp store** in Cunningham Falls State Park, but it's designed to serve only the park's William Houck Campground. It has limited supplies but a plentiful assortment of souvenirs.

ATMS There are two 24-hour banking facilities in Thurmont. One is at **NationsBank** at the intersection of Routes 77 and 806 in the center of town. The other, **F&M Bank Center,** is south, next to the Roy Rogers restaurant just east of Route 77's exit for Route 806.

ARRIVING AND DEPARTING Catoctin Mountain Park is not a "destination" park. The typical length of stay is only two or three days, usually on a weekend. Even during a short visit, you'll probably want to travel outside the park. To do so you'll need a car. If you're traveling here by air or rail, head for Baltimore or Washington, where you can rent a car. Bus service will get you as close as Frederick, where you can also rent a car.

By Plane. The Baltimore–Washington region is served by three major airports. **Baltimore/Washington International Airport,** just south of Baltimore, and **Dulles International Airport,** west of Washington, have national and international flights. **Washington National Airport,** south of Washington, has national flights only. Among the major carriers at BWI are USAir, United, and American; at Dulles, United, American, and TWA; at National, USAir, Delta, and Continental. The major car rental companies can accommodate you at all three airports. The drive to Catoctin from any of them will vary between one and two hours—longer if local traffic conditions are poor. (Baltimore is less likely to be congested than Washington.) You can avoid rush hour traffic by driving away between midmorning and midafternoon.

By Car and RV. From **Baltimore,** take I–70 west to Frederick, about 40 miles. In Frederick, get on Route 15 heading north; in Thurmont (another 20 miles), exit onto Route 77 heading west. The entrance to Catoctin is on the right in about 3 miles; the entrance to Cunningham Falls is .25 mile farther on the left.

From **Washington,** take I–270 north to Frederick, about 40 miles. In Frederick take Route 15 north and continue as above.

From **Gettysburg,** Pennsylvania, take Route 15 south for about 15 miles; exit onto Route 77 in Thurmont and continue as above.

By Train. Amtrak (tel. 800/523–8720) provides service to Pennsylvania Station in Baltimore, to BWI Airport Train Station, and to Union Station in Washington. **Avis** (tel. 410/685–6000) will pick you up at the Baltimore station and take you to its nearby office. In Union Station, **Avis** (tel. 202/789–0742) and **National** (tel. 202/842–7454) both have desks.

By Bus. Greyhound (tel. 800/231–2222) operates service to Frederick, where you may rent from **Hertz** (tel. 301/662–2626).

EXPLORING

Catoctin has 30 miles of hiking trails, which range from the easy (wheelchair-accessible) to the strenuous (steep and rocky). Some of the trails are educational, posted with interpretive signs for children and adults. Others

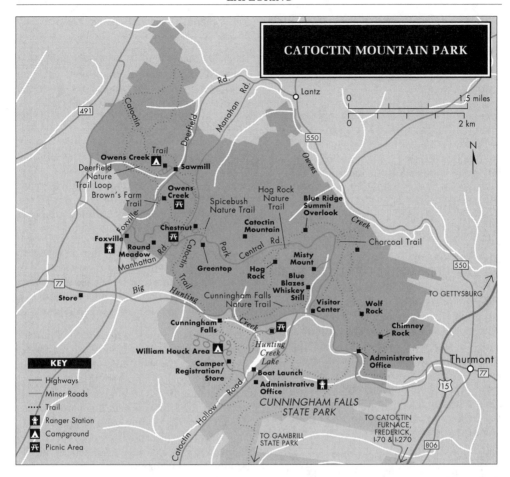

CATOCTIN MOUNTAIN PARK

are exhilarating, with eye-popping views and plenty of opportunities to see wildlife.

THE BEST IN ONE DAY One good thing about a small park: You can experience it intimately even if you're there for only a few hours. If you have a single day to spend in Catoctin, try to spend it on foot. Devote the morning to hiking. Most of the trails are short, so you'll want to string several of them together to form a loop. The trails are not marked with blazes, but the paths are quite visible, and all the trailheads and trail junctions have signs.

To reach many of the park's most scenic areas, walk the Blue Ridge, Hog Rock, and Cunningham Falls trails—the 5.1-mile total will require just over three hours if you take time to enjoy the scenery. The **Blue Ridge Trail** begins at the visitor's center and roughly parallels Park Central Road until you get to the Hog Rock Trail. Around the 1-mile mark you may want to take a brief side trip to the **Thurmont Vista,** which affords a view east toward the Monocacy River valley. After the trail turns westward, you'll be greeted by another vista, the **Blue Ridge Summit Overlook.** Cross Park Central Road and hook up with the **Hog Rock Trail.** If you're still feeling leisurely, pick up a printed guide at the trailhead and take the 1.5-mile Hog Rock Nature Trail loop. From Hog Rock, the highest point you can reach in Catoctin, hike down to Route 77; cross over the road to **Cunningham Falls,** the most popular natural attraction in the area. Return to the north side of Route 77 to catch the **Cunningham Falls Nature Trail**; in about a mile you'll be back at the visitor's center. Drive to Chestnut or Owens Creek for a picnic lunch.

The season will dictate how you spend the afternoon. In the spring you may want to try your hand at fly-fishing in Big Hunting Creek (*see* Fishing *in* Other Activities, *below*). In the middle of summer you'll more likely want to head for the beaches of Hunting Creek Lake (*see* Boating *and* Swimming *in* Other Activities, *below*). In the fall, you may want to take a second hike, a mile shorter than the morning one but more strenuous: the **Wolf Rock/Chimney Rock loop.** Start at the parking lot .5 mile north of the visitor's center. Take the trail 1.8 miles to Wolf Rock. The trail climbs 400 feet and the rock outcroppings can be slippery. (Rappelling is allowed in the area, but only with a permit issued at the visitor's center.) Continue up to Chimney Rock. After you catch your breath from the ascent and the view of the colorful countryside, head down the steep trail toward the administration building, then swing back to the parking lot. Allow about three hours to complete the loop.

ORIENTATION PROGRAMS AND GUIDED TOURS
There are no formal orientation programs or guided tours at Catoctin, but a variety of interpretive programs are offered year-round.

SCENIC DRIVES AND VIEWS Only one road, **Park Central,** winds through the park. It travels mostly east and west, between the visitor's center at Route 77 and Foxville-Deerfield Road at the park's western border. There are parking lots at the start of trails to two scenic views, **Blue Ridge Summit Overlook** and **Thurmont Vista.** Getting to either view requires a 15-minute hike.

HISTORIC BUILDINGS AND SITES At the end of the **Blue Blazes Whiskey Still Trail,** a .5-mile self-guided walk, is an example of the type of still settlers used in the late 18th and 19th centuries to make corn whiskey. Many of the farmers operated stills unlawfully, not because moonshine was illegal but because they didn't want to pay the required excise tax.

The **Charcoal Trail** is a .5-mile loop that traces the process of cutting timber, drawing it to a hearth, and charring it. You'll see the remains of a charcoal pit along the trail.

At **Round Meadow** are the park's oldest and fourth-oldest buildings. The oldest, once the park's general store, is now its resource-management office. The blacksmith shop, which was constructed to help build the park in the 1930s, is open to the public; demonstrations of the blacksmith's trade are given on three Sundays during the summer.

Along Owens Creek near the entrance to Owens Creek Campground is an example of the **sawmills** once used by loggers in the area. The structure is made of stone and houses a vertical saw that turned logs into lumber.

The stone structure that housed the **Catoctin Furnace Iron Works** between 1774 and 1903 is at the southeastern edge of Cunningham Falls State Park, 3 miles south of Thurmont along Route 806. A .5-mile self-guided trail between the ironworks and the state park's Manor Area, accessible from Route 15, puts the region into historical perspective. Pick up a printed guide at the trailhead or at the Manor Area visitor's center.

NATURE TRAILS AND SHORT WALKS Catoctin Mountain Park has six self-guided trails. The **Blue Blazes Whiskey Still Trail** describes the making of moonshine, and the **Charcoal Trail** highlights the important local industry of a bygone era (*see* Historic Buildings and Sites, *above*). The **Spicebush Trail,** a wheelchair-accessible path, teaches forest ecology.

The other three offer printed guides at their trailheads. **Hog Rock Trail,** named after the rock outcropping where farmers used to bring their hogs to feed on acorns and chestnuts, introduces you to 14 species of trees. **Deerfield Nature Trail,** 1.3 miles in length, details the habits and habitat of the white-tailed deer. **Brown's Farm Environmental Study Area Trail,** a .5-mile trail often used by school groups, points out relationships between human beings, animals, plants, and the land.

LONGER HIKES Most of Catoctin's trails are designed for the casual hiker, but there are some challenging ones for the more adventuresome. For a full day of hiking that will take you to the park's vistas and up its steepest trails, combine the Blue Ridge, Hog Rock, and Cunningham Falls trails loop with the Wolf Rock/Chimney Rock trails loop (*see* The Best in One Day, *above*). You'll cover 8.2 miles. With time for side trips and a stop at the falls, expect the trip to take between five and six hours.

An alternative is to hike into Cunningham Falls State Park—or beyond. The state park has four strenuous trails, each more than a mile long. The **Cliff Trail** is the shortest, at 1.5 miles round-trip, and arguably the most beautiful; it starts above the park's maple-syrup demonstration area and takes you through stands of hemlock and to rock outcroppings. **Old Misery Trail** switches back and forth and leads to some beautiful views; it's 4 miles round-trip but can be extended by continuing on the Cat Rock–Bob's Hill Trail. **Cat Rock–Bob's Hill** is a trail (7.5 miles one way) between the parking lot across Route 77 from Catoctin's administration building and the state park's Manor Area. Cat Rock affords a 360° view in winter, and Bob's Hill, at an elevation of 1,765 feet, is the highest accessible point in Cunningham Falls. None of these trails is a loop.

If you're itching to really stride out, take the **Catoctin Trail,** maintained by the Potomac Appalachian Trail Club. The trail runs 27 miles from Catoctin Mountain Park through Cunningham Falls State Park to Gambrill State Park. If you hike this trail, plan to start early; camping is not permitted along the way.

OTHER ACTIVITIES **Biking.** Cyclists are permitted to use the roads in the park, but there are no designated bike lanes, and shoulders are either narrow or nonexistent. No vehicles of any kind, including bicycles, may be taken on the trails.

Bird-Watching. Nearly 150 species of birds—from woodcocks to woodpeckers to wood warblers—have been sighted here. Birders can get a brochure from the visitor's center that lists all the species in the park.

Boating. There is no boating in the national park, but boaters are allowed to put craft into Hunting Creek Lake from the launch off Catoctin Hollow Road in Cunningham Falls State Park at no charge. Only electric motors of less than one horsepower or 33 pounds of thrust may be used. Canoes may be rented at the boathouse on the lake for $4 an hour, aqua-cycles for $6 a half hour or $10 an hour. The boathouse is open daily 10–5. Call the park manager's office (*see* Visitor Information *in* Essential Information, *above*) to inquire further.

Cross-Country Skiing. During the winter the gravel section of Manahan Road—a stretch of about 1.5 miles—and all of Park Central Road are left unplowed and made available for cross-country skiing. Skiing is allowed on hiking trails as well, but often the snowfall is insufficient to cover the rocky paths. The park does not groom the road or the trails for skiing.

Fishing. Big Hunting Creek is a challenge: The trout are easier to spot here than they are to catch. The creek was the first stream in Maryland to be reserved solely for fly-fishing and the first to be restricted by a catch-and-return policy. Before casting for the brook, brown, and rainbow trout, pick up the park's fly-fishing guide at the visitor's center. Fly-fishing is also allowed at Owens Creek, where the catch-and-return restriction does not apply. In Cunningham Falls State Park, fishing is permitted in Little Hunting Creek and Hunting Creek Lake, as well as in Big Hunting Creek. A Maryland fishing license and a trout stamp, which can be purchased at the camper registration office or the administrative office in the state park, are required for angling in either park. A license costs $10 for a Maryland resident, $20 for a resident of another state; the trout stamp is $5.

Horseback Riding. Horseback riding is allowed on 6 miles of the Catoctin Trail in the national park, except during the winter when the trail is closed. The trail winds through woods, crosses creeks, and traverses mountainous terrain. Horse trailers may be parked in the lot (the maximum capacity is five trailers) across from the entrance to Camp Greentop. From the parking lot, take the trail marked with signs bearing a horseshoe symbol. A map and detailed riding regulations are available at the visitor's center.

Hunting. There is no hunting in Catoctin Mountain Park, but hunting deer, wild turkey, squirrel, grouse, and quail is allowed in parts of Cunningham Falls State Park. With a few exceptions, the seasons extend from October 15 to February 28. A Maryland hunting license is required of all hunters. For more information, contact the State Forest and Parks Service at Cunningham Falls State Park (14039 Catoctin Hollow Rd., Thurmont 21788, tel. 301/271–7574).

Rope and Rock Climbing. Basic or beginning rock climbing with ropes is popular at Wolf Rock, which has a substantial stone outcropping with deep crevices. To climb, you must obtain a permit—no fee charged—from the visitor's center.

Swimming. In summer Cunningham Falls State Park marks off three areas of Hunting Creek Lake for swimming and puts lifeguards on duty there; it has two sandy beaches for sunbathing. Picnic areas, a snack bar, and showers are nearby. There's a day-use fee of $2 per person to use the lake between April and October; children in car seats and people with Golden Age/Access passes are admitted without charge.

CHILDREN'S PROGRAMS During the summer, Catoctin offers a program series called "Kid Stuff." Led by the park's interpretive specialists, the series introduces children to the forest's plants and animals. The programs are generally held on Saturday afternoons and Sunday mornings. There's an up-to-date calendar of events at the visitor's center, where the programs are held.

EVENING ACTIVITIES Between late May and early September, the park's interpretive staff holds campfire sessions every Saturday evening at the Owens Creek Campground amphitheater. The topics cover the region's culture and the park's ecology. Check at the visitor's center or with the campground host for specifics.

DINING

Although there are no restaurants within Catoctin Mountain Park, you won't starve for lack of eateries. The state park has a snack bar by the lake that's open daily 9:30–5:30 during the summer. Thurmont has a number of establishments that offer quick or hearty meals. Nearby Gettysburg and Frederick, prime tourist spots in Pennsylvania and Maryland respectively, offer an even greater variety, including fine-dining restaurants.

NEAR THE PARK **Dobbin House Tavern.** The 20-minute drive north will take you back 200 years. The stone Dobbin House, built in 1776, has been restored inside and out, with antiques similar to the original owner's furnishings, and is listed on the National Register of Historic Places. Colonial and Continental cuisine (the recipes have been published in *Bon Appétit* and *Cuisine*) is served in six 18th-century rooms. Try the hunter's chicken (with tomatoes, mushrooms, and brown sausage), the prime rib, or the roast duck. The adjacent Springhouse Tavern, with two working fireplaces, offers salads and sandwiches in the atmosphere of an alehouse. *89 Steinwehr Ave., Gettysburg, PA, tel. 717/334–2100. Reservations advised at dinner. Dress: casual. AE, MC, V. No lunch in restaurant. Moderate–Expensive.*

Tauraso's/Victor's Saloon. If you're indecisive, stay away from this renovated factory and warehouse near the center of Frederick—it offers too many choices. There are three dining areas: the saloon, with exposed brick and ductwork and a freestanding circular bar; a formal candlelit dining room with marble tables; and a garden with a fountain and wrought-iron tables. The menu starts with the Italian basics (including pizza from a wood-burning stone oven) and ranges to New York strip steak, rack of lamb, and a large selection of seafood. The rigatoni with shrimp and broccoli is extremely popular, as is the veal cutlet with arugula and tomatoes. *6 East St., Everedy Sq., Frederick, tel. 301/663–6600. Reservations advised at dinner. Dress: casual (casual chic evenings in the dining room). AE, DC, MC, V. Moderate–Expensive.*

Cozy Restaurant. In Thurmont it seems as if there's a billboard for the Cozy at every turn. The signs must be effective, for the restaurant, which has been in business since 1929, is usually bustling. It's decorated in an eclectic mix of country and Victorian, and it serves up serious down-home cooking. The main attraction is the buffet, where you can find everything from barbecued beef ribs to Alaskan snow crab. There's even a vegetarian buffet. On Friday and Saturday nights the restaurant lays out 100 different items. *103 Frederick Rd., Thurmont, tel. 301/271–7373. MC, V. Inexpensive–Moderate.*

Mountain Gate Family Restaurant. Just down the road from the Cozy is Thurmont's other buffet ("family-style" is what they call it in Thurmont) restaurant. The parking lot is big, to accommodate tour buses, and the interior is bright, spacious, and a little weird; the foyer is done up with splashes of artificial flowers and a large collection of troll dolls. The menu features home-style cooking (liver and onions, pork chops, fried chicken), and the selection is even more extensive at the lunch and dinner buffets. No one seems to dispute the restaurant's claim of having the area's largest salad bar. There's a weekend breakfast buffet from 8 AM, but you can order breakfast any time any day, starting at 5 AM. *133 Frederick Rd., Thurmont, tel. 301/271–4373. D, MC, V. Inexpensive–Moderate.*

Fast Food. There's a cluster of fast-food and chain restaurants—including **Roy Rogers, Pizza Hut,** and the omnipresent **McDonald's**—south of the Mountain Gate Family Restaurant (*see above*) in Thurmont, at Route 77's exit for Route 806.

PICNIC SPOTS Picnic facilities are available at Chestnut and Owens Creek. Many of the sites at Chestnut are wheelchair-accessible. Additional picnic sites can be found in the

William Houck and Manor areas of Cunningham Falls State Park; the state park charges a fee during the summer and on some weekends in the spring and fall for use of the facilities in the William Houck Area.

LODGING

The only lodging within Catoctin Mountain Park is Camp David. Unless you're a head of state or a close friend of the president, you'll have to look to Thurmont, which has a limited selection of accommodations, or to the Gettysburg and Frederick areas, where lodging ranges from truck-stop motels to historic inns and bed-and-breakfasts to major chain hotels. The **Gettysburg Travel Council** (35 Carlisle St., Gettysburg, PA 17325, tel. 717/334–6274, fax 717/334–1166) and the **Tourism Council of Frederick County** (19 E. Church St., Frederick 21701, tel. 301/663–8687 or 800/999–3613, fax 301/663–0039) can assist you in selecting a place to stay.

NEAR THE PARK **Bluebird on the Mountain.** Ten minutes northwest of Catoctin Mountain Park is this bed-and-breakfast in a 1900 manor house. All the rooms have been renovated recently; all are sunny and airy and decorated with antiques, white linens and lace, and Oriental carpets; and all have their own baths, although some are a couple of steps down the hall. A Continental breakfast, included in the rate, is served in your room or on the back porch. *14700 Eyler Ave., Cascade 21719, tel. 301/241–4161 or 800/362–9526. 4 suites. Facilities: fireplaces in 2 suites, Jacuzzis in 3; golf nearby. MC, V. Expensive.*

The Brafferton Inn. A few steps from downtown Lincoln Square is one of Gettysburg's outstanding B&Bs. The stone structure was built in 1786 and fired upon during the Civil War. (You can still see a bullet lodged in the mantel of one of its upstairs fireplaces.) The original house, which is on the National Register, has rooms with fireplaces and brass beds; there are more guest rooms in an adjacent clapboard building. All the rooms are furnished with antiques. A full breakfast is included in the rate. *44 York St., Gettysburg,*

PA 17325, tel. 717/337–3423. 8 rooms with bath, 2 suites. MC, V. Moderate–Expensive.

Cozy Inn. The inn and cottage complex, near the center of Thurmont and next to the Cozy Restaurant (*see* Dining, *above*), has been used by presidential families, Cabinet members, and the media. Many of the rooms and suites (named after presidents) have recently been renovated in Victorian style; some feature fireplace, Jacuzzi, waterbed or canopy bed, and kitchenette. Nonsmoking rooms are available. A Continental breakfast is served Sunday through Thursday. *103 Frederick Rd., Thurmont 21788, tel. and fax 301/271– 4301. 21 rooms, suites, and cabins. DC, MC, V. Inexpensive–Expensive.*

Rambler Motel. This motel at the northern edge of Thurmont offers clean and simple rooms, each with individually controlled air-conditioning, color television, telephone, and wall-to-wall carpeting. All units are on the ground floor; nonsmoking rooms are available. *Rtes. 15 and 550, Thurmont 21788, tel. 301/271–2424. 30 rooms with bath. AE, DC, MC, V. Inexpensive–Moderate.*

Super 8 Motel. The new Super 8 in the southern part of Thurmont is clean and convenient. The rooms have cable TV; nonsmoking and wheelchair-accessible rooms are available, as are rooms with waterbeds or microwaves and refrigerators. In the morning there's toast and coffee in the lobby. *300 Tippin Dr., Thurmont 21788, tel. and fax 301/271–7888, reservations tel. 800/800–8000. 46 rooms and suites with bath. AE, D, DC, MC, V. Inexpensive.*

CAMPING

Camping in either park is allowed only in designated campgrounds. There are almost always sites available during the week throughout the year, but the campgrounds fill up rapidly on weekends, especially between late spring and fall. Don't arrive at Catoctin on a Saturday night in June, July, or August thinking you'll find a place to pitch the tent or park the trailer.

Owens Creek Campground. The Catoctin Mountain Park campground provides a wooded setting for its sites, each of which is equipped with a picnic table and a fireplace or grill. There are flush toilets and hot showers in the campground's comfort stations. All sites are available on a first-come, first-served basis. You must self-register at the campground entrance by filling out a form and depositing a fee into a receptacle. Camping is limited to 7 consecutive days and a total of 14 days per season. Trailers longer than 22 feet are prohibited. (There's no length restriction on motor homes.) *Foxville-Deerfield Rd., no tel. 51 campsites. Fee: $10/night per site ($5 with Golden Age/Access pass). Open Apr. 15– 3rd Sun. in Nov.*

Camp Misty Mount. This group of rustic wood-and-stone cabins (for 3–6 people) and one lodge (for up to 8) is a National Historic District, with the buildings listed on the National Register of Historic Structures. Each cabin is furnished with metal cots and mattresses; you'll find a picnic table, a grill, and a fire circle outside—no cooking is allowed inside. Campers must provide bedding and cookware. Flush toilets and hot shower facilities are centralized nearby. No pets are allowed. A dining hall and kitchen may be rented separately. A swimming pool is available during limited hours. *Off Park Central Rd., tel. 301/271–3140 (camp manager). 27 cabins, 1 lodge. Fee: cabins, $35/night; lodge, $70/night; dining hall, $150/day ($200 for those not renting cabin or lodge). Open May– Oct.*

Adirondack Shelters. The national park maintains two shelters for camping in the woods along the Catoctin Trail. To reach them, you must hike about 2 miles from the Owens Creek Campground. They are available on a first-come, first-served basis, but you must obtain a permit at the visitor's center. (Be sure to have someone at the center give you good directions; the shelters aren't marked on the maps provided by the park.) Pitching a tent in the area or along the Catoctin Trail is forbidden.

William Houck Campground. The main campground in Cunningham Falls State Park has sites distributed over five loops. Each site has a table, a grill, and a parking area. Flush toilets and hot showers are centrally located. You'll find two dumping stations next to the camp registration building, but none of the campsites has electric or water hookups. No pets are allowed. Camping is limited to 14 days. The fee includes use of Hunting Creek Lake. *Off Catoctin Hollow Rd., tel. 301/271–7574. 149 sites. Fee: $12/site weeknights, $16/site weekends (some discounts available). Reservations may be made by phone for an additional $5. Open Apr.– Oct.*

Camper-Ready Sites. In 1993 Cunningham Falls State Park introduced camper-ready tent and cabin sites in the Houck Campground *(see above).* The park has several sites equipped with six-person tents and dining canopies and furnished with camp stoves, Ensolite pads, lanterns, and firewood. It also has rustic cabins with porches available. Each cabin has electrical outlets, a double bed, and a bunk bed (bedding not provided). Cooking must be done outdoors. You can't bring pets here, either. *William Houck Campground, tel. 301/271–7574. 4 tent sites, 4 cabins. Fee: tents, $25 weekdays, $30 weekends; cabins, $35 weekdays, $40 weekends. Call the park to reserve. Available Apr.–Oct.*

Manor Campground. Within this campground operated by Cunningham Falls State Park, flush toilets and hot showers are centrally located; a visitor's center, picnic shelters, and trailheads are nearby. There are no hookups. A stay is limited to 14 days, and you can't bring pets. *Off Rte. 15. 31 sites. Fees as at William Houck (see above). No reservations. Open year-round; bathhouse open Apr.–Oct.*

Cumberland Island National Seashore

Georgia

By Jeffrey R. Young

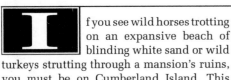

If you see wild horses trotting on an expansive beach of blinding white sand or wild turkeys strutting through a mansion's ruins, you must be on Cumberland Island. This largest of Georgia's barrier islands is one of nature's last stands against the development of coastal lands. As peaceful as it is unlikely, the island remains defiantly wild despite countless human efforts to tame it, and its best and virtually only amenities are serenity and solitude. In many parts of the island, regardless of the direction you strike out in, you probably won't encounter another person all day.

The peace and beauty of the island have not gone unnoticed. Timucuan Indians, its first known inhabitants, lived and thrived in peaceful isolation here, growing as tall as 6 feet on a diet of protein-rich marine life. In the 16th century, both the Spanish and the British became interested in Cumberland's military and agricultural value and fought each other for control of it. Georgia's founding father, General James Edward Oglethorpe, eventually won the island, named it in honor of the duke of Cumberland, and built a hunting camp, Dungeness, on its south end. Soon colonists arrived from England and cleared the hardwood forests to make way for plantations. Majestic live oaks gave unusual strength to battleships, and it's reputed that this wood was used in the USS *Constitution,* known as "Old Ironsides." After the Civil War, the cotton plantations were abandoned, and horses began to roam the deserted fields and beaches, as they do to this day.

Wilderness has been reclaiming the island since the end of the plantation era, and fields are once again sprawling hardwood forests. The only human intrusion since then came when Thomas Carnegie, brother and partner of Andrew, the steel magnate, bought much of the island for a private family playground. The haunting, overgrown ruins that symbolize the island are the remains of a newer

Dungeness that he built. Three Carnegie mansions still stand. Two remain in private hands; one of these, Greyfield, is now an inn and offers the island's only accommodations.

Only 20 years ago, the fate of Cumberland Island was far from certain. Much of what was a Carnegie land trust passed to individual landowners, who began selling off their holdings. Sea Pines Development Company, the developer of Hilton Head Island in South Carolina, decided to establish a modern executive resort on Cumberland and bought much of the land. In an effort to preserve the island, the Johnston family (one of the Carnegie heirs) donated Plum Orchard mansion to the National Park Service, which in turn reclaimed Sea Pines's land and founded the national seashore in 1972.

Technically, the island has a population of one—a naturalist who is Cumberland's last retained-rights holder (this is the legal term for someone who has sold the property to the government but retained the rights to use it). The National Park Service limits the number of visitors to 300 per day and offers only basic camping and public facilities. Nature dominates the island and provides more than enough enjoyment for one or even several days.

ESSENTIAL INFORMATION

VISITOR INFORMATION For information about the island, contact the Superintendent, **Cumberland Island National Seashore** (Box 806, St. Marys 31558, tel. 912/882–4335; open weekdays 10–4). For help organizing your stay on or near the island, contact the **St. Marys Tourism Council** (Box 1291, St. Marys 31558, tel. 800/868–8687).

Since only 300 people per day are allowed on the island, reservations are advised, especially in peak seasons (Mar.–May and weekends in the fall), although walk-ins are accepted if space permits. Reservations can be made up to 11 months in advance by calling the Cumberland Island National Seashore reservation line (tel. 912/882–4335, Mon.–Fri. 10–4) or stopping in at the visitor's

center in St. Marys (on the waterfront, where Route 40 meets the coast, open Mar. 15–Oct. 15., daily 8:15–6:15; Oct. 16–Mar. 14, daily 8:15–4:30). The only access to the island is by passenger ferry, so the most important thing to remember is: Don't miss the boat! The northern part of the island is closed to visitors four or five times each winter when managed deer hunts are scheduled.

FEES The cost of a round-trip on the ferry to either of the island's mail docks, including tax, is $10.07 for adults, $7.95 for senior citizens, and $5.99 for children under 13. There are no entrance or camping fees, and the park service's annual passes do not cover the ferry charge.

PUBLICATIONS The most popular work about Cumberland is a coffee-table book entitled *Cumberland Island Treasure,* published by World Publications. This beautiful collection of the photography of three Cumberland visitors is a great way to remember the island, but it's short on information. It can be purchased at almost any bookstore in St. Marys or at the visitor's center.

The **Eastern National Park and Monument Association** publishes several general guides to the island, including the useful *Cumberland Island Handbook.* This small booklet, handy to have while exploring, describes the island's various habitats and most memorable wildlife, and can be purchased at the visitor's center. Though the booklet does contain a map, the one in the free park service brochure—"Cumberland Island Official Map and Guide"—is larger and more detailed.

GEOLOGY AND TERRAIN Stretching 18 miles long and spanning 3 miles at its widest, Cumberland is nearly one-third larger than Manhattan. It's believed that millions of years ago Georgia's sea islands were once part of the continent. Gradually worn down and cut off from the mainland, they have become a front line in the ongoing battle between land and water. On Cumberland, wind and surf constantly shape and reshape the mostly unsheltered, unjettied shoreline and the fragile, rolling dunes. With the exception of these dunes, the land is flat, and in many places the beach seems to extend to the horizon.

Not far behind the dunes, life has taken root in a rich maritime forest. Pines, cedars, hawthorns, hollies, dogwoods, junipers, and magnolias stand amid the moss-crowned royalty of live oaks. In some places, however, dunes have migrated back, and the line between dune and forest is blurred in a tangle of sand and greenery. Nevertheless, dunes are such successful barriers to the sea that rainwater has formed ponds and even a freshwater lake in basins behind them.

On the back side of the island, sediment buildup has created salt marshes, which incubate marine life. Cordgrass grows from soil that is richer in nutrients than the richest Iowa farmland. Tidal creeks slither through the tall marsh grasses, and life pulses with the rise and fall of the tides.

FLORA AND FAUNA Cumberland's various habitats are home to an almost endless array of plant and animal life. Visitors are practically guaranteed to see feral horses, deer, and other exotic and native wildlife any time of year. So abundant are the deer and hogs that organized hunts and other measures must be taken each year to ensure that they don't overgraze and overpopulate the island. Turkeys, raccoons, and armadillos thrive in the extensive forests and clearings. Alligators can be spotted in small pools in isolated spots. On the beach, shorebirds, such as sandpipers, pelicans, and seagulls, feast in the unusually calm surf, and oysters, clams, crabs, and shrimp are just some of the valuable sea life living and maturing in Cumberland's salt marshes.

Live oaks, draped with Spanish moss and intertwined with wild grapevines, dominate the island's vegetation. Lower to the ground, palmettos spread their fan-shape fronds beside every trail and road, dotting the land well into the backcountry. Pine trees tower where oaks have not taken root, and in the saltier ground, marsh grass thrives where no other vegetation can even survive.

WHEN TO GO The same subtropical climate that supports Cumberland's rich vegetation makes it almost unbearably hot and humid in the summer, when average high temperatures are in the 90s. March, April, and May, when daytime temperatures are in the mid-80s, are the ideal months for visiting Cumberland; they're also the most popular, so reservations must be made well in advance. Winter is the least crowded season. Temperatures are mild; the average low for January is a breezy 44°F. Fall is pleasant, with daytime temperatures in the 70s, cooling to 50s–60s in the evenings.

WHAT TO PACK A trip to Cumberland, whether for one or many days, requires careful planning, since any man-made comfort must be brought with you. Whatever else you take, be sure you include bug spray. Mosquitoes, ticks, and other biting insects thrive in the forests and dunes, but proper protection can keep them from feeding on you. Locals have found that Avon's Skin-So-Soft can be very effective against "sand gnats" and other pests. Small bottles of the strong-smelling bath oil can be purchased at the visitor's center in St. Marys for about a dollar. Warmer months bring ticks, which carry Lyme disease and other maladies. To help avoid them, spray insect repellent on pant legs and shoes, and stay on cleared trails.

Since ferry service limits arrival and departure times, you'll probably be on the island for at least a day. Wear comfortable clothes and shoes, and bring sunblock. Sudden weather changes necessitate a windbreaker or light rain gear. Though overpacking can make for a heavy burden, bringing along water bottles and a small cooler with a picnic lunch or small snack is strongly recommended. Don't forget a camera and lots of film, as the scenery and wildlife almost always prove breathtaking.

Campers should also keep the island's limited facilities in mind. Ground fires are prohibited in the primitive campgrounds. Sea Camp sites have fire grates designated for campfires, so bring a camping stove. First-aid kits and flashlights are also suggested. Rope is needed to suspend packs and litter bags, as raccoons and other scavengers frequently make off with the supplies of unwary visitors.

GENERAL STORES St. Marys, site of the ferry landing, offers the nearest shopping—a range of grocery, hardware, and convenience stores are within short driving distance of the ferry dock. **Kings Bay Shopping Center** (2603 Osborne St., tel. 912/882–1877), only 5 miles away on Route 40, has more than 40 stores, including a **Piggly Wiggly** grocery store (tel. 912/882–6014), a **Belk Hudson** department store (tel. 912/882–1900), and a **Wal-Mart** (tel. 912/882–0772).

ARRIVING AND DEPARTING **By Boat.** The only way to reach Cumberland Island is by boat. A private **passenger ferry** (for reservations, tel. 912/882–4335) travels from St. Marys, along the St. Marys River and Cumberland Sound, stopping at each of the island's two public docks, Sea Camp and Dungeness. The docks are about a mile apart at the southern end of Cumberland. The *Cumberland Queen* runs daily March 15 to October 1 and Thursday through Monday the remainder of the year. Boats depart St. Marys at 9 and 11:45, returning from Cumberland at 10:15, 2:45 (Wednesday through Saturday of peak seasons only), and 4:45. The trip to Dungeness dock takes about 45 minutes each way, about 10 minutes longer for Sea Camp dock, and no pets or bicycles are allowed. A longer trip to Plum Orchard mansion is offered on Sunday (*see* Guided Tours *in* Exploring, *below*).

The one commercial vendor licensed to transport visitors and cargo to Cumberland is **Lang's Seafood** (100 E. St. Marys St., tel. 912/882–4452, fax 912/882–6292). A roundtrip charter from St. Marys costs $65 for up to four people, plus $10 for each additional passenger and $5 for each bicycle. Arrival and departure times can be arranged and do not have to be on the same day. The small boat takes only about 15 minutes for the trip.

By Plane. The nearest commercial airport is **Jacksonville International Airport** in Florida, 30 miles south of St. Marys on I-95. It's roughly a one-hour drive to the ferry station.

Car rentals at the airport are available through **Avis** (tel. 904/741–2327 or 800/331–1212), **Budget** (tel. 904/720–0246 or 800/527–0700), **Dollar** (tel. 904/741–4614 or 800/800–4000), **Hertz** (tel. 904/741–2151 or 800/654–3131), and **National** (tel. 904/741–4580 or 800/328–4567).

By Car and RV. Whether you're coming from Jacksonville, 30 miles to the south, or Savannah, about 100 miles north, take I–95 to Exit 2, the St. Marys exit. Then head east for 8 miles on Route 40 to the waterfront. From the Okefenokee Swamp National Wildlife Refuge, take Route 40 east for about 25 miles from Folkston to St. Marys.

By Train. Jacksonville, Florida, also has the nearest train depot. **Amtrak** (tel. 800/872–7245) service runs daily from points along the East Coast and three days a week from the West Coast. The station is 6 miles northwest of downtown Jacksonville, about 30 miles from St. Marys.

By Bus. Greyhound Lines (tel. 912/729–4820 or 800/231–2222) serves Kingsland, about 11 miles west of St. Marys. There is no car rental nearby, but **Kings Bay Taxi** (tel. 912/673–6900, $12–$14 first person, $1 each additional) offers taxi service to the ferry dock.

EXPLORING

Be prepared for a day of walking and casual exploration on Cumberland's beaches and foot trails. Take it nice and easy. Wildlife and scenery are everywhere, and there aren't many prescribed sights to clutter your itinerary. The 1-mile "Footsteps Tour" and the 3-mile walking tour (*see* Guided Tours *and* Nature Trails and Short Walks, *below*) include a variety of natural and historic sights, but neither covers more than a small sampling of what the island has to offer. Because of ferry schedules, longer hikes generally require backpacking and camping, but the farther in you trek, the more isolation and unspoiled scenery you can enjoy. Allow two to three days to hike the 18-mile length of the island. It is possible to make the 10-mile hike to the northernmost campsite in a single day.

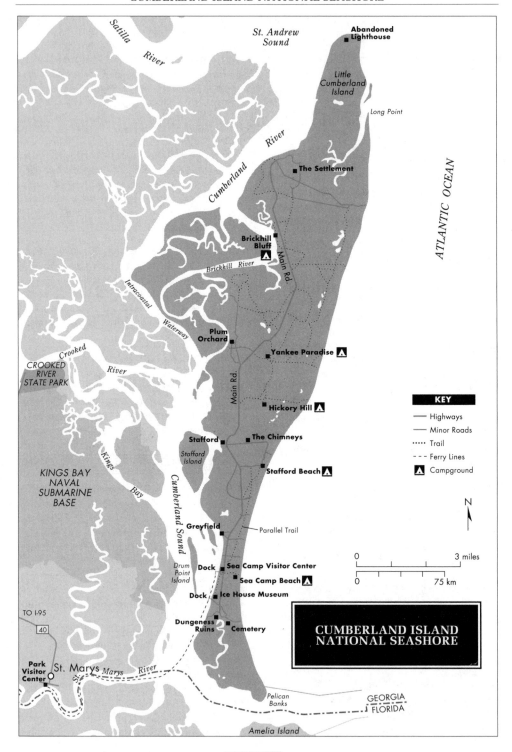

Satilla River

St. Andrew Sound

Abandoned Lighthouse

Little Cumberland Island

Long Point

Cumberland River

ATLANTIC OCEAN

The Settlement

Brickhill Bluff

Brickhill River

Main Rd.

Intracoastal Waterway

Plum Orchard

Yankee Paradise

Crooked River

CROOKED RIVER STATE PARK

Main Rd.

Hickory Hill

Stafford

Stafford Island

The Chimneys

Kings Bay

KINGS BAY NAVAL SUBMARINE BASE

Stafford Beach

KEY
⋯⋯ Highways
—— Minor Roads
⋯⋯⋯ Trail
– – – Ferry Lines
▲ Campground

N

Cumberland Sound

Greyfield

Parallel Trail

0 — 3 miles
0 — 75 km

Drum Point Island

Dock

Sea Camp Visitor Center

Sea Camp Beach

Dock

Ice House Museum

TO I-95

40

Dungeness Ruins

Cemetery

Park Visitor Center

St. Marys

Marys River

St. Marys River

CUMBERLAND ISLAND NATIONAL SEASHORE

Pelican Banks

GEORGIA
FLORIDA

Amelia Island

Bicycles let you cover more ground in less time, but it's not easy to get one on the island.

THE BEST IN ONE DAY Since the ferry docks are on the south end of the island, you are pretty much restricted to this area by time and distance. Start at the Dungeness dock and take the Footsteps Tour (*see* Guided Tours *and* Nature Trails and Short Walks, *below*) with or without a guide. The remainder of the day can quickly slip away walking on the beach, gathering seashells, fishing, swimming, or just sunning yourself. Then, walk up the beach to the trail leading to the Sea Camp dock and catch the ferry back.

ORIENTATION PROGRAMS A brief orientation lecture is given on the park service ferry. The emphasis is on catching the boat at the end of the day. A 10-minute video about Cumberland is available upon request at the visitor's center in St. Marys. The video offers a good overview of the island's offerings and is worth asking for. It isn't shown during busy seasons, when the small visitor's center is crowded.

GUIDED TOURS The park service offers daily guided tours of Cumberland's historic district. Led by a ranger, the **Footsteps Tour** includes stops at the Dungeness ruins and the Greene-Miller cemetery. It usually starts from the Dungeness dock when the ferry arrives and offers a good look at some of the island's most memorable sights. The tour is free and open to all visitors.

HISTORIC BUILDINGS AND SITES At the Dungeness dock, the **Ice-House Museum** offers a variety of artifacts—from Native American pottery shards to Spanish coins to Carnegie china—that chronicle people's attempt to civilize Cumberland. The building once held tons of ice shipped in from the North for the Carnegie family, but today its lack of air-conditioning offers little relief from the summer heat. The one-room museum is free, self-guiding, and open daily 8:30–4:30.

The **Dungeness ruins** are all that remain of several attempts to build a large mansion on the south end of the island. First, General James Oglethorpe constructed a hunting lodge, named after the duke of Cumberland. General Nathaniel Greene ordered his home built on the same site. Though he didn't live to see it, his wife, Catherine Littlefield Greene, had it completed according to his plans—that is, all except several of the fourth-story rooms. She had a superstition that a finished house would cause bad luck to its inhabitants. Despite her precautions, this home also burned. Thomas Carnegie built the last and largest Dungeness just beside the ruins; but in 1959 it, too, caught fire, and today its large, overgrown walls are a reminder of nature's victory over human encroachment.

Near the Dungeness ruins is the **Greene-Miller cemetery,** a small family plot enclosed by a tabby fence. The oak-shaded cemetery includes the original gravestone of General Henry "Light-Horse Harry" Lee, erected by his son, General Robert E. Lee. The elder general was on his way home to Virginia after having lived in the West Indies. Because of illness he interrupted his journey, stopping on Cumberland to visit old friends, members of the Greene family. Lee died shortly after his arrival. Legend has it that the bamboo now growing on the island originated with a single stalk he brought from the West Indies. The general's remains have since been relocated to Washington and Lee University to lie beside his son's.

Constructed in the late 1800s as a wedding present from Lucy Carnegie to her son, **Plum Orchard mansion** is now owned by the National Park Service. Though the 30-room Georgian Revival–style home's exterior was recently refurbished, many of the rooms remain empty and unrestored. The house is just north of the Yankee Paradise campsite and can be reached by foot.

The dozen or so bare chimneys marking Cumberland's once-busy slave quarters are known simply as **the Chimneys.** Located at the island's midsection, near Stafford mansion, they are more than 5 miles from the Dungeness dock. Backpackers can swing by the sight on their way to Hickory Hill or more northern campsites. The story goes that these homes were burned by planters after the Civil War to force the freed slaves off the island. With no other remnants of the houses that once stood, the smokestacks are stirring reminders of Cumberland's plantation era.

NATURE TRAILS AND SHORT WALKS Although there are many trails on Cumberland, virtually the only choice for one day is the self-guiding trail marked with signposts that leads from the Dungeness dock to the ruins and beach (this is the same route taken on the ranger-led Footsteps Tour). This well-marked path is flat and mostly shaded, making it an easy walk for almost anyone. It takes about an hour for the 1-mile tour.

For those wanting to explore elsewhere, the main road, Grand Avenue, leads north to the **Parallel Trail,** a foot trail that's shaded and closed to vehicles. If you aren't backpacking or camping, however, you can't get far before having to turn back and catch the afternoon ferry. Another option is simply to walk along the beach.

LONGER HIKES There are over 50 miles of small roads and trails, and all are on flat terrain in areas mostly well shaded by a canopy of live oaks. Campsites are spread out along the island, and there are few other destinations to aim for. The northernmost trails are only lightly traveled, so venturing this far can give you the satisfaction of being in wilderness areas rarely visited by humans.

OTHER ACTIVITIES **Biking.** While biking is allowed on the island, bicycles cannot be brought on the ferry, only by charter boat. Beach-cruiser or mountain bikes with large tires and low gears are necessities on the sand-and-shell roads and beaches. Even with the proper bike, however, road conditions can be difficult. Plan on slow going on the trails, but even at about 5 miles per hour, bicycles provide access to almost any place on the island in a day's ride.

Bird-Watching. Approximately 300 species of birds have been identified on Cumberland Island. What you see depends on the season, but the best times are March and April, when many migratory birds visit. Different spots are better for different birds, but the wide-open space of the beach commands a sure view of shorebirds, as well as birds nesting among the dunes and shrubs. Gulls, pelicans, sandpipers, ospreys, and owls are some of the island's most visible year-round inhabitants.

Boating. Cumberland has no public boat ramp, but the **Crooked River State Park** (*see* Camping, *below*) in St. Marys does. Opportunities for boating in the area are found in the sound between Cumberland and the mainland, part of the Atlantic Intracoastal Waterway, and on the Crooked River and other smaller rivers. Unfortunately, no boat rentals are available in the area, because the high tides make it difficult to store boats.

Fishing. Cumberland's weak surf makes for unusually good salt-water fishing, and no license is needed to fish from the beach. Bluefish, red drum, and small sharks are among the fish most often caught here. State fishing regulations apply in the freshwater lakes and ponds (Georgia fishing licenses can be purchased for about $3 for a one-day permit from Wal-Mart or other nearby stores), and though there are fish to be had, these fishing holes are difficult to reach. Whitney Lake, the largest freshwater lake on any Georgia island, is at Cumberland's northeast end, about 15 miles from the Sea Camp dock.

Swimming. Cumberland's calm, shallow waters are great for swimming and wading. In the summer there are almost no discernible waves; in winter, surf is slightly rougher. Water temperatures are very comfortable most of the year, with an average of 60°F in the spring, warming to 84°F by August. There are no lifeguards. Public rest rooms are available a short walk from the Dungeness beach and at Sea Camp, where there are also cold showers.

EVENING ACTIVITIES A campfire lecture by one of the rangers is sometimes given at the Sea Camp campground, but program availability depends on staffing. Talks are generally given twice a week during spring and early summer on topics ranging from alligator facts to island folklore. Schedules are posted at Sea Camp.

DINING

There are no restaurants or food vendors open to the public on Cumberland, so plan on a picnic lunch, either packed yourself or ordered from a mainland restaurant. Near the St. Marys dock, however, several dining options exist, and, not surprisingly, seafood is the specialty. Fresh catches, especially shrimp, are recommended. Most of these restaurants are fairly low-key in decor and ambience, but the food quality more than compensates. The I–95 interchange in nearby Kingsland has almost every fast-food franchise you could imagine.

NEAR THE ISLAND **Borrell Creek.** Located off a small dirt causeway, this elegant country restaurant overlooks one of the many rivers winding through expansive marshland. Inside the weathered cabin are finished oak and pine from floor to ceiling, white tablecloths, and candles flickering in the breeze created by ceiling fans. Cajun-style cooking makes steak and seafood, especially shrimp scampi and fresh catches, come alive. *Rte. 40 E, St. Marys, tel. 912/673–6300. Reservations accepted. Dress: casual. AE, MC, V. Closed Sun. Moderate.*

Papa Luigi's. A sign outside reads ITALIAN SPOKEN HERE, and in fact, this quaint waterfront restaurant offers the area's most authentic Italian cuisine. Seafood and pasta combinations are the best dishes, and there are fresh catches daily. Shelves stocked with wines and garnishes provide the practical decor. Though there are only a handful of tables in the small dining room, additional seating is available outside under a vine-entangled sunshade and red, white, and green umbrellas. Despite its small size, the restaurant is much brighter and more festive than Seagle's (*see below*), but it can be crowded with families and couples, especially in spring, requiring long waits. *102 Osborne St., St. Marys, tel. 912/673–6557. No reservations. Dress: casual. MC, V. Closed lunch and Sun. Moderate.*

St. Marys Steak and Seafood. One of the only places in town open on Sunday, this popular family restaurant is not much to look at but offers some of the best seafood around. Wood paneling embossed with seagulls is adorned with fishing paraphernalia. Crab legs and the Saints' Platter for two (scallops, shrimp, oysters, snapper, deviled crab, cole slaw, and hush puppies) are the top choices. For dinner, there's usually about a 15-minute wait, but it can run as long as 30. *1837 Osborne St., St. Marys, tel. 912/882–6875. No reservations. Dress: casual. MC, V. Inexpensive–Moderate.*

Seagle's. Right across from the ferry dock and the visitor's center, this popular, family-run spot in the Riverview Hotel (*see* Lodging, *below*) is simple and homey, with old black-and-white town photos adorning the walls. Catering to Cumberland visitors, it offers box lunches (*see* Picnic Spots, *below*) and a breakfast special you can eat before the early morning boat. Locals say the fried shrimp is the best in St. Marys. Service is friendly, but the small dining room and colorless decor can feel a bit gloomy. *105 Osborne St., St. Marys, tel. 912/882–4187. Reservations for parties of 6 or more. Dress: casual. D, DC, MC, V. Inexpensive–Moderate.*

Trolley's. Also across from the ferry dock, this restaurant/bar plays piped-in popular music and attracts a younger crowd. Decks on two floors offer views of the water. The eatery is especially busy on Tuesday night, when it features all-you-can-eat chicken wings. Its best fare is the shrimp basket and shrimp salad. *109 W. St. Marys St., St. Marys, tel. 912/882–1525. No reservations. Dress: casual. MC, V. Closed Sun. Inexpensive.*

PICNIC SPOTS Picnicking is a necessity on Cumberland, and there are plenty of tables in the Dungeness and Sea Camp areas, as well as at Plum Orchard and along the main road. The best bet, however, is to bring a towel and eat on the beach.

You can order a picnic-basket lunch from a nearby restaurant the night before your trip and pick it up in the morning. **Seagle's** (*see* Near the Island, *above*) offers the most popular take-out picnic. These lunches include a ham or turkey sandwich, cheese and crackers, fruit, chips, lemonade, and cookies, as well as a tablecloth. The cost is $10 for two baskets or $19 for four.

LODGING

On the island itself, Greyfield Inn is the only option, but there are two bed-and-breakfasts and a hotel on the St. Marys waterfront and several motels within a short drive. Advance reservations are usually required for a spring visit to St. Marys, whereas winter, when the interstate is full of traffic for Florida, is the busy season for Kingsland motels.

ON THE ISLAND **Greyfield Inn.** Staying on Cumberland allows you to explore much more of the island, see the beautiful sunsets, and just get away from it all. However, don't expect shopping, TV, or even phone service, though a radio phone is available for emergencies. You'll have to content yourself with reading a book from the library, chatting with other guests, or sitting on the front porch and watching wild horses graze on the lawn. Families often stay at the inn, but children under six are not allowed. Built for Lucy and Thomas Carnegie's daughter in 1901, the house is much as it was at the turn of the century. Guest rooms are not air-conditioned but are comfortable most of the year, cooled by ceiling fans and a sea breeze. Many of the original period furnishings come from Dungeness, including the mahogany table in the small but elegant dining room. Here are served delicious breakfasts and dinners, including fresh-squeezed orange juice, homemade muffins, eggs, and pancakes for the former and fresh seafood, Cornish game hen, homemade breads, and fine wines for the latter. Casual attire is appropriate for breakfast and the basic brown-bag lunch, but dinner is more formal: jackets for men and dresses for women.

A ferry service to the island is offered for guests. Operating daily out of Fernandina Beach, Florida, it leaves the mainland at 9:30, 11:45, and 5:30 and returns from Cumberland at 10:45 and 3:30. This schedule is subject to change, so verify travel times when making reservations. The inn also offers jeep tours of Cumberland led by knowledgeable natural-ists. The safari-style ride along narrow, palmetto-lined sand-and-shell roads covers more than 20 miles of unforgettable back-country and is the best way to explore varied ecosystems and historic sites in a short time (about three hours). One-speed, beach-cruiser-style bikes are also available. However, they are well used and squeaky (making the already difficult roads even tougher) and are not allowed on the beach because of the corrosive salt water. Bicycles are permitted on the inn's ferry, but you should notify Greyfield of any extra cargo in advance. The cost of all activities is included in the room charge. *8 N. 2nd St., Box 900, Fernandina Beach, FL 32035, tel. 904/261–6408. Inn located 2 mi north of Sea Camp dock. 11 rooms, 8 with shared bath. Facilities: dining room, bar. MC, V. Closed Aug. Expensive.*

NEAR THE ISLAND **Goodbread House.** A restored Victorian home, this B&B is within walking distance of the ferry dock. Like most houses in the historic district, it has a comfortable front porch on the second floor and plenty of old rocking chairs, making you feel more as if you're in someone's home than in a public lodging. Each bedroom has a fireplace and antique furnishings, and there's air-conditioning throughout. Since the home is small, it's often filled in the spring and fall. Full breakfast is offered daily. *209 Osborne St., St. Marys 31558, tel. 912/882–7490. 4 rooms. Facilities: breakfast room. Moderate.*

Riverview Hotel. Directly across from the ferry dock, this hotel offers convenient access to Cumberland and to downtown shops and restaurants. Guest rooms and a common living room are furnished with turn-of-the-century antiques but no TVs. For those not wanting to lose all contact with the rest of the world, there's a big-screen TV in the bar and lounge downstairs, but you could easily find enough entertainment watching shrimp boats on the sound from the rocking chairs on the front porch. *105 Osborne St., St. Marys 31558, tel. 912/882–4187. 18 rooms. Facilities: lounge. AE, D, DC, MC, V. Moderate.*

Spencer House Inn. The historic Spencer House Inn, built as a hotel in 1872, has been operating as a B&B since its renovation in 1990. The many-windowed house is bright and breezy, with large porches and verandas. Like all the homes on the waterfront, it's within walking distance of the ferry dock, but in contrast to Goodbread House (*see above*), across Osborne Street, it's larger and more polished. Despite the antique furnishings throughout, the place feels new and modern, complete with air-conditioning and TVs in all guest rooms. Bountiful Continental breakfast is served each morning. *101 E. Bryant St., St. Marys 31558, tel. 912/882–1872. 14 rooms. D, MC, V. Moderate.*

Charter House Inn. This independently owned motel offers slightly better accommodations than the chains. It's also the closest to the waterfront, about 5 miles away at the intersection of Route 40 and Spur 40. Microwaves and refrigerators are found in most rooms. Charter House Inn also offers special discounts at the nearby Osprey Cove golf course. *2710 Osborne St., St. Marys 31558, tel. 912/882–6250 (call collect for reservations), fax 912/882–4471. 120 rooms. Facilities: restaurant, lounge, banquet rooms, pool. AE, D, DC, MC, V. Inexpensive–Moderate.*

Mariners Suites Inn. For a change from the standard motel room, try one of these spacious 600-square-foot rooms with full kitchens, including cookware and utensils. Designed for contractors working at the nearby naval base, the inn has 36 studio units available for single nights. The suites are about a 10-minute drive from the waterfront along Route 40. *2343 Village Dr., St. Marys 31558, tel. 912/882–3004, fax 912/882–6891. 48 rooms. Facilities: pool, locker rooms. AE, D, DC, MC, V. Inexpensive–Moderate.*

Kings Bay Lodges. Located at Spur 40 and San Bar Drive, near the Kings Bay Naval Submarine Base and about 6 miles from the St. Marys waterfront, this motel was designed for longer stays but can be comfortable for one night. All rooms have kitchenettes with a microwave, refrigerator, and small stove, and a free Continental breakfast is served. Since many navy families use them, the lodges can feel like an apartment complex, and the thin walls make it perhaps too domestic. Discount coupons available at the St. Marys visitor's center yield a price comparable to those of the nearby national chains. *603 San Bar Dr., St. Marys 31558, tel. 912/882–8900, fax 912/882–8908. 120 rooms. Facilities: pool, volleyball, basketball, playground, cookout shelter, Laundromat. AE, D, DC, MC, V. Inexpensive.*

At the I–95 interchange in Kingsland, 8 miles from the waterfront on Route 40, are several national chain motels. Most are only a few years old or else recently remodeled, and prices are Inexpensive to Moderate, typically varying $10–$15 depending on the season. The best ones include **Best Western** (tel. 912/729–7666 or 800/528–1234), which offers a free Continental breakfast, a pool, and microwaves and refrigerators in rooms; **Comfort Inn** (tel. 912/729–6979 or 800/228–5150), with a pool, sauna, Jacuzzi, and fitness room; **Days Inn** (tel. 912/729–5454 or 800/325–2525), which has a free Continental breakfast, a pool, and microwaves and refrigerators in rooms; **Hampton Inn** (tel. 912/729–1900 or 800/426–7866), with a free Continental breakfast, pool, and health spa; **Holiday Inn** (tel. 912/729–3000 or 800/322–6866), featuring a restaurant and lounge, a pool, and a country store; and **Ramada Inn** (tel. 912/729–4363 or 800/272–6232), containing a restaurant, lounge, and pool.

CAMPING

ON THE ISLAND Cumberland has one campground with facilities and four primitive campsites, of which three are in wilderness areas and one is near the beach. There is no backcountry camping, so all wilderness camping must be done in designated campsites. Since wilderness campsites don't have cleared spots, you'll have to set up among the vegetation. Camping is limited to seven days, and you'll need a reservation (available by calling the national seashore reservation line, tel. 912/882–4335, Mon.–Fri. 10–2) and a permit (obtained in person from the Sea Camp Visitor Center, located at Sea Camp dock). Permits are not site specific and only 20 campers are allowed at each one, so be prepared to hike to the next campsite if a closer one fills up. That could mean a 10.4-mile trek to Brickhill Bluff if you don't check in early enough. Most of the year, however, only Sea Camp reaches full capacity.

Sea Camp, about .25 mile from Sea Camp dock, offers the only camping with facilities: rest rooms and cold showers. The numbered sites have small clearings large enough for a couple of tents.

Stafford Beach is the next nearest campsite, about 3.5 miles north of Sea Camp. It provides easy access to the beach. Water is available, but it *must* be boiled or treated.

Hickory Hill and **Yankee Paradise,** 5.5 and 7.4 miles north of Sea Camp dock, respectively, do not have their own water sources, but they're served by a shared well, about .5 mile from each. Both are in the middle of Cumberland's vast forest.

Brickhill Bluff is the northernmost campsite, 10.6 miles from Sea Camp dock. It is situated on the Brickhill River in the heart of the salt marshes on the sound side of the island. This site also has its own water source, but, again, the water must be boiled or treated.

NEAR THE ISLAND About 10 miles from the St. Marys waterfront, **Crooked River State Park** (3092 Spur 40, St. Marys 31558, tel. 912/882–5256) offers full-service camping facilities and RV hookups. Its 500 acres on the south bank of the Crooked River include 60 tent and trailer sites, 11 cottages, a public boat ramp, an Olympic-size pool, and a bathhouse. Reservations are only offered for major holidays.

KOA (off I–95 Exit 1, tel. 912/729–3232) is also about 10 miles from the waterfront. It has 140 shaded pull-through tent and trailer sites with water and electric hookups for RVs. About half of the sites also offer sewer hookups. Facilities include a pool, TV and game rooms, basketball goals, horseshoe pits, and two bathhouses. LP gas is available. Reservations are accepted up to a year in advance, but campers must leave a credit card number to hold a site, or send a $10 deposit.

Delaware Water Gap National Recreation Area

New Jersey, Pennsylvania

By M. T. Schwartzman

inety minutes by car from both New York and Philadelphia, the Delaware River forms a dramatic gap, cutting the Kittatinny Ridge into twin peaks. The native Lenape (pronounced *len*-uh-pee) Indians' name for this ridge means "big mountain." Today the ridge crowns the largest national recreation area in the Northeast.

Since the 1800s, city folk have come to vacation in the area. In the early days, families stayed for weeks at a time or even the whole summer. Now, weekend outings are more popular among the park's 4 million annual visitors. But there is still enough to keep you busy for longer: You can picnic along the shores of the river, scan the trees for migrating birds, photograph the dramatic landscape, or even swim in the Delaware, which the park service calls one of the cleanest rivers in the East. Hikers can choose from among more than 60 trails, including a 25-mile stretch of the Appalachian Trail. Some paths offer just

a stroll in the woods; others issue a challenge to climb the area's highest points.

Encompassing nearly 70,000 acres, this 40-mile-long preserve extends along both banks of the Delaware River, which separates Pennsylvania from New Jersey. The park's boundary stretches north nearly to the point where Pennsylvania, New York, and New Jersey meet, and runs 1.5 miles south of the bend at Kittatinny Point. The lower part of the park surrounds New Jersey's Worthington State Forest.

It is here that the Delaware slices the Kittatinny Ridge in two. The notch in the landscape created when a river crosses a mountain range in this way is known as a water gap, and the National Park Service calls this one the greatest in the world. How it formed is open to debate. Some scientists believe that the river was here before the mountains were, flowing along a flat coastal plain. Gradual folding in the earth's crust led to uplifting, but the river fought back—carving a gorge through the ridge that sought to block its path. Others contend that the mountains came first, and that only a shift in the river's course led to erosion of the ridge.

In 1962, Congress authorized construction of a dam and reservoir at Tocks Island, 6 miles north of the gap. In 1965, to generate public support for the project, Congress established the Delaware Water Gap National Recreation Area with the reservoir as its centerpiece. Ironically, the park became the most convincing argument against building the dam: Its construction would have submerged 80% of the recreation area's land. In 1978, the Delaware was designated a Wild and Scenic River and put under park service control. In 1992, the Tocks Island Dam project was officially de-authorized.

ESSENTIAL INFORMATION

VISITOR INFORMATION To find out about recreational opportunities, contact the Superintendent, **Park Headquarters** (Delaware Water Gap National Recreation Area, Bushkill, PA 18324, tel. 717/588–2451). The park's main switchboard (tel. 717/588–2435) is staffed 24 hours a day and is the best place to call. There are also visitor's centers at Kittatinny Point in New Jersey (tel. 908/496–4458; open May–Oct., daily 9–5, and Nov.–Apr., weekends 9–4:30) and in Pennsylvania at Dingmans Falls (tel. 717/828–7802; open May–Oct., daily 9–5, and Nov.–Dec., weekends 9–4:30). The hot line for emergencies is 800/543–4295. For information on New Jersey's **Worthington State Forest**, contact the Superintendent (HC 62, Box 2, Columbia, NJ 07832, tel. 908/841–9575).

For information on lodging and dining outside the park, and other local tourist facilities, contact the **Pocono Mountains Vacation Bureau** (1004 Main St., Box P, Stroudsburg, PA 18360, tel. 717/421–5791 or 800/POCONOS).

FEES Admission to the Delaware Water Gap National Recreation Area, its attractions, and all ranger-led activities is free. Fishing licenses cost $20.50 for a trout stamp, in Pennsylvania (Fish Commission, tel. 717/657–4518) and $15 for seven days, plus $14 for a trout stamp, in New Jersey (Fish, Game and Wildlife, tel. 609/292–2965). Hunting licenses cost $15.75 for a seven-day small game permit in Pennsylvania (Game Commission, tel. 717/787–6286) and $25 for a two-day small game permit in New Jersey, also from Fish, Game and Wildlife. Camping in Worthington State Forest costs $8 for sites with a pit toilet, $10 for sites with bath and shower facilities; permits are available from the superintendent (*see* Visitor Information, *above*).

PUBLICATIONS Pick up the **National Park Service map and guide** to the recreation area at visitor's centers and park headquarters, as well as the newspaper-style "Discovering the Delaware River" for children and "Spanning the Gap," which cover current events. Also available are a river guide for canoeists and boaters showing access points and distances between them, maps of hiking and cross-country ski trails, a list of hunting regulations, and a handout from the park service identifying recommended spots for bald-eagle viewing.

Also for bird-watchers, a field checklist is available from the visitor's centers or the **Pocono Environmental Education Center** (RD 2, Box 1010, Dingmans Ferry, PA 18328, tel. 717/828–2319).

The bookstores at the **Kittatinny Point** and **Dingmans Falls visitor's centers** (*see* Visitor Information, *above*) stock a library of titles on the area's history, geology, and flora and fauna. They also sell bound transcripts of the recreation area's 25th anniversary symposium, which is also available from the park service by mail.

The Eastern National Park and Monument Association, in cooperation with the park service, maintains a mail-order list of trail maps, topographical maps, and children's titles and histories relating to the water gap. Of special interest to park visitors interested in the area's Colonial era are *Old Mine Road*, which tells the story of one of America's oldest highways, and *A Place Called Home*, a history of the Van Campen Inn—one of the park's oldest buildings. Contact park headquarters for an order form. The **Walpack Historical Society** (Box 3, Walpack Center, NJ 07881, tel. 201/948–6671) sells reprints of *The Minisink*, a book chronicling the water-gap area from its prehistoric settlement to the Tocks Island Dam project.

■ GEOLOGY AND TERRAIN ■ The Delaware Water Gap is a monument to water's erosive power. The river follows a tight S-turn through the Kittatinny Ridge; to the west Mt. Minsi rises 1,463 feet, and to the east Mt. Tammany climbs to 1,527 feet—the remains of what may once have been a continuous highland that filled the 1,400-yard-wide gap.

The Kittatinny Ridge stretches diagonally across the park for 10 miles. Along its crest runs the Appalachian Trail. Visible from either side of the river, the ridge dominates the park's landscape north of the gap before veering to the east.

■ FLORA AND FAUNA ■ The mixed hardwood and softwood, coniferous and deciduous forest supports 43 known species of mammals. Hikers are most likely to encounter white-tailed deer, beaver, and an occasional black bear foraging through the woods. The eastern coyote is making a comeback, and bobcats are sighted from time to time. On the water, you may also see river otters. Among the 263 species of birds identified in the area are hawks and other raptors that make a semi-annual migration through the park. As many as 10 to 15 bald eagles winter along the river.

A new danger to the park now comes from a sap-sucking insect, the woolly adelgid, which threatens to destroy the area's stands of hemlock forest. Believed to have been spread to the region by Hurricane Gloria in 1985, it was first detected in 1989. To date, no effective control method or natural predator has been found.

■ WHEN TO GO ■ The water gap's face reflects the seasons. In this mid-Atlantic climate, the changes are distinct and sometimes dramatic. January highs hover around freezing and nighttime lows drop into the teens. July days

average in the upper 70s–lower 80s, but occasional heat waves can drive those figures into the 90s. Temperatures during the warm months bottom out in the mid-50s. From the first break of spring to the fall of autumn's leaves, parking areas are filled on weekends; weekdays provide a break from the crowds. Most day-trippers stick to the short trails that lead to and from the parking areas. So the farther you hike into the park, the fewer humans you are likely to meet.

Swimming in the river is popular in summer. Lifeguards are on duty at Pennsylvania beaches from mid-June to Labor Day. In winter the ponds and lakes often freeze solid enough for ice-skating. Nine miles of snowmobile trails and 13 miles of cross-country ski trails are marked and maintained. Ice-climbing challenges the adventurous and experienced. Bird-watchers may want to consider a trip in January or February, when bald eagles can be seen.

■ SEASONAL EVENTS ■ **Third Sunday in May: Walpack Day** (tel. 201/948–6671), an open house sponsored by the ghost town's historical society, gives visitors the chance to inspect the buildings of abandoned Walpack Center. **Last weekend in July:** The juried **Peters Valley Crafts Fair** (tel. 201/948–5200) attracts 13,000 people and 150 exhibitors. **Weekend after Labor Day: Celebration of the Arts** (contact the Deerhead Inn, tel. 717/424–2000) brings some 4,000 music fans to the tiny town of Delaware Water Gap, Pennsylvania, for live jazz and other performances Friday evening through Sunday afternoon. **First weekend in October: Millbrook Days** (tel. 717/588–2451) celebrate turn-of-the-century rural life. **Third Sunday in November: Van Campen Day** (tel. 201/948–6671) re-creates the area's Colonial period with living history demonstrations and a Revolutionary War encampment. **Fall/Winter: Crafts & Holiday Weekends** (tel. 201/293–7350) at the Neldon-Roberts Stonehouse explore spinning and weaving, stained-glass making, surveying, lace making, and other folk crafts.

■ WHAT TO PACK ■ Be prepared for changeable conditions; bring T-shirts from spring through fall, but don't forget a sweater—June lows in the 40s have been recorded. If you plan to hike, bring sturdy shoes. Rock-strewn trails are common—and muddy during spring runoff. If you plan to bring your own canoe or tube, don't forget life preservers; the river can be deceptively deep and swift. The park service recommends that you wear a wet suit anytime the water and the air temperatures add up to less than 100°F.

GENERAL STORES If you arrive from the east by way of I–80, you can stock up on cold cuts, soft drinks, and snacks—plus western boots at good prices—at the 24-hour **Columbia Service Complex** (tel. 908/496–4124), a convenience store inside the Country Pride Restaurant off Exit 4, 5 miles east of the park. If you're coming from points west and traveling up or down the Pennsylvania side of the river, you'll find groceries, tackle, and bait at the **Shawnee General Store** (tel. 717/421–0956). At the deli there, you can pick up a sandwich for later, or you can eat in either the little country store–style dining room or on the outdoor deck. Shawnee General Store is on River Road, just north of the Shawnee Inn, and is open daily 6:30 AM–7:30 PM, later on Saturdays. Heading north you'll find everything from bait to barbecue meats at **Abby's General Store** (tel. 717/588–6617). Abby's is just inside the park boundary on U.S. 209, and is open Monday–Thursday 7–7, Friday and Saturday 7 AM–8 PM, and Sunday 7–6.

ATMS There's an ATM at the **Columbia Service Complex** in New Jersey (I–80, Exit 4). On the Pennsylvania side, you'll find ATMs at **First Eastern Bank** (U.S. 209, 1.5 mi south of the park border), the **PNC Bank** (Foxmoor Village at U.S. 209, 3 mi south of the park border), and at **Shawnee Square** (Buttermilk Falls Rd., .1 mile off River Rd.).

ARRIVING AND DEPARTING A network of interstates, federal highways, and state routes leads to, through, and around the park from every direction. Because driving is so easy, and public transportation limited, most visitors arrive by private vehicle.

By Plane. The closest commercial airports, both 40–45 miles away, are **Allentown-**

Bethlehem-Easton International (Allentown, PA, tel. 215/266–1946), served by Delta, Northwest, United, and USAir plus a number of regional and commuter lines; and **Wilkes-Barre/Scranton International** (Avoca, PA, tel. 717/457–3445), served by Delta, USAir, and a few regional and commuter lines. Car rentals are available at both airports from Avis (tel. 800/331-1212), Budget (tel. 800/527–0700), Hertz (tel. 800/654-3131) and National (tel. 800/328–4567).

By Car and RV. I–80 runs right through the Delaware Water Gap. On the New Jersey side, the highway hugs the river at the water's S-turn, and a toll bridge crosses the river within sight of the gorge. On the Pennsylvania side, I–84 leads to U.S. 209, which runs north–south through the park from Milford to I–80.

By Train. There is no train service to or near the park.

By Bus. From New York City, **Martz Trailways** (tel. 800/223–8604) operates one local run daily with a stop in Delaware Water Gap, Pennsylvania; they also run several buses a day to the Stroudsburg station on Route 611, 5 miles from the water gap. From Philadelphia, **Greyhound Lines** (tel. 800/231–2222) runs two buses daily to Stroudsburg.

EXPLORING

Where you go will depend upon your interests. Historic sites lie mostly in New Jersey, beaches and snowmobile trails in Pennsylvania. Scenic roads line both sides of the river. You can drive between the main recreation sites and then explore deeper into the wilderness on foot. Three toll bridges connect the New Jersey and Pennsylvania sides of the park. Boaters may want to explore the park by river. A day trip to the area should include a visit to the water gap, a picnic, and a hike in the woods. A two-day itinerary might add water sports or a tour of New Jersey's back roads and hamlets.

THE BEST IN ONE DAY The place to start is at the park's centerpiece, the water gap. Stop in at the Kittatinny Point Visitor Center, and pick up the free map and guide. Ask for a talk on the geology of the area, essential for understanding its ecological importance (*see* Orientation Programs, *below*). Walk around to the back of the visitor's center, where a balcony provides views of the gap, and then continue down to the riverbank. After a picnic alongside the river, walk either the hiking trail to the peak of Mt. Tammany or the trail to Sunfish Pond (*see* Longer Hikes, *below*).

ORIENTATION PROGRAMS The Kittatinny Point Visitor Center presents a slide show introduction to the water gap; rangers give free geological talks upon request from May to October, by reservation only the rest of the year. At Millbrook Village, on Route 602 north of I–80, exhibits provide a look at life on a 19th-century settlement in the water-gap region. At Slateford Farm, at the southern tip of the park, interpreters lead guided tours of the grounds first worked in the 1800s. Tours generally run from noon to 5 late spring or early summer through late summer or early fall. Contact park headquarters for schedules (*see* Visitor Information *in* Essential Information, *above*).

GUIDED TOURS This is a do-it-yourself park except for ranger-led nature walks, hawk watches, and campfire storytelling. The only bus tour is the hour-long trip by some of the park's overlooks on the **Water Gap Trolley** (tel. 717/476–0010; $4 adults, $2.50 children under 12).

SCENIC DRIVES AND VIEWS One of the best ways to gain a sense of the park is simply to drive through it. More than 200 miles of roads wind through scenic valleys, over ridges, and past historic buildings.

The **Old Mine Road** traces its roots nearly to the beginning of American history. Built in the 17th century and stretching 104 miles between New York State and Pennsylvania, this was one of America's first commercial highways. Though most of the road is now paved, an unmaintained section at the water's edge appears much as it did in Colonial days. As you travel down this section's sometimes muddy surface, imagine Massachusetts dele-

DELAWARE WATER GAP NATIONAL RECREATION AREA

KEY
Highways
Minor Roads
Unpaved Road
Trail
Ranger Station
Campground
Picnic Area

gate John Adams traveling this route by stage-coach, stopping at the Van Campen Inn for the night before continuing to Philadelphia and the Continental Congress (*see* Historic Buildings and Sites, *below*).

To get there, take the last exit off I–80W, on the New Jersey side. Drive north alongside the river past Millbrook Village. At the bridge (Rte. 615), make a right, continue past Wal-pack Center (*see* Historic Buildings and Sites, *below*), and make a left at Peters Valley Crafts Center. This leads you to the unpaved portion of Old Mine Road, which you can follow for about 5 miles. To return to the 20th century, make a right once you reach paved highway again, and make another right at the bridge. Follow this road back to I–80. The whole loop is about 50 miles.

For a 4-mile drive to some high vantage points along the river, take I–80 Exit 53 in Pennsylvania and follow Route 611 south through the historic town of Delaware Water Gap. Just down the road, Mt. Tammany stands high above the **Point of Gap** and **Arrow Island** overlooks.

HISTORIC BUILDINGS AND SITES One of the park's oldest buildings reflects the succession of Dutch to English rule during the Colonial period. On the unmaintained section of Old Mine Road (*see* Scenic Drives and Views, *above*), the **Van Campen Inn**, built in 1746, is a prime example of vernacular architecture—a local combination of traditional styles that reflects an area's history and culture. Look for the Dutch details, notably the curved wooden eaves, which contrast with the formal Georgian symmetry of the stone facade.

Walpack Center, on nearby Route 615, is a genuine ghost town. A single-lane country road leads from its post office, at one end of town, to a white steepled church at the other. The town was abandoned during the 1970s in anticipation of the Tocks Island Dam project and the flooding that would follow. You can wander around the grounds, peeking in the church and post office windows, but you can go inside only on Walpack Day (*see* Seasonal Events, *above*).

Where the paved section of Old Mine Road and Route 602 meet lies **Millbrook Village,** 12 miles north of I–80. A gristmill was built here in 1832, and a community grew up around it and flourished until 1900. The village has since been re-created to illustrate rural life of a century ago. Some original buildings remain, others were moved to the site, and still others were reconstructed. The historical society recently added a replica of the mill, destroyed 50 years ago.

APPALACHIAN TRAIL The Appalachian Trail enters the national recreation area below the gorge and runs through the town of Delaware Water Gap, Pennsylvania. Signs guide hikers through its historic downtown district to the river's edge. The trail picks up on the far bank at the Kittatinny Point Visitor Center, and runs along the Kittatinny Ridge before exiting at Stokes State Forest. Along the way, it par-allels and connects with many of the water gap's most popular hiking paths (*see* Nature Trails and Short Walks *and* Longer Hikes, *below*).

NATURE TRAILS AND SHORT WALKS The Ap-palachian Trail forms the spine of the recrea-tion area's primary trail network. Secondary paths lead between the Appalachian Trail and trailheads on the park roads. Alternative paths parallel the Appalachian Trail. In addi-tion there are short trails around other natural and historic attractions.

Easy trails lead from visitor's centers in both New Jersey and Pennsylvania. To find water-falls, start at the **Dingmans Falls Visitor Cen-ter** (.8 mi off U.S. 209), where a mostly shady .5-mile loop leads through a ravine and past wildflowers and hemlocks to Silver Thread Falls, an 80-foot spring-fed cataract, and on to Dingmans Falls, a thundering 130-foot cas-cade. You can hike this in 30–45 minutes.

Three more waterfalls—big, bigger, and big-gest—are at the **George W. Childs Recreation Site** (3 mi off U.S. 209). Wooden steps and bridges lead to the bottom of the cataracts—Factory Falls, Fulmer Falls, and Deer Leap Falls. Paths follow both banks of woods-shaded Dingmans Creek, with crossing points at each falls. At Factory Falls, don't miss the ruins of a wool mill built in 1825. Allow at least an hour to complete the 1.8-mile loop, which is steep and rocky at points.

If you want to climb very high in a very short distance, take the .5-mile **Table Rock Spur Trail.** The broken remnants of a paved road lead past water lily–filled Lake Lenape, where the going gets steeper. At the top, a right turn leads to a bare rock terrace. Beyond the treetops loom the twin peaks of Mt. Tammany and Mt. Minsi. Allow an hour for the 1-mile round-trip.

LONGER HIKES **Sunfish Pond,** a 44-acre glacial lake, lies at the end of a 3.75-mile section of the Appalachian Trail (*see above*). To get there, begin at the Dunnfield Creek parking area in Worthington State Forest, or follow the Appalachian Trail under I–80 from the Kittatinny Point Visitor Center. The route to the pond runs along the creek and past veils of water tumbling over fallen trees, then climbs to the top of the ridge. Sunfish Pond, in a clearing at the path's end, is encircled by another 1.5-mile loop. Look for newly chewed-through tree trunks—signs of the resident beavers. Hiking time on the 7.5-mile trek from the Dunnfield Creek parking area and back is four to five hours.

OTHER ACTIVITIES **Air Parks.** The Hialeah Air Park, on River Road north of Smithfield Beach, is reserved for operators of radio-controlled model aircraft. For complete rules and regulations on its use, contact the Academy of Model Aeronautics (AMA, 5151 E. Memorial Dr., Muncie, IN 47302, tel. 317/287–1256). Or stop by the field and talk to members of the Roxbury Area Model Airplane Club (RAMAC). There's usually somebody around on warm, sunny days, and you can watch as the pilots maneuver their planes into the air, perform aerobatic tricks, then land. It's a demonstration not only of flying skill, but a sight you're not likely to see at most national parks.

Biking. The park service recommends the paved sections of Old Mine Road in New Jersey for a moderately hilly bike tour. Mountain bikes are allowed in the park only on ungated roads. Mountain bikes may be rented

from the **Starting Gate** (U.S. 209, 1.5 mi south of the park border, Bushkill, PA, tel. 717/588–9164; $10 for 2 hours, $25 all day) or from **Shawnee Mountain** (U.S. 209, Bushkill, PA, tel. 717/421–7231; $10 for 1 hour, $15 for 2 hours).

Bird-Watching. Raptors and other birds may be seen during their semiannual migrations in the fall, when they head south for the winter, and in the spring, when they return to their summer breeding grounds. Scavengers can often be seen feeding on roadside carrion. Bald eagles may be seen during January and February. Midmorning or late afternoon when the birds are preening is the best time to look for their white heads against the bare brown branches of the forest. Also look for the eagles over the river, as they swoop down to hook a fish with their talons.

Boating. Forty miles of the Delaware River run through the park, and there are access points every 8–10 miles. Boating information and regulations and detailed maps are available at visitor's centers and at park headquarters.

Canoeing, Rafting, and Tubing. Enthusiasts have been canoeing the Delaware River at least since 1876, and the native Lenape used it for fishing and transportation long before that. Spring is the best time for rafting the Delaware, when water flow is the swiftest and conditions for rapids are best. Summer is ideal for canoeing and tubing—the river is calm and you don't need a wet suit. Equipment rental is available just outside the park at **Pack Shack Adventures** (88 Broad St., 4 mi north of Slateford Farm, Delaware Water Gap, PA 18327, tel. 717/424–8533 or 800/424–0955), **Shawnee Canoe Trips** (River Rd. at the Shawnee Inn, Shawnee-on-Delaware, PA 18356, tel. 717/421–1500 or 800/742–SHAWNEE), **Adventure Sports** (U.S. 209, 2 mi north of I–80 at Exit 52, Marshalls Creek, PA 18335, tel. 717/223–0505 or 800/487–BOAT), and **Kittatinny Canoes** (Rte. 739, 6 mi west of U.S. 209, Dingmans Ferry, PA 18328, tel. 717/828–2338 or 800/FLOAT–KC). Guided trips also may be arranged. A complete list of operators licensed to offer runs down the Delaware is available from the park superintendent (*see* Visitor Information *in* Essential Information, *above*).

Fishing. The 20 natural lakes and ponds within the recreation area are home to panfish, bass, and pickerel. Rainbow, brook, and brown trout are found in most streams. In the Delaware River, anglers may catch American shad, smallmouth bass, walleye, eel, catfish, and muskellunge. In all, 33 species are known to inhabit the area's waters. For information on licenses, *see* Fees *in* Essential Information, *above.*

Horseback Riding. Trail rides through the foothills begin at **Shawnee Stables** (River Rd., .25 mi north of I–80 at Exit 53, tel. 717/421–9763; $18 for 45–60 minutes).

Hunting. Sport hunting is permitted on public land away from populated recreation sites. Like model airplane flying, this is one of the activities allowed within the recreation area that distinguishes it from a national park.

Off-Road Driving. Certain ungated park roads that are not maintained lead to secluded sites within the park and are good choices for exploring in four-wheel-drive vehicles.

Photography. The water gap, with its bookend peaks, is nature's perfect photographic composition. For unobstructed views and good angles, try the Point of Gap and Arrow Island overlooks on Route 611 south in Pennsylvania (*see* Scenic Drives and Views, *above*). A wide-angle lens, tripod, and slow-speed film always yield the best landscape portraits. For a different view, use a medium telephoto to isolate one or both of the peaks against the sky. To get a clear shot, try the bare rock terrace at the end of the Table Rock Spur Trail (*see* Nature Trails and Short Walks, *above*).

Rock Climbing. Both climbing up and rappelling down Mt. Tammany and Mt. Minsi have become popular sports, but specialized training and equipment are necessary. Instruction is available from **Pack Shack Adventures** (88 Broad St., 4 mi north of Slateford Farm, Delaware Water Gap, PA, tel. 717/424–8533 or 800/424–0955; private lessons $95, group lessons $50).

Skiing. Winter visitors can cross-country ski along sparsely used park roads. Off road, the **Slate Quarry Trail** in Pennsylvania (Slateford Farm, south of the water gap) offers 5 miles inside the park for beginners. Cross-country ski rentals, guided tours into the park, and lessons are available from nearby **Pack Shack Adventures** (*see* Rock Climbing, *above*); daily rental $12–$15 adults, $10–$12 children). Skis may also be rented at the **Starting Gate** (U.S. 209 1.5 mi south of the park border, Bushkill, PA, tel. 717/588–9164; daily rental $15). In the park's midsection on the New Jersey side is the challenging 8-mile **Blue Mountain Trail.**

Snowmobiling. A 3-mile loop circles Hidden Lake Recreation Site; at Zion Church, snowmobilers may pick up a connecting 6-mile loop.

Swimming. You can take a dip in the waters of the Delaware at the small, grassy areas at **Milford Beach,** near the park's northern end, and at **Smithfield Beach,** just above the water gap. Both have bathhouses and picnic tables, as well as lifeguards who are on duty from mid-June through Labor Day. Another option is the **Hidden Lake Recreation Site,** just above Smithfield Beach, where trees shade a grassy lawn and more picnic tables. All are on the Pennsylvania side of the river.

Waterskiing. Two areas of river have been designated for waterskiing: 2 miles at the Smithfield Beach boat access and the .5-mile stretch of river between Schellenberger and Shawnee islands. At both these sites, from April through September, you can go up to 35 miles per hour (compared to the 10 miles per hour allowed on the rest of the river during these months). A 35-mile-per-hour speed limit is posted riverwide the rest of the year.

CHILDREN'S PROGRAMS As part of its Junior Ranger program, the park service distributes a Discovery Pack containing a compass, magnifying glass, plant and animal identification cards, and other educational items; sign up at visitor's centers. At the **Peters Valley Crafts**

Center (19 Kuhn Rd., Layton, NJ 07851, tel. 201/948–5200), residents practice and teach crafts. Three-day workshops for kids are offered in May ($40 ages 7–13, $50 ages 14–17). The **Pocono Environmental Education Center** (RD 2, Box 1010, Dingmans Ferry, PA 18328, tel. 717/828–2319) sponsors nature-oriented, weeklong, summer day camps ($45 per week or $10 per day) and weekend and weeklong vacation retreats for families year-round ($79–$149 per person, children under 4 half price).

EVENING ACTIVITIES Rangers lead campfire programs at the Dingmans Campground in Pennsylvania and the Worthington State Forest Campground in New Jersey (*see* Camping, *below*).

DINING

The small town of Delaware Water Gap, Pennsylvania, has become a local culinary center, with at least seven restaurants for only 700 inhabitants. The local specialty seems to be salad dressings: Each establishment has its own varieties, with honey mustard, Dijon vinaigrette, and poppy seed among the many options.

INSIDE THE PARK **Walpack Inn.** The only restaurant within the park's boundaries has been at this location since 1949. Lobster comes solo (two tails), or with steak or teriyaki steak. The Swedish brown bread is so popular it's sold by the loaf, and the fresh fruit pie is the dessert of choice. Dining is in a skylit greenhouse, facing the Kittatinny Ridge. Deer occasionally prance by in the open field outside. The rustic piano bar, adorned with mounted moose, bear, and deer heads, is worth the trip—if only for a drink beside the fieldstone fireplace. *Rte. 615, .5 mi from the Walpack Center Historic District, Walpack Center, NJ, tel. 201/948–9849 or 201/948–6505. Dress: casual but neat. AE, MC, V. Dinner only. Closed Mon.–Thurs. Moderate–Expensive.*

NEAR THE PARK **Brownie's.** The latest in a string of eateries that have occupied this site since the 1890s, this country pub serves burgers, sandwiches, steaks, and seafood all day, plus two or more dinner specials nightly. Fresh clams are steamed year-round, with clambakes on weekends in summer. The Famous Hot Wings live up to their billing, and the 16-ounce steak special will satisfy any hungry hiker fresh off the Appalachian Trail, two blocks away. *Corner of Main and Oak Sts., Delaware Water Gap, PA, tel. 717/424–1154. Dress: casual. AE, MC, V. Closed Mon. Moderate.*

Mimi's Streamside Cafe. In this lively joint next door to the Shawnee Inn (*see* Lodging, *below*) on a stream that feeds the Delaware, there are really three establishments: the front bar, where rock music fills the air; the quaint main dining room; and the outdoor deck built around and under a big, old pine tree. Specialties include Pocono Mountain brook trout and chicken, beef tips, and veal Marsala. *River Rd., Shawnee-on-Delaware, PA, tel. 717/424–6455. Dress: casual, AE, D, DC, MC, V. Moderate.*

Stroudsmoor. The restaurant at this turn-of-the-century inn (*see* Lodging, *below*), situated high on a hilltop, takes great pride in its theme menus. Weekdays is the soup-to-nuts meal, a five-course dinner with a choice of entrée. Friday evening brings an Italian feast, Saturday a grand buffet, and Sunday a champagne brunch and American harvest dinner. *Stroudsmoor Rd. off Rte. 191 (6 mi from the park), Stroudsburg, PA, tel. 717/421–6431. Dress: casual but neat. Reservations advised. AE, MC, V. Moderate.*

Trail's End Cafe. The food is healthful at this cozy storefront bistro one block from the Appalachian Trail. Dinner specials include halibut and tuna steaks plus roast half duckling in sweet and peppery Dijon sauce. Breakfast features homemade granola, and gourmet pizza stands out at lunch. *Main St., Delaware Water Gap, PA, tel. 717/421–1928. Dress: casual. No credit cards. No dinner Sun.–Sat. Moderate.*

American Cookery. At this upscale diner with contemporary decor, you'll find some interesting regional fare, such as Pennsylvania Dutch pot pie and American filet mignon smothered in a Jack Daniels–spiked brown sauce. Other choices range from roast Vermont turkey and Yankee pot roast to Maui and Monterey chicken, New England scrod. For starters, try Louisiana wings, Tennessee corn fritters, or Texas chips. *Rte. 611, Delaware Water Gap, PA, tel. 717/420–0481. Dress: casual. Reservations advised. AE, D, DC, MC, V. Inexpensive–Moderate.*

Country Pride Restaurant. This 24-hour diner, part of the service complex off Exit 4 on I–80 in New Jersey, is a good place to fill up before or after a hike. The best values are the "all you can eat" breakfast buffet and all-day dinner buffet; the regular menu offers still more choices. Western boots are bargain-priced in the adjacent Truck Stops of America outlet, which has a definite urban cowboy feel. Every table has a telephone where you can make toll-free, collect, or credit card calls. *I–80 at Exit 4, Columbia, NJ, tel. 908/496–4124. Dress: casual. AE, D, MC, V. Inexpensive.*

Delaware Water Gap Diner. This 24-hour spot offers a typical diner menu with thick slices of hot, home-baked challah on the side. Hand-painted photos, dating to the early 1900s, decorate the walls. There's a pool table in back. *55 Broad St., Delaware Water Gap, PA, tel. 717/476–0132. Dress: casual. DC, MC, V. Inexpensive.*

PICNIC SPOTS One of the best is at the **Kittatinny Point Visitor Center,** in view of the water gap at the water's edge. At the **Dingmans Falls Visitor Center** and **George W. Childs Recreation Site,** the sound of rushing water serenades alfresco diners (*see* Nature Trails and Short Walks, *above*). **Watergate Recreation Site** on the New Jersey side is a favorite of a gaggle of Canada geese, who make their warm-weather home in and around two ponds. Picnic and barbecue supplies are available at nearby markets (*see* General Stores *in* Essential Information, *above*).

LODGING

From the late 19th century to the early 20th century, at least 25 resorts were built in and around the town of Delaware Water Gap, Pennsylvania. Only one, the Glenwood, remains. As the Poconos west of the area have eclipsed Delaware Water Gap as a vacation center, the town remains better known for its antiques shops and jazz scene.

Within the national recreation area, only a youth hostel offers overnight accommodations. Lodging immediately bordering the park ranges from B&Bs and inns to motels and sprawling resorts.

High season in the water gap is whenever the weather is good. A dry spring lures hikers, a sunny summer brings people to the river, and a snowy winter draws skiers. Rooms can be scarce on weekends. The only off-season is between fall foliage and winter's first snow. This rainy and muddy time is lousy for outdoor recreation. Because it's also hunting season, hikers should wear bright orange vests or jackets.

INSIDE THE PARK **Old Mine Road Youth Hostel.** The sole indoor accommodation is a secluded two-story, 1930s house at the end of a dirt road in the very northern reaches of the park. The common and sleeping rooms are homey and furnished with some handsome old furniture, braided rugs, and plants. Social activity centers around the wood-burning stove in the common room. *Box 172, Layton, NJ 07851, tel. 201/948–6750. 12 beds. No credit cards. Inexpensive.*

NEAR THE PARK **Shawnee Inn.** The only resort on the banks of the Delaware dates to 1912. While the decor is more motel than hotel, rooms are pleasant and clean, and a Victorian gentility prevails, from the immaculately manicured grounds to the expansive porch facing the Kittatinny Ridge. A handful of motel-style units also are on the grounds. Request a room in the main inn with a river view. *Shawnee-on-Delaware, PA 18356, tel. 717/421–1500 or 800/SHAWNEE, fax 717/424–9168. 84 rooms in inn, 19 rooms in motel building. Facilities: 27 holes of golf,* putting green, miniature golf, driving range, canoeing, horseback riding, athletic field, court for basketball or volleyball, lighted tennis court, shuffleboard court, horseshoes, playground, 2 game rooms, 2 outdoor pools, indoor pool, exercise room, jogging paths, 3 restaurants, lounge. AE, D, DC, MC, V. Moderate–Expensive.

Eagle Rock Lodge. Like Shawnee Inn (*see above*) but on a smaller scale, Eagle Rock has views of the Delaware River and the Kittatinny Ridge from its 80-foot-long, screened-in porch. Guest rooms are furnished in an eclectic mix of country antiques. Rooms 3–5 in back have the best views of the river and ridge; Rooms 6 and 7 each have two double beds. The bathrooms have vintage tubs, not showers. The aforementioned porch provides the setting for full breakfasts. Beyond the early 19th-century house, a landscaped lawn slopes steeply down to the river, where guests often relax on a wooden bench and chairs. *River Rd., Box 265, Shawnee-on-Delaware, PA 18356, tel. 717/421–2139. 5 rooms share 2 baths, 1 suite with private bath. Facilities: volleyball, badminton, croquet. AE. Closed weekdays Labor Day–July 4. Moderate.*

Glenwood Hotel & Resort Motel. The last of the golden age resorts in Delaware Water Gap now caters to tour-bus groups, and appeals to a mainly older crowd with its resident social director to arrange activities by day, and floor shows to entertain the guests each night. No guests under 21 are permitted. The main inn evokes the spirit of a hunting lodge. Rooms upstairs are old-fashioned, while those in the surrounding motel units are quite up-to-date. The Overlook building, the latest addition to the property, houses an indoor pool, exercise room, and fireplace lounge. In all, the property's buildings span 137 years. Buses modeled like old-time trolleys depart daily from the hotel for guided tours, stopping at local points of interest and some dramatic water-gap overlooks. *Rte. 611, Delaware Water Gap, PA 18327, tel. 717/476–0010, 800/833–3050, or 800/822–2054 in PA; 122 rooms. Facilities: 9-hole golf course, miniature golf, volleyball, tennis, archery, shuffleboard, ping-pong, horseshoes, game room*

with pool tables, card room, outdoor pool, indoor pool, excercise room, saunas, coffee shop, dining room, 2 lounges, nightclub. AE, MC, V. Moderate.

Ramada Inn. Predictably clean and comfortable, rooms here are also unexpectedly elegant with their mix of contemporary and antique reproduction furnishings—a combination you would expect to find at a place like the Shawnee Inn. Second-floor rooms have balconies. Suites have a king-size bed, sofa, sitting area, and writing table. Continental breakfast is included. *Broad St., Box 270, Delaware Water Gap, PA 18327, tel. 717/476–0000 or 800/228–4897; fax 717/476–6260. 104 rooms. Facilities: indoor pool, outdoor pool, restaurant, lounge, game room. AE, D, DC, MC, V. Moderate.*

Shepard House. A pretty-in-pink bed-and-breakfast that's rosy-hued right down to the closets, this circa-1910 three-story house is one block from the Appalachian Trail. Electric candles in the windows beckon travelers to a wraparound veranda; inside, a chess board flanked by tapestried armchairs awaits a match. The queen-bedded Forsythia Room features a bay window with a writing table, while a round stained-glass window highlights the Wisteria Room. The Tea Rose Room carries the pink color scheme into the guest accommodations, and the spacious Queen Anne Room is furnished with two double beds and a sitting area. Ask the innkeeper if she's baked any zucchini bread that day. *108 Shepard Ave., Box 486, Delaware Water Gap, PA 18327, tel. 717/424–9779. 2 rooms with bath, 4 rooms share 2 baths. Facilities: picnic and barbecue area. No credit cards. Moderate.*

Stroudsmoor. A classic country inn surrounded by cottage units, turn-of-the-century Stroudsmoor sits high on a ridge 6 miles from the park. Rooms in the main inn mix period antiques with floral wall coverings and plush carpeting. Guests can relax hearthside in the lobby's armchairs and rockers, in the piano lounge, or at the pub's horseshoe bar. Rooms 9 and 15 offer four-poster beds and sitting areas; Room 17 is furnished with a canopy bed.

Cottage accommodations are more spacious, but lack the one-of-a-kind furnishings that lend character to rooms in the main building. *Stroudsmoor Rd. off Rte. 191, Box 153, Stroudsburg, PA 18360, tel. 717/421–6431, fax 717/421–8042. 14 rooms in the main inn, 16 cottage units. Facilities: restaurant (see Dining, above), lounge, outdoor pool, indoor pool with Jacuzzi, shopping village. AE, MC, V. Moderate.*

Daystops of Columbia. This two-story motel, within view of the water gap on the New Jersey side, is part of the service complex off I–80 that includes the Country Pride Restaurant (*see* Dining, *above*). Standard doubles are nicely appointed with exposed brick walls. Two deluxe rooms (Nos. 17 and 37) add a queen bed, lounge chair, and drip coffeemaker. *I–80 at Exit 4, Columbia, NJ 07832, tel. 908/496–8221 or 800/325–3820. 35 rooms. Facilities: restaurant, convenience store. AE, D, DC, MC, V. Inexpensive–Moderate.*

Deerhead Inn. This lodge at the intersection of Main Street and the Appalachian Trail, built in 1869, has been known to locals as the home of jazz for 40 years, and there are live shows here on Wednesday, Friday, and Saturday evenings, and on Sunday afternoons; and an annual jazz festival every September. The guest rooms are worn-to-battered, but the location and the price are right. *Main St., Delaware Water Gap, PA 18327, tel. 717/424-2000. 12 rooms share 1 bath. Facilities: tavern. AE. Inexpensive.*

CAMPING

Camping options within the recreation area are limited. The few organized campgrounds are the best choice for those who drive to the park and want to set up a base for exploring. Primitive campsites are intended only for visitors traveling along the river or on the Appalachian Trail.

INSIDE THE PARK Dingmans Campground on U.S. 209 in Dingmans Ferry, Pennsylvania, offers wooded sites for tents, trailers, and RVs on its high ground, plus partially wooded sites along the river for tents. The river sites adjoin a softball field, volleyball court, and horseshoe pits. Recreational facilities at the upper section include a playground, basketball, and more volleyball courts. *RD 2, Box 20, Dingmans Ferry, PA 18328, tel. 717/828–2266. Closed Oct. 15–Apr. 15. No credit cards. Tent sites $11.50–$14, RV and trailer hookups $13.50–$16. 125 sites, 50 with water and electrical hookups. Two bathhouses with flush toilets plus 6 pit toilets.*

The privately held **Walpack Valley Campground,** facing the Kittatinny Ridge in New Jersey's Walpack Valley, is like a little town, since RV owners stay long enough to landscape their sites and even erect toolsheds and decks. But streamside overnight tent sites are available along the Flatbrook, which is stocked with trout spring and fall. *Rte. 615, Walpack Center, NJ 07881, tel. 201/948–4384. No credit cards. Tent sites $15 (1 tent per site, up to 4 campers); no transient RVs permitted. Pit toilets only; no showers.*

By permit, campers in Worthington State Forest may pitch their tents in an open field along the Delaware River near the **Douglas Parking Area.** Sites at the river's edge are better than those bordering the access road. There is a charge of $8 for sites with a pit toilet, $10 for sites with bath and shower access (up to six campers per site); the season runs from April through December. For permits, contact the forest superintendent (*see* Visitor Information *in* Essential Information, *above*).

Primitive camping is allowed in designated areas along the river on a first-come, first-served basis and is strictly limited to boaters traveling a route between two access points that is too great to cover in one day. No permits are required and no fee is charged, but there's a one-night limit.

Hikers traveling the Appalachian Trail must camp within 100 feet of the trail in the national recreation area. You must be traveling two or more days and must move on after each night's stay. Along the section of the trail that crosses through Worthington State Forest, campers are restricted to two sites just south of Sunfish Pond. For other guidelines and restrictions, contact the park headquarters (*see* Visitor Information *in* Essential Information, *above*), or the **NY–NJ Trail Conference** (232 Madison Ave., Box 2250, Room 401, New York, NY 10016, tel. 212/685–9699) or the **Appalachian Trail Conference** (Box 807, Harpers Ferry, WV 25425, tel. 304/535–6331).

NEAR THE PARK A list of campgrounds within a 40-mile radius of the recreation area is available from the park superintendent (*see* Visitor Information *in* Essential Information, *above*). Two of the most convenient are within minutes of the recreation area.

Stokes State Forest, on the New Jersey side of the river (1 Coursen Rd., Branchville, NJ 07826, tel. 201/948–3820), has three areas for tent camping and RVs: Steam Mill Camping Area (open Apr.–Oct., weekends) and Shotwell Camping Area and Lake Ocquittunk (both open year-round). All are just outside the recreation area and near the Appalachian Trail. There are no bathhouses, dump stations, or hookups, and flush toilets only at Shotwell. Sites cost $8–$10 depending on the campground ($7 extra for reservations).

River Beach Campsites is in Milford, Pennsylvania, on the banks of the Delaware bordering the recreation area's northern boundary. Some tent sites have water and others have electricity as well. RV sites are equipped with both plus cable-TV hookups. There also is a campground store and an arcade. Canoes may be rented for trips to Dingmans Ferry, 12 miles downriver ($21 per person weekdays, $24 per person weekends, including return transportation). *U.S. 209 & Rte. 6, Box 382, Milford, PA 18337, tel. 717/296–7421 or 800/356–2852. Closed mid-Nov.–March. 101 tent sites, 5 lean-tos, 30 RV sites. 2 bathhouses with flush toilets. All sites $3 plus $8 per person.*

Everglades National Park and Big Cypress National Preserve
Florida

By Donna L. Singer

hink of the Everglades as a vast, shallow "river of grass" that covers much of the lower half of the Florida peninsula, fanning out from Lake Okeechobee and creeping southward to Florida Bay and the Gulf of Mexico. Out of some 4.3 million acres of subtropical, watery wilderness, more than 1.5 million belong to Everglades National Park, a mere 18 miles from Miami. Visitors can move from the open saw-grass prairies to dense hardwood hammocks. Watery sloughs teem with fish, salt marshes are sprinkled with wildflowers, and coastal mangroves harbor nesting birds and sea turtles. The 100 keys of Florida Bay are home to pelicans, ospreys, and bald eagles; the Ten Thousand Islands of the Gulf Coast, to the gentle manatee. The park is also the last refuge for many rare and endangered species, among them the Florida panther, American crocodile, great white heron, and paurotis palm tree.

The park is accessible year-round. The prime tourist season is winter, when temperatures are moderate, rainfall minimal, and mosquito activity low. Summer, with its high temperatures, torrential rains, and bugs, sees fewer visitors. There is one 38-mile road in the park, with several offshoot walking trails. Flamingo, on Florida Bay at the end of the road, is an outpost resort providing lodging, dining, a store, and even a post office. The park's visitor's centers offer pamphlets and information on everything. The nearest towns are Homestead–Florida City on the east coast and Everglades City on the Gulf of Mexico.

Ancient Calusa shell mounds in the backcountry bear silent witness to the importance of the Glades in the lives of the early Native Americans. Some of the hiking and canoe trails date from the Seminole Wars (1818–42), when the U.S. government tried to forcibly relocate the region's Native Americans. Today, many members of the Miccosukee and Seminole tribes still live as their ancestors did on the hardwood hammocks in the Glades.

After thousands of birds were killed for their plumage and alligators were poached nearly to extinction for their hides, conservationists pushed efforts to save the Everglades and their inhabitants. In 1947 the southwestern corner became Everglades National Park; the Ten Thousand Islands area was added in 1957. Today Everglades is the country's third-largest national park and, as a wetland of international importance, an International Biosphere Reserve and a World Heritage Site.

Everglades is also our most endangered national park. Its fragile environment has been polluted and its water flow disrupted by nearby agriculture, industry, and urban development. Outside water-management policies have changed the balance within the ecosystem, in which freshwater is critically needed in the right quantities at the right seasons, resulting in loss of habitat and potential extinction for many plants and animals. Fortunately, the alarm has been sounded, and efforts are under way to restore the ecological balance.

Some 40% of what is commonly called Big Cypress Swamp was established as Big Cypress National Preserve in 1974, to protect the watershed of Everglades National Park. Another watery wilderness, Big Cypress was initially devoted to preservation and research. Now the preserve is beginning to focus on visitor's facilities and services, including some activities not allowed in most national parks, such as hunting, off-road vehicle use (airboats, swamp buggies), and cattle grazing. The preserve's policy is "use without abuse."

In August 1992, Hurricane Andrew left a path of devastation through the Glades and Big Cypress. In addition, 1992–93 was the wettest winter on record, severely upsetting the mating cycle of the parks' wildlife. Most facilities, such as boardwalks, overlooks, and trails, have been restored, but the destroyed hardwood hammocks, for example, will take much longer to grow back.

ESSENTIAL INFORMATION

VISITOR INFORMATION The main sources for maps, guidebooks, and visitor's information are **Everglades National Park** (40001 SR 9336, Homestead 33034, tel. 305/242–7700) and the **Tropical Everglades Visitors Association** (160 U.S. 1, Florida City 33034, tel. 305/245–9180). There are five on-site visitor centers: the **Main Visitor's Center** (tel. 305/242–7700), **Royal Palm** (tel. 813/695–2945), **Flamingo** (tel. 813/695–2945), **Shark Valley** (tel. 305/221–8776), and **Gulf Coast** (tel. 813/695–3311).

Information on Big Cypress National Preserve can be obtained at the **Visitor Center** (U.S. 41, Ochopee 33943, tel. 813/695–4111) or by writing or calling **Big Cypress National Preserve** (HCR 61, Box 11, Ochopee 33943, tel. 813/695–2000).

Backcountry-use permits are required for all overnight camping (except aboard boats) and may be obtained in person, free of charge, up to 24 hours before the day your trip begins from the **Flamingo Visitor Center** (Flamingo 33090, tel. 813/695–2945) or the **Gulf Coast Ranger's Station** (Rte. 29, Everglades City 33929, tel. 813/695–3311). *See* Backcountry Camping *in* Camping, *below*.

FEES The Everglades entrance fee, valid for seven consecutive days, is $5 per private car, van, or motor home, or $3 per person on foot or bicycle. Entrance to Big Cypress National Preserve is free; however, all off-road vehicles (such as airboats and swamp buggies) need permits, which cost $35 per year and can be obtained at the Oasis Visitor's Center.

PUBLICATIONS An informative brochure with a detailed map of the park; a plethora of excellent trail guides for hiking, biking, canoeing, and bird-watching; and informative booklets on flora and fauna, endangered species, and park preservation are available free at the Everglades visitor's centers or by writing the park (*see* Visitor Information, *above*). Other publications, videos, and nautical charts are available from the **Florida National Parks & Monuments Association, Inc.** (10

Parachute Key, #51, Homestead 33034, tel. 305/247–1216).

A must-read is the classic *Everglades—River of Grass* ($17.95 cloth, $5.95 paper), a witty and poetic history of the Glades by the pioneering conservationist Marjory Stoneman Douglas. For an informative account of the park's natural history, try the *Everglades Wildguide* ($5.95) by Jean Craighead George, which is the official National Park Service handbook. Wildlife biologist William B. Robertson, Jr.'s *Everglades—The Park Story* ($8.95) is a readable guide to flora, fauna, and history. Birders will find *Florida's Birds* ($19.95) by Herbert W. Fell and David S. Maehr and the *Everglades National Park Bird Checklist/Habitat Guide* helpful. So is *Trees of Everglades National Park and the Florida Keys* by George Stevenson ($2.95). The trail-by-trail photo story *Let's Take a Trip—The Everglades* by Cheryl Koenig Morgan ($2.95) is interest-grabbing for children of all ages. For boaters and canoeists, the *Guide to the Wilderness Waterway of the Everglades National Park* ($9.95) contains maps and helpful information on the 100-mile inland Wilderness Waterway, which connects Everglades City on the Gulf of Mexico to Flamingo on Florida Bay. The history of Florida's Seminole Indians and their special relationship to the Everglades is explored in Merwyn S. Garbarino's *The Seminole* ($17.95).

A selection of publications on Big Cypress National Preserve, a brochure with a detailed map of the park, and a video are all available at the Visitor's Center or by writing the preserve (*see* Visitor Information, *above*). In addition, the park service publishes the biannual *National Parks and Preserves of South Florida*, which contains information on Everglades and Big Cypress as well as Biscayne and Dry Tortugas national parks.

GEOLOGY AND TERRAIN The Everglades is really a shallow, freshwater river 50 miles wide and 6 inches deep that is slowly moving south. During the summer months as much as 93% of the park can be underwater. A patchwork of six distinct ecosystems, the park boasts vast expanses of freshwater saw-grass prairies punctuated by tropical hardwood hammocks (tree islands), pinelands, thickets of willows in deeper freshwater areas called "sloughs," cypress-tree islands, and coastal prairies and mangrove swamps. The Ten Thousand Islands region along the Gulf Coast is a labyrinth of passages, channels, tide-swept islets, mud shallows, and oyster bars where freshwater from the Barron River and salt water from the gulf intermingle in Chokoloskee Bay.

The gently sloping, mostly level landscape was once an ancient sea bottom. As the glaciers expanded, they consumed the shallow sea, and the land emerged; as they melted, the seas returned, again submerging the peninsula. The process occurred at least four times, forming the porous, spongelike limestone bedrock on which the Everglades rests.

The more than 2,400 square miles of the Big Cypress Swamp encompass marshlands, wet and dry prairies, hardwood hammocks, sandy islands of slash pine, estuarine mangrove forests, and strands of cypress trees. It rests on the same limestone aquifer as the Everglades. About a third of the preserve is covered with cypress trees, primarily the dwarf cypress; these edge the wet prairies, line the sloughs, and form the cypress domes unique to the preserve. Looking like bubbles on the open landscape, cypress domes have tall trees in the center of an island, reaching to the deeper water of the slough, and shorter trees tapering to the edges of the island.

FLORA AND FAUNA The Everglades has become the last haven for such rare and endangered species as the American crocodile, Florida panther, manatee, brown pelican, southern bald eagle, and loggerhead turtle. Alligators sun themselves along riverbanks and ponds and at "gator holes," watery oases that alligators have excavated with their feet, tails, and snouts. Gator holes also attract other wildlife, such as raccoons, otters, snails, herons, and egrets. The more elusive, lighter-colored and narrow-snouted crocodile can be seen only around the mangrove swamps in the Florida Bay area. Look for the gentle sea cows, or manatees, in the mangrove swamps and in Chokoluskee Bay in the park's Ten Thousand Islands area. The few Florida panthers that roam Everglades and Big Cypress—the nation's last—are extremely difficult to spot; consider yourself fortunate if you see their paw prints in the moist ground.

As for the park's abundant birdlife, 347 species have been identified. Among them are two found only in Florida's southernmost tip: the Cape Sable sparrow and the great white heron (look for them in the Flamingo–Florida Bay area). Hundreds of herons, egrets, wood storks, and other waterbirds flock to the ponds, like Mrazek and Eco ponds near Flamingo, to feed. Look for the white ibis, with its long, curving bill, especially in February. The Anhinga Trail is a prime bird-watching area. Observe the anhinga drying its wings or diving for a fish, which it spears, flips in the air, then swallows whole. Or watch the peacock-hued purple gallinule, with its bright yellow legs, walk across lily pads in search of insects. Look for barred owls and the endangered short-tailed hawk, as well as deer, marsh rabbits, and bobcats in the hardwood hammocks. From your car window you may see tall, red-crowned sandhill cranes moving through the grasslands.

The most prevalent plant in the park's freshwater areas is saw grass, an ancient sedge, which sprawls over 8 million acres and is tough and difficult to penetrate. Its sharp barbs can easily slash bare skin and thin clothing. Several species of palm grow within the park, including the royal palm, which can be seen in its greatest numbers at the Royal Palm Visitor's Center, and the rare paurotis palm, best seen from the Mahogany Hammock Trail. Such tropical trees as the gumbo-limbo and the massive mahogany grow harmoniously alongside the more familiar willows, slash pines, and oaks draped in Spanish moss. Among the most beautiful plants are the bromeliads and orchids, air plants that grow on trees. In Big Cypress Preserve, look for the few remaining great bald cypresses, some of which are 600 to 700 years old.

Remember that the animals are wild: Don't disturb them, feed them, or get too close. Alligators may look slow and awkward, but they are amazingly fast. Watch for poisonous snakes—diamondback and pygmy rattlers, water moccasins, and coral snakes. Some plants, such as poisonwood and manchineel, are also poisonous. Check at the visitor's centers for the latest precautions.

WHEN TO GO The parks really have two seasons: wet (the mosquito season) and dry (the tourist season). The ebb and flow of life has been controlled for centuries by this deluge-and-drought pattern. The dry winter months (mid-November to mid-April) are the most popular time to visit, since the "skeeter meter" records bearable levels and the temperatures range from the 40s at night to the 80s during the day. Lower water levels make the trails drier and easier to navigate, and wildlife viewing is at its peak. In Everglades, ranger-led activities and special programs are in full flush during the winter—but so are the prices and the crowds.

The short "hump" seasons of spring and fall can be good times to visit. The summer season (June to October) brings sudden daily torrents of rain—as much as 12 inches in one day, high humidity, intense sun, and temperatures in the 80s and 90s. The mosquito population burgeons. (The pamphlet entitled "The Mosquito and You" is worth picking up.) But if you arm yourself with insect repellent, sun protection, and rain gear, the summer season can have its upside. Crowds thin out and the less expensive, off-season rates go into effect.

SEASONAL EVENTS The Miccosukee tribe holds two annual festivals at the Miccosukee Culture Center and Indian Village on U.S. 41, the Tamiami Trail, about 25 miles west of Miami, near the Shark Valley entrance to Everglades. **December 26–January 1:** The **Indian Arts Festival** is a weeklong celebration of Native American dance, crafts, and foods, featuring artisans from all over the country. **Fourth weekend in July:** The **Everglades Music and Crafts Festival** focuses on American Indian heritage and celebrates the many ethnic cultures in the Miami area through music, crafts, arts, and food. Contact the Miccosukee tribe (Box 440021, Tamiami Station, Miami 33144, tel. 305/223–8380).

WHAT TO PACK Bring casual, comfortable, loose-fitting clothes and hiking boots or sturdy walking shoes, and be prepared to get your feet wet (especially in summer) on the marshy hiking trails. If you plan to do a lot of hiking, cycling, or canoeing, pack socks, lightweight long pants, T-shirts to be worn under long-sleeved cotton shirts, and a rain slicker (a must for summer months). If you camp in the Everglades during the fall or winter, be sure to bring a jacket, a lightweight sweater, and a heavier sweater, as temperatures can dip to the mid-30s at night.

Regardless of the season, the south Florida sun is always strong, so bring sunglasses, a hat, and plenty of sunscreen (with at least a 15 SPF if you burn easily). Be sure to pack lots of powerful mosquito repellent. Also, bring a canteen for summer hiking, biking, or canoeing.

GENERAL STORES The only general store within Everglades National Park is the **Flamingo Marina Store** (Box 428, Flamingo, tel. 305/253–2241 from Miami area, 813/695–3101, ext. 304, from Gulf Coast area), which is part of the Flamingo Lodge complex 38 miles from the Main Visitor Center. The Marina Store is open daily 7–7 and sells groceries, camping supplies, souvenirs, bait, tackle, and fuel for boats and autos. Several general stores in Homestead and Florida City, only 11 miles from the park entrance, carry supplies for campers, boaters, and hikers.

Serving Big Cypress and the Gulf Coast portion of Everglades is **Glades Haven** (800 S.E. Copeland Ave./Rte. 29, Everglades City, tel. 813/695–2746), 24 miles from the Big Cypress National Preserve Visitor's Center and directly opposite the Gulf Coast entrance to Everglades. Open daily 6 AM–9 PM, this convenience store and full-service deli offers groceries, camping and RV supplies, bait, tackle, fishing licenses, maps and charts, and canoe rentals. Next door is a tent and RV campground (*see* Camping, *below*).

ATMS The nearest automated teller machines are at banks in Florida City and Homestead.

ARRIVING AND DEPARTING Everglades National Park is virtually in the backyard of the Miami metropolis, and vacationers with limited time can sample the park on a one-day excursion from the city by car. **Metrobus** (tel. 305/638–6700 for schedule) runs on Route 1A from the airport to Homestead during peak weekday hours (6:30–9 and 4–6:30), but it's another 12 miles from Homestead to the park entrance. There is no public transportation from Miami to Big Cypress or the Gulf Coast Everglades entrance. The best way to get to either park is by car or RV.

By Plane. From Miami International Airport (tel. 305/876–7000) it's 34 miles to Homestead/Florida City, 83 miles to the Flamingo Visitor's Center, and 60 miles to the Big Cypress National Preserve Visitor's Center. Super Shuttle vans (tel. 305/871–2000) operate 24 hours a day between the airport and Homestead–Florida City, leaving from outside most luggage areas on the lower level. Depending on the destination, the cost is $33–$37 for the first person, and $6 for each additional person traveling together.

By Car and RV. The main highways from Miami to Homestead/Florida City are U.S. 1, the Homestead Extension of the Florida Turnpike, and Krome Avenue (Rte. 997/old U.S. 27). To reach the Main Visitor's Center at Everglades, 11 miles from Homestead, turn right (west) from U.S. 1 or Krome Avenue onto Route 9336 in Florida City and follow the signs to the park entrance. Flamingo is another 38 miles. To reach the Shark Valley entrance (a 45-minute trip from Miami), take U.S. 41 (the Tamiami Trail) west.

To reach the park's western gateway, take U.S. 41 west for 77 miles, turn left (south) onto Route 29, and travel another 3 miles through Everglades City to the Gulf Coast Ranger's Station. From Naples on the Gulf Coast, take U.S. 41 east for 35 miles, then turn right onto Route 29.

Big Cypress National Preserve Visitor's Center is on U.S. 41, 60 miles west of Miami and 60 miles east of Naples.

By Train. Amtrak (tel. 305/835–1200 or 800/USA–RAIL) serves Miami. You can get a taxi from the station (8303 N.W. 37th Ave.) to Homestead/Florida City or to the Greyhound/Trailways terminal (*see* By Bus, *below*).

By Bus. Greyhound/Trailways makes three trips daily from its Miami depot (4111 N.W. 27th St., Miami, tel. 305/871–1810) to the Homestead Bus Station (5 N.E. 3rd Rd., tel. 305/247–2040). You can take an ARTS (Airport Region Taxi Service) cab from the airport to the depot for about $5. From Homestead, you'll need a bike or a taxi to travel the 12 miles to the park entrance.

EXPLORING

A drive-hike combination is the best way to see the east-coast area of the Everglades. The only way to explore the mangrove islands and estuaries of the Gulf Coast region is by boat or canoe. Hiking, canoeing, and off-road vehicles provide the best access to Big Cypress, since the roads cover only a little of the preserve. Keep in mind that Big Cypress is remote and has only limited services. Have a full tank of gas and plenty of food and water before you enter, since you won't find any there.

THE BEST IN ONE DAY Here are two different itineraries. Beginning at the Main Visitor's Center (pick up a map here), take the 38-mile drive (Rte. 9336) to Flamingo, stopping along the way to walk several short trails (each takes about 30 minutes) that will give you an overview of the park's six ecosystems: the Anhinga Trail and the junglelike Gumbo-Limbo Trail at Royal Palm Visitor's Center; the Pinelands Trail, where you can see the limestone bedrock that underlies the park; the Pahayokee Overlook Trail, which ends at an observation tower; and the Mahogany Hammock Trail with its dense growth. Have lunch at the Flamingo Resort, or picnic at Paurotis Pond, Nine Mile Pond, or Flamingo.

After lunch you can take the Pelican backcountry cruise (two hours) or the Bald Eagle–Florida Bay cruise (90 minutes) from the Flamingo Marina, or rent a canoe and explore one of several short canoe trails in the area. Or you can take the two-hour Wilderness Tram along the Snake Bight Trail (winter only), or rent a bike and cycle that or one of the other short trails. The Flamingo Visitor's Center has pamphlets on the canoe, hiking, and biking trails. To return, retrace your way.

The second itinerary starts at Shark Valley. Take the tram tour around the 15-mile Loop Road (two hours), or rent a bike and travel the Loop Road. There's an observation tower midway on the loop, as well as two short nature trails. For lunch, cross over U.S. 41 to the Miccosukee restaurant (*see* Dining, *below*) or bring a picnic. Continue west for 40 miles on U.S. 41, observing the birds and alligators along the Tamiami Canal. Turn left (south) onto Route 29 and travel another 3 miles to the Gulf Coast Visitor's Center, where you can take a boat tour around the Ten Thousand Islands area. If you are based in Naples, you can take this trip in reverse order.

A good sampling of the Big Cypress wilderness is available in one day by combining some driving, hiking, and a tour in an off-road vehicle. Coming from the direction of Miami and Shark Valley on U.S. 41 (Tamiami Trail), turn left (south) onto Route 94, the 26-mile unpaved Loop Road Scenic Drive. Stop for a short walk along the Tree Snail Hammock Nature Trail. When the road hits the Tamiami Trail again at Monroe Station, double back (turn right) to the Big Cypress Visitor's Center and have a picnic lunch there. Return to Tamiami Trail, heading west again. Turn right into the H. P. Williams Roadside Park, where the 17-mile Turner River Road/Birdon Road Trail begins. You can drive, hike, or bike this trail, which brings you back to Tamiami Trail near preserve headquarters. Conclude your tour with a swamp buggy or airboat tour from one of the concessionaires along Tamiami Trail. If you are beginning in Naples, simply reverse the order of the itinerary.

EVERGLADES NATIONAL PARK

Gullivan Bay

Cape Romano

Ten Thousand Islands

TO NAPLES

Barron River

Chokoloskee Bay

Ochopee

Monroe Station

Oasis Ranger Station

Everglades City

Gulf Coast Ranger Station

Chokoloskee

Turner River

41

BIG CYPRESS NATIONAL PRESERVE

Loop Road Interpretive Center

Wilderness

Waterway

EVERGLADES NATIONAL PARK

Highland Point

Broad River

Harney River

Shark River

Ponce de Leon Bay

Whitewater Bay

Hell Canoe

Wilderness

Waterway

Northwest Cape

Cape Sable

Mr

Middle Cape

East Cape

Flaming Visitor Cent

KEY

▬ Expressways
— Highways
— Minor Roads
⋯⋯ Trail/Canoe Trail
Ranger Station
Campground
Primitive Camp
Picnic Area
Restaurant
Lodge

N

0 _____ 10 miles

0 _____ 15 km

GULF OF MEXICO

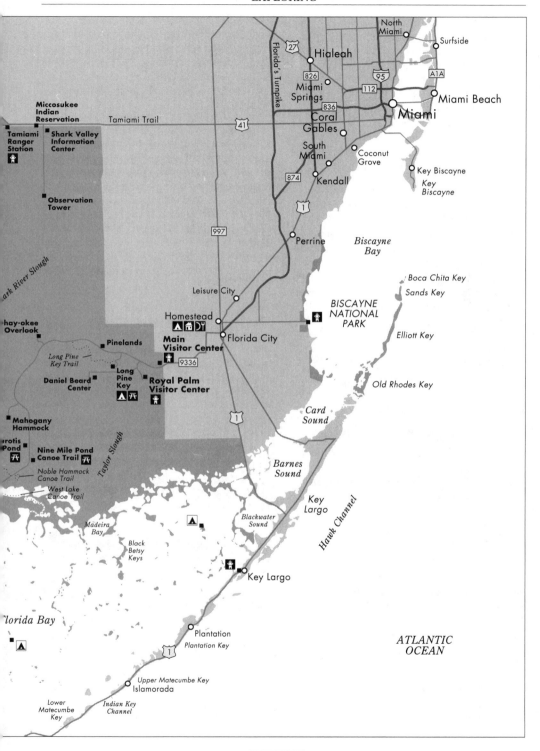

ORIENTATION PROGRAMS Everglades's Main Visitor's Center has limited interpretive materials in the facility that is standing in for the one severely damaged by Hurricane Andrew. The new center, scheduled to open in the fall of 1995, will have an introductory film as well as other pertinent exhibits. There is a small museum on the park's ecosystems at the Royal Palm center, and an audio diorama at the Flamingo center. The 15-minute film at the Oasis Visitor's Center is a great introduction to the flora and fauna of Big Cypress.

GUIDED TOURS Everglades National Park offers free ranger-led hikes, bicycle tours, bird-watching tours, and canoe trips year-round, although the number and variety are greatest from mid-December through Easter, and some (such as the canoe trips) are not offered during the summer months. Among the more popular are a 50-minute walk around the Taylor Slough (departing from Royal Palm Visitor's Center); a 15-mile, two-hour tram tour to view wildlife at Shark Valley; and a 90-minute "Early Bird Special" focusing on bird life (from Flamingo at 7:30 AM). You can get your feet wet on "Slough Slogs" through the saw-grass marshes (from Royal Palm and Shark Valley; wear long pants and lace-up shoes). The canoe trips leave from Flamingo and the Gulf Coast. For monthly listings of ranger tours and information on reservations, contact the park (*see* Visitor Information *in* Essential Information, *above*).

TW Recreational Services offers three naturalist-guided tours at Flamingo (Flamingo Lodge Marina and Outpost Resort, Flamingo 33034, tel. 305/253–2241 from Miami or 813/695–3101, ext. 180, from the Gulf Coast; reservations recommended). Two are boat trips—one into the backcountry, one into Florida Bay—and one is a wilderness tram tour. Prices range from $8 to $12 for adults.

TRF Concessions operates the popular two-hour tram tour at Shark Valley; reservations are recommended December–March (Shark Valley Tram Tours, Box 1729, Tamiami Station, Miami 33244, tel. 305/221–8455. Cost is $7.30 adults, $3.65 children).

Everglades National Park Boat Tours offers several cruises from the Gulf Coast Visitor's Center in Everglades City (Rte. 29, Box 119, Everglades City 33929, tel. 813/695–2591 or 800/445–7724 in FL). They last $1^3/_4$ hours and cost $10.60 for adults, $5.30 for children.

Although airboats and swamp buggies are not permitted in the park, plenty of concessions along U.S. 41 (Tamiami Trail) offer these rides into nonpark areas. One of the best is **Miccosukee Indian Airboat Rides** (adjacent to the Miccosukee Indian Village and Culture Center, U.S. 41, Box 440021, Miami 33144, tel. 305/223–1011; $7 adults and children). Closer to the Gulf Coast try **Wooten's Everglades** (U.S. 41, Ochopee 33943, tel. 813/695–2781 or 800/282–2781), which offers both airboat and swamp buggy rides, as well as an alligator and crocodile farm and a snake exhibit.

For personal guided tours through the Gulf Coast Everglades area and Big Cypress Preserve, contact **North American Canoe Tours** (Outpost at Glades Haven RV Park, 800 S.E. Copeland Ave./Rte. 29, Box 5038, Everglades City 33929, tel. 813/695–4666), which offers tours ranging from day trips up to six nights, by canoe, airboat, and swamp buggy (Dec.–Mar.; reservations required). **Swampland Airboat Tours** (Box 619, Everglades City 33929, tel. 813/695–2700 or 800/344–2740) also offers personalized tours of the Everglades or Big Cypress, starting at $60 per hour for one to three people; reservations are required.

SCENIC DRIVES AND VIEWS The **Main Road to Flamingo** (Rte. 9336) from the Main Visitor's Center in Everglades traverses six distinct ecosystems in its 38 miles. You'll drive through a sea of sharp-toothed saw grass with islands of dwarf cypress forests and the taller, denser hardwood hammocks of live oak, mahogany, and gumbo-limbo. Look for the ecotone, or transition zone, between saw-grass prairie and salt water–loving mangrove forests as you get closer to Flamingo. Interpretive placards en route will help you understand this diverse wilderness. Be sure to stop at one of the ponds (Mrazek, Nine

Mile, Eco) in the early morning or late afternoon to view the hundreds of wading birds gathered to feed. And keep a sharp eye out for wildlife.

The 80-mile stretch of the **Tamiami Trail** (U.S. 41) crosses the Everglades and Big Cypress Preserve. The canal that parallels the road attracts flocks of wading birds (especially in winter), and alligators can frequently be seen sunning themselves along the rocky banks. You will pass through a variegated landscape of wet prairies, sloughs and marshlands, and hardwood hammocks.

The **Loop Road Scenic Drive** (Rte. 94) in Big Cypress is a single-lane road with unimproved surface—and lots of potholes. This is a good drive for viewing such hard-to-see animals as deer, otters, and wild turkeys, as well as wood storks and red-cockaded woodpeckers. The **Turner River Road/Birdon Road Drive** is a U-shaped trail of graded dirt (rough riding), ideal for viewing the wildflowers that periodically flood the grass prairie (especially in the rainy season), besides slash pine islands and bald cypress stands.

NATURE TRAILS AND SHORT WALKS The **Anhinga Trail** (.5 mile; 30 minutes) at the Royal Palm Visitor's Center is one of the nation's best wildlife-viewing trails. A combination of pavement and boardwalk, it cuts through the Taylor Slough—a marshy river that's home to alligators, turtles, marsh rabbits, anhingas, herons, purple gallinules, and hundreds of fish. Scan the saw grass for the white jagged arms of the swamp lily.

In contrast, the **Gumbo-Limbo Trail** (.5 mile), which also originates at Royal Palm, meanders through a shaded hammock of royal palms, wild coffee, gumbo-limbo, lush ferns, and orchids. The colorful gumbo-limbo has been called the "tourist tree" because its peeling red bark resembles a visitor who's stayed out in the Florida sun too long.

The **Pahayokee Overlook Trail** (.25 mile; 15–30 minutes), 9 miles south of Royal Palm on the main road, ends at an observation tower, from which you can see a sweeping vista. Look for indigo snakes, vultures, and red-shouldered hawks among the wildlife in this area.

The **Mahogany Hammock Trail** (.25 mile), 7 miles south of Pahayokee on the main road, leads you into a cool, dark hardwood hammock. On this boardwalk trail you'll see the largest living mahogany tree in the United States, as well as huge mahogany and palm trees that were toppled like matchsticks by Hurricane Donna's 180-mile-per-hour winds in 1960. Look carefully in the trees for the tiny, jewel-hued Liguus tree snails.

Another 11 miles on the main road will bring you to the **West Lake Trail** (.25 mile), which winds through a mangrove forest along the edge of a large, brackish lake. Here you can see the four types of mangroves—red, black, white, and buttonwood—that thrive in the saltier water near Florida Bay and protect the state's fragile coastline.

The **Bayshore Loop** (2 miles) begins at the rear of Loop C in the Flamingo campground and veers left at the trail junction to the bay. It takes you along the Florida Bay shoreline, where you can look for remnants of the old fishing village of the 1800s.

LONGER HIKES Longer hikes in the Everglades range from 4 miles and two to three hours round-trip to 14 miles and one to two days. All of the longer trails begin near Flamingo and lead into the coastal prairies of the southwestern section. The terrain is flat and the trails are relatively easy to navigate. **Snake Bight Trail** (4 miles round-trip) takes you through a hardwood hammock filled with dozens of tropical tree species to a bird-watcher's heaven on the end-of-the-trail boardwalk. The **Rowdy Bend Trail** (5 miles), along an overgrown old roadbed shaded by buttonwoods and across an open coastal salt prairie, begins at the Main Road just before Flamingo and joins with the Snake Bight Trail.

The **Coastal Prairie Trail** (14 miles) begins at the rear of Loop C in the Flamingo campground. The old road was used by wild-cotton pickers and fishermen when Flamingo was a fishing village in the 1800s. Here you'll find such salt-tolerant succulents as cactus and yucca. Sections of this trail are submerged during the rainy summer season (and at other wet times if there is much rainfall), so check with the ranger at Flamingo for its status. You'll need a backcountry permit for overnight camping (*see* Visitor Information *in* Essential Information, *above*).

The only marked hiking trail in Big Cypress is a section of the **Florida Trail,** which begins at the Oasis Visitor's Center parking lot and stretches 31 miles (one way) north to I–75 (Alligator Alley) or 8 miles south to the Loop Road Scenic Drive. Hikers should be prepared for wet areas from ankle- to waist-deep during the summer; feet may even get wet during the winter. The trail is rocky in spots, and as a precaution against insects and snakes you should wear sturdy shoes that cover your feet completely. There are two primitive campsites along the trail, but no potable water. If you are hiking during one of the hunting seasons, wear bright colors and stay alert. This trail is for more experienced hikers. You can purchase a book on the Florida Trail at the visitor's center, or contact the Florida Trail Association (Box 13708, Gainesville 32604, tel. 904/378–8823) for more information.

OTHER ACTIVITIES Biking. The best areas in the Everglades are Shark Valley and Flamingo. You can rent bikes at Shark Valley for $2 per hour from **TRF Concessions** (*see* Guided Tours, *above*) and ride the 15-mile paved Loop Road; the trip takes two or three hours. Rentals are also available from **TW Recreational Services** (*see* Guided Tours, *above*) at Flamingo for $2.50 per hour or $12 per day. Ask the rangers at the visitor's center about the biking trails, and inquire about water levels and insect conditions before you go. For a relatively easy ride take the Snake Bight Trail (3.2 miles) through a mangrove forest. A more strenuous trip is the Coastal Prairie Trail (*see* Longer Hikes, *above*).

You can cycle in the preserve along the 26-mile Loop Road Scenic Drive. The paved road is rough and has lots of potholes, but the up-close views of plant and animal life are worth the jolting. There are also hard-packed roads (designated as off-road vehicle trails) in the Bear Island area of the preserve north of I–75, through pinelands, hardwood hammocks, and freshwater sloughs. Check with the visitor's center for maps of the trails that are best for bicycles.

Bird-Watching. Be sure to ask at the visitor's centers for an up-to-date bird checklist, which notes the abundance and seasonal occurrence of each species. Winter is the optimum season, when many species cluster around the ponds and gator holes. During the summer heat, the best hours are sunrise and sunset. The **Anhinga Trail** is one of the best bird-viewing areas in the park. **Mrazek Pond,** just off the main road before Flamingo, and **Eco Pond,** between the Flamingo Visitor's Center and the campgrounds, are excellent sites for waterbirds. The boardwalk along the coastal prairie at the end of the **Snake Bight Trail** (particularly at low tide) and the Loop Road at **Shark Valley** also offer good bird-watching. Head for the breezeway at the **Flamingo Visitor's Center** at sunset to watch flocks of birds fly to the mangrove islands of Florida Bay. Telescopes and interpretive placards are there to help you identify the birds more easily.

In the **Ten Thousand Islands** region, you can see ospreys nesting on the mangrove islands or channel markers, white egrets dotting tree branches like balls of cotton, and perhaps the endangered brown pelican.

In **Big Cypress National Preserve**, birds congregate in trees and along the banks of the canal that parallels U.S. 41 (Tamiami Trail). Along the **Loop Road Scenic Drive** and the **Turner River Road** you may see wood storks nesting, as well as a variety of other birds.

Boating and Canoeing. The best canoeing is in winter, when the rainfall is minimal, the mosquitoes tolerable, and the temperatures moderate. Canoe trails vary in length and in the skill and experience required to navigate them. Check with a ranger before departure to determine water levels, weather predictions, and insect problems, and file a float plan with the ranger as a precautionary measure. You can obtain free trail maps at the visitor's centers and buy navigational charts at the Flamingo Marina, Main Visitor's Center, or Gulf Coast Visitor's Center.

Most canoe outfitters rent aluminum canoes—mainly 17-foot Grummans. Try the **Flamingo Marina** (Box 428, Flamingo 33090, tel. 305/253–2241 from Miami or 813/695–3101, ext. 180, from the Gulf Coast; $25 full day, $20 half day; open winter, daily 6–7, and summer, daily 7–6); **Everglades National Park Boat Tours** (Gulf Coast Ranger's Station, Everglades City 33929, tel. 813/695–2591 or 800/445–7724 in FL; $20 full day, $15 half day; open daily 8:30–4:30); or **North American Canoe Tours** (*see* Guided Tours, *above*; open Dec.–Mar., daily 8–5).

The 99-mile inland **Wilderness Waterway** between Flamingo and Everglades City is open to motorboats as well as canoes, although powerboats may have trouble navigating the route above Whitewater Bay. There are six canoe trails available from the Flamingo area. They vary from the short **Noble Hammock Trail** (2-mile loop) through a maze of mangrove-lined creeks and ponds to the more challenging **Hells Bay** (5.5 miles one way) and the lengthy **West Lake Trail** (7.7 miles one way), known as an alligator and crocodile habitat. In the Gulf Coast area, canoeists enjoy exploring the nooks and crannies and mangrove islands of **Chokoloskee Bay,** as well as the many rivers near Everglades City. The **Turner River Trail** through part of the Everglades and Big Cypress provides a good day trip through mangrove, dwarf cypress, coastal prairie, and freshwater slough ecosystems.

Small powered boats can explore the shallow waters of Florida Bay, the waters around the Ten Thousand Islands, and the Wilderness Waterway and some canoe trails. The **Flamingo Marina** (*see above*) rents 10 small powered skiffs, 5 houseboats, and several private boats available for charter. The marina also has 50 boat slips and provides ample boat trailer parking and free launch access via two ramps, one for Florida Bay, the other for Whitewater Bay and the backcountry.

Fishing. Largemouth bass are plentiful in freshwater ponds, while snapper, redfish, and sea trout can be caught in Florida Bay. The mangrove shallows of the Ten Thousand Islands along the Gulf of Mexico yield tarpon and snook. Whitewater Bay is also a favorite spot. Lobstering and spearguns are prohibited. Freshwater fishing and saltwater fishing require separate Florida licenses. Saltwater licenses may be purchased at the Flamingo Marina, and in Everglades City at the Town Hall on the traffic circle or Glades Haven store (*see* General Stores *in* Essential Information, *above*). No freshwater licenses are sold in the park; they may be purchased at Everglades City Town Hall or Glades Haven. Or contact the **Greater Homestead–Florida City Chamber of Commerce** (550 U.S. 1, Homestead 33030, tel. 305/247–2332) for information on where to purchase licenses in those towns. Possession limits vary, so request a copy of the parks' fishing regulations. Also, a new mercury limit has been issued in Big Cypress Preserve, so check with the park rangers for particulars (*see* Visitor Information *in* Essential Information, *above*).

Boats can be rented or chartered at **Flamingo Marina** (*see* Boating and Canoeing, *above*). Everglades City has boat rentals, chartered fishing trips, and fishing guides in abundance. For U.S. Coast Guard–licensed fishing guides, try **Fishing on the Edge** (tel. 813/695–2322) or **Capt. Clint Butler** (tel. 813/695–4103).

Hunting. Unlike most national parks, Big Cypress National Preserve permits hunting and trapping. Wild turkeys, hogs, and deer can be hunted, but special Florida Game Management Area regulations apply. Contact the park rangers at the Big Cypress Visitor's Center (*see* Visitor Information *in* Essential Information, *above*) for details.

Off-Road Vehicles. Everglades does not permit off-road or all-terrain vehicles, but Big Cypress does. All off-road vehicles, such as airboats, swamp buggies, and ATVs, must have a permit from the National Park Service.

Information about trails, vehicle requirements, and regulations is provided with the permit (*see* Fees *in* Essential Information, *above*).

CHILDREN'S PROGRAMS There are no specific programs for children at either park. At the Flamingo Visitor's Center, the ranger-led "Naturalist's Knapsack" allows kids to pull alligator skulls, flamingo feathers, or a sea turtle shell from the knapsack during a 30-minute talk. For a monthly activity schedule, contact the Flamingo center (*see* Visitor Information *in* Essential Information, *above*).

At the **Miccosukee Indian Village** on U.S. 41 next to the Shark Valley entrance to the Everglades (Box 440021, Miami 33144, tel. 305/223–8380; open daily; $5 adults, $3.50 children), guides take you on a tour through the tribe's history, culture, and lifestyle, and you see demonstrations of doll making, basket weaving, beadwork, and alligator wrestling.

EVENING ACTIVITIES You can attend ranger-led evening programs at Flamingo, Shark Valley, or the Gulf Coast visitor's centers during the winter season only. Contact the respective centers for schedules and topics (*see* Visitor Information *in* Essential Information, *above*). Shark Valley hosts the ranger-led Sunset Tram Tour (5:30 PM) and the Full Moon Tram Tour (6:30 PM) on various nights; both last 2¹/₂ hours, a fee is charged, and reservations are recommended.

DINING

Casual but neat attire is the rule when dining in or near the park. While there are fast-food places and varied cuisines in Homestead–Florida City, the primary offerings are fresh seafood and Native American dishes. South Florida specialties include dolphin (mahi-mahi), grouper, yellowtail snapper, stone crab claws, and swordfish; conch chowder and conch fritters; fried alligator; and Key lime pie. Many restaurants will pack a picnic for you, and several will prepare your catch with all the trimmings if you fillet it first.

INSIDE THE PARK **Flamingo Restaurant.** Picture windows on two sides of the only restaurant in Everglades National Park allow diners to savor the beauty of Florida Bay. Dine at sunset or breakfast at sunrise to catch the best bird show. The tables are a bit close, and the service can be slow in the winter. Vegetarian pizza, sandwiches, and complete dinners—including such specialties as fried marlin and pork loin roasted Cuban-style with garlic and lime—are all on the menu. Picnic boxes are available, and the chef will prepare your catch. From April until mid-October there is buffet service only. *Flamingo Visitor's Center, tel. 305/253–2241 from Miami, 813/695–3101, ext. 275, from the Gulf Coast. Dinner reservations advised. AE, DC, MC, V. Moderate.*

EVERGLADES CITY **The Oyster House.** Cold drinks served in jelly jars add to the down-home atmosphere at this rustic seafood restaurant. Specialties include fried blue crab fingers, fresh Chokoloskee Bay oysters, and the Everglades platter (fried gator, frogs' legs, catfish, deviled crab). A variety of Florida wines is offered, and your catch will be prepared to order. Large portions and friendly service make for a happy experience. *Rte. 29 (across from the Gulf Coast Visitor's Center), tel. 813/695–2073 or 813/695–3423. Reservations accepted. MC, V. Inexpensive.*

Susie's Station. You can't miss this white, green, and yellow restaurant on the traffic circle in Everglades City. Vintage photos, leather armchairs, and booths with oilcloth-covered tables give this spot the feel of a bygone era. The menu includes burgers, subs, pizza, seafood, steaks, and a tempting cold seafood plate with lobster salad. The Key lime pie is a winner (whole pies to go cost $12). *103 S.W. Copeland Ave., tel. 813/695–2002. Reservations accepted. No credit cards. Beer and wine only. Inexpensive.*

HOMESTEAD–FLORIDA CITY For restaurants in Homestead and Florida City, *see* Dining in the Biscayne National Park chapter.

TAMIAMI TRAIL **Garden Court Restaurant.** This light and airy restaurant opens into the lobby of the Port of the Islands Resort on one side and overlooks the pool on the other. Pink walls, faux bamboo furnishings, and floral prints create a tropical ambience. The food—American and Continental, with local specialties—is good, the service impeccable. Try the seafood baguette with fresh fruit, the fresh local grouper, or, as an appetizer, the alligator fingers. *Port of the Islands Resort, 25000 Tamiami Trail E, Naples, tel. 813/394–3101 or 800/237–4173. Reservations accepted. AE, DC, MC, V. Moderate.*

Miccosukee Restaurant. The murals depict Miccosukee village life, and waitresses in colorful woven skirts serve such Miccosukee dishes as pumpkin bread, catfish breaded and deep-fried in peanut oil, Indian fry bread (dough deep-fried in peanut oil), and an "Indian burger" (ground beef in fry bread). *Tamiami Trail near Shark Valley entrance to the park, tel. 305/223–8380, ext. 332. No reservations. AE, DC, MC, V. Inexpensive.*

PICNIC SPOTS **Everglades.** The picnic area at the **Flamingo Visitor's Center** overlooks Florida Bay and its keys. Bird- and wildlife-watching are the main attraction at the **Paurotis Pond** and **Nine Mile Pond** picnic sites (on the road from the Main Visitor's Center to Flamingo). There are sites with grills and rest rooms at the three campgrounds within the park: **Flamingo, Long Pine Key, Chekika**.

Big Cypress. There are two wayside picnic areas along U.S. 41 (Tamiami Trail) as you drive west from the Big Cypress Visitor's Center. They have grills and concrete tables and benches but no rest rooms. The **Kirby Storter Roadside Park** has a short interpretive trail through a freshwater prairie and cypress stand adjoining the picnic site. The **H. P. Williams Roadside Park** provides a picnic site along the Turner River. There is also a picnic area with grills at the **Visitor's Center**. Supplies can be obtained in Homestead–Florida City or at the Flamingo Marina Store or Glades Haven (*see* General Stores *in* Essential Information, *above*).

LODGING

If you plan to spend several days exploring the Everglades, stay either in the park itself (at the Flamingo Resort or one of the campgrounds) or 11 miles away in Homestead–Florida City, where there are reasonably priced motels and RV parks. If you plan to spend only a day in the Everglades, you may prefer the Greater Miami–Fort Lauderdale area. Lodgings and campgrounds are also available on the Gulf Coast in Everglades City or Naples. Accommodations near the parks range from inexpensive to moderate and offer off-season rates during the summer months. For those who crave luxury and lots of extras, head for Miami or Naples—where you'll pay more. For information, contact the Tropical Everglades Visitors Association (*see* Visitor Information *in* Essential Information, *above*).

INSIDE THE PARK **Flamingo Lodge Marina and Outpost Resort.** This rustic strip of civilization plunked into the wilds is for serious nature lovers. The accommodations—a two-story motel and several cottages—are basic but attractive and well kept. The motel rooms, which face Florida Bay, have paneled walls, contemporary furniture, floral bedspreads, and bird prints. The cottages are in a wooded area where you can wake up to a flock of ibis on the lawn or eye a curious heron through the sliding glass doors. The setting and the amiable staff compensate for the lack of amenities. If you plan to stay in winter, make your lodging, restaurant, tour, and canoe reservations well in advance. *Box 428, Flamingo 33090, tel. 305/253–2241 from Miami, 813/695–3101 from Gulf Coast. 102 motel rooms, 24 kitchenette cottages (2 disabled-accessible), 1 2-bath suite. Facilities: pool, restaurant, lounge, marina, store, coin laundry. AE, D, DC, MC, V. Moderate.*

EVERGLADES CITY **The Captain's Table Resort.** This Spanish-style resort (red tile roofs, yellow walls, flowers), renovated in 1990, lies along a waterway about a mile from the Gulf Coast entrance to Everglades. It has a boat dock and ramp, and the staff will gladly book charters and fishing guides for you. It offers three styles of accommodation. The compact motel rooms have white furnishings with blue rugs and a sink/refrigerator in an alcove. Suites have screen porches with wicker table and chairs, tiled kitchenettes, and living-bedroom areas with pink rugs and blue couches. Villas have a boat- and carport underneath. *Rte. 29, Drawer B, Everglades City 33929, tel. 813/695–4211 or 800/741–6430, fax 813/695–4211. 20 motel rooms, 22 suites, 27 villas. Facilities: Continental breakfast, pool with bar, 8-slip boat dock plus ramp. AE, MC, V. Moderate.*

The Rod & Gun Club. The public rooms, with their dark wood walls and animal heads, and the wraparound screen porch overlooking the river take you back to the '20s and '30s, when U.S. presidents and the Barrymore dynasty came to this landmark inn on the banks of the Collier River for hunting, fishing, and boating. Although the old guest rooms upstairs are no longer in use, there are several plain but serviceable cottages. Cottage rooms are spacious, with hardwood floors, green-and-pink paisley spreads and curtains, and bird prints. The plumbing is old, so be prepared for drips. *200 Riverside Dr., Everglades City 33929, tel. 813/695–2101. 25 cottage rooms. Facilities: restaurant, lounge, pool, tennis courts, boat dock. No credit cards. Moderate.*

Ivey House. At this homey bed-and-breakfast, set on blocks, you'll find lots of local flavor and backcountry expertise, since it's run by the folks who operate North American Canoe Tours (*see* Guided Tours *in* Exploring, *above*). Afternoon tea is served in the spacious living room, and the front and back decks are pleasant on balmy evenings. Rooms are small and plain but impeccable, with twin beds, nightstand, luggage rack, and towel bar. Men's and women's baths with multiple showers and toilets are down the hall. *107 Camellia St., Everglades City 33929, tel. 813/695–3299, fax 813/695–4155. 10 no-smoking rooms share baths. Facilities: breakfast room, small library, coin laundry. Open Nov.–Apr. MC, V. Inexpensive.*

HOMESTEAD-FLORIDA CITY For accommodations in Homestead and Florida City, *see*

Lodging in the Biscayne National Park chapter.

TAMIAMI TRAIL **Port of the Islands Resort & Marina.** With a pink-and-turquoise Spanish Mission–style hotel as its focal point, this 500-acre resort, just 12 miles from Everglades's Gulf Coast entrance and 20 miles from Big Cypress's Oasis Visitor's Center, offers luxurious accommodations and several special services. The resort has its own nature trail, cruise boat, and airstrip. Charter fishing trips and trap/skeet shooting are also available. The high-ceilinged lobby with its windowed tower and huge fireplace sets a tone of relaxed elegance. Rooms are in the hotel proper, an annex, and in courts around the pool area; each is done in a soothing seafoam color scheme. Ask for one that overlooks the harbor or the pool. *25000 Tamiami Trail E, Naples 33961, tel. 813/394–3101 or 800/237–4173, fax 813/394–4336. 154 rooms, 23 with kitchenettes; 5 suites. Facilities: restaurant, lounge, grill, 2 heated pools, fitness room, 6 tennis courts (4 lighted), boat and bike rentals, 137-slip marina and marina store, playground, shooting, 3,500-ft private airstrip, 99 full hookup RV sites. AE, DC, MC, V. Moderate.*

CAMPING

Everglades National Park offers three developed campgrounds—Chekika, Flamingo, and Long Pine Key—for tents and RVs, plus 48 primitive backcountry campsites. The developed campsites have no hookups for water, electricity, or sewage; but modern rest rooms and showers, picnic tables, grills, tent and trailer pads, drinking water, and sanitary dump stations are all available. Camping is on a first-come, first-served basis, so come early, especially in the winter season when the camps fill up quickly. Both Chekika and Long Pine Key were heavily damaged by Hurricane Andrew; check with park headquarters (tel. 305/242–7700) for availability. The stay at all three campgrounds is limited to 14 days from December through March and to a total of 30 days per year.

Chekika. This small, cozy, and somewhat isolated campground, set in a hardwood hammock surrounded by open prairie, was added in 1991. It offers a nature trail, fishing lake, and the park's only lake for swimming. It's also the only site with hot showers. The site was closed during the 1993 season because of damage from Hurricane Andrew; check with park headquarters for current availability. *$8 nightly in winter, free in summer.*

Flamingo. The largest and most popular campground is located along Florida Bay, with easy access to hiking and canoe trails and good fishing in the bay. The marina and marina store, restaurant, and post office are nearby, too. Try to get a site in Loop A, because that's where the two cold showers are. *235 drive-in sites ($8 nightly in winter, free in summer), 60 walk-in sites ($4 winter and summer).*

Long Pine Key. The pine forest and much of the network of connecting nature trails here were destroyed by Hurricane Andrew; the key and campground were closed for the 1993 season. The key is currently set to reopen for hikers and campers in 1994. Check with park headquarters to see what's available. *$8 nightly in winter, free in summer.*

Backcountry Camping. Everglades offers 48 backcountry campsites—2 accessible by land, the others only by water. Fourteen are chikee sites (raised wooden platforms with thatched roofs); the rest are beach and ground sites. All have chemical toilets. Four chikee sites and 9 ground sites are within an easy day's canoeing from Flamingo; 5 ground sites are within an easy day's canoeing from Everglades City. Free backcountry camping permits are available from the rangers at Flamingo or the Gulf Coast Ranger's Station (*see* Visitor Information *in* Essential Information, *above*). Permits are issued for a specific site on a first-come, first-served basis; capacity and length of stay are limited. You can obtain the "Backcountry Trip Planner" from a visitor's center, or write the Flamingo

Ranger's Station (Backcountry Reservations Office, Box 279, Homestead 33034) for more information.

Big Cypress National Preserve. The primitive campsites in Big Cypress have no water or facilities. All allow tent camping; most accommodate RVs. **Dona Drive Campground** (5 mi east of Rte. 29 off U.S. 41) has the only dump station with potable water. Further campsites along U.S. 41 and the Tamiami Canal are **Burns Lake, Midway,** and **Monument Lake.** Other sites can be found in the backcountry. Contact the Oasis Visitor's Center (*see* Visitor Information *in* Essential Information, *above*).

RVs. Since there are no RV hookups in Everglades National Park, RVers must go to sites outside the park. The parks discussed below have rest rooms, shower/bath facilities, and liquid propane gas available. For sites in Homestead–Florida City, *see* Camping in the Biscayne National Park chapter.

Glades Haven Recreational Resort. This is located across the street from the Gulf Coast Visitor's Center of Everglades and is 40 miles from the Oasis Visitor's Center of Big Cypress. The 60 RV sites cost $15–$20 each (depending on season) per day, with full hookup. The resort has a marina and docks, a convenience store, and full-service deli. Tent sites are also available at $12.50–$15 per day. *800 S.E. Copeland Ave./Rte. 29, Box 443, Everglades City 33929, tel. 813/695-2746. AE, MC, V.*

Outdoor Resorts at Chokoluskee Island. This campground lies 3 miles south of the Gulf Coast Visitor's Center at Everglades and across a causeway. It offers 150 RV sites with full hookups for $20–$35 each daily, depending on season and whether the site is on the water and with or without a dock. The campground has a convenience store, recreation hall, and boat and canoe rentals, as well as some RV trailers and motel efficiencies for rent. *Box 429, Chokoluskee Island 33925, tel. 813/695-2881. MC, V.*

Fire Island National Seashore
New York

By Jonathan Siskin

A slender 32-mile-long strip of land, Fire Island runs parallel to Long Island—a battered pawn in the South Shore's frequent battles against gale-force winds, fierce nor'easters, and constant beach erosion. Only 50 miles from Manhattan (about 90 minutes by car and ferry), Fire Island is, like its wealthier Long Island cousins to the east, the Hamptons, synonymous in the minds of Manhattanites with summer shares, beach parties, and sun-worshiping. It is also home to a vibrant gay and lesbian community. But people often forget that much of this bastion of fun and frolic is a precious and wonderful national seashore. It contains the only federally designated wilderness area in New York State and is one of the few unspoiled stretches of seashore along the northeastern seaboard.

In 1964 Congress named 26 miles of Fire Island a national seashore—about 6,200 of its 20,000 acres fall under park service jurisdiction. The beaches and parking lots of Robert Moses State Park occupy the westernmost 8 miles of the island, while those of Smith Point County Park cover the same amount of land on the island's eastern tip. Between the two parks lies the 26-mile-long national seashore, interspersed with 17 tiny communities, strips of private property that span the quarter mile to half mile from the Great South Bay (which separates the island from Long Island) to the restless Atlantic Ocean. These communities, many of which date from the turn of the century, were allowed to remain and to continue to grow within designated confines after the island became part of the National Park System; today they occupy about 1,000 acres. About 1.5 million people visit the island each summer, some to spend a day, others the whole season.

Composed largely of white-quartz sand mixed with mineral deposits of magnetite and garnet, Fire Island acts as a natural barrier protecting part of the Long Island coast against the combined forces of heavy surf and strong winds. Without any protection itself, Fire Island is especially vulnerable to storms coming off the Atlantic.

As recently as February 1993, a devastating nor'easter ripped across the island, tearing away a couple of dozen homes and portions of several boardwalks (i.e., "roads" in Fire Island vernacular) and pushing the beach back a good distance. The storm scattered flotsam and jetsam, and cost the park service tremendous time and effort in cleanup and rebuilding.

To help steer vessels away from the island, the first Fire Island Lighthouse was built in 1826. The lighthouse that stands today was completed in 1858. It has become a major tourist attraction; part of the National Seashore, it has its own staff of rangers and exhibits on island history.

During Prohibition, rumrunners were able to operate without fear of the authorities due to the island's isolation from the mainland (there were no bridges connecting it to Long Island in those days).

Most visitors today are day-trippers, coming to spend a weekend afternoon at the beach, to take nature walks, and to explore the island's wilderness areas. The absence of roads and cars on most of the island, though perhaps slightly inconvenient, makes it a terrific escape, especially for those fleeing the hustle and bustle of New York City. As it has just a few small hotels and limited camping facilities, you'll probably want to rent a house or cottage if you plan to stay more than two nights.

ESSENTIAL INFORMATION

VISITOR INFORMATION Contact the Park Superintendent (Fire Island National Seashore, 120 Laurel St., Patchogue 11772, tel. 516/289–4810, open daily 8–4:30).

For information on dining and lodging, house and apartment rentals, and local sights, contact the **Fire Island Tourism Bureau** (49 N. Main St., Sayville 11782; tel. 516/563–8448; open Memorial Day–Labor Day, daily 9–5).

From west to east, the island's four visitor's centers are at the **Fire Island Lighthouse,** .5 mile east of Robert Moses State Park (tel. 516/321–7028), and by the ferry terminals at **Sailors Haven** (tel. 516/597–6183), **Watch Hill** (tel. 516/597–6455), and **Smith Point West** (just west of Smith Point County Park, tel. 516/281–3010). The centers at the lighthouse and Smith Point are open year-round, while Sailors Haven and Watch Hill are open only from Memorial Day through Labor Day (rest rooms there are open mid-May–mid-October). During peak season from late June through Labor Day weekend, visitor's centers open earlier and close later depending on staffing.

Backcountry campers must obtain a free permit at the Watch Hill ranger's station; Watch Hill also has 25 campsites for which you must have a reservation (*see* Camping, *below*).

FEES There is no entrance fee regardless of where on the island you disembark or park. The only cost you will incur getting onto the island is the charge to park, board the ferry from Long Island, or dock your own boat.

PUBLICATIONS Contact the park headquarters for maps and brochures (*see* Visitor Information, *above*). The best island paper is the *Fire Island Tide* (tel. 516/567–7470), which has news and features on island life and events, and listings of services available to visitors.

GEOLOGY AND TERRAIN The Fire Island National Seashore's wilderness area, a 7-mile stretch between Smith Point West and Watch Hill, looks not much different than it did to the Algonquian, Sagtikos, and Shinnecock Indians who staged great hunts and spiritual rituals here, or to the settlers who arrived here from Europe 400 years ago.

The terrain's most notable feature is the complex series of sand dunes that rise behind the ocean beach. Heading north from the Atlantic, you encounter first the primary dunes, then, behind them, a row of secondary dunes.

Shaped over the centuries by the combined action of winds and tides, these ever-shifting piles of sand are held together by plants and grasses. Beach grass traps the windblown sand and binds the dunes together. Extremely fragile, they may take years to form and can be destroyed in a single day by careless visitors. For this reason, signs around the island warn against leaving the boardwalk trails and walking on the dunes. Thoroughfares in these beach communities are wooden boardwalks. Never venture off them.

Another perennial concern is beach erosion, which is likely to occur during high spring tides and winter storms when wave action, tidal currents, and wind are especially potent. Fortunately, the beach is able to rebuild itself in summer, when the action of tides and waves is at a minimum.

FLORA AND FAUNA The roots of the beach grass, also called sea grass, are essentially the glue that holds the dunes of Fire Island together and stabilizes erosion. The greenish gray flowers of false beach heather grow above the dune line, along with beach shrubs, holly, phragmites, sassafras, bayberry, shadblow, stunted pitch pine, oak trees, and wild cherry trees. Beach peas, found primarily in the wilderness area, yield an edible vegetable that islanders recommend with pasta. The pretty pinkish white blossoms of beach plums decorate the island in the springtime; in summer, the plant replaces its flowers with edible fruit. Salt spray roses bear red and pink blossoms that islanders gather and dry in the fall to use for soothing rose-hip tea during the colder months. Reeds flourish in both freshwater and salt water, overwhelming other plant life.

A short distance from the Sailors Haven Visitor Center, you'll encounter the Sunken Forest, a primeval maritime hardwood forest hidden behind the dunes with more than a dozen different types of trees, plants, and shrubs growing below sea level, including black oak, cattail, sassafras, holly, tupelo, ferns, and inkberry. The term "sunken" derives from the fact that, due to the force of winds driving the salty air over the top of the

dunes, vegetation has been forced to grow horizontally instead of vertically. No tree is able to grow higher than the level of the dunes. The resulting low forest canopy is extremely dense, forming a shady habitat for rabbits, foxes, and deer. One major drawback: There's also plenty of poison ivy here.

Despite its proximity to the most heavily populated section of the United States, Fire Island is surprisingly rich in wildlife. Situated along the migratory route known as the Atlantic flyway, the island is a favorite destination for local bird-watchers in spring and fall.

In the spring, populations of migratory waterfowl including mallard ducks nest on the waters of the Great South Bay; along with the ducks, geese also breed on the island's sheltered waters. Other members of the duck family that can be spotted here include black ducks, gadwalls, and blue-winged teals. Hawks can be observed on their way south in late September and early October.

The tidal marshes on the bay side of the island draw piping plovers, named for their distinctive bell-like whistle. Watch these small, stocky, sandy-colored birds, which resemble sandpipers, jerk idiosyncratically along the beach, starting and stopping every few steps. Often heard before they are seen, these birds, declared an endangered species in 1986, are a Fire Island treasure, their arrival celebrated in late March to early April, their departure lamented in early September. You'll also see plenty of common terns, elegant snowy egrets, stately green herons, and black-crowned night herons; the latter nest in the bayside forests. Four different kinds of gulls, as well as mourning doves and whippoorwills, summer here; soaring sparrow hawks occasionally pass overhead; and hairy woodpeckers are sometimes heard hammering away in forests.

The waters surrounding the island teem with marine life. Mussels are plentiful, and observant visitors wandering along the beach often notice starfish washed up on the sand. The ubiquitous horseshoe crab is difficult to miss. Closely related to spiders, ticks, and scorpions, it uses its spiked tail for navigation. While its durable shell serves as protection from predators, its legs are used to grind food.

Fish abound in the waters surrounding the island, and the Great South Bay is a favorite spot for anglers in search of bluefish, flounder, and striped bass; surf casters go for bass as well as bluefish and mackerel. Sea trout can be caught anywhere.

It is not uncommon to see white-tailed deer meandering through the woods or even alongside boardwalk trails. They're used to people and appear tame, but keep your distance: Allow them to roam as freely as possible. Rabbits, red foxes, raccoons, and colorful monarch butterflies inhabit the island as well. Less appealing are the island's three varieties of ticks: dog ticks, lone star ticks, and northern deer ticks (be especially wary of the last, as it is a carrier of Lyme disease).

WHEN TO GO Fire Island is primarily a spring and summer destination. Two of the four visitor's centers are closed from Labor Day to Memorial Day; ferries generally are in service from early spring until late fall, with peak season falling approximately between Memorial Day and Labor Day. Ferries continue to make crossings in the wintertime, but far less frequently and to fewer destinations. Beaches are especially crowded on weekends, less congested on weekdays.

Wind and proximity to the sea keep temperatures reasonable all summer; ferry crossings can even be a bit chilly. Fog and mist loom often in early morning and late afternoon.

In summer, daytime temperatures range from the 70s to low 80s, falling back into the 60s and upper 50s at night. Spring is rainy.

SEASONAL EVENTS The arrival of the peak season on Fire Island marks the beginning of a series of annual events. Participants in the **March for Parks Walk-a-thon** make the trek from Robert Moses State Park to Kismet every April. In spring and summer Cherry Grove, Saltaire, Fair Haven, Davis Park, Point o' Woods, Kismet, and Ocean Beach host theater productions and art exhibits (contact the Fire

Island Tourism Bureau, tel. 516/563–8448, or check the *Fire Island Tide* for more information), and at Watch Hill and Sailors Haven the national seashore sponsors photography contests and sand castle–building competitions. Many communities celebrate the Fourth of July with parades. The Barefoot and Blacktie Gala in front of the lighthouse on the first Saturday in August always draws a fun-loving crowd, while the highlight of any year for the gay and lesbian population is the renowned **Miss Fire Island Contest,** a notorious and wonderful drag competition held the second Saturday after Labor Day at the Ice Palace, a nightclub in Cherry Grove (tel. 516/597–6600).

WHAT TO PACK Sunbathing is the name of the game: Bring sunglasses, sunscreen, a hat, swimsuits, and towels. You'll need a jacket, windbreaker, or sweaters for ferry crossings and for evenings. With poison ivy and ticks prevalent, it's wise to wear long sleeves, slacks, and socks when hiking. Lightweight hiking shoes are best for walking on sand or along the wooden boardwalks. No matter where you go, restaurants and food stores are usually close to the ferry landing, though picnic supplies are cheaper on the mainland.

GENERAL STORES While there are no large supermarkets on the island, there are several small, well-stocked general stores and groceries selling deli foods, soft drinks, juice, beer, and wine. **Davis Park:** Davis Park Harbor Store, tel. 516/597–6956. **Fire Island Pines:** Pines Pantry, tel. 516/597–6200. **Cherry Grove:** The Associate II, tel. 516/597–9210. **Ocean Bay Park:** Ocean Bay Park Market, tel. 516/583–8431. **Seaview:** Seaview Market, tel. 516/583–8482. **Ocean Beach:** Ocean Beach Trading, tel. 516/583–8440. **Fair Haven:** Pioneer Market, tel. 516/583–8435. **Saltaire:** Saltaire Market, tel. 516/583–5522. **Kismet:** tel. 516/583–8449. Food and supplies can also be bought prior to boarding the ferries in the Long Island towns of Sayville, Patchogue, and Bay Shore.

Bring plenty of cash, because there are no ATM machines on the island. Around the ferry stations on Long Island, however, there are several.

ARRIVING AND DEPARTING On sunny summer mornings multitudes of cars, ferries, and private boats carry visitors to the island, an overwhelming majority traveling from no farther than Long Island or New York City.

By Plane. If you are coming from outside the greater New York City area, consider that MacArthur Airport in Islip on Long Island is less than 10 miles from Fire Island as the crow flies. (You will likely have to make a connection at either La Guardia or Kennedy Airport in Queens, at the western tip of Long Island.) Car rental companies at MacArthur Airport include **Avis** (tel. 800/331–1212), **Budget** (tel. 800/527–0700), and **Hertz** (tel. 800/654–3131).

By Car. To reach the east end of Fire Island, take the William Floyd Parkway to the Smith Point West Visitor Center; to reach the west end, take the Robert Moses Causeway to Robert Moses State Park. If you are coming from New York City or western Long Island, you can either travel east on the Long Island Expressway (I–495) and then follow the Sagtikos Parkway south to Exit 53, or you can follow the Southern State Parkway east to Exit 40. Either route will lead you to the Robert Moses Causeway, which traverses Captree Island and brings you to Robert Moses State Park on the west end of the island, where you can leave your car in parking field Number 5 for $4. To reach the east end of the island, take the Long Island Expressway as far as the William Floyd Parkway, then go south, crossing the Narrow Bay, to Smith Point County Park, where parking costs $6.50 on weekends, $5.50 on weekdays. The drive from Manhattan to the island's western end is usually a little over an hour, but could take up to two hours if you hit traffic.

There are no roads for driving on Fire Island. Park either at Smith Point, Robert Moses State Park, or the ferry terminals on Long Island at Patchogue, Sayville, and Bay Shore.

By Ferry. Ferries leave from Patchogue for Davis Park (Davis Park Ferry Co., West Ave.,

$1/2$ block from Division St., tel. 516/475–1665) and Watch Hill (Davis Park Ferry Co., Brightwood St., tel. 516/475–1665); from Sayville for Cherry Grove, Fire Island Pines, and Sailors Haven (Sayville Ferry Service, 41 River Rd., tel. 516/589–8980); and from Bay Shore for Ocean Bay Park, Seaview, Ocean Beach, Atlantique, Dunewood, Fair Harbor, Saltaire, and Kismet (Fire Island Ferries, Inc., 99 Maple Ave., tel. 516/665–2115). During peak season (April or May until September or October), ferries run every hour or two. Ferries run only to Cherry Grove, Fire Island Pines, Ocean Beach, and Saltaire in the wintertime, and only on a very limited basis (call in advance for schedule information). Fares range from $7.50–$10 round-trip ($4.75–$6 for children under 11), and parking costs up to $10 a day.

In July and August, a ferry also runs between Kismet and Ocean Beach.

By Water Taxi. Water taxis run among the communities on the island. Fares vary; most trips cost around $3–$6 ($3 is the minimum fare). Although it is possible to take a water taxi across the Great South Bay to Long Island, the trip could run you $100 or so. The three water taxi services are **Island Water Taxi** (tel. 516/363–2121 or 516/665–8885), **South Bay Water Taxi** (tel. 516/272–4363), and **Aqualine Water Taxi** (tel. 516/639–9190). It's best to call in advance; even at the ferry stations, there is no guarantee that a water taxi will be waiting for you.

By Boat. Private boats are another possible means of transportation to the island. Docking fees, charged everywhere on the island, vary according to the length of your boat and whether or not you require an electrical hookup. Anyone can dock at Watch Hill or Sailors Haven, whereas town residents have priority at Davis Park and Atlantique. (*See also* Boating *in* Exploring, *below.*)

By Train. The Long Island Railroad (tel. 516/822–5477) has regular service from Manhattan's Penn Station to stations near each of the three ferry terminals. Trips cost more during peak hours, which are 6 AM–10 AM westbound and 4 PM–7 PM eastbound. To Bay

Shore: 1 hour, $6 each way ($8.75 peak). To Sayville: 1 hour, 20 minutes; $6 each way ($8.75 peak). To Patchogue: 1¹/₂ hours, $6.75 each way ($9.75 peak). Another option is to take the LIRR to Babylon (1¹/₄ hours, $5.25 each way, $7.75 peak), then catch the S47 bus to Robert Moses State Park.

EXPLORING

With no roads, you can either hike around the island on foot, shuttle around by water taxi, or use your own private boat. With ferry landings well apart, you'll have to decide before you leave where you want to spend the day. Beach bums will probably head for one of the lifeguarded beaches near Watch Hill and Sailors Haven. The beach at Robert Moses State Park, accessible by car, is quite crowded.

To visit the federal wilderness area, start at the Watch Hill Visitor Center at the western end of the preserve (tel. 516/597–6455) or at the Smith Point Visitor Center at the eastern end (tel. 516/281–3010). You can explore only this region on foot.

Although the national seashore, Robert Moses State Park, and Smith Point County Park are all public resources, bear in mind that tourists are not especially welcome in the island's communities. To maintain privacy and discourage day-trippers, some communities (particularly those toward the western end of the island) issue inexpensive tickets for minor infractions, such as walking shirtless on the boardwalk, drinking water from a container on the beach, or riding a bicycle after dark.

THE BEST IN ONE DAY Visitors seeking to experience the island in a day might want to start at the **Smith Point Visitor Center,** where you can take a tour of the virtually untouched **federal wilderness area.** From there, catch a water taxi to **Sailors Haven** and take a guided tour of the primeval **Sunken Forest.** The Seashore Inn at Sailors Haven is a good bet for a tasty lunch of seafood, meat, or pasta. After your meal you might be ready to spend a lazy hour or two relaxing in the sunshine at Sail-

ors Haven's lifeguarded beach. End your day with a visit to the **Fire Island Lighthouse,** with its keeper's quarters and visitor's center, east of Robert Moses State Park on the island's western end (tel. 516/321–7028) (*see* Historic Buildings and Sites, *below*). For a terrific view, climb the nearly 200 steps to the top (be sure to call the national seashore for reservations, tel. 516/661–4876). Linger to watch a beautiful sunset over the water before hiring a water taxi to take you back to Sailors Haven to catch the ferry back to Sayville, or to your car at Smith Point County Park.

For a day on the beach, families with young children will find plenty of company near the family-oriented communities of Ocean Bay Park and Ocean Beach. Sailors Haven and Watch Hill attract couples and other families, gays gravitate to Cherry Grove and Fire Island Pines, and Davis Park and Fair Harbor draw the singles.

The 1.5-mile boardwalk trail through the Sunken Forest provides a close-up look at the single most unusual natural phenomenon on the island.

The protected wilderness between Smith Point West and Watch Hill is recommended for hikers. This 7-mile section of the island remains the least developed, and is an ideal spot for day visitors who want to immerse themselves in nature and momentarily escape the trappings of civilization.

ORIENTATION PROGRAMS Ranger-led nature walks depart from the Smith Point West visitor's center (tel. 516/281–3010) from mid-May to mid-October. Among the topics covered are Fire Island history (with a discussion about shipwrecks) plus information on shells and edible plants.

The visitor's center at Watch Hill (tel. 516/597–6455) offers canoe trips, fishing expeditions, bird-watching hikes, and nighttime star-gazing talks.

The visitor's center at Sailors Haven (tel. 516/597–6183), gateway to the Sunken Forest, also regularly conducts naturalist activities, including evening campfire programs at

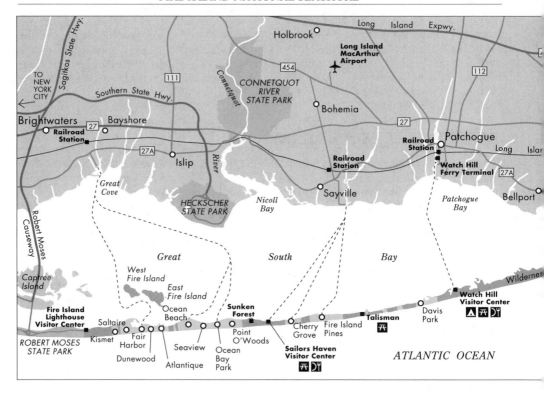

which rangers talk about astronomy, some of the island's ancient legends, and the storms that have visited the island over the years.

GUIDED TOURS Other than the brief orientation walks listed above, the park service conducts no guided tours of the park. National seashore rangers give 1-hour tours of the Sunken Forest. They will also guide you through the nature trails by Watch Hill, where you can see salt marshes that serve as nurseries for marine life.

SCENIC VIEWS Visitors who climb the 192 steps to the top of the Fire Island Lighthouse (reservations required; call the national seashore, tel. 516/661–4876) are rewarded with a spectacular view of the island and the surrounding area (on a clear day you can pick out the World Trade Center). Also, day-trippers shouldn't be in too much of a hurry to leave the island at the end of the day, because from any dock or pier the sunset is magnificent.

HISTORIC BUILDINGS AND SITES The **Fire Island Lighthouse and Visitor Center** (tel. 516/321–7028), .5 mile east of Robert Moses State Park, offers a glimpse into the lives of the dedicated lighthouse keepers who ran this station starting in the mid-19th century. The lighthouse closed in 1974 and was slated to be demolished. Fortunately, a swell of popular support for its preservation altered these plans, and it was relit in May of 1986. At the visitor's center, rangers show slides on the lighthouse's construction and on the daily duties required of its keepers. You'll also learn about the island's cultural history and some of the peoples who have lived here, including Native Americans and pirates. The Lighthouse Visitor Center was closed during 1993 due to construction and restoration of the stone terrace surrounding the facility. At press time, the lighthouse was scheduled to be open in summer 1994, at least on weekends, and probably three other days a week as well. Admission is free, but donations are welcome.

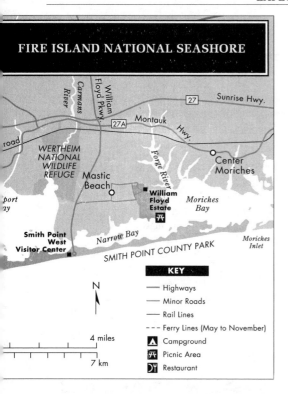

FIRE ISLAND NATIONAL SEASHORE

KEY

— Highways
— Minor Roads
— Rail Lines
--- Ferry Lines (May to November)
▲ Campground
☗ Picnic Area
))ī Restaurant

4 miles
7 km

a leaflet identifying 35 significant points along the trail. (There are such pamphlets for all Fire Island nature trails.) Some of the sturdy holly trees that thrive in this unusual forest are more than 200 years old. You can walk the trail on your own or, on weekends, take a ranger-led tour (*see* Orientation Programs, *above*).

The .75-mile loop from the **Smith Point West Visitor Center** takes you past beach plum and sassafras trees. Be on the lookout here for deer, foxes, and raccoons, which frequently scamper across the path.

The **boardwalk trail** near Smith Point West is nearly a mile long (one-way) and leads past massive sand dunes, cranberry bogs, and patches of pitch pine and bearberry.

LONGER HIKES A path called **Burma Road** runs through the federal wilderness area, but rangers do not recommend hiking it in its entirety because it is overgrown in many places and infested with ticks and poison ivy. Part of it is accessible, however. Stop at the Watch Hill Visitor Center (tel. 516/597–6455) or the South Point Visitor Center (tel. 516/281–3010) for more information.

OTHER ACTIVITIES **Biking.** Biking on the island is limited. No bikes are permitted on the ferries, but you can rent one at Island Hardware in Ocean Beach (tel. 516/583–5090) and pedal along a 3-mile cement path nearby.

Bird-Watching. This is serious bird-watching country: The tidal marshes on the bay side provide some of the finest waterfowl habitats in New York State. The nature trail around Smith Point, in particular, attracts birdwatchers intent on sighting some of the island's graceful herons, red-winged blackbirds, egrets, lapwing terns, sandpipers, mallards, wild geese, and even an occasional snowy owl. Spring and fall, when birds migrate, are the best time to watch; the lighthouse and Watch Hill are two popular vantage points during these seasons.

Boating. Nowhere on Fire Island can visitors rent boats; if you wish to get around this way,

The **William Floyd Estate** (tel. 516/399–2030), near Fire Island on Long Island in the town of Mastic Beach, was donated to the National Park Service in 1976 by a descendant of its namesake, and subsequently was placed under the administration of Fire Island National Seashore. William Floyd was a signer of the Declaration of Independence and one of the original members of the U.S. House of Representatives. It is a short drive from the Smith Point West Visitor Center (take Rte. 46 N and turn right on Neighborhood Rd.). Tours of the estate, which comprises more than 600 acres, are conducted from April to September. Call ahead; it is possible that the estate will be closed to the public in the summer of 1994 because of budget cuts.

NATURE TRAILS AND SHORT WALKS The 1.5-mile loop through the **Sunken Forest** allows great views of the forest canopy and the treetops' horizontal slants. Begin near the Sailors Haven Visitor Center, where you can pick up you will have to rent a boat on Long Island or hire a water taxi (*see* Arriving and Departing, *above*). The most convenient marinas are adjacent to the communities of Watch Hill (150 slips) and Sailors Haven (36 slips). Electric power is available at both marinas and boats up to 50 feet long are accommodated. There is also a marina at Ocean Bay Park (20 slips) and a boat basin for day use at Robert Moses State Park.

A few cruise operators offer sails to various points around the island. A tourist favorite is the four-hour, $25 luncheon cruise on Wednesdays aboard the *Evening Star* (tel. 516/666–3601). Guests have lunch on the boat, then dock at Ocean Beach for two hours. There is dessert, coffee, and dancing during the leisurely return trip. Special deals are offered in conjunction with the Long Island Railroad (tel. 516/822–5477). The *Evening Star* also runs 3¹/₂-hour dinner cruises three or four times a week ($40 and up), and a three-hour Sunday brunch trip ($27). All cruises operate from May to the end of October and depart from the Bay Shore Marina. The *Bay Mist,* which leaves from the national seashore headquarters in Patchogue (tel. 516/475–1606), offers dinner cruises nightly from Valentine's Day to New Year's Eve (3¹/₂–4¹/₂ hours, $29.75–$39.75), as well as four-hour lunch cruises Monday–Friday ($25) and a 2¹/₂-hour Sunday brunch trip ($28.75); and on Thursdays the *Fishtale* sets sail from Captree State Park on Captree Island, just across the bridge from Robert Moses State Park (tel. 516/226–8882 days, 516/669–5343 evenings).

Fishing. In the Atlantic off the coast of the national seashore anglers can go after bluefish, mackerel, and striped bass, while winter flounder, blowfish, and fluke lurk in the shallow waters of the bay. Fire Island's grocery stores carry a limited amount of fishing supplies (*see* General Stores *in* Essential Information, *above*).

Swimming. From about Memorial Day until about Labor Day there are lifeguards on duty at Robert Moses State Park, Ocean Beach (no rest rooms), Sailors Haven, Davis Park, Watch Hill, and Smith Point County Park.

CHILDREN'S ACTIVITIES A special children's program for kids 3–10 features seaside tales and crafts, while a Junior Ranger program geared for the needs of older children is offered every Wednesday during the summer. Visitor's centers also have specific ranger-led children's activities on Sunday.

EVENING ACTIVITIES Sailors Haven and Watch Hill visitor's centers organize various events. A few times each summer, guest speakers are invited to the centers to instruct stargazers on the wonders of the night sky. Specialists from Long Island's Theodore Roosevelt Bird Sanctuary give occasional talks on the island's birds of prey. Other lecture topics include endangered species, the deer population, and beach erosion. Call the visitor's centers or the national seashore headquarters for more information (*see* Visitor Information *in* Essential Information, *above*).

DINING

There are restaurants in every town on Fire Island, usually just a short walk from the ferry landings (but without addresses, since there are no roads). Seafood caught fresh daily is on most menus. Reservations are always advisable during weekends, and dress is always casual.

IN THE PARK There are park-sanctioned eating establishments in Watch Hill and Sailors Haven. At Watch Hill, **Watch Hill Concessions** runs a restaurant and bar (Seashore Inn), a snack bar, a pizza place, a general store, and a marina.

Seashore Inn. Watch Hill Concessions runs this eatery overlooking the marina; you can eat at umbrella-shaded tables out on the deck or inside. The menu is varied, heavy on seafood, but with a good selection of meat and pasta dishes; there's a limited, less expensive "Mellow Yellow Weekend" menu after 4 on Saturday and Sunday. *In Watch Hill, tel. 516/597–6655. Reservations advised. AE, DC,*

MC, V. Closed Labor Day–mid-May. Moderate.

Sailors Haven Snack Bar. The breakfast menu is basic—eggs, pancakes, French toast—but lunchtime ranges beyond the expected burgers and hot dogs to salads, platters, and occasional specials such as spaghetti. Beer and wine are also available. The best part is the setting: a deck overlooking the marina and Great South Bay. *Sailors Haven Walk, tel. 516/597–6171. No reservations. No credit cards. Closed mid-Oct.–Apr. Inexpensive.*

OUTSIDE THE PARK **Leja Beach Casino.** This singles-oriented beachfront establishment is part restaurant, part bar and dance spot. It's one of the only restaurants on the island that's right on the ocean, and the seafood is accordingly fresh. The specialty is baked clams; other comestibles include clam chowder and blackened swordfish. *Davis Park, tel. 516/597–6150. Reservations advised. MC, V. Moderate–Expensive.*

The Monster. This fixture of the Fire Island scene, on the boardwalk by the ocean, is definitely the place to go for steak and seafood; don't miss the obscenely stuffed lobster, bursting with a half pound of shrimp, crab, and scallops. Among the tastiest appetizers are lobster bisque, clams Casino, and steamed mussels with garlic. The main floor has a romantic dining room, a bar, and a disco that draws a gay crowd, and there's a raw bar and piano lounge upstairs. *Ocean Walk, Cherry Grove, tel. 516/597–6888. Dinner reservations required. AE, D, MC, V. Closed Oct. 15–Apr. 20. Moderate–Expensive.*

Top of the Bay. Refreshing ocean breezes sweep through this open-sided dining room on the second floor of a dockside building overlooking Great South Bay. In addition to the great sunsets, it offers one of the island's more sophisticated menus. For starters, try a bowl of clam chowder or steamed mussels. Specialties include crabcakes, swordfish, and tuna steak. *Dock Walk, Cherry Grove, tel. 516/597–6699. Reservations advised. AE, DC, MC, V. Closed last Sun. in Sept.–first Fri. in May. Moderate–Expensive.*

Flynn's Casino. Every Sunday afternoon, this landmark buzzes for the weekly "it's not over yet" party. On Tuesday, Wednesday, and Thursday evenings in summer, there's a deluxe hot and cold buffet, and a special boat runs from Captree Boat Basin for the event. The regular menu is à la carte, with fresh fish and other specials daily and Flynn's special baked clams. The restaurant, which seats about 200, sprawls onto a deck, and on nice days you might find a bar out there, too. Lunch and dinner are served daily, and there's breakfast on weekends. *Ocean Bay Park, tel. 516/583–5000. Reservations accepted for parties over 6 (required for boat). AE, DC, MC, V. Closed the week after Labor Day until Memorial Day weekend. Moderate.*

Kismet Inn. It's vintage Fire Island. The building that houses the bar and restaurant was built in 1925 and withstood the 1938 hurricane; restaurateur Larry Cole has owned the place for over 35 years and now serves lunch and dinner daily and breakfast from June through August. Shrimp scampi and broiled bluefish accompany the view of the half-mile-distant lighthouse and the bay. *Oak Walk, Kismet, by Bay Shore ferry terminal, tel. 516/583–5592 or 800/785–6477. Reservations advised. AE, MC, V. Closed Nov. 1–Apr. 15. Moderate.*

Pines and Dunes Yacht Club. This section of the Fire Island Pines Botel (*see* Lodging, *below*) is the Pines' favorite gathering place for its great harbor view and convivial atmosphere. Grilled salmon, broiled filet mignon, and chicken breast stuffed with shiitake mushrooms exemplify the culinary approach here. *Fire Island Pines, tel. 516/597–6500. Reservations advised. AE, DC, MC, V. Moderate.*

Michael's. The outdoor tables at this funky local hangout make it a fine spot for people-watching. There are weekly specials such as grilled swordfish, London broil, and steamed mussels, and on Tuesday there's a budgetwise all-you-can-eat pasta dinner, which includes salad, bread, ziti with meatballs, and ice cream. The regular dinner menu offers everything from prime rib and fried flounder to meat loaf and mashed potatoes. Breakfast and lunch are also available. *Dock Walk, Cherry Grove, tel. 516/597–6555. Reservations accepted. MC, V. Inexpensive–Moderate.*

PICNIC SPOTS There are established picnic areas at Watch Hill, Talisman, Davis Park, and Sailors Haven. You can also picnic on the beach at the national seashore; if you want to eat on the beach in other areas, check local regulations first.

LODGING

There are just a handful of hotels on Fire Island, and they aren't luxurious—the island prides itself on being rustic. Rooms are basic with minimal amenities. Hotels are open from May through September or October; high season is June through August. Since most visitors are day-tripping, the vast majority of those who do stay overnight rent houses, cottages, or apartments by the month or the season; these are completely furnished, and some have linens and towels. Properties that are unrented as of March may become available for weekly rentals. For information on rentals, contact **At the Bay Realty** (Cherry Grove, tel. 516/597–9797), **Dana Wallace** (Ocean Beach, tel. 516/583–5596), **Etheland Realty** (Davis Park, tel. 516/597–9735), **Fire Island Land Company** (Cherry Grove, tel. 516/597–6040), **Larson Realty** (Kismet, tel. 516/583–9100), **Island Properties** (Pines, tel. 516/597–6360), **Arlene Jaffe** (Ocean Beach, tel. 516/583–8158), and **Pines Harbor Realty** (Pines, tel. 516/597–7575).

ON THE ISLAND **Belvedere Guest House.** Corinthian columns, fountains, reflecting pools, ceiling frescoes, statues, and urns put this vaguely Venetian-style structure jutting high above surrounding buildings in a class by itself. Rooms are furnished with antiques, and some have terraces; all rooms share a bath. Most guests are gay. *Cherry Grove 11782, tel. 516/597–6448. 26 rooms. AE, MC, V. Moderate–Expensive.*

Cherry Grove Beach Hotel. The largest swimming pool on the island is here, minutes from the ferry landing and right off the Main Walk.

A few deluxe rooms have VCRs and wet bars. Catering to a largely gay clientele, it's next to the Ice Palace disco, home of the renowned Miss Fire Island Contest. *Main Walk, Box 537, Sayville 11782, tel. and fax 516/597–6600. 58 rooms with bath. Facilities: outdoor pool. AE, MC, V. Moderate–Expensive.*

Fire Island Hotel and Resort. This former Coast Guard residence now consists of several motel-style buildings surrounding a pool. It's clean, pleasant, family-run, and just a short walk from the ocean. The simply furnished rooms are outfitted with TV's, table, and chairs. *Cayuga Walk, Ocean Bay Park 11770, tel. 516/583–8000, fax 516/583–7413. 50 rooms plus 4 2-bedroom cabins. Facilties: heated outdoor pool, restaurant, playground, laundry. AE, D, MC, V. Moderate–Expensive.*

Fire Island Pines Botel. Rooms in this three-story cinderblock hotel are small and no-frills, but you've got to appreciate the view: a harbor full of yachts. Some rooms share baths. *Fire Island Pines 11782, tel. 516/597–6500. AE, MC, V. Moderate–Expensive.*

Four Seasons Bed & Breakfast. Down pillows and comforters, Egyptian cotton sheets, and beachy decor set the tone at this rustic beach house—the only hotel on the island that's open year-round. A hearty breakfast of lox, bagels, fresh cinnamon buns, and juice, if you feel like squeezing it, prepares you for the day, whether you choose to lounge in the spacious living area, walk to the beach, or take off on a bike and explore. Room rates include breakfast and, from May through October, afternoon tea. *468 Denhoff Walk, Ocean Beach 11770–0748, tel. and fax 516/583–8295. 10 rooms, 3 with bath, 2 apartments, 1 cottage. Facilities: Jacuzzi, fishing rods, bicycles. AE, D, DC, MC, V. Moderate-Expensive.*

NEAR THE ISLAND Since there are so few hotel accommodations on Fire Island, many visitors stay at hotels on Long Island and take ferries over for the day. Some hotels even offer special packages for people who plan to visit Fire Island.

Holiday Inn Ronkonkoma. This Holiday Inn, acquired in 1993 by the owners of New York City's luxurious Parker Meridien hotel, aspires to be the finest Holiday Inn in the country; $2.5 million has been put into renovating everything from the box springs to the bathroom tiles. With the ferry just 7 miles away, this is the closest full-service hotel to Fire Island. Reasonably priced packages come complete with Fire Island ferry tickets. *3845 Veterans Memorial Hwy., Ronkonkoma 11779, tel. 516/585–9500 or 800/422–9510, fax 516/585–9564. 287 rooms with bath. Facilities: restaurant, bar, lounge, outdoor pool, gift shop. AE, D, DC, MC, V. Moderate.*

Inn at Medford. This inn, near the Long Island Expressway and MacArthur Airport, caters to vacationers as well as a business crowd. The Patchogue ferry terminal is nearby—just take Route 112 S into town and follow the signs—making for convenient day trips to Fire Island. A southwestern motif prevails—there are southwestern paintings and bedspreads in the rooms and southwestern tapestries in public spaces. *2695 Rte. 112, Medford 11763, tel. 516/654–3000 or 800/626–7779, fax 516/654–1281. 76 rooms with private bath. Facilities: hot tub, health club, sauna, indoor pool, laundry, lounge. AE, D, DC, MC, V. Moderate.*

Summit Motor Inn. This no-frills economy lodge was built in the '60s and renovated in the '80s. It has the advantage of being just a mile from the Bay Shore ferry terminal, and it's just 10 minutes away from MacArthur Airport and the Brentwood station of the Long Island Railroad. *501 E. Main St., Bay Shore 11706, tel. 516/666–6000, fax 516/666–6002. 42 rooms, 5 suites, all with bath. AE, D, DC, MC, V. Inexpensive.*

CAMPING

Backcountry camping is allowed, away from the dunes and the beach. **Watch Hill Campground** is the national seashore's only official campground. The maximum stay is four nights; required free permits are available at the ranger's station. The 25 sites are much in demand, and reservations, available by lottery only, are required; in February and March, submit your application (available by sending an SASE to the superintendent; *see* Visitor Information *in* Essential Information, *above*) for the drawing in April. No-shows are common, however, so if your number doesn't come up, you may be able to snag a site by calling the campground (tel. 516/597–6633) at the last minute. Wood fires are not allowed anywhere on the island, so you'll need a camp stove.

Suffolk County residents and their guests may camp in county parks with a Green Key Pass, a three-year pass available at any county park when you show picture I.D. and proof of residence. At **Smith Point County Park** (tel. 516/852–1316) on Fire Island, there are 150 sites on the barrier beach, open year-round. Five sites are first come, first served, and 145 are by reservation only (tel. 516/244–PARK).

Great Smoky Mountains National Park

North Carolina, Tennessee

By Eddie Nickens

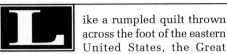 ike a rumpled quilt thrown across the foot of the eastern United States, the Great Smoky Mountains sprawl across a half-million acres of ancient terrain, the largest wilderness sanctuary in the East. The park is a patchwork of virgin forest and high mountain meadow, its diverse habitats stitched by mountain streams and roaring rivers.

Encompassing nearly equal portions of Tennessee and North Carolina, the Great Smoky Mountains National Park is a land of superlatives. Here are the largest stands of virgin forest in the eastern United States, the greatest mountains east of the Rockies (boasting 16 peaks that shoulder into the sky higher than 6,000 feet above sea level). But often, words pay poor homage to a park whose beauty also lies in the details of bloodroot and bluet, trillium and Turk's cap lily. A United Nations International Biosphere Reserve and World Heritage Site, the park contains about 100 species of trees, more than 200 species of

birds, even 27 different species of salamanders.

These rugged mountains were once sacred to the Eastern Band of the Cherokee, who in 1838 were brutally removed from their ancestral home by government action and forced to march to Oklahoma. Thousands died along the Trail of Tears, but small groups of Cherokee held out in the North Carolina high country, and in 1889 the 56,000-acre Qualla Indian Reservation was formed. It now shares part of the park's southern border.

The high mountains that attracted rugged pioneer settlers in the 18th and 19th centuries were discovered by the timber industry in the early 1900s. A librarian and writer named Horace Kephart documented the changing fortunes of the southern Appalachian mountain peoples in the classic *Our Southern Highlanders,* and sparked a national movement to declare the Smokies a national park.

On June 15, 1934, the park was officially established.

Today the interior is managed as a wilderness preserve: There are extensive camping facilities and interpretive programs, but few other services. The park is traversed by two main roads, a portion of U.S. 441 called the Newfound Gap Road and the Little River/Launch Creek Road, which leads to Cades Cove. On the perimeter of the park the resort towns of Gatlinburg, Tennessee, and Cherokee, North Carolina, offer extensive visitor facilities, while smaller towns around the park, such as Townsend and Bryson City, afford a more limited array of services.

This melding of services and sights makes the park a popular place. There are more than 8 million recreational visits to the park each year, more than twice the number of visits to any other national park. The oft-cited statistic that the park is within a day's drive of two-thirds of the nation's population shouldn't deter visitors, for solitude is often found just a short hike from the blacktop. Step off the paved road and the true heart of the park opens itself. Here you'll find hollows and coves and ridges rarely seen by human eyes. In the space of a few dozen feet, quietness pervades, all sounds muffled by moss and fern, stream and forest. Birds call. Brooks trickle. Rain drips. Tiny unseen streams seep from the undergrowth. Welcome to *Shaconage* (Place of Blue Smoke), the land held sacred by the Cherokee, a land whose wildness is still celebrated today.

ESSENTIAL INFORMATION

VISITOR INFORMATION For information on the park, contact the Superintendent, **Great Smoky Mountains National Park** (107 Park Headquarters Rd., Gatlinburg, TN 37738, tel. 615/436–1200).

There are three main visitor's centers (to reach any of them, tel. 615/436–1200). The **Oconaluftee Visitor Center** is near Cherokee, 2 miles north of the main park entrance; the center's **Pioneer Farmstead** is a living history exhibition area where park interpretive staff demonstrate pioneer trades and skills in farm buildings moved from other areas of the park. Near the northern entrance to the park is the **Sugarlands Visitor Center**, 2 miles south of Gatlinburg on Newfound Gap Road. Here a 10-minute park-produced film, *Sanctuary*, is full of evocative footage and narrative, but short on nuts and bolts. The **Cades Cove Visitor Center** is on Cades Cove Road, 12 miles south of Townsend, Tennessee. Here are many fine preserved farms and historic buildings. *Sugarlands and Oconaluftee visitor's centers open Nov.–mid-Mar., daily 8–4:30; mid-Mar.–Oct., variable longer hours. Cades Cove Visitor Center open mid-Mar.–Nov., daily 9–7.*

For information on lodging, dining, and local attractions, contact the **Swain County Chamber of Commerce** (Box 509, Bryson City, NC 28713, tel. 704/488–3681); **Cherokee Visitor Center** (Box 460, Cherokee, NC 28719, tel. 704/497–9195 or 800/438–1601); **Jackson County Travel & Tourism Authority** (18 N. Central St., Suite G, Sylva, NC 28779, tel. 800/962–1911); **Gatlinburg Chamber of Commerce** (Box 527, Gatlinburg, TN 37738, tel. 615/430–4148 or 800/568–4748); and the **Townsend Visitor Center** (Smoky Mountain Visitors Bureau, Dept. TT, 7906 Lamar Alexander Pkwy., Townsend, TN 37882, tel. 615/448–6134 or 800/525–6834).

Free backcountry permits are required for overnight stays in the 86 backcountry campsites and 18 trail shelters (*see* Publications *and* Camping, *below*).

FEES Admission to the park is free. Camping at the 10 developed campgrounds in the park costs $6–$11 per site per night.

PUBLICATIONS Brochures, booklets, maps, and guides are sold at the three visitor's centers. The free *Smokies Guide* newspaper, available at visitor's centers and from the superintendent (*see* Visitor Information, *above*), publishes park news and schedules of special events and ranger-led activities. The *Great Smoky Mountains Trail Map and Guide,* sold in the park, gives details on all backcountry campsites and trail shelters.

The **Great Smoky Mountains Natural History Association** (115 Park Headquarters Rd., Gatlinburg, TN 37728, tel. 615/436–7318) sells a number of great publications and tapes through its catalog, "Books & Things." Among the best are Rose Houk's *Exploring the Smokies,* an 80-page full-color book that details recreational and educational opportunities; *Mountain Roads & Quiet Places,* by Jerry DeLaughter, a detailed guide to the less-traveled back roads that burrow through dense forest and skirt tumbling rivers and streams; *Smoky Mountains Audio Tour,* a 120-minute double cassette of natural history commentary, interviews with park rangers and former residents, and Cherokee legends, all keyed to highlights along Newfound Gap Road; and, for the kids, Ed Dodd and Jack Elrod's *Mark Trail in the Smokies!* a 48-page full-color comic strip volume that educates children about local plants and animals.

GEOLOGY AND TERRAIN Some 200 million years ago the ancient continents of Africa and North America collided, crushing and grinding together over a period of tens of millions of years. A result of this sustained tension, the Appalachian Mountains were gradually thrust upward. A 2,000-mile belt of folded and faulted rock that stretches today from Maine to Georgia, the Appalachians were originally as high as the Rockies. Additional millions of years of wind and rain have whittled the mountains down to their present more modest though still awe-inspiring size.

The Great Smoky Mountains are the crowning glory of the Appalachian mountain chain, rising 4,000 and 5,000 feet above the surrounding valley floors, flecked by rocky outcrops and crisscrossed by 732 miles of river and mountain stream. Even though glaciers never reached the Smokies, their effects were felt in the primordial Appalachians. Cyclical freezing and thawing sheared from the cliffs huge chunks of rock and sent them crashing into the valleys below. Today, trout swim in the deep pools below these house-size boulders, and park visitors squeal as they "tube" over small waterfalls formed by rocks that once capped mighty mountains.

The crest of the Great Smokies forms the Tennessee–North Carolina border, a high-altitude horizon punctuated by Thunderhead Mountain, Clingmans Dome, Charlies Bunion, and Mount Guyot. From Newfound Gap, the geographic center of the park, the Little Pigeon River falls toward the Tennessee gateway town of Gatlinburg, while the Oconaluftee River tumbles across North Carolina on its way to downtown Cherokee. On the southwestern border of the park a series of flood control dams form a 30-mile chain of mostly undeveloped waters known as the "Finger Lakes of the South." This least-accessible corner of the park is one of its most spectacular regions.

FLORA AND FAUNA A visit to the Great Smokies is a visit to ecosystems found from Georgia north to Canada. In the lowlands are mixed deciduous-coniferous forests common to the South, but atop the high peaks are boreal forests like those of Canada. In between are the oak–hickory–red maple forests common to Virginia and the hardwood stands reminiscent of the north woods. More than 1,500 species of vascular plants have been documented in the park.

Some 95% of the park is forested, and a quarter of that is considered virgin or old-growth—a 110,000-acre treasure that represents more than 80% of the remaining old-growth forest in the eastern United States. Many of those stands are in "cove hardwood forests," a forest type that most commonly grows in topographic flats and mountain hollows, and is the result of millions of years of forest evolution. Huge trees form a dense canopy in the cove forests, shading an understory of mosses and ferns.

Other unusual plant communities are the park's grass and heath balds, treeless patches found on several Smokies mountaintops. Along the highest ridges in the park is found the southernmost example of the red spruce–Fraser fir forest. Nearly 75% of all spruce-fir forest found in the Southeast grows here, but these dense forests are far from protected from outside peril. The balsam woolly adelgid, an exotic insect introduced from Europe, has killed more than 95% of the mature Fraser firs in the Smokies, and air pollution is suspected of killing large stands of red spruce. For the unprepared, the skeletons of firs and dying spruce lining the ridgetops at Clingmans Dome is a startling sight, and a sobering reminder that our lifestyles have implications far beyond our backyards.

Among the park's favorite creatures are its 400 to 600 black bears, which feed on berries, nuts, and animal carrion. For many, seeing a black bear is a highlight of a park visit, and whenever a bear lumbers up to the roadsides, so-called "bear jams" are inevitable. All bears, however, should be considered potentially dangerous and viewed from a distance. Feeding the bears turns them into "panhandlers," and they become prime targets for poachers or prime candidates for highway accidents.

As many as 2,000 hybrid wild hogs are found in the park, with concentrations in the park's western reaches. The largely nocturnal hogs feed on just about everything, and their habit of "tilling" up the forest floor with their tusks has been linked to the destruction of rare plants and the contamination of streams. Perhaps the most intriguing animal in the park is the red wolf. Once common throughout the Southeast, an experimental population of *Canis rufus* has been released around Cades Cove and Tremont. These largely nocturnal predators average only 60 to 70 pounds and are very shy. Chances of spotting a red wolf are slight, but best bets are early and late in the day along field edges, where the wolves hunt small rodents.

While not an uncommon species, white-tailed deer in Cades Cove are uncommonly cooperative when it comes to wildlife viewing. In the summer, white-spotted fawns are a common sight, while the months of late October and November bring the breeding bucks out of the deep woods.

WHEN TO GO Weather is both the park's beauty and its bane. The same fog that cloaks mountaintops in an eerie, otherworldly mist also blocks the views. Icy weather that sheathes waterfalls in crystal closes roads.

April showers bring May trilliums. Frequent visitors learn to embrace the seasonal changes and wear a good waterproof hat.

Elevations in the park range from 800 feet to 6,643 feet, so generalizations regarding weather are difficult. In the Smokies, every 1,000-foot gain in elevation is equivalent to traveling 400 miles north; average temperatures fall 3°F. It can be 10°F–15°F cooler at Newfound Gap than it is in the lowlands. Rainfall varies as well, from an average of 55 inches per year in the valleys to a drenching 85 inches per year at Clingmans Dome.

Although as in most parks, visitation peaks in summer, more and more visitors are discovering that spring in the Smokies rivals any other season. The months of April and May still find much of the park unpeopled. March to May, low temperatures average 42°F; highs average 61°F. By mid-April daytime highs occasionally crest in the 80s. By summer, however, even the Smokies aren't immune to the region's stifling heat and humidity. August afternoons in the lower elevations peak in the 90s, with evening lows dropping to the comfortable mid- to upper 60s. When summer heat drives visitors to the mountains, one place is a cool head taller than the rest: Mt. LeConte, where no temperature above 80°F has ever been recorded (*see* Lodging, *below*).

During September and early October, the humidity and crowds disappear, a welcome respite before the onslaught of the fall color season. September highs are in the 70s, with cool nights and first frosts by the end of the month. A second peak travel season occurs in October, as the park's hardwood forests turn to their autumn colors. Entire hillsides erupt in explosions of yellows, reds, and oranges, punctuated by the daggerlike dark evergreens. It's a fantastic time to visit the park, but only if you're prepared for the crowds. By early November, daytime highs fall to the 50s and 60s. Soon it is winter, a generally moderate season, with daytime highs in the 50s about half the time, but with bitter outbreaks of severe weather and temperatures that plunge below 0°F.

SEASONAL EVENTS Contact the visitor's centers (tel. 615/436–1200) for details on the following festivals and events.

Late June: The **Annual Storytelling Afternoon** at Cades Cove brings to life the rich southern Appalachian Jack tales and ghost stories. **July: Cherokee Indian Heritage Day** fills the Cherokee Ceremonial Grounds with Native American song, dance, and skills competitions. **Late July:** The **Annual Quilt Show** in Cades Cove presents traditional quilt-making skills and patterns. **August: Women's Day** at Ocanaluftee Farmstead celebrates the past and present contributions of women in southern Appalachia. **Mid-September:** The **Mountain Life Festival** at Oconaluftee Pioneer Farmstead focuses on the skills early pioneers needed to carve a life from the rugged mountains. **May and late September:** At the two **Old Timers' Days** at Cades Cove, mountain music with banjos, dulcimers, and harmonicas is a featured event. **Early October:** **Sorghum molasses–making demonstrations** at Cades Cove fill the air with the heavy, sweet aroma of this Appalachian favorite. **Late October: Apple butter making** at Cades Cove is a peak-season activity. **December:** The **Festival of Christmas Past** at Sugarlands Visitor Center turns back time to Yuletide traditions of the pioneers.

WHAT TO PACK These are among the most rugged mountains of the eastern United States, and even easy trails have stretches of rough, rocky, rutted terrain. More important than any camera or camcorder is a good pair of lightweight hiking boots or trail shoes. And all that lush greenery grows with a price: There are frequent rain showers in the Smokies, so pack a lightweight rain jacket to layer over light clothing in summer and heavy wool sweaters in winter. Many trails require frequent stream crossings, so hikers should pack plenty of polypropylene-type sock liners and consider carrying a walking staff. Backpackers should also pack 40 to 50 feet of light rope to hoist packs at least 10 feet above the ground, out of the reach of bears. Instructions are printed on the back of the *Great Smoky Mountains Trail Map and Guide* (*see* Publications, *above*).

GENERAL STORES **North Carolina.** Grocery stores, fast-food outlets, and gas stations are clustered in Cherokee, Sylva, and Bryson City on the North Carolina side of the park. Stores are few and far between on Route 28 from outside of Bryson City to Fontana Village. The **General Store at Fontana Village Resort** (Fontana Dam, tel. 704/498–2211) stocks picnic supplies and a good selection of trail maps. It's open Sunday–Friday 9–6, Saturday 9–8.

One-half mile south of the park entrance on Newfound Gap Road, Cherokee's **Gas N Groceries** (tel. 704/497–5515) sells liquified petroleum gas, lots of snacks, and a few staples—soups, juices, detergent, baby foods—but few other camping supplies. Just .25 mile south is the **Cherokee Food Mart** (tel. 704/497–5524), with shelves of food, sandwich meats, and a good supply of frozen food; it also carries the kind of camping supplies easily forgotten—coffeepots, Coleman fuel, rain tarps—but no LP gas. Both stores are open daily 6 AM–11 PM (until 9 PM in winter). The closest full-service grocery market is the **Qualla Market** (U.S. 441, 1.5 mi south of park entrance, tel. 704/497–7597). Summer hours are weekdays 7 AM–10 PM, Saturday 8 AM–9 PM, and Sunday 10–6; November–May hours are weekdays 7 AM–8 PM, Saturday 8–7, and Sunday 10–6.

Tennessee. In Gatlinburg, the **Mountain Market** (U.S. 441, 100 yards north of park entrance, no phone) is open daily 7 AM–midnight. The store's old wooden floors hold up a small produce and fresh meats display, plus picnic staples and a well-stocked hardware section. Across the parking lot is the **Parkway Market** (tel. 615/436–6364) with similar goods; it's open daily 7 AM–1 AM. In Townsend, **Pat's Cedar Bluff Market** (U.S. 321, .5 mi north of park, tel. 615/448–2266), open Sunday–Thursday 7 AM–11 PM, Friday–Saturday 7 AM–midnight, has cardboard boxes of local onions and potatoes, picnic staples, dry goods, and the early morning aroma of bacon frying on the small grill where you can buy breakfast biscuits and lunch sandwiches. There's a better selection of hardware and camping supplies, including

LP gas, in addition to the usual picnic goods, at the **Little River Village Campground** (Rte. 73, just outside the park entrance, tel. 615/448–2241); open mid-February–November, daily 7 AM–10 PM.

ATMS Automated teller machines are located throughout Cherokee to the south of the park, along Parkway in Gatlinburg to the north, and in Townsend near the Cades Cove area in the park's northwest region.

ARRIVING AND DEPARTING A car is essential to exploring the park, which is traversed by two main roads: Newfound Gap Road (U.S. 441) runs north–south across the middle of the park, connecting the two primary park entrances: Cherokee, North Carolina, and Gatlinburg, Tennessee. Little River/Launch Creek Road runs for 24 miles along a stream between the Sugarlands Visitor Center and Cades Cove. U.S. 321 threads its way along the northern border of the park, connecting the Cades Cove–Townsend area with Gatlinburg and Cosby in the little-traveled northeastern corner of the park. I–40 parallels the park's eastern border, with few interchanges. On the southern border of the park, four-lane highways ferry traffic from Waynesville west to Sylva, Dillsboro, and Bryson City. From Bryson City west to Fontana Village, Route 28 is a scenic, windy road with views of deep forest and wide-open lake.

By Plane. The nearest major airport is **McGhee Tyson Airport** (tel. 615/970–2773), 45 miles west of Gatlinburg and near Knoxville, Tennessee. From the airport take U.S. 129 south to Maryville, Tennessee, then U.S. 321 north to Townsend. From the **Asheville Regional Airport** (tel. 704/684–2226) in North Carolina, about 60 miles east of the park, take I–26 north to I–40 west, then U.S. 19 south to U.S. 441 north to the park's entrance at Cherokee. All major rental cars are available at both airports.

By Car and RV. From Knoxville and points north and west, follow directions from McGhee Tyson Airport (*see* By Plane, *above*). From points east, follow directions from Asheville Regional Airport (*see* By Plane, *above*). From points south, follow U.S. 441

north to the park entrance at Cherokee. The park is approximately one hour's drive from both Knoxville and Asheville.

By Train. There is no direct train service to the park. The closest cities served by **Amtrak** (tel. 800/872–7245) are Toccoa, Georgia, 170 miles away, and Greenville, South Carolina, 120 miles away.

By Bus. Greyhound Lines serves Knoxville (100 Magnolia Ave., tel. 615/522–5144) and Asheville (2 Tunnel Rd., tel. 704/253–5353).

EXPLORING

Most visitors enjoy what one park publication calls a "windshield experience" of the Great Smokies: More than 16% of park visitors never turn the car ignition off during their visit, and most never venture farther than a few hundred yards off the road. Granted, the views from Newfound Gap Road are incomparable, and the less crowded scenic routes through the valleys are valuable for those with little time to spend or inclination to hike. Still, the Great Smokies reveal their secrets only to those who take the time to walk away from the crowds and into the heart of the forest, where all seems silent until the ears are retuned to the seeping of a spring, the chatter of a "boomer" squirrel, and then the full chorus of the living wilderness.

THE BEST IN ONE DAY Rise early for a one-day tour of this gigantic slice of wilderness. You'll need to depart Gatlinburg in the dark to make the 45-minute drive to Cades Cove by sunrise, but save your groans: There's scheduled nap time in this dawn-to-dusk itinerary.

Cades Cove in the far western reaches of the park preserves the historic structures and open pastoral landscape of the region as it appeared at the turn of the century. The 11-mile loop through Cades Cove can be very crowded, which is half the reason for arriving at sunrise. The other half is the valley at dawn. Fields are seas of golden flame in warm early light. Deer feed in the meadows. Drive slowly, stop often, and find an open pasture where you can take a long walk.

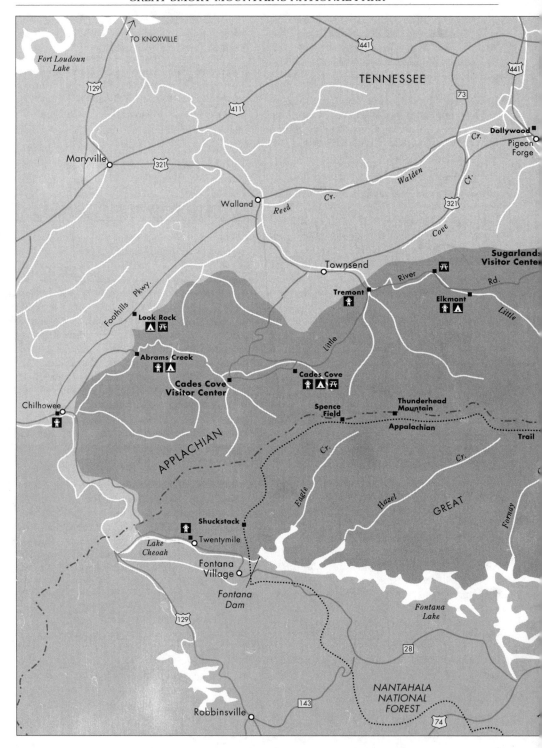

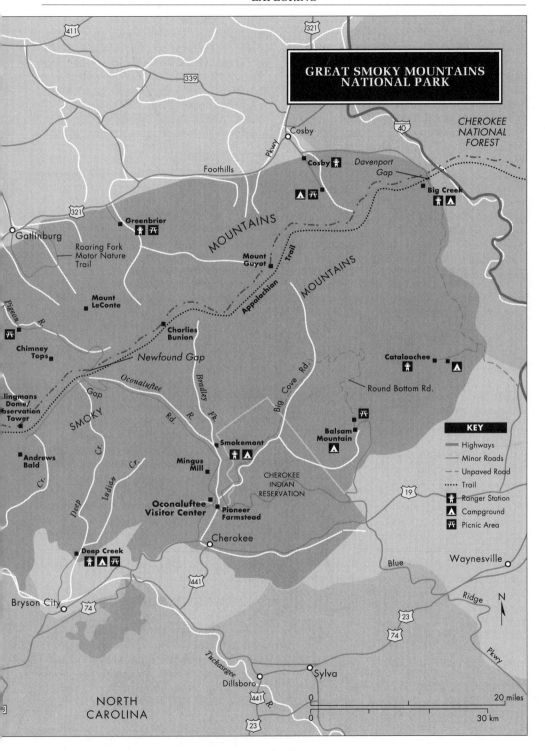

GREAT SMOKY MOUNTAINS NATIONAL PARK

CHEROKEE NATIONAL FOREST

Cosby

Cosby

Davenport Gap

Foothills Pkwy

Big Creek

MOUNTAINS

Greenbrier

Gatlinburg

Roaring Fork Motor Nature Trail

Mount Guyot

Appalachian Trail

MOUNTAINS

Mount LeConte

Pigeon R.

Charlies Bunion

Cataloochee

Chimney Tops

Newfound Gap

Round Bottom Rd.

Clingmans Dome/ Observation Tower

SMOKY

Gap

Oconaluftee Rd.

Bradley Fk.

Big Cove Rd.

Balsam Mountain

KEY

Andrews Bald

Indian Cr.

Deep Cr.

Cr.

Smokemont

Mingus Mill

CHEROKEE INDIAN RESERVATION

19

Highways
Minor Roads
Unpaved Road
Trail
Ranger Station
Campground
Picnic Area

Oconaluftee Visitor Center

Pioneer Farmstead

Deep Creek

Cherokee

Blue

Waynesville

Bryson City

74

441

Ridge

23

74

Pkwy

N

Tuckasegee R.

Sylva

Dillsboro

441

NORTH CAROLINA

23

0   20 miles

0   30 km

By midmorning, find Missionary Baptist Church on the northern part of the Cades Cove loop. Directly across from the church pick up the gravel Rich Mountain Road; follow it 8 miles over the mountain, with fantastic views of the Cades Cove valley and the spine of the towering Smokies above, then out of the park. Turn right on U.S. 321 just outside Townsend; keep right where U.S. 321 turns north, load up on picnic supplies in Townsend, then follow the road south back through the park entrance. Turn left on Little River Road and follow this scenic route to Sugarlands Visitor Center, 2 miles south of Gatlinburg. (Rich Mountain Road is closed in winter; at that time, take Laurel Creek Road from Cades Cove to Tremont, and continue straight on Little River Road, following the rest of this itinerary.)

From Sugarlands, turn south on Newfound Gap Road and follow this primary Smokies thoroughfare toward its highest point at Clingmans Dome. Picnic along the way, perhaps at the Chimney Tops Picnic Area. From Chimney Tops, continue south on Newfound Gap Road to Newfound Gap. About .2 mile south of the gap, turn right on the road to Clingmans Dome and follow the 7-mile scenic route to the parking lot. It's a .5-mile walk on a steep, serpentine, asphalt walkway that loops over itself and rises above the treetops for a spectacular panoramic view.

After Clingmans Dome, you'll likely be in search of solitude. Continue south on Newfound Gap Road to Cherokee and turn right on U.S. 19 toward Bryson City. Once in town, follow the signs to the Deep Creek area of the park, 3 miles north of town. If there's time, rent an inner tube for a late afternoon float downriver. If not, find a nice smooth boulder, soothe your feet in the cool stream, and take a well-deserved nap. If all goes as planned, you'll be awakened by the flutelike calls of the wood thrush at dusk, with just enough time to find your way back to the car by dark.

ORIENTATION PROGRAMS The three main visitor's centers present a variety of interpretative programs (*see* Visitor Information, *above*). Ranger-led hikes, slide shows, fire-side talks, and living history demonstrations are offered by the score. Check the *Smokies Guide* (*see* Publications, *above*) and kiosks at visitor's centers, ranger's stations, and campgrounds for details. Ranger's stations are at Greenbrier, Cosby, Big Creek, Cataloochee, Smokemont, Deep Creek, Twentymile, Chilhowee, Abrams Creek, Cades Cove, Tremont, and Elkmont.

GUIDED TOURS Step-on bus tours depart from the Cherokee and Gatlinburg areas to Cades Cove, Newfound Gap, Clingmans Dome, and Roaring Fork. Rates are $12–$18, depending upon destination. Choose from tours offered by **Acorn Vacations Step-On Guide Service** (Box 121, Gatlinburg, TN 37738, tel. 615/436–8898 or 800/736–8898), **Mountain Tours Inc.** (Box 1134, Pigeon Forge, TN 37868, tel. 615/453–0864), **Smoky Mountains Guide Service** (Box 1334, Gatlinburg, TN 37738, tel. 615/436–2108), and **Smoky Mountain Tours** (Box 278, Gatlinburg, TN 37738, tel. 615/436–3471, or 2756 Middle Creek Rd., Pigeon Forge, TN 37863, tel. 615/428–3014 or 800/962–0448).

Guided backpacking expeditions can be booked through **Back of Beyond Expeditions** (Box 856, Gatlinburg, TN 37738, tel. 615/436–0481). Naturalist and writer George Ellison (Box 1262, Bryson City, NC 28713, tel. 704/488–8782) offers guided wildflower hikes, wildlife workshops, and southern Appalachian natural history seminars. The **Great Smoky Mountains Institute at Tremont** (Rte. 1, Box 700, Townsend, TN 37882, tel. 615/448–6709) offers two- to six-day courses in backpacking, mountain crafts, wildlife photography, Appalachian history, and mountain ecology.

SCENIC DRIVES AND VIEWS Driving is the most popular way of sightseeing in the park, with its 170 miles of paved road and more than 100 miles of gravel road. Common in summer are cars and trucks pulled along the roadside, hoods open and radiators boiling over. It's a good idea to carry an extra gallon of coolant and an extra quart of brake fluid. Driving in the park requires that you pump your brakes, use lower gears, and be patient.

There's always someone slower than you just around the next bend. Turn your headlights on in the fog, and remove sunglasses before entering tunnels.

The indispensable guide to scenic drives in the park is *Mountain Roads & Quiet Places* (*see* Publications, *above*). A copy of the brochure "Auto Touring" is available at visitor's centers. These publications also tell you which roads are unpaved, closed in winter, or unsuitable for RV traffic.

The most popular auto tour in the park is the 11-mile **Cades Cove Loop Road,** which skirts the edge of a broad valley with open pastures and a preserved pioneer settlement. Cades Cove can be extremely crowded, but its pleasures are worth the trouble. If traffic sends your blood pressure skyward, pull the car off midway around the loop and hit the trail to Abrams Falls, a 5-mile round-trip.

The **Cataloochee Auto Tour** begins in a secluded valley where historic structures dot the hillsides. Take Exit 20 off I–40, drive .2 mile, turn right onto Cove Creek Road, an 11-mile windy, sometimes paved, sometimes gravel, route that ferries you to the entrance to Cataloochee. You'll follow the right fork of Cove Creek through hardwood forests to Cove Creek Gap, the park boundary, where the road dips sharply for the descent of Cataloochee Divide. In the valley you'll pass restored and unrestored homes, churches, and schools (without the crowds prevalent at Cades Cove).

The 5-mile **Roaring Fork Motor Nature Trail** begins in Cherokee Orchard and follows a rushing creek through a young forest. A highlight of the loop is the Place of a Thousand Drips, where tiny underground seeps and springs turn a mountainside into an unusual sort of waterfall.

Clingmans Dome Road clings to the crest of the Smokies for 7 miles, offering unparalleled views of ridges piled upon ridges. A short walk along the Spruce-Fir Self-Guiding Nature Trail will get you away from the crowds (*see* The Best in One Day, *above*).

There are two sections of the **Foothills Parkway.** The western 17 miles of the alternate route, just outside the park boundaries, is known by Smokies insiders for its spectacular fall color. The eastern 6 miles connects U.S. 321 to I–40, and serves as a shortcut to Big Creek and Cataloochee. It's a shorter route than the western parkway and is closed in winter.

If you're willing to get your tires wet, **Parson Branch Road** heads south from the Cades Cove Visitor Center for an 8-mile climb up Hannah Mountain and a plunge down Parson Branch. You'll ford several small streams along this one-way road. Turn right on U.S. 129 for a 10-mile trip with outstanding views of Chilhowee Lake; another right on the Foothills Parkway brings you back to Townsend. Parson Branch Road is closed in winter and shouldn't be attempted by RVs or trucks with high-top campers.

From Bryson City, **Lakeview Drive,** is a 6-mile climb high above Fontana Lake. This is a prime spot for viewing fall colors. The road crosses numerous streams before dead-ending at Laurel Branch. Before returning to Bryson City, stretch your legs on the .75-mile walk through the tunnel.

HISTORIC BUILDINGS AND SITES The park's wealth of preserved pioneer settlements features white churches glistening jewel-like in distant valleys, working mills, and cabins whose varied dovetail corner-notches speak volumes of the heritage of their long-forgotten builders. There are 77 historic structures in the park, many clustered in **Cades Cove, Cataloochee,** and the **Pioneer Farmstead** at Oconaluftee Visitor Center.

About .75 mile north of Oconaluftee Visitor Center is the picturesque **Mingus Mill,** built in 1886. Even when Pioneer Farmstead is teeming with visitors, Mingus Mill is a good bet for a quiet walk around a restored historic site. Here you can listen to the sound of water dripping from the flume and purchase stone-ground flour from a costumed interpreter who explains how the mill works. *Admission free. Open mid-Apr.–Oct., daily 9–5.*

One of the park's best-kept secrets is the ruins of the logging town of tiny **Proctor.** Reachable only by boat, the crumbling remains of industrial sites, mill foundations, and a few standing structures along scenic Hazel Creek make a day trip to Proctor a private and personal glimpse of life in the Great Smokies long before it was a national park. For boat rentals or ferry service to Hazel Creek, contact **Fontana Village Resort** (tel. 704/498–2211 or 800/849–2258).

■■■ **NATURE TRAILS AND SHORT WALKS** Scores of short trails and interpretative walks beckon from nearly every curve in the park's roads. **Quiet Walkways** are short strolls of .5 mile or less that meander from the main roads into deep forests or skirt laurel-lined streams. Parking areas for Quiet Walkways hold only two or three cars, so even in the most crowded areas of the park these accessible trails offer a quick route to peace and quiet. Watch for the signs.

None of the 10 self-guiding nature trails in the park is longer than 2.5 miles except the 5-mile Alum Cave Bluffs Nature Trail (*see* Longer Hikes, *below*). The paved 2.5-mile **Laurel Falls Self-Guiding Nature Trail** is a good introduction to the park's varied habitats and terrain. Three miles west of the Sugarlands Visitor Center, on Little River Road, the trail wends through laurel thickets, pine-oak forests, and a cove hardwood forest before tunneling through a ridgetop wood and down to Laurel Falls. It's a good choice for wildflower lovers who don't like to venture far from the road. Though the terrain on this trail is moderate, you soon learn that the lush vegetation that cloaks these mountainsides can hide very rugged country. If you're ready for a bigger challenge, continue past the falls for a steeper, more rugged .5 mile to a virgin hardwood forest.

The .75-mile **Noah "Bud" Ogle Place Self-Guiding Trail** is a different sort of interpretive walk. The trail skirts abandoned fields and apple orchards as you walk past the old Ogle homestead, a large log barn, and the stone foundation of the "weaner" cabin, where Ogle's sons each spent the first year of

their newly married lives. The trailhead is on the Cherokee Orchard Road, 3 miles south of Gatlinburg via Airport Road.

The 4-mile round-trip hike to Andrews Bald via **Forney Ridge Trail** is a superb choice in May and June. From the Clingmans Dome parking area the trail first traverses a steep, rocky section, then meanders through a spruce-fir forest. Keep bearing left and you soon reach the bald, which soaks up the springtime sun, returning the energy in the form of early blooming wildflowers that poke their pastel blossoms through the mountain oat grasses. By mid-June, flame azalea and rose-purple catawba rhododendron light up the bald's shrubby edges.

If you like your mountain streams crashing over waterfalls, the **Deep Creek–Indian Creek Loop** fits the bill. The trail, just under 4 miles long, begins north of the Deep Creek Campground, 3 miles north of Bryson City. In less than .5 mile you come to Tom Branch Falls, which cascades over rock ledges that shatter the falling water into shimmering veils of mist. Another .5 mile brings you to a fork in the trail; take the left fork and follow Deep Creek Trail. Cross the creek at the top of the trail, climb Sunkota Ridge, and pick up Indian Creek Trail back to the fork. Indian Creek Falls is visible near the stream's confluence with Deep Creek.

■■■ **LONGER HIKES** Veteran park visitors know that the more time spent on the trail, the better. But be honest about your hiking skills; don't attempt more than you are comfortable with. Trails in the Smokies can get very steep quickly and stay slippery for a day or two after a brief shower or heavy dew.

There are no interpretative signs along the popular 5-mile **Alum Cave Bluffs Self-Guiding Nature Trail.** This special area has been spared the logger's saw, and even today, the physical reminders of man's presence are kept to a minimum. The first 1.5 miles to Arch Rock is heavily forested with hemlock and yellow birch. Past Arch Rock, the trail gets steeper and climbs the dry mountain slopes above the creek, eventually breaking into open heath balds. The bluffs above are nearly

100 yards long. If you catch a second wind, continue on for the 2.5-mile climb to Mt. LeConte, home of the famous LeConte Lodge (*see* Lodging, *below*). In early June the rhododendron blooms along the trail are a highlight, but this trail doesn't fall under any best-kept-secret category. If the parking lot is packed, you may want to choose a different trail for solitude's sake.

The 8-mile round-trip hike to **Charlies Bunion** offers easy access, spectacular views, and relatively small elevation gain, which makes it a very popular trail. From the Newfound Gap parking area, take the Appalachian Trail north, where you'll walk literally on the spine of the Appalachian chain. All along are sweeping vistas of the Little Pigeon and Oconaluftee watersheds. About 2.5 miles down the trail is the Boulevard Trail; bear right, remaining on the Appalachian Trail, and continue to the best view of all, from the rocky knob of Charlies Bunion, perched atop sheer 1,000-foot cliffs.

The 8-mile round-trip **Ramsay Cascade Trail** offers a double bonus. First, you walk through the park's largest old-growth forest, a cathedral of tuliptrees and Eastern hemlock trunks like giant temple columns. A bit farther on, the park's highest waterfall awaits: the 100-foot Ramsay Cascade. It's a strenuous pull, with an elevation gain of 2,375 feet in 4 miles, but worth every drop of sweat. The trailhead is in the Greenbrier area of the park, 6 miles east of Gatlinburg off U.S. 321.

In the wild, less-visited southwest corner of the park, there are peaks much higher than the 4,020-foot **Shuckstack,** but few offer its diversity of sights. There are two routes: the 4.5-mile one-way trip up **Twentymile Trail** or the 3.4-mile stretch of **Appalachian Trail** from Fontana Dam to Shuckstack, which has a 2,200-foot elevation gain. Both are challenging. The blue-green waters of Fontana Lake and Lake Cheoah twinkle along the valley floors, while the great ridgeline of the Smokies forms a high-altitude horizon, flecked with heath and grass balds. The trailhead at Fontana Dam is located off Route 28, near Fontana Village, 50 miles west of Chero-

kee. Twentymile's trailhead is another 7 miles west.

APPALACHIAN TRAIL For 68 miles the famed **Appalachian Trail** (also called AT) bumps and grinds over the crest of the Great Smokies. Entering the park from the south at Fontana Dam, it climbs the 4,020-foot Shuckstack, then hops along ridgetops from Spence Field to Thunderhead Mountain to Clingmans Dome, and heads northeasterly until it exits the park at Davenport Gap near Big Creek. Sections of the trail near Newfound Gap are heavily traveled, but the remote southwest and northeast corners of the park offer a chance at great stretches of solitude.

Backcountry permits are required for overnight stays (*see* Camping, *below*). While the AT boasts the best views over the longest route, there is a price to be paid: Campers must stay in trailside shelters, so you'll share bunk space with strangers. Still, for many the best way to see the park is from the familiar white-blazed trail. For more information on the entire length of the trail, contact the **Appalachian Trail Conference** (Box 807, Harpers Ferry, WV 25425, tel. 304/535–6331).

OTHER ACTIVITIES Arts and Crafts Galleries. While cheap souvenir shops abound in the area, fine arts and crafts that meld utility and aesthetics are also an Appalachian hallmark. At the foot of the Arrowmont School of Arts and Crafts campus, **Arrowcraft** (576 Parkway, Gatlinburg, TN, tel. 615/436–4604) carries fine weaving, pottery, woodworking, and jewelry from Arrowmont artists and others. Tours of the **Arrowmont** campus (Box 567, Gatlinburg, TN, tel. 615/436–5860) are available by appointment. **Elizabeth Ellison Watercolors** (Main St., Box 1262, Bryson City, NC, tel. 704/488–8782) is a great find up a flight of narrow, creaky stairs above the 1920s Clampitt Hardware Store. Ellison's watercolors of native flora and landscapes often incorporate papers handmade from native plants such as yucca, iris, and mulberry. In the tiny historic hamlet of Dillsboro, **Oaks Gallery** (Riverwood Shops, Box 310, Dillsboro, NC, tel. 704/586–6542) carries the work of full-time artisans. Here, Gordon Batten's hand-thrown, hand-painted porcelain and stoneware sinks are festooned with Victorian primrose patterns and cartoonlike streetscapes. In the surrounding **Riverwood Shops** are working pewtersmiths and other artisans. In Cherokee, the **Qualla Arts & Crafts Mutual** (Rte. 441–N Box 310, Cherokee, NC, tel. 704/497–3103) is part museum, part gallery, owned and operated by Cherokee craftspeople. A best bet might be a Cherokee split-oak basket, accented with rivercane and honeysuckle.

Back-Road Driving. No off-road driving is allowed in the park.

Biking. Bicycles are not allowed on most trails or in the backcountry, and the park's narrow, windy roads are unsuitable for bicycles, but there are a few possibilities. From early May to mid-September the 11-mile Cades Cove Loop Road is closed to automobile traffic until 10 AM. Rent cycles at the **Cades Cove Campground Store** (tel. 615/448–9034; open Apr.–Oct.). A 10-mile round-trip via the Deep Creek Loop is a good way to log bike time; mountain-bike rentals and route maps are available at **NOC Bryson City Store** (Everett St., Bryson City, NC 28713, tel. 704/488–2446).

Bird-Watching. More than 20 different kinds of warbler breed in the park, just a sampling of the more than 200 bird species in the Smokies. The excellent *Birds of the Smokies,* available from the Great Smoky Mountains Natural History Association (*see* Publications *in* Essential Information, *above*), is a pocket-size guide with checklists and tips.

Boating. Fontana Lake on the southwestern border of the park is a superb boating site, with the surrounding mountains reflected in the clear blue-green waters. **Fontana Village Resort Marina** (*see* Lodging, *below*) rents jonboats, bass boats, and houseboats, and offers launching facilities for private craft.

Cross-Country Skiing. In winter, Roaring Fork Motor Nature Trail, the eastern portion of the Foothills Parkway, and Parson Branch, Rich Mountain, Clingmans Dome Road, and the Balsam Mountain Road to Round Bottom

are closed. Each offers fine cross-country skiing. Rental equipment is not available in the park.

Fishing. The cold, pure waters of these mountains offer some of the Southeast's finest trout fishing. Rainbow and brown trout are common in most park streams, and the protected native brook trout frequents high headwater streams. There is no open season on brook trout, and only single-hook, artificial lures are permitted. To fish, you'll need a Tennessee or North Carolina license—either one covers the whole park. Guided fishing and fly-fishing instruction are available through **McLeod's Highland Fly Fishing** (191 Wesser Heights Dr., Bryson City, NC 28713, tel. 704/488–8975) and **Old Smoky Outfitters** (511 Parkway, Gatlinburg, TN 37738, tel. 615/430–1936). Fishing for lake trout, largemouth and smallmouth bass, muskellunge, and walleye is big sport in Fontana Lake and Lake Cheoah. Guided fishing trips can be booked through **Fontana Village Resort Marina** (*see* Lodging, *below*). There are more than 30 miles of stocked trout streams on the **Cherokee Indian Reservation.** Required tribal permits are $4 per day, available at most campgrounds in Cherokee. No other license is needed.

Horseback Riding. Guided horseback trips are offered by **Cades Cove Riding Stables** (4035 Lamar Alexander Pkwy., Walland, TN, tel. 615/448–6286), **Deep Creek Riding Stables** (Rte. 1, Box 78, Whittier, NC, tel. 704/497–7503), **Davy Crockett Riding Stables** (234 Stables Dr., Townsend, TN, tel. 615/448–6411), **Fontana Riding Stables** (*see* Lodging, *below*), **McCarter's Riding Stables** (1102 Steeple Way, Box 132, Gatlinburg, TN, tel. 615/436–5354), **Smokemont Riding Stables** (Box 72, Cherokee, NC, tel. 704/497–2373), **Smoky Mountain Stables** (729 Kear Ln., Gatlinburg, TN, tel. 615/436–5634), and **Wonderland Stables** (3889 Wonderland Way, Sevierville, TN, tel. 615/436–5490).

Indian Reservation. The 56,000-acre **Cherokee Indian Reservation** shares miles of the park's southern border. There are fine educational facilities that explain the history and culture of the Cherokee Indian, but much of the town of Cherokee is lined with "tomahawk shops" filled with plastic spears and stuffed bears. Children go bonkers over the main town drag, where they can have their picture taken with "street chiefs" in gaudy feathered headdresses beside tin tepees. The saddest sights are the caged bears. Pay not a penny to view these exploited creatures. Highlights of a visit to Cherokee include the wildly popular and impressive *Unto These Hills* outdoor drama; the historically accurate re-created Oconaluftee Indian Village; the Museum of the Cherokee Indian, where those even slightly interested in Native American culture can get lost for hours; and the Qualla Arts & Crafts Mutual (*see* Arts and Crafts Galleries *in* Other Activities, *above*). For further information, contact the **Cherokee Visitor Center** (Box 460, Cherokee, NC 28719, tel. 704/497–9195 or 800/438–1601).

Rafting. Numerous outfitters offer white-water floats on nearby rivers. The best known include **Nantahala Outdoor Center** (41 U.S. 19 W, Bryson City, NC 28713, tel. 704/488–6900 or 800/232–7238), **Nantahala Rafts** (Gorgarama Park, Bryson City, NC 28713, tel. 704/488–2325 or 800/245–7700), and **Rolling Thunder River Co.** (U.S. 19/W 74, Bryson City, NC 28713, tel. 704/488–2030 or 800/344–5838).

Railway Touring. Since 1988 the **Great Smoky Mountains Railway** (1 Front St., Box 397, Dillsboro, NC 28725, tel. 704/586–8811 or 800/872–4681) has been a don't-miss option during a park visit. These brightly painted diesel-electric and steam trains offer enclosed cabooses and open cars. Choose between a Dillsboro departure and return, which includes a three-hour excursion along the Tuckaseegee River with a 45-minute layover in Bryson City; or a 4¹/₂-hour Bryson City departure and return excursion through the stunning Nantahala Gorge with an hour layover in the gorge. All-day "Raft & Rail" trips are a favorite.

Swimming. Park officials "tolerate" swimming in the park's many streams and rivers, but it is not encouraged. Waters are swift and

cold, and despite posted warnings, people climb waterfalls, and some have slipped and fallen to their deaths. To be safe, choose one of the more popular swimming holes. There are lots of paved pull-offs along **Little River Road** between Gatlinburg and Cades Cove; one great spot is **The Sinks. Deep Creek** is also popular (*see* Tubing, *below*) as is **Bradley Fork Creek** as it flows through Smokemont Campground, near Cherokee.

Tubing. Pilot your very own inner tube down scenic **Deep Creek** as many times as you like. Commercial tubing centers are clustered at the park entrance at Deep Creek, 3 miles north of Bryson City. Most charge the same $5 for a tube with a wooden seat, $3 without, but vendors located farther away from the entrance charge a few dollars less. Deep Creek can be very crowded in July and August. Try it earlier in spring when there are fewer people and, due to the spring rains, faster water.

Wildlife Photography. The Smokies exact particular techniques from those wanting to put their treasures on film. Dark forests and fog fool light meters, while streams are sunlit only in the middle of the day. Tripods are required equipment if you want to photograph wildflowers or blur the water in a mountain river. Mecca for photography buffs in the Smokies is **Beneath the Smoke** (467 Parkway, Gatlinburg, TN, tel. 615/436–3460), a gallery/store with a huge selection of prints, from backlit deer feeding in fog-shrouded meadows to black bear cubs clinging to trees to dew-dappled wildflowers. The store also has the most complete natural history book selection around, with more than 4,000 titles, and offers free photography programs. Store personnel can handle technical questions and point you to the best overlooks for sunrise shots. Spring and fall photography workshops are offered, plus 10 one-day workshops inside the park.

CHILDREN'S PROGRAMS From sing-alongs with interpretive staff to dozens of walks, talks, and tall-tale times, the park's rangers and interpretive staff offer enough children's programs to tire the most animated tyro; all are outlined in the park newspaper, *Smokies*

Guide, or posted on kiosks at ranger's stations, campgrounds, and visitor's centers. The **Junior Ranger program,** run by the park service (tel. 615/436–1200), is for kids 8–12. Participants qualify for Junior Ranger status and the official badge when they've completed a natural history workbook, attended a special ranger-led activity, visited one of three Junior Ranger special areas, and picked up one bag of litter or turned in one bag of recyclables.

EVENING ACTIVITIES Several ranger-led activities explore the park after dark. Best bets are "Owl Calls and Wolf Howls" on summer nights June–August in Cades Cove, and the one-hour "Twilight Strolls" that depart from the Elkmont, Cosby, and Smokemont campgrounds each night April–Labor Day. Consult the *Smokies Guide* or kiosks at ranger's stations, campgrounds, and visitor's centers for details.

DINING

Southern home-style cooking is the pride of the region, and meals at restaurants are often served family style, with heaping plates of vegetables and mountains of rolls and cornbread. The rule is, come hungry: Portions are plenteous. Mountain trout is a favorite, and a sort of culinary one-upmanship has resulted in at least 15 different ways to cook this delicate fish, often served with head and tail attached. There are no public dining facilities inside the park, but plenty are nearby.

NEAR THE PARK **The Burning Bush.** You can't beat the views: Velvet-antlered bucks graze in the forest beyond glass walls in the Wonderland and Park Porch dining rooms. Inside, exotic finches call from large aviaries. If you'd rather not dine with the animals, a spacious wood-paneled dining room is available. Specialties include fillet of beef Rossini, a center-cut filet mignon sautéed in butter with mushrooms and Madeira sauce, and the small but tempting quail braised with brown sauce, peas, and mushrooms. *1151 Parkway, Gatlinburg, TN, tel. 615/436–4669. Reservations advised in summer and fall. Dress: cas-*

ual but neat. AE, D, DC, MC, V. Moderate–Expensive.

Lulu's Cafe. If you need a break from the Smokies' traditional trout-ham-gravy food groups, this gourmet American diner is considered by many locals the region's finest restaurant. It's certainly the only restaurant that has a red-white-and-blue barber pole mounted by the front door on mauve columns. Inside, chic mauve-and-black walls make an elegant statement, although ladder-back chairs and black-and-white checked cloths keep the mood casual. Menu favorites include pasta primavera with garlic, herbs, sun-dried tomatoes, and pine nuts; and scallops oreganata (scallops baked with basil, oregano, and Parmesan bread crumbs). There are also daily specials reflecting seasonal ingredients and eight homemade salad dressings. Come early on summer weekends. *18 W. Main St., Sylva, NC, tel. 704/586–8989. No reservations. Dress: casual but neat. MC, V. Moderate.*

Ruby Tuesday. This chain eatery doesn't put on airs: It's a good steaks, burgers, fajitas, and salad-bar kind of place with lots of neighborhood appeal and a fair-size local following. There are tables over the Little Pigeon River, but you'll be staring straight at the hotel across the water. A half-dozen blocks from the center of town, it makes a good meeting place after a day of shopping. *449 Parkway, Gatlinburg, TN, tel. 615/436–9251. No reservations. Dress: casual. AE, D, MC, V. Moderate.*

The Chestnut Tree. This hotel restaurant is a consensus favorite for dining in Cherokee, even though it's located on the highway bypass outside of town. On weekend nights, there is prime rib and seafood, with at least six types of fish. Sunday brunch is a heavy meal, and the breakfast and lunch buffets are popular with families. *Holiday Inn, U.S. 19, Cherokee, NC, tel. 704/497–9181. Reservations accepted. Dress: casual but neat. AE, D, DC, MC, V. Inexpensive–Moderate.*

De La Paz. Though this family-owned diner is sparsely furnished with the trappings of typical Mexican eateries, its menu is extensive. There are literally dozens of choices of south-of-the-border favorites, from fajitas to taquitos to burritos. It's a good bet for a quick and filling change-of-pace lunch. *459 Parkway, Gatlinburg, TN, tel. 615/436–0380. No reservations. Dress: casual. MC, V. Inexpensive.*

Dillsboro Smokehouse. A wide-open, wooden-floor dining room with walls festooned with farm implements sets the tone: This is the place for old-fashioned eatin'. Hickory-smoked pork, beef, ribs, chicken, and turkey are piled on the plates, served with no less than four side dishes. Choose between five varieties of barbecue sauce lined up on each table. Go for the combo platter or risk eating off your neighbor's plate. The baby back ribs are marinated in a peach-laced barbecue sauce before doing time over the coals, and the result is fork-tender meat suffused with a sweet-smoky taste. Order a box lunch for your trip on the nearby Great Smoky Mountains Railway. *267 Haywood St., Dillsboro, NC, tel. 704/586–9556. No reservations. Dress: casual. MC, V. Inexpensive.*

Ogle's Buffet Restaurant. The name says it all: Why order from the menu when buffet tables sag with fried chicken, roast beef, two kinds of fish, and a fifth meat? Sunday buffets feature country ham, turkey and dressing, and chicken, while Friday night seafood feasts feature five kinds of fish plus the requisite chicken and roast beef. The best seats in the house are in the glassed-in dining room that doubles as a walkway over the Little Pigeon River. *539 Parkway, Gatlinburg, TN, tel. 615/436–4157. No reservations. Dress: casual. MC, V. Inexpensive.*

Pancake Pantry. Inside, tall windows overlook Gatlinburg's finest shopping area and a waiting line outside that can be 100 deep. With 24 varieties of pancakes, this is the area's favorite breakfast house, with copper highlights and century-old brick exterior. Austrian apple-walnut pancakes are a hit, and all are served with whipped butter and syrup or fruit compote and whipped cream. Gourmet sandwiches can be boxed for picnicking in the park. *628 Parkway, Gatlinburg,*

TN, tel. 615/436–4724. No reservations. Dress: casual. No credit cards. Inexpensive.

PICNIC SPOTS The park service maintains 11 developed picnic grounds (Big Creek, Deep Creek, Collins Creek, Balsam Mountain, Cosby, Greenbrier, Look Rock, Chimney Tops, Little River, Metcalf Bottoms, and Cades Cove), but any flat rock, flowering meadow, or streamside gravel bar makes for a fine place to spread a tablecloth. Along **Little River Road** between Sugarlands and Cades Cove are innumerable picturesque possibilities. Better yet is to load grub into a day pack and strike out for **Andrews Bald, Charlies Bunion,** or **Cataloochee.**

LODGING

Years ago, fine old lodges and inns were built to house visitors who arrived by train and bus. Today, some of those lodges are still among the best places to stay around the park. Large enough to provide privacy, but small enough to offer personality and personal service, these inns run the gamut from rustic to elegant. One word of caution: Any place that advertises "natural air-conditioning" is actually admitting to a lack of mechanical air-conditioning. Nights in the Smokies are generally comfortable throughout the year, but these hills aren't immune to stifling heat. Weigh the advantages.

There are hundreds of hotels, motels, and mom-and-pop motor courts in the area, and they vary considerably in quality. Contact local chambers of commerce for information (*see* Visitor Information *in* Essential Information, *above*). The safest bets are recognized chain establishments, but many locally owned hostelries offer charming and sometimes nostalgic accommodations. Almost all rooms can be booked up during the high seasons; many guests book rooms in fall a year in advance.

INSIDE THE PARK **LeConte Lodge.** The only overnight lodging in the park, this rustic mountaintop retreat is considered by many the highlight of their visit to the Smokies. There are five ways to get there, but all have one thing in common: hiking boots. The shortest route to the lodge is the 5.5-mile Alum Cave Self-Guiding Nature Trail, a four-hour hike for a fit hiker. Other trails stretch out as far as 8 miles, but all are at least moderately steep. Couch potatoes beware. At the summit you'll find rooms in cabins or group sleeping lodges, with kerosene lanterns and heaters and bunk beds sporting colorful Hudson Bay blankets. Supplies are brought in by llama three times per week, and meals are served family style. A fact-filled brochure is available with suggestions on gear and trail routes. *250 Apple Valley Rd., Sevierville, TN 37862, tel. 615/429–5704. Capacity: 50 guests per night. No electricity, no private baths, no showers. Flush toilets. No credit cards. Closed late Nov.–mid-Mar. Moderate.*

NEAR THE PARK **Hippensteal's Mountain View Inn.** Wide double porches run the entire length of this secluded mountaintop B&B designed by one of the Smokies' best-known watercolorists. Built in 1990, rooms have a Victorian feel: There are painted iron beds, floral wallcoverings, fireplaces framed by white marble, and well-lighted reading chairs. White wicker furniture is scattered about a large lobby with a fireplace, whose walls are a virtual gallery of Vern Hippensteal's works. *Grassy Branch Rd., Box 707, Gatlinburg, TN 37738, tel. 615/436–5761 or 800/527–8110. 8 rooms. Facilities: Jacuzzi baths. AE, D, MC, V. Expensive.*

Balsam Mountain Inn. Guests seldom believe their eyes when they glimpse this sprawling neoclassical inn. Opened in 1991 after an exacting restoration to National Register guidelines, the old railroad hotel commands attention from the top of a small mountain in the Balsam range. Built with 10-foot-thick walls and rooms for 100 guests, everything is big about the inn, except for its ambience, which the owner manages to keep personal and very attentive. Quilts, rockers, and bent willow-branch furniture fill the common rooms, while green wicker furniture and white iron beds lend an open, bright feel to the guest rooms, with original art and antiques throughout. Located 20 miles east of the park off U.S. 23/74, the inn isn't as nearby as many other lodges, but none of them can match the 225 windows. *Balsam Mountain Inn Rd., Box 40, Balsam, NC 28707, tel. 704/456–9498. 34 rooms. Facilities: restaurant, library, game room with board games. MC, V. Moderate–Expensive.*

Best Western Fabulous Chalet Inn. In a quiet residential neighborhood a few blocks above the main downtown drag, this secluded mountain lodge is situated amid rose gardens, native plantings, and stone terraces. From the woods beside the parking lot, birds sing their sunset serenade. Choose between rooms with views of Mt. LeConte and downtown Gatlinburg or rooms with a hot-tub. Some larger rooms have two full bathrooms. There are woodburning fireplaces in some rooms; one- and two-bedroom town houses and private villas are available. *516 Sunset Dr., Gatlinburg, TN 37738, tel. 615/436–5151 or 800/933–8675, fax 615/523–8363. 38 rooms. Free Continental breakfast in summer. Facilities: heated outdoor pool. AE, D, DC, MC, V. Moderate–Expensive.*

Best Western Great Smokies Inn. With its milled log-cabin exterior and stone floor, this is among the most attractive chain hotels in the area. Grounds meticulously landscaped with native plants keep the pool very private. Inside, attractive wallpapers and mountain art in each bright room are a welcome break from the usual chain-hotel decor. One block off the main drag through town, the hotel is next door to the tribal bingo facility and electric lotto-style gambling. *Follow U.S. 441 and turn north at Acquani Rd. Box 189, Cherokee, NC 28719, tel. 704/497–2020 or 800/528–1234. 152 rooms. Facilities: pool, hot-tub rooms available. AE, D, DC, MC, V. Closed Jan.–Feb. Moderate.*

Best Western Twin Island. Overlooking a fork in the Little Pigeon River at the base of Gatlinburg's main shopping district, this sprawling hotel offers a few rarities in the downtown area. Picnic tables and grills line a small grassy lawn overlooking the river, hemmed in by tall rock walls. It's no wilderness area, but a pleasing change. Federal-style reproductions in the rooms are a nice touch. *At the intersection of U.S. 441 and U.S. 321, Box 648, Gatlinburg TN 37738, tel. 615/436–5121 or 800/223–9299. 107 rooms. Free Continental breakfast. Facilities: Jacuzzi baths. AE, DC, MC, V. Moderate.*

Folkestone Inn. This B&B is filled with fine Empire antiques, but you needn't worry about feeling comfortable here. Hikers dry their boots by an enormous ornate Victorian woodstove in the parlor while trading tall tales with the innkeepers. The English-cottage ambience is charming: The innkeepers brought from England painted porcelain doorknobs and English china on which a full breakfast is served. There are four landscaped acres with white benches by a field left unmown to attract birds, a stone bridge over a small brook, a croquet set waiting on the porch, and an English herb and perennial garden with a lattice arch. Upstairs rooms have private balconies with views of the Alarka Mountains, while the downstairs rooms in the English basement are smaller, but very cozy, with stone floors and walls, pressed-tin ceilings, and views of cattle in the neighboring fields. Located 3 miles from Bryson City and a scant .1 mile from the park entrance at Deep Creek, the country setting is a pleasing change from many area accommodations. *101 Folkestone Rd., Bryson City, NC 28713, tel. 704/488–2730 or fax 704/488–8689. 9 rooms. No TVs or phones. No credit cards. Closed Jan.–Feb. Moderate.*

Fryemont Inn. Covered with the bark of huge poplar trees cut in the 1920s, this rustic lodge was built by a timber baron, and it shows. Exposed wood is everywhere, from the rooms paneled with chestnut to the gleaming hardwood floors to the large timbers that support a high vaulted ceiling in an open dining room. Small windows in each room open for an aromatic, evergreen-suffused breeze. The ambience is a bit more reserved than that at the Hemlock Inn (*see below*); guests here tend to gather in small groups on the wide wooden porch with its paddle fans and muse over the view of mountain ridge and the Bryson City streetscape far below. In the lobby during the winter, a fire roars from a stone fireplace large

enough for eight-foot logs. If you're a light sleeper, ask for rooms away from the stairs, kitchen, and dining room. Nonguests are welcome in the restaurant, which features southern cooking and a superb trout Eugenia, a whole trout butterflied and lightly fried with mushroom stuffing. *1 Fryemont Rd., Box 459, Bryson City, NC 28713, tel. 704/488–2159 or 800/845–4879. 37 rooms, 3 cottage suites. Facilities: restaurant, outdoor pool, full bar. No TVs or phones. MC, V. MAP plan required. Closed Nov.–third week of Apr. Moderate.*

Hampton Inn Gatlinburg. With its high ceilings and airy lobby this hotel sets itself apart from many downtown chain establishments. Opened in July 1992, rooms are furnished with natural-finish pine beds and dressers and brass floor lamps and wall sconces. First-floor rooms on LeConte Creek have private balconies right on the water. *967 Parkway, Gatlinburg, TN 37738, tel. 615/436–4878, fax 615/436–4088. 96 rooms. Free Continental breakfast. Facilities: outdoor pool, fireplaces, wet bars, Jacuzzis. AE, D, DC, MC, V. Moderate.*

Hemlock Inn. While waiting for the dinner bell, guests gather on the flagstone porches of this mountaintop lodge to trade fish tales and tell of secret hiking spots. Perched high above three deep valleys on its own 44 secluded acres, the inn offers a real getaway. The only thing that separates you from the looming Alarka Mountains is a split-rail fence and a few bluebird boxes. There are no phones or TVs in the rooms, each furnished with simple country accents and beds and tables made by area artisans. Breakfast and dinner are served family style at large tables with lazy Susans laden with seasonal vegetables. *911 Galbraith Creek Rd., Bryson City, NC 28713, tel. 704/488–2885. 19 rooms, 4 cottages. MAP plan required. No credit cards. Closed mid-Dec.–mid-Apr. Moderate.*

Mid-Town Lodge. Chalet-style town houses are a favorite here: Each has a large stone fireplace, a loft bedroom with king-size bed, and a full bathroom tucked under cathedral ceilings. Downstairs is a complete kitchen and sofa bed. Other options in this heart-of-downtown hotel include poolside rooms, luxury rooms, suites, and efficiencies. Granted, the short red shag carpeting is a bit worn, but these are still great deals. Downstairs is a small gift mall, so there's plenty of bustle just outside the door; or opt for rooms in the newer, quieter Tower Building, with larger rooms with microwaves and small refrigerators and balconies overlooking the Little Pigeon River and the surrounding mountains. *805 Parkway, Gatlinburg, TN 37738, tel. 615/436–5691 or 800/633–2446. 133 rooms. Facilities: Jacuzzis, pool. AE, MC, V. Moderate.*

Squire Watkins Inn. Just a few blocks from historic Dillsboro, this secluded Queen Anne–style B&B has rooms filled with antiques, pineapple four-poster beds, and iron beds. Heirlooms from the innkeepers' families are in the large common areas, and a wide porch with swing and rockers overlooks 3 landscaped acres with towering white pines. For the best evening breezes, try the Dogwood or Rose rooms. Two Cape Cod–style housekeeping cottages with stone fireplaces and knotty pine woodwork are nearby. You'd expect to pay far more for an inn of this quality. *Box 430, Dillsboro, NC 28725, tel. 704/586–5244. No TVs or phones. No credit cards. Moderate.*

Wonderland Hotel. Those who loved the old Wonderland Hotel, which until 1992 was located inside the park at Elkmont, will find much to love about the new Wonderland. Clinging to a freshly cleared mountainside 1.5 miles from the Metcalf Bottoms Picnic Area off Little River Road, this sprawling lodge with its rough-sawn knotty pine exterior re-creates the rustic appeal of the time-worn original. Some of the old lodge's rocking chairs and swings line the 165-foot porch with a spectacular view of Cove Mountain and a constant breeze afforded by more than a dozen whirring paddle fans, but the latest Wonderland incarnation has some weathering to do. An exposed cinderblock foundation doesn't help, and rooms are furnished with reproduction antiques that seem strangely out of character with the rustic interiors. But its location and remote setting are

hard to beat, for now, at least. Lots are being sold and developed near the hotel, so it's likely the sound of bulldozers will mar the ambience for a few years. *3889 Wonderland Way, Sevierville, TN 37862, tel. 615/436–5490 or 615/428–0779, fax 615/429–4752. 29 rooms. Facilities: restaurant, stables for horses. No TVs or phones. Closed Jan.–mid-Mar. MC, V. Moderate.*

Fontana Village Resort. Originally built in the 1940s to house construction workers for the nearby Fontana Dam, this clustered community of cabins, cottages, a hotel, marina, and recreational facilities is a jewel of a find. Far in the wild, untrammeled western reaches of the park, there is no finer family vacation spot in the Smokies; and if you hike, fish, or consider yourself a champion porch rocker, you'll be happy you made the $1\frac{1}{2}$-hour drive out of Cherokee. This is casual country, nothing fancy. Rooms in the Fontana Inn are the typical motel offering; opt instead for one of the recently remodeled cottages, which are very cozy and comfortable, with fireplaces and kitchens. Once you've arrived, you'll be torn between utilizing as many of the area's considerable outdoor opportunities as possible, or perfecting your porch-rocking form. Tough choices. *Rte. 28, Box 68, Fontana Dam, NC 28733, tel. 704/498–2211 or 800/849–2258. 80 rooms, 100 cottages. Facilities: 2 restaurants, tennis courts, miniature golf, horseback riding, boating, fishing. AE, D, MC, V. Inexpensive–Moderate.*

Lloyd's on the River. Located halfway between Cherokee and Bryson City, and only 5 miles from each, this family-owned motor lodge caters to those searching to get away from the frenetic Cherokee downtown. Double porches, a nicely landscaped L-shaped pool, updated exteriors, and meticulous maintenance lend much charm to the 1950s appeal. Rocking chairs are full of guests swapping family photos. Rooms 1–12 have back porches overlooking the river. Carpeted rooms with wood paneling are very clean. Loaded with personality, this is a super dollar value. *Box 429, Bryson City, NC 28713, tel. 704/488–3767. 21 rooms. Facilities: outdoor* pool. D, MC, V. Closed Nov.–Mar. Inexpensive–Moderate.

Newfound Lodge. This clean, comfortable hotel is only .25 mile from the hub of Cherokee's activity, but it feels far more removed. Private balconies overlook the Oconaluftee River, with a small, well-maintained riverside lawn lined with maple and river birch trees. You can fish from your porch, if you're hungry enough. *34 U.S. 441 N, Cherokee, NC 28719, tel. 704/497–2746. 73 rooms. Facilities: outdoor pool. AE, D, MC, V. Closed Nov.– mid-Mar. Inexpensive–Moderate.*

Jarrett House. A regional landmark, this historic railway hotel with triple porches and a tin roof is located right in the middle of the bustling tourist district. It's a nice change of pace if you want to try a local B&B without breaking your budget. Floors creak and roll in the Victorian bedrooms. Light sleepers should request rooms off the street and away from the famous dining room, where the table is loaded up with southern-style veggies— butter potatoes, harvest peas—served family style. Old hands save valuable stomach space for the real stuff: country cured ham and trout, fried in a light, peppery batter, served with head and tail attached, with "trout refills" a mere $1.50 extra. *1 Haywood St., Dillsboro, NC 38725, tel. 704/586–0265 or 800/972–5623. 22 rooms, 4 with shared bath. Facilities: restaurant. No credit cards. Closed mid-Dec.–mid-Apr. Inexpensive.*

CAMPING

The wild backcountry of the park is an acclaimed backpacker's paradise: More than 800 miles of trails climb forested summits, cross open grassy balds, and plunge into mist-shrouded valleys. Most sites are available by self-registration at any of the 10 ranger's stations; others, including all Appalachian Trail shelters, are rationed due to heavy use and require telephone registration via the **Backcountry Reservation Office** (tel. 615/436–1231; open daily 8–6). Reserve these sites at least a month in advance.

INSIDE THE PARK There are 997 campsites at 10 park service campgrounds. Some are large complexes; others are tiny little nooks scattered about a creek; still others are tucked under the boughs of high elevation spruce-fir forests. Choose your campsite well, for the quality of your park experience will rest heavily on your decision. And choose it early if you're traveling in summer or fall, or you'll have your choice dictated by availability. Advance reservations for campsites are taken only at Elkmont, Cades Cove, and Smokemont campgrounds from May 15–October 31, and for any group campsite. For reservations, contact **HSN Mistix** (tel. 800/365–CAMP). All other park campgrounds are operated on a first-come, first-served basis.

There are no electrical hookups, water hookups, or showers at any of the park service campgrounds. Cold running water, fire grills, picnic tables, and flush toilets, however, are available at **Cades Cove** (161 sites main season, 19 off-season; disposal station, wood for sale, small grocery store, and bicycle rental); **Elkmont** (220 sites main season, 29 off-season; disposal station nearby, wood for sale); **Smokemont** (140 sites main season, 35 off-season; disposal station, wood for sale); **Balsam Mountain** (46 sites, closed mid-Oct.–late May; wood for sale); **Cosby** (175 sites, closed Nov.–early May; disposal station); **Deep Creek** (108 sites, closed Nov.–early May; disposal station, wood for sale); **Look Rock** (92 sites, closed Nov.–late May); **Abrams Creek** (16 sites, trailers limited to 12 feet, closed Nov.–mid-Apr.); **Big Creek** (12 sites, tents only, closed Nov.–mid-Apr.); and **Cataloochee** (27 sites, closed Nov.–mid-Apr.).

For family-oriented activities and accessibility to ranger's stations and interpretive programs, Cades Cove, Elkmont, and Smokemont campgrounds are a best bet. Elkmont is closest to Gatlinburg, while Smokemont is closest to Cherokee. Deep Creek is near superb creek tubing and hiking; Balsam Mountain is a remote campground with the highest elevation of all; and Big Creek, Cataloochee, and Abrams Creek offer the most solitude.

NEAR THE PARK Commercial campgrounds are clustered at the primary park entrances at Cherokee, North Carolina, and Gatlinburg and Townsend in Tennessee. On Big Cove Road outside of Cherokee are several large, popular campgrounds that largely cater to RVs, among them **Yogi-in-the-Smokies** (Star Rte., Box 54, Cherokee, NC 28719, tel. 704/497–9151) and **Cherokee KOA Campground** (Star Rte., Box 39, Cherokee, NC 28719, tel. 704/497–9711 or 800/825–8357).

Halfway between Cherokee and Bryson City, on U.S. 19, **Ela Campground RV Park and Grocery** (5100 Ela Rd., Bryson City, NC 28713, tel. 704/488–2410) packs RVs in close, but it's a super clean, well-maintained campground with friendly owners and 33 pull-through sites. Flower beds are maintained by the "seasonal residents." Bonuses are bicycle rentals, a mile-long walking trail, river access and tube rentals, an LP tank repair facility, and more than 1,000 movies for rent. The store's creaky wooden floors and board-and-batten exterior are reminiscent of an old country store. Inside is a game room and a popcorn machine, in addition to picnic and camping staples.

If convenience to facilities is a factor, or the park campgrounds are full, the tent sites in the "Riverwalk" section of the **Little River Village Campground** (8533 Rte. 73, Townsend, TN 37882, tel. 615/448–2241) rival park campgrounds for a pleasing woods setting and privacy. Just .2 mile from the park entrance, there are clean bathhouses, picnic tables with cement decks, inner-tube rentals, and complete hookups for RVs.

Halfway between Bryson City and the park's Deep Creek entrance, the **Deep Creek Tube Center Campground** (1090 W. Deep Creek Rd., Box 105, Bryson City, NC 28713, tel. 704/488–6055) is a pleasant full-hookup RV facility with two restored log cabins available as camping cabins. Rent inner tubes and ride the creek all the way back to the campground. There are only 23 sites, so reservations are strongly suggested.

Green Mountain National Forest
Vermont
By Tara Hamilton

Although they possess neither the craggy pitch of New Hampshire's White Mountains nor the rugged wilderness expanse of New York's Adirondacks, Vermont's Green Mountains work their own potent magic. Surging and swelling rather than slicing and jutting, they are mountains of wisdom and subtle elegance, asserting a modest grandeur. The landscape and wildlife are as richly diverse as the mountains are old. Just beyond the next rise might be a great blue heron standing nimbly beside a shimmering pond, the engineering marvel of a beaver dam, a cool stand of towering eastern hemlock, or a pair of awkwardly beautiful moose.

The mountains, though themselves rounded and softened with age, display the stark contrasts of the seasons. The sumptuous verdant tones of summer illustrate how the mountains got their name, while autumn's harvest is a vibrant palette of color known worldwide. Winter, both exquisite and ruthless, can cover the forest floor with hushed, deep snows or strand you in a nasty blizzard. Spring flourishes with new growth and a brilliant display of wildflowers.

One of 158 national forests, Green Mountain is divided into two sections, northern and southern. Together they cover 339,000 acres and stretch across nearly two-thirds of the state's length. Over the past few centuries, the landscape has seen dramatic changes. In the mid-1800s, logging had reduced Vermont's forest cover to a mere 20%, and much of the cleared land was used for grazing sheep. By 1900, however, westward migration and a weakened economy left pastures abandoned and fields fallow. Gradually, through the natural succession of plant communities, the state has been reforested, and now 80% is woodland. Though the national forest is still used for timbering, the focus is primarily on recreational pursuits: camping, wildlife viewing, hunting, fishing, skiing, snowmobiling, and, of course, hiking.

The centerpiece of the national forest's extensive trail network is the Long Trail (LT), the oldest long-distance hiking trail in the country and the prototype for the Appalachian Trail (with which it coincides for about 100 miles). For 265 miles from Massachusetts to Canada, the LT balances on the north–south central ridge-line—the spine of the Green Mountains— traversing 142 miles of the national forest and connecting with 175 miles of side trails. It's maintained cooperatively by the United States Forest Service and the Green Mountain Club, a nonprofit organization founded in 1910 and devoted to maintaining this "footpath in the wilderness."

As national parks and forests continue to attract more and more outdoor enthusiasts, the Green Mountain National Forest has managed to maintain a sense of solitude and peacefulness in six wilderness areas, comprising almost 60,000 acres. The result of the National Wilderness Preservation Act of 1964, these areas differ from the rest of the forest in their designated purpose: to provide large blocks of mature and old-growth trees for wildlife in need of undisturbed habitat and to offer visitors, lured only by the song of the birds and a sense of adventure, a chance to experience the remoteness and beauty of the deep woods.

ESSENTIAL INFORMATION

VISITOR INFORMATION For information about the national forest, contact the Forest Supervisor, **Green Mountain National Forest** (231 N. Main St., Rutland 05701, tel. 802/747–6700, TDD 802/747–6765). For information on specific regions, contact the **Manchester Ranger District** (Rte. 11/30, RR 1, Box 1940, Manchester Center 05255, tel. 802/362–2307), **Middlebury Ranger District** (U.S. 7, RR 4, Box 1260, Middlebury 05753, tel. 802/388–4362), or **Rochester Ranger District** (Rte. 100, RD 1, Box 108, Rochester 05767 tel. 802/767–4777).

Contact the **Green Mountain Club, Inc.** (Rte. 100, RR 1, Box 650, Waterbury Center 05677, tel. 802/244–7037) for information on the Long Trail; the **Appalachian Trail Conference** (Box 807, Harpers Ferry, WV 25425 tel. 304/535–6331) about the Appalachian Trail; the **Vermont Department of Forests, Parks, and Recreation** (Agency of Natural Resources, 103 S. Main St., Waterbury 05676, tel. 802/241–3655) concerning state parks; and the **Vermont Chamber of Commerce, Department of Travel and Tourism** (Box 37, Montpelier 05602, tel. 802/223–3443) or **Vermont Travel Division** (134 State St., Montpelier 05602, tel. 802/828–3236) for other travel information.

The U.S. Forest Service has suspended a previously imposed permit requirement and now allows dispersed camping on national forest lands. In return, campers are expected to follow strict fire-safety guidelines and "no trace" camping procedures: Sites should be at least 200 feet from any trail, stream, or pond; never use streams or ponds for washing dishes or clothes (water should be used and disposed of well away from a water source); remove all traces of having been at a site, including a fire; and don't camp where someone has clearly camped before, unless it is an established site. In addition, backpackers are urged to use the Long Trail's 62 cabins and lean-tos, each about a day's hike apart, to minimize camping impact. Certain restrictions, which are prominently posted, apply to fires and camping in designated recreation areas.

FEES There are no entrance fees for the national forest, although state parks and some recreation areas within its boundaries do charge admission for day use. Fees are also charged at the following staffed shelters and tenting areas: Battell, Skyline Lodge, Peru Peak, Lula Tye, Bigelow, and Vondell.

PUBLICATIONS An assortment of maps, pamphlets, and fact sheets covering an array of areas and topics—from day hikes and wheelchair-accessible interpretive trails to the latest moose management plan—is available from the forest service by mail or at any of the ranger district offices (*see* Visitor Information, *above*). Maps and brochures can also be obtained at state park visitor's centers. For in-depth explanations of the myriad trails in the Green Mountains, pick up a copy of *Day Hikes in Vermont* or *Guide Book of the Long Trail,* both put out by the Green Mountain Club (available in bookstores). *The Guide to the Appalachian Trail in New Hampshire and Vermont* is available from the Appalachian Trail Conference (*see* Visitor Information, *above*).

GEOLOGY AND TERRAIN In a number of episodes that occurred approximately 400 million years ago, massive continental and oceanic plates collided slowly but steadily, pushing up the earth's crust along a line roughly parallel to the East Coast. The result was the Appalachians, of which the Green Mountains are a part. The metamorphic rocks produced during the collision—greenstone, quartzite, gneiss, and the most common, schist—can be seen cropping out in numerous places, especially atop some of the higher peaks.

As a result of the east–west movement of the tectonic plates, the Green Mountains are oriented in three long, parallel, north–south ranges. The first, or front, range includes the Hogbacks and Taconics in the western portion of the state. To the east, the second, or main, range has most of the taller peaks and is often thought of as Vermont's spine. The third range, including the Northfields and Worcesters east of Route 100, are in the state's northern half and not within the national forest.

The Green Mountains' other great reshaping occurred during the most recent ice age, from 3 million to 10,000 years ago. Sheets of glacial ice up to 2 miles thick gouged and scraped at the mountains. When the glaciers retreated, they left behind a mishmash of boulders, rocks, pebbles, sand, and clay called till. The scouring action of the ice is largely responsible for the subtlety of the Greens: gentle, rounded peaks; broad, sloping valleys; and the sprinkling of mountain ponds and lakes.

FLORA AND FAUNA Most of the Green Mountains are covered by northern hardwood forests, in which sugar maple, American beech, and yellow birch predominate. Higher eleva-

tions, between 2,400 and 3,000 feet, are covered by a transitional forest consisting mainly of yellow and white birch and red spruce. Above 3,000 feet, red spruce and balsam fir dominate the landscape.

There is very little old-growth forest left in the Green Mountains due to the heavy logging and clearing of the 19th century, but just as forests have reemerged in the last 100 years, so too have several animal species previously driven from the state. Coyotes, pine marten, beavers, and moose have restaked their claim; in fact, moose have proliferated enough that a controversial hunting season was recently instituted. These species join the white-tailed deer, black bear, red fox, snowshoe hare, and bobcat as some of the national forest's larger mammals.

Also staging the beginnings of a comeback, with the help of a recovery plan formulated in 1979, is the peregrine falcon, endangered since the 1960s by the use of several "long-lived" pesticides, including DDT. Efforts to hatch and raise young peregrines in captivity and then release them in the wild have been successful; small populations are taking hold on Mt. Horrid and on the cliffs in the White Rocks National Recreation Area.

The U.S. Forest Service subscribes to a management plan that includes various methods of logging for equally various purposes: providing a diverse wildlife habitat, maintaining open areas for viewing animals, enhancing berry-bush growth, and, of course, producing high-quality timber for profit, which in turn helps promote and protect local jobs. The grassy clearings and heterogeneous forests that result provide good habitats for a majority of the 323 wildlife species, which require a mix of nonwooded areas and young forests for many of their activities.

WHEN TO GO If you plan to venture into the woods on foot, the best and most popular time is mid-June through October. Excursions in mid-April to late May, also known as mud season, will likely result in serious confrontations with snowmelt mire. In fact, many trails at higher elevations are officially closed until Memorial Day to prevent excessive erosion. More likely to be the bane of a spring sojourn, however, are the bugs: Mosquitoes and blackflies can be downright ferocious until mid- or late June, enough to intimidate even the most seasoned backpacker.

Whether on foot or in your car, crowds are not usually an issue except during peak foliage season, when the number of "leaf peepers" can be more than a bit disconcerting and accommodations hard to come by. If you can withstand the hordes, though, the astounding explosion of colors makes this an exceptional time to visit.

With snowfall often beginning as early as late October and lasting into April, winters are long, but there's certainly no shortage of outdoor recreational opportunities. Cross-country and downhill skiing, snowmobiling and snowshoeing, and, for the heartiest of souls, winter camping are all exceedingly popular. The tranquillity of winter in the woods, though alluring, should be approached with prudence, given the possibility of hypothermia and frostbite.

SEASONAL EVENTS The **Vermont Department of Forests, Parks, and Recreation** helps sponsor an annual summer arts and entertainment series in state parks near the national forest (*see* Evening Activities *in* Exploring, *below*).

WHAT TO PACK Although the Northeast may seem tame compared to the more rugged West, don't be lulled into complacency by the lack of towering peaks, grizzly bears, or unrelenting sun. The Green Mountains have their own temperament, and weather is weather no matter where you are. Unless you're only venturing on a very short hike, always carry provisions for cold and wet—even in summer. Bring good rain gear, and be sure to layer clothing made of wool, silk, or a synthetic material that wicks moisture well, such as polypropylene. In addition to standard wilderness gear (e.g., sunscreen, pocketknife, maps), pack some high-energy food for extended excursions, and never hike without an adequate water supply (*see* Staying Healthy and Safe *and* Hiking and Camping Equipment *in* the Essential Information *chapter*).

Sturdy walking shoes or hiking boots are a must, and if your plans include some porch sitting, bring a couple of good books.

GENERAL STORES In the south, the **Three Mountain Grocery** (Rte. 100), north of Jamaica, will fulfill food and other shopping needs, as will the larger grocery stores, pharmacies, and sport shops in Bennington, Manchester, Londonderry, and Wilmington. Bondville's **Winhall Market** (Rte. 30) carries choice meats, cheeses, and other picnic fixings. The **Newfane Country Store** (Rte. 30), in historic Newfane village, has been offering a wide range of high-quality goods, from Vermont-made food products to handcrafted gifts and toys, for nearly 120 years.

Rimming the northern section of the forest, small mom-and-pop grocery stores in Pittsfield, Stockbridge, Rochester, and Hancock provide such basics as toothpaste and picnic supplies. Head for the **Warren Store** (just off Rte. 100) in Warren for savory baked goods, ingredients for a gourmet meal in the woods, or its good selection of wines and newspapers; the emporium upstairs rivals some big-city boutiques. For more serious shopping, Waitsfield and Middlebury proffer **Grand Union supermarkets** (Rte. 100 and U.S. 7, respectively) and a variety of sporting goods and hardware stores. If you're stocking up for camping or backpacking, stop in the **Bristol Market** (North St.) or the **Natural Food Coop** (1 Washington St., Middlebury) for bulk goods and other munchies.

ATMS You'll find cash machines in the following towns in or near the national forest: Bennington, Brattleboro, Wilmington, Manchester, Ludlow, Rutland, Brandon, Middlebury, and Waitsfield.

ARRIVING AND DEPARTING The most practical means of reaching your destination in the Green Mountain National Forest is by car. Most trailheads and campsites are a fair distance from public transportation, though buses access some trailheads near major crossroads.

By Plane. Burlington International Airport (tel. 802/863–2874) is served by several major airlines, and smaller companies fly into the **Rutland, Springfield, Barre–Montpelier,** and **Stowe–Morrisville** airports. West of Bennington and convenient to southern Vermont, **Albany–Schenectady County Airport** in New York State is also served by several major carriers.

By Car and RV. Meandering their way along both the southern and northern sections of the Green Mountain National Forest, U.S. 7 and Route 100, on the western and eastern edges of the forest, respectively, make much of the area quite accessible. Several east–west roads cross the forest, some of which afford views worth the grumbling protests issued from your struggling vehicle. In the south, Route 9, otherwise known as the Molly Stark Trail, connects Bennington and Wilmington and passes by the trailhead for the George D. Aiken Wilderness. Route 140 passes through Wallingford, the northern boundary of the southern section, and accesses the White Rocks National Recreation Area. U.S. 4 heads from the New York border past Rutland, the southern boundary of the forest's northern section, and the Pico and Killington ski areas. Route 125 passes by the Robert Frost Interpretive Trail and near the Bread Loaf Wilderness, while the Lincoln Gap Road and Route 17, heading over the Appalachian Gap, access northern areas of the national forest.

By Train. Amtrak's (tel. 800/872–7245) *Montrealer,* an overnight train connecting New York City and Montreal, stops at Brattleboro, Bellows Falls, Claremont, White River Junction, Montpelier, Waterbury, Essex Junction, and St. Albans in Vermont. The *Adirondack,* which runs from New York City to Albany and Glens Falls, New York, and then to Montreal, is convenient for western and southern Vermont.

By Bus. In addition to providing limited access to trailheads, **Vermont Transit Lines** (tel. 802/864–6811 or 800/451–3292; in VT, 800/642–3133) connects Bennington, Brattleboro, Burlington, Rutland, and other cities in Vermont with Boston, Springfield (Massachusetts), Albany, New York City, Montréal,

and cities in New Hampshire. Call for information regarding particular drop-off points.

EXPLORING

The forest is well served by a combination of state highways and national forest roads, but it's outside your car's confines that you can best appreciate the beauty of the place. With 512 miles of hiking trails winding through the forest, leg power is ultimately the best way to experience the Green Mountains.

THE BEST IN ONE DAY If all you've got is one day to take it all in, you'll need a car and some energy. Start with a sumptuous breakfast at one of the many country inns or bed-and-breakfasts in southwestern Vermont. Then— preferably with picnic provisions stowed in a cooler—head east from Arlington on the Kelley. Stand Road (also called the Arlington–West Wardsboro Road and Forest Road 6) for quick entry into the backwoods. At the 12-mile mark, turn right into the Grout Pond Recreation Area (*see* Nature Trails and Short Walks, *below*), where you'll find easy hiking trails and opportunities for fishing, taking a dip, or paddling a canoe. (You can rent in Arlington or at nearby Stratton Mountain Village.) If you'd like to see the forest without putting on hiking boots, try it on the back of a horse. Trail rides are offered at the Stratton Mountain Ski Area (*see* Horseback Riding *in* Other Activities, *below*).

After exploring the area, continue east to West Wardsboro and head north on Route 100. Take your time enjoying the mountain scenery and the sleepy villages of Jamaica, Peru (just off Rte. 100), and Weston. Time for lunch? Take a break at either the Greendale Campground (Forest Rd. 18, 2 mi north of Weston) or at the peaceful Weston Priory (.1 mi north of junction of Rtes. 100 and 155), a Benedictine monastery. If you don't have picnic provisions already, pick them up at the general stores in Peru or Jamaica or the cheese shop in Weston.

After lunch, continue north on Route 100 for a meandering 50-mile foray through the heart of central Vermont, stopping for an afternoon

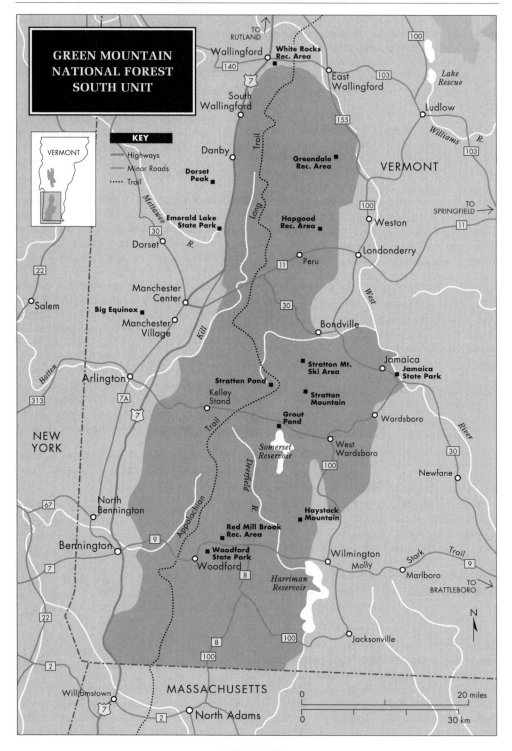

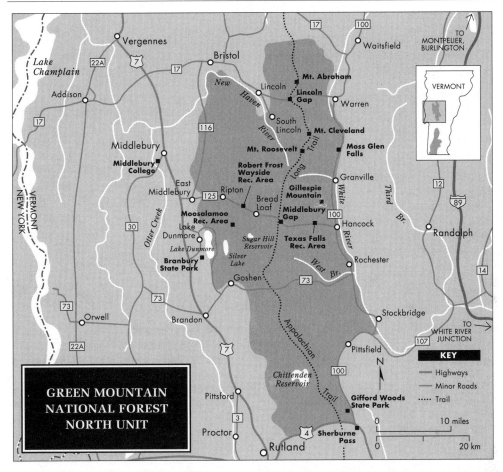

GREEN MOUNTAIN
NATIONAL FOREST
NORTH UNIT

dip (weather permitting) in any of the lakes or rivers along the way. Turn left on Route 125 in Hancock and, after 3 miles, right into the Texas Falls Recreation Area. Here Texas Brook has gouged a small chasm out of the surrounding rock. There's a 1.2-mile nature trail loop worthy of the time it takes. Continue west on Route 125 up to the top of Middlebury Gap, where you can access the Long Trail. A half-mile hike to the south brings you to Lake Pleiad, one of the highest lakes in the state.

Down the other side of the ridge, Route 125 passes through the historic Bread Loaf Campus of Middlebury College (*see* Historic Buildings and Sites, *below*) and past the Robert Frost Wayside and Interpretive Trail

(*see* Nature Trails and Short Walks, *below*). Here you can enjoy the gathering dusk while acquainting yourself with Frost's poems in the woods and fields that inspired him. Continue through the tiny hamlet of Ripton and on to East Middlebury, Middlebury, or Bristol for dinner in a fine restaurant and a well-deserved rest in one of the many B&Bs.

ORIENTATION PROGRAMS The **Vermont Department of Forests, Parks, and Recreation** (*see* Visitor Information *in* Essential Information, *above*) sponsors **summer naturalist programs** at state parks, many of which are within or adjacent to the borders of the national forest. Programs include workshops or talks on such subjects as astronomy, natural history, and Native American and early American crafts.

A few miles north of the national forest's northern section, the **Green Mountain Audubon Nature Center** (Huntington–Richmond Rd., RD 1, Box 189, Richmond 05477, tel. 802/434–3068) is bursting with great things to do, see, and learn and is a wonderful place to orient yourself, get comfortable in the woods, expand your knowledge, and pique your interest in the natural world. The center's 230 acres of diverse habitats are a sanctuary for wild things, and 5 miles of trails encourage the visitor, through trail maps and self-guiding materials, to explore and understand the workings of various natural communities. The center regularly offers events such as dusk walks, wildflower and birding rambles, nature workshops, and other community events and educational activities for both kids and adults.

GUIDED TOURS **Vermont Hiking Holidays** (Box 750, Bristol 05443, tel. 802/453– 4816) runs hiking trips of varying lengths that combine learning about the natural world with the comforts and good food of cushy country inns. **North Wind Country Hiking Tours** (Box 46, Waitsfield 05673, tel. 802/496–5771) offers various outings and excursions, as does **Vermont Country Walkers** (89 S. Main St., Waterbury 05676, tel. 802/244–1387), which touts trips designed to "please your senses, not test your endurance."

The **Vermont Department of Forests, Parks, and Recreation** (*see* Visitor Information *in* Essential Information, *above*) conducts guided nature walks and hikes as well as canoe and boat outings in the state parks.

SCENIC DRIVES AND VIEWS Following **Route 100** as it pokes in and out of the eastern edge of the national forest is as pleasurable as a leisurely drive in the country can get. You'll move through pastoral valleys, forested tunnel-like stretches, and quiet country villages of sparkling white houses with their obligatory green shutters. One particularly fine section snakes through **Granville Gulf;** this "natural reservation" is free of man-made structures and boasts the origins of the Mad

River, which heads north, and the White River, which runs south, as well as the 70-foot Moss Glen Falls.

As far as chin-dropping views go, it's hard to top those from the **Appalachian Gap,** the crest of **Route 17,** which connects the towns of Waitsfield and Bristol and skirts the forest's northern border. Crossing the Green Mountain's spine at the **Brandon, Middlebury, and Lincoln gaps,** also in the northern section, yields gorgeous serpentine drives. Due to Lincoln's tight curves and steep grade, some might want to choose a less menacing route, and it's closed during the winter.

In the southern section, **Kelley Stand Road,** which reaches 2,726 feet on its exciting traverse of the forest, and **Forest Road 10** between Danby and Peru, immerse you in the solitude of the wilderness without your even getting out of the car.

HISTORIC BUILDINGS AND SITES On the hillside of Mt. Moosalamoo near Lake Dunmore is **Ethan Allen's Cave,** a huge hollowed-out boulder that was used as a hideout and storage spot by Vermont's favorite son and his Green Mountain Boys during the land-grant disputes between Colonial New Hampshire and New York, each of which claimed Vermont for its own. Although Vermont ultimately declared itself an independent nation, from 1776 to 1791, Allen and his cohorts diligently participated in the American Revolution by capturing Fort Ticonderoga, across Lake Champlain, without firing a shot. The cave is marked with a carving by the local chapter of the Daughters of the American Revolution. Follow the Ethan Allen Trail from the Falls of Lana on Route 53.

Just to the east of the Robert Frost Wayside on the north side of Route 125 in Ripton is an unmarked road leading to the **cabin** the poet used for 23 summers. It lures those who want to poke around his old haunts in hopes of absorbing the enchantment and solitude that no doubt inspired many of his poems. Owned by Middlebury College, the site has been kept deliberately obscure to prevent the casual passerby from marring its tranquillity.

One-half mile to the east on Route 125 is the sprawl of mustard-yellow buildings that make up the **Bread Loaf Campus** of Middlebury College. The campus's veranda-and-flapping-screen-door country simplicity makes it look like a Shady Acres–type home for the aged, but that's the idea. For more than 70 years, these serene meadows, bordered by the national forest, have fostered aspiring writers attending the Bread Loaf Graduate School of English and the Bread Loaf Writers' Conference, started by Robert Frost.

NATURE TRAILS AND SHORT WALKS **Robert Frost Interpretive Trail** (2 mi east of Ripton on Rte. 125) is an easy 1-mile loop through swamps, woods, and blueberry and huckleberry bushes. Plaques along the trail carry smatterings of his writings. The first .3 mile, which runs along a beaver pond, is accessible by wheelchair.

Seven miles to the east across the Middlebury Gap is the **Texas Falls Nature Trail** (3 mi west of Rte. 100 on Rte. 125), an easy 1.2-mile loop along the cascading Texas Brook. The trail begins just across a footbridge near the base of the falls.

A favorite easy hike to a dramatic spot is the one-hour, 1.5-mile round-trip jaunt to **Sunset Ledge.** From Lincoln Gap head south on the Long Trail. It climbs steeply at first, affording fine views to the east, and then levels off fairly quickly, revealing stunning panoramas of the Adirondacks and Lake Champlain to the west.

The **Grout Pond Recreation Area** (12 mi east of Arlington off Kelley Stand Rd.) maintains a series of pleasant, short loop trails totaling about 8 miles. They encircle Grout Pond and access the north end of nearby Somerset Reservoir.

Little Rock Pond, reached via the **Homer Stone Brook Trail** (east of South Wallingford on U.S. 7), is one of the most popular (i.e., heavily used) areas on the Long Trail. It's a moderate 5-mile round-trip hike to the pond.

The **Natural Bridge Trail** begins just west of U.S. 7 at the entrance to Emerald Lake State Park. It passes two old dams, veers right, and begins a short but steep and winding climb, before descending to a natural bridge spanning a brook's narrow gorge. The round-trip is about 3 miles.

LONGER HIKES The long spine of the Green Mountains' main ridge is the national forest's dominant feature, and the **Long Trail,** which runs along it, makes for satisfying long-distance hikes. In addition, a whole network of side trails, some of them loops, provides plentiful options for climbing peaks or traversing the spine and returning to lower elevations. Pick up the LT at any gap crossing and head north or south to the next one; these gap-to-gap jaunts can provide one to three or more days of backwoods repose. Arrange to leave a vehicle at your destination.

Southern Section. More trail networks offer a greater variety of loop options here than in the northern section. From U.S. 7, 2 miles north of Emerald Lake State Park, the **Lake Trail** follows an old carriage path that once brought folks from the valley to an inn on **Griffith Lake.** Two miles up the trail, turn left on the **Baker Peak Trail,** which ascends the peak, providing views of the valley and the marble quarries on Dorset Peak, and meets up with the Long Trail. Take the LT south, back to the lake, and from there take the Lake Trail back to where you started. The whole trip is about 6 miles. For another loop in this area, start at Forest Road 10, just east of a suspension bridge, and take the Long Trail south to Griffith Lake. Return via the **Old Job Trail,** which runs northeast along several old logging roads, past an extensive clearing where the village of Griffith once stood (a shelter occupies the spot now), and back to Forest Road 10.

The **Stratton Pond** area, bounded by Route 11/30 in the north, Stratton Mountain in the east, the Kelley Stand Road in the south, and the Lye Brook Wilderness in the west, has an array of options for long day hikes or extended backpacking trips. Because several trails intersect, many combinations of routes and loops are possible, and all are enjoyable. What follows is only a sampling.

If you begin from Kelley Stand Road, you can choose from three northbound trails: the **Branch Pond Trail,** the **Long Trail,** and the **Stratton Mountain Trail** (the most strenuous). The latter two converge at Stratton Pond—the largest body of water on the Long Trail—where you can circle the pond before heading either north on the LT or west toward **Bourne Pond.** There you can continue west into the Lye Brook Wilderness or take the Branch Pond Trail south, passing **Branch Pond** before returning to Kelley Stand Road. (Of course you can also make the loop in a clockwise direction.)

From the north, try the **Lye Brook Trail.** (To reach the trailhead, take Route 11/30 east ½ mile from U.S. 7 in Manchester Center, head south for 1.3 miles on Richville Road, and then east on Lye Brook Road for about ½ mile.) The trail follows an old logging road before beginning a steady climb to Lye Brook Hollow. There the path levels off, meanders along old railroad beds and logging roads and past a dramatic waterfall, and finally meets up with the upper end of the **Branch Pond Trail.** (From the trailhead to Bourn Pond is 7.3 miles.)

For a different approach from the north, drive east on Route 11/30 from Manchester Center for 2½ miles, and turn right on Rootville Road, following it ½ mile to its end, where there's limited parking. (Be careful not to obstruct private driveways.) Ascend about 2 miles along a flumelike stream to a junction with the Long Trail. About 200 feet east via the LT is **Prospect Rock,** an aptly named vantage point towering above Downer Glen, with an excellent view of Mt. Equinox, Dorset Mountain, and the valley below. To make a loop, walk south on the Long Trail about a mile to the Branch Pond Trail, from which you can pick up the Lye Brook Trail north (*see above*). From its trailhead, just go east on the logging road to get back to your car.

Northern Section. The climb to the summit of **Mt. Abraham** can be approached in two ways: heading north from the Lincoln Gap via the Long Trail or heading east from a trailhead at the end of Mosley Road in the town of Lincoln via the **Battell Trail.** Mt. Abe's rocky summit, well above timberline, boasts some of the best views in the Green Mountains— the panoramic expanse of New York's Adirondacks to the west, the Greens' three ranges stretching to the north and south, and on a clear day, the White Mountains of New Hampshire 80 miles to the east. Either before or after being blown away by the 360° view, look down and take note of the summit's rare and fragile community of arctic-alpine vegetation. Be especially careful to protect this endangered plant life by staying on the marked trail or rock outcroppings when hiking above tree line.

A full-day 12.5-mile circuit into the heart of the **Bread Loaf Wilderness**—at 58,000 acres, the largest of the six wilderness areas—begins and ends at the **Cooley Glen** trailhead (Forest Road 54 between South Lincoln and Ripton). The trail starts with a gentle climb, crosses a tributary of the New Haven River several times, and intersects the Long Trail. Head south on the LT over the summits of Mts. Cleveland, Roosevelt, and Wilson (the latter two have terrific views to the south and east) before taking the **Emily Proctor Trail** back down to your starting point.

Appalachian Trail. The Appalachian Trail (AT) runs for 2,100 miles from Springer Mountain, Georgia, to Mt. Katahdin in Maine. Since it was modeled after the Long Trail, it's curious that today one of its least celebrated sections is the 136 miles in Vermont, including nearly 100 miles along the Long Trail.

From the Massachusetts border, the AT follows the LT through hollows, brook crossings, and beaver ponds before gaining substantial elevation north of Route 9. It then makes its way across peaks and valleys, skirting Stratton Pond and the northern boundary of Lye Brook Wilderness. Griffith Lake, Little Rock Pond, and Spring Lake beckon the hiker to swim or picnic.

A half mile north of Sherburne Pass on U.S. 4, the AT diverges from the LT and heads east. A mile later, it enters Gifford Woods State Park, with one of a handful of virgin hardwood stands in Vermont. Next the AT crosses

Route 100 and leaves the national forest; for much of the rest of its way in Vermont, it passes along old logging roads and still-used "town highways." (More than half of Vermont's roads are gravel, so it's not surprising that some are designated highways of sorts.) The intrepid traveler may find this part of the AT lacking in awe-inspiring views and challenging terrain, but those looking for gentle hiking options along tranquil backcountry roads will find it pleasant and steeped in the spirit of New England.

OTHER ACTIVITIES **Back-Road Driving.** In addition to those already mentioned, a host of forest roads provide backcountry access. In the southern section, **Forest Road 71,** whose scenery is well worth the rough ride, connects Kelley Stand Road with Somerset Road, Somerset Reservoir, and Route 9. In the northern section, **Forest Road 42** (Bingo Road), off Route 73, is a long climb with lots of vistas. **Forest Road 55,** near Granville, follows the White River's headwaters and gets well up Gillespie Mountain. **Forest Road 32** (Ripton–Goshen Road) runs north–south along the western edge of the mountains' spine and has several scenic spots; a side trip leads to Voter Brook overlook, where you can see to the Adirondacks. Near Forest Road 32's terminus, **Forest Road 224** heads east into open expanses. Several back roads between Lincoln and Ripton, including **Lincoln–Ripton Road, Forest Road 59,** and **Forest Road 54** (Natural Turnpike), are ideal for exploring the woods.

Biking. Thanks to its quiet backcountry roads, rolling countryside, quintessential New England towns, and friendly people, Vermont teems with cyclists during warm weather. They range from muddy, single-track mountain-bike racers to pampered inn-to-inn tour guests. Since the national forest covers the state's hilliest terrain, cyclists should be prepared to sweat at least a little.

Given the shortage of paved roads in the national forest, pedaling on a sturdy mountain bike or hybrid is your best bet. All of the roads listed above under Back-Road Driving are excellent choices. The **Woodford** area,

south of Route 9 off Forest Road 273, has an extensive network of ridable trails and roads, and the **Green Peak** area, north of Manchester off Dorset Hill Road, has some challenging rides up to a couple of abandoned quarries. **Forest Roads 25** and **55,** off Route 100 between Warren and Granville, and **Forest Roads 60, 30,** and **279,** off Forest Road 10 between Danby and Peru, access old logging roads and hefty climbs; they're perfect for getting you and your bike as grungy as your soul desires.

For those on road bikes, there are countless options just outside the forest's borders. Pick up a copy of *25 Bicycle Rides in Vermont,* by John Friedin, for suggestions.

The **Mad River Bike Shop** (Rte. 100, Waitsfield, tel. 802/496–9500), **Green Mountain Bikes** (Rte. 100, Rochester, tel. 802/767–4464), **Vermont Pedal Pushers** (Rte. 11/30, .5 mile east of U.S. 7, tel. 802/362–5200), and **Mountain Bike Peddler** (954 E. Main St., Bennington, tel. 802/447–7968) all rent and repair bikes and provide maps and information.

Bird-Watching. With at least 150 species living in and around the national forest, there's plenty going on overhead. Among them are seven species of hawk, eight sparrows, five owls (including the great horned and long-eared), and at least 15 varieties of warbler. Keep an eye out for nesting loons on quiet, undeveloped ponds, and for turkey vultures and the recently reintroduced peregrine falcon on cliffs at higher elevations. Spring and autumn offer the added bonus of migratory species, as the honking of Canada or snow geese flying in formation can attest.

The **Vermont Institute of Natural Science** (Church Hill Rd., R.R. 2, Box 532, Woodstock 05091, tel. 802/457–2779), a nonprofit organization dedicated to environmental education and research, hosts a variety of bird-related workshops and talks, including banding demonstrations. Its **Raptor Center** provides top-quality medical care and rehabilitation for injured birds of prey, with the goal of releasing them into the wild. Permanently disabled birds are kept in spacious habitats accessible to visitors.

Boating. Boating in the national forest is best pursued in the southern section. **Grout Pond** is ideal for canoeing, although the state does allow electric motors. **Hapgood Pond** and **Somerset, Harriman,** and **Adams reservoirs** are also nice. Northern options include **Chittenden Reservoir,** east of Pittsford off U.S. 7, and **Silver Lake** and **Sugar Hill Reservoir,** accessed by Forest Road 32. Canoeing down the **White River** along Route 100 is a popular pastime, too.

Umiak Outfitters (Gale Farm Center, Mountain Rd., Stowe, tel. 802/253–2317 or 800/479–3380) offers customized instruction and tours, including day trips and longer excursions, in addition to a comprehensive retail shop. **Batten Kill Canoe Ltd.** (Rte. 7A, Manchester, tel. 802/362–2800) is a complete paddler's shop with rentals, sales, lessons, tours, and a shuttle service.

Cross-Country Skiing. The 280-mile **Catamount Trail** runs the length of the state on old logging roads, groomed cross-country trails, and snowmobile trails and passes through more than 20 ski-touring centers and by many inns and B&Bs. Much of it traverses the national forest. The **Catamount Trail Association** (Box 1235, Burlington 05402, tel. 802/864–5794) provides maps and information for self-guided skiing and sponsors guided trips ranging from day tours on gentle terrain to longer, more challenging backcountry tours. Other trail networks can be found just north of the **Moosalamoo Campground** (near Goshen on Forest Rd. 32), at the **Chittenden Brook Campground** (off Rte. 73), and at **Grout Pond Recreation Area** (off Kelley Stand Rd.).

Caroll and Jane Rikert Ski Touring Center (Rte. 125, Ripton, tel. 802/388–2759) has 50 kilometers of varied machine-tracked trails that meander through the forest; instruction, rentals, and repairs are provided as well. **Blueberry Hill** (Ripton–Goshen Rd., Goshen, tel. 802/247–6735), in the heart of the national forest, offers 75 kilometers of trails, 50 of them machine tracked; instruction; rentals;

repairs; and dining and lodging in the adjacent country inn. Though outside the national forest, **Camel's Hump Nordic Ski Center** (Handy Rd., R.D. 1, Box 422, Huntington, tel. 802/434–2704) has the most spectacular setting of any Vermont ski center. It's worth the few extra miles to get there. In the foothills under the shadow of the Green Mountains' most distinguished peak, has 65 kilometers of trails, 40 of which are machine tracked; instruction; rentals; and repairs on premises. **Hermitage Cross-Country Ski Area** (Coldbrook Rd., Box 457, Wilmington, tel. 802/464–3511) has 50 kilometers of trails, 40 of them machine tracked, including a ridgetop trail with spectacular views of the Mt. Snow valley. Instruction, rental, repairs, and excellent dining and lodging in the fine inn are also available.

Fishing. Vermont has ample angling opportunities in mountain streams and undeveloped lakes and ponds. Their limestone bottoms have helped spare them the destruction by acid rain wrought on the waters of the nearby Adirondacks. Brook and rainbow trout, landlocked salmon, yellow perch, northern pike, bass, bullhead, and panfish are common catches.

In the southern section, the **Batten Kill,** the state's most well-known trout stream, originates above Dorset and flows for about 25 miles through Manchester and Arlington before emptying into the Hudson River in New York. Despite many years of heavy fishing, the river's consistently cool waters yield quality brown and brook trout. Access is from Route 313 and River Road just south of Manchester. If you're looking for good backwoods fishing, head for **Stratton, Branch,** or **Bourne ponds** (*see* Longer Hikes, *above*). The nearby **Somerset** and **Harriman reservoirs** offer boating access to both warm- and cold-water species.

Pickings are slimmer in the northern section. Four-mile-long **Lake Dunmore,** just west of the forest, produced the state's record rainbow trout. Beautiful walk-in ponds along the Long Trail network and **Chittenden Reservoir** offer up fish as well.

The **Vermont Fish and Wildlife Department** (103 S. Main St., Waterbury 05676, tel. 802/244–7331) can supply license applications, a pamphlet outlining fish and wildlife laws, and a list of organizations that provide guided fishing trips. Licenses, required of anyone 15 or older, can also be purchased at local sporting goods and general stores as well as many town clerk's offices.

Junction Sports (U.S. 7, New Haven, tel. 802/453–3555) and, in Waitsfield, **Inverness Sports** (Rte. 100, tel. 802/496–3343) and **Bisbee's Hardware** (Mad River Green, tel. 802/496–3635) supply fishing equipment.

Horseback Riding. In the southern section, **Horses for Hire** (167 South Rd., Peru, tel. 802/824–3750) and **Stratton Stables** (behind the base lodge at Stratton Mountain, tel. 802/297–2200) offer mountain trail rides in the national forest. Just outside the northern section, **Cobble Hill Farm** (Painter Rd., Middlebury, tel. 802/388–7027) and **Icelandic Horse Farm** (Common Rd., Waitsfield, tel. 802/496–7141) provide riding and instruction.

Rope and Rock Climbing. Due to the soft nature of a lot of the rock in the Green Mountains, climbing opportunities are limited. However, if the need to get vertical overwhelms you, contact **Climb High** (U.S. 7, South Burlington, tel. 802/985–5055), where you can buy or rent equipment, use an indoor climbing wall, or get tips on where to find some solid rock.

Snowmobiling. Nearly 2,000 miles of groomed snowmobile corridors and 1,500 miles of secondary trails run along designated unplowed roads and trails as part of an extensive statewide system, developed and maintained by the Vermont Association of Snow Travelers. Within the national forest, snowmobiling is permitted only on these trails, which are marked on the winter Recreation Map, available for $2 at district ranger offices.

Snowshoeing. The trails and roads listed in previous sections are also great choices for winter use, provided you know what you're doing. If you're not entirely comfortable in the woods in the winter, stick to shorter, easier trails close to roads, and no matter what, carry extra food and clothing and notify others of your whereabouts. Many ski centers (*see* Cross-Country Skiing, *above*) rent snowshoes.

Swimming. Just jump in! There are plenty of places to get your feet wet in the national forest. Most of the rivers in and around the forest, including the **White, Mad,** and **West rivers** and the **Batten Kill,** have many a swimming hole. Or try a recreation area: **Grout Pond,** a popular unsupervised swimming and canoeing spot, or **Hapgood Pond** (*see* Camping, *below*), where, for a fee, you get a full-fledged camping and day-use area with toilets and hot showers.

Other local favorites include **Bartlett's Falls** (off Rtes. 17 and 116, Lincoln), famous for its numerous cascading pools, and a good **swimming hole** at the edge of East Middlebury (near Rte. 125 bridge, where the road begins to climb).

CHILDREN'S PROGRAMS The national forest doesn't sponsor activities for kids, but many of the state parks' evening events and nature programs are suitable for children (*see* Evening Activities, *below, and* Orientation Programs, *above*). The **Green Mountain Audubon Nature Center** (*see* Orientation Programs, *above*) holds several ecology day-camp sessions as well as preschool programs.

EVENING ACTIVITIES The Vermont Department of Forests, Parks, and Recreation offers **campfire programs** in the state parks and, along with the Vermont Council on the Arts and the Vermont Youth Conservation Corps, sponsors the **Summer Series,** an arts and entertainment program. Performances and workshops, which have included fables, storytelling, puppetry, and folk and jazz music, are hosted at the Branbury, Emerald Lake, and Jamaica state parks, bordering the national forest. Shows, for which there's no additional charge, generally begin at 7. Contact the Department of Forests, Parks, and Recreation (*see* Visitor Information *in* Essential Information, *above*) for dates and locations.

DINING

SOUTHERN SECTION Because of the large number of former city dwellers turned innkeepers and restaurant owners, as well as the presence of the New England Culinary Institute in Montpelier, dining in and around the Green Mountain National Forest is about as varied as that in more populated urban areas. You'll find everything from New York City–style pizza to the newest of nouvelle cuisine. Dress is casual, unless noted otherwise.

Main Street Café. Since it opened in 1989, this small storefront with polished hardwood floors, candlelit tables, fresh flowers, and northern Italian cuisine has drawn raves. The rigatoni tossed with Romano, Parmesan, broccoli, and sausage in a cream sauce and the chicken stuffed with ham, provolone, and fresh spinach and served in a Marsala-onion sauce are favorites. *Rte. 67A, North Bennington, tel. 802/442–3210. Reservations advised. AE, DC, MC, V. Closed lunch and Mon., Tues., Thanksgiving, Christmas. Expensive.*

Wildflowers. The dining rooms of the Reluctant Panther have long been known for elegant cuisine, and the new owner is upholding that tradition. A huge fieldstone fireplace dominates the larger of the two dining rooms; the other is a small greenhouse with five tables. Glasses and silver sparkle in the candlelight, the service is impeccable, and the menu, which changes daily, might include boneless stuffed chicken with spinach, Gruyère, and chardonnay-thyme sauce or fricassee of lobster with Nantucket Bay scallops and Gulf shrimp. *West Rd. at Rte. 7A, Manchester, tel. 802/362–2568. Reservations required. Dress: casual but neat. AE, MC, V. Closed Tues., Wed. Expensive.*

Alldays and Onions. A deli and restaurant, this place does both well. Ingredients are fresh and recipes creative for both take-out items and a dinner menu that changes daily. Innovative dishes include sautéed scallops and fettuccine in a jalapeño-ginger sauce and

rack of lamb with a honey-thyme sauce. Pastries and other desserts are baked on the premises. *519 E. Main St., Bennington, tel. 802/447–0043. Reservations accepted. MC, V. Closed Sun. Inexpensive–Moderate.*

Quality Restaurant. Gentrification has reached this down-home neighborhood eatery, which was the model for Norman Rockwell's *War News.* The restaurant now has Provençal wallpaper and polished wood booths; such sturdy New England standbys as grilled meat loaf and hot roast beef or turkey sandwiches have been joined by the likes of tortellini Alfredo with shrimp and smoked salmon. *Main St., Manchester, tel. 802/362–9839. Reservations accepted. AE, MC, V. Inexpensive–Moderate.*

Blue Benn Diner. Breakfast is served all day in this authentic diner, and the eats are as down-home as turkey hash and as off-the-wall as breakfast burritos (scrambled eggs, sausage, and chiles wrapped in a tortilla). There can be a long wait. *U.S. 7 N, Bennington, tel. 802/442–8977. Reservations advised. No credit cards. Closed Sun.–Tues. dinner. Inexpensive.*

NORTHERN SECTION **Swift House.** The white paneled wainscoting, elaborately carved mahogany and marble fireplaces, and cherry paneling give a formal elegance to the dining room in this Georgian home, which once belonged to a 19th-century governor and his philanthropist daughter. An attentive staff serves an adventurous menu that might include angel-hair pasta with imported mushrooms and macadamia pesto sauce or smoked pheasant salad with vinaigrette. *25 Stewart La., Middlebury, tel. 802/388–9925. Reservations advised. Dress: casual but neat. AE, D, MC, V. Expensive.*

Mary's. Walking off the sleepy streets of Bristol and into this little storefront restaurant is like finding a precious antique in a dusty attic. It's earned a reputation as one of the most inspired dining experiences in the state. Seasonal offerings include Vermont rack of lamb with a rosemary mustard sauce, Norwegian salmon Szechuan style, and venison au poivre. For dessert try the Bailey's white-chocolate-chip cheesecake. *11 Main St., Bristol, tel. 802/453–2432. Reservations advised. AE, MC, V. Moderate–Expensive.*

Woody's. Peach walls with diner-deco fixtures, abstract paintings, and cool jazz can be a bit off-putting after a long hike in the woods. Lack of warm hues and comfortable booths aside, the food is worthy and the view of Otter Creek isn't bad either. Nightly specials often include Vermont lamb; charbroiled strip steak with smoked Cheddar nachos and salsa butter might be another choice. *5 Bakery La., Middlebury, tel. 802/388–4182. Reservations advised. DC, MC, V. Moderate–Expensive.*

Back Home Cafe. Wooden booths, black-and-white linoleum tile, and exposed brick give this second-story café the air of a hole-in-the-wall in New York City, where the owners come from. Dinner might be baked stuffed fillet of sole with spinach, mushrooms, feta cheese, and tarragon sauce or any number of Italian favorites. Daily lunch specials consist of soup, entrée, and dessert for less than $6. *21 Center St., Rutland, tel. 802/775–2104. Reservations accepted. MC, V. Inexpensive–Moderate.*

Miguel's. Subtle flavors, ample portions, and a hopping cantina make this local favorite a good bet when satisfying an appetite is of prime importance. In addition to burritos and the like stuffed with a wide choice of fillings, there are daily specials that might include grilled salmon with mango or black-bean-and-corn salsa. For the faint of heart, there's always a gringo option. Everything's made from scratch, including the chips and salsa. *Sugarbush Access Rd., Warren. tel. 802/583–3858. Reservations accepted. MC, V. Inexpensive–Moderate.*

PICNIC SPOTS In the southern section, have a picnic at **White Rocks Recreation Area** (follow signs on Rte. 140 in Wallingford) for great views of towering cliffs, or at **Grout Pond Recreation Area** (*see* Nature Trails and Short Walks *in* Exploring, *above*) and explore the trails before, during, or after your meal. For more solitude, just head out on any trail or back road and pick your spot.

There are several picnic areas along Route 100 in the northern section, including **Branden Brook Picnic Area** (8.4 mi west on Rte. 73); **Texas Falls Recreation Area** (3 mi west on Rte. 125), which has a few relatively short trails in addition to tables and a falls observation site; and **Peavine** (near Stockbridge). Picnic facilities under a red pine grove make the **Robert Frost Wayside** (Rte. 125) a pleasant spot. For a more rugged experience (sans picnic tables), head for **Lake Pleiad** (.5 mi south of Rte. 125 on the LT), **Sunset Ledge** (.5 mi south of Lincoln Gap Rd. on the LT), or **Abby Pond** (2.5 mi west of Rte. 116 on a blue-blazed trail, East Middlebury).

LODGING

Lodging in and around the national forest runs the gamut from chain motels and ski lodges to cozy bed-and-breakfasts and elegant country inns. Availability depends on season and location. Take your pick on a quiet spring weekend, but you'll have to take your chances near a major ski area in February or anywhere during peak foliage time (late September to early October) without a reservation. Choices are usually plentiful, though, especially in the larger towns, and almost every village, however small and remote, has a generations-old inn or a newly sprouted B&B. Be aware that some lodgings close during the slower seasons, April–May and late October–early December.

SOUTHERN SECTION **The Reluctant Panther.** In a town full of outlet and off-price stores, this inn is about as removed from the woods as you can get, but it's great for those in search of a little shopping and a lot of indulgence. Spacious rooms each have goose-down duvets, a complimentary half-bottle of wine, and an eclectic mix of antique, country, and contemporary furnishings. Ten rooms have fireplaces, and the four suites have whirlpools. The best views are from rooms B and D. *West Rd., Box 678, Manchester 05354, tel. 802/362–2568 or 800/822–2331. 20 rooms. Facilities: restaurant, lounge, conference room. AE, MC, V. Expensive.*

Nutmeg Inn. This cozy inn has all the Colonial touches you'd expect in a two-centuries-old farmhouse: an old butter churn, antique dressers, rag rugs, mason jars with dried flowers, and hand-hewn beams in the low-ceilinged living room. Three suites in the barn are larger and get less road noise, and the king suite has a private balcony with a terrific view of Haystack Mountain. Rates include a full breakfast. *Rte. 9W, Wilmington 05363, tel. 802/464–3351. 13 rooms. AE, MC, V. Moderate–Expensive.*

Darling Family Inn. The rooms in this renovated 1830 farmhouse have baskets of apples and hand stenciling, and some have folk art or an antique silver pitcher. Cottages in back are less meticulously furnished (twin beds, a refrigerator, and a shower stall) and allow pets. Full breakfast is included. *Rte. 100, Weston 05161, tel. 802/824–3223. 5 rooms, 2 cottages. Facilities: outdoor pool. No credit cards. Moderate.*

Hill Farm Inn. This homey inn right next to the famed Batten Kill still has the feel of the country farmhouse it used to be. The mix of sturdy antiques and hand-me-downs, a spinning wheel in the upstairs hall, paintings by a family member, the beefalo (yes, beefalo) that roam the 50 acres, jars of homemade jam, and loaves of fresh-baked bread convey a relaxed, friendly atmosphere. Room 7 has a beamed cathedral ceiling and a porch with a view of Mt. Equinox; rooms in the 1790 guest house are very private. Rates include full breakfast. *U.S. 7, Box 2015, Arlington 05250, tel. 802/375–2269 or 800/882–2545. 13 rooms, 5 share bath; 4 cabins in summer. Facilities: restaurant. AE, D, MC, V. Moderate.*

Molly Stark Inn. Tidy blue plaid wallpaper, gleaming hardwood floors, and a wood-burning stove in the sitting room's brick alcove, combined with the innkeeper's charisma, give country charm to this recently renovated 1860 inn. The first-floor Rockwell Room is spacious but opens on the sitting room; Molly's Room, in the back, gets less noise from Route 9. There's no smoking, and a full breakfast is included. *1067 E. Main St., Ben-*

nington 05201, tel. 802/442–9631. 6 rooms, 4 share bath. MC, V. Inexpensive–Moderate.

NORTHERN SECTION **Blueberry Hill Inn.** Here, tucked on a backcountry road in the hushed woods of the national forest, you can pamper yourself while "roughing it." Access to trails doesn't come any easier, and the two fireplaces, solarium, and pond are ideal spots in which to indulge yourself. *Ripton–Goshen Rd., Goshen 05733, tel. 802/247–6735 or 800/448–0707. 12 rooms. Facilities: restaurant, cross-country ski center, sauna. MC, V. Expensive.*

Churchill House Inn. First, walk down the road to check out the llamas. Then settle into the sauna or read a book on the screened porch until dinner's ready. With access to 25 kilometers of trails, a help-yourself kitchen, and homey country decor, this place is very casual—perfect for the outdoor enthusiast. Rooms are furnished with antiques; some have whirlpools. *Rte. 73, RD 3, Box 3265, Brandon 05733, tel. 802/247–3300. 8 rooms. Facilities: outdoor pool, sauna. MC, V. Moderate–Expensive.*

Waybury Inn. If this inn looks familiar, it's because it appeared as the "Stratford Inn" on TV's "Newhart." Guest rooms, some of which have the awkward configuration that can result from converting a building of the early 1800s, have quilted pillows, antique furnishings, and middle-aged plumbing; the Robert Frost Room has a four-poster bed. Comfortable sofas around the fireplace create a homey living room, and the pub serves the best variety of beer in the area. *Rte. 125, East Middlebury 05740, tel. 802/388–4015 or 800/348–1810. 14 rooms. Facilities: restaurant, pub. AE, D, MC, V. Moderate–Expensive.*

Beaver Pond Farm Inn. The expansive views of mountains and beaver ponds from the inn's huge deck and the charming, romantic rooms are lure enough, but the real attraction is the nearly effortless access to hiking and cross-country ski trails and to the first tee of the championship Sugarbush Golf Course next door. Rates include a full breakfast. *Golf Course Rd., Box 306, Warren 05674, tel.*

802/583–2861. 6 rooms, 2 share bath. MC, V. Moderate.

Crystal Palace B&B. In this small, cozy inn with Old World elegance, rooms are decorated delicately with antiques, cut crystal, and lace. Ideally located, it's just two blocks north of the village green and a quick drive away from the Appalachian and Lincoln gaps and the Long Trail. The gazebo and goldfish pond in back make for pleasant spots to put your feet up. Breakfast is Continental. *48 North St., Bristol 05443, tel. 802/453–4131. 6 rooms share bath. Facilities: gazebo. MC, V. Inexpensive–Moderate.*

Long Run Inn. Across the street from the New Haven River and its numerous swimming holes and down the road from the Lincoln Gap and the Long Trail, this inn is just the thing for the outdoor lover who doesn't feel like camping. Sitting on the inn's wraparound porch facing the subdued little town's main street brings illusions of lazy summer afternoons spent by generations past. Food is the specialty here: hearty country breakfasts, afternoon hors d'oeuvres, and ample family-style dinners. You can even get a packed lunch. *Lincoln Gap Rd., Lincoln 05443, tel. 802/453–3233. 8 rooms share bath. No credit cards. Closed Nov.–Apr. Inexpensive.*

CAMPING

The national forest campgrounds listed below tend to provide fewer facilities (e.g., showers, electricity) than private campgrounds, but they offer immediate access to the ruggedness of the forest while still being close to the comforts and perceived refuge of your vehicle. Except at Hapgood, camping is on a first-come, first-served basis. Campgrounds are accessible by gravel or paved road, and sites have gravel surfacing that can accommodate RVs up to 18 feet. Water hand pumps and nonflush vault toilets are provided, and fees are $5 at all areas, except at Hapgood, where the toilets flush and the fee is $10.

Chittenden Brook (6 mi west of Rte. 100 on Rte. 73) has 17 sites and provides easy access to the Long Trail via the Chittenden Brook Trail. **Greendale** (2 mi northwest of Rte. 100 on Forest Rd. 18, near Weston) has 14 sites and is near hiking and fishing. The most heavily used, **Hapgood Pond** (north of Peru on Forest Rd. 3, tel. 802/244–5045 before mid-May, 802/824–6456 thereafter, for reservations) has 28 sites, a self-guided nature trail, swimming, fishing, boating, and hot showers. **Moosalamoo** (3.2 mi south of Rte. 125 on Forest Rd. 32) offers 19 sites (three wheelchair-accessible), a wheelchair-accessible toilet, and great hiking and is close to Sugar Hill Reservoir's fishing and canoeing. **Red Mill** (north of Rte. 9 on Forest Rd. 274, near Bennington), with 16 sites, is a good spot if you're arriving late from points south.

With 1,600 acres of semiprimitive land, a 79-acre pond, and 8 miles of multipurpose trails, **Grout Pond Recreation Area** (*see* Nature Trails and Short Walks *in* Exploring, *above*) is another option. There are five designated hike-in campsites (four accessible by canoe) and three lean-to–type shelters. The water spigots are turned off in winter.

For a list of private campgrounds and state parks with camping facilities, contact the **Vermont Department of Forests, Parks, and Recreation** (*see* Visitor Information *in* Essential Information, *above*).

Gulf Islands National Seashore
Florida, Mississippi
By Dick Pivetz

amilies and beach bums
day-trip to Gulf Islands National Seashore, RVers trek
between its Florida and Mississippi districts,
and walkers and bird-watchers stroll along
the many nature trails. Sometimes it seems as
much a beach resort as a national park, except
that instead of dense crowds and high-rise
hotels you find acres of soft sand and sea oats
that wave gently in the breeze.

The park, comprised of 11 sections, sprawls
along 150 miles of Gulf of Mexico coastline
from Fort Walton Beach in the Florida Pan-
handle to Gulfport, Mississippi. Six sections
are in Florida: Okaloosa (19 acres on
Chochtawhatchee Bay), Santa Rosa (1,598
acres), Ft. Pickens (1,742 acres), Naval Live
Oaks (1,378 acres), and Fort Barrancas and
Advanced Redoubt (64 acres), and Perdido
Key (1,041 acres). Five sections are in Mississippi: Davis Bayou (401 acres), Horn Island
(3,650 acres), Petit Bois Island (1,466 acres),

East Ship Island (362 acres), and West Ship
Island (555 acres).

Spanish explorers recognized the strategic
significance of the islands that are now part
of the national seashore. Power changed
hands regularly for 300 years, as the land was
claimed alternately by Spain, Great Britain,
and France, until 1821, when the United
States flag first flew here. Established in 1971,
Gulf Islands is a relative newcomer to the
National Park Service family.

In the Florida district there are beaches at the
Santa Rosa, Okaloosa, Perdido Key, and Ft.
Pickens areas. All offer fishing, and rangers
at Fort Pickens can recommend good spots for
scuba diving. You can jet ski in the waters
near Okaloosa, Santa Rosa, Ft. Pickens, and
Perdido Key. Only Ft. Pickens has camping,
but all areas have picnic facilities. History
buffs can explore Ft. Pickens and Ft. Barrancas, 19th-century brick fortresses, on their
own or on a ranger-led tour. Nature lovers

find diverse flora and fauna, and stargazers delight in clear nights—the glare of city lights is absent.

On the Mississippi side are West Ship, East Ship, Horn, and Petit Bois islands, each about 12 miles offshore, accessible only by boat. (There were three islands before Hurricane Camille's 240-mile-per-hour winds cut Ship Island in two in 1969.) West Ship Island, accessible by excursion boats from Gulfport and Biloxi in the spring, summer, and fall, has picnic facilities, 19th-century Ft. Massachusetts, and sand—lots of soft, white sand. Ferry service isn't available to the other three islands, two of which, Petit Bois and Horn, were declared wilderness areas by an act of Congress in 1978; to reach them you must have your own boat or charter one licensed by Gulf Islands National Seashore. At the Mississippi section's sole mainland area, Davis Bayou, in Ocean Springs, you can ride through the salt marsh in a johnboat or camp for a few days amid stands of live oaks. Fishing and boating are also popular, but, with alligators aplenty, swimming is not allowed.

ESSENTIAL INFORMATION

VISITOR INFORMATION Both districts can provide information about the entire national seashore; when contacting the park, be sure to specify the type of information you need.

Florida District. Contact the Superintendent, **Gulf Islands National Seashore** (1801 Gulf Breeze Pkwy., Gulf Breeze 32561, tel. 904/934–2600) or stop by the Naval Live Oaks Visitor Center on Santa Rosa Island (tel. 904/934–2600; open Apr.–Oct., daily 8:30–5; Nov.–Mar., daily 8:30–4:30). For information about Pensacola, contact the **Pensacola Convention & Visitor Information Center** (1401 E. Gregory St., Pensacola 32501, tel. 904/434–1234, 800/874–1234, or 800/343–4321 in FL); the **Santa Rosa Island Authority** (Drawer 1208, Pensacola Beach 32561, tel. 904/932–2259); or the **Pensacola Beach Visitor Information Center** (Box 1174, Pensacola Beach 32561, tel. 904/932–1500).

Mississippi District. Contact the Superintendent, **Gulf Islands National Seashore** (3500 Park Rd., Ocean Springs 39564, tel. 601/875–0821). You can also stop at the **William M. Colmer Visitor Center** in Davis Bayou (tel. 601/875–0821; open June–Labor Day, daily 9–6; Labor Day–Oct. and Mar.–May, daily 8–5; Nov.–Feb., daily 8–4:30). For information on coastal Mississippi, contact either the **Biloxi Visitors Center** (710 Beach Blvd., Biloxi 39530, tel. 601/374–3105); the **Mississippi Gulf Coast Chamber of Commerce** (1401 20th Ave., Drawer FF, Gulfport 39502–0950, tel. 601/863–2933); or the **Mississippi Beach Convention and Visitor's Bureau** (Box 6128, Gulfport 39506–6128, tel. 601/896–6699 or 800/237–9493).

FEES Admission is free to all park areas except Ft. Pickens and Perdido Key, where entrance fees are $4 for a seven-day permit. No permits or fees are required for primitive camping where it is available (for more information, *see* Camping, *below*).

PUBLICATIONS Free National Park Service Site Bulletins covering all aspects of the park are available at visitor's centers.

Bird-watchers will look to *Birds and Birding of the Gulf Coast*, by Judith Toups (University Press, $22.95). Birders in the Florida district will want *The Birds of Escambia, Santa Rosa, and Okaloosa Counties, Florida*, by Robert A. Duncan (published by the author and available from him at 614 Fairpoint Dr., Gulf Breeze, FL 32561; $10.95).

GEOLOGY AND TERRAIN Gulf Islands National Seashore preserves three landscapes: southeastern deciduous forests, bayou marshes, and barrier islands, which protect the mainland from storms. The barrier islands—West Ship, East Ship, Horn, and Petit Bois islands in Mississippi, and, in Florida, Perdido Key and Santa Rosa Island—are made of shifting sand, unstable sand dunes, and salt marshes. Here, the beaches are flat and the soil sandy. Backing the beaches, parallel to the Gulf of Mexico, are the primary dunes, whose vegetation slows wind erosion. Still farther inland is another set of dunes, the so-called secondary dunes, which may stand alone or be connected to the primary dunes. They are anchored by vegetation. As a result of gulf currents that bombard their eastern shorelines and dump sand on their western coasts, the barrier islands actually "move." Over the years, the western tip of Santa Rosa Island has moved several hundred yards father west; more fragile Ft. McRee, which once stood on the eastern point of Perdido Key, has been washed away entirely.

At Mississippi's Davis Bayou, a typical bayou salt marsh, the Mississippi Sound meets the mainland, and shallow water and plentiful vegetation nurture fish, migratory birds, and other wildlife. The soil is more stable than in beach areas and able to support the root systems of the live oaks, magnolias, and pine trees that grow along the bayou shore.

FLORA AND FAUNA Vegetation on the islands and in the bayous and salt marshes is determined primarily by a species's tolerance for salt. The primary dunes support only sea oats and the occasional beach morning glory, beach pea, sea purslane, sea rocket, and pennywort. As primary dunes give way to secondary dunes, more species flourish: jointweed, woody goldenrod, golden aster, rockrose, rosemary, and evening primrose. In summer, look for white arrow-leaf morning glories, yellow St. John's wort, and pink meadow beauties between the dunes and the forest.

Still farther inland are slash pines, scrub live oaks, and palmettos. Near freshwater marshes, cattails and saw grass proliferate. Slash, loblolly, and sand pines dot the landscape, and immense live oaks, many cloaked in Spanish moss, reach towering heights on the mainland. Never touch the moss in summer unless you want to battle the itch of chiggers, which live in the fragrant green stuff.

Animal life along the coast ranges from fish and shellfish to the American alligator. In the gulf, Florida pompano, sea trout, red drum, sharks, cobia, redfish, and sheepshead are plentiful. Shrimps, crabs, and southern flounder have found homes in the gentler waters of Mississippi Sound. Bird life includes ospreys, brown pelicans, and great blue herons. Horn Island has a large rabbit population. Watch out for less friendly creatures: Eastern diamondback rattlesnakes, water moccasins, and alligators reside in the area. Although the latter are sometimes seen on the barrier islands, they prefer the freshwater of the bayous. Raccoons seem to be everywhere in the park; campgrounds are a favorite target of these bandits.

All plants and animals on the national seashore are protected by law, and to help preserve the natural habitat, visitors are asked to stay on established trails.

WHEN TO GO Gulf Islands National Seashore is popular year-round, so don't think you'll find bargains in the low season at the many beach resorts of the Florida district.

Summers are warm and sunny, and winters are temperate. Summer coastal temperatures creep into the high 80s, and although offshore breezes temper the heat, midsummer can be unbearable for hiking and exploring. Spring and fall are the most inviting seasons, with daytime highs in the 70s and nighttime lows in the 50s. In winter, expect the mercury to dip into the upper 30s to mid-40s. This is the season when surf anglers, bird-watchers, and beachcombers use the beaches. Bird-watchers arrive for the spring and fall migratory periods.

Storms come and go year-round, but early summer through fall is the time for hurricanes. Although they're infrequent, you should keep abreast of changing weather patterns if you visit during this time. There isn't a defined rainy season, but brief, heavy rainstorms are common in spring and summer, as pressure systems sweeping across the country pull gulf moisture onshore, and winter is fairly wet.

SEASONAL EVENTS Gulf Islands has no scheduled events of its own, but nearby communities offer plenty. Any celebration related to coastal seafood delicacies is hotly attended.

Florida District. Late January: Artificial snow is imported to Pensacola Beach on

Santa Rosa Island for **Snow Fest** (tel. 904/932–2259), much to the delight of everyone who misses northern winters. **Early June:** The annual **Fiesta of the Five Flags** (tel. 904/932–2259) features a sand castle contest, children's treasure hunt, parades, and a fishing rodeo and other water-related sporting events. **Mid-September: The Pensacola Seafood Festival** (tel. 904/433–6512) draws shellfish junkies from around the world. **Mid-November:** The navy's **Blue Angels** (tel. 904/452–2311), the famed aerial demonstration team, star in an annual air show held at Sherman Field, near Pensacola's National Museum of Naval Aviation.

Mississippi District. Early April: Many of the antebellum homes (tel. 601/432–5836) of Ocean Springs and Gulfport open their doors to visitors. **Early May:** Biloxi hosts a **Shrimp Festival** (tel. 601/435–5578), serving thousands of pounds of what some visitors swear is the best boiled crustacean ever savored. **Early July:** Gulfport is the center of the action for the annual **Deep-Sea Fishing Rodeo** (tel. 601/863–2933). **Mid-September:** In the Gulfport area, what is said to be the world's largest **Sand Sculpture Contest** (tel. 601/896–2434) attracts many teams, who use sand, water, and hand tools to sculpt objects relating to an assigned theme.

WHAT TO PACK Pack for a beach resort—swimsuits, shorts, and T-shirts—because casual wear is the order of the day, even in most restaurants. If hikes are on your itinerary, pack a rain poncho in your knapsack. Don't forget sunscreen and a hat—the sun's rays are especially intense when reflected off the water and sand, and there are few trees for cover. Take comfortable, lightweight walking shoes for climbing around the 19th-century forts or strolling the nature trails. Cool evening breezes on your sun-scorched skin will make you glad to have a windbreaker. If you're camping, venturing onto Davis Bayou, or fishing from the docks, pack insect repellent.

GENERAL STORES Well-stocked stores are virtually nonexistent within the park boundaries; only **Perdido Key, Ft. Pickens,** **Santa Rosa,** and **Okaloosa** have snack stores, and they carry a minimal supply of food and beach and picnic supplies—hot dogs, sandwiches, soft drinks, and the like. The **campground store** at Ft. Pickens Campground (tel. 904/932–3275; open Apr.–Oct., daily 8–8) has the best selection. Outside the park boundaries on the Florida side, where park areas are interspersed with bustling beach communities, shopping is not a problem. The Davis Bayou Campground in Mississippi has no campground store, but there's plenty of shopping in nearby Ocean Springs.

ATMS In Florida, look for the Bank of the South on Santa Rosa Island, as well as other banks in Pensacola and Gulf Breeze. In Mississippi there are banks in Gulfport, Biloxi, and other towns and cities along the coast.

ARRIVING AND DEPARTING **By Plane. Pensacola Municipal Airport** (tel. 904/435–1745), about 13 miles from the Florida district's Ft. Pickens, is served by most major airlines, including **Delta, NW Airlink, Continental, USAir,** and **American Eagle.** You'll probably need to rent a car; there's no local bus transportation to the park. Companies with offices at Pensacola's airport include **Avis** (tel. 904/433–5164), **Budget** (tel. 904/474–3721), and **Thrifty** (tel. 904/477–5553). Mississippi visitors can fly to **Gulfport/Biloxi Regional Airport** (tel. 601/863–5951), which is served by **Delta, Northwest, Continental Express,** and **American Eagle.** You can rent a car from **Avis** (tel. 601/864–7182), **Budget** (tel. 601/864–5181), or **Hertz** (tel. 601/863–2761).

By Boat. West Ship, East Ship, Horn, and Petit Bois islands are accessible only by boat. Most people visit West Ship via **Ship Island Excursions** boats from March through October (Gulfport tel. 601/864–1014, Biloxi tel. 601/432–2197). The trip takes 55 minutes from Gulfport, 75 minutes from Biloxi. Boats leave at about 9 and noon and return from West Ship at about 3:45 and 6:45; round-trip tickets are $12 for adults, $6 for children.

To reach East Ship, Horn, and Petit Bois and to get to West Ship between December and February, you must charter a boat; contact the

Colmer Visitor Center (tel. 601/875–0821) for a list of licensed operators.

By Car and RV. From Pensacola, U.S. 98 will take you to Gulf Breeze. The Naval Live Oaks area is just east of Gulf Breeze on U.S. 98. To reach Fort Pickens and Santa Rosa, take Route 399 from Gulf Breeze to Pensacola Beach. From there, Fort Pickens is 9 miles west, Santa Rosa is 10 miles east. The Okaloosa area is on U.S. 98 east of Fort Walton Beach. To reach Ft. Barrancas and the Advanced Redoubt, take Route 292 from Pensacola, then turn left onto Route 295, which will lead you to the Pensacola Naval Air Station, in whose confines both areas are located—you must stop at the gate to obtain a pass (free). For Perdido Key, take Route 292; on the island, turn left onto Johnson Beach Road.

In Mississippi, take the Ocean Springs exit from I–10, then drive south to U.S. 90, which runs past the park entrance at Davis Bayou. Gulfport and Biloxi are off U.S. 90.

By Train. Amtrak (tel. 800/872–7245) runs the *Sunset Limited* between California and Florida via the southern United States. Three trains per week travel east and three west, stopping at Pensacola, Gulfport, and Biloxi.

By Bus. In Florida the **Escambia County Transit System** (tel. 904/436–9383) and **Greyhound Lines** (Pensacola tel. 904/476–4800) offer fairly extensive service throughout the area. In Mississippi, Greyhound has stations in Biloxi (tel. 601/436–4335) and Gulfport (tel. 601/863–1022). This area is also served by **Coastliner** (tel. 800/647–3957) and **VIP Mobile Shuttle Service** (tel. 800/738–5466).

EXPLORING

To experience Gulf Islands, you can explore on foot or by bicycle, or you may just sit still on a soft spot on the sand. Ft. Pickens, Ft. Barrancas, and Ft. Massachusetts can be visited on foot, either on your own or with a ranger-led tour. The many nature trails are neither long nor difficult. You'll find them in Mississippi at Davis Bayou and in Florida at Fort Pickens, Naval Live Oaks, Perdido Key, and Fort Barrancas.

You can take a scenic boat ride to West Ship Island and tour Ft. Massachusetts. At Davis Bayou, rangers offer a free evening johnboat trip on summer weekends. Space is limited to the first 20 visitors in line by 5 PM at the Colmer Visitor Center (tel. 601/875–0821); call in advance to make sure the trip will be run on the day you plan to take it.

THE BEST IN ONE DAY **Florida District.** Fort Pickens offers a sampling of Gulf Islands activities. You can take a break from sunning or fishing to learn about the national coastal-defense system or stroll along a nearby nature trail. Two short trails reveal the diverse ecosystem of a barrier island; a longer trail leads around the western tip of Santa Rosa Island. The small **Fort Pickens Museum** (tel. 904/934–2635; open Apr.–Oct., daily 9:30–5; Nov.–Mar., daily 8:30–4), near the fishing pier at the Fort Pickens area, has excellent dioramas on park wildlife and military history. You can picnic at the beachfront pavilion or in one of the park's shaded picnic areas.

Mississippi District. Taking in this side of Gulf Islands in a day is a little tricky. Catch the excursion boat to West Ship Island (*see* Arriving and Departing by Boat *in* Essential Information, *above*). The 75-minute ride takes you across Mississippi Sound, busy with shrimp boats, intracoastal barges, and oceangoing freighters (some full of chickens and chicken parts bound for Russia); dolphins are often spotted during the ride. Spend some time examining brick Ft. Massachusetts (*see* Historic Buildings and Sites, *below*) and strolling the island's 7-mile beach. West Ship's snack bar sells hot dogs, sandwiches, fruit, and soft drinks; if you want anything else, pack a lunch. If you like to fish, bring your own tackle and you can go for sheepshead, which are often caught from the dock near the fort. The return ride often includes a view of a lipstick-hued gulf sunset.

ORIENTATION PROGRAMS Campfire talks give an overview of Gulf Islands National Seashore and explain the delicate balance of its flora and fauna and the history of the National

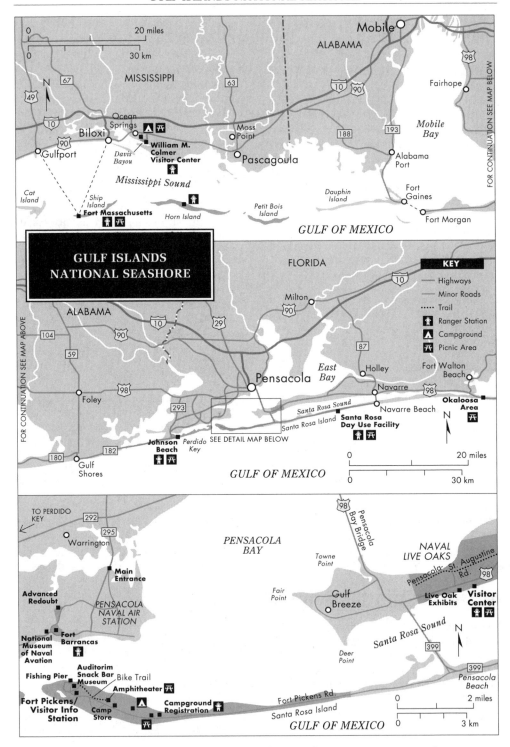

GULF ISLANDS
NATIONAL SEASHORE

Park Service's attempts to preserve it. The talks are erratically scheduled in spring and fall at the Fort Pickens amphitheater (tel. 904/934–2635 for information); at Davis Bayou they are held in the campground amphitheater on Saturday evening from November through February (tel. 601/875–0821). In the auditorium at the Naval Live Oaks Visitor Center (tel. 904/934–2600) you can ask to see a 12-minute slide show on the park, and at the **Colmer Visitor Center** at Davis Bayou (tel. 601/875–0821) you can ask to see a video.

GUIDED TOURS Rangers conduct tours of three of the park's forts: **Ft. Massachusetts** (summer, daily 10:30 and 4); **Ft. Pickens** (year-round, weekdays at 2 and weekends at 11 and 2); and **Ft. Barrancas** (summer, weekdays at 2 and weekends at 11 and 2). Candlelight tours are also occasionally scheduled at Ft. Pickens. Confirm schedules for ferries and tours with one of the two main visitor's centers before you make plans (tel. 904/934–2600 in Florida or 601/875–0821 in Mississippi).

SCENIC DRIVES AND VIEWS Driving toward Ft. Pickens on narrow Santa Rosa Island provides a sparkling glimpse of the gulf. Also take in the view from atop **Ft. Pickens** across Pensacola Bay to the naval air station, Ft. Barrancas, and Lighthouse Point; the view of Pensacola Bay from **Ft. Barrancas**; the breezy sea scene from the beaches at **Okaloosa**, **Santa Rosa**, and **Perdido Key**; and the dramatic boat approach to narrow **West Ship Island** (don't be intimidated by the massive brick fort near the dock—the cannons haven't been fired in years).

HISTORIC BUILDINGS AND SITES Florida District. The **Water Battery of Ft. Barrancas** (in Spanish, the Bateria de San Antonio) is the last of four remaining Spanish fortifications overlooking the entrance to Pensacola Bay. Built in 1797, it came under U.S. control in 1821. American engineers built a new fort—today's Ft. Barrancas—into the bluff above the old Water Battery (1839–44) and linked the two with a tunnel. **Ft. Pickens** was built on the western tip of Santa Rosa Island between 1829 and 1834 and **Ft. McRee** on the

eastern tip of Perdido Key between 1834 and 1839. These forts are part of an extensive coastal-defense system launched following the War of 1812. From 1845 to 1849 the army constructed the **Advanced Redoubt** to protect the mainland flank of Ft. Barrancas; it was used only once, however—as an ordnance depot during the Civil War.

The **Pensacola Naval Air Station** (Naval Blvd., off U.S. 98, tel. 904/452–2311) houses about 120 historic aircraft, a spectacular collection that includes planes used by renowned World War II marine Major Greg "Pappy" Boyington, Lieutenant Junior Grade George Bush, and the navy's Blue Angels Aerial Demonstration Team. Exhibits and films document naval aviation. The free 250,000-square-foot **National Museum of Naval Aviation** (Naval Air Station, tel. 904/452–3604, open daily 9–5) complements the collection of planes with exhibits and films on aeronautical topics.

Mississippi District. West Ship Island's **Ft. Massachusetts,** never used much militarily, is an excellent example of a restored coastal masonry fort. Its 15-inch Rodman cannon and carriage are capable of firing a 15-inch-diameter cannonball weighing more than 300 pounds as far as 3 miles. Ft. Massachusetts, begun in 1859, was completed in 1866.

NATURE TRAILS AND SHORT WALKS Excellent trails traverse both districts. When you hike, watch out for fellow travelers—particularly snakes, chiggers, and ticks— as well as cactus and poison ivy.

Florida District. Naval Live Oaks has two short trails and one longer one. The **Visitor Center Trail** winds .7 mile (one way) along Santa Rosa Sound and through a forest of Spanish moss–draped live oaks. The mile-long (one way) **Beaver Pond Trail** runs along the area's northern boundary, passing a large pond with an active beaver lodge. The 2.2-mile (round-trip) **Pensacola–St. Augustine Trail,** originally part of the Pensacola–St. Augustine Road used by early Spanish explorers, passes through woods of sand pines, longleaf pines, pignuts, southern magnolia, and scrub oak. The only interpretive trail markers here are along the Visitor Center Trail.

The **Blackbird Marsh Trail** meanders through the marshes and forests behind the campground of the Ft. Pickens unit. The .25-mile (one way) **Dune Nature Trail** passes through primary and secondary dune systems. Perdido Key's .25-mile (one way) **Johnson Beach Nature Trail** takes you through a marsh on the sound side of the key, where you'll see the short-growth shrub environment typical of maritime forests, with lots of sea oats, palmettos, slash pine, and scrub live oak.

Mississippi District. At Davis Bayou the .5-mile (one way) **Nature's Way Trail** edges the bayou, leading through dense forests. Stop by the small pond across the street from the trailhead to see the resident alligator (hands off!).

LONGER HIKES Although there are no designated longer trails at Gulf Islands, you can hike for miles along the beaches. On **Perdido Key** in Florida, the trek from the end of Johnson Beach Road to the jetties on the northeastern tip of the key and back is 12 miles round-trip. There's not a lot to see except surf and sand dunes—but you can count on good surf fishing and plenty of privacy. In Mississippi you can circumnavigate **West Ship Island**—it's a sandy 7 miles. A shorter, more leisurely hike of 2 miles from the swimming area around the west tip of the island to Ft. Massachusetts takes about 1¹/₂–2 hours. Remember to bring water and wear sunscreen and a hat.

OTHER ACTIVITIES Biking. In Florida, Ft. Pickens is popular for cycling. A 2-mile bike path connects Battery Langdon near the ranger station with the fort. Rentals are available for $2 per hour from the **campground store** (tel. 904/932–3275). Pensacola Beach has a 4.5-mile trail, and many cyclists ride the highway between the beach and the bike trail at the Ft. Pickens area. The **Live Oak Bicycle Trail** in Ocean Springs, Mississippi, goes into the Davis Bayou area; you can get a map at the Colmer Visitor Center (tel. 601/875–0821).

Bird-Watching. Visitor's centers in both districts distribute handouts identifying birds and the best times to spot them. With its diverse habitats, the park attracts an eclectic avian population, including more than 280 species. In Florida the Naval Live Oaks area, Ft. Pickens, and Perdido Key (particularly the self-guided trail to the overlook above the marsh), and, in Mississippi, Davis Bayou and West Ship Island are on migratory-bird routes. In addition to the ever-present seagulls and terns, you may spot ducks, gallinules, coots, indigo buntings, warblers, and, if you're lucky, nesting ospreys.

Boating. In the Florida district, several small docks along Pensacola Bay rent and charter boats, including the **American Boating Club** (tel. 904/932–2992), **Mel's Marina** (tel. 904/934–1005) in Gulf Breeze, **Moorings of Pensacola Beach** (tel. 904/932–0305), and **The Marina** (tel. 904/932–5700) in Pensacola. Pensacola Bay, Santa Rosa Sound, Big Lagoon, and the Gulf of Mexico are favorite cruising grounds; the Okaloosa, Santa Rosa, Ft. Pickens, Perdido Key, and Naval Live Oaks areas are directly accessible by boat. Launch areas on Santa Rosa Sound are on the right side of Ft. Pickens Road, before the Fort Pickens Area sign, and at the large area on Pensacola Beach Boulevard after the tollbooth at Quietwater Beach on the sound side. There are no launch sites on the gulf side.

In Mississippi you can cruise to all four of the offshore barrier islands, anchoring near beaches on the leeward side. Rangers can tell you where it's safest to anchor; the boat dock at West Ship can be used by private boats during daylight hours March 1 to October 31. You can also anchor at Davis Bayou. Depart from Biloxi or Gulfport for East or West Ship, from Pascagoula for Petit Bois, and from Pascagoula or Ocean Springs for Horn. The **Gulfport Small Craft Harbor** (tel. 601/863–7711) and **Biloxi Small Craft Harbor** (tel. 601/436–4062) supply names and numbers of contacts for chartering and renting boats. **Ross Tours** (tel. 601/864–6801) in Biloxi rents boats, as does **Shearwater** (tel. 601/875–3511) in Ocean Springs. **Biloxi Schooner** (tel. 601/435–6320) in Biloxi docks a handcrafted schooner, available for charters and tours along the waterfront, to the right of the Isle of Capri Casino. Charter prices on the coast range from about $200 for a half-day to $600 for 10 hours, depending on the craft. Only charters licensed by the Gulf Islands National Seashore are authorized to travel to East Ship, Horn, and Petit Bois islands; charters are not permitted to dock at West Ship Island. Contact the Mississippi District office for names and numbers of official charter services (tel. 601/875–0821).

Fishing. You can wet your line from docks, piers, boats, and beaches just about anywhere in the Florida district. You can surf cast off Perdido Key for redfish, blues, pompano, and cobia. The small inlet between the tip of Perdido Key and the mainland is a good spot; the nearest bait and tackle shop is **Gray's** (tel. 904/492–2666) in the Winn Dixie Shopping Center at the intersection of Sorrento Boulevard and Gulf Beach Highway, .5 mile east of the bridge leading to the key. Another good bet is the western end of Santa Rosa Island. At Ft. Pickens you can fish for mackerel, groupers, amberjack, and red snapper, depending on the season; fishing is best in spring and summer. There's also a small fishing pier in Pensacola Bay at the Fort Pickens area; the **Firehouse,** a snack bar near Ft. Pickens (tel. 904/932–3274 for information) sells bait and tackle. Licenses are available at most bait and tackle shops and, in Gulf Breeze, at **Delchamps** (334 Gulf Breeze Pkwy., tel. 904/932–0115), a food store off U.S. 98 on the east side of the 3-mile bridge spanning Pensacola Bay. For fishing charters try **Mel's Marina** (tel. 904/934–1005), **Moorings of Pensacola Beach** (tel. 904/932–0305), and **The Entertainer** (tel. 904/932–0305), in Gulf Breeze; charters for as many as six people cost $300–$400 for four hours and $600 for 8–10 hours. Your catch may include red snapper, grouper, triggerfish, and amberjack.

In the Mississippi district, Davis Bayou's pier is the hot spot for mullet and blue crabs; get bait and tackle on the mainland at the **Fort Bayou Bait Shop** in Ocean Springs (tel. 601/875–6252). On West Ship Island you can catch sheepshead and redfish from the dock;

buy bait from the Fort Bayou Bait Shop. Charters take more serious aficionados into the gulf in search of large red snappers, groupers, and amberjack; for information, contact the **Gulfport Small Craft Harbor** (tel. 601/863–7711), **Biloxi Small Craft Harbor** (tel. 601/436–4062), **Seaspace Dive Center** in Gautier (tel. 601/497–1381), or **Point Cadet Marina** (tel. 601/436–9312).

Golf. There are no courses in the park, but the area on both sides of the Florida–Mississippi state line is full of courses. Greens fees range from $25–$45 including cart, and many resorts and motels offer golf packages (contact the **Fairways Group,** tel. 800/477–4833, for information). In Florida a few of the top-rated courses are **Tiger Point Country Club** (tel. 904/932–1333 or 800/447–4833) in Gulf Breeze, **Scenic Hills** (tel. 904/476–0611) in Pensacola, and the **Club at Hidden Creek** (tel. 904/939–4604 or 800/239–2582), 17 miles east of Pensacola on U.S. 98. In Mississippi try Biloxi's **Sunkist Country Club** (tel. 601/388–3961) or **Tramark Golf Course** (tel. 601/863–7808) in Gulfport.

Kite Flying. Wide-open beaches, brisk gulf breezes, and the absence of trees and utility lines make for ideal conditions. You'll see a variety of shapes and styles darting across the sky, especially at Pensacola Beach and the Santa Rosa day-use area. Bring your own kite, since there are no kite stores in the area.

Sailing. In Florida, sailing to Ft. Pickens, Perdido Key, and Okaloosa is popular, but you can't launch a boat in the park, only at public launches along the beaches. Contact **Gulf Islands Sailing Center** (tel. 904/664–6710) at Okaloosa or **Key Sailing** (tel. 904/932–5520) or **Bonifay Water Sports** (tel. 904/932–0633), both in Pensacola Beach. In Mississippi, rentals are not common, but you can try **Biloxi Sailboat Rental** (tel. 601/863–8677) and **Mid South Sailing & Charter** (tel. 601/863–6969), both in Gulfport, and **Coast Cat Sailboat Rentals** (tel. 601/452–9564) in Long Beach. Sunfish rentals cost $5–$10 per hour, and two hours on a four-person catamaran can cost as much as $60, a little more if you need instruction.

Scuba Diving and Snorkeling. The Naval Live Oaks Visitor Center has handouts covering local diving locations and regulations. The best areas are the grass beds at the Naval Live Oaks area or the end of Shoreline Park in Gulf Breeze (2–5 feet deep) and at the east end of the Big Lagoon (7–10 feet deep) in the Perdido Key area, the diving jetties (15–50 feet deep) at Ft. Pickens. From June through early August, Gulf Islands National Seashore sponsors snorkeling programs at **Naval Live Oaks** and **Ft. Pickens;** call 904/934–2600 for tour times for both sites. Florida has more dive sites per mile of coastline than almost any other state on the gulf. For scuba- and snorkeling-equipment rental and supplies in Florida, try **Southwind Dive Charters** (tel. 904/932–2224) and **PSI Diving Company** (tel. 904/934–5009), both in Gulf Breeze, and **Scuba Shack** (tel. 904/433–4319) and **Gulf Coast Pro-Dive** (tel. 904/456–8845), both in Pensacola. In Mississippi call **Seaspace Dive Center** (tel. 601/497–1381) in Gautier and **Dive Five** (tel. 601/385–7664) in Biloxi for excursions in Mississippi, Alabama, and Florida waters. One-week, accelerated certification courses are available, and scuba-equipment rental costs about $15–$35 per day; charters cost $40–$50 per half-day, $60–$70 per full day, and group dives $30–$60, depending on how far out you go and how many tanks you consume. Fish, particularly red snapper, are abundant throughout the area, and in deep waters you see angelfish, butterfly fish, and other tropical fish, as well as the occasional lobster. Sites include wrecks, marine ballast, and artificial reefs.

Water Sports. Swimming, waterskiing, and windsurfing are popular throughout the Florida district and on the Mississippi islands. There is no swimming at Davis Bayou. Lifeguards are on duty in summer at the public beach in Pensacola. Many businesses outside the park rent water-sports equipment, including **Bonifay Water Sports** (tel. 904/932–0633) and **Surf And Sail Windsurfing** (tel. 904/932–7873) in Pensacola Beach; **Monkey Business** (tel. 601/896–5673) in Gulfport; and **Life's a Beach** (tel. 601/385–1488), **Wet & Wild** (tel. 601/374–7962), and **Biloxi Beach Rentals** (tel. 601/388–3310) in Biloxi.

CHILDREN'S PROGRAMS It won't be easy tearing your kids away from sand castle construction and seaside gamboling. Just tell them that if they participate in the Junior Ranger program, they'll earn a park button and special certificate. In both the Florida and Mississippi districts, park rangers conduct hour-long programs on natural and cultural history for children aged 5–12 from June through early August. Call the visitor's centers (tel. 904/934–2600 in FL, 601/875–0821 in MS) to confirm schedules.

EVENING ACTIVITIES In the true spirit of southern living, evenings along the coast are typically spent perched on the beach lazily watching the sun set over the Gulf of Mexico—the surf is a soothing backdrop. In Ft. Pickens, members of the Escambia Amateur Astronomers Association (c/o Dr. Wayne Wooten, Pensacola Junior College, tel. 904/484–1600) gather for stargazing on clear evenings; they usually allow nonmembers to gaze through their telescopes. Campfire programs with an illustrated slide show on park ecology and history are held in October and March at the Ft. Pickens amphitheater (tel. 904/934–2635) and November through February at the Davis Bayou amphitheater (tel. 601/875–0821). The Colmer Visitor Center hosts free johnboat tours of the Davis Bayou on summer weekend evenings. Show up at the visitor's center well before 5 PM; tickets are issued free to the first 20 people in line at that time. For more information, call 601/875–0821.

DINING

The only places that serve food inside the park are the snack bars at Perdido Key, Ft. Pickens, Santa Rosa, Okaloosa, and West Ship Island, which are open March through Labor Day weekend. Outside the park you'll have no problem finding great food. Shellfish is essential eating. Just about every restaurant serves baked oysters, broiled grouper, and the like, and there are plenty of sandwich shops and pizza joints. On the Mississippi side, Creole and Cajun flavors abound. Casual attire is fine in the restaurants reviewed below, unless noted otherwise.

NEAR THE FLORIDA DISTRICT **Boy on a Dolphin.** The Greek-influenced seafood at this water's-edge eatery on Santa Rosa Sound at Pensacola Beach is among the best in the Pensacola area. Chef Spero Athanasios and his family have been pleasing locals and visitors for three decades. Steak, prime rib, and pasta dishes are available, along with a huge selection of delicious seafood. Whether charcoal-grilled Greek-style or baked in a traditional Athenian marinade, the catch of the day is always superb; it could be grouper, snapper, flounder, or triggerfish. For dessert, try the honey-drenched baklava, a multilayered triangular pastry, and *kadaif,* shredded wheat covered with custard, topped with whipped cream, and sprinkled with toasted almonds. *400 Pensacola Beach Blvd., Pensacola, tel. 904/932–7954. Reservations advised summer weekends. AE, MC, V. Moderate.*

Lighthouse Point. A wall of picture windows at this restaurant, formerly the Pensacola Naval Air Station Chief's Club, allows daytime diners to gaze across Pensacola Bay at Ft. Pickens and Perdido Key. The all-you-can-eat buffet changes daily, but there are always Tex-Mex dishes, build-your-own sandwiches, and gumbos and other soups. The Thursday buffet table is all pasta dishes and salads. On any day, you can also order hot entrées and sandwiches à la carte. *Lighthouse Point, Pensacola Naval Air Station, tel. 904/452–3251. No reservations. MC, V. Closed weekends, dinner. Inexpensive.*

Peg Leg Pete's Oyster Bar & Restaurant. Visitors to this easygoing beachside spot on Ft. Pickens Road are in for a treat. For starters, try baked oysters casino or Cajun-style. Chase them down with red beans and rice, jambalaya, or shrimp Orleans (sautéed with rice, onions, and peppers). Or try the Pirate Platter, which includes a little of everything on the menu. Jazz guitarists entertain Thursday, Friday, and Saturday nights from June through September. *1010 Ft. Pickens Rd., Pensacola Beach, Pensacola, tel. 904/932–4139. No reservations. MC, V. Inexpensive.*

NEAR THE MISSISSIPPI DISTRICT **La Casa de Elva.** The pink stucco and rounded arches at this large restaurant say Mexico, but the woodsy views are definitely Gulf Coast. Specialties include marinated shrimp stuffed with cheese and jalapeño, wrapped in bacon, and broiled with a cheese topping; shrimp baked in a butter sauce perfumed with cilantro and citrus; and Mexican dishes such as beef strips in *ranchero picante* salsa and boneless breast of chicken baked in a flavorful sauce with orange and chicken broth colored by annatto. A pianist plays until midnight, and there's dancing. *U.S. 90, 1 mi east of Biloxi–Ocean Springs Bridge, tel. 601/875–0144. Reservations not necessary. MC, V. Closed Sun. Moderate.*

Vrazel's. Hurricane Camille blew away the venerable restaurant here in 1969; the brick building that replaced it gets its charm from soft lighting and dining nooks with large windows facing the beach. Added attractions include the finny fare—red snapper, gulf and sea trout, flounder, and shrimp prepared every which way: amandine, blackened, étouffée, or au gratin à la Cajun (blackened, spicy, and grilled). Seafood à la Vrazel piles crabmeat, shrimp, and scallops over pilaf or spaghetti, and seafood Pontchartrain meunière is sautéed red snapper fillet and softshell crabs topped with lemon butter. Snapper Lenwood, another specialty, teams broiled fish with a topping of crabmeat and crayfish in a Cajun sauce. Or try veal Aaron (tender veal medallions in a lemony sauce chunky with crabmeat and mushrooms). *3206 W. Beach Blvd. (U.S. 90), Gulfport, tel. 601/863–2229. Dinner reservations advised. Jacket and tie required. AE, MC, V. Moderate.*

Jocelyn's. Locals come here often to celebrate birthdays and anniversaries. Soft music, bare wood floors, fireplaces, and walls hung with prints by Mississippi son Walter Anderson create a casually refined atmosphere. Specialties include broiled steak, calves' liver, chicken pot pie, baked beans, and baked and broiled seafood served with white sauce, butter sauce, or wine sauce. Every so often Jocelyn adds an idiosyncratic dish to the menu, maybe an entrée of boiled cabbage au gratin or a dessert of cranberry-peach crisp with oatmeal. *U.S. 90, opposite Sunburst Bank,*

Ocean Springs, tel. 601/875–1925. Reservations advised. No credit cards. Closed Sun. Inexpensive–Moderate.

Robby's Seafood. Nautical signs, boating memorabilia, paddles and oars, ship bells, neon seagull signs, running lights, and other nautical trappings decorate this spot, which you might call tacky. But for giant shrimp, oyster, beef, and ham po' boys on thick French bread (9 or 14 inches long), Robby's is tough to beat. Try fried soft-shell crabs or fried oysters your first time around. Regulars know to go for the enormous seafood platters— either of stuffed crab and fried catfish, shrimp, and oysters, or, in season, boiled shrimp, crabs, or crayfish. The gumbo is excellent. *U.S. 49, across from Norwood Village Shopping Center, tel. 601/831–1160 or 601/831–1161. No reservations. AE, MC, V. Inexpensive.*

PICNIC SPOTS In the **Okaloosa** area, on the shores of Choctawhatcee Bay, a shady picnic area overlooks the bay. The **Santa Rosa day-use area,** on Route 399 between Navarre Beach and Pensacola Beach, and the **Johnson Beach pavilion,** at Perdido Key, offer gulf-side picnic settings. **Ft. Pickens** has two wooded picnic groves with views of Pensacola Bay, both well protected from offshore breezes. In Mississippi, **Davis Bayou** has a large picnic area with a playground. But far more scenic is **West Ship Island**'s small pavilion and snack stand. You can bring picnic fixings, but keep things modest, because ferries to and from the island can accommodate only small or medium-size coolers.

LODGING

Although there's no lodging in the park, the surrounding area is full of beach resorts, hotels, and motor lodges. Rooms are more expensive from April through October, high season; a gulf view will set you back another $10–$15. Because Mississippi has recently legalized gambling, once-quiet Biloxi is fast on the way to becoming a neon showcase of bustling casinos and nightclubs. Hotels are shooting up everywhere—and so are room rates.

NEAR THE FLORIDA DISTRICT **Best Western Pensacola Beach.** In this beachside motel built in 1991, guest rooms are large and brightly decorated in coral and turquoise, with a tropical-fish motif enlivening the bedspreads and watercolors on the walls; windows overlook the Gulf of Mexico or Pensacola Bay. All rooms have one king- or two queen-size beds plus a microwave oven, refrigerator, coffeemaker, and wet bar. Free Continental breakfast is served in the lobby each morning. The pool is a sand dollar's throw from the gulf and has a cabana bar open on weekends. The clientele includes families, businesspeople, and some conferences. *16 Via de Luna, Pensacola Beach 32561, tel. 904/934–3300 or 800/528–1234, fax 904/934–4366. 124 rooms. Facilities: restaurant; 2 pools; poolside bar; beach-chair, -umbrella, -cushion rentals. AE, D, DC, MC, V. Moderate.*

The Dunes. This beachfront motel, which looks like a sand castle emerging from the dunes, is close to Ft. Pickens and the Naval Live Oaks Visitor Center and has panoramic views of Santa Rosa Island and the gulf. The place was new in 1988 and still looks good, but rooms in the eight-story tower are particularly fresh, with a beige, sea green, and pale blue color scheme. The clientele includes businesspeople and families, with some conference traffic. *333 Ft. Pickens Rd., Pensacola Beach 32561, tel. 904/932–3536 or 800/833–8637, fax 904/932–9088. 140 rooms and suites. Facilities: café; bar; 2 pools; croquet; volleyball; beach chairs, umbrellas, tents. AE, D, MC, V. Moderate.*

Holiday Inn Pensacola Beach. This renovated hotel with spectacular gulf views is on the beach and near several park areas. The rooms are done in soft, beachy tones of seafoam green, pale blue, and peach. The ninth-floor penthouse lounge overlooks the Ft. Pickens area to the west and Santa Rosa Sound to the north. *165 Ft. Pickens Rd., Pensacola Beach 32561, tel. 904/932–5361 or 800/465–4329, fax 904/932–7121. 150 rooms, 18 suites. Facilities: restaurant, tennis, racquetball, outdoor pool, beach chairs and umbrellas. AE, D, DC, MC, V. Moderate.*

NEAR THE MISSISSIPPI DISTRICT **Best Western Beachview Inn.** The Best Western is just across the street from the Gulfport marina, where you can catch the excursion boat for West Ship Island, and a couple of blocks from Gulfport's excellent beaches. Because the motel is even closer to the Grand Casino, one of the Gulf Coast's biggest and newest, opened in early 1993, you must reserve rooms three to four weeks in advance. None of the rooms overlooks the marina, but they are cheerful, decorated in bright blues and greens, and have two double or one king-size bed. *2922 W. Beach Blvd., Gulfport 39501, tel. 601/864–4650 or 800/748–8969, fax 601/863–6867. 150 rooms. Facilities: restaurant, lounge, pool, room service, airport transportation. AE, DC, MC, V. Moderate.*

Holiday Inn Biloxi Beachfront. This is just across the street from the beach, halfway between Gulfport and Biloxi, 6 miles from the Davis Bayou area and the dock for excursion boats going to West Ship Island. There are some 15 types of rooms, from standard doubles and king-size bedrooms with Jacuzzis to bilevel, condominiumlike suites with hot tubs and gulf views. Rooms are decorated in floral patterns of coral, sand, and seafoam green. *2400 Beach Blvd., Biloxi 39531, tel. 601/388–3551 or 800/441–0882, fax 601/385–2032. 268 rooms, 6 suites. Facilities: restaurant, lounge, pool bar, pool, children's pool, playground. AE, DC, MC, V. Moderate.*

CAMPING

The park maintains only two campgrounds, one in each district, with 251 sites between them. Both are open year-round; in summer they're especially crowded and fill quickly. However, there are some other options near both districts.

FLORIDA DISTRICT The **Ft. Pickens Campground** (tel. 904/934–2621 for 24-hour recorded message), in a grove of tall pines, has 200 sites; they're picturesque, well maintained, and popular with tenters and RVers. All sites have water hookups, and 135 have electricity as well; none has a sewage hookup, but there's a dump station near the well-stocked campground store. Sites with electricity cost $14 a night; sites without electricity, $10. The showers are great, with plenty of hot water and good water pressure. Pets are allowed in the campground with a 6-foot leash, but not at the beach. No reservations are accepted; it's first-come, first-served. If all sites are taken when you arrive, your name will be put on a waiting list for the following day.

Primitive camping is allowed on the eastern end of **Perdido Key,** beginning .5 mile east of the end of Johnson Beach Road. You are asked to avoid the dunes and vegetated areas, and must pack out what you pack in. Most campers arrive by small boat (land on the northern side of the island). A permit is required if you plan on leaving a vehicle overnight in the parking lot or along the stabilized road shoulder.

NEAR THE FLORIDA DISTRICT **Big Lagoon State Recreation Area** (Rte. 292A west of Pensacola, tel. 904/492–1595), just across the Intracoastal Waterway from Perdido Key and a few miles from Ft. Barrancas, has 75 sites, 49 with electric and water hookups. Sites are large and the bathhouses outstanding, built of cedar with roomy rest room–shower units. A boardwalk meanders through the lagoon, where you'll probably see raccoons, opossums, squirrels, rabbits, and a lone resident alligator. Sites cost $11 per night with electricity and water hookups, $9 without.

Gulf State Park (22050 Campground Rd., Gulf Shores, AL, tel. 205/948–7275), about 15 miles west of Perdido Key, Florida, and a mile from the gulf, is enormous and one of the best places for camping in the country. Every one of its 468 roomy sites has electric and water hookups, and many have views of freshwater lakes, two of them in the park: It's not unheard of for campers to cast fishing lines from their site's picnic table. The park also offers saltwater angling, golf, and tennis. Campsites cost $14–$20 with electric and water hookups, depending upon location, $11 without hookups.

Closer to Ft. Pickens and Naval Live Oaks is the **Navarre Beach Family Campground**

(U.S. 98, tel. 904/939–2188). Of its 99 sites, 60 have full hookups (complete with cable-TV outlets); you'll also find a pool, playground, laundry room, fire grates, and readily available firewood. Fees are $14–$16 per day, $12 for tenters.

MISSISSIPPI DISTRICT **Davis Bayou Campground** (tel. 601/875–0821) is relatively small, but its 51 sites, all with electricity and water hookups, are spacious and protected by live oaks. It's first-come, first-served; reservations are not accepted, and there is no waiting list. You will pay $14 for sites with electricity and water, $10 if you're tenting. The showers are hot and have good water pressure. There is a dump station near the bathhouse.

With their dunes, gulf surf, slash pines, palmettos, occasional live oak trees, and wax-myrtle bushes, **Horn, Petit Bois,** and **East Ship** islands are popular with primitive campers. Permits are not required, but it's wise to check in with the rangers who patrol the islands. Horn Island has a ranger's station, but there are no structures on Petit Bois and East Ship islands. Fires are not allowed above the extreme high-tide line, and you must pack out what you pack in.

NEAR THE MISSISSIPPI DISTRICT The **Southern Comfort Camping Resort** (U.S. 90, Biloxi, tel. 601/432–1700), one of several campgrounds near the beach in the Biloxi area, is neat and clean. All 112 sites have water and electricity, and 65 of them have full hookups. Fees are $16–$20, $15 for the 25 tent sites. A pool, showers, a game room, laundry facilities, a Jacuzzi, a sauna, picnic tables, and grills are on the premises.

The **Cajun RV Park** (U.S. 90, Biloxi, tel. 601/388–5590), another reliable choice, is 300 yards off the highway, so it's quiet. Because the beach is across the road, this campground is also convenient. The handful of long-term sites, which have phone hookups, lend a feeling of permanence you don't find everywhere. There are 100 sites and lots of amenities, including picnic tables, showers, propane, a laundry room, a par-3 golf course, a playground, and a convenience store. Fees are $19 for full hookups ($15 with electricity and water only) and $14 for tents.

Hot Springs National Park and Ouachita National Forest
Arkansas, Oklahoma
By Robert S. McCord

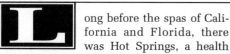 ong before the spas of California and Florida, there was Hot Springs, a health resort whose main attraction was and is a collection of 47 thermal mineral springs. In the last 50 years, as bath therapy gave way to modern drugs, long-distance travel became easier, and newer resorts sprang up, Hot Springs and its bathhouses became less popular. Recently, however, a native son, who grew up in Hot Springs, became president of the United States, and interest has been rekindled, both in Arkansas and in the Hot Springs area. With its moderate climate and proximity to the lakes, streams, and mountains of the Ouachita National Forest, it's Arkansas's favorite vacation site, drawing visitors year-round.

Though some residents, fearing crowds and higher prices, aren't crazy about increased tourism, travelers are nevertheless discovering Hot Springs and the nearby Ouachita National Forest in greater numbers. Visitors are coming not just to see where Bill Clinton grew up but also to take advantage of the diverse opportunities available where a major national forest is so close to an urban national park. An hour after hiking or canoeing in a wilderness area, you can be eating in a fine French restaurant, watching some of the country's best thoroughbred racing, or immersing yourself in a hot mineral bath.

Hot Springs the city (population 32,462) and Hot Springs the national park are inextricably linked. Geographically, the city and park are not so much adjacent as they are intertwined; parts of the park are nearly surrounded by city and vice versa.

Functionally, they are interdependent as well. For years each bathhouse had its own spring, but today the National Park Service collects the approximately 850,000 gallons of water that flow each day from the 44 springs and distributes it to concessionaires, including the bathhouses, a rehabilitation center and health spa that specializes in treating arthritis, and four hotels that operate their own bathhouses. The park service also operates thermal jug fountains, from which individuals can carry off as much water as they want at any hour of the day and at no charge.

Town and park are joined historically, too. People have been coming to the area for hundreds of years. The first visitors were Native Americans, attracted by the healing thermal waters that bubbled to the surface. De Soto, on one of his explorations, was the first European here, followed by French hunters and trappers who used the springs to ease and rejuvenate their weary bodies.

By the time of the Louisiana Purchase in 1803, when the area now called Arkansas became part of the United States, the springs were widely known, and in 1832, the federal government designated four sections of land that contained hot springs as a federal reservation. Soon the sick and the lame were coming in great numbers from all over the country. Regular stagecoaches traveled roads not only rough but treacherous, beset by bandits, who knew that visitors often carried great amounts of cash. In 1874, the railroad was extended to Hot Springs.

At first the bathhouses were little more than huts open to the public. Later, private bathhouses were built as concessions and operated under the supervision of the federal government. By the early 20th century, Hot Springs's bathhouses were at the height of their popularity, being used to treat almost everything, from arthritis and rheumatism to gonorrhea and syphilis. "The spa," wrote Dee Brown in his book *The American Spa,* "had won wide acceptance among the trend setters of America, travelers who were comparable to the jet set of today. . . . It became fashionable to visit the Springs for a series of baths regardless of whether one was ailing or not."

As the springs' popularity grew, so did the town's. Casinos, though illegal, flourished, while several governors, pleased with the dollars they generated, turned a blind eye. Finally, Governor Winthrop Rockefeller shut them down for good in 1967, but thorough-

bred racing remains at Hot Springs's Oaklawn Park, one of America's premier tracks.

At 4,900 acres, Hot Springs is the country's smallest national park and still the only government-owned and -operated hot springs. Though not officially designated a national park until 1921, Hot Springs likes to claim that it's the oldest one, since Congress "reserved" the springs in 1832. (Yellowstone was actually named the first national park in 1872.)

A study in contrasts, nearby Ouachita National Forest, at 1.6 million acres, is the largest in the South, stretching from west-central Arkansas to southeast Oklahoma. It, too, was first explored by Hernando de Soto in 1541. In 1907 it was set aside as the Arkansas National Forest and renamed the Ouachita National Forest in 1926 in recognition of the mountains that run through it. "Ouachita," or "Washita" as it was spelled originally, is a Native American word that means "happy hunting ground."

Most of the 63,000 acres of wilderness in the national forest are on the slopes of the Ouachita Mountains. In addition to abundant and varied forestland, there's plenty of water, ranging from those intimate little lakes that anglers think of as private ponds to the 48,300-acre Lake Ouachita, one of the cleanest in the United States. As a result, the national forest and its 33 recreation areas offer a wide range of outdoor experiences—camping, canoeing, fishing, hunting, backpacking, crystal mining, swimming, horseback riding, and hiking—as well as historical sites and excavations.

ESSENTIAL INFORMATION

VISITOR INFORMATION For information about the park, contact the Superintendent, **Hot Springs National Park** (Box 1860, Hot Springs 71902, tel. 501/624–3383). Also check with the **Fordyce Visitor Center** on Bath House Row in Hot Springs (tel. 501/623–1433). For information on the forest, contact the Public Affairs Office, **Ouachita National Forest** (Box 1270, Hot Springs 71902, tel.

501/321–5202). Information about the city of Hot Springs and nearby areas can be obtained from the **Department of Parks and Tourism** (1 Capitol Mall, Little Rock 72201, tel. 800/NATURAL) and the **Hot Springs Advertising and Promotion Commission** (Box K, Hot Springs 71902, tel. 800/SPA–CITY).

Though not allowed at Hot Springs, backcountry camping is a popular pastime in the Ouachita National Forest and is allowed anywhere unless posted.

■ FEES ■ There is no entrance fee for the national park. Entry to most of the 33 recreation areas in the national forest costs $3 per vehicle.

■ PUBLICATIONS ■ The **Hot Springs National Park brochure** is free and lists general rules; it also has a map and information on trails, campgrounds, and hiking resources. A short (100 pages) and very readable history of Hot Springs is *The American Spa,* sold at the visitor's center bookstore and written by Dee Brown, author of the best-seller *Bury My Heart at Wounded Knee.* In addition, special folders on Hot Springs, such as "Tour of President Clinton's Hot Springs," are available from the city advertising commission (*see above*). The best publication about the Ouachita National Forest is the *Recreation Area Directory,* a compendium of rules, names and addresses of ranger's districts, campsites, trails, and map; there is also a trails packet, which describes forest trails in great detail.

■ GEOLOGY AND TERRAIN ■ Hot Springs National Park is nestled in a valley formed by four small mountains in the Ouachita range. The hot springs' water, which averages 143°F, begins as precipitation. Over the course of 4,000 years, it percolates through layers of chert and novaculite (a rock found in greater quantity in the Ouachitas than anywhere else) to a depth of 6,000 to 8,000 feet. It heats up and picks up dissolved minerals, and finally, in the span of about a year, it rushes back to the surface. Old tufa masses, which look like tan stalagmites, are visible on Hot Springs Mountain and mark the presence of the springs.

The Ouachita Mountains are the tallest between the Appalachians and the Rockies. The highest point, Rich Mountain, rises to 2,681 feet near the Arkansas–Oklahoma border. The mountains are composed of sandstones, shales, and cherts that are 300 to 500 million years old. Like many other ranges, they were formed when sediment was deposited in a deepwater setting and then folded and faulted by continental collision. Unlike most others, however, the Ouachitas run east–west.

■ FLORA AND FAUNA ■ The warmth of the earth's interior, brought to the surface by the springs, allows for the year-round growth of plants in Hot Springs National Park. Herbs and ferns live near the two open springs, and Trelease's blue-green algae, found in only three other places worldwide, exist in the springwater itself. The algae fascinated early scientists, who could not believe anything could survive in the hot water.

The mountains of the national park are filled with oak, hickory, and pine, and many of the trees are 200 years old or more, despite quite a bit of clearing by homesteaders in the early 20th century. Ozark chinquapin, a native tree made very rare by the chestnut blight, is found in 12 park areas. Stately magnolias, introduced along Central Avenue in Hot Springs years ago to mark the border of Bathhouse Row, are most impressive.

The national forest has an interesting mixture of plant life, an estimated 2,500 species. On the northern slopes of these east- to west-running mountains, there's a dominance of oak and hickory; on the southern slopes you'll find pines—this is an uncommon combination. Patient visitors can find beautiful orchids and ferns growing out of acid seeps. Two plants, the Cossatot leafcup and Browne's waterleaf, are found nowhere else. The forest contains 60 species of trees, both hardwoods and pines, including the largest expanse of short-leaf pine in the nation. Especially noteworthy is Rich Mountain's elfin forest of 300-year-old, 3-foot-high, lichen-covered white oaks.

Because Hot Springs National Park is an urban park, the only creatures seen regularly are squirrels and pigeons. However, the fauna once common to the springs are still found in the nearby national forest.

Arkansas used to be known as the Bear State because of the abundance of black bears. Over the years, almost all were killed, but they're now being reintroduced in the Ouachitas. Foxes, white-tailed deer, turkeys, coyotes, bobcats, and mountain lions roam the forest, but because it is so dense they are seldom seen. There are even alligators. Game fish, such as bass, bluegill, sunfish, crappie, catfish, and walleye, abound in lakes and streams, and there are at least three fish—the paleback darter, the Ouachita darter, and the Caddo madtom (catfish)—that are endemic. Among the forest's endangered animals are the Indiana bat, the red-cockaded woodpecker, and the bald eagle.

WHEN TO GO The weather in southwestern Arkansas is moderate, though there are four distinct seasons. Many visitors come to see the vibrant fall foliage or the bright profusion of spring wildflowers. Summer is a bit humid; winter is mild and still fine for hiking.

The 30-year average high is 73.1°F and the low is 50°F. The annual precipitation is 56.5 inches. Summer is hot and humid; the average high in July is 93.3°F. Spring and fall are short but very pleasant. The average high and low in April are 74.3°F and 50°F, but it is also a month of thunderstorms and an occasional tornado. The two coldest months are December and January, with lows averaging around freezing and light snow not unusual.

SEASONAL EVENTS Late January to mid-April: Hot Springs's **Thoroughbred racing season** includes Oaklawn Park's popular **Arkansas Derby** (on the final day of the season)—second only to the Kentucky Derby in the size of the winner's purse (tel. 501/623–4411 or 800/722–3652). **June:** The **Miss Arkansas Pageant** is always held in Hot Springs. **October:** The **Festival of Arts** is very popular: Local and international artisans display and sell their wares, ranging from photography to sculpture. The event is capped off by an acclaimed documentary film festival. In the middle of the month is **Oktoberfest,** where the large German population re-creates this famed Munich pastime: Two bands from Germany appear, arts and crafts demonstrations are featured, and revelers take part in German dancing, eating, and beer drinking. The Mount Ida Chamber of Commerce (Box 6, Mount Ida 71957, tel. 501/867–2723) sponsors a **Quartz Crystal Dig;** amateur miners pay a fee and dig for crystals at any of about 10 commercial mines in the national forest.

WHAT TO PACK If you're heading for the national forest, bring basic outdoor clothes and gear, including first-aid equipment and insect repellent. A good pair of walking shoes and casual clothes are all you'll need to explore the national park. Informal dress is acceptable almost anywhere in town, but during the racing season, men often wear jackets and women dress up more in the evening.

GENERAL STORES There are more than 100 small towns in and around the Ouachita National Forest, and virtually all of them have a service station or a general store that can provide basic supplies. For major purchases, you'll have to travel to Fort Smith, to the northwest, or Little Rock, due east of both the park and the forest. Of course Hot Springs has ample shopping facilities, too. In a pinch, try **Dillard's Department Store** (Hot Springs Mall, 4501 Central Ave., tel. 501/525–4501) or **Wal-Mart** (on the way to Lake Ouachita, 1601 Albert Pike, tel. 501/624–2498).

As in most American cities, retailing has moved out of downtown Hot Springs to suburban shopping malls. In the last 10 years, the old Victorian buildings, many of them dating to the late 1800s, have been taken over by artists, who have added another dimension to the old city. Many live and work on the upper floors and display their art in galleries on the first floor. On the first Thursday and Friday of each month, from 5 PM to 9 PM, there are gallery walks on Central Avenue, where you can take a self-guided tour of the myriad exhibit openings.

ATMS Banks with automatic teller machines are located in Hot Springs, Little Rock,

Fort Smith, and Mena, Arkansas, and in Poteau, Oklahoma.

ARRIVING AND DEPARTING **By Plane.** Hot Springs's **Memorial Airport** is served by **Lone Star Airlines** (tel. 800/877–3932) only; most major airlines fly into **Little Rock Regional Airport** (tel. 501/372–3439), 60 miles northeast. The **Hot Springs/Little Rock Airport Shuttle Service** (tel. 800/643–1505) operates several times daily between the Little Rock airport and downtown Hot Springs and costs $18 per person. All major car-rental agencies can be found at Memorial Airport.

By Car and RV. The easiest way to get to Hot Springs from the northeast is to pass through Little Rock on I–30 West, exiting at U.S. 70 west; if you're coming from points south, take the U.S. 270 exit. From here, the Ouachita National Forest is to the north and west. U.S. 270 and 70 both access the forest, and both continue into Oklahoma. North of the forest, I–40 runs from Fort Smith, at the Oklahoma border, east to Little Rock, where you can pick up I–30 West.

By Train. Amtrak (tel. 800/872–7245) serves Little Rock from Chicago and San Antonio. To get to Hot Springs, take the **Hot Springs/Little Rock Shuttle** (*see* By Plane, *above*).

By Bus. Greyhound Lines (tel. 501/372–1861) runs two buses daily between Little Rock and Hot Springs.

EXPLORING HOT SPRINGS

Because the national park is so compact, both it and the city can be seen in one day, but two days would be better. Walking is the easiest and best way to explore downtown Hot Springs and its environs as well as park trails. Motorized trolley cars can take you to other places, including the 216-foot mountain tower on Hot Springs Mountain. You'll need a car to drive the mountain roads; see the Lake Hamilton area, which is like another city of hotels, restaurants, marinas, condominiums, and private homes; and take the self-guided Bill Clinton tour.

THE BEST IN ONE DAY A good way to get oriented to the area is to take one of the early morning Duck Tours (*see* Guided Tours, *below*). Once back downtown, you might want to visit some of the art galleries on Central Avenue. Explore Bathhouse Row (*see* Historic Buildings and Sites, *below,* for both), including the outdoor spring behind it. Climb to the Grand Promenade (*see* Nature Trails and Short Walks, *below*) for a stroll, and then head north to Fountain Street. Across from the Arlington Hotel, the park service allows steaming water to splash down the side of a mountain in an interesting cascade; it's a great spot to take off your shoes and soak your feet. Walk through the historic hotel, and perhaps have lunch there or at the Cafe New Orleans across the street (*see* Dining, *below,* for both). After lunch, sample one of the famous baths. If you're not staying at a hotel with a bathhouse, the easiest way to do this is to go to the Buckstaff (*see* Historic Buildings and Sites, *below*). Finish exploring by car. For scenery, drive to the Hot Springs Mountain Tower atop Hot Springs Mountain, and, for a glimpse of President Clinton's childhood and an interesting view of the city, take the Clinton retrospective tour (*see* Scenic Drives and Views, *below,* for both). At the end you'll then be in easy reach of restaurants either downtown or in the Lake Hamilton area.

ORIENTATION PROGRAMS The Fordyce Visitor Center in the middle of Bathhouse Row in Hot Springs (*see* Historic Buildings and Sites, *below*) runs a 17-minute movie on the park and a 4-minute video on the thermal baths.

GUIDED TOURS Rangers lead 40-minute walking tours from March to Thanksgiving (eight daily in summer; four daily at other times). These free tours leave the Fordyce Visitor Center and teach visitors about the geology of the cascades and open springs. Call one day ahead to let the rangers know you're coming. Two commercial operators, **Duck Sightseeing** (tel. 501/623–1111) and **Duck Tours** (tel. 501/321–2911), use World War II amphibious vehicles known as Ducks to conduct interesting tours of the city and park as well as Lake Hamilton, the resort area

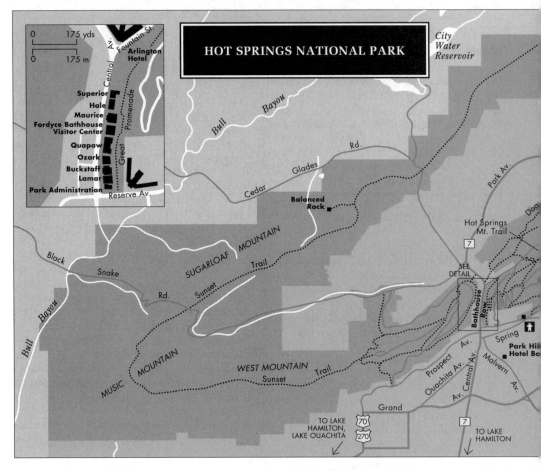

10 minutes from downtown Hot Springs. A motorized—though not guided—trolley service, operated by the city of Hot Springs, provides a good way to see the city. You can get off and on all day for $2.

SCENIC DRIVES AND VIEWS The self-guided **"Tour of President Clinton's Hot Springs"** is the most popular drive in town. Along the way, you'll see the president's two homes and other places from his childhood, including his favorite drive-in, the site of his senior prom, and the hall where his dance band performed. Pick up a map at the Hot Springs Convention Center (134 Convention Blvd.).

For more scenery, the National Park Service maintains roads and overlooks on Hot Springs and North mountains overlooking downtown Hot Springs and the Ouachita National Forest. Views are dominated by short-leaf pine, but flashes of color are provided by oak and hickory in the fall and redbud and dogwood in the spring. Drive up Hot Springs Mountain Road to the Hot Springs Mountain Tower, and take the elevator to the top for a great view of the park, the city, and the national forest.

HISTORIC BUILDINGS AND SITES There are 17 structures in Hot Springs on the National Register of Historic Places. The best known are the eight elegant bathhouses on Central Avenue's **Bathhouse Row.** Built in the early 1900s to replace earlier ones, they range in style from California modern to Spanish Renaissance. Such notables as F. W. Woolworth,

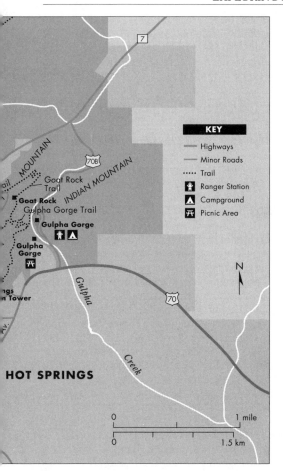

KEY
— Highways
— Minor Roads
····· Trail
⛑ Ranger Station
⛺ Campground
🏕 Picnic Area

N

HOT SPRINGS

0 ⊢———⊢———⊢———⊢ 1 mile
0 ⊢———⊢———⊢———⊢ 1.5 km

William Jennings Bryan, Andrew Carnegie, Helen Keller, Jack Dempsey, Babe Ruth, and Al Capone were frequent visitors.

Only one of the bathhouses, the handsome neoclassical **Buckstaff** (Bathhouse Row, tel. 501/623–2308), circa 1912, is still operating. For the complete treatment ($26.25) including massage and whirlpool, allow 1¹/₂ hours; a bath ($12.20) takes nearly an hour. It's closed Sunday.

The largest of the bathhouses, the three-story **Fordyce** (369 Central Ave., tel. 501/623–1433) has been turned into the national park's visitor's center and museum at a cost of more than $5 million. When built in 1915, it was advertised as the most complete and luxurious bathhouse in the United States. Today

volunteers conduct tours of the building, which contains bizarre devices once used in "mechano-therapy." The National Park Service is in the process of leasing the other bathhouses to private concerns that will turn them into spas, restaurants, clinics, and the like.

Unfortunately, many of the truly historic buildings in the city have been destroyed or remodeled in the name of progress, but some of the old Victorian mansions remain. **Wildwood House** (808 Park Ave., tel. 501/624–4267), built in 1884, has a 300-pound front door and is now a bed-and-breakfast (*see* Lodging, *below*). The **Ohio Club** (336 Central Ave., tel. 501/623–4554), across from Bathhouse Row, was one of the original casinos during Hot Springs's gambling days. Supposedly, Harry Truman, before becoming president, came by once or twice to play the piano and a little draw poker. The club has been restored and is now a restaurant and blues club. Evidence of the illegal racing telegraph and bullet holes from a police raid can be seen in the walls.

NATURE TRAILS AND SHORT WALKS The very popular .5-mile (one way), red-and-tan-brick **Grand Promenade** runs behind Bathhouse Row on Hot Springs Mountain. Along this trail you'll walk by stately historic buildings fronted by landscaped shrubbery.

The .5-mile (one way) **Red Trail** was the least strenuous of a series of exercise trails, of which only this one remains—the others have been cut up by roads; some of them have even become roads. It runs from the Fordyce Visitor Center up Hot Springs Mountain to the Hot Springs Mountain Tower. This steep walk cuts through a forest of pine and hardwood trees.

The 3-mile (round-trip) **Gulpha Gorge and Goat Rock Trail** starts by Hot Springs National Park campground, where the Gulpha Creek ripples by. Begin on the Gulpha Gorge span, then, after .8 mile, pick up the Goat Rock Trail, which reaches a wildflower-filled prairie; its rock surface is a terrific spot for picnicking. The pinnacle of Goat Rock juts up at the edge of this unusual mountain prairie.

LONGER HIKES There are 28 miles of trails—which all link up with one another—in the national park, leading from downtown to the top of the four Ouachita mountains that cradle Hot Springs. You can lengthen or shorten just about any hike you embark on—all trail junctions are marked. Most of them pass through dense forests of hickory and shortleaf pine; flowering trees are also common, and successive seasons show off colored leaves and abundant flowers. Redbud and dogwood bloom in the early spring, gracing the understory of the pine and hardwood woodlands. Songbirds and small animals are abundant on these trails.

From the West Mountain Overlook parking area, the 9.5-mile (round-trip) **Sunset Trail** runs along the rocky ridge that loops around the peak of Music Mountain, the highest point in the small mountain system. This is the center of a horseshoe-shape ridge whose ends are Sugarloaf and West mountains. It then heads down a small saddle across Black Snake Road and around Sugarloaf Mountain, where Balance Rock stands precariously before you. This vantage point offers one of the best views in the park. Continue on to Cedar Glades Road, from which it's an easy mile of hiking back to the parking area.

From the Hot Springs National Park campground it's also possible to take Gulpha Gorge to Goat Rock (*see* Nature Trails and Short Walks, *above*) and then continue on to the **Dogwood Trail**, which runs along the north slope of North Mountain and is blanketed with redbuds and dogwoods, which blossom in spring, and a fair sprinkling of pines mixed in with the predominant hardwoods. The Dogwood Trail hooks up with the Hot Springs Mountain Trail, which loops around Hot Springs Mountain. From this loop, cut down the incline of Gulpha Gorge Trail and return to the creek and campground. The entire hike is about 5 miles.

EXPLORING OUACHITA

The national forest has seven wilderness areas and 33 recreation areas, accommodating a variety of interests. Trails range from 1 to 192 miles; 22 are for hiking, five for horseback riding, 10 for mountain biking, and one (Wolf Pen Gap) for all-terrain vehicles. Lakes and rivers are popular for canoeing, fishing, and swimming. How long you stay will depend on how much you want to do, but it would take four or five days to really get a feel for the forest—and you will need a car.

THE BEST IN ONE DAY From Little Rock take scenic Route 10 and stop at the Winona Visitor Information Center (north of Perryville) to get maps and information about the forest. Head south on Route 9, and turn on Forest Service Road 324 to reach Lake Sylvia, a serene 14-acre mountain lake perfect for swimming and fishing. Hiking and interpretive trails (including one for the disabled) run through the area. Continue west on Road 324 until you reach Winona Forest Drive. The 25-mile route through the Flatside Wilderness Area provides panoramic views of Lake Winona, Chinquapin and Crystal mountains, the Alum Creek Experimental Forest, and a 1,550-foot rock outcrop. Drive south on Route 7 to the Iron Springs Recreation Area, a wooded roadside setting where you can wade in a beautiful mountain stream and walk the 4-mile Hunt Loop Trail, one of the prettiest in the forest. From here it's a 4.5-mile drive to the Jessieville Visitor Information Center. Walk the .7-mile bench-lined, asphalt trail; it's designed for the disabled but is very popular with all visitors. You can also feed the forest service's goats, part of an experiment in vegetation control. If you're interested in Ouachita crystals, make your last stop Ron Coleman Mining (Little Blakely Creek Rd., off Rte. 7, tel. 501/984–5396) in the village of Jessieville. Here you can see examples of the rocks and crystals found in the forest, including amethysts and agates, and dig for your own in the mine's tailings. From Jessieville you're 19 miles from Hot Springs and 52 miles from Little Rock.

ORIENTATION PROGRAMS Orientation in the national forest is usually provided on an individual basis at the 12 visitor information centers, formerly called ranger's stations.

GUIDED TOURS Guided tours are available for large groups only through special arrangement with the superintendent (tel. 501/321–5202).

SCENIC DRIVES AND VIEWS The national forest contains two U.S. Scenic Byways: **Route 7,** a 60-mile road that passes through some of the most spectacular scenery in both the Ouachita and the smaller Ozark national forests, and the **Talimena Scenic Byway,** a 54-mile road that winds along mountain crests between Mena, Arkansas (70 miles west of Hot Springs), and Talihina, Oklahoma. Interesting stops along the latter include the Queen Wilhelmina State Park and the Kerr Nature Center, an interpretive center and outdoor forest laboratory. The forest service has also designated seven scenic areas, most of them accessible by primitive forest roads.

HISTORIC BUILDINGS AND SITES There are many historic sites along the Talimena byway, including the **Queen Wilhelmina Inn** (*see* Lodging, *below*), built originally in 1896 for a visit by Holland's queen that never quite materialized and rebuilt after a 1973 fire, a **pioneer cemetery,** and the original **survey marker for the Indian Territory,** which became the Oklahoma border. Several Civilian Conservation Corps buildings, dating back to the 1930s, are preserved in the forest. Archaeologists have found evidence of **Caddo Indian villages** in two digs near the Albert Pike and Shady Lake recreation areas, outside Langley. For hundreds of years, Native Americans and mountain people made pilgrimages to what is now the **Bard Springs Recreation Area,** near Mena, for what are supposed to be medicinal waters.

NATURE TRAILS AND SHORT WALKS In addition to interpretive trails for the disabled at Lake Sylvia and Jessieville (*see* The Best in One Day, *above*), try the interesting, pretty, and family-oriented **Serendipity Interpretive Trail,** near the Oden Visitor Information Center on Route 88. Access is easy, the surface is gravel, and it's only .8-mile long.

LONGER HIKES The 4-mile (one way) **Athens Big Fork Trail,** near the town of Oden, has spectacular vistas but is so rugged that mules had to be used when it was a mail route. Get there by taking Route 246 west from Glenwood to the small town of Athens. The trail is strenuous and passes through some very dense forest; it's best done in fall and winter.

Also difficult and exceptionally beautiful is the 12-mile (round-trip) **Black Fork Mountain Wilderness Trail,** which straddles the Arkansas–Oklahoma border and passes huge rockslides and an elfin forest.

The **Ouachita National Recreational Trail** begins north of Little Rock and extends 192 miles west to Talihina, Oklahoma. Elevation on this trail ranges from 600 to 2,600 feet; the trail passes over the Ouachita Mountains, through valleys, across streams and rivers, and through hardwood and pine forests. Hundreds of old logging roads, which are shown on U.S. Forest Service maps, access the forest, even in areas where there are no formal trails.

OTHER ACTIVITIES Boating. Canoeing is very popular on the **Ouachita** and **Little Missouri rivers.** A 45-mile trip on the Ouachita starts at **Dragover Float Camp** (*see* Camping, *below*); it passes narrows, rapids, and rock bluffs. A 3-mile float at a bend in the river here is also possible. Starting at the **Albert Pike Recreation Area** (*see* Camping, *below*) on the Little Missouri River, canoeists can travel 20 miles over challenging rapids past massive bluffs and tree-covered banks. Commercial outfitters in the Mount Ida (Rte. 27 and U.S. 270), Oden (Rte. 88), and Langley (Rte. 84) areas rent canoes.

The **Lake Ouachita State Park Marina** (5451 Mountain Pine Rd., Mountain Pine, tel. 501/767–9366) and **Taylors Water Toys** (on Lake Hamilton, tel. 501/525–4146) rent boats, water-sports equipment, and party barges.

Crystal Hunting. Rangers allow you to look for Ouachita crystals, admired around the world, anywhere in the forest if you aren't going to sell them, but the quickest and easiest way to find some is to go to one of the 30 or so commercial mines in the national forest and dig around in the tailings (*see* The Best in One Day, *above*).

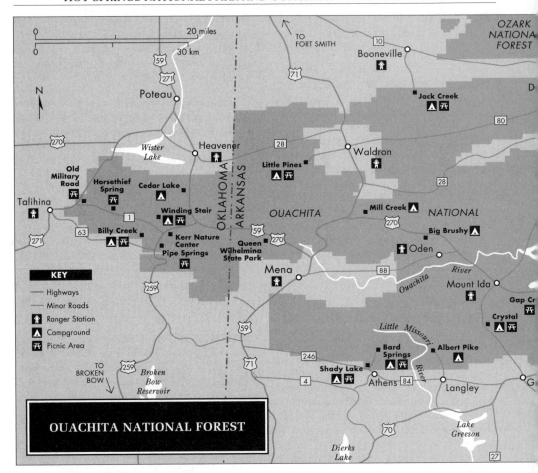

Fishing. The national forest is full of great fishing spots (Lake Ouachita, Cedar Lake, Shady Lake, Lake Sylvia, Lake Hinkle, Lake Hamilton, and the Ouachita and Little Missouri rivers) and fish (*see* Flora and Fauna *in* Essential Information, *above*). Common catches are sunfish, crappies, smallmouth bass, and catfish; Hinkle is stocked by the game department. Oklahoma and Arkansas licenses are required and are sold at most stores and service stations inside the forest and on its borders.

Horseback Riding. The modern, peaceful camping facility at **Cedar Lake** in Oklahoma (*see* Camping, *below*) features a large equestrian camp and more than 200 miles of riding

trails around the lake and picturesque Holson Valley.

Swimming. Many of the national forest's lakes and rivers have excellent spots for swimming (*see* Camping, *below*).

EVENING ACTIVITIES During camping season, rangers give free interpretive talks at night at many of the campgrounds (*see* Camping, *below*).

DINING

Neither the national park nor the national forest operates dining facilities, but commercial operations are found in Hot Springs, in the forest, and on its periphery. Hot Springs has some of the best restaurants in Arkansas.

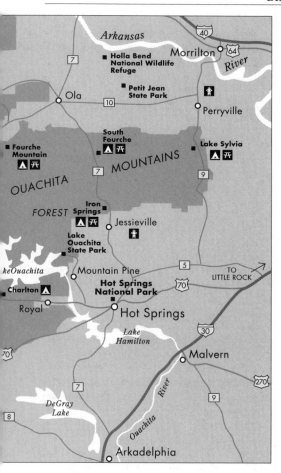

130 Van Lyell Dr., tel. 501/525–2727. Reservations advised. Dress: casual but neat. AE, D, DC, MC, V. Closed lunch and Sun. Expensive.

Arlington Resort Hotel and Spa. Of the three dining rooms in this, one of the last of the grand hotels, the Venetian Room is the most elegant. Known for its Sunday brunch and seafood buffets, it has a full menu and excellent service provided by liveried waiters. The informal Captain's Tavern, in the Arlington Mall, serves light meals and sandwiches. *Central Ave. at Fountain St., tel. 501/623–7771. Reservations required. AE, D, MC, V. Moderate–Expensive.*

Agostino's. This rather formal French-Italian restaurant in the heart of downtown attracts many tourists. It has a full bar and is known for its fish and veal dishes. *510 Central Ave., tel. 501/624–5500. AE, MC, V. Moderate.*

Mollie's. Since 1946 this has been Hot Springs's favorite deli and kosher-style restaurant. The Reuben is superb, as is most everything, especially the steaks and seafood. In what used to be a private home, it offers dining in an outdoor courtyard in good weather. *538 W. Grand Ave., tel. 501/623–6582. Reservations accepted. AE, D, DC, MC, V. Closed Sun. Moderate.*

Mrs. Miller's. Specializing in home-cooked dishes like fried quail and chicken pot pie, this is where the home folks eat. This town landmark is just a block or two from Lake Hamilton in what looks like a white frame country home. *4723 Central Ave., tel. 501/525–8861. Reservations advised Jan.–Apr. MC, V. Closed Mon. Inexpensive–Moderate.*

Cafe New Orleans. Tourists like this restaurant, with its black-and-white decor, because it's handy, usually filled with characters, and open late. It also serves food that you can't get everywhere—red beans and rice, gumbo, beignets, and café au lait. Most popular are the giant and sloppy po' boys. Beer and wine are available. *210 Central Ave., tel. 501/624–3200. D, MC, V. Inexpensive.*

Most have full bars or at least beer and wine, but in rural areas, you'd best bring your own. Dress is informal everywhere, although it gets a little dressier in Hot Springs during the racing season. Reservations are not generally necessary.

IN HOT SPRINGS **Hamilton House.** Hot Springs's finest restaurant is in the manor house of an old estate, and tables are scattered in rococo rooms and niches on four levels. Situated on a peninsula in Lake Hamilton, it's accessible by boat or car (off Route 7). The extensive menu includes beef and fresh seafood, and one of the most popular dishes is trout Marshall (spicy trout stuffed with crab and baked in parchment). An excellent domestic wine list complements the full bar.

McClard's. Barbecue aficionados say this white, squat building is the best of the city's many barbecue restaurants, and there are continuing arguments over whether the ribs or the sandwiches are better. Since there's always a line and no one to seat you, you have to jostle the crowd. *505 Albert Pike, tel. 501/625–9586. No reservations. No credit cards. Closed Sun., Mon. Inexpensive.*

IN AND AROUND THE NATIONAL FOREST **Tommy's.** After briefly closing for renovation, this town favorite reopened with a new bar and a new front entrance, but the same good food, mostly steak and seafood. Fans also praise its blue cheese dressing and home-baked rolls. *2428 Midland Blvd., Fort Smith, tel. 501/783–9523. AE, MC, V. Closed lunch and Sun. Moderate–Expensive.*

Mountain Harbor Restaurant. In the rustic registration and office building of Mountain Harbor Resort and Condominiums 25 miles west of Hot Springs (*see* Lodging, *below*), this restaurant has a commanding view of Lake Ouachita. The fare is more varied than what you find at other restaurants near the national forest and consists of salads, sandwiches, steak, and seafood. Weekend buffets are especially popular. *On the shores of Lake Ouachita, 2.5 mi off U.S. 270, near Mt. Ida, tel. 501/867–2191. Reservations advised. AE, D, DC, MC, V. Moderate.*

Taliano's. This authentic Italian restaurant is located in a beautifully restored mansion. Steak and seafood are on the menu, but devotees seem to like the homemade pasta and sauces, including cannelloni, fettuccine Alfredo, and chicken cacciatore. *201 N. 14th St., Fort Smith, tel. 501/785–2292. AE, DC, MC, V. Closed Sun. Moderate.*

Chopping Block. A butcher shop for 20 years, this downtown establishment switched gears and became an unusual and popular log-cabin restaurant a few years ago. Naturally steaks are featured, and rib eyes are the house specialty. *U.S. 71 S, just south of Mena, tel. 501/394–6410. Reservations advised. MC, V. Closed Sun. and dinner Mon., Tues. Inexpensive–Moderate.*

Fish Net. The emphasis is on catfish at this 15-year-old restaurant atop a hill in the national forest. Steak is also served, Wednesday there's all-you-can-eat shrimp, and Cajun night is Thursday. *3 mi south of Mena on U.S. 71 S, tel. 501/394–4079. AE, MC, V. Closed Mon. and lunch Tues.–Sat. Inexpensive–Moderate.*

B&J's Charles Wesley's Restaurant. In business since 1911, this downtown restaurant is proud of its home cooking. The salad and potato bar is very popular. *U.S. 259, Broken Bow, OK, tel. 405/584–9229. No reservations. MC, V. Inexpensive.*

Black Angus. This family restaurant in a motel of the same name (*see* Lodging, *below*) features a seafood buffet on Friday and charbroiled steaks on Saturday. *U.S. 270, Poteau, OK, tel. 918/647–8080. Reservations advised on Fri. D, MC, V. Inexpensive.*

Crystal Inn. Chicken-fried steak with white gravy is a favorite, catfish is also popular, and prime rib is available several days a week. The breakfast buffet and fruit bar attract a lot of anglers. It's next door to the Crystal Motel (*see* Lodging, *below*). *6 mi east of Mount Ida on U.S. 270, tel. 501/867–2643. Reservations advised. MC, V. Inexpensive.*

Cypress Barn Family Restaurant. As you might expect, this two-story barn in the middle of town is made of cypress. Though the specialty of the house is catfish, many customers prefer the chicken-fried steak. On Thursday night there's a Mexican buffet. *U.S. 71 bypass, Waldron, tel. 501/637–3369. MC, V. Inexpensive.*

LODGING

Hot Springs has many motels and hotels, and cheaper rates are often available from mid-April to mid-January, when it's not racing season. Since the national forest provides only campgrounds, many visitors to the forest stay in Hot Springs, though lodging is also available along the highways and in the small towns in and around the forest.

IN HOT SPRINGS **Arlington Resort Hotel and Spa.** Since 1875, this landmark has stood at the head of Bathhouse Row. Its newest version (the first two were destroyed by fire) rises 11 stories and has two 7-story wings. Although accommodations vary from large and elaborate to small and modest, the resort offers all the accoutrements of a grand hotel: a shopping mall, twin cascading swimming pools, dancing to a jazz trio in the lobby bar most nights. Water from the hot springs is piped into the complete bathhouse, and golf and tennis facilities are available to hotel guests at the Hot Springs Country Club. *Central Ave. and Franklin St., Hot Springs 71902, tel. 501/623-7771 or 800/643-1502, fax 501/623-6191. 500 rooms. Facilities: 3 restaurants, bar, mall, 2 pools, bathhouse. AE, D, MC, V. Moderate–Expensive.*

Hot Springs Park Hilton. This newest downtown hotel was built in anticipation of a statewide vote to legalize gambling. It didn't happen. (Ask to see where the casino was going to be.) Rooms are small but modern, and the hotel has its own bathhouse with piped-in thermal waters. Waldo Pepper's Lounge, in the lobby, is bustling. *1 Convention Plaza, Hot Springs 71902, tel. or fax 501/623-6600 or 800/844-7275. 200 rooms. Facilities: restaurant, lounge, bathhouse. AE, D, DC, MC, V. Moderate–Expensive.*

Avanelle Motor Lodge. At the junction of Route 7 and U.S. 70/270, on the way to the national forest, the motor lodge is well known, convenient, and very popular with regular visitors to Hot Springs. Rooms vary in size, and some have kitchenettes. The Sirloin Room has a good reputation for its strip sirloins. *1204 Central Ave., Hot Springs 71901, tel. 501/321-1332. 88 rooms. Facilities: 2 restaurants, pool. AE, DC, MC, V. Moderate.*

Holiday Inn Lake Hamilton. Most of the rooms in this high-rise on Lake Hamilton have balconies overlooking the lake. The restaurant has the usual Holiday Inn fare, but the lounge, the Soc Hop, may be the liveliest spot in town on weekends. Entertainment is provided by DJs and karaoke sing-alongs. There are boat docks and a fishing area, too.

Rte. 7, Hot Springs 71901, tel. 501/525-1391 or 800/238-8000, fax 501/525-0812. 105 rooms. Facilities: restaurant, lounge, pool, tennis court. AE, D, DC, MC, V. Moderate.

Wildwood 1884. Built by a physician who was one of the city's first settlers, this impressive peach-color Victorian mansion with cream-and-green trim opened in the summer of 1993 as Hot Springs's newest bed-and-breakfast. (The date in its name is the year it was built.) This antiques-filled home is on the National Register of Historic Places. A full breakfast is included. *808 Park Ave., Hot Springs 71901, tel. 501/624-4267. 5 rooms. Facilities: dining room, parlor. MC, V. Moderate.*

IN AND AROUND THE NATIONAL FOREST **Mountain Harbor Resort.** The largest facility on Lake Ouachita comprises motel rooms, lakefront cabins with kitchens, and two- and three-bedroom, luxury, time-share condominiums—all available by the day or week. Campgrounds accommodate tents and trailers. The resort is 3 miles off U.S. 270, 26 miles west of Hot Springs. Recreational facilities range from a game room and playground to a full-service marina with rental boats and marine repair. *On Lake Ouachita, 2.5 mi off U.S. 270 near Mount Ida, Mount Ida 71957, tel. 501/867-2191. 75 units. Facilities: restaurant, 2 outdoor pools, tennis courts. AE, D, DC, MC, V. Moderate–Expensive.*

Country School Inn. Until 1987, this was the Langley public school, but when falling enrollment forced consolidation with a school in another town, it became a bed-and-breakfast. The classrooms are now bedrooms with private baths, and the old gym next door is available for guests to use. It's near the Albert Pike Recreation Area and the Little Missouri River. A full breakfast is included. *Rte. 84, Langley 71952, tel. 501/356-3091. 6 rooms. Facilities: dining room, gym. D, MC, V. Moderate.*

Holiday Inn Fort Smith Civic Center. The unusually large rooms in this downtown hotel face a nine-story atrium, and a wide range of recreational and dining facilities are available. *700 Rogers Ave., Fort Smith 72901,* *tel. 501/783–1000. 255 rooms. Facilities: 3 restaurants, bar, indoor pool, sauna, whirlpool baths, exercise room. AE, D, DC, MC, V. Moderate.*

Queen Wilhelmina Inn. Built in 1896 for the visit of a queen who never came, the inn was rebuilt following a fire in 1973. The modern facility is operated by the Arkansas Department of Parks and Tourism and is situated atop Rich Mountain, 20 miles west of Mena on the Talimena Scenic Byway. Many of the rooms have spectacular views, and two have massive stone fireplaces. The restaurant is admired for its catfish and steaks. *Rte. 7, Box 53A, Mena 71953, tel. 501/394–2863. 38 rooms. Facilities: restaurant, petting zoo, miniature railroad. AE, D, MC, V. Moderate.*

Beaver Bend State Park. This sprawling compound, 15 miles north of Broken Bow, Oklahoma, consists of cabins on the bank of the Mountain Fork River. Canoes can be rented nearby, but entry to the river must be made outside the park. A nine-hole golf course is close by. *Rte. 259A, Box 10, Broken Bow, OK 74728, tel. 405/494–6538. 47 cabins. Facilities: restaurant. D, MC, V. Inexpensive.*

Best Western Lime Tree Inn. The better rooms at this typical chain motel are in the new addition. Rooms have king-size beds; some have refrigerators and coffeemakers. *U.S. 71 N, Mena 71953, tel. 501/394–6350. 78 rooms, 2 suites. Facilities: restaurant, pool, fitness room. AE, D, MC, V. Inexpensive.*

Black Angus Motel. The standard motel was built in 1958, but the newest units are in sections 20 and 30. *U.S. 59/270, Poteau, OK 74953, tel. 918/647–3246. 100 rooms. Facilities: restaurant, pool. AE, D, DC, MC, V. Inexpensive.*

Charles Wesley's Motor Lodge. Ask for rooms in the newer D section; others at this mid-size motor lodge with western-style cedar decor are a bit drab. *U.S. 259, Broken Bow, OK 74728, tel. 405/584–3303. 50 rooms. Facilities: restaurant, pool. AE, D, DC, MC, V. Inexpensive.*

Crystal Inn and Motel. Close to Lake Ouachita, this small motel has recently been modernized. It's operated in connection with the popular restaurant by the same name next door. *6 mi east of Mount Ida on U.S. 270, Mt. Ida 71957, tel. 501/394–6410. 12 rooms. Facilities: restaurant. MC, V. Inexpensive.*

Green Country Inn. Recently remodeled, the motel has no restaurant, but there are several nearby. *U.S. 59, Heavener, OK 74937, tel. 918/653–7801. 27 rooms. AE, D, MC, V. Inexpensive.*

CAMPING

IN THE NATIONAL PARK The **Gulpha Gorge Campground,** 2 miles east of Hot Springs, has 47 disabled-accessible paved pads, tables and grills, and a dump, but no showers or hookups. Interpretive programs are given at the amphitheater on summer evenings. The fee is $6 per night for tents or trailers.

IN THE NATIONAL FOREST Backcountry camping is allowed anywhere in the forest unless posted otherwise. Pack out what you pack in, stick carefully to trails during hunting season (November 13–December 6), and use only fallen wood to build your campfire. There are more than a dozen campgrounds in the forest, and though none has a sewer hookup, some have electric hookups. Fees range from $2 to $12 per night, depending upon facilities and the season. There are no reservations; it's first come, first served. The following are some of the most popular.

In the mountains on the bank of the Little Missouri River, **Albert Pike Recreation Area** (6 mi north of Langley, tel. 501/356–4186) has good fishing and a beach for swimming. (Albert Pike was a widely known mystic, Freemason, soldier, and lawyer, who holed up here to write *Morals and Dogma,* the compilation of Masonic philosophy.) There are 46 sites, with showers and drinking water but no hookups. The fee is $7 a night.

The **Cedar Lake Recreation Area Campground** and equestrian camp in Oklahoma (Forest Service Rd. 269, 1 mi north of Rte. 5, tel. 918/653–2991) is often booked up way in advance, so call ahead. There's a 90-acre lake for swimming and fishing, but no boat motors over 7.5 horsepower are allowed. A half-mile interpretive trail and the 2.9-mile Old Pine Trail circle the lake, providing views of a waterfall and wading birds. Showers and drinking water are available, and 27 of the 86 sites have electric and water hookups. The fee is $6 to $10 per night.

Near Mount Ida, **Dragover Float Camp** (Rte. 58 to Country Rd. 1.5 mi south of Rte. 88, tel. 501/326–4322) is a good entry point and camp for those who want to float the Ouachita River (*see* Other Activities *in* Exploring Ouachita, *above*). There are no hookups at the eight sites, but there is drinking water. Camping is free.

Nestled in the mountains, the **Lake Sylvia Recreation Area Campground** (Forest Service Rd. 324, 4 mi west of Rte. 9, tel. 501/889–5176) offers excellent swimming and fishing from the 14-acre lake's shore. No motors are allowed. There are also a number of trail-heads (*see* The Best in One Day *and* Nature Trails and Short Walks, *above*). The 19 sites with electric hookups cost $8 per night, and showers and drinking water are available.

The 1,000-acre Lake Hinkle at **Little Pines Recreation Area** at Lake Hinkle (Rte. 248, 11 mi west of Waldron, tel. 501/637–4174) is run by the Arkansas Game and Fish Commission. The campground has 21 sites, some with electric hookups; showers; water; and excellent fishing. The fee is $5 per night.

Shady Lake Recreation Area Campground (Forest Service Rd. 538, north of Rte. 84, tel. 501/394–5313) is in a remote mountain area near Langley. The 25-acre lake is great for fishing and swimming, but no motors are allowed. A 3-mile interpretive hiking trail is used by mountain bikers, too, and the Tall Peak Trail is a rugged, 3.2-mile climb to an old fire tower. Facilities include 96 sites (no hookups), showers, drinking water, a beach, and a playground, and the cost is $7 a night.

Isle Royale National Park

Michigan

By Gene Rebeck

hough Isle Royale (many locals pronounce it plain "royal" rather than "roy-AL") was made a national park in 1940, it's still one of the least accessible parks in the system. You can't get there by car or even by small boat. There are no roads on the island, no telephones, and only the most minimal of sewage systems. There are no real tourist attractions and no RV campgrounds, and the two grocery stores are open for only three months of the year. This is as wild as a park gets.

And no doubt it will remain so. The United Nations has designated Isle Royale an international biosphere reserve (one of several hundred around the world) under its Man and the Biosphere program. This means that the island's plants and animals are recognized as a natural community that must be preserved. Some 99% of the park is legally recognized wilderness. In many respects, Isle Royale is more a nature park than a people park.

It's a wild place, and even wild creatures have trouble settling here for very long. The life on this island is simply too arduous, the land too difficult, the passage across Lake Superior often too stormy and uncertain, the winters too bitter and too long. Many people consider it too far north, too far from urban areas—just too far. But it's this distance, this wildness, that draws people to Isle Royale.

Not that they stay long. The Ojibwe, the first known human beings to arrive here, came only in the summer to fish and mine copper, and wisely shoved off by October. White settlers came to mine copper and to log in the latter 1880s. They had disappeared by the early 20th century, and Isle Royale became a summer retreat for the wealthy, who built cottages and even a golf course. But out of all this human activity, only a few structures and a cemetery remain.

Then there are the animals: Caribou, lynx, coyotes, and white-tailed deer have come and gone. The island's best-known beasts, the moose and the timber wolf, have arrived only in the past 70 years, and their numbers fluctuate wildly. They, too, often seem to be on the verge of disappearing from this beautiful, difficult place.

Solitude and the rhythms of nature rule here, and whoever comes to gather his or her spiritual fruits has to work hard. Yes, one can hang around the ranger's stations at Windigo and Malone Bay or relax in the domesticated lodge at Rock Harbor, using these places as base camps for little ambles into the woods. But even ambling is difficult here. The rocky, winding trails climb up steep ridges. The bogs and marshes that ooze up from between stands of cedar and pine soon put a halt to daydreamy Wordsworthian wanderings.

No, the best way to experience the island is to plunge into its wildness with a pack on your back. You'll need good, sturdy boots, a strong heart, and a careful plan. You'll also need to know your limits: Once you get beyond the environs of the four ranger's stations, you're pretty much on your own. If you're prepared, the actual dangers are few. There are no venomous snakes or insects, no bears. But the trails are challenging, and even if you're hiking in a T-shirt and shorts during the day, the temperatures can dip below freezing at night. (Residual ice on the shoreline often doesn't melt until summer.) What's more, the weather can turn wild in a hurry, so much so that you might find yourself stranded for a day or more.

But if you're willing to meet this place on its own terms, the rewards will astonish you. The trails beside Lake Superior offer epic views; the many inland lakes provide tranquillity (and excellent fishing). The loon's cry, the serenade of warblers, the woods' deep richness, the wildflowers—the sheer variety of life in such a small space amazes its visitors. This is beauty you have to earn, but once you do, it stays with you for the rest of your life.

ESSENTIAL INFORMATION

VISITOR INFORMATION Contact the **Superintendent, Isle Royale National Park** (Houghton 49931, tel. 906/482–0984) for an information packet, which includes a general map and description of the park, as well as information on boats to the island and a brochure of available publications. For reservations, rates, and other information on the Rock Harbor Lodge and housekeeping facilities during the summer season, write **National Park Concessions, Inc.** (Box 405, Houghton 49931). Off-season lodging information is available from **National Park Concessions, Inc.** (Mammoth Cave, KY 42259).

Backcountry camping permits, which are free, must be picked up at any of the ranger's stations before you hike in. Campsites cannot be reserved in advance.

If you're also interested in traveling on Minnesota's North Shore or Michigan's Upper Peninsula (the two regions closest to Isle Royale), contact the **Minnesota Office of Tourism** (375 Jackson St., 250 Skyway Level, St. Paul, MN 55101–1848, tel. 612/296–5029 or 800/657–3700) or the **Upper Peninsula Travel & Recreation Association** (Box 400, Iron Mountain, MI 49801, tel. 906/774–5480 or 800/562–7134 for IL, MI, MN, and WI residents).

FEES Entrance to the park is free (though the boats to the island are not; *see* Arriving and Departing, *below*). Michigan fishing licenses are required if you fish in Lake Superior. No licenses are needed to fish the inland lakes and streams, but Michigan rules still apply there (*see* Other Activities *in* Exploring, *below*).

PUBLICATIONS The **Isle Royale Natural History Association** (800 E. Lakeshore Dr., Houghton 49931, tel. 800/678–6925) includes its publications catalogue in the information packet available from the park superintendent (*see* Visitor Information, *above*). The catalogue offers an almost overwhelming selection of books, brochures, children's books, videos, cassettes and CDs, games, posters, and T-shirts. Most of the publications discuss the flora and fauna of the island. Those of special note include *Isle Royale: Moods, Magic and Mystique* by Jeff Rennicke ($8.95, 1989)—40 pages of color photographs of the island in all its variety of season, weather, and light. King Huber's *The Geological Story of Isle Royale National Park* ($9.95, 1983) is a classic study of the park's landscape and land shapes, of general more than scholarly interest. Lake Superior is infamous for its shipwrecks; in *Above and Below: A History of Lighthouses and Shipwrecks of Isle Royale* ($5.95, 1985), Thom Holden details the 10 great wrecks known to be lost near Isle Royale. For naturalists, *101 Wildflowers of Isle Royale* by Robert A. Janke ($2.50, 1962) comes complete with drawings and descriptions; *Wildlife of Isle Royale* by P. Shelton and P. Jordan ($2.95, 1982) features checklists of animals in the park. The history-minded should look into *Borealis: An Isle Royale Potpourri* ($7.95, 1992), a collection of works covering the island's cultural history, from the logging and mining days to the rise and fall of the resorts. Ingeborg Holte's *Ingeborg's Isle Royale* ($7.95, 1984) and Dorothy Simonson's *Diary of an Isle Royale School Teacher* ($7.95, 1992) offer tales of the struggles that women settlers faced.

The Isle Royale Natural History Association also offers a "Hiking Package" ($18), which includes a folded waterproof topographic map and a detailed description of foot trails and water routes. Seven Great Lakes navigation charts (including one of Isle Royale and surrounding waters) are also for sale at $14 each.

GEOLOGY AND TERRAIN The island is 45 miles by 9 miles and encompasses some 210 square miles, not counting its inland waterways. Geologists believe the patterns of ridges and valleys began to form even before Lake Superior itself, perhaps as early as a billion years ago, when the earth's crust tore from a spot close to the present-day island all the way down to the Gulf of Mexico. This great rift produced cracks through which lava oozed, and it was from this lava that Isle Royale's volcanic, sandstone, and conglomerate bedrock began to form. Copper deposits

formed within the hills of cooling rock. Meanwhile, the land along the rift sank to form the Superior Basin.

The island itself is probably much younger. Its striations—ridges and troughs that become clear as you move inland—are the handiwork of glaciers and are (at least in geological time) quite recent. Isle Royale's landform rose from the ice about 10,000 years ago. The last major glacier, the Wisconsin, receded even more recently—only a few thousand years ago—and as it dragged itself northward, it ripped, tore, and crushed the rocky land. It also smoothed many of the land's sharper edges, making the hilltops rounder. In the southwestern part of Isle Royale you'll find small, long, slim hills, more linear than round, formed from deposits the glacier left behind in its retreat.

As the glacier scraped across the land, it formed the series of ridges that run the island's length: Minong, Oak, Stanley, and the island's so-called "backbone," Greenstone, which stretches from Windigo in the west all the way to Blake Point on the eastern tip. It's on Greenstone Ridge that the island's highest points are found: Mt. Desor (1,349 feet), Ishpeming Point (1,377 feet), Mt. Siskiwit (1,250 feet), and Mt. Franklin (1,074 feet); they decline in height as you head from west to east. The many inland lakes (notably Siskiwit, Desor, Chickenbone, and Richie) and the numerous rivers, ponds, creeks, bays, and basins formed from water that collected in the troughs between the ridges. Isle Royale is a moist island—so wet that at least one trail has been closed because it was too onerous to maintain it. As you walk amid the bogs and sloughs (plank bridges traverse the wettest spots), you may feel as if the land is sinking back into the lake it rose from. (A stiff climb up one of the ridges will dispel that notion.)

The western part of the island is woodsy, the soil richer and deeper. On the eastern side, around the appropriately named Rock Harbor, the ground is stubbled with outcroppings of rock.

FLORA AND FAUNA The plant life here can tolerate the island's extremes—its wet yet rocky soil, its bitter winters, the winds that blow in on all sides from Lake Superior.

Two woodland communities meet here. The northern part of the island falls within the southern reaches of the northern boreal forest, a community of, primarily, spruce and balsam fir. Its southern half marks the northernmost boundary of the great hardwood forest. Here the most common trees are maple, yellow birch, and white birch. You can find the loveliest stands of sugar maple on the higher points of Greenstone Ridge, especially around Sugar Mountain. (The Ojibwe set up a sugaring camp on the mountain.) Stands of oak can be found (naturally enough) on Oak Ridge. These maples and oaks make the island lovely in late September. You'll also find cedar and white pine. Few of the trees here are old-growth (19th-century logging practices saw to that), but they've been here long enough to *seem* ancient.

The Ojibwe called the island Minong, the "berry place," for its wild strawberries and thimbleberries. Its wildflowers are mostly those that tolerate heavy shade and wetland conditions, such as wild columbine and marsh marigold (which you'll see beside the island's myriad small creeks and runs); they bloom mostly in the late spring, though wood anemone and Michigan lily add touches of white and deep orange in the summer. Poison ivy is very rare: You'd have to bushwhack far off the trails to run into it.

What visitors most want to see, of course, are the moose and the wolves. Remarkably, these mammals, so important to the island's ecosystem, are very recent arrivals. The moose came first, swimming over from the mainland early this century. They came at the right time: The white settlers' arrival had rid the island of caribou and lynx, and such mainland creatures as black bears and deer never made the crossing. So they faced no competition and no real predators. From those first few newcomers the population exploded, changing the island's ecology forever; on the forest floor, for instance, American yew was soon browsed away, and thimbleberry, carried via moose scat, took over.

Then, during the brutal winter of 1948–49, a small pack of eastern timber wolves crossed over the ice from Canada. Like the moose, they found life here to their liking—in no small part because of the moose themselves. The wolves found an excellent source of food, and the moose gained a form of population control that kept illness in check (since wolves take the weak and infirm) and their browse in good supply (by lowering the number of moose). It's primarily because of the wolves that pets are forbidden on the island: Dogs may bring canine diseases wolves often can't fight off.

You'll be lucky if you see a wolf during your stay, but you probably won't have any problem spotting a moose, especially near campgrounds. Many campgrounds are also visited by a "camp fox," a feral red fox that campers have fed so often that it will curl up near the spot where you're eating and patiently wait for a treat. (Feeding wildlife, by the way, is absolutely forbidden.) Other island animals include hares (the foxes' favorite wild food), beavers (whose dams promote the growth of aquatic vegetation that moose enjoy), red squirrels, bats (rarely seen), and nonvenomous snakes.

Gulls and cormorants, along with mergansers and other ducks, are the first birds you'll see as your boat approaches the harbor. You may spot common loons in the harbor, too, though they prefer the solitude of the inland lakes. Hikers will be serenaded by ovenbirds, white-throated sparrows, and a wide variety of warblers, of which the easiest to spot are the yellow-rumped and the bay-breasted. They make lovely (and, after a while, monotonous) alarm clocks.

WHEN TO GO The only stretch of time you can come to Isle Royale is between April 15 and November 1, the park's opening and closing dates. Not that you'd want to visit any other time: The island is really too cold to visit until about mid-May, when the ferries begin to run. They stop around mid-October, and that's about as late as you'd want to visit.

By the summer, temperatures have usually stabilized. Daytime highs rarely exceed 80°F, though the humidity (and the weight of a backpack) can make it seem warmer. Evenings are cool (sometimes cold), so bring a warm sleeping bag. While summer is the busiest season, Isle Royale is still one of the least busy parks in the national system, and the crowds are rarely oppressive. Camp inland and solitude shouldn't be hard to find. The only drawback to a summer visit is that the central part of the park is closed then, to allow the wolves to den and whelp. This renders many of the best trails (including the one that follows Greenstone Ridge) and many good fishing lakes off-limits.

You might therefore prefer the spring or fall. There's more solitude and just as much beauty (especially in fall, when the maples flare and flame), but there's also a lot more cold weather. Temperatures often dip below freezing, even in late May. And throughout the open season, fog and thunderstorms are regular visitors. In each season the rule remains: Be prepared.

WHAT TO PACK Layered clothing is the rule; you should be ready for every kind of weather. Even in spring and fall, bring warm gloves and long underwear, just in case (especially if you're backpacking). Keep rain gear handy. Shorts are nice in warmer months, but you may want to keep long pants on: Weather can change, and because trails tend to be quite narrow, low-lying branches can scratch painfully. The rocky, difficult, sometimes boggy terrain makes sturdy, waterproof hiking boots a must. In the summer, the marshes and woods become rich breeding grounds for mosquitoes, gnats, and black flies, so bring a deep-woods insect repellent.

In addition, backpackers should bring a self-contained camp stove, toilet paper, and a little more food than they might need, just in case weather slows them down. (Also, the island's grocery stores aren't open outside the summer months.) Since there are no medical services on the island, make sure your first-aid kit is complete and includes sunscreen. Another must: a water filter capable of filtering down to 0.4 microns. Though the water on the island is generally clean, some sources

may be contaminated with hydatid tapeworm eggs (courtesy of animal droppings). Chemical purification won't kill these eggs. All water in the park (except those clean sources by ranger's stations and inside the lodge) should be either filtered or boiled for at least two minutes.

GENERAL STORES There are stores near Windigo and Rock Harbor ranger's stations on the west and east ends of the island, respectively. They're open from about mid-June to Labor Day, and carry a limited supply of groceries and meats, as well as fishing equipment, water filters, and souvenirs. Windigo has no public phone; Rock Harbor can be reached via the Rock Harbor Lodge (tel. 906/337–4993; *see* Lodging, *below*).

ATMS The nearest ATMs are in Grand Marais, Minnesota, about 40 miles southwest of the Grand Portage boat dock, at the Holiday Gas Station and Store on U.S. 61 downtown. In Michigan, there's an ATM behind the Houghton National Bank in central Houghton.

ARRIVING AND DEPARTING The only ways you can get to Isle Royale are by boat or by seaplane. Since there are no big cities nearby, you'll need to drive or bus to the boat docks. The Minnesota docks are in Grand Portage, the state's northeasternmost municipality; in Michigan, they're at Houghton and Copper Harbor on the Upper Peninsula. Grand Portage is the nearest mainland port of departure; the boat ride from there is half the length of one from the Michigan ports. The Twin Cities of Minneapolis and St. Paul lie about 300 miles to the south—a six-hour drive, the last half of which, hugging the Lake Superior shore, winds through woods, across small but spectacular rivers, and through tiny north woods towns. The Twin Cities also have the nearest international airport and Amtrak station.

By Plane. The nearest large airport is the **Minneapolis–St. Paul International Airport** (tel. 612/726–5555). Daily flights via **Mesaba Airlines/Northwest Airlink** (tel. 612/726–1234) connect it with **Duluth International** (tel. 218/727–2968), 180 miles to the north and that much closer to Grand Portage and Isle Royale. Car rental agencies at the Twin Cities airport include **Alamo** (tel. 612/726–5323), **Avis** (tel. 612/726–5220), **Budget** (tel. 612/727–2000), **Hertz** (612/726–1600), and **Thrifty** (tel. 612/854–8080). At the Duluth airport, there's **Avis** (tel. 218/727–7233), **Budget** (tel. 218/727–7685), and **Hertz** (tel. 218/722–7418).

Another option is to fly from Minneapolis–St.Paul to **Thunder Bay Airport** (tel. 807/475–0006) in Ontario, only 45 miles north of Grand Portage. The airline you need is **Bearskin** (tel. 800/776–3000), an Air Canada linkup. Flights are daily, and you'll have to deal with customs. Bearskin can arrange rental cars for you, or you can call **Avis** (tel. 807/473–8572) or **Hertz** (tel. 807/475–3330), both at the airport.

By Car and RV. Driving up from the Twin Cities, take I–35 to Duluth, where it ends. Follow the exits for U.S. 61 (NORTH SHORE), which will take you all the way to Grand Portage—keep your eyes peeled for signs reading ISLE ROYALE BOAT LAUNCH. Parking ($3 per day) is available at the dock.

Interstate 75 is the main north–south route through Michigan, from Detroit to Sault Ste. Marie. Exit on the Upper Peninsula and follow Route 28 westbound for 150 miles until it hooks up with U.S. 41. Follow U.S. 41 about 125 miles, driving up the Keweenaw Peninsula through both Houghton and Copper Harbor. Copper Harbor is about 45 miles farther, but the boat ride from there to Isle Royale is at least an hour shorter, depending on lake conditions (*see* By Boat, *below*).

If you're coming through Canada, the nearest major town is Thunder Bay, Ontario, through which U.S. 11 and U.S. 17 pass. Once in town, take Route 61 south to Grand Portage, a 45-mile drive.

RVs and trailers will have to park at the docks also. If you're carrying a canoe or kayak, contact the boat companies in Grand Portage, Houghton, or Copper Harbor to see if they can carry your craft.

By Train. The closest that **Amtrak** (tel. 800/872–7245) comes is St. Paul (tel. 612/644–1127). Two daily trains—one eastbound, the other westbound—stop at the station; each is an *Empire Builder*, on the Chicago–Seattle route. A taxi to downtown St. Paul can take you to the Greyhound terminal (*see* By Bus *below*).

By Bus. The nearest **Greyhound** station is in Duluth (tel. 218/772–5591). The trip there from stations in either downtown Minneapolis (tel. 612/371–3311) or St. Paul (tel. 612/222–0509) takes about three hours. You can rent a car in Duluth (*see* By Plane, *above*).

By Boat. However you get to the mainland ports, the last leg of the journey has to be either by boat or seaplane. The boat is less expensive. Whether you sail from Grand Portage, Copper Harbor, or Houghton, reservations are required.

Service from Grand Portage is offered by **Grand Portage–Isle Royale Transportation Line, Inc.** (1507 N. First St., Superior, WI 54880, tel. 715/392–2100). There are two boats. The smaller, faster, and slightly more expensive *Voyageur II* runs approximately every other day from early May through late October, making various stops on the island—Windigo, McCargoe Cove, Belle Isle, Rock Harbor, Daisy Farm, Chippewa Harbor, and Malone Bay. It's a 1^{1}/2- to 2-hour ride to the Windigo ranger's station and campground ($40), but around 6^{1}/4 hours to Rock Harbor ($46 one way). The company also offers trips (between Grand Portage and Windigo only) on the larger, slower *Wenonah* from mid-June to early September ($30 adults, $15 children under 12). Both boats will transport canoes, kayaks, and other hand-loaded boats for a $15–$20 charge. Car parking at the Grand Portage docks is $3 per day.

For a shorter trip to Rock Harbor, board at Copper Harbor on the *Isle Royale Queen III*, operated by the **Isle Royale Ferry Service** (Box 24, Copper Harbor, MI 49918, tel. 906/289–4437 summer, 906/482–4950 offseason). This 100-passenger vessel runs about 4^{1}/2 hours between the two harbors, and is available twice a week from mid-May to late September ($35 adults, $17 children under 12). The *Queen* will also transport canoes and kayaks ($12), hand-loadable motorboats ($25) and motors ($5–$10), and air tanks ($5). To get to the dock, just follow U.S. 41 north all the way to its end and watch for the signs. Parking is free.

The park service operates its own 123-passenger vessel, the *Ranger III.* It runs between Houghton and Rock Harbor from early June to mid-September, every other day during the summer and twice a week at other times. The trip takes about 6$^{1}/_{2}$ hours ($42.50 adults, $20 children under 12). The boat will also carry canoes and kayaks ($15), outboard motors (fuel tanks empty—$8.25), and larger boats ($45–$80). For more information, contact the superintendent's office (*see* Visitor Information, *above*). To get to the dock, follow the signs on U.S. 41 in downtown Houghton. Parking is free.

If you own a Superior-worthy vessel, you can sail over to Isle Royale yourself. (For information on mainland docks, contact the tourist offices listed under Visitor Information, *above.* For information about docks on the island, *see* Other Activities *in* Exploring, *below.*) The National Park Service recommends that all boaters visiting the island carry Lake Survey Chart 14976 (Isle Royale). Copies can be purchased at Windigo and Rock Harbor. Boaters should also have an FM radio strong enough to reach shore. (Channel 16 Marine Band is monitored at Mott Island and Windigo ranger's stations during the day, by the Coast Guard 24 hours a day.) Boats smaller than 29 feet should *not* voyage between Isle Royale and Michigan's Keweenaw Peninsula—they should be transported on the *Ranger III.*

By Seaplane. Seaplanes, faster but more expensive than ferries, are available between Houghton and both Rock Harbor and Windigo from May through September via **Isle Royale Seaplane Service** (Box 371, Houghton 49931, tel. 906/482–8850 mid-May–Sept.). The seaplane flies daily except Sunday and accommodates up to five persons; the fare is

$100 one way, $150 round-trip. Parking is free.

EXPLORING

Because it's no easy feat to get to Isle Royale (and the boats back usually run only every other day), plan on spending at least a couple of days here. There are two ways to explore: by foot or by foot and canoe. Indeed, many of the campgrounds are accessible only by boat. If you're bringing a canoe or kayak, get ready to lug it around without wheeled portages.

There are no touristy sights. The area around Rock Harbor, with its lodge and housekeeping facilities, is the most popular, but it takes a hike to reach even the "sights" (the Siskowit mine, Scoville Point) on this part of the island. If you have a motorized boat, you can cruise around Rock Harbor, stopping off at Cemetery Island, the Edisen Fishery, and other points of interest. But the real sight here is the island itself.

THE BEST IN ONE DAY Because boats come only once daily, there are no day trips here as such. If you're staying at the Rock Harbor Lodge, however, you can use it as a base for short, hearty hikes, such as the interpretive trips conducted by Rock Harbor's rangers (*see* Guided Tours, *below*) and the **Stoll Trail,** a 4-mile loop that shows you a good cross-section of ecosystems on the rockier eastern side of Isle Royale.

There are also a few overnight options. Other than the self-propelled boat trips mentioned above, they'll require foot power and camping gear. (Note, too, that an overnight trip isn't cheap, given the cost of getting to and from the island, so you'll have to consider whether a one-night stay is worth the money.)

Landing at Windigo on the island's **western side,** stop in the ranger's station and pick up a map of the **Huginnin Loop.** This 10-mile tramp will give you a good idea of some of the island's chief ecological communities, its woods, marshes, ponds, creeks, ridges, and Lake Superior itself. The loop follows Washington Creek for .5 mile, then crosses a bridge and begins an irregular, challenging ascent

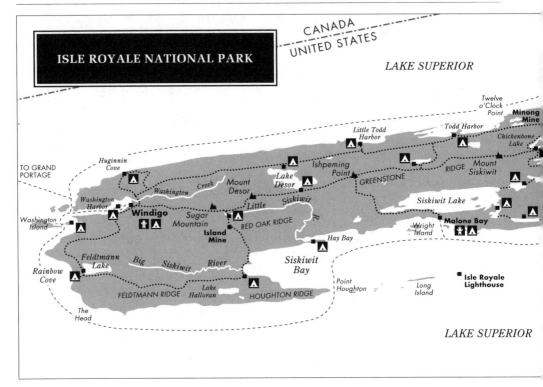

onto the Minong Ridge. Once on the ridge, you can take either the east or west loop. The east loop, which is .5 mile longer, passes some small mine ruins deep in the woods, winds through stands of pine, cedar, and birch, and crosses through some lovely little meadows, with its final leg following the wooded shores of Lake Superior. Camp overnight at the small Huginnin Cove "rustic" campground (no running water or other conveniences, a pit toilet). The cove offers a secluded view that's perfect for an evening's contemplation. Get an early start the next morning and hit the west loop, which veers away from the lake and requires some serious climbs here and there. By the time you reach Minong Ridge, you'll be rewarded with a lovely view of Washington Harbor and a (mostly) downhill hike. You'll get back for a cool shower (summer only) near the Windigo campground and the noontime boat back to Grand Portage.

On the **eastern side** of the island, you can use Rock Harbor as your starting point and follow the shoreline to the Three Mile campground. The next day you can follow the trail into the island toward the tip of Tobin Harbor, then hike back toward Scoville Point and Rock Harbor. Compared to the Huginnin Loop, this is a shoreline tour, and slightly more level. For a more ambitious variation on this theme, overnight at Three Mile, then continue west on the shore 5 miles to Daisy Farm, where the Grand Portage boat will pick you up midmorning.

Heartier backpackers can jump off the Grand Portage boat at McCargoe Cove and follow the river past Chickenbone Lake, camping there or a few miles down the trail at Lake LeSage. The next morning (early), a 4-mile-plus hike will take you to Chippewa Harbor, where the boat picks you up around midmorning. This route crosses several ridges, meaning many beautiful views and a great deal of work. Though many have done Isle Royale this

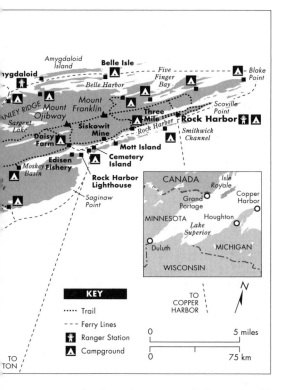

KEY

····· Trail

--- Ferry Lines

🔥 Ranger Station

⛺ Campground

commercial fishing operation maintained in historic condition. A guide lives at the fishery throughout the summer, providing tours and answering visitors' questions. The tour also includes a guided walk to the oldest lighthouse (1855) on Isle Royale. It costs $9 per person.

A number of guided boat trips around Rock Harbor are offered at various times throughout the week. These trips go to the lovely little islands and points that hiking can't take you to; they cost $9–$14 per person. You can obtain a list and a schedule of interpretive activities from any ranger's station.

HISTORIC BUILDINGS AND SITES Besides the Edisen Fishery (*see* Guided Tours, *above*), there are a number of points of human-made interest. Outside of the **copper mining ruins** (buildings, equipment, and so on) that dot the island, these sites are accessible only by boat. The island's four **lighthouses,** dating to at least the turn of the century, are closed to the public but are of great visual and historic interest. Boaters can also venture to **Cemetery Island** near Rock Harbor, where many of the island's old settlers are buried. It's a richly spooky place—if you like a good scare, come at dusk.

NATURE TRAILS AND SHORT WALKS Besides the guided walks (*see* Guided Tours, *above*), there is a trail loop at Windigo you can hike while you follow along with a printed guide to the island's flora and other natural phenomena. Several trails emanate from both Windigo and Rock Harbor, and rangers at both locations can offer tips on what you'll see and what to look for. On most of them, you'll have to double back to return.

LONGER HIKES If you're going for more than an overnight trip, you have plenty of choices. Isle Royale has some 166 miles of hiking trails, all of which should be considered challenging. In choosing a route, consult with park administration ahead of time to determine when and where you'll meet the boat taking you off the island. If you're hoping to get in some fishing, find out which trails go

way, only those in *very* good shape should attempt to do it overnight. And no matter what shape you're in, have an alternate plan handy in case the weather turns.

ORIENTATION PROGRAMS The information centers at Windigo and Rock Harbor show a number of short videos on large-screen TV; these cover a variety of subjects, notably the island's history and wildlife. All are professional and informative.

GUIDED TOURS From approximately mid-June through Labor Day, several tours depart daily from both Rock Harbor ("At a Glance") and Windigo ("Windigo Nature Walk"). Most take visitors on short trail walks to view the island's plant life. Besides walking tours, which are free, Rock Harbor (through the lodge) offers a daily water-borne expedition on the *Sandy* tour boat, which explores various points of interest hikers can't get to, including the **Edisen Fishery,** a former by the best lakes. Officials can also tell you if any trails will be closed, either for maintenance or because they traverse wolf-denning areas.

Remember that you'll have to be flexible in case of bad weather. Bring sufficient food. And stay on the trails. Because of Isle Royale's wilderness status, off-trail bushwhacking, while not exactly discouraged, is not a good idea, especially if you're not handy with a compass. In any case, the bogs and dense vegetation can make off-trail travel extremely difficult, even dangerous.

OTHER ACTIVITIES Outside of boating on Lake Superior, no motorized sporting activities of any kind are allowed on Isle Royale. Bicycles, horses, and skis are forbidden, too. And except for boats, there are no vehicles or equipment to rent.

Bird-Watching. If you're looking for water birds, you'll have luck near the ranger's stations. Cormorants and mergansers are regular visitors; even common loons and some less common species of duck (buffleheads, redheads) stop by. Be quick with your binocs—the water birds here are divers, not dabblers. Loons also frequent the inland lakes, where you're much more likely to hear their haunting wails and yodels. Woodland birders face a stiffer challenge, since the dense trees and underbrush make excellent hiding places for warblers and sparrows. Both types (warblers, especially) move through the woods in small packs, so keep your ears open: If you hear singing, look at the treetops for flitting forms. Glades and small open areas often yield the best sites for spotting these birds.

Boating. The Rock Harbor Lodge marina is open from about mid-May through mid-September. Diesel fuel, gasoline, and oil are available. There is a smaller dock at Windigo, which has gas and oil only. Holding-tank pump-out stations are available at both locations. (Discharging human waste into Lake Superior is a violation of state and federal laws.) Most park docks can accommodate cruisers of moderate draft. All boats must obtain a permit from rangers upon arrival at Isle Royale. (For more information on boating

between Isle Royale and the mainland, *see* Arriving and Departing *in* Essential Information, *above.*)

Both Rock Harbor and Windigo rent 14-foot aluminum craft, motors, and 15- to 17-foot canoes. Both motorized boats and canoes can be taken on hourly, half-day, daily, and weekly bases. Motorized rates range from $12 to $200; canoes, $4.50 to $90. Boats with motors are not allowed on inland waters. Canoes are allowed, but not wheeled vehicles for portaging.

Fishing. Lake, brook, and rainbow trout draw the main interest, but most anglers will happily settle for the northern pike, walleye, and yellow perch that frequent the island environs. Fishing is good all season long, but spring and fall bring in the biggest catches. A Michigan fishing license (available at Rock Harbor, Windigo, Amygdaloid, and Malone Bay ranger's stations) is required for those who want to fish Lake Superior. A daily license costs $5.35; the seasonal fee is $9.85 for state residents, $20.35 for out-of-staters. If you want to fish for trout or salmon, you'll also need a trout/salmon stamp, which costs an additional $9.85. No license is required for inland lakes and streams, but Michigan rules regarding catch, size, and season still apply. A list of these rules is available at any ranger's station.

Fish disposal requirements must be strictly adhered to. At Rock Harbor, use the fish cleaning station. At Windigo, you must bag the remains in plastic and put them in the station's trash cans. Otherwise, fish remains must be cut into pieces of less than four inches and the air bladders punctured. If you're fishing in Lake Superior, the remains should be discarded in waters more than 50 feet deep. On the island itself, remains should be placed on shore (above wave action and below the vegetation line) and at least 100 feet from campgrounds, docks, trails, and other development.

Scuba Diving. The sport has some popularity here because of the 10 boat wrecks around the island. Divers must preregister (there is no fee) at a ranger's station. Scuba is not discouraged, but you should sign up with an organized charter, since there is no place on the island to fill up air tanks.

Swimming. Forget it. Lake Superior is too cold, and the inland lakes are loaded with leeches.

EVENING ACTIVITIES Both Rock Harbor and Windigo offer slide programs and demonstrations at the ranger's stations every evening in the summer. Each year the park designates an artist-in-residence, who often participates in evening presentations, displaying work and discussing how the island has influenced it.

DINING

The rule around here is decent food, good prices. Steak and walleye are as gourmet as things get, but remember, this is the north woods, not SoHo. In Minnesota, most of the worthwhile restaurants in the Grand Portage area are in Grand Marais (pop. 1,300), 35 miles to the southwest. In Michigan, Houghton is the nearest hot spot, but don't discount places in and around Copper Harbor. Dress at all these restaurants is casual; at dinnertime, suits and dresses often intermingle with hiking boots and shorts.

INSIDE THE PARK **Rock Harbor Lodge.** The lodge houses Isle Royale's only restaurant, and staff prefer to call it a "dining room." Like the lodge, the decor is part woodsy, part modern motel. The food is classic north woods fare: hearty breakfasts and, for dinner, chicken and steaks. Seafood is probably the best choice, since it's usually fresh from Lake Superior. The quality depends on how good the summer cooks are, but the preparation, while not particularly imaginative, is never poor. If you're staying at the lodge (*see* Lodging, *below*), you can get your meals in the dining room as part of its American Plan. *Rock Harbor, tel. 906/337–4993. No reservations. AE, DC, MC, V. Closed mid-Sept.–early June. Moderate.*

NEAR THE PARK: MINNESOTA **Angry Trout Cafe.** A typical good North Shore restaurant—casual, meat and fish menu, nice view of Lake Superior. If you want a taste of north woods cuisine, you can hardly do better. The specialty is coal-grilled lake trout, and they do it up angrily indeed. *U.S. 61, Grand Marais Harbor, Grand Marais, tel. 218/387–1265. No reservations. MC, V. Moderate.*

Birch Terrace. This local tradition opened in 1945 (in a log mansion built before the turn of the century) and is one of the few good restaurants around here that doesn't have a lakeside location. It serves well-prepared steak and fish, and there's a wine list. If you like a place that's a little more than camper-casual, this is it. *W. 6th Ave. at U.S. 61, Grand Marais, tel. 218/387–2215. Reservations accepted. Dress: casual but neat. MC, V. Moderate.*

Grand Portage Lodge. Part of the lodge and casino complex in the Grand Portage Indian Reservation (*see* Lodging, *below*), it's the restaurant nearest the Grand Portage boat docks. If you're expecting Native American cuisine in a room decorated with Ojibwe art, you'll be disappointed: The food is standard north woods cuisine (steaks, walleye, and so forth), and the ambience, though rather "newish," is comfortable. *U.S. 61, Box 307, Grand Portage, tel. 218/475–2401 or 800/543–1384. Reservations accepted. AE, D, DC, MC, V. Moderate.*

Naniboujou Lodge. Inside the magnificent Great Hall of this National Historic Register hostelry (*see* Lodging, *below*) is what may be the best restaurant on the North Shore. The emphasis is on regional food—yes, good trout and walleye, but also roast pork with cranberries, and Naniboujou's own "trapper flatbread." For a touch of elegance, come between 3 and 5 for afternoon tea. And if you eat too much, stroll beside the lake or cross the road and hike it off in Judge Magney State Park. *U.S. 61 (18 mi south of Grand Portage), Grand Marais, tel. 218/387–2688. Reservations accepted for parties of 5 or more. D, MC, V. Closed mid-Oct.–Mother's Day and weekdays Dec. 26–mid-Mar. Moderate.*

Betty's Pies. From the outside it's a modest place, but step inside and you enter one of Minnesota's holy places. You can get more than pie here—mostly straightforward Main Street café fare, plus lake fish—but the pies (sweet, not savory) are what people journey long distances for. Fruit, cream, pumpkin—just about any kind of pie you've ever heard of is for sale. Betty's isn't very close to Grand Portage—about 130 miles to the southwest, down the North Shore. Still, if you're coming to Isle Royale via Duluth, don't miss it. *U.S. 61, 4 mi north of Two Harbors, tel. 218/834–3367. Closed mid-Oct.–Apr. and weekdays in May. No credit cards. Inexpensive.*

Blue Water Cafe. A typical small-town Minnesota café, except that it's a bit bigger; it's the kind of place locals come to drink coffee and shoot the breeze. You can fill up on a quick, hot breakfast early in the morning before running up to Grand Portage to catch the Isle Royale boat. It's open 6 AM–8 PM. *Wisconsin St. at 1st Ave. W, Grand Marais, tel. 218/387–1597. D, MC, V. Inexpensive.*

NEAR THE PARK: MICHIGAN **Harbor Haus.** You'll find this homey spot up at the tip of rugged Keweenaw, just a stone's throw from the Copper Harbor docks. Along with fish fresh from Lake Superior, which the place overlooks, the Harbor Haus offers German favorites such as sauerbraten and schnitzel. The ambience is gemütlichkeit topped with a dollop of schmaltz—when the ferry arrives in the harbor, the waitresses greet it by running out to the dock and folk dancing. *1 block off U.S. 41, Copper Harbor, tel. 906/289–4502. Reservations for groups of 10 or more only. AE, D, DC, MC, V. Moderate.*

Northern Lights. This restaurant atop the Best Western Franklin Square Inn (*see* Lodging, *below*) is perhaps the most elegant spot in this rustic region. It provides steak and fish (lake trout is the specialty; lobster and shrimp are also on the menu), as well as well-prepared (but rather standard) chicken and pasta. Paintings and watercolors by local artists decorate the walls, but the best local color is the lake, from seven stories up. *820 Shelden Ave., Houghton, tel. 906/482–4882. Reservations accepted. AE, D, DC, MC, V. Moderate.*

Fitzgerald's. The tiny town of Eagle River, on the northern shore of Keweenaw about midway between Houghton and Copper Harbor,

is home to this highly regarded little dining room. You can get good, fresh lake trout and whitefish here, as well as pork ribs. But the restaurant is also known for its innovations—the basil-cream and curry sauces with which it dresses the fish, the Thai and vegetarian dishes that appear from time to time. The nautical decor (it's named for the ill-fated oar boat *Edmund Fitzgerald*, immortalized by Gordon Lightfoot) is pleasant, but the outdoor deck is nicer, especially toward sunset. *100 Front St., Eagle River, tel. 906/337–0666. Reservations advised. MC, V. Inexpensive–Moderate.*

Armando's Douglas Saloon. This restaurant and bar are housed in downtown Houghton's Douglas House Building, which, like the Naniboujou (*see above*), is on the National Register of Historic Places. The saloon has retained its original arched ceiling and Tiffany-style chandeliers. The attached restaurant doesn't have quite the charm, and its Italian menu (Americanized lasagna and pasta) isn't really inspired. But it does offer cheap eats beyond the standard steak and walleye. On Friday night there's a fresh-fish buffet; Saturday is all-you-can-eat Italian night. *517 Shelden Ave., Houghton, tel. 906/482–2003. Reservations accepted. MC, V. Inexpensive.*

Gemignani. Just across the bridge from Houghton is Hancock, home to this hole-in-the-wall spaghetti joint, which has the best Italian-style food around. Southern Italian, that is: gnocchi and pasta smothered in red sauce and served with homemade bread. It's collegiate, but a good place to bring a family hungry from hiking, camping, or driving many miles. *512 Quincy St., Hancock, tel. 906/482–2920. No reservations. No credit cards. Inexpensive.*

Suomi Home Bakery and Restaurant. *Suomi* is the Finnish word for Finland, and this cheerful place is testimony to Keweenaw's Finnish heritage. People come primarily for the breakfasts, which you can get all day long. The emphasis is on big, white, puffy food smothered in fruit. Case in point: the large Finnish pancake with fruit sauce. There's

Finnish French toast, too, plus omelets and other breakfast fare. (The lunches are typical midwestern café fare.) *54 Huron St., Houghton, tel. 906/482–3220. No credit cards. Open weekdays 6–6, Sat. 6–5, Sun. 7–2. Inexpensive.*

LODGING

The tourists who come to the North Shore and the Upper Peninsula are a hardy breed; they are up here to get their clothes dirty. So while there are no fancy resort hotels here, there are plenty of pleasant, unfussy cabins, lakeside resorts, strip motels, lodges, and B&Bs. Most of them are mom-and-pop operations, which means they are very friendly (though a few have gone to seed). There's also a handful of chain operations, especially in Michigan, which tend to be more up-to-date but a bit more sterile. Prices are reasonable, though there is sometimes a bit of tourist-gouging during the summer. Rooms aren't generally hard to get. This may soon change, especially in increasingly popular Houghton. The season does heat up around July 4, so it's best to call a few weeks ahead, just in case.

INSIDE THE PARK **Rock Harbor Lodge.** This lodge offers the only accommodations on the island that don't require you to bring your own sleeping bag. Inside its woodsy-cum-Craftsman exterior, the rooms are up-to-date with little touches of rusticity: comfortable, but by no means city-slicker plush. You can choose between the lodge proper, whose 60 hotel-style rooms all face the lake, and 20 separate cottages. Meals (*see* Dining, *above*) are included if you stay in the lodge; the cottages each have housekeeping facilities. You're near a number of attractions, as well as a number of tourists, since this is the crowded side of Isle Royale. Those boating to the island can dock at the marina (*see* Other Activities *in* Exploring, *above*). *Box 405, Houghton 49931, tel. 906/337–4993 (summer); National Park Concessions, Mammoth Cave, KY 42259 (off-season). 60 rooms with bath, 20 cottages. Facilities: restaurant. AE, D, MC, V. Closed mid-Sept.–early June. Moderate–Expensive.*

NEAR THE PARK: MINNESOTA **Best Western Superior Inn.** This is a centrally located Grand Marais chain motel, but its woodsy exterior gives it the look of a slightly upscale lodge. The interior is more in the semi-sterile chain style, but the inn is on Lake Superior, which gives all the rooms excellent views. The larger second-floor rooms also have balconies. *U.S. 61 E, Box 456, Grand Marais 55604, tel. 218/387–2240. 50 rooms. Facilities: whirlpool, private beach. AE, D, DC, MC, V. Moderate.*

Grand Portage Lodge. The town of Grand Portage lies inside the Grand Portage Indian Reservation, and the lodge (the nearest accommodations to the Minnesota access to the park) is tribal property. This means that it can legally include a casino—which it does, with blackjack, keno, bingo, and slot machines being the big draws. As casinos go, it isn't Caesar's, but it isn't sleazy either. If you just want a place to stay, you can avoid the gambling scene entirely. The lodge was built in 1975, and it's far more a hotel for whites than a tribal center; the rooms are new, comfortable, and just this side of sterile. *Box 307, Grand Portage 55605, tel. 218/475–2401 or 800/543–1384. 100 rooms with bath. Facilities: restaurant (see Dining, above), lounge, casino, pool, sauna. AE, D, DC, MC, V. Moderate.*

Naniboujou Lodge. About 20 miles south of Grand Portage down the North Shore, this historic inn offers a taste of the area's glory days, when Lake Superior was a tony sports paradise. It went up in 1928 (early visitors included Babe Ruth and Jack Dempsey) and is now listed on the National Register. Its lovely Great Hall features a 200-ton native rock fireplace, oak beams, and Indian-inspired designs. The rooms, most of which face the lake, are small, but their pine furnishings offer a cheerfully civilized rusticity. *U.S. 61 (HC 1, Box 505), Grand Marais 55604, tel. 218/387–2688. 25 rooms with bath. Facilities: restaurant (no alcohol; see Dining, above), basketball and volleyball courts, fireplaces in 4 rooms. D, MC, V. Closed mid-Oct.–Mother's Day and weekdays Dec. 26–mid-Mar. Moderate.*

Pincushion Mountain Bed & Breakfast. Three miles up the Gunflint Trail from Grand Marais is this small, woodsy B&B. It's a new-ish (1986) place, but north woods touches are everywhere, from the wood stove in the dining room to the fir beams on the ceiling. From the house, set on a ridge, you get gorgeous views of the forest and of Lake Superior. The room with the best view is the Pine, which also has an extra single bed (the other rooms are doubles). *220 Gunflint Trail, Grand Marais 55604, tel. 218/387–1276 or 800/542–1226. 4 rooms with bath. MC, V. Moderate.*

The Shoreline. Grand Marais is primarily a north woods tourist town, but it's also something of an artists' colony with pleasant restaurants, motels, shops, and even a natural foods co-op. The Shoreline, on Lake Superior, is one of the nicer motels, with lakeview rooms and cable TV. It's unexceptionally decorated—clean and quiet, little more. Consider it a wayside, not a destination. *U.S. 61, Box 667, Grand Marais 55604, tel. 218/387–2633 or 800/247–6020 (MN only). 30 rooms with bath. Facilities: room refrigerators. AE, D, DC, MC, V. Moderate.*

Trovall's Inn and Resort. It's comfortable and a bit woodsy, in a very North Shore mix; it's been around awhile, it has cabins, and the facilities (grocery, laundry) lean toward campers more than honeymooners. But it's been updated. The old campground facilities are gone, the rustic inn has been freshened up into a B&B, and the gift shop offers locally smoked fish. *U.S. 61 (18 mi south of Grand Portage), Box 98-B, Hovland 55606, tel. 218/475–2344. 4 rooms share 3 baths, 5 cabins. Facilities: coin laundry, grocery, gift shop. MC. V. Moderate.*

NEAR THE PARK: MICHIGAN **Best Western Franklin Square Inn.** One sign that Houghton is becoming more and more of a tourist mecca is this fairly recent addition to its downtown skyline. Indeed, at seven stories, it *is* the skyline. The decor is standard chain hotel, but the proprietors have added touches that recall local copper mining history, from photographs and artwork to copper-colored room numbers. The inn is centrally located and near the boat docks. *820 Shelden Av., Houghton 49931, tel. 906/487–1700. 77 rooms with bath. Facilities: restaurant (see Dining, above), lounge, indoor pool, whirlpool, sauna. AE, D, DC, MC, V. Moderate.*

Eagle's Nest Bed & Breakfast. This cedar-log house, 20 miles south of Copper Harbor and 25 north of Houghton, is perched on a 300-foot ridge over Lake Superior. It's a pleasant north woods retreat, with such touches as brass wall lamps and stained-glass windows. The bedrooms are done up with rustic cedar furnishings. A hand-carved birch fireplace holds court over the living room. The tab includes a full breakfast. *Garden City Rd., Box 14, Eagle River 49924, tel. 906/337–4441. 3 double rooms share 2 baths. MC, V. Moderate.*

Laurium Manor Inn. Built by a copper baron during the mining boom at the turn of the century, this amazing neoclassical pile is now a B&B run by two former Silicon Valley engineers, and it surely offers the most elegant lodging near an Isle Royale access. The walls of the breakfast room (where a Continental breakfast is served) are covered in gilded elephant hide, and the kitchen's built-in icebox was crafted of marble, tile, and oak. The rooms are huge, the biggest being the Laurium Suite, which features a hand-carved oak fireplace. Laurium is about 10 miles up U.S. 41 from Houghton. *320 Tamarack St., Laurium 49913, tel. 906/337–2549. 8 doubles with bath, 2 doubles share bath, 4 suites. Facilities: fireplaces in 2 rooms. MC, V. Moderate.*

Houghton Super 8. A good location (downtown, near boat docks) and, for the tourist-minded town of Houghton, good cheap accommodations. It's not as inexpensive as many other Super 8s, but Houghton knows what it can get during the season. *1200 E. Lake Shore Dr., Houghton 49931, tel. 906/482–2240. 40 rooms (2 wheelchair-accessible). AE, D, DC, MC, V. Inexpensive-Moderate.*

Downtowner Motel. A typical "nice" motel—clean, comfortable, and somewhat nondescript. Its virtues are its proximity to the boat docks (only five blocks away), its low price, and its central location in downtown Houghton. It has cable TV, sun decks overlooking the Portage Lake Lift Bridge, and not much else. *110 Shelden Ave., Houghton 49931, tel. 906/482–4421. 27 rooms. AE, D, DC, MC, V. Inexpensive.*

CAMPING

INSIDE THE PARK Only tent camping is available. There are 36 campgrounds in the park, most of which are designated "rustic," with the only facilities offered being pit toilets. Only a few allow open campfires. Since there are no trash cans except at ranger's stations, you must carry out whatever you carry in. Needless to say (perhaps), dumping soapy or otherwise soiled water into any lake or stream is prohibited. Washing should be done at least 50 feet from natural water sources. Quiet time at campgrounds is 10 PM–6 AM.

Camping in groups of more than 10 is prohibited. Groups of 7 to 10 may camp only at group tent sites; 17 of the campgrounds have them. A number of campgrounds are accessible only by boat. Several have both trail and water access. Each of the boat-accessible campgrounds has a dock. These spots offer the most solitude, especially since few of them have group sites. Hikers can also find group-free campgrounds on the Minong Ridge Trail between Windigo and McCargoe Cove.

In addition to the bare-minimum campsites, about half the campgrounds provide three-sided sleeping shelters. These pleasant wooden units provide excellent protection from bad weather. The front of each shelter also features screening that offers protection from biting insects. As with all the campsites, the shelters are available on a first-come, first-served basis. Though it costs you nothing to camp here, you do need a permit, which you can get at any ranger's station.

Because families with young children rarely move inland, the best spots for quiet are in the backcountry, away from Windigo and Rock Harbor. (This doesn't mean that campgrounds closer in, such as Huginnin Cove, can't be *very* private during the spring and fall.) For beauty, it's hard to make a bad choice. If you want scenic vistas, stay on the rocky eastern side of the island. If it's forests you prefer, head west. All the campgrounds face water, be it a quiet inland lake or Lake Superior. Most of the spots on Superior are set on attractive coves and bays. The campgrounds are spaced far enough apart to accommodate a good day's hike.

OUTSIDE THE PARK If you want to camp off-island either before or after your trip, there are options on both the Minnesota and Michigan shores. In Minnesota, **Judge Magney State Park** (U.S. 61, Hovland 55604, tel. 218/387–2929) has a spacious drive-in campground with room for campers and RVs, as well as hiking trails with beautiful views of the tempestuous Brule River. In Michigan, **Ft. Wilkins State Park** (Copper Harbor 49918, tel. 906/289–4215) and **McLain State Park** (Hwy. 203, Hancock 49930, tel. 906/482–0278) have campgrounds (with room for RVs, but no hookups) and trails near the Superior shore. Admission ($3.50–$4) and camping fees ($7–$11 per night) are charged at all three parks.

Mammoth Cave National Park
Kentucky

By John Filiatreau

Mammoth Cave National Park, in south central Kentucky, has something you won't see anywhere else: a hole in the ground with 330 miles of winding subterranean passages. It's a first-class natural wonder, as reliably awe-inspiring as that other famous hole in the ground, the Grand Canyon. (The second-longest cave, Optimisticeskaya, in Ukraine, is barely a quarter as long as Mammoth.)

The cave's marvels range from 192-foot-high Mammoth Dome to 105-foot-deep Bottomless Pit; from a rugged climb called Mt. McKinley to a drifting voyage on the River Styx, 360 feet down, where eyeless fish swim; from a salt-peter mine abandoned after the War of 1812 to a tuberculosis hospital abandoned after an ill-advised experiment in 1843; from an un-forgiving passage called Fat Man's Misery to a vaulting chamber known as—what else?—the Grand Canyon.

Legend has it that the cave was discovered in the 1790s by a doughty buckskin-clad hunter who pursued a wounded bear through the gaping arch now known as the Historic Entrance. Actually, prehistoric Native Americans had been using this entrance and several others for shelter for at least 3,000 years and had even explored about 20 miles of cave passages in search of flint, minerals for medicinal or ceremonial use, and, presumably, adventure. The cave's first private owners brought in slaves to mine saltpeter (nitrates) for making gunpowder. It was only after the War of 1812, when that market dried up, that Mammoth Cave became a tourist destination. Twenty-six years later, Franklin Gorin, the first of the great Mammoth Cave entrepreneurs, bought the cave and 1,300 surrounding acres and put up a resort hotel. The venture failed, but one of Gorin's black slaves, Stephen Bishop, became America's first great cave explorer and guide. Bishop's legendary crossing of Bottomless Pit on a thin cedar log opened up vast new sections of the cave. (His grave is in the Old Guides Cemetery near the present-day hotel.) Gorin sold the property in 1839 to Dr. John Croghan, who built several little huts in the cave for the treatment of tuberculosis and kept 15 patients there for four to six months.

Even with many other beautiful and interesting caves in the area, by 1875 Mammoth Cave was pulling in 25,000 tourists a year. It had no serious commercial rival until the 1895 opening of Colossal Cave, which was nearly as big as its name suggested and conveniently near the L&N Railroad. Unknown Cave, discovered in 1900, was explored for only a short distance, despite its intriguing name—or perhaps in deference to it; six decades later it would be a keystone in linking all the major caves into one giant system. In 1915, Great Onyx Cave was opened to the public, which trooped in to see it for 50 years. (The early cave tours were not for the faint of heart; between 1895 and 1910, lantern-carrying visitors to Colossal Cave were invited to cross a rickety narrow boardwalk over a chasm 125 feet deep.)

Between 1916 and 1924, an ambitious nearby landowner blasted open three new entrances to Mammoth, two of them closer to the main highway than the Historic Entrance, and started offering tours. The ensuing ownership dispute gave rise to resentments that would smolder for years. By the mid-1920s at least four rival commercial caves were battling for tourists in what later came to be known as the Kentucky Cave War. Healthy competition yielded to hucksterism and increasingly brazen advertising, then escalated to midnight vandalism, brawls, feuds, and shoot-outs. In 1926, when Congress authorized the creation of a Mammoth Cave National Park, the action was perceived locally as a sort of cease-fire— although the warfare didn't end for good until the park was officially dedicated in 1941.

One of the least successful of the cave warriors became the most famous. Floyd Collins, a farmer's son and weekend cave crawler, found a pretty cave on his family's property, named it Great Crystal Cave, and opened it to

the public in 1917. Nobody came; the attraction was too far off the beaten path. Undaunted, Collins set out to find an entrance closer to the main highway. By 1925, he thought he'd found it in what he called Sand Cave, a narrow tunnel that opened on some large, promising passages. But on one exploratory trip a small boulder fell on Collins's ankle, pinning him in a cramped passage deep underground. He was found the following day, and a heroic rescue effort was soon organized. Newspaper and radio reporters flocked to the cave to broadcast eyewitness accounts of poor Floyd's misadventure, his pluck, his family's heartbreak, and the rescuers' bravery—and their melodramatic stories caught the nation's attention.

Collins's long, cold, brave death took two weeks to play itself out on the airwaves and front pages. Historians now identify the attendant circus as one of the first global "media events." Ironically, his death proved to be just what the Great Crystal Cave needed to lure visitors away from the distant main roads. A promoter bought the cave and put poor Floyd's coffin on display in its main chamber, and tourists came in droves. Great Crystal Cave remained open to the public until 1961, when it became part of Mammoth Cave National Park.

In 1925, the known extent of Mammoth Cave was just 45 miles and it was considered the world's third-longest. A mere half-century later Unknown Cave had been surveyed and mapped, and Mammoth, at about 215 miles, was undisputedly the world's longest cave. (In 1985, when a team of cavers snaked through a long-sought connection to Roppel Cave to the east, they added another 53 miles.) By that time explorers had determined that many if not all of the area's caverns were part of one gigantic network, which is now known as the Mammoth Cave System. Exploration, and discoveries, continue to this day. No one expects the current 330 miles to be the final figure.

The cave lives up to its name. It really is mammoth, and its size will impress you. But what comes as a surprise to most "topsiders" is the peculiar beauty of the subterranean world. The 14 miles of passages open to the public include underground "rooms" festooned with delicate, snow-white gypsum-crystal "flowers"; decorative features known as flutes, scallops, popcorn, and soda straws; amber waves of flowstone; vast hanging draperies of multicolored limestone; and glistening colonnades of stalactite and stalagmites.

The temperature underground is all but constant, fluctuating between about 54°F and 60°F—which makes the cave a refreshing destination in summer, when outside temperatures in the region are likely to hover in the 90s. (Even in August, you'll want to bring a sweater.)

The 52,830-acre park that surrounds the cave is a wilderness of second-growth oak and hickory woodlands, open barrens with prairie vegetation, and modest wetlands. National Park Concessions, Inc., manages a hotel and an assortment of low-tech cottages. The National Park Service operates the campgrounds and has laid out an extensive series of hiking trails. Like the cave tours, they range from easy (and wheelchair-accessible) to quite strenuous.

This is no luxury vacation. Hikers and campers are likely to encounter chiggers, ticks, mosquitoes, and horseflies, depending on the season; copperheads and rattlesnakes are also indigenous to the park. Timing is a crapshoot: Spring and fall can be wet and chilly; summers are apt to be hot, humid, and stormy; and the weather in all seasons is notoriously changeable. Some cave tours are dirty, difficult, and tiring. Dining and lodging alternatives are relatively primitive, and the cave area offers no Disney-style Xanadus of entertainment. What you will find instead are mom-and-pop gift and souvenir stands; roadside rock shops selling quartz, geodes, and cave deposits (actually imported from other caves in other countries); small-scale animal and curiosity exhibits; private museums of cave lore and history; scattered boardwalk-style entertainments such as bumper boats and miniature golf; and '50s-style theme campgrounds. These enterprises are mostly remnants of the old tourist industry that took root here before the arrival of the National Park Service.

ESSENTIAL INFORMATION

VISITOR INFORMATION **Mammoth Cave National Park** (Park Office, Mammoth Cave 42259, tel. 502/758–2328). **Edmonson County Recreational Tourist & Convention Commission** (Box 353, Brownsville 42210, tel. 502/597–2819 or 800/624–8687). **Cave City Tourist & Convention Commission** (400 Mammoth Cave Rd., Cave City 42127, tel. 502/773–3131 or 800/346–8908). **Kentucky Department for Travel Development** (2200 Capitol Plaza Tower, Frankfort 40601, tel. 800/225–8747).

Backcountry permits are required and are available at the park office at no charge. Some caving expeditions require special permits; contact the chief ranger's office (tel. 502/758–2251) for details. Tune your radio to AM 530 for tourism, travel, and weather information.

FEES Cave tours run $3.50–$25 for adults, $1.75–$8 for children 6–15 years old. Modest fees are charged for some campgrounds in the park, but most are free.

PUBLICATIONS The park service rangers at the visitor's center have an extensive collection of free pamphlets, maps (including topographical maps), and data sheets on various facets of the cave and the park. A newspaper, *Inside Out,* chronicles daily park activities for children and adults. A bookstore is amply stocked with volumes about Mammoth Cave and its history, geology, and biology. Especially recommended are *A Visitor's Guide to Mammoth Cave National Park,* by Deane Oliva and Karen Genter ($4.95), and *A Geological Guide to Mammoth Cave National Park,* by Arthur N. Palmer ($6.95).

GEOLOGY AND TERRAIN The topography of south central Kentucky is unusual. The cave country is part of a low, rugged plateau with abrupt hills and secluded valleys—a ridge-and-gully landscape carved out of limestone by flowing water. The limestone originated from deep beds of shell fragments at the bottom of a shallow sea that covered the area until about 200 million years ago. The water acts as a weak acid, slowly but relentlessly dissolving the limestone, creating fissures, sinkholes, caves, and underground streams. Scientists have assigned the name *karst* to this kind of topography; the word is derived from the Serbo-Croatian *jars,* meaning "stone," and was first used to describe the northern Adriatic region. The same water that slices and dices the limestone eventually loses carbon dioxide and takes on calcium carbonate, which it then deposits to create the stalagmites, stalactites, and other stone sculptures that dazzle visitors.

FLORA AND FAUNA The park is literally crawling with wildlife: 23 kinds of snakes and an assortment of frogs, toads, lizards, and turtles; a full complement of mammals, including the white-tailed deer, which you almost certainly will see, and the bobcat, which you almost certainly will not; 200 species of birds (including the wild turkey, reintroduced in 1983); 30 ferns; and 872 flowering plants. About 200 species of animals live in Mammoth Cave itself, including 42 troglodytes—animals adapted to living exclusively in darkness, among them eyeless cave fish and crayfish, and crickets with extralong, see-in-the-dark antennae. You are unlikely to see these exotic creatures when you visit the cave, though.

Although most of the forest is dominated by second-growth hickory and oak trees, the park supports a number of unique communities of plants. Hemlocks and other northern plants grow in cool, moist ravines; prairie vegetation thrives on open barrens; and aquatic and bog plants colonize scattered wetlands. Twenty-one plant species in the park are listed as endangered, threatened, or of special concern. The 7 miles of forest trails radiating from the visitor's center are lined with some very old, unusually large sycamores, beeches, and tulip poplars. The Big Woods, off Little Jordan Road, is considered virgin forest. Wildflowers bloom throughout the park from March through September; the floral show is at its best in April.

The park was designated a World Heritage Site in 1981 and an International Biosphere Reserve in 1990.

WHEN TO GO Many people think the best time to visit the park is mid-March to mid-April, when the redbud and dogwood trees are in bloom. Springtime temperatures average 65°F; but they may range from the 30s to the 80s, and spring is the rainy season. The park is only moderately crowded in early spring, and the cave tours are not fully booked (although reservations are always advisable). Hotels offer off-season rates at least through April 15.

If you're interested only in viewing the cave, winter is when the tours will be underbooked and you'll have the voluble National Park Service guides to yourself. If you're interested mainly in the park, you might consider the fall, when the weather cools, the crowds thin out, and the trees are ablaze with color. As mentioned, the cave has a delightful air-conditioned ambience on hot summer days, but the park is packed and the tours are all sold out.

SEASONAL EVENTS **April: Wildflower Month** at Mammoth Cave National Park; nature walks, bus tours and special programs. **Weekend after Memorial Day: Glasgow Highland Games** at Barren River Lake State Resort Park (35 mi south on U.S. 31E); a gathering of Scottish clans with such sporting events as battle-ax throwing and tossing the caber. **Early August: Cave City Arts & Crafts Fair** (9 mi east of the park on Rte. 70); artisans from across the nation display and sell their wares. **Early September: Watermelon Festival,** Tompkinsville (40 mi southeast on Hwy. 63); crafts, live entertainment, and ripe thumpers. **Last weekend in October: Hart County Tobacco Festival,** Munfordville (15 mi northeast on I–65); farm-machinery displays, crafts, live entertainment. **Mid-December: Christmas Sing in the Cave;** subterranean music performed by soloists or choirs.

For more information on seasonal events, contact the Mammoth Cave National Park Office, the Cave City Tourist & Convention Commission, or the Kentucky Department for

Travel Development (*see* Visitor Information, *above.*)

WHAT TO PACK For cave tours, be sure to have long pants, a sweater or light jacket, and comfortable walking shoes (sneakers are good for most of the public tours). For park activities, let the season be your guide: In summer, bring loose cotton clothing, a sun hat, and sunscreen; in spring and fall, you'll want layers that you can don and doff as changeable temperatures require; and in winter, be prepared for snow. A raincoat is apt to be handy at any time of year. Except in the dead of winter, you'll want insect repellent. You will never need formal clothing. You may want to bring a bathing suit for hotel pools, but river waters in the park are unsafe for swimming (or drinking).

GENERAL STORES You'll find well-stocked markets in all the surrounding towns. The **Houchens** grocery chain has stores (bigger and less pricey than convenience-type stores, smaller than supermarkets, and all open daily) in Cave City (34 1st St., tel. 502/773–3818), Glasgow (31-E Bypass, tel. 502/651–5011, and others), Horse Cave (U.S. 31-W, tel. 502/786–2639), and Leitchfield (Indian Hills Shopping Center, Hwy. 61, tel. 502/259–3397). The collection of two dozen stores at **Mammoth Cave Factory Outlets** (Horse Cave, I–65 Exit 58, tel. 502/786–4446) offers bargains on everything from books to sportswear to shoes to kitchen equipment.

ARRIVING AND DEPARTING **By Plane.** Two major airports serve the area: Louisville's Standiford Field (tel. 502/367–4636) and Nashville International Airport (tel. 615/275–1675) in Tennessee. Each is about 90 miles from the park. You'll need to rent a car; both airports have **Alamo, Avis, Budget, Dollar, Hertz, National,** and **Thrifty** branches. From Standiford Field, drive west on I–264 to I–65 (5 mi from downtown Louisville), take I–65 south to Exit 53 at Cave City, then follow Route 70 west about 9 miles to the park. From Nashville, take I–65 north to Exit 48 at Park City, then follow Route 255 west about 8 miles to the park.

By Car and RV. If you're coming from north or south, I–65 offers the best access. (Three rest areas—north of Exit 53, south of Exit 43, and north of Exit 28—provide bathrooms and tourist information.) A more scenic southerly route is the Cumberland Parkway, a toll road that runs roughly east–west through hardwood ridge country.

By Train. There is no rail service to Mammoth Cave National Park.

By Bus. Greyhound Lines (tel. 502/733–2200 or 800/231–2222) offers service to Cave City, about 10 miles east of the park. There is no public transportation to the park, but you can get a taxi from **Pedigo Cab Company** (tel. 502/773–3531); the one-way fare runs about $15. (Don't count on getting a cab on Sunday.) Alternatively, you can get the taxi to take you to nearby Glasgow (also about $15), where you can rent a car at **BETMAR** (416 Columbia Ave., tel. 502/651–6699, open weekdays 9–5).

EXPLORING

It's possible to see the cave in half a day and be on your way, but there's no reason not to linger in the park and explore the "surface world" a bit. The countryside is largely unspoiled and the topography is interesting; check out some of the thousands of sinkholes in an area once promoted as the "Land of 10,000 Sinks."

A few words of caution: Kentucky's unpredictable weather can create hazards for drivers in any season. Patches of fog or mist sometimes settle along the roads, and thunderstorms can cut visibility to nearly zero. In winter, ice and snow are just unusual enough to compromise well-intentioned plans for their removal. Drive with appropriate caution. Most roads in the park are well maintained, but those in remote areas may be mud or gravel, and secondary routes outside the park may be in rough shape.

From early spring until mid-autumn, ticks and chiggers run rampant. Newly hatched seed ticks appear in early summer and persist until a killing frost. Because they are so tiny,

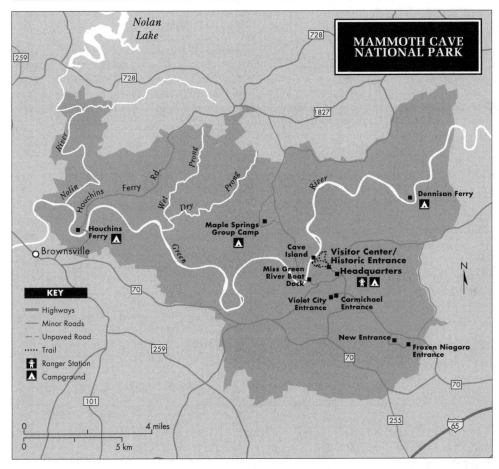

MAMMOTH CAVE
NATIONAL PARK

KEY

▬ Highways
— Minor Roads
-- Unpaved Road
···· Trail
🧍 Ranger Station
⛺ Campground

it is possible to pick up several hundred at a time. To avoid infestation, wear high boots, socks, and long pants, the latter preferably of a light-colored, closely woven cotton. Apply tick repellent to your clothes. (The park store sometimes runs out, so it's best to bring your own.) Try to walk mostly on the designated trails, which are kept clear of vegetation. And check your body carefully for ticks at the end of the day.

Also keep an eye out for copperhead snakes. These poisonous creatures are found throughout the park (so are rattlesnakes, although you are much less likely to encounter one). If you see a snake of any kind, leave it alone. Don't kill it—all the animals and plants in the park are protected by federal

law. Skunks and raccoons are attracted by picnic remains, so be sure to store all food in sealed coolers or containers. (Raccoons are a nuisance, but skunks can be a disaster.)

If you're planning to travel the backcountry, take along a compass. Some of the trails are not clearly marked, and it's easy to make a wrong turn. Let someone outside your party know where you are going and when you expect to return.

THE BEST IN ONE DAY If you're passing through on a tight schedule and have time for only one cave tour, take the "Historic Tour" (two hours, 2 miles). You'll see Native American artifacts, the remains of the saltpeter-mining operation, Fat Man's Misery, Bottomless Pit, and Mammoth Dome.

ORIENTATION PROGRAMS Two films, *Voices of the Cave* and *Bats of America,* are shown in the visitor's center auditorium. The waiting areas near the center are sprinkled with instructional displays on the history and geology of the cave region.

GUIDED TOURS Guided tours of Mammoth Cave start from the visitor center's daily at various times from 8 to 5:30. They last from a little over an hour to six hours, and their difficulty ranges from relatively easy to very hard. All except the "Tour for the Mobility-Impaired" involve some stair-climbing and stooping, and the official park service line is that all the tours are relatively strenuous. Flashlights, cameras, and walking sticks are allowed in the cave; smoking, tripods, and baby strollers are not. Tour prices range from $3.50 to $25 for adults; children under 6 are admitted free, those under 16 at half-price. Group rates are available. For 24-hour information on cave tours, call or, if you prefer, write to the superintendent (Mammoth Cave National Park, Mammoth Cave 42259, tel. 502/758–2328). To make reservations up to two months in advance, contact Mistix Customer Service (Box 85705, San Diego, CA 92186–5705, tel. 800/365–2267; D, MC, V); the company charges a $1-per-ticket fee. You can also buy tickets one day in advance at the cave, or just show up at the visitor's center and take your chances. Reservations are always advisable, though, and are a must in summer.

Tour options include the **"Historic Tour"** (two hours, 2 miles), which takes you through the more famous passages, past mining operations from the War of 1812 and prehistoric artifacts; the **"Frozen Niagara Tour"** (two hours, .75 mile), culminating at a spectacular rock formation that resembles a giant multicolored waterfall; and, during the summer, the **"Lantern Tour"** (three hours, 3 miles), which recaptures the eeriness of cave exploration in the days before electricity and is tailored to visitors with an interest in archaeology (including relics of early Native American Indian explorers of the cave). The **"Tour for the Mobility-Impaired"** is a 90-minute, .5-mile tour for those who, for physical reasons (including wheelchairs), can't participate in other tours.

Spelunking Tours. These exploratory tours are seasonal. Group size is limited, reservations are required, and good health is essential. Participants can expect to get muddy. Recommended: old clothes, knee pads, gloves, sturdy lace-up shoes or boots; and long pants with a belt loop for a battery pack. Helmets with light and battery pack are provided. The six-hour, 6-mile **"Wild Cave Tour"** is limited to 14 participants, all aged 16 or older; the very strenuous nature of the excursion is suggested by the fact that chest size is limited to 42 inches. The three-hour **"Trog Tour"** is for children 8 to 12; they must be accompanied by parents for the first 15 minutes, and they get to keep their helmets at tour's end. The instructional 3½-hour **"Explorer Tour"** is for older children (13–15).

The park also offers alternative caving experiences for qualified spelunkers; the required permits may be obtained from the office of the chief ranger (tel. 502/758–2251). It is illegal to enter any cave not open to the public unless you are engaged in approved research. To forestall temptation, off-limits cave entrances are fenced or covered by rocks. **Ganter Cave** is the park's only choice for small groups to explore on their own. It's about .5 mile off the Sal Hollow Trail in the backcountry, and can be reached by boat or canoe or on foot. The cave is about 8,000 feet long. All Ganter groups must have between four and nine people, with at least one experienced caver for every two novices. Essential equipment includes a first-aid kit, helmets with chin straps, and sturdy boots. Each caver must have three independent sources of light. Reservations, permits, and 8 AM–9 AM check-ins with a ranger are required. For details, call the chief ranger's office (502/758-2251).

Organized Excursions. The **Cave Research Foundation** (Box 443, Yellow Springs, OH 45387, tel. 513/767–9222) regularly leads experienced cavers on expeditions into Mammoth and surrounding caves. In addition, each summer Western Kentucky University and Mammoth Cave National Park conduct field studies combining caving with lectures and surface activities; contact the park office (*see* Visitor Information *in* Essential Information, *above*) for details.

SCENIC DRIVES AND VIEWS The **Joppa Ridge Trail,** southwest of the visitor's center, is a one-way, 2-mile dirt and gravel road once used by farm families; it's also an excellent place to catch a glimpse of wild turkey and the ubiquitous white-tailed deer. It's not open to trailers or motor homes. Any stretch of road from which one can see Green River is likely to be scenic. For an unusual aerial view of cave country scenery, try the chairlift to a ridgetop at **Kentucky Action Park** (off I–65 at Cave City, tel. 502/773–2636), and use its .25-mile "Alpine slide" to come back down.

HISTORIC BUILDINGS AND SITES A community of celibate religious cultists known as Shakers established a settlement at **South Union** in Logan County in 1807. In the 1850s the group included as many as 300 people scattered over 6,000 acres; the group was disbanded in 1922. The South Union Shakers were known throughout the region as expert furniture and tool makers, artists, and craftspeople. In Tompkinsville, the **Old Mulkey Meeting House** (40 mi southeast of the park on Rte. 63), built in 1804, is one of the oldest wood churches west of the Alleghenies; Daniel Boone's sister is buried in the church cemetery. Near Tompkinsville, between Gamaliel and Flippin on Rte. 100, is the **Mount Vernon African Methodist Episcopal Church,** built prior to the Civil War by a group of freed slaves and long used as a school for blacks. Six neighborhoods of **Bowling Green** are on the National Register of Historic Places, including the **Brinton B. Davis Thematic Resource,** 11 structures designed by a noted Louisville architect between 1910 and 1937.

NATURE TRAILS AND SHORT WALKS The available park trails (70 miles in all) are divided into three areas—Headquarters, Backcountry South (of the Green River), and Backcountry North. Headquarters trails are reachable on foot from the visitor's center and are the shortest and easiest. Try **Cave Island Nature Trail,** a mile-long path that begins at the mouth of the cave and winds through the woods past the River Styx Spring, named for its black water. Or take the **Heritage Trail,** a .75-mile stroll (well lit, disabled-accessible, and open until midnight), and whistle past the Old Guides Cemetery, where many early cave explorers are buried.

Most Backcountry South trails are paved and/or graded and are well delineated, while those to the north (some reachable by ferry) are rough, uneven, hard to follow, and generally more adventurous. Most backcountry north trails are open to horses. All hikers, campers, and riders must sign in and out at one of three trailheads in the park. Every hiker is strongly advised to bring a map (available at the visitor's center) and a compass. Recommended South trails include the .75-mile **Cedar Sink Trail,** a pleasant amble to the region's largest sinkhole, where a babbling stream disappears into the earth; the .5-mile **Echo River Loop Trail,** which offers a surface view of majestic Mammoth Dome; and the .1-mile **Sand Cave Trail,** which leads to the sealed-up entrance of the cave where Floyd Collins died.

LONGER HIKES You can design your own backcountry hike, but be sure to let the rangers know where you're going and how long you expect to be gone.

OTHER ACTIVITIES **Inside the Park.** The National Park Service organizes a variety of daily activities for children and adults, ranging from nature walks (lasting 30 minutes to 2 hours) to mini-lectures to evening campfire programs. The hotel complex includes two asphalt tennis courts and four concrete shuffleboard courts; you don't have to be a hotel guest to use them, although guests get first dibs (make arrangements at the registration desk).

Outside the Park. The area is thick with options, starting with several privately owned caves that are open to tourists. At **Crystal Onyx Cave,** a one-hour tour features a Native American burial ground (dated 680 BC) and cave formations (2 mi east of I–65 at Exit 53, tel. 502/773–2359; $5 adults, $3 children 5–

12; open Feb.–Dec., daily 9–4, and summer, daily 8–6). **Buzzard's Roost Badlands Historical Cave** offers a one-hour, disabled-accessible tour with flowstone and other formations (2 mi west of I–65 at Exit 53, tel. 502/773–4598; $4 adults, $3 children under 12; open May–Oct., daily 10–dark). The 1¹/₂-hour tour at **Kentucky Diamond Caverns Show Cave** starts in a building constructed over the cave entrance (1.25 mi west of I–65 at Exit 48, tel. 502/749–2891; $5.25 adults, $3.85 children 12–17, $2.75 children 6–11; open Mar.–Dec., daily 9–4:15). **Mammoth Onyx Cave** has an easy, 45-minute guided tour that is disabled-accessible and includes admission to the **Kentucky Down Under** theme park (.1 mi east of I–65 at Exit 58, tel. 502/786–2634 or 800/762–2869; cost in-season, $11.50 adults, $6.50 children 5–14; out-of-season, $6.50 and $4.50; open Jan.–Mar. and Labor Day–Dec., daily 9–4, and summer, daily 8–6; closed Christmas and New Year's). The Down Under park (open Apr.–Oct.) is a 75-acre wildlife refuge representing the Australian Outback and populated by kangaroos, emus, and lorikeets. There are also sheep-shearing demonstrations. Cave country's newest attraction is **Onyx Cave,** opened in 1973 (Rte. 70 at I–65, tel. 502/773–3530; tours available Memorial Day–Labor Day).

Other attractions tend to be touristy and high camp. **Mammoth Cave Wax Museum** (Cave City, tel. 502/773–3010) has wax portraits of about 100 famous people (including "Jesus of Nazareth") presented in costume and detailed settings along a timeline. **Mammoth Cave Wildlife Museum** (tel. 502/773–2255) features representations of 1,600 mammals, birds, fish, and reptiles from around the world posed in models of their natural habitats. **Bush's Zoo** (tel. 502/773–3791) has a variety of exotic animals, including Japanese sika deer, nilgai antelope, and African pygmy goats. The **Floyd Collins Museum** (tel. 502/773–3366), on the site of the defunct Mammoth Cave Souvenir Shop from the early 1930s, uses pictures, artifacts, and spelunking equipment to tell the story of the ill-fated cave explorer; next door is the Wayfarer Gift Shop. The **American Cave and Karst Museum** (Horse Cave, tel. 502/786–1466) is an environmental education center (run by the nonprofit American Cave Conservation Association) that offers exhibits on the cultural and natural resources associated with caves.

Back-Road Driving. Traveling 50 miles on **historic 68/80,** a meandering convergence of U.S. 68 and Route 80, is like stepping back 150 years. This stretch of the highway moseys through six small and smallish towns, passing more than 100 designated historic landmarks, scores of antiques shops, and thousands of 19th-century homes and commercial buildings. It's a good way to experience the antebellum atmosphere of this part of Kentucky. The tour starts in **Glasgow,** perhaps with a visit to the **Museum of the Barrens** (tel. 502/651–9792), and proceeds westward through **Smiths Grove,** an antique town full of antiques shops; **Bowling Green,** which has six neighborhoods on the National Register of Historic Places; **South Union,** where the Shakers conducted their century-long experiment in community and craftsmanship (*see* Historic Buildings and Sites, *above*); **Auburn,** another town that has exploited its antiquity to become a marketplace of antiques; and finally, **Russellville,** which is much as it was in 1868, when Jesse and Frank James supposedly held up its Southern Bank of Kentucky. Russellville was known as the Confederate capital of Kentucky (which did not secede from the Union) during the Civil War; a monument to Confederate President Jefferson Davis, a Kentuckian, stands a few miles farther along on 68/80, which continues west all the way to the Land Between the Lakes recreational area.

If you're tending east, take the **Cumberland Parkway** to the **Bluegrass.** The famous horse-farm country is about a half-day's drive from Mammoth Cave. Drive the scenic route: south on I–65 to Cumberland Parkway (a toll road), east on the Cumberland to I–75, then north on I–75 to Lexington. The route connects with several points of interest. South of I–75, near Middlesboro, is the **Cumberland Gap,** the historic gateway to the West, where early pioneers thrust their way through the mountains into Tennessee. Nearby **Cumberland Falls** (tel. 606/528–4121) is one of two places in the world where you can see—but only when the moon is full—a moonbow: a rainbow formed by moonlight striking the waterfall; it's a pretty place to visit anytime. Return to I–75 and take Exit 95 for **Fort Boonesborough State Park** (tel. 606/527–3131 or 800/255–7275), where you'll find a replica of the fort where Daniel Boone fought. Inside the cabins, artisans in period dress will be using period tools as they work on 18th-century crafts. Just north of Lexington on I–75, detour to the **Kentucky Horse Park** (tel. 606/233–4303), which features an equestrian museum, a "parade of breeds," and displays on many of the riding arts.

Biking. A gentle-grade, mile-long bike trail runs from Headquarters Campground to Carmichael Entrance Road, skirting the edge of a bluff and passing through shaded woodlands. No bicycles are for rent in the park, however, so visitors must bring their own. At Barren River State Resort Park (about 20 mi south on U.S. 31E), you can sign on for a 2-mile pleasure ride (rentals available).

Bird-Watching. Any part of the park might prove a worthy spot. Many species seem to be attracted to the human activities around the visitor's center, but the areas nearest the Green River are best for variety and diversity. The cave country is particularly rich in warblers (37 varieties), woodpeckers (8, including the seldom seen red-cockaded), and New World sparrows (18). Common inhabitants include the great blue heron, the red-tailed hawk, the spotted sandpiper, and the belted kingfisher. Rare visitors include the snow goose, the double-crested cormorant, the bald eagle, the osprey, and the snowy owl. In the summer, most birds find daytime temperatures just as oppressive as humans do; so unless the bird you want to watch is a soaring vulture (black or turkey), the best time to unpack your field glasses is sunrise.

Boating. Almost 30 miles of the Green and Nolin rivers are open to boaters and canoers in the park. Unfortunately, there are no boats to rent (for canoes, *see* Canoeing, *below*); visitors must provide their own. The most popular boat trip launches at Dennison Ferry

Campground (*see* Camping, *below*) and floats down the Green to Houchins Ferry. The six-hour voyage carries guests past scenic woodlands and dramatic bluffs. No launch fees or permits are required for boating. However, you do need a Coast Guard–approved life preserver for each person on board.

The park includes a 25-mile stretch of Green River, whose waters shaped the colossal cave beginning about 300 million years ago. **Ferries** operate daily, except under high-water conditions. The hours of operation at Houchins are 9:45–5:15; at Green River, 6–9:55. From April through October, the 63-foot twin-diesel *Miss Green River II* (tel. 502/758–2243 Apr.–Oct., 502/758–2563 Nov.–Mar.) makes several hour-long cruises daily. Tickets ($4 adults, $2 children under 12) may be purchased at the visitor's center.

Canoeing. Canoe rentals, shuttle service for your car, and guided canoe trips are available from private outfitters in the area; ask for brochures at the visitor's center. **Canoe Kentucky** (7265 Peaks Mill Rd., Frankfort 40601, tel. 800/552–6631) rents canoes and provides guides for everything from two-hour excursions to two-day trips. You can pick from several sections of Green River.

Fishing. You can fish year-round on both the Green and Nolin rivers. Within the park, you don't need a fishing license, but all other Kentucky state regulations apply. Check at the visitor's center for specifics. If you drop a line, you might catch muskellunge, bass, white perch, or catfish. The tailwaters of Nolin Lake (just north of the park) are a primary stock-and-catch point for nonnative rainbow trout; contact the Edmonson County Recreational Tourist & Convention Commission (Box 353, Brownsville 42210, tel. 502/597–2819 or 800/624–8687).

Golf. There are 10 public courses within an hour's drive of the park. One of the best and most convenient is the 18-hole course at **Park Mammoth Resort** (Park City, tel. 502/749–4101).

Horseback Riding. Sixty miles of park trails north of the Green River (all except the Ganter

Cave Trail) are open for riding. Four of seven campsites at the park's **Maple Springs Group Campground** (3 mi north of the Green River ferry) can accommodate up to 24 people and eight horses each; a site costs $10 per night, and reservations are required. Four parking areas are provided for trailers belonging to day-use horseback riders, and a free map of the trails is available in the park newspaper. Contact the chief ranger's office (tel. 502/758–2251).

Several private contractors offer guided rides. **Jesse James Riding Stables** (Rte. 70W, Cave City 42127, tel. 502/773–2560) has half-day guided rides through the backcountry for $25 per person. You can also rent horses by the hour ($10) or half hour ($7) for trail rides on the 300 acres of property adjoining the stables. **Barren River State Park Riding Stables** (Glasgow, tel. 502/646–2151 or 800/325–0057) offers one-hour guided horseback tours of scenic Barren River Lake at $8 a head. **Crain's Riding Stables** (Park City, tel. 502/749-4101) has guided tours ranging from 30 minutes to two hours and from $6 to $20.

Swimming. Green River in Mammoth Cave National Park is unsafe for swimming. If you're eager for a dip, there's Barren River Lake Resort State Park, 25 miles to the east, or Nolin Lake, 15 miles to the north. Jellystone Park (*see* Camping, *below*) has a public pool and water slide.

CHILDREN'S PROGRAMS Children will enjoy the nightly **Campfire Circles** in the summer, when the rangers give free talks about the region's plants and animals and the cave's history. For a leisurely 90-minute stroll, join in one of the **"Wildflower Walks"** offered free to acquaint visitors with the park's seasonal blossoms. The park's extensive nature trails are free, of course, but would be a bargain at twice the price.

EVENING ACTIVITIES **Music.** The **Mammoth Jamboree** (Rte. 70, Cave City, tel. 502/773–3314) features live country bands and singers year-round on Friday ($4) and Saturday ($5) nights and on major holidays at 8 PM. **Plaza Theater & Country Music Show Place** (Glasgow, tel. 502/651–0446) has stage shows at 8

on Saturdays year-round ($5 adults, $4 senior citizens; free for children under 12 accompanied by an adult).

Theater. The **Horse Cave Theater** (Main St., Horse Cave, tel. 502/786–2177), one of only eight rural professional theaters in the nation, produces five plays in rotating repertory from June through November, performed by professional players in historic Thomas Opera House—whose lobby is designed to resemble a tobacco-curing barn ($10–$14 adults, $7 students, $5 children). **Green River Amphitheater** (Brownsville, tel. 502/597–3818) offers *The Death of Floyd Collins,* an outdoor drama, from Memorial Day weekend through Labor Day (Fri. and Sat. 8 PM; $6 adults, $4 children under 12).

DINING

Friendly southern restaurants with short, unambitious menus dominate the area. Most of them have the short-order, hurry-up-and-eat atmosphere that commonly prevails in heavily trafficked tourist areas. Visitors on low-cholesterol or special diets may have a problem finding restaurants to accommodate their needs. Most visitors rely on the fast-food chains, such as Wendy's and McDonald's, which are scattered throughout nearby towns, but wiser travelers follow the locals to roadside barbecue pits that serve up beef and pork slathered with distinctive regional sauces. Truly picky diners may want to drive to Nashville or Louisville.

All the restaurants in the area fall into the Inexpensive category; the price per person, excluding 6% tax, service, and drinks, is under $15. All are casual, and reservations are unnecessary.

INSIDE THE PARK **Mammoth Cave Hotel Restaurant.** This pleasant, busy restaurant at the inn features southern fare, such as country ham, and generous, country-style breakfasts. *Mammoth Cave, tel. 502/758–2225. AE, DC, MC, V.*

NEAR THE PARK **Bolton's Landing.** The distinctive Kentucky fare includes catfish fried in cornmeal and the Hot Brown sandwich—

turkey and chicken topped with cheese, tomatoes, and bacon, baked to perfection and served open-faced. *U.S. 31E, Glasgow, tel. 502/651–8008. AE, DC, MC, V. Closed Sun.*

Hickory Villa Restaurant. Tourists and locals come here for the barbecued beef and chicken, slathered with a sauce allegedly made from a 100-year-old recipe. *Rtes. 70 and 90, Cave City, tel. 502/773–3033. AE, DC, MC, V.*

Watermill Restaurant. Casual country food is served in casual country surroundings. Southern fried chicken is the house specialty. There's also an all-you-can-eat buffet. *Rte. 70 west of Cave City, tel. 502/773–3186. AE, DC, MC, V.*

PICNIC SPOTS The extensive picnic area near the visitor's center has grills, rest rooms, and covered shelters. Most campgrounds in and near the park have grills and picnic tables. Except on high-summer holidays, you'll probably have no trouble finding a comfortable, convenient place to unpack and chow down.

LODGING

IN THE PARK The park boasts a single hotel, which resembles an inn. There are three other lodging options associated with the hotel, arranged rectangularly around a (free) parking lot; they have no dining facilities but are all within easy walking distance of the main hotel's restaurant. The hotel, food service, bus transportation, and souvenir and crafts shops at the park are all run by National Park Concessions, Inc. (Mammoth Cave 42259, tel. 502/773–2191), which plays a comparable role at four other national parks—Big Bend (Texas), Blue Ridge Parkway (Virginia–North Carolina), Isle Royale (Michigan), and Olympic (Washington). Cabins, campsites, and motels are also available in nearby towns.

Mammoth Cave Hotel. This simple but clean two-story inn, within steps of the visitor's center, offers the park's most luxurious lodging. The rooms are quite pleasant. Group meeting facilities are available September–April. *Mammoth Cave 42259, tel. 502/758–*

2225. 38 rooms. Facilities: restaurant, private patios and balconies. AE, DC, MC, V. Moderate.

Mammoth Cave Hotel Cottages. These one-room cottages furnished in Early American style are .25 mile from the main hotel. They have air-conditioning and electric heat. *Mammoth Cave 42259, tel. 502/758–2225. 10 cottages. AE, DC, MC, V. Open Mar.–Nov. Moderate.*

Sunset Point Motor Lodge. Built like an old-fashioned motor lodge around an open court, Sunset Point offers generously sized, air-conditioned rooms and is recommended for families and larger groups. Reservations can be made through the Mammoth Cave Hotel Cottages. *Mammoth Cave 42259, tel. 502/758–2225. 20 rooms. AE, DC, MC, V. Moderate.*

Woodland Cottages. Also .25 mile from the main hotel, these one- and two-bedroom New England–style cabins are for those who favor rustic lodgings. They're not in great shape, but they're air-conditioned and they're cheap. *Mammoth Cave 42259, tel. 502/758–2225. 23 rooms. AE, DC, MC, V. Open May–Oct. Inexpensive.*

NEAR THE PARK Cave City has more motels than either Horse Cave or Park City. Prices for double occupancy, excluding 9% tax, are all either Moderate ($50–$100) or Inexpensive (under $50).

Moderate. Best Western Kentucky Inn (Box 356, Cave City 42127, tel. 502/773–2321 or 800/528-1234). 51 rooms; pool, coin laundry. MC, V. **Best Western–Mammoth Resort** (Park City 42160, tel. 502/749–4101). 93 rooms; restaurant, pool, tennis court. AE, D, DC, MC, V. **Days Inn–Cave City** (Box 2009, Cave City 42127, tel. 502/773–2151 or 800/325–2525). 110 rooms; pool, coin laundry. AE, D, DC, MC, V. **Heritage Inn** (Box 2048, Cave City 42127, tel. 502/773–3121 or 800/264–1514). 116 rooms; pool. AE, D, DC, MC, V. **Interstate Inn** (Box 397, Cave City 42127, tel. 502/773–3101, fax 502/773–6082). 140 rooms; pool. AE, D, DC, MC, V. **Quality Inn** (Box 547, Cave City 42127, tel. and fax 502/773–2181 or tel.

800/228–5151). 100 rooms; adjoining restaurant, pool. AE, D, DC, MC, V.

Inexpensive. Budget Host Inn (Box 332, Horse Cave 42749, tel. 502/786–2165 or 800/888–CAVE, fax 502/786–2168). 80 rooms; coin laundry. AE, D, DC, MC, V. **Cave Land Motel** (Box 242, Cave City 42127, tel. 502/773–2321). 14 rooms; pool. MC, V. **Holiday Motel** (U.S. 31W, Cave City 42127, tel. 502/773–2301). 25 rooms; pool. AE, D, MC, V. **Jolly's Motel** (Box 327, Cave City 42127, tel. 502/773–3118, fax 502/773–7151). 24 rooms; pool. AE, D, MC, V. **Wigwam Village** (U.S. 31W, tel. 502/773–3381). 15 tepees; grills, covered picnic area. MC, V.

CAMPING

There are four campgrounds within Mammoth Cave National Park that allow you to sleep near your car. Twelve additional backcountry sites (all primitive, some very hard to find) are available to hikers. All are in beautiful, natural settings and near water (although drinking water should be carried in or treated before being consumed). Like the park itself, the campgrounds are less crowded before Memorial Day and after Labor Day; even in summer, however, they are managed on a first-come, first-served basis. The exception is Maple Springs Group Campground, which accommodates horses and requires reservations through the chief ranger's office (tel. 502/758–2251). The address and phone for all four campgrounds is Mammoth Cave National Park, Mammoth Cave 42259, tel. 502/758–2212. Backcountry sites require a permit, obtainable free at the Visitor's Center.

INSIDE THE PARK **Headquarters Campground.** One-quarter mile from the visitor's center, Headquarters is larger and less rugged than the other campgrounds. It's the only one in the park suitable for RV camping, though there are no hook-ups. *111 tent sites, RV parking, showers, bathrooms, liquid propane gas available, picnic tables and barbecue areas. No reservations. Fee: $6 per night. No credit cards.*

Maple Springs Group Campground. Because of the hitching posts, which lend an Old West flavor, these campgrounds, north of Green River, are the park's most popular. *6 tent sites, chemical toilets, picnic tables and barbecue areas, parking for horse trailers. Reservations required. Fee: $10 per night. No credit cards.*

Houchins Ferry Campground. Your car is the only reminder of civilization at this small campsite, 14 miles from headquarters, on the west side of the park. *12 tent sites, 2 chemical toilets, picnic tables and barbecue areas. No reservations. No fee.*

Dennison Ferry Campground. This secluded, primitive campground is on the east side of the park, 7 miles from the visitor's center, and borders Green River. *4 tent sites, 1 chemical toilet, picnic tables and barbecue areas. No reservations. No fee.*

OUTSIDE THE PARK **Jellystone Park.** At this 200-site campground west of the park, visitors are greeted by TV-cartoon star Yogi Bear and introduced to "Bacon, the world's most-photographed pig." The park has full RV service, bunkhouse camping, secluded tent sites, and a disabled-accessible rest room and shower. *1.5 miles west of Cave City on Rte. 70, tel. 502/773–3840. Fee: $16 per night; with water and electric, $21; with water, electric, and sewer, $23. D, DC, MC, V.*

The Natchez Trace Parkway
Mississippi, Alabama, Tennessee
By Sylvia Higginbotham

he Natchez Trace Parkway is unusual in the national park system in that it's a two-lane highway with approximately 400 feet of adjoining timberland, streams, and occasional pastures on either side. It's a long, thin patchwork of forests and fields, hills and vales—a clean, green historic route that cuts through what may be the most serene and scenic parts of the rural American South. Beginning in Natchez, it crosses Mississippi diagonally from southwest to northeast, touches the northwestern tip of Alabama, and continues through south-central Tennessee before winding up near Nashville. The parkway is currently about 30 miles short of the 445-mile route it will cover when finished.

Visitors on the Trace, as it's called by those who know it, will appreciate the direct route and the absence of traffic lights, billboards, commercial vehicles, and buildings to obstruct the view. In fact, there's only one gas station on the entire Trace, although it's easy to fill up in nearby towns. Part of the parkway's appeal is that it's unhurried and (usually) uncrowded, as it must have been in earlier times, when it encouraged the exploration and settlement of a vast section of the country.

Long before the Natchez Trace became a paved highway connecting Natchez and Nashville, buffalo hooves and Native American moccasins created a number of well-trod pathways through the wilderness. Beginning in the late 1700s, boatmen who arrived in Natchez or New Orleans via the Mississippi River would sell their flatboats and rafts there along with their wares. Then, instead of attempting a trip upriver, they would use these trails to return to "Kaintuck" or wherever they had begun their journey.

The Trace became a dangerous route, with bandits waiting to ambush rivermen and other travelers who hadn't lost their holdings at "Natchez-under-the-Hill," the town's notorious red-light district. But it remained a popular route because it saved miles—and time. In 1800 Congress named it a post road for mail delivery. During the War of 1812, General Andrew Jackson marched his troops along the Trace en route from New Orleans, where he had soundly defeated the British and launched his political career. He returned to the Trace many times and married Rachel Robards at Springfield Plantation, which still stands today northeast of Natchez. (Jackson defended her "sacred name" by dueling men who questioned her honor because she was divorced.)

Over the years, with so many Americans either walking the Trace or riding it on horseback, the soft loess soil wore down in places, creating deep trenches. The Sunken Trace, near Milepost 41.5, is a good example of the deeply eroded old trail.

In the mid-1930s, a project to create a scenic road in the southeast began. President Franklin D. Roosevelt established the Natchez Trace Parkway in 1938, although work had actually begun in 1937. The National Park Service has done an excellent job of providing Old Trace exhibits, nature trails, picnic areas, campgrounds, and a beautiful 400-plus-mile drive. Bring a camera and lots of film, for in addition to outstanding scenery you'll probably see deer, turkeys, and other wild game. The drive is so peaceful and undisturbed that you may feel as though you discovered it.

ESSENTIAL INFORMATION

VISITOR INFORMATION The **Natchez Trace Parkway Visitor Center** (RR 1, NT-143, Tupelo, MS 38801, tel. 601/680–4025; open daily 8–5) provides a good introduction to the parkway and its offerings. Six miles north of Tupelo at Milepost 266.0, the visitor center offers a 12-minute audiovisual orientation program, free brochures, information sheets, and a good selection of regional books for sale.

FEES There are no entrance fees, user fees, or tolls for National Park Service facilities on the Natchez Trace Parkway.

PUBLICATIONS The visitor center in Tupelo (*see* Visitor Information, *above*) provides free, detailed maps and sells literature pertaining to the Natchez Trace and the region through which it passes. The free "Official Map and Guide," which contains history, a milepost gazetteer, campground locations, a list of facilities, and other general information, is essential. Also at the visitor center are free sheets on hiking trails, bicycling, cultural resources, and foliage seasons.

The center sells a variety of books on the region's architecture, history (including Native Americans and the Civil War), natural phenomena, and cookery. You might want to check out *Devil's Backbone, Story of the Natchez Trace* ($4.25) or *The Natchez Trace: Pictorial History* ($9.95). For a complete listing and an order blank, contact the visitor center and request the Eastern National Park and Monument Association's sheet of sale items.

GEOLOGY AND TERRAIN Along its 445-mile route between Natchez and Nashville, the Natchez Trace Parkway—an 800- to 1,000-foot-wide strip of land with a two-lane highway running down its center—winds through six major forest types and eight major watersheds, with elevations ranging from 70 to 1,100 feet. A combination of latitude, soil, and geological formation creates an ever-changing landscape. The Trace crosses flats and ridges, swamps and meadows, encompassing 51,742 acres (81 square miles), with Mississippi claiming most of the land.

From Natchez, which stands on a bluff 100 feet above the Mississippi River, the parkway enters forests draped with swaying Spanish moss, climbs through pine hills, and continues through the lush greenery around the Ross Barnett Reservoir. North of Jackson it passes through the rich alluvial soil of the Black Belt prairie, where agriculture flourishes, then, in northeast Mississippi, through the foothills of the Appalachian Mountains. After traversing the Tennessee River Valley of northwestern Alabama, with its red clay soil, the Trace reaches its highest elevation in the oak- and hickory-dominated forests of Tennessee's Highland Rim.

The more fertile lands along the parkway are devoted to milo, soybeans, corn, and cotton, and marginal agricultural lands are used for cattle grazing.

FLORA AND FAUNA Evergreen trees—pine, juniper, magnolia—add luster to the parkway year-round. In May and June the fragrant white magnolias are at their peak. Along the low-lying bayous at the south end of the Trace, cypress trees with their knees and moss-laden limbs cast an air of mystery over lakes and streams. The Trace's thick forests are populated with sycamore, black walnut, and silver maple. To that add 16 different oaks, six hickories, three elms, sweet gums, tupelos, willows, and some 800 other plant species. (One of them is poison ivy, which grows heartily here. Keep in mind the saying "Leaflets three, let it be.")

Expect to see white-tailed deer, armadillos, raccoons, opossums, foxes, squirrels, and rabbits. Don't expect to see black bears, bobcats, or beavers, although they live here, too. Be alert; animals can wander into the path of oncoming cars.

Among the resident reptiles and amphibians, especially in damp forest areas, are alligators, 16 kinds of turtles, and an assortment of lizards and snakes. More than 200 species of birds take wing over the three-state area—among them geese, ducks, hawks, and owls, along with the more common warblers, sparrows, and wrens.

WHEN TO GO Given the moderate year-round climate and lack of seasonal crowds, the best time to go is up to you. Spring offers the pink and white blossoms of redbud, dogwood, magnolia, and wild honeysuckle. April and May also bring a sea of red clover and big fields of bright yellow smooth groundsel. Fall is just as colorful. Sumac and red maple turn bright red, red oaks and sassafras turn orange, and hickories become bright gold.

Average temperatures for Mississippi are 44°F in winter (50° downstate—in other words, south of Jackson), 62° in spring (64° downstate), 79° in summer (81° downstate), and 63° in fall (66° downstate). Summer and early fall seem hotter here because of the high humidity. Temperatures are basically the same in Alabama and a few degrees cooler in Tennessee.

SEASONAL EVENTS The South is a region that celebrates. Most weekends, festivals and fairs are in progress in towns along and just off the Trace.

March–early April: Natchez Spring Pilgrimage features tours of the town's grand historic mansions (tel. 601/446–6631 or 800/647–6742). **Last Saturday in April: Natchez Trace Festival** is held on the courthouse square of Kosciusko, Mississippi, with big crowds enjoying a fiddlers' contest and children's theater (tel. 601/289–2981). **Second weekend in May: Gumtree Festival,** a juried crafts show and sale in Tupelo, Mississippi, is also a place for songwriters to compete (tel. 601/841–6521 or 800/533–0611). **Last weekend in June: Helen Keller Festival,** held in the Shoals area of Alabama, features an outdoor production of *The Miracle Worker,* plus arts, tours, and more (tel. 205/383–0783). **First full week in August: W. C. Handy Music Festival,** also in the Shoals, celebrates the life of this Alabama native (1873–1958), often called the "father of the blues" (tel. 205/760–6434). **Second Thursday in October: Canton Flea Market** brings hundreds of dealers in antiques and folk art to this Mississippi town's courthouse square (tel. 601/859–8055). **Third Saturday in October: Pioneer and Indian Heritage Festival,** at the Mississippi Crafts Center in Ridgeland (Milepost 102.4 on the parkway), offers such collectibles as Choctaw baskets (tel. 601/856–7546).

WHAT TO PACK Unless you attend a high tea at a Greek Revival showplace in Natchez or go into Jackson for dinner and a concert, dress along the parkway is casual. If it's summer and hiking or bicycling is on the agenda, shorts and a T-shirt will do nicely—and don't forget insect repellent, sunscreen, and water.

Winter weather is generally mild, though a "norther" can make the temperature drop quickly. Be prepared with a heavy sweater and a good windbreaker.

GENERAL STORES There's little commercial activity (and no general stores) on the parkway, although supplies are readily available in small towns and cities nearby. Plot a stock-up stop on your map, and plan to enjoy the many picnic areas and historic sites along the Trace.

ARRIVING AND DEPARTING An automobile is essential for this 400-mile-plus journey. The major highways near the Trace are I–20 (east–west), at Jackson, Mississippi; I–55 (north–south), also at Jackson; U.S. 78 and 45, at Tupelo, Mississippi; U.S. 72, in the Shoals area of Alabama; and I–40, I–65, and I–24, at Nashville. You probably won't want to spend much time on any of them, though, because highways and interstates are plentiful and common. There's only one Natchez Trace.

If you arrive via commercial transportation, plan to rent a car at the nearest rental counter. If you're planning to start at the south end of the Trace near Natchez, consider flying into the **Baton Rouge Metropolitan Airport** in Louisiana (tel. 504/355–0333) on American, Delta, or Northwest. Rent a car at the airport from **Avis** (tel. 504/355–4721), **Budget** (tel. 504/355–0312), **Hertz** (tel. 504/357–5992), **National** (tel. 504/355–5651), **Payless** (tel. 504/356–1892), or **Thrifty** (tel. 504/356–2576). Then head to Natchez, 90 miles north, on U.S. 61.

If you're beginning at the northern terminus—currently Leipers Fork, Tennessee—fly into **Nashville International Airport** (tel. 615/275–1675) on American, Delta, Northwest, Southwest, United, or USAir, and rent a car from **Alamo** (tel. 615/275–1050), **Avis** (tel. 615/361–1212), **Budget** (tel. 615/366–0800), **Dollar** (tel. 615/275–1081), **Hertz** (tel. 615/275–2600), **National** (tel. 615/361–7467), **Payless** (tel. 615/275–4280), or **Thrifty** (tel. 615/275–4257). **Amtrak** does not serve Nashville or Baton Rouge, but **Greyhound Southeast** (tel. 800/231–2222) serves both.

EXPLORING

Even with its speed limit of 50 miles per hour (strictly enforced by uniformed park rangers), the Natchez Trace Parkway can be driven in its entirety in one long, long day—but that's obviously not the best way to experience the scenery. Plan on frequent stops to observe and photograph the colorful foliage and wildlife and to explore the many historic sites. Hiking trails, long and short, abound, and there are even trails for horseback riders.

THE BEST IN ONE DAY If you're limited to a single day on the Natchez Trace Parkway, concentrate on the southern end between Natchez and Jackson. Enjoy a quick drive through the antebellum grandeur of **Natchez,** then pick up U.S. 61 heading north, which leads you to the parkway. Stop at **Emerald Mound** (Milepost 10.3) to inspect the country's second-largest Native American ceremonial mound. The **Mount Locust Inn** (Milepost 15.5), the last inn left standing on the Trace, is one of the oldest surviving structures in Mississippi. Next, detour into **Port Gibson** to visit a lovely little town full of fine old homes and churches. At the **Sunken Trace** (Milepost 41.5) you can walk on a section of the original Trace that travelers gradually wore down. The **Rocky Springs Site** (Milepost 54.8) marks the location of a town that vanished after the Civil War; here you'll find interpretive trails, an information station, campsites, and picnic tables. (For fuller descriptions of all these places, *see* Historic Buildings and Sites, *below.*)

By this time, your day should be about over, and you'll be nearing Jackson. The Trace is interrupted through Mississippi's capital city. You can pick up I–20 east to I–55 north, where you'll find restaurants and accommodations. If you're planning to continue, I–55 will return you to the Trace just north of Jackson at Ridgeland.

ORIENTATION PROGRAMS The **Natchez Trace Parkway Visitor Center,** 6 miles north of Tupelo (*see* Visitor Information *in* Essential Information, *above*) provides the Trace's official orientation. It's also the source for

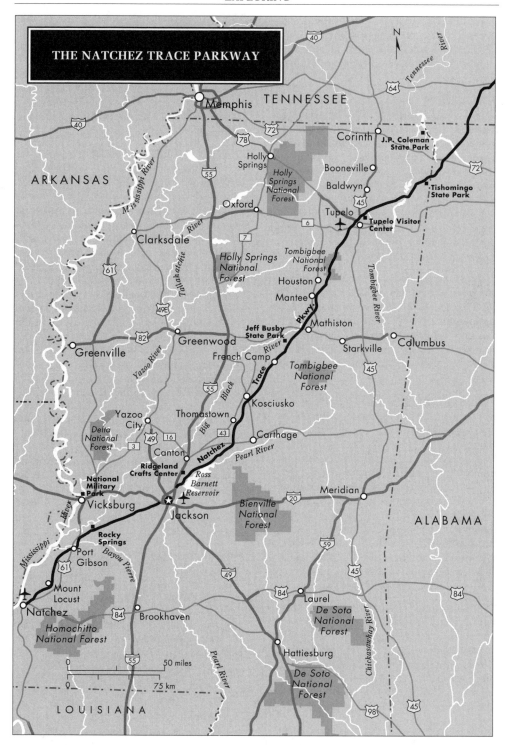

THE NATCHEZ TRACE PARKWAY

maps, historic and educational literature, artifacts, displays, and a continuously running 12-minute video that depicts the development of the Old Trace and the modern parkway.

GUIDED TOURS There are no officially sanctioned guided tours of the Natchez Trace Parkway, though bus tours are welcome. At Mount Locust (*see* Historic Buildings and Sites, *below*), park service employees conduct free tours of the historic property. Convention and visitor bureaus in Natchez (tel. 601/446–6345 or 800/647–6724), Jackson (tel. 601/960–1891 or 800/354–7695), and Tupelo (tel. 601/841–6521 or 800/553–0611) can tell you about tour organizers and guides in these Mississippi cities.

In the Alabama portion, contact the **Chamber of Commerce of the Shoals** (tel. 205/764–4661) or the **Mountain Lakes Tourist Association** (tel. 205/350–3500 or 800/648–5381). The new **Tennessee Natchez Corridor Association** (112 E. Main St., Hohenwald, TN 38462) can provide information on the upper Trace.

SCENIC DRIVES AND VIEWS The entire parkway is a scenic drive replete with pastoral landscapes and seasonal foliage. (In fact, the Natchez Trace Parkway, as a unit of the National Park Service system, will administer the Natchez Trace National Scenic Trail, which has been legislated—for hikers, bikers, and horseback riders—but at press time was not yet in place.) Expect to see rural America the way it was before the days of Styrofoam litter, billboards, and traffic signals. One of the prettiest walks along the Trace is the **Cypress Swamp Nature Trail** (*see* Nature Trails and Short Walks, *below*).

Cypress Swamp is in the **Ross Barnett Reservoir** area. The popular and picturesque 30,000-acre reservoir, built in the early 1960s to prevent flooding in the Jackson area, parallels the parkway for about 8 miles starting north of Jackson at Ridgeland. There's an overlook at Milepost 105, and picnic spots and pull-over places all along the stretch.

The following are among the many other noteworthy overlooks: in Mississippi, **Black Belt Overlook** (Milepost 251.9) and **Twenty-mile Bottom Overlook** (Milepost 278.4); in Alabama, **Freedom Hills Overlook** (Milepost 317.0); in Tennessee, **Swan Valley Overlook** (Milepost 392.5), **Baker Bluff Overlook** (Milepost 405.1), and **Water Valley Overlook** (Milepost 411.8).

HISTORIC BUILDINGS AND SITES The city of Natchez, Mississippi, which will someday mark the beginning of the Natchez Trace Parkway, lies 8 miles south of what is currently the start. The city is a mecca for architectural historians. As you drive in from the Trace on U.S. 61 or U.S. 84 (the two roads merge near Natchez), stay straight as the highways veer left, and you'll be on D'Evereux Drive. On your left you'll soon see **D'Evereux.** The stately antebellum mansion is open for tours only during Pilgrimage (*see* Festivals and Seasonal Programs and Events *in* Essential Information, *above*), but many others are open year-round—among them **Auburn, Dunleith, Longwood, Magnolia Hall, Monmouth, Rosalie,** and **Stanton Hall.** Others can be viewed by appointment, and many offer bed-and-breakfast accommodations. Maps, information, and tour tickets are available from **Natchez Pilgrimage Tours** (200 State St., Natchez, MS 39121, tel. 601/446–6631 or 800/647–6742). The **Natchez Convention and Visitors Bureau** offers information as well as a handy "Historic Natchez Guide" to attractions, dining, and lodging (422 Main St., Natchez, MS 39121, tel. 601/446–6345 or 800/647–6724).

Melrose, one of Natchez's grandest homes, is the first of three sites that will constitute Natchez National Historical Park, established by Congress in 1988. A lavish Greek Revival planter's home from 1845, it features the original furnishings, including rare Victorian pieces. *1 Melrose–Montebello Pkwy., tel. 601/446–5790. Admission with guided house tour: $4 adults, $2 senior citizens, children under 12 free. Open daily 9–5 except Christmas.*

Also a part of the Natchez National Historical Park is the **William Johnson House,** the home of a prominent free black man in antebellum Natchez. It's currently being restored as a black history museum and should open, at least on a limited basis, in 1994. For information, call the historical park headquarters, tel. 601/442–7047.

On the parkway itself, **Emerald Mound** (Milepost 10.3) is, at nearly 8 acres, the second-largest Native American mound in the country (the largest is Monks Mound near Cahokia, Illinois). The flat-topped ceremonial mound was built by a tribe believed to have been the ancestors of the Natchez Indians to accommodate a religious structure or leader's dwelling; it was probably used AD 1250–1600. A trail leads to the top.

A few miles farther on you'll arrive at the **Mount Locust Inn** (Milepost 15.5), the last remaining inn along the Trace and one of the oldest surviving structures in Mississippi. The house was constructed around 1780 as a family dwelling, but because of its location on the trail used by homeward-bound Kentucky boatmen, it became a "stand," or inn— one of nearly 50 that stood along the Trace in its heyday. (In the peak year of 1810, some 10,000 travelers headed north on the trail.) The inns were so crowded that some travelers had to sleep on the floor or in the yard; that was preferable to facing the marauding gangs who rode the Trace. After 1812, steamboats from New Orleans and Natchez ferried travelers north, providing a faster and a safer journey. By 1825 the Mount Locust Inn had become a respite for planters who wanted to escape the party circuit in nearby Natchez. Today park service workers offer free interpretive programs from February through November (tel. 601/445–4211, open daily 8:30–5).

Port Gibson (Milepost 39.2) is a treasure—a quiet town with a tree-canopied main thoroughfare lined with lovely old homes and churches. During the Civil War, when Union general Ulysses S. Grant was leaving scorched ruins in his wake, he declared that Port Gibson was "too beautiful to burn"; it still is.

At the **Sunken Trace** (Milepost 41.5) you'll see how the old trail looked. It takes about five minutes to walk along this deeply eroded section of the original Trace, worn down over the years by buffalo and Indians, settlers and soldiers. It's one of the most beautiful and most photographed spots along the parkway.

Rocky Springs (Milepost 54.8) was once a prosperous community; now it has disappeared. Beginning in the late 1790s, settlers drawn by the rich soil and the numerous springs cleared the land, planted cotton, and built homes and an impressive brick church. At the outbreak of the Civil War in 1861, Rocky Springs was a burgeoning rural community of more than 2,600, with a post office, a Masonic lodge, and several stores. The devastation of the war, a yellow fever epidemic, a boll weevil infestation, and land erosion all contributed to the town's demise. Today the only evidence that Rocky Springs existed is the 1837 church, a cemetery, and an old safe that was once filled with the proceeds from the vast cotton crops. The area also includes an information station, 22 campsites, and picnic tables. Supplies are available at either Port Gibson (*see above*) or Utica, both about 15 miles away.

You'll have to get off the Trace in the Clinton/Jackson area (take the Lakeland Drive exit from I–55 north) to visit the **Jim Buck Ross Mississippi Agriculture and Forestry/National Agricultural Aviation Museum.** It's a living-history museum that depicts life on a 1920s farm and in a turn-of-the-century small town that includes a general store, a church, and a cotton gin. The aviation museum features very small crop-dusting airplanes. *1150 Lakeland Dr., Jackson, just east of I–55 north, tel. 601/354–6113. Admission: $3 adults, $2.75 senior citizens, $1 children 6–18. Open Mon.–Sat. 9–5, Sun. 1–5.*

In the Shoals section of northwestern Alabama, you can visit **Ivy Green,** the birthplace of Helen Keller and the house where the teacher Annie Sullivan taught the blind and deaf child to communicate. The house and grounds are now a museum. *300 W. North Commons, Tuscubia, tel. 205/383–4066. Admission: $3. Open Mon.– Sat. 8:30–4, Sun. 1–4. Closed Labor Day, Thanksgiving, Dec. 24 and 25.*

Close to the Trace's northern terminus in Leipers Fork, Tennessee, is the charming town of **Franklin,** where the entire 15-block old downtown area is listed on the National Register of Historic Places. Among other attractions is the nearby **Carnton Plantation;** the house, built in 1826, served as a hospital during the Civil War. *1345 Carnton La., Franklin, tel. 615/794–0903. Admission: $5. Open summer, Mon.–Sat. 8–5, Sun. 1–4; winter, Mon.–Sat. 9–5.*

Civil War Battlefields and Sites. Battlefields and cemeteries near the Trace draw Civil War buffs and historians all year long. Exit near Jackson onto I–20 heading west to reach the **Vicksburg National Military Park,** where cannons, graves, and monuments from each of the states that lost soldiers in battle line a 16-mile drive. The visitor center is a mile north of I–20, Exit 4B (3201 Clay St., Vicksburg, tel. 601/636–0583; admission, $2 per individual or $4 per carload; open daily 8–5). **Tupelo National Battlefield,** 1.2 miles east of the Trace at Milepost 259.7, is a grim reminder of the July 1864 encounter. **Brice's Crossroads National Battlefield Site** saw a bloody battle in June 1864; to get there, exit the Trace at Milepost 266 heading north on U.S. Highway 45 (business) to Baldwyn and then west on Route 370. Several exits from the Trace will take you to **Shiloh National Military Park,** just across the Mississippi state line in Tennessee, where you can take a self-guided auto tour and visit a national cemetery where some 4,000 soldiers lie buried. A film at the visitor center helps explain this supremely important battle (tel. 901/689–5275; admission, $2 adults, children under 17 and senior citizens free; open fall–spring, daily 9–5, and summer daily 9–6).

Parkway rangers at the visitor center in Tupelo (*see* Visitor Information *in* Essential Information, *above*) can provide additional information on Civil War sites.

NATURE TRAILS AND SHORT WALKS There are 14 nature trails and 8 hiking trails along the parkway. The hiking trails are short by serious hikers' standards, for the longest is a 10-mile loop, the next-longest 4.6 miles. Though comfort stations are available, take water (there are no fountains) and, perhaps, insect repellent.

The **Old Trace** hiking trail (Milepost 16.8, at Rte. 553, about 20 miles north of Natchez) follows the original Trace. This 3.5-mile one-way trail is a good walk for spotting birds and small game.

There's much to ponder on the **Rocky Springs** hike around the now-vanished community (*see* Historic Buildings and Sites, *above*). It begins at Milepost 54.8 with a 1.5-mile trail over the old Trace; a separate trail is the 10-mile loop between Rocky Springs and the Owens Creek area (Milepost 52.4), which boasts a small waterfall. This hike is on rolling terrain and should take about four hours to complete.

Some 21 miles north of the parkway entrance at Jackson (Milepost 122.0), the 2,200-foot **Cypress Swamp Nature Trail** offers one of the prettiest short walks along the Trace. Its 22 interpretive stops explain what's what in a typical cypress swamp. There's a sturdy wooden bridge over the dark water, where cypress knees and tupelo trees cast an air of mystery. The bridge is a good place to photograph whatever comes up from the glistening water—perhaps an alligator, certainly a turtle or two.

The **Jeff Busby Site** (Milepost 193.1) offers a hiking trail up 600-foot Little Mountain, one of the highest points on the parkway. A scenic overlook is the payoff for the fairly easy mile-long hike from the Jeff Busby Campground. Along the way, markers at 28 interpretive stops draw attention to the importance of protecting the natural environment. (Jeff Busby was the Mississippi congressman who in 1934 introduced a bill authorizing a survey of the old Natchez Trace; four years later, the Natchez Trace Parkway became a reality.)

In Tennessee, the **Glenrock Branch** (Milepost 364.5) is a 1-mile trail (one way) along a clear, fast stream. Once you're in Tennessee you'll notice a slight change in the terrain. At the **Meriwether Lewis Site** (Milepost 385.9), it's hilly and forested, with less undergrowth than you'll have seen at the southern end of the Trace. The site's namesake—the Lewis of Lewis and Clark (the explorers who first charted the American West)—died in 1809 at Grinder's Inn here. A 2.3-mile trail takes you past the grave site to the Little Swan picnic area. There's a ranger's station near the grave site.

This is waterfall country, and the final trail on the Trace is at **Jackson Falls** (Milepost 404.7). The trail descends steeply to the falls (named for Andrew Jackson), which empty into the Duck River. You can hike to Baker's Bluff Overlook and see a picturesque farm in the distance. The fairly easy trail is less than a half-mile long.

OTHER ACTIVITIES **Biking.** Mountain bikes and trail bikes are not allowed on parkway trails. Otherwise, bicycling along the Trace is governed by Title 36, Code of Federal Regulations. Each bicycle must exhibit a white light on the front and a red light or reflector on the rear. Obviously, you need to be extremely cautious about automobiles. Keep to the right, in single file; never carry other riders; use proper hand signals; and be off the parkway by sundown. For further information, contact the visitor center in Tupelo (*see* Visitor Information *in* Essential Information, *above*).

The width of the parkway varies—it is wider at historic and recreational sites. All lands outside the parkway right-of-way (except Tishomingo State Park and Tombigbee National Forest, both in northeastern Mississippi) are privately owned, and it's up to the owners to grant permission for use.

Bird-Watching. Despite the absence of designated observation points for bird-watching, the parkway offers ample opportunities; the variety of environments attracts an equal variety of species. A host of woodland birds perch in the forested areas of the **Meriwether** Lewis, **Jeff Busby,** and **Rocky Springs** sites (*see* Nature Trails and Short Walks, *above*). During September, the ruby-throated hummingbird makes its annual migration through the **Rock Spring Nature Trail** in Alabama; bluebirds, hawks, and vultures keep their watchful eyes on the parkway's trails year-round. Travelers in northern Mississippi and Alabama are occasionally greeted by wild turkeys feeding along the roadside.

Horseback Riding. Though riding is prohibited along the parkway proper, there are four designated horse trails. The visitor center in Tupelo (*see* Visitor Information *in* Essential Information, *above*) has information on the established trails. The **Lonesome Pine Horse Trail,** a wooded, one-way trail northeast of Jackson at Milepost 114.9, is 15 miles long; you get onto it at Route 43. It does not provide rest rooms. The **Tombigbee Horse Trail,** in the Tombigbee National Forest, is an elongated figure eight, 15 miles in length (or just 9 if you stick to one loop). Enter it at the Witch Dance Picnic Area at Milepost 233.2; there's a comfort station nearby. The **Tupelo Horse Trail** at Milepost 259.7 is a 3.5-mile loop; you access it at Route 6. Finally, near the northern terminus of the parkway (Milepost 427.5) is the 25-mile-long **Garrison Creek Trail.** Enter the trail at the comfort station; you'll stay parallel to the parkway until you reach Route 7.

Running. It's permitted, but there are no special provisions or locations. Be careful. Traffic can be heavy, especially near Jackson and Tupelo, and it gets worse during holiday periods and the foliage seasons. Wear colorful, high-visibility clothing. You are required to run against the traffic, on the shoulder (which is mowed and stable). And be prepared for the high humidity from May through September!

Swimming. The beach on the parkway at Colbert Ferry, Alabama, no longer has a lifeguard. Swim with caution.

CHILDREN'S PROGRAMS Park rangers at the **Mount Locust Inn** (*see* Historic Buildings and Sites, *above*) offer projects for children through a Junior Ranger program. The kids, generally ages 8–12, work alongside the rangers with cleanups and other activities and participate in special events, learning about conservation, preservation, and history. At the **Mississippi Crafts Center** (Milepost 102.4, tel. 601/856–7546, open daily 9–5), children enjoy watching artisans at work, especially weavers and quilters. Children are fascinated by the **Cypress Swamp Nature Trail** (*see* Nature Trails and Short Walks, *above*), though parents must watch them carefully, since the place really is a swamp. The **visitor's center** in Tupelo (*see* Visitor Information *in* Essential Information, *above*) has a good selection of children's literature, educational games, and "hands-on" exhibits of Trace-related artifacts.

EVENING ACTIVITIES The Trace is fairly desolate at night. There isn't even much traffic. Campgrounds observe quiet time from 10 PM till morning, so if you're looking for action— such as it is—check out the nearby towns for movie theaters or lounges. Natchez, Jackson, and Tupelo have many more options.

DINING

Those who don't want to leave the parkway had best plan to bring their own food and take advantage of the cook-out grills along the way, for there are no restaurants directly on the Trace. There are, however, some very good restaurants in Natchez, Jackson, and Tupelo. Smaller towns generally have fast-food franchises and a locally owned café or two, though the latter may have limited hours and a menu heavy on fried items—from chicken and catfish to little fried peach or apple pies. The exits are well marked, and except for Jackson, the towns are small enough to get around in easily.

NEAR THE PARKWAY: MISSISSIPPI Brother's. This Natchez favorite is relatively small and crowded, and it can be noisy. But it has a bar and courtyard out back, and they add authenticity to the New Orleans–style atmosphere. Among the Cajun and Creole specialties there's usually spicy seafood served over angel-hair pasta or rice. *209 Franklin St., Natchez, tel. 601/442–1777. Reservations ac-*

cepted. Dress: casual. AE, MC, V. Moderate–Expensive.

Ralph & Kacoo's. Another Cajun restaurant, this one in Jackson, Ralph & Kacoo's offers upscale decor and seafood fresh from south Louisiana. The crayfish étouffée is excellent, shrimp and red snapper are delicious, and the gumbos are the best around. There's steak, too, cooked to perfection. *100 Dyess Rd., I–55 and E. County Line Rd., Jackson, tel. 601/957–0702. Reservations advised. Dress: casual but neat. AE, D, MC, V. Moderate–Expensive.*

Harvey's. This innovative Tupelo restaurant now has branches in four cities. Amid the dark wood enlivened by green plants, you can order grilled chicken and fish along with big, filling salads such as the Southland, an extravagant chef's salad. The dressings are homemade. *424 S. Gloster, Tupelo, tel. 601/842–6763. Reservations not required. Dress: casual. AE, MC, V. Closed Sun. Inexpensive–Moderate.*

Primos Northgate. Primos has been serving Jackson families for years. The atmosphere is quiet, somewhat French country in style; outside there's a patio. Count on fresh seafood, prime rib, and big, delicious salads. *4330 N. State St. (exit I–55 at Northside Dr.), Jackson, tel. 601/982–2064. Reservations accepted. Dress: casual but neat. AE, DC, MC, V. Inexpensive–Moderate.*

The Carriage House. Lunch on the grounds of the magnificent Stanton Hall, one of the grandest antebellum mansions in Natchez, is a true southern experience. This open, paneled restaurant is managed by the same garden club that owns the mansion. The ladies of the club offer such plantation specialties as southern (delicately) fried chicken, baked ham, tiny biscuits with homemade preserves—and mint juleps. *401 High St., Natchez, tel. 601/445–5151. Reservations advised on weekends and during Pilgrimage. Dress: casual but neat. AE, DC, MC, V. No dinner. Inexpensive.*

Redbud Inn. This gracious old Victorian house (circa 1885) is also an antiques shop and a B&B (*see* Lodging, *below*). Every day at lunch the Redbud serves up a chicken or a seafood entrée, with lots of fresh vegetables, salads, and a secret-recipe hot fudge cake. Private candlelight dinners ($15–$20 per person) may be arranged in advance. *121 N. Wells St., Kosciusko, tel. 601/289–5086. Reservations advised. Dress: casual but neat. MC, V. Lunch weekdays 11:30–1:30, weekends for groups of 8 or more with reservation; dinner by previous arrangement only. Inexpensive.*

NEAR THE PARKWAY: ALABAMA Old Rocking Chair Restaurant. The down-home country cookin' here—ribs, chicken, steaks, cobblers—fits nicely with the rocking chairs on the front porch. The restaurant, which serves three meals every day, stands across the highway from the Alabama Music Hall of Fame. *800 U.S. 72 W, Tuscumbia, tel. 205/381–6105. Reservations not necessary. Dress: casual but neat. AE, D, MC, V. Inexpensive.*

NEAR THE PARKWAY: TENNESSEE Choice's Restaurant. This local favorite is housed in an old hardware store. Top lunchtime choices from the eclectic menu include the salad sampler and a vegetarian burrito; at dinner the star is the stuffed chicken breast. Among the popular desserts is the chocolate peanut-butter GooGoo cluster cake with chocolate mousse icing; if you've ever listened to the Grand Ole Opry, you won't need "GooGoo" translated. *108 4th Ave. S, Franklin, tel. 615/791–0001. Reservations not required. Dress: casual. AE, MC, V. No Sun. dinner. Moderate.*

Merridee's Bakery-Restaurant. You'll sniff the aroma before you see the place. There are omelets at breakfast and soups, sandwiches, and salads at lunch, but the real star is the baked goods. (Take a loaf with you.) The regulars hang out here for hours at a time. *110 4th Ave., Franklin, tel. 615/790–3755. No reservations. Dress: casual. MC, V. Closed Sun. Inexpensive.*

PICNIC SPOTS The Natchez Trace Parkway maintains 35 designated picnic sites along its 435 miles. All have tables; some have grills and rest rooms; all are marked. (See Explor-

ing, *above*, for more information on these sites.) The most picturesque and popular sites for alfresco dining are **Rocky Springs** (Milepost 54.8; *see* Historic Buildings and Sites, *above*), the **Mississippi Crafts Center** (Milepost 102.4), **River Bend** (Milepost 122.6), **Jeff Busby** (Milepost 193.1; *see* Nature Trails and Short Walks, *above*), **Witch Dance** (Milepost 233.2), **Colbert Ferry,** Alabama (Milepost 327.3), **Meriwether Lewis** (Milepost 385.9; *see* Nature Trails and Short Walks, *above*), **Jackson Falls** (Milepost 404.7; *see* Nature Trails and Short Walks, *above*), and **Garrison Creek** (Milepost 427.9; *see* Horseback Riding *in* Other Activities, *above*).

LODGING

Because of the isolation, it's a good idea to be off the Trace by dark. There are no hotels or motels directly on the parkway, but accommodations are plentiful within a short distance. You won't find pricey hotels, but you will find chains with quite reasonable rates. A more intimate but somewhat costlier alternative is a bed-and-breakfast.

CHAIN HOTELS AND MOTELS Ramada Renaissance Hotel. A relatively new and popular high rise, with a convention or two usually in progress. *1001 County Line Rd. (at I-55), Jackson, MS 39201, tel. 601/957–2800 or 800/272–6232. 300 rooms. Facilities: restaurant, bar, gift shop. AE, DC, MC, V. Moderate–Expensive.*

Best Western River Park. It's close to downtown and the new *Lady Luck* dockside riverboat casino. *645 S. Canal St., Natchez, MS 39120, tel. 601/446–6688 or 800/274–5532, fax 601/442–9823. 146 rooms. Facilities: restaurant, lounge, pool, Jacuzzi, gift shop. AE, DC, MC, V. Moderate.*

Cabot Lodge. This place has a homey, comfortable feel even though it's new. *120 Dyess Rd. (off I-55 at County Line Rd.), Jackson, MS 39120, tel. and fax 601/957–0757. 208 rooms. V. Moderate.*

Holiday Inn. Like most of the others in this chain, this is a comfortable, dependable, and bland establishment. *1307 Murfreesboro Rd.,*

Franklin, TN 37064, tel. 615/794–7591 or 800/HOLIDAY, fax 615/794–1042. 100 rooms. Facilities: restaurant, lounge, pool. AE, D, DC, MC, V. Moderate.

Holiday Inn. While this represents the usual Holiday Inn fare, the people working here make guests feel very welcome. 4900 Hatch Blvd., Sheffield, AL 35660, tel. 205/381–4710 or 800/HOLIDAY, fax 205/381–4710, ext. 403. 205 rooms. Facilities: restaurant, lounge, pool. AE, D, DC, MC, V. Moderate.

Holiday Inn, Downtown. The rooms on the east side overlook a lovely park and the fine Cathedral of St. Peter the Apostle. 200 E. Amite St., Jackson, MS 39120, tel. 601/969–5100 or 800/HOLIDAY, fax 601/969–5100, ext. 1350. 359 rooms. Facilities: restaurant, lounge, pool. AE, DC, MC, V. Moderate.

Ramada Hilltop. The hotel sits high on a bluff overlooking the Mississippi River. 130 John R. Junkin Dr., Natchez, MS 39120, tel. 601/446–6311 or 800/256–6311, fax 601/446–6321. 172 rooms. Facilities: restaurant, lounge, pool, gift shop, free in-house movies. AE, DC, MC, V. Moderate.

Ramada Inn. The Ramada's best feature is its Café Bravo, with outstanding food and service. 854 N. Gloster, Tupelo, MS 38801, tel. 601/844–4111 or 800/228–2828. 230 rooms. Facilities: restaurant, lounge, 2 pools, sauna, game room, hair salon. AE, DC, MC, V. Moderate.

Comfort Inn. This no-nonsense motel emphasizes value. 1190 N. Gloster St., Tupelo, MS 38801, tel. 601/842–5100 or 800/228–5150. 83 rooms. Facilities: complimentary Continental breakfast, exercise room. AE, D, DC, MC, V. Inexpensive.

Ramada Inn. This is standard but comfortable and favored by visitors to the nearby Saturn plant. 1208 Nashville Hwy. (U.S. 21 N), Columbia, TN 38401, tel. 615/388–2720 or 800/2-RAMADA, fax 615/388–2360. 155 rooms. Facilities: restaurant, lounge, pool. AE, D, DC, MC, V. Inexpensive.

BED-AND-BREAKFASTS For accommodations in an antebellum mansion, expect to pay $75 to $125 for one or two persons. For reservations, contact **Natchez Pilgrimage Tours** (Box 347, Natchez, MS 39121, tel. 601/446–6631 or 800/647–6742) or **Lincoln, Ltd., B&B Reservations** (Box 3479, Meridian, MS 39303, tel. 601/482–5483 or 800/633–6477).

The Burn. This elegant 1832 Greek Revival mansion is a treasure trove of 19th-century antiques. There's also a pool. 712 N. Union St., Natchez, MS 39120, tel. 601/442–1344 or 800/654–8859. 6 rooms with bath. AE, MC, V. Moderate–Expensive.

French Camp Academy Bed and Breakfast. A B&B formed by joining two log cabins together, this comfortable inn has iron beds, handmade quilts, and other rustic amenities. The Huffman Cabin visitor's center and gift shop stands nearby. French Camp, MS 39745, tel. 601/547–6835. 4 rooms with bath, 1 suite. MC, V. Moderate.

McEwen Farm Log Cabin Bed & Breakfast. This is actually a trio of (modernized) cabins on a farm 2 miles from the Trace, just north of the crossroads community of Duck River. It's popular with Trace walkers and cyclists, and the privacy is splendid. Bratton La., Box 97, Duck River, TN 38454, tel. 615/583–2378. 3 cabins. MC, V. Moderate.

Redbud Inn. A pretty 1885 Queen Anne house, the Redbud also has a popular restaurant (see Dining, above). Each room is decorated with period antiques. 121 N. Wells St., Kosciusko, MS 39090, tel. 601/289–5086. 4 rooms with bath. MC, V. Moderate.

CAMPING

In addition to the numerous private campgrounds near the trace, there are three campgrounds directly on (and administered by) the Natchez Trace Parkway. The designated campsites are free, available on a first-come, first-served basis, and crowds are almost never a problem. Uniformed parkway rangers patrol the campgrounds periodically. Cutting plants and digging are both prohibited; fires may be built in fireplaces only, with dead or downed wood; pets must be leashed or otherwise restrained. Quiet hours last from 10 PM to 6 AM. Organized groups should make arrangements in advance by writing the superintendent at the visitor's center in Tupelo (*see* Visitor Information *in* Essential Information, *above*).

Each campsite is outfitted with a picnic table, a fireplace with grill, and a level tent site. Drinking water and rest rooms are provided at the campgrounds, but not hot water, showers, or electrical or sanitary hookups. RVs will find drive-through spaces but no pull-ins and no hookups at the parkway sites; for other options, *see below.*

Rocky Springs Campground (Milepost 54.8, tel. 601/535–7142) provides 22 sites, two comfort stations, water, and a hiking trail (*see* Historic Buildings and Sites *and* Nature Trails and Short Walks *in* Exploring, *above*). Camping and picnicking supplies are available at Port Gibson or Utica, both about 15 miles away.

Jeff Busby Campground (Milepost 193.1, tel. 601/387–4365) offers 18 campsites. A conces-sionaire operates a camp store and service station at the site. There's a rest room and good hiking on Little Mountain (*see* Nature Trails and Short Walks *in* Exploring, *above*).

Meriwether Lewis Campground (Milepost 385.9, tel. 615/796–2675) has 32 campsites, a rest room, and hiking. Camping supplies and gas can be found 7 miles west of the parkway on Route 20 in Hohenwald.

Other Campgrounds and RV Camping. If the drive-through spaces in the public campgrounds are not sufficient, there are other options. **The Elvis Presley Lake Campground** (Rte. 4, Box 387-E, Tupelo, MS 38801, tel. 601/841–1304), operated by the city of Tupelo, has 16 RV sites; one is a pull-through, the others pull-in. The cost is $11 per night for RVs; tent camping is $5 for 2 people. The 350-acre lake is a popular fishing spot. **Tishomingo State Park** (Box 880, Tishomingo, MS 38873, tel. 601/438–6914) has 62 RV sites, some paved, some slag. Tishomingo, one of Mississippi's prettiest parks, lies in the Appalachian foothills. RV camping and tent camping both cost $10 per night here.

Okefenokee National Wildlife Refuge
Georgia

By Jeffrey R. Young

 trip into the refuge feels like you've been transported to another, or at least an earlier, world. Swamp is everywhere—growing out of endless water and hanging in impossibly tall trees with wide, exposed stumps. Native Americans named this land Okefenokee ("Land of Trembling Earth") because when they stomped the unfirm peat, cypress trees swayed and shrubs quivered.

Animals, some of which have probably never seen a human, still rule this primitive area. Alligators—10,000 to 20,000 strong and up to 17 feet in length—reign, and birds representing 235 species wade through flooded marshes and glide from island to island in the muggy air. This is also the land of possums, as anyone familiar with Walt Kelly's comic strip "Pogo" can attest.

The swamp has been marked by human hands, however. Native Americans lived here as early as 2500 BC and remained a presence until the Seminoles were driven out in 1850. Next, the timber industry took an interest in the swamp's giant hardwood forests and cut most of the virgin timber in the early 1900s. Some of the trees taken were as much as 2,000 years old and 18 feet in diameter.

In the 1960s, a dam was built on the swamp's southwestern edge. It was intended to protect the adjacent private timberland from fire by controlling drainage into the Suwannee River and storing more water in nearby areas. In recent years, however, scientists have called into question the wisdom of interfering with the swamp's natural processes; fire, it seems, is necessary to burn away sediment and allow new growth.

Since 1937, Okefenokee has been under the protection of the federal government, but as a national wildlife refuge rather than a national park. As such, it has more restrictions on camping and fewer recreational activities than a national park, but if you plan carefully, these limitations can become advantages. The refuge is less crowded, and fewer people mean less trash and other human evidence. Still, there are plenty of opportunities to explore and camp in this magic country of bogs, islands, and marshes.

Entrances to the swamp are at its northern, eastern, and western edges, and though all enable you to tour the swamp by boat or boardwalk, each provides a slightly different experience. The east entrance, near Folkston, offers the most quiet, undisturbed view of the swamp. For a quick look, your best bet is the north entrance, near Waycross, which has the Okefenokee Swamp Park, a private, nonprofit attraction. The west entrance, outside Fargo, accesses the 80-acre Stephen C. Foster State Park, one of few state parks within a national wildlife refuge.

ESSENTIAL INFORMATION

VISITOR INFORMATION For information about the refuge, contact the Refuge Manager, U.S. Fish and Wildlife Service, **Okefenokee National Wildlife Refuge** (Rte. 2, Box 3330, Folkston 31537, tel. 912/496–3331). For information about the parks, contact the Park Manager, **Stephen C. Foster State Park** (Fargo 31631, tel. 912/637–5274), or the Manager, **Okefenokee Swamp Park** (Waycross 31501, tel. 912/283–0583).

Canoeing offers the only access to camping in the heart of the swamp, and raised platforms for tents and some pit toilets are the only facilities, so full wilderness camping supplies are needed. Reservations and permits, available from the refuge manager up to two months in advance, are required for use of canoe trails, which begin at the east and west entrances and by a small boat-ramp access point at the northeastern corner of the swamp. No more than one party can use each trail at a time.

FEES Entrance fees for the Okefenokee National Wildlife Refuge are $4 per car at the east and west entrances. Admission at the north entrance's Okefenokee Swamp Park is $8 for adults and $6 for children 6–12. For canoeing and camping, the fee is $6 per person per night.

The Golden Eagle Pass, Golden Age Passport, Golden Access Passport, and Duck Stamp, valid at all national wildlife refuges, can be used at the east and west entrances but not at the private swamp park.

PUBLICATIONS The refuge provides several free, information-packed brochures, including "Okefenokee National Wildlife Refuge," which includes month-by-month listings of the wildlife visible in the swamp. A small hardcover book, *History of the Okefenokee,* by McQueen and Mizell, is the best record of the swamp's past. "The Okefenokee Swamp," a colorful, magazine-size pamphlet put out by Dot Gibson Publications, gives information on swamp wildlife and folklore. These and other publications are available at the visitor's centers at all three entrances.

The best canoe trail map is in a canoeing brochure put out by the refuge. This small guide, which includes all public boat trails, is sent out along with overnight canoe permits, and is also available at the eastern and western entrances for only 48¢.

GEOLOGY AND TERRAIN The 396,000 acres (about 620 square miles) of swampland in the Okefenokee, part of the Suwannee and St. Marys river watersheds, make it one of the largest swamps in the United States, but it wasn't always as it is today. During the Pleistocene epoch the sea level rose, and what is now the southeastern United States was covered by ocean, reaching up past the Georgia–Florida state line. As the waters receded, a low-level basin trapped water in this inland bog. Rainwater eventually washed out the sea water and created a large freshwater lake. Gradually, decaying plant material filled it in, producing nutrient-rich soil in which other plants took root.

Neither will the Okefenokee remain as it is. A swamp is an evolving ecosystem, constantly growing and changing, working to complete the transition from water to land. Some areas of the swamp are already mature forests still bounded by water. The swamp as a whole contains examples of almost every in-between stage of lake to forest—from open "prairies" of marsh grasses and shrubs to islands clustered with trees.

The swamp has 60 lakes large enough to be named. They are shallow (most only a few feet deep), small (100 to 250 yards wide), and teeming with fish. Because of the dark background of decayed plants on the bottom, the tea-colored water looks almost black, and the dark, still waters cast almost perfect reflections of the trees towering above the surface.

Dividing the many lakes are some 60,000 acres of "prairies," so called because of their resemblance to the prairies of the American Midwest. These expanses of tall grasses would more correctly be called marshes. Here, aquatic plants stand on a bed of peat that dislodged from the nutrient-rich bottom to float in 1 to 2 feet of water. Swamp "prairies" are home to such wading birds as herons, egrets, ibises, cranes, and bitterns.

Small clusters of trees and underbrush in the swamp's prairies were called "houses" or "hammocks" by early settlers. Over time, some of these small, isolated groupings grew and combined to form larger islands. There are approximately 70 islands in the Okefenokee, 60 of which are big enough to have names.

FLORA AND FAUNA Whether you're looking at the plants of a lake, a prairie, or an island, you'll notice one striking similarity. Species grow on top of species in an interwoven tangle of life. A giant cypress at the water's edge grows "knees," extra stumps jutting up from the root system. Biologists still don't know what to make of these outgrowths, but plants do, taking root on the raised surfaces, which provide a firm footing out of standing water. Such symbiotic relationships are common in the swamp community, and sometimes it's difficult to see where one plant ends and another begins.

When talking about the teeming swamp life, people generally give numbers instead of names. In addition to the 621 species of plants, there are 39 types of fish, 37 amphibians, 64 reptiles, 235 birds, and 50 mammals. If local naturalists are pressed for names, they sound like they're at an auction, running down a list so fast you can hardly follow it—fish: bowfin, pickerel, bluegill, mosquito fish, pirate perch, flier, warmouth, largemouth bass, eel, scalyhead darter, swamp darter, brook silverside . . . and they're just getting started. There are hundreds of rare and endangered species; the gopher tortoise, ivory-billed and red-cockaded woodpeckers, and bald eagle are just a few of the better-known ones. If you ask the right question, you can get a smaller list; for instance, there are only five species of poisonous snakes.

Since the swamp's sprawling plant growth provides cover for creatures great and small, a quick glance may reveal no animal life at all. You could be a few yards away from a 10-foot alligator and not notice its dark body swimming in the water. It doesn't take long to feel life all around you, however. Frogs, birds, and insects sing together in an unending background accompaniment; fish pop up here and there; and squirrels and other animals rustle in the foliage.

The real action of the swamp occurs at night, though, when predators take advantage of the extra cover darkness brings. Opossums can be seen looking for their dinner on an island, and alligators, bats, raccoons, and foxes also do their hunting.

WHEN TO GO To avoid the bugs and heat, visit during October to mid-May. June through September, the 90°F heat and high humidity keep even the sun-loving alligators from venturing out into the open. Summer is also the swamp's rainy season, and afternoon rain and thunderstorms are typical. Daytime winter temperatures average in the 50s and 60s but can be as low as 40°F or as high as 80°F. Winter nights are much colder, with temperatures dipping below freezing and often accompanied by high winds.

SEASONAL EVENTS Third week of April: During **National Wildlife Week,** several educational programs and lectures are given at the east entrance visitor's center. Speakers generally bring along rare animals and discuss topics of wildlife preservation. **Second week of October:** The **Okefenokee Festival,** at the east entrance's Chesser Island Homestead, celebrates early swamp settlers. Descendants of the Chesser family lead living-history demonstrations that include wood carving, meat smoking, soap making, and cotton weaving.

WHAT TO PACK If you're just coming for the day, bring along sunblock and a hat or visor to protect against the sun, and plenty of insect repellent. For wilderness camping, add drinking water, mosquito netting, rain gear, a first-aid kit, a flashlight and extra batteries, litter bags, rubber boots, rope for pulling your canoe, a pup tent or jungle hammock, and a sleeping bag. Pack binoculars if you want to get the most benefit from the observation towers.

GENERAL STORES Basic foods and supplies can be purchased from the concessionaires at any of the swamp's entrances. In Stephen C. Foster Park, the concessionaire is in the same building as the visitor's center; at the east entrance, it's adjacent to the visitor's center (the only other building). In addition, camping equipment, such as tents, sleeping bags, and portable toilets and stoves, can be rented from the concessionaire at the east entrance.

The town of **Folkston,** near the east entrance, has pretty limited shopping. **Okefenokee Sportsman** (411 N. 2nd St., tel. 912/496–7286) and **Big J. Grocery** (U.S. 301, tel. 912/496–7093) offer some basic food and camping supplies. Fargo has even less in the way of shopping, but **Waycross** has the **Hatcher Point Mall** (off U.S. 1, about 10 mi north of the swamp park, tel. 912/285–1431) with over 20 stores, and a **Wal-Mart** (2425 Memorial Dr., tel. 912/283–9000) next door. There are also several large grocery stores nearby, including a **Winn Dixie** (1803 Knight Ave., tel. 912/285–7750) and a **Piggly Wiggly** (1312 Plant Ave., tel. 912/285–7530), both in Waycross.

ARRIVING AND DEPARTING The first decision you have to make is which entrance to visit. All feature a visitor's center, boardwalks, viewing towers, and boat tours, but each of-

fers distinctive opportunities and styles of viewing the vast swampland. From the east (main) entrance, which has a number of educational and recreational facilities, the man-made Suwannee Canal reaches more than 10 miles into the swamp, and several canoe trails branch off it. The Okefenokee Swamp Park, at the north entrance, is set out like a small amusement park. Containing exhibit pavilions and fenced-in swamp life, it's entertaining, educational, and great for children. There are even reptile shows with live snakes; however, there is only one small canoe trail. The east entrance is open 7 AM–7:30 PM in spring and summer and 8–6 during fall and winter. The west entrance's Stephen C. Foster State Park, where the Suwannee River snakes into the center of the swamp, offers fewer interpretive activities but more options for boating and camping, including the only in-swamp campground.

By Plane. Jacksonville International Airport, southeast of the refuge over the Florida border, is the nearest major commercial airport. From here, the only way to get to Okefenokee is by car. Take I–95 north to Exit 2, and head west on Route 40 to Folkston. From here, the directions vary, depending on which entrance you'd like to visit (*see* By Car or RV, *below*).

Car rentals at the airport are available through **Avis** (tel. 904/741–2327 or 800/331–1212), **Budget** (tel.904/720–0246 or 800/527–0700), **Dollar** (tel.904/741–4614 or 800/800–4000), **Hertz** (tel.904/741–2151 or 800/654–3131), and **National** (tel. 904/741–4580 or 800/328–4567).

By Car and RV. If you're coming on I–95 either from Jacksonville and the south or Savannah and the north or from Cumberland Island National Seashore, you'll probably want to take Route 40 (Exit 2 off I–95) west to Folkston. From here it's about 8 miles south on Route 121/23 to the refuge's east entrance. The west entrance and the Stephen C. Foster State Park are, quite frankly, in the middle of nowhere and can only be reached by small highways running around the swamp's perimeter. Continue on Route 121/23 past the east entrance to Route 94 west, which cuts through a corner of Florida before reaching Fargo. Route 177, a 17-mile causeway, leads to the state park. To get to the north entrance from Folkston, drive northwest on U.S. 1 to Route 177 (not connected to the west entrance causeway), which runs south to the swamp park.

However, if you're coming from the north on I–95 and bound for the north entrance, take Exit 6. U.S. 84 stretches west to Waycross, a little more than 50 miles, from which U.S. 1 heads southeast to Route 177 and the swamp park. If you want to continue on to the west entrance from Waycross, drive southwest on U.S. 84 to Homerville and south on U.S. 441 to Fargo and the causeway.

By Train. Jacksonville, Florida, also has the nearest train depot. **Amtrak** (tel. 800/872–7245) service runs daily from points along the East Coast and three days a week from the West Coast. The station is 6 miles northwest of downtown Jacksonville, about an hour's drive from the swamp.

By Bus. Greyhound Lines (tel. 912/729–4820 in Kingsland, 912/283–7211 in Waycross, or 800/231–2222) serves Kingsland and Waycross. The Kingsland station is about 22 miles east of Folkston. There is no car rental nearby, and though there are cabs (Kings Bay Taxi, tel. 912/729–6569), the distance makes it an expensive ride. The Waycross depot is downtown, about 8 miles from the swamp park. Taxi service from **Waycross Cab** (tel. 912/283–8889) is available for $15 for the first passenger, $2 for each additional person, and so are car rentals through **Hertz** (tel. 912/285–8412), located along U.S. 1 about a mile from the bus terminal. It's possible to have a car waiting for you at the station upon your arrival.

EXPLORING

There is no single best way or place to see the Okefenokee. Only about 80% of the swamp is within the national wildlife refuge, so even before you reach the visitor's centers you're already in the swamp. Along large ditches beside the roads, you can sometimes spot alligators and wading birds.

Once you reach one of the visitor's centers, the best way to continue into the swamp is by boat. There are few opportunities for hiking, biking, or driving, as the waterlogged "trembling earth" is too unstable. The limited boardwalks, viewing towers, and trails at the visitor's centers can all be undertaken in a single day, whereas boat trails are numerous and can take days to explore. Most trails are only a few miles, but combinations of trails can pose real challenges to all levels of boaters. Day-use sections average about 5 miles, and a round-trip can be accomplished in about six to eight hours. However, some trails allow you to cross the swamp, which takes three to four days one way. While some areas are deep enough for small motorboats, the longer trails can be navigated only by canoe.

THE BEST IN ONE DAY Arrive at one of the visitor's centers early in the morning and do everything. Start off in one of the museums and watch any of the short documentaries to learn what to look for in the swamp. Take a guided boat tour to immerse yourself in the swamp environment. Then strike out onto the boardwalk and climb an observation tower, binoculars in hand. If you're at the north or east entrance, visit the restored homesteads.

ORIENTATION PROGRAMS Brief films are shown at the east and north entrances. The best is a National Geographic film entitled *A Swamp Ecosystem*. The 22-minute film is entertaining and informative and features great nature footage of some truly memorable swamp creatures in action. The swamp park generally shows the film at 10:30, 12:30, 2:30, and 4:30; the east entrance visitor's center gives screenings on request.

GUIDED TOURS Guided boat tours are offered at all three entrances: At the eastern entrance, contact the concession manager (Rte. 2, Box 3325, Folkston 31537, tel. 912/496–7156) for information about tours and equipment rentals. For tour and concession information at the other entrances, call or write the park manager (*see* Visitor Information *in* Essential Information, *above*).

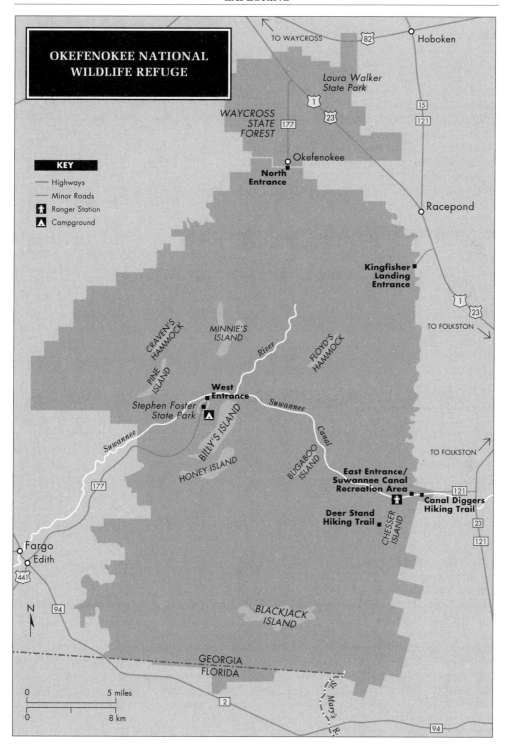

OKEFENOKEE NATIONAL WILDLIFE REFUGE

KEY
— Highways
— Minor Roads
🛉 Ranger Station
⛺ Campground

TO WAYCROSS

82 — Hoboken

Laura Walker State Park

1

15

121

WAYCROSS STATE FOREST

177 — 23

Okefenokee
North Entrance

Racepond

Kingfisher Landing Entrance

1
23

TO FOLKSTON

CRAVEN'S HAMMOCK

MINNIE'S ISLAND

River

FLOYD'S HAMMOCK

PINE ISLAND

West Entrance

Stephen Foster State Park

Suwannee

BILLY'S ISLAND

Suwannee

Canal

TO FOLKSTON

HONEY ISLAND

BUGABOO ISLAND

East Entrance/ Suwannee Canal Recreation Area

Canal Diggers Hiking Trail

121

Suwannee

177

Deer Stand Hiking Trail

CHESSER ISLAND

23

121

Fargo
Edith

441

N

94

BLACKJACK ISLAND

GEORGIA
FLORIDA

St. Mary's R.

0   5 miles
0   8 km

2

94

At the east entrance, one- and two-hour motorboat tours are led by one of the concessionaire's naturalists. There are no scheduled tours, but guides are generally available between 8 and 4:30 and will take a group out as soon as there are enough people. (Four are required for a one-hour trip, six for two hours.) Costs for one hour are $7.50 for adults, $3.75 for children 5–12, and $2.50 for preschoolers; for two hours, it's $15 for adults, $7.25 for children 5–12, and $4.75 for preschoolers. Night tours, by reservation only, are available for a minimum of six people and cost $15 per person. Night tours should be arranged with the concession manager at least a week in advance.

At the north entrance, half-hour boat tours are included in the admission price. Park guides, often college students, lead small motorized tour boats with about nine people around a circular boat trail that was artificially deepened to accommodate the boats. Since the swamp park feeds its wildlife, there are always plenty of alligators and other animals en route. Tours start on the hour and half hour all day long.

At the west entrance, tours of roughly an hour are given at 10, 1, and 3. A pontoon boat takes up to 17 passengers out on Billy's Lake and the Suwannee River. Led by state park rangers, the tours are very interactive, and guides are eager to answer questions or stop the boat to watch alligators or other wildlife. The charge is $7 for adults, $5 for children 6–12.

Wilderness Southeast (711 Dandtown Rd., Savannah 31410-1019, tel. 912/897–5108), a nonprofit educational organization in Savannah, offers extended tours. A five-day canoe trip takes visitors from the eastern side of the swamp to the western side, beginning at the Suwannee Canal Recreation Area. A less-demanding four-day cabin trip at the Stephen C. Foster State Park lets guests spend their days paddling through the western parts of the Okefenokee and their nights in the comfort of cabins. Offered October through November and February through May, both trips are led by trained naturalists and focus on the swamp's wildlife. The cost, $450 per person

for the five-day trip and $420 for the cabin trip, includes all entrance and permit fees.

SCENIC DRIVES AND VIEWS Other than the causeways and roads leading to the swamp entrances, there is little in the way of driving tours. At the east entrance, the 4.5-mile scenic **Swamp Island Drive** leads to the boardwalk and trailheads on Chesser Island, including a path to the Chesser Island Homestead (*see* Historic Buildings and Sites, *below*). The scenery here is not much different from that on the causeway leading up to the refuge, but the 15-mile-per-hour speed limit allows for a closer look at forests and ditches.

HISTORIC BUILDINGS AND SITES There is no additional charge for visiting any of the following sites. Be aware, however, that the Swamp Island Drive, the road you need to use to reach most of these attractions, closes earlier than the main gate. *Main gate, east entrance, open Sept.–Feb., daily 8–6; Mar.–Aug., daily 7 AM–7:30 PM.* Swamp Island Dr., open Sept.–Feb., daily 7–5:30; Mar.–Aug., daily 8–4:30.

At the east entrance, **Chesser Island Homestead,** first established in 1858, offers a glimpse of how early settlers lived off the riches of the land. The existing five-bedroom pine and cypress main house was built by the Chesser family in the late 1920s. Although you're not allowed inside it, you can peek in its windows to see some of the original furnishings. Walking around the dirt yard, you'll see the large family's grindstone, hog pen, chicken coop, sugarcane mill, and smokehouse. The homestead is accessible by a short path off the Swamp Island Drive. The 4.5-mile scenic drive is the only way to get to the homestead entrance and to the boardwalk/observation tower.

Indian mounds can be found in various spots in the Okefenokee, but the only easily accessible one is a few steps from the Chesser Island Homestead. This raised area marks a burial ground once used by the Timucuan people, who were known for their extreme height (up to 7 feet tall).

The **Pioneer Homestead,** at the north entrance, is a reconstructed pioneer cabin, complete with many of the tools used by early settlers to make their living from the swamp.

Billy's Island, one of the largest islands in the Okefenokee, was once headquarters for a large timber operation on the west side of the swamp. The Hebard Cypress Company developed the island for its employees, building an office, commissary, barber shop, and even a movie theater. Today the island is abandoned, and fresh timber grows around the ruins of the old company town. It's a short boat ride from the Stephen C. Foster State Park and is open to the public for day use only.

NATURE TRAILS AND SHORT WALKS Boardwalks, located at all three entrances, provide one of the best and easiest ways to access the wet swamp. Each boardwalk is less than a mile long. The east entrance also offers a few nature trails through drier areas, including the .5-mile **Deerstand** and **Homestead trails.** These easy walks are flat and shaded, winding through forests of pine and palmetto. Another .5-mile walk, the **Canal Digger's Trail,** is slightly more difficult since it runs along uneven terrain. It circles around the eastern end of the Suwannee Canal and is accessible from Swamp Island Drive.

OTHER ACTIVITIES **Biking.** Bicycling is allowed on the roads of the east and west entrances. Bikes can be rented through concessionaires (about $1.50 per hour) at both entrances. The beach cruiser–style bicycles are in relatively good shape and allow a calm, leisurely ride through the drier areas of the swamp. Bike rentals are offered on a first-come, first-served basis, but there are usually enough to go around. You may also bring your own bike.

Bird-Watching. Observation towers at the east and west entrances provide the best perch for bird-watchers. Two photo blinds along the east entrance's boardwalk also have great views over the marshes and prairies, and a checklist of hundreds of swamp birds is available at the visitor's center. The best time for birders is the winter and spring, when migratory birds, both those en route

and arriving to nest, are in the area. The morning is the best time to view pileated and redheaded woodpeckers, as well as egrets, blue herons, and sandhill cranes, from the swamp observation towers.

Boating. You may bring your own boat, launching it from public boat ramps at the east and west entrances, or rent a small motorboat or canoe for fishing and exploring (about $10 a day for a canoe, $20–$30 a day for a motorboat). Motors above 10 horsepower are prohibited, however, and there are launching fees of $2.50 at the east entrance and $1 at the west. Contact the concessionaire at the eastern entrance (*see* Guided Tours, *above*), or the visitor's centers (at the manager's address) at other entrances (*see* Visitor Information *in* Essential Information, *above*) for more information about boat use and rentals.

Fishing. The swamp's fishing holes, prized by many locals, offer up largemouth bass, warmouth, chain pickerels, bowfins, and sunfish, to name a few. The canal offers the best fishing. State fishing regulations apply, so a valid Georgia fishing license is required. Licenses can be purchased (about $3 for a one-day permit) from the concessionaires or at almost any nearby convenience stores.

CHILDREN'S PROGRAMS Unfortunately, there's little in the way of children's activities, though the visitor's center does show an upbeat 10-minute film called ***Our Untamed Wilderness.*** Available upon request, it's a great way to get kids interested in the swamp.

DINING

There are no restaurants in the refuge. For a cooked, sit-down meal, your best bet is one of the inexpensive eateries in Folkston or Waycross.

INSIDE THE REFUGE The small concessionary shops at each entrance, which sell basic supplies and run the tours and equipment rentals, offer the only food within the swamp. At the east entrance, five different box lunches, including a sandwich, chips, a dessert, and a drink, are available for $6.50 each.

At the west and north entrances, sandwiches and snacks can also be purchased. There are no sit-down eateries inside the refuge.

NEAR THE EAST ENTRANCE **Okefenokee Restaurant.** Located on U.S. 1, Folkston's main drag, this simple, down-home restaurant is the closest eating spot to the east entrance, about 9 miles away. It serves up southern-style meals that taste home cooked, and locals and tourists alike flock here, especially for the lunch buffet. Although it's known for steaks and seafood, everything is good. Booths and hanging plants constitute the basic and comfortable decor. *103 S. 2nd St., Folkston, tel. 912/496–3263. No reservations. Dress: casual. MC, V. Closed last Sun. of month. Inexpensive.*

Tahiti Restaurant. Located at the Days Stop/Tahiti Motel, this is one of the best, and only, places in town. The small restaurant has almost no atmosphere; but, like the Okefenokee, it offers real southern cooking and a popular lunch buffet. Specialties include country-fried steak and the big mamma platter, which has one of the biggest hamburgers you've ever seen. *U.S. 301 S, Folkston, tel. 912/496–2519. Reservations accepted. Dress: casual. No credit cards. Inexpensive.*

NEAR THE NORTH ENTRANCE **Caitlyn's Courtyard.** The only bed-and-breakfast in Waycross also offers the most elegant dining in the area. The restored Victorian dining rooms sport bright window and table dressings. Located near the business district downtown, about 7 miles from the swamp park, the restaurant is generally frequented by local executives and couples. Stuffed flounder is one of the standouts on the steak-and-seafood menu. *602 Gilmore St., Waycross, tel. 912/284–1755. Reservations accepted. Dress: casual. AE, MC, V. Closed for lunch weekends, Sun.–Wed. dinner. Inexpensive–Moderate.*

Christopher's. Right across the railroad tracks from downtown, this restaurant and lounge offers fine casual dining. Subdued lighting and a dark-wood interior make for calm and comfort. Steaks and pasta are good choices. *140 Lee Ave., Waycross, tel. 912/283–5260.*

Reservations accepted. Dress: casual. AE, MC, V. Closed Sat. lunch, Sun. Inexpensive–Moderate.

Maurice's Steak House. This new downtown restaurant has a bright, open, and friendly atmosphere and a style that's out of the '50s and '60s with some country thrown in. It dishes up grilled food and hot wings and hosts local bands and DJs on weekends. *410 Plant Ave., Waycross, tel. 912/285–8032. Reservations accepted. Dress: casual. AE, MC, V. Closed lunch and Sun., Mon. Inexpensive–Moderate.*

Whitfield's. Likening itself to a neighborhood English pub, this downtown restaurant has three floors, each with a different ambience. From the sports bar on the lower level, casual sunroom and "Cheers"-style bar on street level to more formal dining on the top level, the eatery draws a varied and lively clientele. Grilled and broiled fish, rib-eye steak teriyaki, and fresh pasta are specialties. The "formal" dining area (slacks and a sport shirt, or skirt and blouse are fine) is open only for dinner. *514 Mary St., Waycross, tel. 912/285–9027. Reservations accepted. Dress: casual. AE, MC, V. Closed Sat. lunch, Sun. Inexpensive–Moderate.*

PICNIC SPOTS Since the Okefenokee is a national wildlife refuge, you won't find picnic tables sprinkled in remote locations. Each entrance has a group of tables clustered near the visitor's center, usually under a shelter— the only picnic areas in the swamp. If you're taking a boat out, you can enjoy a packed lunch on the calm, secluded swamp waters.

LODGING

There are no accommodations within the refuge itself. Instead, visitors can choose from a number of relatively inexpensive options, mostly motels, nearby. Since there is no real peak season, prices and room availability remain about the same year-round.

NEAR THE EAST ENTRANCE **Days Stop/Tahiti Motel.** This basic motel offers the cleanest accommodations in the Folkston area. Located off U.S. 1, it's about 11 miles from the refuge entrance. The no-frills rooms are clean, and the amenities are adequate. *U.S. 301 S, Folkston 31537, tel. 912/496–2514, fax ext. 141. 37 rooms. Facilities: restaurant, pool. AE, D, DC, MC, V. Inexpensive.*

NEAR THE NORTH ENTRANCE **Caitlyn's Courtyard.** This B&B is a restored Victorian home downtown. Though furnished with antiques, guest rooms have such modern conveniences as air-conditioning and TVs. A sitting room with a fireplace is a pleasant place to sit and read, while breakfast is served in the public dining rooms downstairs. *602 Gilmore St., Waycross 31501, tel. 912/284–1755. 3 rooms. Facilities: restaurant. AE, MC, V. Moderate.*

Jameson Inn. This Georgia chain motel, off Memorial Drive, offers slightly better accommodations than the national chains, and usually with friendlier service. A complimentary Continental breakfast is served daily. *950 City Blvd., Waycross 31501, tel. 912/283–3800. 40 rooms. AE, D, DC, MC, V. Inexpensive–Moderate.*

A few national chains in Waycross offer basic rooms at inexpensive prices. The best include **Days Inn** (U.S. 1 S, at 2016 Memorial Dr., Waycross 31501, tel. 912/285–4700 or 800/325–2525), which has a swimming pool; **Holiday Inn** (1725 Memorial Dr., Waycross 31501, tel. 912/283–4490 or 800/322–6866), with a pool, restaurant, lounge, and game room; and **Red Carpet Inn** (1740 Memorial Dr., Waycross 31501, tel. 912/283–6134 or 800/251–1962), which features the lowest rates and no frills, though it does have a small pool.

CAMPING

INSIDE THE REFUGE Aside from the raised wooden tent platforms (*see* Visitor Information *in* Essential Information, *above*), the only campsites within the swamp itself are in the **Stephen C. Foster State Park.** The park offers 68 tent and trailer sites, nine cottages, and two picnic shelters; 66 of the sites have water and electric hookups for RVs. Campsite reservations can be made up to 90 days in advance, and cottages, which are usually full year-round, can be reserved up to 11 months in advance. *Fargo, GA 31631, tel. 912/637–5274.*

NEAR THE EAST ENTRANCE The only camping in the Folkston area is found at **Traders Hill Park Campground and Recreation Area** (7 mi south of Folkston on Rte. 23/121; for information, call the Board of Commissioners, tel. 912/496–2549). About 8 miles from the visitor's center, this 32-acre park along the St. Marys River has 24 tent and trailer sites with water and electric hookups, virtually unlimited walk-in tent sites, a boat ramp, a fishing pier, picnic tables and shelter, and rest rooms. The park is run by the county, and costs per night are $9.50 for sites with hookups and $5 for other sites. There are no reservations, but the park is rarely crowded.

NEAR THE NORTH ENTRANCE The **Laura S. Walker State Park** (5653 Laura Walker Rd., Waycross 31501, tel. 912/287–4900) is 306 acres on the outskirts of the Okefenokee Swamp. Just 8 miles from the swamp park, the state park offers 44 tent and trailer sites, a 120-acre lake, swimming pool, fishing dock, boat ramp, canoe rentals, and picnic shelters. Water and electric hookups are available at all sites, and a disposal station is provided. Reservations are not available, except during major holidays, but the park is rarely filled to capacity.

Shenandoah National Park
Virginia
By Paul Calhoun

henandoah National Park drapes the backbone of Virginia's northern Blue Ridge Mountains like one of the region's famous handcrafted quilts—a mosaic of hardwood and evergreen forest accented by rocky crags, open meadows, crystal streams, and roaring waterfalls.

The birth of the Blue Ridge traces back a billion or more years, when shiftings and upheavals in the earth thrust skyward a granitic ridgeline. Over the eons, trees have advanced up the slopes and claimed most of the peaks; only a few rocky summits still stand barren.

Shenandoah National Park claims a much shorter history. It is, in essence, a massive recycling and reclamation project. What is now a scenic and nearly wild landscape was in the 1920s a badly eroded patchwork of overcut timberland and subsistence farms. Unlike most areas that became national parks, the lands were privately owned, and when Congress authorized creation of the park in 1926, it did so with the stipulation that no federal funds could be used to buy these properties. The parcels were acquired—by sale, donation, and condemnation—with private contributions and an appropriation by the state of Virginia. The park's wandering border is a testimony to limited funding and the ability of some persistent landowners to keep their farms. There were some 500 families on the land when Congress set it aside for the park. The mountaineers were proud, self-sufficient, and defiant; many of them barely wrested a living from the thin soil, but they bristled at the idea of being evicted. Today battle lines still form when anyone mentions expanding the park's 196,000 acres. But mention it they do: Additional land swaps and purchases are planned as part of the ongoing strategy to enlarge the park and protect more of the area.

Within the park's territory lie an array of historical and recreational enticements. Many are readily accessible from the Skyline Drive, the 105-mile paved roadway that runs the length of the park along the spine of the Blue Ridge. Others require some hiking. Each turn on road and trail reveals stunning scenery, always with the chance of spotting white-tailed deer, black bears, and other wildlife. More than 200 species of birds have been identified in the park. Wildflowers are plentiful.

Unfortunately, Shenandoah is not the pristine, ecologically secure preserve that was envisioned when it was established in the 1920s. It is suffering two kinds of degradation—one the by-product of fossil fuels, the other of human folly. The former is the airborne sulfates blown in from the coal-fired power plants of the Ohio Valley, and from Washington, D.C., and other heavily trafficked, highly industrial urban areas. They contribute to limited visibility, dangerous ozone levels, and the acid rain that is slowly killing many of the park's streams. The latter is the gypsy moth, a native of France that escaped from a New England silkworm experiment in the late 1800s. It spread across much of the Northeast and mid-Atlantic and reached the park in 1983, where it is devouring more and more foliage each year.

Note: Mileposts (MP)—small gray concrete markers with black mileage indicators—are numbered from north to south on Skyline Drive. For this reason, most park literature (and this chapter) refers to locations in terms of miles from the northern end of the park. In the case of Loft Mountain (79.5), for example, the designation means this popular area is 79.5 miles from the northern end of Skyline Drive, but only 25.5 miles from the southern end.

ESSENTIAL INFORMATION

VISITOR INFORMATION For general information on the park, including developed campsites and backcountry camping, contact the Superintendent, **Shenandoah National Park** (Rte. 3, Box 348, Luray 22835–9051, tel.

703/999–2266). Travel information—reports about weather and road conditions, interesting events, wildlife sightings, and more—is also available at several waysides, general stores, campgrounds, and two major visitor's centers along Skyline Drive.

Wilderness hikers must possess valid backcountry camping permits, which are free and available in advance from park headquarters or at entrance stations, visitor's centers, and park headquarters during normal business hours.

The area surrounding the park is rich in attractions, too. For specific information contact: **Charlottesville/Albemarle Convention & Visitors Bureau** (Box 161, Charlottesville 22902, tel. 804/977–1783)—Thomas Jefferson country, including Monticello and the University of Virginia; **Foothills Travel Association** (37 Beckham St., Warrenton 22186, tel. 703/347–4414)—Virginia's horse country; **Front Royal–Warren County Chamber of Commerce** (501 S. Royal Ave., Box 568, Front Royal 22630, tel. 703/635–3185)—Shenandoah and Skyline caverns, Shenandoah River; **Harrisonburg–Rockingham Convention & Visitors Bureau** (191 S. Main St., Harrisonburg 22801, tel. 703/434–2319)—Central Shenandoah Valley, including Massanutten, Endless, and Grand caverns, Natural Chimneys, Massanutten Resort; **Lexington Visitors Bureau** (102 E. Washington St., Lexington 24450, tel. 703/463-3777)—Civil War history (Robert E. Lee and Stonewall Jackson), the Virginia Horse Center, Natural Bridge; **Page County Chamber of Commerce** (46 E. Main St., Luray 22835, tel. 703/743–3915)—Luray Caverns; **Shenandoah Valley Travel Association** (Box 1040, New Market 22344, tel. 703/740–3132)—the entire region and Civil War history and battlefield reenactments; and **Staunton–Augusta Travel Information Center** (1301 Richmond Ave., Staunton 24401, tel. 703/885–8504)—birthplace of Woodrow Wilson and Cyrus McCormick and Museum of American Frontier Culture.

FEES Entrance fees are $5 per vehicle and $3 per hiker, bicyclist, or bus passenger aged

16–62. An annual Shenandoah Passport is $15. Entry is free if you have an Annual Golden Eagle Passport, Golden Age, or Golden Access permit (*see* Before You Go *in* Chapter 1, Essential Information).

PUBLICATIONS A full-color map and guide labeled simply *Shenandoah* is available for only a quarter at visitor's centers. The text addresses everything from geology to history; the map includes scenic areas, overlooks, and picnic grounds. *Shenandoah National Park Magazine,* a slick, pocket-size, full-color booklet available at park lodges, gives an informative overview. *Shenandoah Overlook,* the park newspaper, can be found at visitor's centers and ranger's stations; it provides seasonal information about the park, a bit of history, and helpful travel hints. "Exploring the Backcountry," a free brochure available at entrance stations and visitor's centers, addresses rules, precautions, and equipment for venturing into the park's remote regions.

For a comprehensive account of the park's history, trails, and more, read *Guide to Shenandoah National Park,* by Henry Heatwole ($6.50). *Herbert Hoover's Hideaway,* by Darwin Lambert ($4.95), is the story of the tiny cluster of buildings built at the headwaters of the trout-rich Rapidan River as a retreat for the president; Camp Hoover stands today much as it did then. Both books are available from the Shenandoah Natural History Association (Rte. 4, Box 348, Luray 22835, tel. 703/999–3581; include $3 for postage and handling) and are also on sale in park visitor's centers and gift shops. So is *Skyland,* by George Freeman Pollock (Chesapeake Book Company, $5.95), the author's account of arriving in the mountains a half-century before the park was founded and of establishing the mountain resort now known as Skyland. Colorful and dryly humorous, the book provides insights into life in the mountains a century ago.

GEOLOGY AND TERRAIN Underlying the mountains of the park are two types of ancient granite: the rare Old Rag, such as that exposed on the face of Old Rag Mountain

itself; and the fairly common granodiorite, visible throughout the park. The granitic core beneath goes back a billion years or more. More recent geologic periods include a time of volcanic eruptions resulting in a dozen or more layers of lava flows; a period during which the park was covered with shallow water; and finally the modern era of the past 225 million years, which saw the uplifting and erosion that created the mountains and valleys as they are today.

Today most of the ancient rocks are draped in vegetation, from low-lying ground cover and wildflowers to the shrublike mountain laurel and rhododendron to the mature oak-hickory and evergreen forest. The rocks here, unlike those in the barren vistas of the West, peer out only on occasion.

The park is comprised mainly of highlands and mountain peaks; only occasionally do its lands work their way down toward the more fertile and gentle terrain below. At the heart of the park are the Blue Ridge Mountains, an eastern flank of the Appalachian Mountains, which run from Pennsylvania to Georgia. The park area runs at a southeast-to-northwest diagonal—from Afton Mountain (just east of Waynesboro) to the northwest terminus at a point just south of Front Royal.

To the east of the park is Virginia's rolling Piedmont. To the west is the Shenandoah Valley, named (like the park) for the Shenandoah River that winds through it. The valley was the setting for several Civil War battles, a history preserved in many of its towns and museums. On the western horizon, far across the Shenandoah Valley, are several prominent Appalachian peaks. Closer, in the valley itself, is the 40-mile-long mountain called Massanutten.

Most of the park's terrain is mountainous, but the extensive flatlands of Big Meadows (51.0) are a rare and interesting exception. The meadow was probably first cleared by fire, set either by lightning or by Native Americans. Subsequent Indian fires, along with grazing by deer, elk, and bison, kept the meadows maintained until the mountaineers arrived with their cattle. The meadows actually suffered from the decision to return the park to its wild state: Without fire or grazing animals, they succumbed to the encroachments of the surrounding shrubs and forest. Once stretching some 3 miles, they have now shrunk to about 150 acres. Today they're maintained by mowing and controlled burning.

FLORA AND FAUNA More than 95% of Shenandoah is now covered by more than 100 species of trees, testimony to nature's ability to heal and reclaim the land if given the opportunity. The reclamation has been so successful that in 1976—a mere 40 years after the park's dedication—Congress designated 40% of it as wilderness.

The sheltering forest is typical of the deciduous oak-hickory blend that blankets most of the region. A few pockets of unusual or specialized trees are interspersed: Evergreens (such as the hemlock, in wet, cool areas, and pines, mostly on dry slopes) are, with rare exceptions, second growth, reclaiming the ground left by their fallen but once-towering ancestors. Black locust is one of the first invaders of fields, abandoned farms, and other open areas such as Big Meadows. Cove hardwoods, including birches, maples, and the tulip poplar, often establish territory at the head of lowland hollows and along low-elevation stream banks.

The abundant wildflowers—200 or more species of interest—are one of the park's most popular attractions. The leafy forest canopy restricts the sunlight that might otherwise contribute to a lavish display, yet the mixture of heavy shade, partial sunlight, and forest fringe fosters a great floral diversity. With the exception of the open fields of Big Meadows, where there can be a veritable blanket of flowers, the sun-loving varieties are easiest to find along trails and roadsides. Furtive species, such as the pink lady's slipper, lurk in the deeper, darker woods. Note that the park rule is very strict: *No collecting!*

Only a few decades ago postcards depicted the eastern black bear *(Ursus americanus)* as a playful buffoon, begging for treats or helping itself to a picnic basket while people smiled and watched. Those days have

passed, and today's emphasis is on discouraging interaction. Why? Because big, strong, *wild* animals and naive tourists are a bad combination. Although the park has one of the highest concentrations of black bears in the region, the animal's natural inclination is to avoid people, lying low during the day and prowling mostly at night. Although it doesn't have the size or the reputation of the western grizzly, it's still a powerful and unpredictable creature. You probably have little to fear from a black bear, but it can harm cars, tents, and people in its quest for food—and it can do a truly serious amount of damage if it sets its mind and muscle to the task. Obey all rules for food storage when camping, and consider yourself fortunate if you do catch a glimpse of a black bear in the wild.

Virginia white-tailed deer *(Odocoileus virginianus)* are likely to be seen at almost any time or place in the park—especially feeding around campgrounds and roadsides where the sun spurs the growth of grasses and shrubs. Although many are used to being around people, they are not tame and should not be fed or approached too closely. It's against park rules and potentially dangerous: Even the most soft-eyed doe can rear and strike unexpectedly with her front hooves. The most common (and dangerous) place to spot a deer is from your car, on the Skyline Drive. Obey the speed limit and *immediately* slow down if you see a deer, especially at night when your headlights might blind or confuse it.

Among wildlife you're likely to see during the daytime are chipmunks and groundhogs; at night, the gray fox, striped skunk, and raccoon. Less common are the red fox, spotted skunk, bobcat, and beaver.

There are more than 200 species of birds in the park (*see* Other Activities *in* Exploring, *below*). A five-year project that began in 1980 on Hawksbill Mountain has been aimed at reintroducing the peregrine falcon to the wilds of the region. Famous as the world's fastest bird (it can dive for prey at over 200 miles per hour), it was once common throughout the East—before DDT and other pesticides contributed to a decline in its reproduction.

There is also a wide variety of snakes, lizards, frogs, salamanders, and other reptiles and amphibians in the park. Happily, only two of the park's snakes, the timber rattler and copperhead, are poisonous, and they are rare.

WHEN TO GO Autumn, when thousands upon thousands of visitors converge on Skyline Drive to view the stunning fall foliage (usually at its peak October 10–25), is the most popular season at Shenandoah National Park.

Only winter, which brings limited lodging options and the possibility of road closings, could be declared off-season at the park. Startling cold and unexpectedly heavy snowfalls can strike anytime from October to April. But the clear views that the cold, crystal winter skies can offer hold a special allure for many.

The park's spring arrives in April or May, depending on the severity and stubbornness of winter in the highlands. Early wildflowers bloom during those two months. The green of new foliage charges up the flanks of the mountains at a rate of 100 feet per day, finally reaching the peaks in late May, just in time for the resplendent display of the pink azalea. The tiny white teacup-shaped blossoms of the mountain laurel follow in June. Rivaling the spring bloom are the vivid, vocal, fast-flying colors of warblers and other mating songbirds.

Summer is a time of nesting birds, spotted fawns, and an explosion of wildflowers. Summer temperatures range from the 40s to the 90s, and are usually 10 to 15 degrees cooler than in the valleys below.

SEASONAL EVENTS Mid-May: During **Wildflower Weekend,** the park sponsors walks, exhibits, slide programs, and other activities that draw attention to the spring wildflowers. **Last weekend in July:** The **Mountain Heritage Festival Days** feature activities and demonstrations relating to mountain life in years gone by, including woodcarving, basket weaving, square dancing, and clogging.

Weekend closest to August 10 (Herbert Hoover's birthday): **Hoover Days** are celebrated with tours and bus shuttles from Byrd Visitor Center to the former president's summer camp at the headwaters of the Rapidan River.

WHAT TO PACK Regardless of the season, you'll probably want sunscreen, sunglasses, a hat or cap, rain gear, and comfortable walking shoes. Long-sleeved shirts and light jackets are often welcome even in July and August. Other handy accessories include field guides and field glasses. The park is relatively pest-free, but pack an insect repellent to ward off ticks and the few chiggers, mosquitoes, or small gnats you might encounter. It's a good idea to bring your own drinks, snacks, et cetera; you may want a different variety (or price) than what's available at park concessions. You might also bring a couple of aerosol tire-inflator cans, should you have a flat you don't want to change on the spot.

GENERAL STORES The park is far removed from malls and grocery stores, though convenience stores are common in the small towns you pass through on your way to the park. The few stores along Skyline Drive are far removed from each other. Note that schedules are subject to change, especially given the concerns over further budget cuts. **Elkwallow Wayside** (24.1) is a camp store with groceries, camping supplies, ice, and gasoline (tel. 703/999–2253; open mid-Apr.–Oct., daily 9–5:30). **Panorama** (31.5, at the Thornton Gap entrance at the U.S. 211 interchange, 4 miles east of Luray) is a combination information center, gift and crafts shop, bookstore, and restaurant; park headquarters is nearby (tel. 703/999–2265; open mid-Mar.–mid-Nov., daily 9–5:30). **Skyland** (41.7) isn't a general store per se, but this lodge with dining room has a mountain crafts shop, newsstand and information center, drink machines, and pay phones (tel. 703/999–2211; most services open late Mar.–late Nov., daily 9–8). **Big Meadows** (51.0) wayside camp store has food, drinks and ice, a gift shop and newsstand, gasoline, and a short-order snack shop (tel. 703/999–2221; open

May–Oct., daily 9–5:30). **Lewis Mountain** (57.6) has a campground store with wood, ice, food and drinks, and other supplies, as well as showers, and washers and dryers (tel. 703/999–2255; open May–Oct., daily 9–5:30). **Loft Mountain** (79.5) offers the same things as Lewis Mountain, plus gasoline (tel. 804/823–4515; open late May–Oct., daily 9–5:30).

ATMS There are no ATMs within the park. The closest are at the East Luray branch of Jefferson National Bank (Business Rte. 211 at East Luray Shopping Center, tel. 703/743–6566), approximately 6.5 miles east of Skyline Drive via U.S. 211; and, in Front Royal, the South Street branch of Jefferson National Bank (432 South St., tel. 703/635–1952). To get to the latter, take Route 340 north from the park entrance into Front Royal and turn right at the second traffic light on South Street/Route 55; the bank is across from the K-Mart. There are also ATMs at Luray, on U.S. 11 near the Thornton Gap entrance; and Waynesboro, on U.S. 250 near the south entrance.

ARRIVING AND DEPARTING There is no rail or air service into the park itself, but several of the park's gateway communities are accessible by air, rail, or bus.

By Plane. Charlottesville-Albemarle Airport (201 Bowen Loop, Charlottesville, tel. 804/973–8341 for Airport Authority Office), 8 miles north of Charlottesville on U.S. 29, is the closest major airport. Airlines serving it include **American Eagle** (tel. 800/433–7300), **Comair/Delta** (tel. 800/354–9822), **United Express** (tel. 800/241–6522), and **USAir Express** (tel. 800/428– 4322). You can rent a car at the airport from **Avis** (tel. 804/973–6000), **Budget** (tel. 804/973–5751), or **Hertz** (tel. 804/973–8349). There is no public transportation to the park; **Yellow Cab** (tel. 804/295–4131) to Big Meadows Lodge runs about $100 one way.

To get to the park from the airport, take U.S. 29 south and then I–64 west to the park's southern entrance at Rockfish Gap; or take U.S. 29 north and then U.S. 33 west to the park's central entrance at Swift Run Gap. Driving time is approximately 30 minutes

either way. The southern access is preferable for a one-way, end-to-end viewing of the park; the central access is the quickest way to the main lodges at Big Meadows and Skyland.

Shenandoah Valley Airport (tel. 703/234–8304), west of Grottoes on Route 256 between Staunton and Harrisonburg, is midway between the Rockfish and Swift Run entrances on the park's west side; you can rent a car there from **Avis** (tel. 703/234–9961) and **Hertz** (tel. 703/234–9411). The much larger **Dulles International Airport** (tel. 703/661–2700), near Herndon, Virginia, and just east of Washington, D.C., is within 1½ hours of the park's Swift Run and Front Royal entrances. Rental agencies at Dulles include **Alamo** (tel. 703/661–8149), **Avis** (tel. 703/661–3500), **Budget** (tel. 703/437–9373), **Dollar** (tel. 703/661–8823), **Hertz** (tel. 703/661–5900), and **National** (tel. 703/471–5278).

By Car and RV. Shenandoah National Park is readily accessible by motor vehicle, although larger RVs may be challenged by the fairly steep climb to the Skyline Drive. From Charlottesville, take I–64 west to the park's southern entrance at Rockfish Gap; or take U.S. 29 north, then U.S. 33 west to the park's central entrance at Swift Run Gap, a 30-minute drive. From Washington, take I–66 west, then U.S. 340 south through Front Royal to the Skyline Drive access at Dickey Ridge, a 1½-hour drive.

Gasoline is available in the park, but not always convenient. Roadside assistance is even harder to arrange, so make sure your car is serviced and top off the tank before you enter the park. The three gas stations along Skyline Drive, each open daily 9–5:30, are **Elkwallow Wayside** (24.1; open early Apr.–Oct.); **Big Meadows Wayside** (51.0; open late Mar.–late Nov.); and **Loft Mountain Wayside** (79.5; open early Apr.–Oct.).

By Train. The nearest major station is the one in Charlottesville (600 E. Water St.) served by **Amtrak** (tel. 800/872–7245). There is no public transportation from the station to the park. A **Yellow Cab** (tel. 804/295–4131) to Big Meadows would cost around $125. A cab to the rental car agencies at the airport (*see* By Plane, *above*) is about $20.

By Bus. Greyhound Lines (tel. 800/231–2222) serves Charlottesville, Harrisonburg, Staunton, and Culpeper—all of which are convenient to the park. Once you reach any of these towns, though, you'll need to rent a car.

EXPLORING

One of Shenandoah's best qualities is that it appeals equally to the most and least adventurous of visitors. The best way to experience the park is to combine car touring with short walks from overlooks and trailheads. Serious hikers can explore the expansive backcountry. Bicycling is allowed, but it's difficult for inexperienced riders because of all the climbs and descents and the narrow-to-nonexistent road shoulders.

THE BEST IN ONE DAY Although the park covers 300 square miles and stretches along the 105-mile Skyline Drive, it is relatively narrow, ranging from 1 to 13 miles in width. By devoting a day (or less) to traveling the Drive and stopping at visitor's centers and some of the 75 overlooks, motor tourists can learn a lot about the park—and enjoy mountaintop views of most of it—without venturing more than 50 yards from their vehicles. By combining a motor tour with a couple of short-to-intermediate walks, you can see a great expanse of nature from a distance, and a fair amount of it up close.

Overlooks along the Drive offer short walks, informative exhibits, expansive views, fabulous sunsets or sunrises—and some even have drinking fountains with treated water tapped from natural springs. **Dickey Ridge** (4.6; open early May–late Oct., daily) and **Byrd** (51.0; open Apr.–late Nov., daily; reduced schedule Dec.–Mar.) visitor's centers are the park's two major information facilities, with historical and cultural exhibits, pamphlets and publications, rest rooms, phones, drinking water, picnic areas, hiking trails, and friendly and helpful staffs that can answer just about any question. While at

Byrd, take time to view the **Big Meadows** area and the exhibit on the loss of the native chestnut trees that once dominated the region's forests; then consider a short detour to see Big Meadows Lodge, a structure built from this ill-fated tree.

Skyland (41.7 and 42.5) was originally established by George Freeman Pollock as Stony Man Camp, after the mountain that towered over it. Pollock had done much to preserve the beauty of the area, and Skyland had become a popular mountain retreat long before his insistent campaigning inspired the creation of the national park.

ORIENTATION PROGRAMS The **Dickey Ridge Visitor Center** (4.6) shows, on request, a 10-minute film that's mainly for first-time visitors. Newcomers nervous about rules, animals, trails, and so on may find it informative and reassuring. The **Byrd Visitor Center** at Big Meadows (51.0) shows hourly (or on request) a 20-minute film about the park's creation, history, and purpose.

GUIDED TOURS There are no commercial tours. Park service rangers conduct free interpretive walks; these walks vary in time (1–4 hours), attendance (5–100 people), subject, and location, but typically they deal with natural or cultural history, or such current management concerns as air quality or the gypsy moth. Details about current and upcoming walks are published in the park newspaper, the *Shenandoah Overlook* (free at park entrance stations and visitor's centers).

SCENIC DRIVES AND VIEWS Skyline Drive, from its northern terminus (just south of Front Royal at U.S. 340) to its southern terminus (at Rockfish Gap, at the I–64/U.S. 250 interchange just east of Waynesboro), was created as a scenic drive. It offers outstanding views, from open panoramas of distant peaks and valleys to roadside foliage and wildflowers, throughout its 105-mile length. The following is a list of the most popular vantage points along the roadway.

Shenandoah Valley Overlook (2.8) provides a soaring view across Shenandoah Valley to

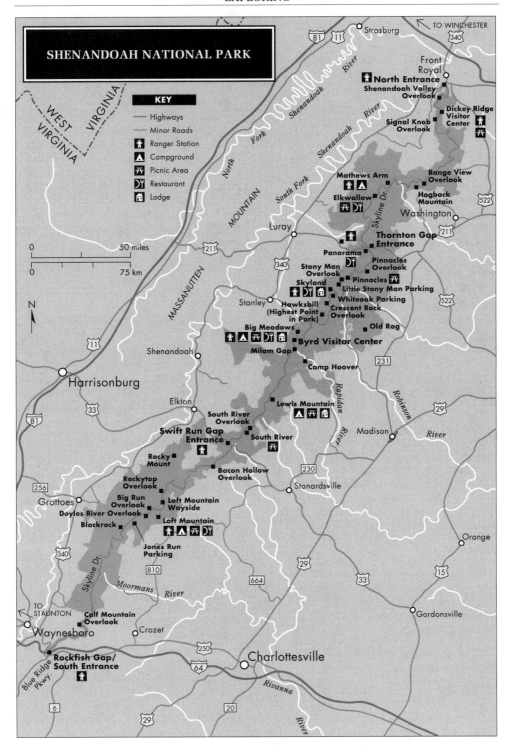

SHENANDOAH NATIONAL PARK

KEY
- Highways
- Minor Roads
- Ranger Station
- Campground
- Picnic Area
- Restaurant
- Lodge

TO WINCHESTER

Strasburg

Front Royal

North Entrance

Shenandoah Valley Overlook

Dickey Ridge Visitor Center

Signal Knob Overlook

Range View Overlook

Mathews Arm

Hogback Mountain

Elkwallow

Washington

Luray

Thornton Gap Entrance

Panorama

Pinnacles Overlook

Stony Man Overlook

Pinnacles

Skyland

Little Stony Man Parking

Whiteoak Parking

Stanley

Hawksbill (Highest Point in Park)

Crescent Rock Overlook

Old Rag

Big Meadows

Byrd Visitor Center

Milam Gap

Shenandoah

Camp Hoover

Elkton

Lewis Mountain

South River Overlook

Madison

Swift Run Gap Entrance

South River

Rocky Mount

Bacon Hollow Overlook

Stanardsville

Rockytop Overlook

Grottoes

Big Run Overlook

Loft Mountain Wayside

Doyles River Overlook

Loft Mountain

Blackrock

Jones Run Parking

Orange

Harrisonburg

WEST VIRGINIA / VIRGINIA

MASSANUTTEN MOUNTAIN

North Fork

South Fork

Shenandoah River

Skyline Dr.

Rapidan River

Robinson River

Gordonsville

TO STAUNTON

Calf Mountain Overlook

Crozet

Waynesboro

Rockfish Gap/ South Entrance

Blue Ridge Pkwy.

Moormans River

Charlottesville

Rivanna River

0   50 miles
0   75 km

N

Signal Knob, a Civil War communications post on Massanutten Mountain.

Range View Overlook (17.1) offers a sweeping expanse of the Blue Ridge from a 2,810-foot elevation.

Pinnacles Overlook (35.1) is an overview of many of the park's peaks, including the distant, rock-studded, lichen-covered ridgeline of Old Rag and the valley beyond.

Stony Man Mountain Overlook (38.6) features a view of Stony Man Mountain to the south and Massanutten Mountain to the west.

Crescent Rock (44.4) has by far the best view of 4,051-foot Hawksbill Mountain, the park's highest peak. The viewpoint is only 25 yards from the Drive, but watch out: Footing can be unstable.

Big Meadows (51.0) is a must-see destination. A walk along the inviting paths in the last of the park's open meadows (*see* Geology and Terrain *in* Essential Information, *above*) puts you among a richness of wildflowers, berries, and songbirds not found in more heavily forested sections. The browsing deer are usually numerous (especially on spring evenings) and uncharacteristically calm and trusting.

Bacon Hollow Overlook (69.3) has views of two drastically different regions of Virginia—the rolling Piedmont to the east, and 3,000-foot-plus peaks to the north and south.

Rockytop Overlook (78.2) offers views of the canyon and wild backcountry of the Big Run watershed.

Big Run Overlook (81.2), one of the park's best views, is another perspective on the Big Run watershed, from the cliffs and talus slopes of Rocky Mountain to distant Massanutten.

Calf Mountain Overlook (98.9) is known for excellent sunsets and 300° views.

HISTORIC BUILDINGS AND SITES Because the park was established to preserve the remaining wilderness and let the elements reclaim what man had wrought, most structures have been allowed to crumble. There are two important exceptions.

Camp Hoover, President Herbert Hoover's version of Camp David, was used by Hoover as a retreat until he donated the dwellings to the park in 1933. It's set at the headwaters of the Rapidan River, one of the best trout streams in the park (now catch-and-release only), and is maintained much as it was in Hoover's time. The camp can be reached by an easy 2-mile walk on the Mill Prong Trail, from mile 52.5 on the Drive, or by a longer one from Milam Gap (*see* Nature Trails and Short Walks, *below*); and, occasionally, by a special-permission carpool from the Byrd Visitor Center.

Corbin Cabin is the only mountaineer's home that has been maintained and kept fully intact, its main distinction. Most of the others (including two near Corbin Cabin) have been reclaimed by nature. Access is by a challenging trail from the Drive at mile 37.9. The cabin is intended mainly for the use of those who rent it; when it's occupied, other visitors are encouraged to keep their distance. For rental information, contact the Potomac Appalachian Trail Club (*see* Appalachian Trail, *below,* for the address).

NATURE TRAILS AND SHORT WALKS If you'd like to take a break from the driver's seat and stretch your legs, the park's options are nearly limitless. The main problem is deciding which trail to take. Consult the park's "Short Hikes" brochures for the northern, central, and southern districts, or Henry Heatwole's wonderful *Guide to Shenandoah National Park* (*see* Publications *in* Essential Information, *above*). Note that pets are not allowed on some trails. The following is an abbreviated and fairly arbitrary list of short hikes.

North Marshall Viewpoint (15.9; .75 mile, 45 minutes round-trip). Follow the Appalachian Trail, on the east side of Skyline Drive, less than 100 yards north of the milepost. The gentle climb, with switchbacks, will bring you to an open ledge with a sheer drop and a fine view. In the distance you can spot the Pinnacle, Marys Rock, Stony Man, Millers Head, and Pass Mountain.

Limberlost (43.0; 1.3 miles, 45 minutes). This easy circuit walk along a dirt-and-rock trail starts at the parking area and circles through a section of old-growth hemlock forest that George Pollock saved by paying a logger *not* to cut it. Some of the ancient hemlocks, 3 feet or more in diameter, still tower; the fallen and decaying trunks of others make for somber but interesting scenery.

Blackrock (84.8; 1 mile, 1 hour round-trip). Parking is on the west side of Skyline Drive, around 100 feet from the road. Take Trayfoot Mountain Trail (a former fire road) up the ridge; continue on the Appalachian Trail. For .3 mile the path is an easy climb through the forest, followed by a gradual descent of 200 yards or so across an open talus slope of rocks that range from small to car-size. Beyond the slope is a stunning panorama over the Madison Run watershed and Dundo Hollow. The trail loops around Blackrock Summit. (There is no trail to the summit, but you can find your way by scrambling uphill over the rocks.) Return via the same route.

LONGER HIKES Experienced hikers can spend weeks exploring the park's 500 miles of trails and still see only a portion of its backcountry. Carry a copy of Heatwole's *Guide to Shenandoah National Park* (*see* Publications *in* Essential Information, *above*), because it's possible to get turned around on some of the trails and end up well away from your intended destination. The longest trail is the approximately 90 miles of the famous Maine-to-Georgia **Appalachian Trail** (*see below*). The following are some other popular trails.

Overall Run Falls (22.2; 3.8 miles, 3–4 hours round-trip). It's an easy descent to—but a challenging climb on your return from—93-foot Overall Run Falls, the park's highest waterfall. From the end of B loop in Matthews Arm campground, take the old Matthews Arm fire road 1.4 miles to Big Blue Trail, then continue 100 yards and take a left on the Big Blue/Overall Run Trail. After another .1 mile, there's a side trail on the left to the upper falls. Continue down the main trail to other side trails to view the main falls.

Whiteoak Canyon (42.6; 4.6 miles, 4 hours round-trip). This popular but strenuous hike takes you to the first and tallest (86 feet) of Whiteoak Canyon's six noted waterfalls. The trailhead lies on the east side of Skyline Drive, just south of the south entrance to Skyland. The trail descends through the towering Limberlost hemlocks, along Whiteoak Run (nearly dry in some seasons, torrential in others), into the heart of Whiteoak Canyon, and, finally, to the waterfalls. The first is the highest; there are five more deeper in the canyon, but the trail is very rough and steep.

Camp Hoover via Mill Prong from Milam Gap (52.8; 4.1 miles, 3³⁄₄ hours round-trip, or well under 3 if you're in practice). If you want just one fairly easy longer walk, here's a great choice. From the south end of the Milam Gap parking lot, follow the Appalachian Trail about 50 yards on the east side of Skyline Drive; then turn left onto the Mill Prong Trail. The single-track dirt trail skirts an old orchard and then meanders across the fern-carpeted floor of second-growth forest. The trail crosses Mill Prong twice as it follows the small stream to Herbert Hoover's summer retreat. In some places the stream is barely a trickle; in others, the holes are large enough to support brook trout and encourage hot-weather hikers to an impromptu (chilly) dip. At times Camp Hoover (*see* Historic Buildings and Sites, *above*) is still used; hikers are expected to stay clear of the area when the camp is occupied.

Pocosin Mission and South River Falls via Pocosin fire road (59.5; 8.5 miles, 7 hours). You reach the crumbling ruins of an early 20th-century Episcopal mission and 83-foot-high South River Falls on this challenging circuit hike. Heatwole's book (*see above*) describes the rather complex route.

Doyles River/Jones Run/Appalachian Trail (81.1; 8 miles, 7 hours). There are three waterfalls, a bunch of tiring climbs and descents, some of the park's biggest trees, and expansive views along this circuit hike. Take the Doyles River Trail downhill from the parking area, crossing the Appalachian Trail and Browns Gap fire road, to the Doyles River

Falls. From there, continue descending to the Jones Run Trail; follow it uphill and take a right onto the Appalachian Trail. It's approximately 3 miles back to the parking area. If you can leave one car at the Doyles River parking lot (81.1) and a second vehicle at the Jones Run parking area (84.1), you can shorten the hike to 4.8 miles by dispensing with the return leg on the Appalachian Trail.

APPALACHIAN TRAIL Some 90 miles of the Maine-to-Georgia **Appalachian Trail** (AT) run within the park's boundaries roughly parallel to Skyline Drive. The park section of the AT is well maintained by volunteers, with, generally, good footing and even grading; it is marked by white blazes on trees and rocks, which make it easy to follow. Wilderness hikers must possess valid backcountry permits (*see* Visitor Information *in* Essential Information, *above*).

The best source of information for AT hikers is the **Potomac Appalachian Trail Club** (118 Park St. SE, Vienna, VA 22180, tel. 703/242–0315, Mon.–Thurs. 7 PM–9 PM, Thurs.–Fri. noon– 2). The club maintains seven trailside huts and six backcountry cabins, which provide good overnight stops. The huts are basically covered sleeping and lounging areas; the fee is $1 per night. The cabins, are better appointed than the huts; each has a table, a fireplace, bunks for up to 11 people, and a door with a lock, not to mention a spring (the water should be treated before drinking) and a pit toilet.

OTHER ACTIVITIES **Biking.** *Experienced* bicyclists will delight in the vistas and in the Drive's 35-mile-per-hour speed limit, but they'll be challenged by the narrow road shoulders, the heavy traffic in high season (particularly October weekends), and the climbs to elevations of 3,680 feet. (Amateurs should forget it.) Off-road or mountain bikes have the ideal gearing for the steep going, but they may be used only on paved areas. During times of limited visibility or at night, each bicycle must have a white light on the front and a red light or reflector on the back. For additional safety, wear gloves and a helmet.

Bird-Watching. Carry a field guide and binoculars and you can rack up an impressive variety of sightings—more than 200 species of birds have been identified in the park. Novice birders can readily spot turkey and black vultures, ravens, crows, robins, and blue jays. Students of the hobby will appreciate the way the park's high altitudes and dense cover attract birds that are usually found farther north, such as the woodcock, junco, wood thrush, and some 35 species of warblers.

While a few birds live in the park year-round—notably the ruffed grouse, barred owl, and wild turkey—late spring and summer are the best times to see the birds that visit the area for breeding and nesting. The park is also an excellent observation area for watching the thousands of raptors (several types of hawks plus the occasional eagle and falcon) that migrate south along the Blue Ridge every autumn.

The open areas of Big Meadows (51.0) support an outstanding diversity of species, especially small songbirds. The small and furtive warblers, flycatchers, and vireos abound in the forest canopy; sharp-eyed birders are likely to spot them at just about any time and place. A popular outside-the-park point for watching the fall migration of raptors is the covered Ballroom Terrace at the Afton/Waynesboro Holiday Inn (*see* Lodging, *below*).

Fishing. Anglers who enjoy pursuing the diminutive but challenging native brook trout will find some 30 streams open to fishing from the third Saturday in March to October 15. Anglers aged 16 and over must possess a valid fishing license, which can be obtained at camp stores within the park. Virginia residents pay $12.50 for a year ($5 for five days); a five-day nonresident license costs $6.

Only artificial flies and lures with single hooks may be used. Rules and regulations are geared toward protecting the trout. On some streams the limit per person is five trout per day, each a minimum of eight inches in length; on the Rapidan, Staunton, and North Fork Moormans rivers, no fish may be kept, and only artificial flies and lures with single barbless hooks may be used. On many of the better streams you have to walk a fair amount to reach the best fishing areas. For further information, consult the park's "Trout Fishing" brochure, available from park headquarters or at visitor's centers.

Hang Gliding. There are three authorized launch sites for hang gliders: Dickey Hill, Hogback Mountain, and Millers Head. You may not launch anywhere else. These sites are neither marked nor maintained by the park, though you may be able to find them on site maps available from park headquarters. You must have at least a Hang 3 rating and must obtain permission to land at an off-mountain site. You'll need a hang-gliding special-use permit, available from park headquarters for $15. There is no place to rent equipment in the area.

Horseback Riding. Horseback riding is allowed on designated trails from April through October. Contact the park superintendent (*see* Visitor Information *in* Essential Information, *above*) for maps and information. **Skyland Stables** (tel. 703/999–2210), near Skyland Lodge (41.7), offers guided trail rides only, April through October ($16 per person per hour); pony rides are available for smaller children ($4 per half hour). Credit cards are not accepted.

Rock Climbing. The most popular routes are on Old Rag Mountain and Little Stony Man Cliff—though the latter was closed during 1992 when peregrine falcons showed an interest in nesting there. You don't need a permit, but you must be familiar with park restrictions: no altering rock faces, no removing plants or lichens, no using motorized drills in designated wilderness areas. The superintendent's office can supply the complete list of regulations.

Swimming. Swimming, at your own risk, is allowed in park streams. However, except during the spring runoff, when they're too cold for comfort, park waters are too shallow for anything but wading. Most streams do feature a few small holes that allow for a modest amount of hot-weather splashing—

for example, Mill Prong, on the hike to Camp Hoover.

CHILDREN'S PROGRAMS Activities for children from preschool age to early teens fall into two categories—summer interpretive programs and the Junior Ranger program.

The schedule of free summer interpretive programs—nature walks, night-sky observation, and so forth—is published in the park newspaper, *Shenandoah Overlook*. There's also a Junior Ranger program, which involves buying a book ($1 in park visitor's centers and gift shops), completing it, and turning it in to earn a Junior Ranger badge. The book has kids working puzzles, learning the names of pictured animals, completing use-your-senses exercises, attending ranger-led walks, and so on.

EVENING ACTIVITIES Park rangers conduct free programs most summer evenings at lodges, campgrounds, and amphitheaters. The programs vary in length and content; most involve slide shows and ranger-led night walks. For a schedule of topics, times, and locations, consult the park newspaper, *Shenandoah Overlook*. Wear comfortable walking shoes and clothes; bring a flashlight and a long-sleeved shirt or jacket. Insects aren't much of a problem in the park, but you might carry bug spray, just in case.

DINING

INSIDE THE PARK The park's six restaurants cater to appetites and attire that suit the outdoors. Meals are filling, the setting casual, the service good, the scenery outstanding. Don't expect bargain prices, vegetarian options, or inventive cooking; the accent is on fried chicken, trout, and meat. In the three larger restaurants (Big Meadows Lodge, Skyland Lodge, Panorama) you can get all three meals: Breakfast and lunch are Inexpensive, with plenty of selections; dinner is Moderate but no bargain. The dining rooms at Big Meadows and Skyland have good wine lists. Reservations aren't taken, and a 30- to 60-minute wait for a table is not unusual. The adjacent taprooms are modest extensions (seating 20–30) of their respective lodges, with sandwiches, snacks, evening entertainment during peak visitor periods, and mixed drinks—some allegedly made with legally distilled "moonshine."

Big Meadows Lodge. The rich tones of native American chestnut dominate the interior of this cozy structure. The exterior features a multitiered roof and spacious windows that provide sunset views from the dining room. The menu is pretty much limited to the same offerings as elsewhere, but Big Meadows generally has superior preparation and snappier service. It's a good place to savor the sunset with a cup of coffee and the specialty dessert, blackberry ice cream pie topped with blackberry syrup. *MP 51.0, Skyline Dr., tel. 703/999–2211 or 800/999–4714. Dress: casual but neat. AE, D, MC, V. Open daily 7:30 AM–8:30 PM; taproom open 4–11. Closed Nov.–early May. Moderate.*

Panorama. Panorama is a multilevel wood-and-stone building with a dining area and, in a separate wing, a general store and gift shop. The menu is basically the same as at Big Meadows and Skyland; service is usually quicker. There is no wine list or taproom—just wine by the glass or draft beer. The hours are shorter, though sometimes during peak visitor traffic they're extended. *MP 31.5, Skyline Dr., tel. 703/999–2265. Dress: casual but neat. AE, D, MC, V. Open daily 9–5:30 (later in high season). Closed mid-Nov.–late Mar. Moderate.*

Skyland Lodge. The rustic stone-and-timber setting and traditional Southern Highlands menu hark back to the era when George Freeman Pollock established Stony Man Camp at this site. If you can procure a window table, you may see deer and rabbits nibbling at the grasses on the narrow strip of lawn between the lodge and a nearby stand of mountain laurel and rhododendron; if not, you can still enjoy the view toward Massanutten Mountain through the spacious glass of the dining room's west wall. The typical dinner entrées—ham, beef, fried chicken—are somewhat overpriced considering the quality, the portions, and the cafeteria-like ambience;

still, the place is usually overcrowded during the busy season, when you can wait an hour for a table. Breakfast offers the best variety and the best prices, though hearty eaters should double their cereal orders and take the tall stack of pancakes over the short. *MP 41.7, Skyline Dr., tel. 703/999–2211 or 800/999–4714. Dress: casual but neat. AE, D, MC, V. Open daily 7:30 AM–8:30 PM; taproom open 4–11. Closed late Nov.–late Mar. Moderate.*

In addition to the above, three inexpensive wayside stops offer snacks, drinks, ice, groceries, and lunch counters serving burgers, fries, and various deli-style sandwiches.

Big Meadows. *MP 51.0, Skyline Dr., tel. 703/999–2221. AE, D, MC, V. Open daily 9–5:30. Closed late Nov.–late Mar.*

Elkwallow. *MP 24.1, Skyline Dr., tel. 703/999–2253. AE, D, MC, V. Open daily 9–5:30. Closed Nov.–early Apr.*

Loft Mountain. *MP 79.5, Skyline Dr., tel. 804/823–4515. AE, D, MC, V. Open daily 9–5:30. Closed Nov.–early Apr.*

NEAR THE PARK The park's gateway communities offer a variety of dining options, from fast to fine. If you're staying the night in the park, the long drive out for dinner may not seem practical, but the restaurants below generally offer faster service, a broader choice, finer preparation, and better prices. Except where noted, dress is casual.

Inn at Little Washington. You can splurge here on the likes of medallions of veal Shenandoah (with grilled local apples, Virginia apple brandy, and fresh fettuccine) and wash it down with wine from the inn's 8,000-bottle inventory. It's *extremely* expensive (*see* Lodging, *below*), but the quality is sky-high. *Middle and Main Sts. (13 mi from the Thornton Gap entrance to Skyline Dr.), Washington, VA, tel. 703/675–3800, fax 703/675–3100. Reservations required. Jacket and tie advised. MC, V. Dinner only (breakfast for guests staying at the inn). Closed Tues. except May and Oct. Very Expensive.*

Captain Sam's Landing. This is a seafood restaurant with decor to match, topped off with antiques, a wooden deck, and a patio. One week each month is devoted to the "shrimp feast"; chicken and steaks are other options. *2323 W. Main St., Waynesboro (on U.S. 250 10 min from the southern entrance to Skyline Dr.), tel. 703/943–3416. No reservations weekends or during shrimp feast. AE, DC, MC, V. Dinner only; closed Sun. except during monthly shrimp feast. Moderate.*

Dean's Steakhouse. The understated wood-and-brick exterior sets the casual, friendly tone for the three interior dining areas and outdoor patio. Specialties include locally raised trout, fresh seafood, and baby back and prime ribs. The extensive wine list features many Virginia and California labels. *701 S. Royal Ave. (.25 mi from the northern entrance to Skyline Dr.), Front Royal, tel. 703/635–1780. Reservations accepted. AE, DC, MC, V. Open daily 11–10 (later during peak season). Moderate.*

Parkhurst Restaurant. The stately white building evokes the air of a country club. The international specialties include chicken dishes (from fried to cordon bleu), steak, and fettuccine with shellfish. There's special emphasis on Virginia wines. *Rte. 1, Box 465, Luray (2 mi west of Luray Caverns on U.S. 211, 10 mi from Skyline Dr.), tel. 703/743–6009. Reservations advised weekends. Dress: casual but neat. AE, D, DC, MC, V. Dinner only. Moderate.*

Brookside Restaurant. This full-service, home-style restaurant offers homemade breads and desserts, a 30-item salad bar, luncheon and dinner buffets, and such specialties as stove-top pan-fried chicken. The dining room decor is country conservative: country curtains, wood-grain tables, carpeting, wood paneling. There are booths in a separate coffee shop section, as well as a gift shop. *Rte. 4, Box 346, Luray (on U.S. 211 4.5 mi from Skyline Dr.; 20 min from Skyland), tel. 703/743–5698. No reservations. AE, D, DC, MC, V. Inexpensive.*

Pano's. A spacious, family-oriented restaurant with a French provincial motif outside that belies the cozy wood paneling and bargain prices within. The huge menu offers 65 entrées at lunch, 96 at dinner. *3190 S. Main St., Harrisonburg (just off I–81 at Exit 243; 30 min west of Skyline Dr. via U.S. 33), tel. 703/434–2367. No reservations. AE, D, DC, MC, V. Inexpensive.*

PICNIC SPOTS Picnicking is an obvious way to enjoy the view, wait for deer and other wildlife to wander by, and savor the outdoors. Box lunches, including a sandwich, fruit, chips, and cookie for around $6, are available from the Big Meadows Lodge, Panorama, and Skyland Lodge dining rooms. You can eat at one of the overlooks (they don't have tables, but you can spread out a blanket on a grassy spot and enjoy the view) or at one of the park's picnic areas: Dickey Ridge (4.6); Elkwallow (24.1); Pinnacles (36.7); Big Meadows (51.0); Lewis Mountain (57.5); South River (62.8); or Loft Mountain (79.5). The designated picnic areas have tables, grills, drinking water, and rest rooms; nearby camp stores offer soft drinks, firewood, snacks, and other supplies.

LODGING

There is a multitude of motels, hotels, bed-and-breakfasts, and country inns close to Shenandoah National Park; within the park itself are several very nice options—from lodge rooms to private cabins. Vacancies are hard to find, especially during the peak summer and fall foliage seasons (when rates are highest—though usually not by more than 10%), so make your reservations as far in advance as possible. If all nearby rooms are booked, the next-closest options are the chain motels in Charlottesville and Winchester. For more information or reservations, contact the ARA Virginia Sky-Line Co., Inc. (Box 727, Luray 22835, tel. 703/743–5108 or 800/999–4714, fax 703/999–2231).

IN THE PARK **Skyland Lodge.** The stone- and-timber main lodge (which does not have accommodations) traces its roots to Stony Man Camp, which George Freeman Pollock established at this site in 1886. Nearby, modern motel-style units offer 163 rooms, and there are an additional 22 small but cozy cabins nestled among the trees. The views are stunning, and everything is within a short walk or drive of the main dining area. *MP 41.7, Skyline Dr., tel. 703/999–2211 or 800/999–4714, fax 703/999–2231. 185 rooms, 182 with bath. Facilities: restaurant, after-hours taproom, crafts shop, newsstand; TV in some rooms but no in-room phones; 4 rooms wheelchair-accessible, some nonsmoking rooms; playground, horseback rides, hiking trails. AE, D, MC, V. Closed late Nov.–early Mar. Moderate–Expensive.*

Big Meadows Lodge. Built in 1939 of native stone and chestnut, the rustically elegant main lodge features 22 rooms with huge windows that yield soaring over-the-valley views. Other accommodations within the complex include 70 rooms in six motel-style units, and 11 less expensive but fully appointed rustic wood or log cabins that each sleep two. *MP 51.0, Skyline Dr., tel. 703/999–2221 or 800/999–4714, fax 703/999–2011. 103 rooms, 99 with bath. Facilities: restaurant and taproom; TV in 10 rooms (but no in-room phones); 2 rooms wheelchair-accessible. AE, D, MC, V. Closed Nov.–early May. Moderate.*

Lewis Mountain Cabins. The least expensive of the park's lodging options, these 1940s-era one-room housekeeping cabins combine modern baths and sleeping spaces with covered picnic areas and outside fireplaces with grills. Basically they're semi-modern motel rooms nestled in an oak forest, with campsite-style cooking facilities—a good way to rough it without making it too rough. *MP 57.6, Skyline Dr., tel. 703/999–2255, fax (reservations) 703/743–7883. 4 single units with bath; 10 double units share 5 baths. No TV or phones; not wheelchair-accessible. AE, D, MC, V. Closed Nov.–early May. Inexpensive–Moderate.*

NEAR THE PARK **Inn at Little Washington.** From its white stucco-and-clapboard exterior to the antiques inside, this remarkable inn, on a two-block expanse in a small Virginia town, has the look and feel of an exquisitely elegant English country house. It caters to the well-off: rates start at $240 per night. The restaurant (*see* Dining, *above*) is one of the best in the country. *Middle and Main Sts., Washing-ton, VA 22747 (13 mi from the Thornton Gap entrance to Skyline Dr.), tel. 703/675–3800, fax 703/675–3100. 12 rooms with bath. Facilities: restaurant, tennis courts nearby. MC, V. Closed Tues. except May and Oct. Very Expensive.*

Cabins at Brookside. Here is a successful combination of rusticity and luxury, privacy and accessibility. While the milled-log exteriors pay tribute to Blue Ridge frontier cabins, interior amenities such as queen-size beds and modern baths (with skylights) provide the comforts of a luxury motel—and there's a grassy distance between you and your neighbors. Private decks overlook a small brook, resident peacocks prowl the grounds, and there's fresh-brewed coffee delivered to your cabin every morning. *U.S. 211 (Rte. 4, Box 346), Luray 22835 (4.5 mi west of Skyline Dr.), tel. 703/743–5698. Six 1- and 2-bedroom cabins. Facilities: restaurant, gift shop, gallery. AE, D, MC, V. Moderate–Expensive.*

Afton/Waynesboro Holiday Inn. This three-story white-brick hotel stands at the southern tip of the Skyline Drive where the roadway joins the Blue Ridge Parkway. The outstanding attraction is the soaring view over Rockfish Valley (36 rooms have a full view and another 36 a partial view). The covered Ballroom Terrace is a popular spot for watching the fall raptor migration. *Junction of I-64 (at Exit 99) and U.S. 250 (Box 849), Waynesboro 22980, tel. 703/942–5201 or 800/HOLIDAY, fax 703/943–8746. 118 rooms. Facilities: restaurant, lounge, banquet/meeting rooms, heated pool, golf privileges on nearby course. AE, D, DC, MC, V. Moderate.*

Quality Inn. This three-level motor inn is very nice by chain-motel standards, from the marble and slate in the lobby to the custom wallpaper and drapes in the rooms. The downtown location is convenient to the Front Royal visitor's center and just 10 minutes from the northern entrance to the Skyline Drive. *10 Commerce Ave., Front Royal 22630, tel. 703/635–3161 or 800/821–4488. 107 rooms. Facilities: restaurant, bar, pool. AE, D, DC, MC, V. Moderate.*

Super 8. This standard motel with signature beige stucco exterior and dark trim sits in a modern retail district between Charlottesville and the regional airport. Carpeted guest rooms have cable TV and phones. *390 Greenbrier Dr., Charlottesville 22901 (1 block off U.S. 29, 5 mi north of the city and 9 mi south of the airport), tel. 804/973–0888, fax 804/973–2221. 66 rooms. AE, D, DC, MC, V. Inexpensive.*

CAMPING

CAMPGROUNDS The park has four developed campgrounds. Each one has a store and rest rooms; all but Matthews Arm have showers and laundry facilities; and each campsite has a table and fire grate. There are no RV hook-ups, but sewage disposal stations are available at all but Lewis Mountain. Camping is permitted for up to a total of 14 days from June through October. Pets are allowed, as long as they're kept on 6-foot (or shorter) leashes and never left unattended. Expect crowded conditions during peak season.

Mathews Arm. The park's northernmost campground may not reopen because of budget cuts, which is a shame because the sites lie farther apart than at the other campgrounds, and there's a quieter, more family-oriented atmosphere. (The A loop sites are the least trafficked and most private.) It's a 4-mile round-trip hike to Overall Run Falls, and a 3-mile round-trip hike to the camp store. There aren't any showers or laundry facilities here. *MP 22.2, Skyline Dr., tel. 703/999–2266 (park headquarters). 180 sites: 10 tent only, 170 tent or RV. Fee: $12/night per site. MC, V. Closed Nov.–May.*

Big Meadows. The largest (and most popular and crowded) of the park's campgrounds has the most convenient access to facilities. The sites in the new section are closer together; X, Y, and Z loops in the old section are at an access to the Appalachian Trail. Reservations (required) may be arranged up to eight weeks in advance from MISTIX (Box 85705, San Diego, CA 92138–5705, tel. 800/365–CAMP). Make them well ahead of time to ensure that you get your tickets before you depart. *MP 51.0, Skyline Dr., tel. 703/999–3231 (or 703/999–2266 for park headquarters). 227 sites: 40 tent, 187 tent or RV. Fee: $14/night per site. D, MC, V. Closed Nov.–late May.*

Lewis Mountain. A smaller, quieter facility than the other campgrounds, heavily wooded with older-growth timber, and staffed mainly by volunteers. (It was a blacks-only area in the era of segregation.) The campground, which operates on a first-come, first-served basis, frequently fills up early with overflow campers from Big Meadows. *MP 57.6, Skyline Dr., tel. 703/999–2266 (park headquarters). 31 sites: 16 tent, 15 tent or RV. Fee: $12/night per site. No credit cards. Closed Nov.–late spring.*

Loft Mountain. The elevated views from the hillside location take in the valley and the surrounding mountains; the sites with the best views vary, though, depending on the state of the foliage. This campground, too, operates on a first-come, first-served basis. *MP 79.5, Skyline Dr., tel. 804/823–4675 or 703/999–2266 (park headquarters). 221 sites: 54 tent, 167 tent or RV. Fee: $12/night per site. MC, V. Closed late Oct.–late spring.*

BACKCOUNTRY CAMPING Backcountry camping has its own set of rules and responsibilities (camp out of sight of trails; stay at least 250 yards away from paved roads; and so on). Permits are required, but they're free (*see* Visitor Information *in* Essential Information, *above*). The "Exploring the Backcountry" pamphlet, available at entrance and ranger's stations and visitor's centers, outlines the rules of wilderness etiquette. The Potomac Appalachian Trail Club operates seven trailside huts and six backcountry cabins (*see* Appalachian Trail *in* Exploring, *above*).

Voyageurs National Park
Minnesota
By Gene Rebeck

oyageurs National Park lies at the top of Minnesota, right on the Canadian border and near the internationally renowned Boundary Waters Canoe Area. It's one of the least known, least visited members of the National Park System. Why? For one thing, it's relatively new, having become a national park only in 1975. While it's a jewel of north woods beauty, it hasn't built up the reputation of a Yellowstone or a Yosemite, and it doesn't have their tourist trappings.

It's also more difficult to get inside than they are. Voyageurs is above all a water park—wilderness locked in by large lakes. Though the four main access points are accessible by car, the bulk of the park consists of four large lakes and the Kabetogama Peninsula, none of which can be traversed by car or RV—you have to have a boat or know someone who does. And even then, once you've crossed the lake and reached the peninsula you'll find yourself in a wilderness area with only a few trails, many of them so rarely traversed that they may be partly obscured by grasses and ferns.

So why come here? Precisely because of that broad blue lake and that wild green peninsula. You come for good fishing, for wilderness hiking, for motorboating, and for camping. You come because it isn't touristy—at least, not yet.

It was hunting and fishing that first brought enthusiasts to Kabetogama (pronounced Kab-uh-TOE-ga-ma, though some locals elide it to Kap-TOE-ga-ma) in the early part of this century. Lumberjacks and gold miners had already discovered the area. By the time the walleye anglers and grouse hunters began to flock here, the miners and most of the loggers were gone—the gold too unprofitable to scratch out of the granite, the old forests clear-cut.

The trees, though second-growth, came back. Small resorts and cabins, most of them family-run, sprang up in clusters on the southern shores of the lake to cater to the seasonal visitors. Those who wanted a woodsier stay crossed over the lake and through tortuous narrows to the Kettle Falls Hotel, a loggers' bordello turned respectable hostelry. (The hotel still exists, as do many of the resorts; *see* Lodging, *below*.)

Hunters and anglers weren't the only visitors. On the other side of the peninsula—on the Canadian border—lies Rainy Lake. With its myriad little islands, woods, channels, and secretive coves, the lake became a popular spot for bootleggers during Prohibition. Boats full of Canadian whiskey and other illicit hootch would cross and continue through the American Channel on the eastern side of the peninsula, moving carefully between the fragments of land.

Before the hunters, loggers, and bootleggers, Rainy Lake and Lake Kabetogama had already been frequented by white men of a very different stripe. These were *les voyageurs,* hardy French Canadians who during the 17th and 18th centuries paddled and portaged their great canoes from Montréal to far northwestern Canada, seeking and transporting the pelts of beaver, fox, wolf, and other animals whose fur was in demand among fashionable Europeans. The voyageurs wore rugged, brightly colored clothing festooned with fur and feathers; they could paddle for up to 16 hours a day; and they sang songs that ranged from the high-spirited to the deeply sorrowful.

You have to come to Voyageurs with something of the voyageurs' spirit. Now that the region is a national park you can no longer hunt here, and fishing is regulated; there are cozier accommodations than tents, if you so choose. But otherwise you'll have to contend with many of the same forces the voyageurs did. Whether you see the park on your own or on a naturalist-led group trip, you need a certain sense of history, an awareness that nothing (except perhaps the fish) will come too easy.

ESSENTIAL INFORMATION

VISITOR INFORMATION Contact the **Superintendent, Voyageurs National Park** (3131 Hwy. 53, International Falls 56649–8904, tel. 218/283–9821) for an information packet, which includes a general map and description of the park as well as information on boat trips, guided tours, park wildlife, hiking, and lodging. A brochure listing available publications is also enclosed.

If you're also interested in traveling elsewhere in northern Minnesota, contact the **Minnesota Office of Tourism** (100 Metro Sq., 121 7th Pl. E, St. Paul 55101, tel. 612/296–5029 or 800/657–3700).

FEES There are no fees to enter the park. However, boats must be licensed (*see* Other Activities *in* Exploring, *below*).

PUBLICATIONS The nonprofit **Lake States Interpretive Association** (3131 U.S. 53, International Falls 56649–8904, tel. 218/283–2103) sells publications, videos, and educational materials on Voyageurs and on the surrounding natural attractions, specifically the Chippewa, Nicolet, and Superior national forests. You can order the following publications from them by phone, using a credit card (MC, V); you'll also be charged for postage and handling.

The publications available deal mostly with the human history of the park region, though some cover natural history as well. The most notable on both is Greg Breining's *Voyageurs National Park* ($7.95, 56 pages, 36 color photos), which won the National Park Service's 1988 Excellence in Publications Award. The text is beautifully written, and the photographs, by J. Arnold Bolz, illustrate it exquisitely. Offering more detail about the park's natural landscape is Jim DuFresne's *Voyageurs National Park: Water Routes, Foot Paths and Ski Trails* ($9.95, 176 pages), which offers such full descriptions of the lakes and trails that it's considered the park bible by many. And for those who want to know more about the colorful men for whom the park is named, Grace Lee Nute's *The Voyageur*

($7.95, 289 pages) offers perhaps the most definitive history.

The Lake States Interpretive Association also sells different maps of the park. (Many are for sale at the park's four visitor's centers.) The choice depends in part on how you'll be traveling. The U.S. Geological Survey's Voyageurs map (VNP-1; $5) has a scale ratio of 1:50,000 and shows lake depths. If you want more detail (and more maps), there are USGS topographical maps ($2.50) at 1:24,000, and McKenzie maps ($5.50) at 1:31,680. For boaters, there are five National Oceanic and Atmospheric Administration (NOAA) navigation charts for canoeists, which do not show depths; there are also NOAA charts for Rainy Lake, which do (all $4). For anglers who want to know depths for Kabetogama, the Lake States Interpretive Association sells a "Fishing Hot Spots" map of the lake ($6.95).

GEOLOGY AND TERRAIN Writer Greg Breining (*see* Publications, *above*) describes the Kabetogama Peninsula landscape, paradoxically but aptly, as "flat but rugged." Overall, the elevations in the park don't vary as greatly as in many other national parks. But the glaciers that came through here several millennia ago scraped numerous ridges and striations into the land, and these give Voyageurs a remarkable variety.

The park's bedrock is very old—several billion years old. Later volcanic action and glacial movement created the structures that shape the park today. The northern part marks the southern edge of the Canadian Shield, a mantle of rock that extends north to Hudson Bay. The predominant material in this mantle is greenstone, a volcanic rock. Farther south, encompassing most of the Kabetogama Peninsula, a layer of granite and biotite schist lies beneath the bedrock. In some places, the two types of rock intermingle to form a swirled-striped formation called migmatite. South of the peninsula, vermilion granite predominates.

It was the glacier that gave the landscape its rumpled appearance as it receded about 11,000 years ago. During its retreat, rocks and mineral fragments caught in its flow dragged across the land like fingertips across sand. As you walk across the peninsula, you'll see the results of this movement in the great boulders that the glacier left behind and in the outcroppings of granite and greenstone that continually interrupt the soil line.

FLORA AND FAUNA The last glacier's recession left the peninsula a huge barren slab of rock. Over the succeeding millennia, vegetation slowly re-established itself, and a thin layer of soil formed over the rock.

While the soil remains shallow—as you'll find out if you try to stake a tent here—it's still deep enough to support a wide variety of trees. Voyageurs falls within the southern boreal forest, what Minnesotans call the "north woods." Trees that make their home here include, notably, black spruce, balsam fir, and northern white cedar, along with hardwoods such as aspen, oak, and paper birch. Red pine and jack pine intermingle with these; on some islands, pines are the only trees you'll find.

The wildflowers are those that can tolerate a great deal of shade or water or both, not to mention hardy conditions and short summers. In early summer, white bunchberry flowers can be seen almost everywhere. Less common but even more exquisite are Indian pipe, fond of mossy habitat, and lady's slipper, which grows amid rocks strewn with pine and spruce needles. As summer progresses, nooks and corners of many park ponds and lakes witness an explosion of water lilies. Tiny wild strawberries appear, to be plucked from the ground by observant visitors.

Then there are the beasts—of the water, land, and air. Northern pike, smallmouth bass, and walleye are the big reason people have come to the region for decades. The great elk and caribou have long since been driven from the area by human encroachment and hunting, but such other north woods denizens as deer, black bear, and beaver remain. There are about 200 bears in the park, and more in the area outside it. They aren't frequently spotted, though careless campers occasionally see their handiwork in the morning when an errant bear has smelled their food. Beavers are easier to spot; they have built lodges in many of the inland ponds and lakes.

Rarely seen but often heard are timber or gray wolves, which number about 30 to 40 in the park. After being nearly wiped out in Minnesota, wolves are making a slow but steady comeback, as human beings realize that *Canis lupus* poses no threat to them and little to their livestock. Wolves remain shy creatures, and they're very susceptible to canine diseases, which is why dogs and other pets are restricted to certain areas in the park. Other less numerous mammals dwelling in the park include bobcats, river otters, minks, and pine martens.

Because of the land's moistness, you'll very likely encounter toads and (nonvenomous) snakes shuffling in the underbrush. The moisture also assures that you'll run into mosquitoes and deer flies (often in clouds), as well as both deer and wood ticks. Be ready for these varmints if you come in late spring and early summer.

Last but not least, there are the birds. The singers you'll hear most are thrushes, white-throated sparrows, and varieties of warblers. Even urban birds liks robins and blue jays pipe up. Bald eagles and ospreys also make their home here, special blessings to the visitor who happens to spot either of them. On the water, mergansers and red-necked grebes are most often seen (and gulls, of course); a few less common ducks, such as goldeneyes, make appearances every now and then. Three birds are worthy of special attention. The common loon (not quite as common as it used to be), Minnesota's state bird, is perhaps the most delightful, and if you pick a campsite with care and a bit of luck, its haunting howls will create a strange, moving lullaby. Out on the big lakes, white pelicans, comical yet dignified, love to cluster on small rocky islands. And if you camp in the middle of the woods, be prepared to hear—and hear, and hear—the monotonous nocturne of the whippoorwill. During the day, fearless Canada jays may stop by your camp to beg. Some especially brazen "whiskey jacks" have been known to make off with morsels when unsuspecting backs are turned.

WHEN TO GO If you're a snowmobiler or cross-country skier, the choice is obvious. January and February are when the snow is at its peak, though it often lasts well into March.

If you're coming up for the fishing, it's at its best in late May and June, tapering off a bit in July and August, then picking up again in September and October. Many people come up in the winter to ice-fish, which in Minnesota is as much (if not more) about fishing-house camaraderie than actually catching anything. If you're up here to boat or canoe, any time but winter is fine, though mid-summer and early fall probably have the nicest weather, and biting bugs are scarcer then, too.

As for hiking, late summer and early fall are prime time. Spring is too humid, and the mosquitoes and black flies are ferocious. Even if you're lathered with insect repellent, their clouding and buzzing can make your jaunt a minor hell. Deer flies and wood and deer ticks are another summer annoyance; the latter can transmit Lyme disease, though cases in Minnesota are not too common. Summer is also when the park is most crowded with folks as well as bugs. Not that this park gets jammed—but the increased numbers can make it more difficult to get your choice of campsite.

WHAT TO PACK Whatever time of year it is, it's good to have a little more clothing on hand than you think you'll need. While T-shirts and shorts are fine most summer days, the weather up here can turn cool quickly. In the spring and fall the temperature can dip below freezing, so it's best to carry extra warm clothing (long underwear, wool socks). If you plan to hike, bring hiking boots that can keep your feet dry; you may go through grassy trails covered with dew. Summer bugs and ticks make deep-woods types of insect repellent, such as DEET, a must. Boaters and all their passengers must wear personal flotation devices (PFDs) when on the water.

GENERAL STORES There are no general stores in the park itself. The store nearest the Kabetogama and Ash River entrances is the **Gateway** (corner of U.S. 53 and Route 122, tel. 218/875–2121; open summer, daily 7AM–11PM, fall–spring, daily 7–6). Gateway not only has a small but broad selection of foodstuffs, it also sells bait and other fishing-related items. The stores closest to the Rainy Lake Visitor's Center are the several grocers in International Falls, among them **Lucca's** (1103 7th Ave., tel. 218/285–7295), and **Super One** (Hwy. 11/71, tel. 218/283–8440).

ATMS There are several automated teller machines in International Falls, about 12 miles from the Rainy Lake entrance to the park, at the **Stop and Shop** on U.S. 53 south of downtown. Downtown there are several more: in the **First National Bank** lobby (419 3rd St.), the **First American Bank** drive-up facility (3rd Ave. between 3rd and 4th Sts.), and the **Boise Employee Credit Union** (501 4th St.); all are open 24 hours a day.

ARRIVING AND DEPARTING By far the easiest way to get to any of the visitor's centers, which also serve as the points of entry, is by car. The nearest major city with both train and regular air service is Minneapolis, 300 miles to the south—a 5½-hour drive. There's plane and bus service to International Falls, but you'll need to get to the park on your own; it's 12 miles from there to the nearest entrance, Rainy Lake. You can rent a car at the airport (*see* By Plane, *below*). Alternatively, you can reserve a limousine from **North Air Service** (tel. 218/283–4422); a one-way ride to the Rainy Lake Visitor's Center is about $50. If you're staying at a resort in the area, the resort's owner may be willing to shuttle you back and forth to International Falls for an agreed-upon sum.

If you're planning to hike and camp, the best point of entry is probably Kabetogama Lake, the one closest to both the main hiking trail in the park and the Woodenfrog State Campground 5 miles away. Boaters will find launches at any entry point.

By Plane. The nearest big-city airport is the **Minneapolis–St. Paul International Airport** (tel. 612/726–5555). Several flights each day on **Northwest Airlink** (tel. 612/726–1234) connect it with **Falls International Airport** (tel. 218/283–4630) in International Falls. Car rental agencies at the Twin Cities airport include **Avis** (tel. 612/726–5220), **Dollar** (tel. 612/854–3003), **Hertz** (tel. 612/726–1600), and **Thrifty** (tel. 612/854–8080). At Falls International, there's **Hertz** (tel. 218/283–3471) and **National** (tel. 218/283–4461).

By Car and RV. Driving up from the Twin Cities, take I–35 to Route 33; then follow Route 33 17 miles north to U.S. 53. Take U.S. 53 north about 130 miles to Route 122, turn right, and follow the signs to Voyageur's Kabetogama Visitor's Center. If you're coming from International Falls, take U.S. 53 south 25 miles to Kabetogama, or Route 11 some 12 miles east to Rainy Lake.

Nearby National Park Service areas are Grand Portage National Monument and Apostle Islands National Lakeshore. If you're coming to Voyageurs from Grand Portage, take U.S. 61 south 90 miles (1½ hours) to Route 1; follow Route 1 north and west 111 miles (2½ hours) to U.S. 53; finally, take U.S. 53 another 70 miles (1½ hours) to Kabetogama.

By Train. The closest that **Amtrak** (tel. 800/872–7245) comes to Voyageurs is St. Paul (tel. 612/644–1127), 275 miles away. Two trains daily—one eastbound, one westbound—stop at the station; each is an *Empire Builder,* on the Chicago–Seattle route. A taxi to downtown St. Paul (about $10) can take you to the Greyhound terminal (*see* By Bus, *below*).

By Bus. Greyhound (tel. 800/231–2222) has a station in International Falls. The trip from stations in either Minneapolis or St. Paul is a long one—about eight hours.

By Boat. Though you can get to the park entrances by car, actually getting *into* this water park is another matter. As part of the deal between landowners and government that established the park, Voyageurs itself does not rent boats; instead it relies on concessionaires and lakeside resort owners to supply water transportation for visitors who haven't brought their own. For information on resorts that rent boats or offer "water taxi" service, contact the resort association nearest the park entrance you plan to use. For **Kabetogama,** contact the **Kabetogama Lake Association** (9707 Gamma Rd., Ray 56669, tel. 218/875–2621 or 800/524–9085); for **Rainy Lake,** the **International Falls Chamber of Commerce** (Box 169, International Falls, MN 56649, tel. 218/283–9400 or 800/325–5766); for **Crane Lake,** the **Crane Lake Visitor and Tourism Bureau** (Box 15 VTB, Crane Lake, MN 55725, tel. 800/362–7405); and for **Ash River,** the **Ash River Commercial Club** (Orr, MN 55771, tel. 218/375–4445 or 800/950–2061). Expect to pay around $40 per day ($120 per week) for a 16-foot runabout with motor—pretty much the standard item, though there are, of course, many options. The more expensive resorts generally have the nicer boats.

EXPLORING

In the three warmer seasons, the best way to get around is by boat. (In the winter, your only real option is a snowmobile.) If you can get over to the hiking trails at Lost Bay on the south central part of the peninsula, you can also spend a day, or several, on foot. Tour boats are available during the summer. Outside of the Kettle Falls Hotel and what remains of the Little American Island gold mine (both accessible only by boat—*see* Historic Buildings and Sites, *below*), there are no "sights" as such beyond the woods and waters.

THE BEST IN ONE DAY The Voyageurs information packet (*see* Visitor Information *in* Essential Information, *above*) contains a schedule of naturalist-guided activities, which are conducted during the summer only (usually mid-June to late August). Every day has a slightly different schedule. Four days a week during the summer you can take a six-hour pontoon boat trip between the Kabetogama Lake Visitor's Center and the historic Kettle Falls Hotel (*see* Guided Tours, *below*). The ride gives you an excellent sense of scenic Kabetogama and Namakan lakes, with

their wooded shores, bays, and many small islands.

If you don't want to spend your whole day on a boat, the best option is a 1½-hour sunset cruise or park-sponsored canoe trip during the day and a naturalist program in the evening (*see* Guided Tours, *below*). This combination, under the auspices of the Kabetogama Lake Visitor's Center, is usually available four days a week. Similar tour boat, canoe, and nature-walk options are available at Rainy Lake. See the activities schedule for exact times and locations.

ORIENTATION PROGRAMS Each of the visitor's centers has an auditorium in which a 15-minute narrated slide show, with lots of beautiful photography, gives an overview of the park and its recreational options. Rainy Lake has the most impressive audiovisual setup, but the show's the same.

GUIDED TOURS Several guided tours—on foot or by boat—are available during the summer at both Kabetogama and Rainy Lake, as well as a beaver-pond hike at Ash River. Nearly all are led by park naturalists. Because of the size and layout of the park, none can claim to give a "complete" view—there are simply too many nooks and crannies here. Boat tourists departing from Rainy Lake board a 49-passenger double-decker; at Kabetogama, the craft is a 19-passenger pontoon boat.

At Kabetogama, three different **Sunset Cruises** are each available once a week. As with all Kabetogama boat tours listed here, you should reserve space at the visitor's center (tel. 218/875–2111). The visitor's center also sponsors 2½-hour boat-hike "adventures," each happening once a week. The **Lost Bay Adventure** travels into Kabetogama Lake's Lost Bay to see its woodsy cliffs. The boat makes a stop at the Cruiser Lake Hiking Trail, where passengers disembark for a mile-long hike inland (passing a bald eagle nest along the way) to Agnes Lake. The **Locator Lake Adventure** combines a boat trip to the nature trail on the southwestern part of the peninsula with a trail hike and a canoe ride

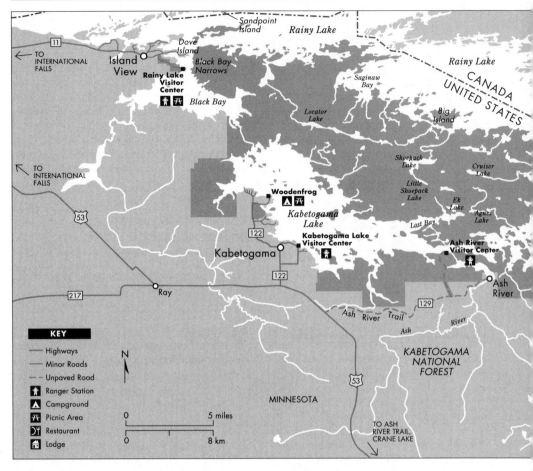

on pretty little Locator Lake ($14 adults, $8 children). Canoes are furnished.

The Kabetogama Lake Visitor's Center also provides canoes for two-hour **guided canoe trips** that travel the waters and explore wooded shores. These accommodate about 12 people. One explores Duck Bay; the other, which leaves from the Woodenfrog State Campground, wends through the Grassy Islands. Both trips are free.

Pontoon-boat trips to Kettle Falls leave Kabetogama Lake Visitor's Center four times a week. They last about six hours round-trip, sailing across Kabetogama Lake, past its lovely wooded shores and myriad small islands, and anchoring near the historic Kettle Falls Hotel, where lunch is served. Reserva-

tions are available through the boat's concessionaire, **Voyageurs National Park Boat Tours, Inc.** (Rte. 8, Box 303, J3, International Falls 56649, tel. 218/286–5470; $31 adults, $19 children).

A similar (and longer) trip to Kettle Falls leaves Rainy Lake Visitor's Center once a week and lasts about 7½ hours round-trip. Voyageurs National Park Boat Tours, Inc. (*see above*) also conducts this trip, at the same cost.

There are many guided tours available at Rainy Lake. The **Rainy Lake Cruise** gives its passengers a trip across the wildly beautiful lake and through its forested islands (4 times a week, $14 adults, $8 children). During August, you can also grab a boat and hike to

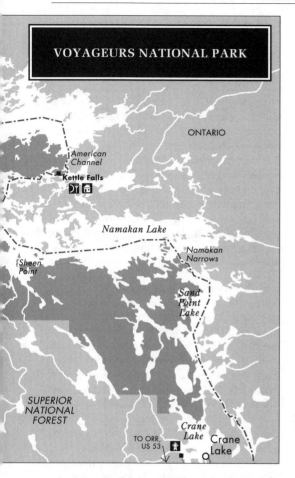

VOYAGEURS NATIONAL PARK

ONTARIO

American Channel

Kettle Falls

Namakan Lake

Namakan Narrows

Sheen Point

Sand Point Lake

SUPERIOR NATIONAL FOREST

Crane Lake

TO ORR, US 53

Crane Lake

cruises departing from the Rainy Lake Visitor Center. The **Natural Adventure Afloat Tour** combines an evening cruise with a naturalist program ($9.50 adults, $6 children). The Out of This World Tour from Rainy Lake explores the sky above the park—the stars, planets, and (with luck) the northern lights (also $9.50 adults, $6 children).

For those who prefer nonmotorized transport, there's the 1¹/₂-hour park-sponsored **North Canoe Voyage.** Twenty passengers travel with a naturalist aboard a 26-foot *Voyageurs North* canoe copied after the vessels of the original voyageurs. Besides a hearty canoe ride, passengers are treated to talks about voyageur life and even a few of their songs. Equipment and tour are free.

SCENIC DRIVES AND VIEWS For obvious reasons, there are no scenic drives (at least not by car) within Voyageurs. The loveliest approach to the park is on Route 11 from International Falls on to the Rainy Lake Visitor's Center. Instead of turning toward the visitor's center, you can take Route 11 2 miles east to Dove Island, a pretty little cabin and resort area with some attractive views of the peninsula.

HISTORIC BUILDINGS AND SITES Nearly all of the park is wilderness—second-growth wilderness, but wilderness nonetheless. Two pieces of the human past do remain, though. You can reach the **Kettle Falls Hotel** only by boat, and even then it's not easy to get to. Set in the farthest northeastern part of the Kabetogama Peninsula, it's accessible from either Rainy or Namakan lakes. The southern approach through Namakan Lake passes through winding wooded narrows to reach it. The route winds so tortuously, in fact, that the hotel is one of the few places in the United States where Canada is actually *south* of the border. It was built around 1910 to accommodate the men working on the nearby Kettle Falls Dam. Its history hasn't always been savory; it once housed a speakeasy and a brothel. But after some years of neglect in the '70s, it has been restored as closely as possible to its 1910 condition (one of the wood floors were kept in their original uneven state). You

a beaver pond ($7 adults, $4 children). All Rainy Lake boat tours can be reserved at the tour-boat concessionaire's office (tel. 218/286–5470).

Those who want to see something of the region's brief history as a gold mining center circa 1893 can take the park's 1¹/₂-hour **Gold Mine Tour** to Little American Island, a 3-acre site that includes several deep mine shafts and a huge 500-pound iron wheel that was used for hoisting ($9.50 adults, $5.50 children). Last but not least, a once-a-week **Grand Tour** combines the Rainy Lake Cruise with the Gold Mine Tour ($20 adults, $11 children).

If you come in July or August you can hook up with either of two two-hour evening can still eat and sleep here (*see* Dining *and* Lodging, *below*); tour boats (*see* Guided Tours, *above*) leave from both Kabetogama and Rainy Lake visitor's centers. *Ash River Trail, Orr 55771, tel. 218/374–3631 or 800/322–0886. Admission free. Open Jan.– Mar. and May–Sept.*

Near the Rainy Lake Visitor's Center is **Little American Island,** focal point of a brief turn-of-the-century gold rush. Nature has all but swallowed up what remains of the mining operation. There was gold here, but the granite and greenstone in which it was encased made it too expensive to dig out. A few shafts and caverns, plus the odd bit of equipment, are all that remain here, but the island and its surroundings comprise the Gold Mine Historic District. It, too, is accessible by boat; a tour boat (*see* Guided Tours, *above*) can take you there.

NATURE TRAILS AND SHORT WALKS Many of the nature trails and short walks at Voyageurs can be traveled with a park naturalist (*see* Guided Tours, *above*). The **Overholzer Trail** (1 mile round-trip) at Rainy Lake and the **Locator Lake Nature Trail** (4 miles round-trip) on the Kabetogama Peninsula can also be done as self-guided tours. Pamphlet guides are available at visitor's centers and at the trailheads. Both trails are of easy to moderate.

If you have a boat, you can get to the two main hiking trails on the peninsula—Locator Lake to the west (*see above*) and the **Cruiser Lake Trail** to the east. The latter comprises the longest trail system in the park, but you needn't hike its entire 15 miles. A pleasant 1-mile (round-trip) jaunt from the trailhead on Lost Bay to Lake Agnes will give you a good sense of the peninsula's terrain. You can also access the trail on Rainy Lake at Anderson Bay and walk the 2-mile Anderson Bay Island Loop.

LONGER HIKES The best hiking trail is the park's only hiking trail of any length—the **Cruiser Lake Trail.** It runs about 9 miles from Lost Bay on Kabetogama Lake to Rainy Lake, but there are a number of side loops you can take if you want a longer adventure. It's a good way to see the variety of the park's terrain, from spruce bogs to rocky ridges to tranquil lakes.

The trail is not terrifically challenging, but if you've got a pack on your back, it won't be a snap, either. Vermilion granite outcroppings pop up constantly, meaning good strong shoes are a must. The little waterways that course through the peninsula create a fair number of hills and valleys. Expect plenty of solitude, especially the deeper inland you go. There's so much solitude, in fact, that the trail can become all but hidden by grasses and ferns. In other words, it's not the beaten path, and you need to stay observant lest you lose the trail. If you do lose it, don't panic: Stacks of rocks, laid out by park staff, will help guide you back.

The hike is worth its small frustrations. There are several beautiful lakes along the way (all of which have small campgrounds), and the pine and spruce woods look and smell gorgeous. And you aren't restricted to the trail. If you're handy with a compass and a detailed map, you can walk nearly anywhere on the peninsula and experience greater solitude. There are several secluded lakes here, many of which also have campsites. One option: Get off the Cruiser Lake Trail system at Jorgens Lake and head to **Little Shoepack Lake.** There's a campsite on the lake, and if you've reserved ahead you can take the park service canoe and paddle it out onto Big Shoepack Lake (*see* Boating *in* Other Activities, *below*).

OTHER ACTIVITIES In the summer, all park activities are pursued either on foot or by boat. In the winter, skis and snowmobiles are the only transportation options.

Bird-Watching. The easiest birds to spot in the park are waterfowl. You'll probably see several species of ducks and mergansers on the big lakes, though the roar of motorboats can keep them away. More fearless gulls and pelicans congregate on small stony islands. Your luck will be better in secluded bays and channels protected from the wind. Wood ducks and common mergansers are typical sightings, and, in the evening, loons.

On land, the woods and the insects make birding more difficult and less pleasant. City birds such as robins, blue jays, and ravens are remarkably common in the park; in the morning, sparrows and warblers often appear. Bald eagles and ospreys are active throughout the day.

Boating. Boating, for fishing or just for pleasure, is the chief summer pastime at Voyageurs. There are boat launches at all the visitor centers, and private docks at most of the lakeside resorts. Most of these resorts rent boats; the fees vary (*see* Arriving and Departing by Boat *in* Essential Information, *above*). However, only experienced boaters should venture onto the lakes in Voyageurs, since they are filled with small islands and many rocks just below the surface. NOAA depth charts (*see* Publications *in* Essential Information, *above*) can help, but if you think you may be out of your league, find out whether the resort offers a guide service.

While the park service leaves most boat rentals to the resorts, it does offer **canoes** on various inland lakes—Locator, Cruiser, Ek, Loiten, Shoepack, and Little Shoepack. Though they are sometimes available the day you come up, it's best to reserve about a week in advance with the Kabetogama Lake Visitor's Center (tel. 218/875–2111). The canoes are locked up at shorelines; keys are available at visitor centers. You'll have to hike in on a trail to get one of the boats, but they'll make a delightful addition to your trip. What's more, they're free.

Motorboaters in the park must make themselves familiar with rules of navigation and the U.S. Coast Guard's numbered buoy system, which is used on the park's lakes. The park service's information packet on Voyageurs (*see* Visitor Information *in* Essential Information, *above*) includes a description of the buoy system and a newspaper that outlines rules of navigation, salient hazards, and safety tips. Plan your route in advance and discuss it with a ranger before you set out. Rangers can also advise you on especially scenic routes.

There is yet another boating option here during the May-to-October season: **houseboating.** Large double-decker craft, which feature sleeping and in most cases kitchen quarters, combine recreation with lodging. The four lessors are **Minnesota Voyageurs Houseboats** (10326 Ash River Trail, Orr 55771, tel. 218/374–3571), near the Ash River entrance; **Voyaguaire Houseboats** (7628 Gold Coast Rd., Crane Lake, MN 56725, tel. 800/882–6287); **Rainy Lake Houseboats** (Rte. 8, Box 408, International Falls 56649, tel. 218/286–5391), near Rainy Lake; and **Northernaire Floating Lodges** (HCR8, Box 510, International Falls, MN 56649), also near Rainy Lake. Depending on the number of people in your party and the size of the boat, rates range from about $200 to $500 per day, less if you rent by the week.

Cross-Country Skiing. The park's terrain—generally flat, with a few easy rolling hills here and there—makes it a good place for cross-country skiing. The park maintains the Black Bay Ski Trail, just across the Black Bay Narrows from the Rainy Lake Visitor Center. The looping trail covers about 8 miles. A map of it is available from the park office (*see* Visitor Information *in* Essential Information, *above*) upon request.

Fishing. Fishing is the chief reason people were coming up to the Voyageurs area before there was even a park. It's best during the months of May, June, September, and October. The most common fish here are yellow perch and northern pike, but the "big lakes" (Rainy, Kabetogama, Namakan, and Sandpoint) also boast black crappie, walleye, rock bass, and smallmouth bass. A few inland lakes offer largemouth bass and lake trout, even the occasional muskie.

During the winter, several of the large lakes are popular **ice-fishing** spots. The only way to get to them is by snowmobile. But you can bring and set up your own ice-fishing house. Houses are often equipped with small generators to run boom boxes, heaters, and TVs—which, along with beer, make the time after you've chopped a hole in the ice and dropped your line through pass more pleasantly. You can rent houses from **Ash Trail Lodge** (Ash River Trail, Orr 55771, tel. 218/374–3131 or 800/777–4513) and **Red Pine Lodge** (Lake Kabetogama, Ray 56669, tel. 218/875–2441 or 800/435–7301).

All visitors wishing to sink a line in the park lakes need to obtain a Minnesota fishing license. The information packet available from the park superintendent's office (*see* Visitor Information *in* Essential Information, *above*) contains information on fishing and fishing licenses; for more information about licenses, contact the **Minnesota Department of Natural Resources** (500 Lafayette Rd., St. Paul 55155, tel. 612/296–4506 or 800/652–9093).

Snowmobiling. This is the park's most popular wintertime sport, and the woodland trails are kept well-groomed. The park doesn't offer snowmobiles for rent, but several nearby resorts do, including **Ash-Ka-Nam** (Ash River Trail, Orr 55771, tel. 218/374–3181) and **Bunt's Bed & Breakfast Inns** (*see* Lodging, *below*). Most resorts open during the winter sell snowmobile gas and oil. Snowmobilers should obtain a snowmobile trail map from the park superintendent's office (*see* Visitor Information *in* Essential Information, *above*).

Snowshoeing. Snowshoeing is not discouraged, but the park does not rent snowshoes, and there are no designated snowshoeing trails.

Swimming. The best time for swimming here is from mid-July to mid-August, when the water warms up (though it will still be too chilly for some). There are no restrictions, but there are no beaches, changing facilities, or lifeguards, either. (There are leeches in some waters, so you should give yourself a once-over when you come out.) A beach with a changing facility is available at Woodenfrog State Campground, about 4 miles from Kabetogama.

CHILDREN'S PROGRAMS Besides its various guided tours (*see above*), Kabetogama Lake Visitor Center also offers a "Northwoods Puppet Show" twice weekly during the summer. The show stars several animals that live in Voyageurs and teaches children how they can help protect their north woods home. Rainy Lake Visitor's Center's various tours and events also include a once-a-week program called "Kids Explore Voyageurs," in which children 7–12, led by a naturalist, take a woodland walk and explore a beaver pond, among other outdoor sights.

EVENING ACTIVITIES Voyageurs offers a number of evening cruises and naturalist programs (*see* Guided Tours, *above*). There are no other social activities in the park.

DINING

Dining around Voyageurs is neither a gourmet affair nor an ethnic one. The food tends toward burgers and chicken, with steak and seafood (especially the locally caught walleye) representing the high end. (Walleye is white and flakey like cod, with a sweet, full flavor reminiscent of trout. It's often breaded and fried.) Most of the restaurants close by are attached to resorts; if you're staying around Rainy Lake, there are other options in International Falls. If you have a taste for something a bit more unusual, drive the 45 miles south to the Country Supper Club (*see below*). Needless to say, none of these places requires jacket and tie; casual but neat is the style.

INSIDE THE PARK **Kettle Falls Hotel.** Accessible only by boat, the Kettle Falls Hotel has had a long, colorful history (*see* Historic Buildings and Sites *in* Exploring, *above*), and it's still the only place that serves food and beverages inside the park. The restaurant is open for all three meals. The atmosphere is rustic, the food traditional northern Minnesota fare—chicken, hamburgers, and, of course, walleye. Dinners are all-you-can-eat with two entrées available. Even if you're a teetotaler, check out the bar; a large part of the floor still bears the marks of loggers' hobnail boots. *Ash River Trail, Orr, tel. 218/374–3631 or 800/322–0886. Reservations accepted. MC, V. Closed Oct. 1–May 15. Moderate.*

NEAR THE PARK **Country Supper Club.** Though it's nearly an hour from Kabetogama (an hour and a half from Rainy Lake), this is the place for some of the most distinctive food in the area. Chef/owner Bill Clazmer came up north after a long career in the Twin Cities, and he brings to this rural spot an unpretentiously but unmistakably urban sense. Sophisticated examples include Sicilian shrimp stuffed with spinach and basil and topped with Italian cheeses; grilled duck breast with green peppercorn sauce; and tasty homemade pizzas. A simpler lunch is served, too. *9257 Olson Rd. (Hwy. 910), Cook, tel. 218/666–5351. Reservations advised. D, MC, V. Moderate.*

Island View Lodge. Inside this cheerful, woodsy lakeside lodge near Rainy Lake (*see* Lodging, *below*) is a dining room with Diamond Willow furniture and wood paneling. The food ranges from typical Minnesota resort fare (walleye, barbecue) to fancier dishes simply prepared—lobster, shrimp, prime rib, filet mignon. *Hwy. 8, International Falls, tel. 218/286–3511. Reservations advised. AE, D, MC, V. Closed Nov. Moderate.*

Sandy Point Lodge. Inside this lodge—one of the newer ones on Kabetogama Lake (*see* Lodging, *below*)—is what many consider the vicinity's gourmet restaurant. It's gourmet, upper Midwest–style. Sure, you can get burgers and walleye here. But you also get steaks taken from specially raised beef brought in from Iowa. And the lodge loves to use northern Minnesota wild rice. Besides steaks, the house specialty is Voyageur chicken, sautéed in herbs, served on a bed of wild rice, then further enlivened with a rosemary cream sauce. Breads and rolls are homemade. The ambience here is a cleaner, newer kind of rustic, with log-paneled walls and a big open fireplace. *10606 Gamma Rd., Ray (Kabetogama), tel. 218/875–2615. Reservations advised. MC, V. Moderate.*

Bait & Bite. This spot near Kabetogama is especially popular with locals and regular visitors for its breakfasts, which are hearty in a Main-Street, Minnesota-café manner. Lunches and dinners are casual, with hamburgers and chicken leading the way. The restaurant's log building also contains a bait and tackle shop. *9634 Gamma Rd., Kabeto-*

gama, tel. 218/875–2281. No reservations. MC, V. Closed Oct.–Apr. Inexpensive.

Bunt's Bar & Grill. With its woody interior and bar-food menu (burgers, fried chicken, pie), Bunt's is in many respects a typical Voyageurs-area restaurant. Its log walls and log bar give it just the right feel for a place to come to after a day of fishing—a good place to have a beer, talk sports, and exchange fish tales. Add a big-screen TV and several pool tables, and it doesn't get any better than this, for what it is. On Sunday there's a substantial all-you-can-eat brunch. *Gappa and Burma Rds., Kabetogama, tel. 218/875–3700. No reservations. AE, D, MC, V. Inexpensive.*

LODGING

Before Voyageurs became a national park, the area had long been popular for its fishing and hunting. Numerous mom-and-pop resorts—cozy, modest, and unfancy—opened to cater to the anglers and hunters and their families. Many still exist, and they comprise nearly all the lodging around the park. A few inexpensive ones consist, in effect, of small trailer homes; most of the rest are made up of campgrounds, cottages, and cabins; and a few small lodges round out the selection. The owners tend to be friendly and very helpful. Nearly all the places fall into the Inexpensive to Moderate categories; most offer boat rental, a boat launch, and even fishing guides. The park's information packet (*see* Visitor Information *in* Essential Information, *above*) includes a list of resorts, the services they offer, and when they're closed. Most are in business only during the May-to-October season, but several stay open year-round.

For visitors looking for something a little different, four vendors offer houseboats for rent (*see* Other Activities *in* Exploring, *above*).

INSIDE THE PARK **Kettle Falls Hotel.** This is the only lodging inside the park, and certainly the most colorful place to stay in the area (*see* Historic Buildings and Sites *in* Exploring, *above*). The exterior is pleasant and unexceptional—something like a barn with a front porch and awnings. The inside is what's special. The hotel closed in the 1970s but was lovingly and painstakingly restored in the mid-'80s—taken apart board by board, cleaned and fixed up, then put back together. "Modernizing" has generally been restricted to plumbing and electricity and new mattresses. Most of the furnishings are early 20th-century originals or reproductions. The one drawback is that you can get there only by boat. However, tour boats do shuttle back and forth from park visitor's centers to the hotel four times a week, and the hotel offers shuttle service from Ash River. *Ash River Trail, Orr 55771, tel. 218/374–3631 or 800/322–0886. 12 rooms share 3 baths. Facilities: restaurant (see Dining, above), boat rental and fuel. MC, V. Closed Oct.–mid-May. Moderate (modified American plan: Rates include breakfast and dinner).*

NEAR THE PARK **Bunt's Bed & Breakfast Inns.** Bunt's represents the high-end option around the park. Located near the Kabetogama entrance, the complex comprises a four-bedroom B&B, a two-bedroom beach house on the lake, and a three-bedroom bungalow. All have kitchens; all are modern, like upper-middle-class suburban homes with a few rustic touches. The B&B is the most private, surrounded by thick woods and connected to the water by a path. The beach house is right on the water and has a boat dock. Wherever you stay, the rate includes a Continental breakfast. *9906 Gappa Rd., Ray 56669, tel. 218/875–2691 or 218/875–3700. Facilities (B&B and bungalow only): sauna, whirlpool, fireplace. AE, MC, V. Moderate–Expensive.*

Thunderbird Lodge. A somewhat newer resort than Island View (*see below*), the Thunderbird nonetheless goes for the woodsy-rustic look that most of the higher-end Voyageurs lodges pursue. It's close to the Rainy Lake Visitor's Center. The comfortable rooms are decorated with a little more warmth than in a good-quality motel, but they don't all face Rainy Lake—so ask. The restaurant and lounge are more elegant than most area places, with high windows looking out onto a broad expanse of blue water. *Hwy. 8, Box 402, International Falls 56649, tel. 218/286–3151, fax 218/286–3004. 15 rooms with bath, 8 cabins. Facilities: restaurant, bar, tennis courts, boat rental. AE, D, MC. V. Moderate–Expensive.*

Island View Lodge. This pleasant little lodge lists its address as International Falls, but it's actually on Dove Island, an old community of summer cabins and resorts beyond the Rainy Lake Visitor's Center. Built in the 1930s (its predecessor, erected at the turn of the century, stands nearby, unoccupied), the double-decked redwood lodge is agreeably rustic, and it faces onto Rainy Lake, so request a lake view. The rooms are decorated in undistinguished (but still pleasant) motel fashion. *Rte. 8, Box 411, International Falls 50649, tel. 218/286–3511, fax 218/286–5036. 9 rooms with bath, 11 cabins. Facilities: beach, restaurant (see Dining, above). AE, D, MC. V. Closed Nov. Moderate.*

Sandy Point Lodge. Set on a narrow spit of land 3 miles west of the Kabetogama Lake Visitor's Center, Sandy Point is one of the newer resorts around Voyageurs. It was built in 1987, but it emulates the old area style with its rustic, log-paneled walls. The log theme is picked up in some of the furnishings, notably the bedsteads. Overall, however, the lodge represents a newer, smoother kind of rusticity. (The resort's housekeeping cabins are some 20 years older, but similar in style.) *10606 Gamma Rd., Ray 56669, tel. 218/875–2615. 8 rooms share 2 baths, 12 cabins. Facilities: restaurant (see Dining, above), bar, canoe and boat rental. MC, V. Moderate.*

CAMPING

All camping in the park is tent camping. There are 120 developed campsites, most of them accessible only by boat. The exceptions are those on the Cruiser Lake Trail, which can be reached only on foot (but you need a boat to get to the trail itself). There are no camping fees. Campsites can't be reserved, which usually isn't a problem early in the season. In July and August, get there soon— or zero in on a part of the park where campsites are numerous, such as the Namakan Narrows or Sheen Point. The sites themselves typically have two 12-foot square sandy tent pads, and each site has a fire grate, a picnic table, and a pit toilet (i.e., without a roof overhead). Many have bear-proof storage lockers. Camping is limited to 14 days at a site. You are not restricted to camping at designated sites, but it's preferred, and it's certainly easier. Some sites may be closed when you visit; check the bulletin boards at park boat ramps.

INSIDE THE PARK All the campsites on the Cruiser Lake Trail are on small, tree-lined lakes—which means great views, a water source (but be sure to filter or boil), and an excellent chance that loons will serenade you to sleep. Don't be alarmed by large splashes; they're far more likely to be caused by beavers or deer than by bears. The campsite on Cruiser Lake itself is on a small island accessible by footboards, hard by a beaver lodge whose residents are fairly unafraid. Pets are not allowed on trails. The trailhead is accessible only by boat.

Boaters have many more choices. All the boat-accessible sites are on the big lakes, many on their own tiny islands or peninsulas.

There are large clusters of campsites around Sheen Point several miles from the Ash River boat access, and around the Namakan Narrows near Crane Lake. Pets are allowed, but they must be leashed at all times.

NEAR THE PARK Campers with cars and RVs can find a place to stay at **Woodenfrog State Campground** (tel. 218/757–3274 for information; fee: $7 per night; no reservations; open year-round), 5 miles from the Kabetogama Lake Visitor's Center. Outside of running water and washrooms, it doesn't have a great many services, but it does have a swimming beach and 60 campsites, some of them overlooking Rainy Lake. Many resorts near each of the entrances also have campgrounds; the resort listings inside the park newspaper, available at visitor's centers and through the park superintendent's office (*see* Visitor Information *in* Essential Information, *above*), can tell you which ones. RVs also are welcome at the **International Voyageur RV Park** (U.S. 53, International Falls, tel. 218/283–4679; open May–Sept.) near Rainy Lake, which offers 60 RV sites, as well as a dump station and bathhouse.

White Mountain National Forest
Maine, New Hampshire
By Tara Hamilton

ubbed "Aqiocochook," Home of the Great Spirit, by the Abenaki, Sokosis, and Pennacock tribes of the Algonquian nation who inhabited what is now the northeastern United States, Mt. Washington is the centerpiece of White Mountain National Forest. This mammoth, brooding peak—the tallest in New England at 6,288 feet—still evokes a sense of awe. Wind velocities of 231 miles per hour, the greatest ever recorded, were measured at its summit, and its Antarctic-like temperatures are the ultimate lows broadcast to New Englanders every winter. Along with its adjacent brethren in the Presidential Range, Mt. Washington presides over 773,000 acres that spread across parts of central and northern New Hampshire and into a small section of western Maine.

The Presidential peaks north and northeast of Mt. Washington extend out into an arc that encompasses the Great Gulf, the largest glacial cirque in the White Mountains; to the southwest, they rise and fall above tree line several times before finally descending into the woods below Mt. Pierce, and form a ridge that reaches 8 miles to the Webster Cliffs above Crawford Notch. The central region of the White Mountains is also dotted with mountains: The Twin and Willey mountain ranges to the north and east form a giant horseshoe with the Franconia Range to the west. Sharper and craggier than the Presidentials, though slightly smaller, the Franconias are no less beautiful.

The White Mountain National Forest is divided into five ranger's districts: Ammonoosuc, Androscoggin, Evans Notch (Maine), Pemigewasset, and Saco. The most heavily visited areas, Mt. Washington Valley along Route 16, the Kancamagus Highway, and Franconia Notch, are worthy of their popularity because of their spectacular terrain, but they are by no means the only compelling places to visit in the forest. Within the patchwork of national forest lands, a number of state parks—among them, Crawford Notch and Franconia Notch—preserve stunning natural formations and provide educational information and programs.

The above-tree-line summits offer magnificent views of the lush forest, but it is not until you've descended from their heights that the essence of the vast woodland is revealed. It is an expanse of towering cliffs and gutted ravines; of narrow, sheer notches etched between masses of ancient mountains; of surging cascades and swiftly flowing rivers. It is a wilderness of moose and bear; of birch, beech, and spruce; of birdsong and howling wind and silence.

That's not to say that White Mountain National Forest is entirely wild and pristine. Just outside its boundaries lie an abundance of hotels, motels, restaurants, factory outlets, miniature golf courses, and tourist attractions, some of the gaudiest kind. And there's plenty of human activity and enterprise within the forest's boundaries, too. A national forest rather than a national park, White Mountain is not maintained solely for preservation, but managed for multiple uses. In addition to recreational activities, these include timber production, watershed preservation, and wildlife habitat management. The forest service manages logging operations so that trails, streams, campsites, and other significant sites are protected—an effort that often has the organization walking the fine line between community interest in development and jobs and environmentalist interest in leaving the forest untouched.

The Wilderness Act of 1964 designated 15% of the forest for special protection. Low-key recreation is encouraged in these wilderness areas; man-made structures are restricted and mechanized equipment and vehicles, including bicycles, are prohibited. The forest service has also established nine scenic areas in the national forest, small preserves in which camping is not allowed: Gibbs Brook, Nancy Brook, Greeley Ponds, Pinkham Notch, Lafayette Brook, Rocky Gorge, Lincoln Woods, Sawyer Pond, and Snyder Brook.

ESSENTIAL INFORMATION

VISITOR INFORMATION For detailed information about the national forest, write to Forest Supervisor, **White Mountain National Forest** (Box 638, Laconia, NH 03247, tel. 603/528–9528, TT 603/528–8722). The following ranger's stations can also help you: **Ammonoosuc** (Trudeau Rd., Box 230, Bethlehem, NH 03574, tel. 603/869–2626); **Androscoggin** (Rte. 16, Gorham, NH 03581, tel. 603/466–2713); **Evans Notch** (Rte. 2, Box 2270, Bethel, ME 04217, tel. 207/824–2134); **Pemigewasset** (Rte. 175, Box 15, Plymouth, NH 03264, tel. 603/536–1310); or **Saco** (Kancamagus Hwy., 33 Kancamagus Hwy., Conway, NH 03818, tel. 603/447–5448, TT 603/447–1989).

The **Pinkham Notch Visitor Center** (Rte. 16, Box 298, Gorham, NH 03581, tel. 603/466–2725), the northern New England regional office headquarters of the nonprofit Appalachian Mountain Club, is an educational and recreational visitor center operating under a special-use permit with the forest service. Open daily 8 AM–10 PM, it provides hikers with information on the Appalachian Trail and all other trails maintained by the organization.

White Mountain Visitor Center (Rte. 112, Box 10, N. Woodstock, NH 03262, tel. 603/745–8720) and **Mt. Washington Valley Visitors Bureau** (Rte. 16, Box 2300-G, North Conway, NH 03860, tel. 603/356–3171) both provide information about the towns in the vicinity of the forest as well as about the forest itself. You can also contact **Franconia/Easton/Sugar Hill Chamber of Commerce** (Box D, Franconia, NH 03580, tel. 603/823–5661), **Lincoln/Woodstock Chamber of Commerce** (Rte. 112, Box 358, Lincoln, NH 03251, tel. 603/745–6621), and **Waterville Valley Region Chamber of Commerce** (Rte. 49, Box 1067, Campton, NH 03223 tel. 603/726–3804 or 800/237–2307) for other area information.

FEES Although there are no entrance or permit fees for White Mountain National Forest, there are admission charges for the state parks, state and national forest campgrounds, and some of the backcountry tent sites and shelters within the forest.

PUBLICATIONS A variety of one-page fact sheets available at the ranger's stations and information centers (*see* Visitor Information, *above*) cover such diverse topics as Native American place-names, alpine plants, and scenic waterfalls in the national forest. Mimeographed handouts about many of the hikes in the forest include information on local flora and fauna. Also available here free of charge are various maps, brochures, and regulation sheets pertaining to mountain biking, snowmobiling, and fishing and boating in the forest.

Available at most bookstores in the Northeast, the *AMC White Mountain Guide,* published by the Appalachian Mountain Club, is the most comprehensive and useful book on hiking in White Mountain National Forest.

GEOLOGY AND TERRAIN By geologic time, the White Mountains, at roughly 300 to 400 million years old, are middle-aged—younger siblings of the nearby Green and Adirondack mountains and older than the youthful ranges of the western United States. Their origins, though, are similar to the East Coast's entire Appalachian family. A series of mountain-building periods caused by tectonic plate collision resulted in a heating, crumpling, and uplifting of the Appalachian geosyncline, sediments piled deep in coastal areas from earlier upland erosion.

Nature's activity became evident again during the most recent ice age, when glaciers carved and sculpted the mountaintops and valleys. Jagged peaks were softened, sharp-cut river valleys were rounded, amphitheater-like cirques and ravines were scoured, and, when the ice receded, rocks and boulders were left scattered willy-nilly across the landscape.

Though still among the tallest mountains in the eastern United States—dozens of peaks rise over 4,000 feet and a handful over 5,000—these peaks have been trimmed by erosion from what may have been twice their current height. With many of the peaks reaching above tree line, the White Mountains' two highest sub-ranges, the Presidential and Franconia, still maintain a decidedly rugged appearance, with granite cliffs and outcroppings. Down below, dense forests hide fast-rushing mountain streams cascading down from the highlands and carrying a cargo of rock and sand to be deposited on the continental shelf in preparation for becoming the mountains of the future.

FLORA AND FAUNA Steep mountainsides, dense forests, and long, harsh winters bear strong influences on the forms of wildlife found in the White Mountain National Forest. Black bears and white-tailed deer roam valley floors in spring in search of food, as do bobcats and fishers, which can occasionally be spotted on open ridges. Mink follow watercourses, and beaver ponds occur throughout the forest. Other species include red fox, porcupine, raccoon, snowshoe hare, weasel, and woodchuck.

Weighing in at about 1,000 pounds and measuring up to 6 feet at the shoulder, the largest animal in the White Mountains is the moose. Its gangly grace and unpredictability make sighting one an unforgettable experience. Often spotted at lower elevations and along roadsides in the spring, where they seek food and refuge from the black flies, moose tend to be active at night, making car–moose collisions an increasing problem.

Those who hike in the White Mountain National Forest to any summit above tree line will pass through a succession of natural zones, from lowland deciduous forest to alpine tundra. Northern hardwoods of American beech, various maples, and yellow and paper birch cover much of the forest at lower elevations, where oaks and white pines may also be seen. Hemlocks dominate in some of the deeper valleys, and red pines often line ledges above 2,000 feet. At 3,000 feet, the forest evolves into a mix of birch, spruce, and balsam fir; and, at 4,000 feet, the trees become twisted and stunted—odd, people-size specimens called krummholz (German for "crooked wood")—and interspersed with dense, low mats of vegetation. Above the timberline, they cease to exist altogether, replaced by the low-lying sedges, grasses, lichens, and mosses that cover the rocky surfaces and isolated patches atop the highest peaks.

With 8 square miles above timberline, this is the largest alpine tundra area in the country east of the Rockies. The alpine vegetation here is well adapted to the harsh wind and cold. Evergreen perennials grow close to the ground and often have leaves that overlap each other or have protective coverings. Often found high up in the Presidential and Franconia ranges, many of these tiny alpine plants flower from early spring to midsummer; they are best seen in late June. Some of the most frequently seen are the five-petaled white diapensia, minuscule pink alpine azalea, white Labrador tea, and pink-magenta Lapland rosebay. Common in the White Mountains, mountain avens is found elsewhere only on a small island off Nova Scotia. Robbins (dwarf) cinquefoil, a fuzzy plant with yellow flowers, grows only in a small area in the Presidential Range and is one of the rarest species in the United States.

WHEN TO GO The highlight of any north country excursion is seeing the wildflowers bloom in May and June. Spring is also an ideal time to explore the national forest unhindered by the summer crowds. Mosquitoes and black flies can be a nuisance, but if you come armed with a good bug repellent and a little determination, this is an inspiring time to be in the White Mountains.

Summer is the most popular season to visit. The national forest is sufficiently vast, however, to afford isolation to those willing to get off the beaten track, and to absorb the hordes of travelers who flock here. If avoiding crowds is a priority, head to the less developed sections of the forest east of Route 16 and north of Route 2, or hike a few miles into the backcountry.

In late September and early October, busloads of leaf peepers can turn the Kancamagus Highway—arguably the most beautiful, and unquestionably the most popular, foliage road in the Northeast—into a virtual parking lot. Make reservations well in advance if you plan to come at this popular time. And consider coming during the few weeks between Labor Day and peak foliage; this period can be the most pleasant, with moderate crowds and temperatures.

Although winter in the northeastern mountains is known for its severity, it rivals the other three seasons for beauty. The mountains also provide a perfect setting for winter sports: Downhill and cross-country skiing are ever popular in the White Mountains, as is snowmobiling.

Be aware, however, that the Presidential and Franconia ranges are subject to some of the worst weather on the planet and Mt. Washington's reputation as the most dangerous small mountain in the world should not be taken lightly. Hurricane-force winds, dense fog, and snow occur even during the summer months, and sudden and extreme weather is common: Winds of 100 miles per hour blow every month of the year.

SEASONAL EVENTS **Fourth weekend in June:** Folks either flock to, or flee from, Mt. Washington Valley during the annual **Auto Road Hill Climb,** when racers turn the Mt. Washington Auto Toll Road into a drag strip. Beware: The mufflerless vehicles can be heard from the other side of the Great Gulf Wilderness! **July–August:** A gigantic tent pitched at Settlers' Green in North Conway provides concerts, dance, and circus acts during the local **Arts Jubilee** (tel. 603/745–8720). **Mid-September:** The **Highland Games** (tel. 603/964–9634 or 603/745–8111) bring fife and drum bands and other music, dance, and athletics to the town of Lincoln at Loon Mountain.

WHAT TO PACK Mountain weather is fickle, so it's best to bring layers of clothing when visiting the area, no matter what the time of year. Hikers and campers in particular should be prepared for anything, especially at higher elevations.

Your day pack should always contain a layer of wool, fleece, or other wicking material; rain gear; long pants; spare socks (not cotton);

wool hat and mittens; flashlight; extra food and water; matches; first-aid kit; sunscreen; a knife; a map and a compass. Good walking shoes or hiking boots are essential, even for short jaunts into the woods. Even if you don't intend to venture into the woods very often, bring along a pair of binoculars to enrich your porch sitting.

GENERAL STORES You can find general stores at all corners of the White Mountains. The larger towns of Berlin, Gorham, Jackson, Glen, North Conway, Conway, Lincoln, North Woodstock, and Franconia all have supermarkets and sporting goods stores on their main streets. The **Holy Cow Market** (tel. 603/846–5541) on Route 302 just east of Route 3 at Twin Mountain is stocked with essentials. **Crawford Notch General Store** (tel. 603/374–2779) on Route 302 south of Crawford Notch State Park is a good place to pick up such last-minute supplies as fishing hooks and Coleman fuel; it also has a minimal selection of food. **Thornton Country Store** (tel. 603/726–8665) on Route 3 in Thornton is amply stocked with groceries and camping gear. **Tripoli Country Store** (tel. 603/745–6421) on Tripoli Road north of Waterville Valley is only open in the summer but has a good selection of sporting goods.

ARRIVING AND DEPARTING By Plane. Laconia **Municipal Airport** (30 mi south of southern boundary of the forest, tel. 603/524–5003) has facilities for charters and private planes; **Lebanon Municipal Airport** (35 mi southwest of the southern boundary of the forest, tel. 603/298–8878) is served by USAir, Northwest, and Delta/Business Express.

By Car and RV. Running north–south from Massachusetts to Quebec, I–93 and Route 3 bisect the White Mountain National Forest at its western end. Route 16, also running north–south, accesses the eastern portion of the forest, slicing through the Mt. Washington Valley. The Kancamagus Highway (Route 112) and Route 2 are the east–west thoroughfares that access the southern and northern regions of the national forest, respectively. Route 302 winds through the central portion

of the forest in a southeast-to-northwest direction.

The official state map, available free from the Office of Travel and Tourism Development (Box 856, Concord, NH 03302, tel. 603/271–2666), has useful directories for each of the tourist areas.

By Train. There is no standard rail service into the White Mountain National Forest or into any of the neighboring towns.

By Bus. Concord Trailways (tel. 603/228–3300 or 800/639–3317 in NH) offers daily service to and from South Station in Boston; one route goes up Route 16 through Conway, North Conway, Jackson, Glen, Pinkham Notch, Gorham, and Berlin; while another travels along Route 93, stopping at Woodstock, Lincoln, Franconia Notch, and Littleton. The **Appalachian Mountain Club** (tel. 603/466–2727 for schedules and rate information) operates a hiker shuttle bus during the summer that runs between Pinkham Notch Visitor Center and most of the major trail heads within the national forest.

EXPLORING

Without a car, exploring the expanses of the national forest is difficult, if not impossible. But investigating every corner of this large region is not necessarily preferable to immersing yourself in a single area. Pedal a bicycle, paddle a canoe, ride a horse, or take a hike for at least part of your stay to really get a sense of the White Mountains. The time spent outside your car will afford a variety of perspectives on the beauty of the forest.

THE BEST IN ONE DAY Start early from North Conway, with breakfast behind you and a picnic lunch in tow, heading north on Route 16; to avoid the congestion caused by the popular outlet stores, take a left off Route 16 in neighboring Conway onto West Side Road, which runs parallel to the more frenetic route through town. About 4 miles north, turn left for the 1-mile drive up to Cathedral Ledge and a rewarding view of the valley below. Then head east to Route 16 and make a left, heading north. Short side trips to the towns of Inter-

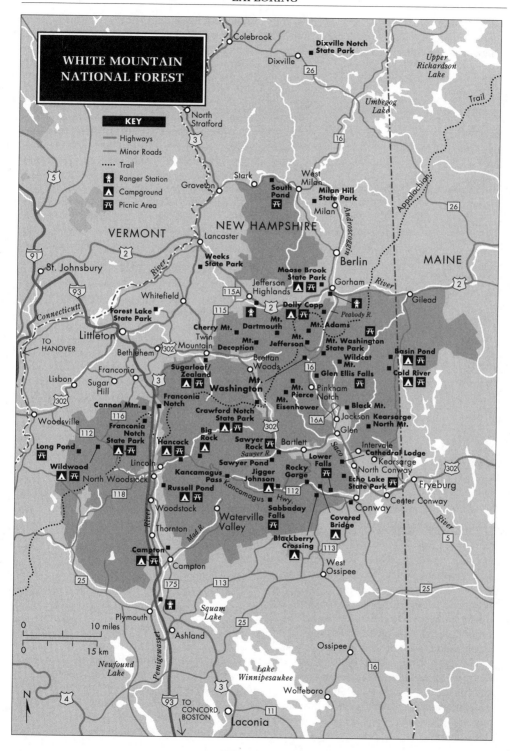

vale, Lower Bartlett, and Jackson will provide a more endearing version of small-town New Hampshire than does North Conway.

Continue north on Route 16 into Pinkham Notch and the heart of the White Mountains' Presidential Range. The Appalachian Mountain Club headquarters and visitor's center here will help get you oriented. If you are interested in a hike, this is the place to ask for suggestions.

After spending some time in Pinkham Notch, head north to Gorham and turn left on Route 2. Fourteen miles to the west in Jefferson Highlands, turn left on Route 115 for a cut through to Route 302 in Twin Mountain and an easterly turn to Bretton Woods and Crawford Notch State Park. Or better yet, in Jefferson Highlands, take the more adventurous Jefferson Notch Road south between Mt. Dartmouth and Mt. Adams and Mt. Jefferson into Bretton Woods and then Route 302 into Crawford Notch. This serene valley is a good place to break out the picnic lunch and to enjoy a short hike afterward.

Backtrack northwest on Route 302, bearing left onto Route 3 south in Twin Mountain for the 10-mile drive into Franconia Notch State Park, where you might take a dip in Echo Lake. Or consider making a detour via Route 18 to the village of Franconia, renting a bicycle, and spending the afternoon riding the 9-mile bike path that slices through the notch.

ORIENTATION PROGRAMS The **Appalachian Mountain Club** offers hundreds of educational programs each year, most of them out of the Pinkham Notch Visitor Center. Among them are day programs covering a wide range of topics, including geology, meteorology, and forest ecology; workshops focusing on outdoor skills, such as backpacking, canoeing, snowshoeing, orienteering, and telemark skiing; and hikes led by skilled guides with extensive knowledge of the natural and cultural history of the White Mountains. For more information, contact AMC Education Programs (Rte. 16, Box 298, Gorham, NH 03581, tel. 603/466–2721).

GUIDED TOURS **Outdoor Bound** (Bear Swamp Rd., Montpelier, VT 05602, tel. 800/223–4172) offers a guided hut-to-hut hiking tour in the Presidential Range. **Great Outdoors Hiking and Walking Vacations** (Stonehurst Manor, Box 1937, North Conway, NH 03860, tel. 603/356–3113 or 800/525–9100) caters programs to various ages and abilities. **New England Hiking Holidays** (Box 1648, North Conway, NH 03860, tel. 603/356–9696 or 800/869–0949) and **Hiking Holidays** (Monkton Rd., Bristol, VT 05443, tel. 802/453–4816) both offer two- to five-day inn-to-inn tours. The **Appalachian Mountain Club** (*see* Orientation Programs, *above*) publishes a catalog, which makes choosing from its daunting array of guided hikes a bit easier.

SCENIC DRIVES AND VIEWS The 34-mile **Kancamagus Highway** (Rte. 112 east of Lincoln) is the most scenic of the many scenic drives in the national forest. Although it can be overrun with sightseers in summer and fall foliage season, it's a photographer's dream. One of the most stunning vistas in the Mt. Washington Valley is from the top of **Cathedral Ledge,** which can be reached via the winding road that heads west off West Side Road, 4 miles north of its junction with Route 16 in Conway. For a tour under a wilderness canopy, take Route 49 east from Campton to Waterville Valley and then **Tripoli Road** back around to I–93. **Routes 112** and **118** in the section of the forest west of I–93 offer panoramic views east toward the higher peaks. **Route 302,** from Glen to Bethlehem via Crawford Notch State Park, affords awesome views of the Presidential Range and makes a convenient loop when combined with the Kancamagus and **I–93** through Franconia State Park; this section of the interstate is a two-lane, reduced-speed "parkway" that was completed after 25 years of haggling between conservationists and those pushing for a north–south transportation corridor.

The **Mt. Washington Auto Road,** a toll road to Mt. Washington open when weather conditions permit, begins at Glen House, 16 miles north of Glen. There are frequent rest stops. The cost is $14 for the car and driver, $5 for each adult passenger, $3 for children 5 through 12; call 603/466–3988 for additional information.

HISTORIC BUILDINGS AND SITES Just outside the bounds of the national forest, the **John Wingate Weeks Historic Site** on the top of Mt. Prospect, off Route 3 near Lancaster, is the estate and mansion of the former U.S. senator and secretary of war who introduced the legislation that led to the establishment of the White Mountain National Forest Reserve. The site is on the National Register of Historic Places and is part of the New Hampshire state park system.

Also outside the confines of the forest is the **Robert Frost Place,** home to the poet for many years. Two rooms contain memorabilia and signed editions of his books, and behind the house a .5-mile nature trail is posted with lines of Frost's verse. On summer evenings, there are readings by visiting poets. *Ridge Rd., off Rte. 116 in Franconia, tel. 603/823–5510. Admission: $3 adults, $2 senior citizens, $1.25 children 6–15. Open Memorial Day–June, weekends 1–5; July–Columbus Day, Wed.–Mon. 1–5.*

NATURE TRAILS AND SHORT WALKS The White Mountains offer a staggering number of short hikes, which provide everything from panoramic vistas to wilderness solitude. In Franconia Notch State Park, the 1.5-mile loop to **Artist's Bluff and Bald Mountain** is an easy hike that culminates in fine views of Cannon Mountain and the notch; the trailhead is on Route 18, just across from the Peabody Base Lodge. Also in Franconia is a slightly more challenging climb to **Lonesome Lake,** nestled 1,000 feet above the valley floor. It's 1.25 miles to the lake from Lafayette Campground via the Lake Trail.

For a view of the 200-foot drop of **Arethusa Falls,** the highest in the state, take the moderate 1.3-mile trail beginning off Route 302, a half mile south of the Dry River Campground in Crawford Notch State Park. Return via the same route, or extend the hike into a 3-mile loop past Frankenstein Cliff.

An abundance of short hikes, leading to cascades, rock formations, and other outstanding views, depart from the Kancamagus Highway. The **Sabbaday Falls Trail** is a .5-mile hike with interpretive signs that leads along a narrow flume; the trail starts at the picnic area 15 miles west of Conway. Five miles east of the picnic area is an easy, 3-mile hike to **Champney** and **Pitcher Falls.** And for great views of the Swift River Valley, try the 4-mile round-trip to the summit of Mt. Potash. Follow the Downes Brook Trail across from Passaconaway Campground and then veer right onto the **Mt. Potash Trail.**

An easy 20-minute walk partway up the **Tuckerman Ravine Trail,** beginning behind the Pinkham Notch Visitor Center, leads to the Crystal Cascade. Walk just across the road from the visitor's center to the trailhead of a half-hour hike to **Lost Pond;** it will take you past beaver ponds, along a mountain stream, and through thick forest.

LONGER HIKES Be sure to choose your route carefully and carry a good map if you plan to take a long hike in the White Mountain National Forest; it's also a good idea to check in with a ranger's station before you leave to get information about possible trail changes. Although conditions are often not hazardous, it is *extremely important* when hiking in the high country to be aware of the weather forecast; stop in at or phone the Pinkham Notch Visitor Center (tel. 603/466–2725, line open 8 AM–10 PM) for weather information. If you hike above the tree line, always stay on the trail. If the weather deteriorates while you are hiking in the Franconia or Presidential ranges, turn back; it will not improve.

An easy, well-marked loop, the **Imp Trail** in the Androscoggin ranger district leads to the "Imp Profile," an intriguing, facelike rock formation. The summit of this countenance offers commanding views of the Presidential Range. From opposite the Dolly Copp Campground, ascend to the profile, continue another mile to the junction with North Carter Trail, and then continue on the Imp Trail for 3.2 miles to Route 6. It's a 6-mile trip in all.

Crawford Path in the Ammonoosuc district is the oldest continuously used mountain trail in the eastern United States. Ascending first to Mt. Clinton and then across the ridge to Mt. Washington, it is a rigorous trail, 5 miles of it above tree line and exposed to the full force of most storm systems that come through the area. Begin on Route 302 after parking in the lot on Mt. Clinton Road; you'll pass Gibbs Falls and the Gibbs Brook Scenic area, where there is a rare virgin stand of spruce and birch. After passing a junction with the Webster Cliff Trail at the 2.9 mile marker, the Crawford Path traverses several ledges, offering magnificent views on its way from Mt. Clinton to Mt. Eisenhower. At 4.8 miles, the trail begins to ascend Mt. Franklin, passing the summit of Mt. Monroe before reaching the Lakes of the Clouds hut and beginning the final ascent of the cone of Mt. Washington. Those intending to attempt this hike should be well prepared and in good physical condition. Remember, if weather conditions deteriorate, turn back. It is 8.2 miles to the summit of Mt. Washington, so make arrangements to stay at one of the shelters or tent sites in the vicinity; call or write the Pinkham Notch Visitor Center (Box 298, Gorham, NH 03581, tel. 603/466–2727) for reservations.

Welch Mountain's bold, rocky peak comprises the western wall of the narrow southern aperture through which the Mad River flows out of Waterville Valley in the Pemigewasset ranger district; Dickey Mountain is a short distance to the northwest. Exposed mountain summits below 4,000 feet are rare, but fire bared the tops of these two peaks; as a result, the views from their summits— which are relatively easy to attain—are outstanding. The **Welch/Dickey Mountain Trail** leaves from a parking area on Orris Road (take Mad River Road—reached 4.5 miles from the junction of Route 49 with Route 175—to Orris Road), quickly reaching the ridge of Welch Mountain at 1.3 miles. Waterville Valley can be seen below from ledges here, but the trail climbs farther through contorted jack pine, blueberry bushes, and dwarfed spruce and birch to reach the summit at 2 miles. After enjoying this panorama, continue on the trail, passing through a wooded col and up a natural staircase, toward the exposed summit of

Dickey and another chance to touch the sky. This hike is 4.5 miles round-trip.

Outstanding views may be had from the top of Caribou Mountain in the Evans Notch ranger district. The **Caribou Trail** leaves Route 113 about 6 miles north of the Cold River Campground and follows Morrison Brook for 2.25 miles, crossing it several times before reaching 25-foot-high Kees Falls at 1.9 miles. At 2.9 miles, turn right on Mud Brook Trail to reach the summit. There is a shelter about halfway between the trail junction and the top of Caribou. It's a relatively easy 3.5-mile hike to the summit, with some steep sections toward the top.

The hike to Mt. Kearsarge North in the Saco ranger district leads to one of the finest vantage points in the White Mountains. Head out from the parking area 1.5 miles east of Route 16/302 on the north side of Hurricane Mountain Road in Kearsarge, just north of North Conway. **Mt. Kearsarge North Trail** begins on an old logging road, becoming progressively steeper and reaching open ledges that afford views of the Saco River Valley and peaks to the west and south; at 2.4 miles, the trail crests the ridge that connects Kearsarge North with Bartlett Mountain and climbs to the summit, which is 3.1 miles from the beginning of the trailhead. To return, retrace your steps back down.

With the passage of the National Trails System Act by Congress on October 2, 1968, the **Appalachian Trail** (AT) became the first federally protected footpath in the United States. The AT traverses the White Mountains for about 17 miles from Hanover, New Hampshire, to Grafton Notch in Maine, crossing many of the major peaks and ranges in the national forest; its most stunning sections are those where it crosses the high ridges of the Franconia and Presidential ranges. For those who would prefer to travel without the weight of a backpack, the Appalachian Mountain Club huts offer a nice alternative to camping. The AMC also manages several rustic shelters and tent sites just off the Appalachian Trail. For detailed information, write to the **Appalachian Trail Conference** (Box 236,

Harpers Ferry, WV 25425) or **Appalachian Mountain Club** (5 Joy St., Boston, MA 02108, tel. 617/523–0636).

OTHER ACTIVITIES Back-Road Driving. **Cherry Mountain Road** is a dramatic drive on a narrow dirt road that runs for 7 miles from Route 302 about 1 mile west of the Fabyan Motel in Fabyan to the junction of Routes 115 and 115A, passing through the high notch that separates Cherry Mountain and Mt. Dartmouth and Mt. Deception of the Dartmouth Range. In the same area, and a logical continuation if you're looking to get in some more four-wheel-drive mileage is **Jefferson Notch Road,** which leads from Jefferson Highlands at the junction of U.S. 115 and U.S. 2 through the mountains to Bretton Woods on Route 302. At over 3,000 feet, the Jefferson Notch crossing is the highest public road in the state. On the far western edge of the national forest, north of Route 112 and west of Route 116, are several dirt roads worthy of exploration. Forest service roads 310A and 353 make their way between Cobble Hill and Moody Ledge. There are no views, but the abandoned **South Landaff Road,** off of Route 112, leads to an area strewn with intriguing stone walls, cellar holes, and other remnants of old abandoned farms; this road continues for another 1.5 miles across private land to Mill Brook Road south of Landaff Center. Conditions on all the above-mentioned roads vary with the season and the weather. Although they may be accessible to regular cars with good tires, four-wheel-drive vehicles are recommended.

Biking. Loon, Waterville Valley, and **Bretton Woods** ski resorts (*see* Skiing, *below*) have opened their trails and surrounding logging roads to cyclists during the summer months, and also offer bike rentals and repairs. Miles of the well-maintained cross-country ski trails in the **Whitaker Woods** area are also accessible to mountain bikers. The **Bartlett Experimental Forest** has various graded dirt roads that lead off Bear Notch Road; the terrain is gentle and ideal for beginners. National Forest Service maps of the extensive trail network open to cyclists on federal land can be purchased at the Pemigewasset and

Saco ranger district offices (*see* Visitor Information *in* Essential Information, *above*). Also, look for "18 Off-Road and Back-Road Routes in Mt. Washington Valley," a pamphlet available at local sporting goods stores.

Opportunities to bike on paved roads are somewhat less plentiful. The Franconia Notch State Park bike path runs for 9 miles from the Flume Visitor Center through some of the most inspiring scenery in the state. For riders in top shape, the Kancamagus Highway affords spectacular views and a 1,200-foot ascent to the top of Kancamagus Pass. Watch out for cars!

Off-Road Cycling Adventures (Box 2055, North Conway, NH, tel. 603/356–2080) offers guided, half-day mountain-biking excursions in the Mt. Washington Valley. Among the many shops that rent and repair bikes are **Franconia Sport Shop** (Main St., Franconia, NH, tel. 603/823–5241), **The Greasy Wheel** (40 S. Main St., Plymouth, NH, tel. 603/536–3655), and **Ski Fanatics** (Campton Plaza, Rte. 49, Campton, NH, tel. 603/726–4327).

Bird-Watching. More than 200 species of birds make their warm-weather home in the White Mountains. A short stroll into the forest may be enough to provide glimpses of gold and purple finch, rose-breasted grosbeak, blackpoll and Canada warbler, scarlet tanager, or wood thrush, and the sound of the hollowed-tree hammering of a yellow-bellied sapsucker or the melody of the song sparrow. At higher elevations, on rock ledges or above tree line, sightings of broad-winged hawks, great horned owls, and other birds of prey are frequent.

Boating. Saco Bound (Rte. 302, Center Conway, NH, tel. 603/447–2177) specializes in guided family canoe and camping trips; rentals are also available here. Also try **Canoe Ring of New England** (Rtes. 16/302, North Conway, NH, tel. 603/356–5280) or **The Ledges** (Rte. 3, Woodstock, VT, tel. 603/745–8433) for rentals and shuttles. In the eastern side of the forest, **River Run** (Brownfield Bridge, Rte. 160, Brownfield, ME, tel. 207/452–2500) offers canoe rentals, shuttles, and camping areas for overnight trips.

Fishing. The White Mountains support 750 miles of streams and 50 freshwater ponds that abound with salmon; lake, brook, and rainbow trout; northern pike, pickerel, black bass, and walleye. The Swift River, flowing in an easterly direction for more than 20 miles along the Kancamagus Highway, is a popular and easily accessible spot for nabbing trout. Healthy brook and rainbow trout can also be found on the Ellis, Wildcat, and Saco rivers.

For those looking for a quieter angling experience, Big and Little Sawyer Ponds—a hike from either the Kancamagus or Route 302—host brook trout, brown bullhead, American smelt, and creek chub. You can angle for chain pickerel, yellow perch, brown bullhead, and white sucker at Elbow Pond, a 1.5-mile hike from Route 118 near Woodstock.

State fishing licenses are available from many area sporting goods and general stores or by writing to the New Hampshire Fish and Game Department (Rte. 3 N, Box 241, Lancaster, NH 03301, tel. 603/788–3164) or the Maine Department of Inland Fisheries and Wildlife (284 State St., Augusta, ME 04333, tel. 207/289–2043).

Horseback Riding. Guided trail rides through the national forest, as well as hay wagon and pony rides, are available from the **Waterville Riding Stable** (north end of Waterville Valley, tel. 603/236–4811) and **Fields at Attitash** (Rte. 302, Bartlett, tel. 603/374–2368).

Rock Climbing. The **EMS Climbing School** (Box 514, North Conway, NH 03860, tel. 603/356–5433), in operation for more than 25 years and accredited by the American Mountain Guides Association, offers many courses, including those geared specifically for women and adolescents.

Skiing. Opportunities for fine cross-country skiing are abundant. The **Jackson Ski Touring Foundation** (Rte. 16A, Box 216, Jackson, NH 03846, tel. 603/383–9355) offers 146 kilometers of trails that wind through the village and out into the surrounding national forest. The **Bretton Woods Ski Area** (Rte. 302, Bretton Woods, NH 03575, tel. 603/278–5181 or 800/232–2972) boasts 86 groomed kilometers and magnificent views of the Presidential Range. With 60 kilometers of trails through evergreen woods and open meadows, **Franconia Ski Touring Center** (Rte. 116, Franconia, NH 03580, tel. 603/823–5542) connects four different inns with Cannon Mountain and Franconia Notch. In Franconia Notch State Park, the 9-mile recreation path is open to skiers in the winter. **Loon Mountain** (RR 1, Box 41, Kancamagus Hwy., Lincoln, NH 03251, tel. 603/745–6281) and **Waterville Valley** (*see below*) have several challenging routes. You'll also find good cross-country skiing on the extensive hiking trail system of the national forest. For details, check with one of the district ranger's offices (*see* Visitor Information *in* Essential Information, *above*).

Many appealing options also exist for downhill skiers. There are eight lift-serviced areas within White Mountain National Forest: **Attitash** (Rte. 302, Bartlett, NH 03812, tel. 603/374–2368); **Balsams/Wilderness** (Dixville Notch, NH 03576, tel. 603/255–3951 or 800/255–0800); **Black Mountain** (Rte. 16B, Jackson, NH 03846, tel. 603/383–4490); **Bretton Woods** (*see above*); **Cannon Mountain** (off I–93, Franconia, NH 03580, tel. 603/823–5563 or 800/552–1234); **Loon Mountain** (Rte. 112, Lincoln, NH 03251, tel. 603/745–8111); **Waterville Valley** (Rte. 49, Waterville Valley, NH 03215, tel. 603/236–8371 or 800/468–2553); and **Wildcat Mountain** (Rte. 16, Jackson, NH 03846, tel. 603/466–3326 or 800/643–4521). Cannon has the highest vertical drop; Waterville Valley offers the most trails, the bulk of them intermediate; and Balsams/Wilderness boasts a huge resort hotel and 13 alpine trails. Bretton Woods, Waterville Valley, and Cannon are full-fledged mega-ski resorts with all the trimmings. **Tuckerman Ravine,** the be-all and end-all of skiing in the East, is accessible only by hiking up from the Pinkham Notch Visitor Center on Route 16, and is open only in spring. Contact Pinkham Notch (*see* Visitor Information *in* Essential Information, *above*) for details.

Snowmobiling. The national forest is laced by 360 miles of corridor trails. The **New**

Hampshire Snowmobile Association (Box 38, Concord, NH 03302, tel. 603/224–8906) can provide maps, snow condition reports, and information on rentals and lodging along these routes.

Snowshoeing. All the trails and roads listed in the hiking, biking, and cross-country skiing sections, *above,* are also great choices for experienced snowshoers. Those not entirely comfortable in the woods in winter should stick to the shorter, easier trails close to the roads. It's important to always carry extra food and clothing and notify others of your whereabouts. Many cross-country ski centers (*see* Skiing, *above*) rent snowshoes.

Swimming. The White Mountains abound in cascades, emerald pools, and brisk mountain water. There are several good swimming spots along Route 302, including the confluence of the **Sawyer** and **Saco rivers;** north of Bartlett on Route 302, follow the well-beaten path that veers left after the bridge over the Sawyer River. Follow Route 16B up the hill past the Wentworth Resort in Jackson to **Jackson Falls;** the large boulders near the many swimming holes here are great for riverside picnics. Other excellent places to get wet are **Profile Lake, Lonesome Lake, Russell Pond, South Pond, Lower Falls,** and the **Peabody River.** Note: Swimming in often-chilly mountain streams and lakes is not for the meek, even in summer.

CHILDREN'S PROGRAMS The **Appalachian Mountain Club** runs a number of creative programs for children out of the Pinkham Notch Visitor Center and eight backcountry huts; they're a fun way to introduce kids to an awareness of the environment. Contact the AMC Education Department (Box 298, Gorham, NH 03581, tel. 603/466–2721) for a list of current offerings.

EVENING ACTIVITIES The **Appalachian Mountain Club** sponsors lectures, slide shows, and natural history programs at the Pinkham Notch Visitor Center (tel. 603/466–2721) nightly throughout the summer and on weekend evenings the rest of the year. The **forest service** also offers a variety of interpretive programs at the Campton, Russell Pond, Jigger Johnson, and Dolly Copp national forest campgrounds throughout the summer; inquire at any of the ranger's stations or write to the forest supervisor (*see* Visitor Information *in* Essential Information, *above*). The **Crawford Notch Hostel** (Rte. 302, Crawford Notch, no phone) occasionally has presentations on outdoor-related subjects such as tracking and hypothermia prevention. Contact the AMC Education Department (*see* Children's Programs, *above*) for times and topics.

DINING

Dining options, from fast food to four star, abound around the forest's perimeter. The New Hampshire towns of Conway, North Conway, Jackson, Gorham, Berlin, Bethlehem, Lincoln, North Woodstock, and Campton each offer a range of culinary possibilities.

Horse and Hound Inn. This wood-paneled dining room is romantic, with its terrace, roaring fireplace, tables set with dogwood-pattern china, and lawn views. The Continental menu has a French emphasis, but also includes English grills. The chef always prepares something special for vegetarians. *Wells Rd., Franconia, tel. 603/823–5501. Reservations required. Dress: casual but neat. AE, MC, V. Expensive.*

Homestead Restaurant. The heavy native timbers and wooden pegs used by Amos Barnes in 1793 to build this old red farmhouse are still visible in the Homestead's Colonial-style dining rooms. The Early American tradition is also carried on in such simple yet satisfying fare as New England fish chowder, Cape Cod cranberry shrub, oven-broiled scallops, and beef kebabs—topped off with hot Indian pudding, of course. *Rte. 16, south of North Conway, tel. 603/356–5900. Reservations suggested. Dress: casual. AE, MC, V. Moderate–Expensive.*

Scottish Lion. The dining room overlooks meadows and mountains, and the copious Sunday brunch attracts locals as well as visitors. The Scottish Lion's menu expanded a decade ago when what was formerly only a restaurant became a bed-and-breakfast. Now the tartan-papered pub offers more than 50 varieties of Scotch whiskey, and the Scottish-American cuisine includes hot oatcakes in the evening bread basket. *Rte. 16, North Conway, tel. 603/356–6381. Reservations advised. Dress: casual. AE, MC, V. Moderate.*

Woodstock Station. It may be hard to choose from the 148-item menu of this converted railroad station, moved to its present site from the neighboring town of Lincoln, but once you zero in on something it's bound to be good. Choices include piled-high sandwiches, pasta dishes, Mexican fare, seafood entrées such as shrimp tempura, and pub-type food. This is a popular and welcoming place. *Rte. 3, North Woodstock, tel. 603/745–3951. Reservations accepted. Dress: casual. AE, D, MC, V. Moderate.*

T.H.E. Thompson House Eatery. This rustic restaurant, with a farm produce stand, a full bar, and a soda fountain, attracts cross-country skiers in winter and hikers in summer. The menu runs the gamut from such simple dishes as chili and frittatas to more sophisticated fare—bay scallops and spinach casserole, say, or tender medallions of pork tenderloin piccata. *Rte. 16A, Jackson, tel. 603/383–9341. Dress: casual. D, MC, V. Closed Apr. and Nov. Inexpensive–Moderate.*

Scarecrow Pub & Grill. Here's the place to go if you're looking for the most food for your money. You'll find everything in this rough-hewn, low-lit setting, from "sweet hearts"—artichoke hearts in a pesto sauce with melted cheese—and baked, stuffed quahogs to hearty burgers and steaks. A good deal. *Rte. 16, Intervale, tel. 603/356–2287. Reservations not required. Dress: casual. No credit cards. Inexpensive.*

PICNIC SPOTS **Long Pond,** a remote body of water on a dirt road off Forest Road 19, is an idyllic spot for an outdoor repast, as is **Beaver Brook Hayside Area,** 4 miles west of Twin Mountain on Route 3. The **Basin** in Franconia Notch State Park features an easy walk to tumbling Cascade Brook and to 20-foot-high Kinsman Falls, two outstanding sites for

lunch in the woods. **Lower Falls Picnic Area, Rocky Gorge Scenic Area,** and **Sabbaday Picnic Area** are all picturesque places for a meal along the eastern length of the Kancamagus Highway. On Route 302, **Sawyer Rock Picnic Area,** near Bartlett, and **Crawford Notch State Park** are both ideal for outdoor dining. Two other popular picnic sites are **Jackson Falls** on the Wildcat River in Jackson and the 70-foot-high **Glen Ellis Falls** in Pinkham Notch.

LODGING

New England is synonymous with country inns and bed-and-breakfasts, and the White Mountain region of New Hampshire has more than its fair share of these tastefully decorated, warmly welcoming accommodations. Inns of vintage Victorian, country comfortable, or a melange of styles may be found here in abundance. Sugar Hill, Lincoln, North Woodstock, Jackson, Bartlett, and North Conway all boast quality accommodations. For those who prefer anonymity and a remote control TV, motels and hotels are also available, most notably in Franconia and North Conway. In all cases, reservations are a must, especially in foliage season.

Darby Field Inn. Every room is different at this cozy inn, but what most have in common is a spectacular mountain view. A fieldstone fireplace is the center of the living room, the dining room is paneled in pine, and the bar features a woodstove and a piano. Room rates include breakfast and dinner. *Bald Hill, Conway 03818, tel. 603/447–2181 or 800/426–4147. 14 rooms with bath, 2 rooms share 1 bath. Facilities: restaurant, cross-country ski trails, pool. AE, MC, V. Closed Apr. and Nov. Expensive.*

Inn at Thorn Hill. One might almost expect Stanford White, the famed architect of the Gilded Age, to turn up at this inn, which he designed in 1895: The rooms still feature the polished dark woods, rose-motif papers and fabrics, and Oriental rugs that were popular in his day. The casual elegance and romantic ambience make the inn an ideal hideaway for couples. *Thorn Hill Rd., Jackson 03846, tel.*

603/383–4242. 13 rooms with bath, 2 rooms share 1 bath, 2 suites, 3 cottages. Facilities: restaurant, pub, pool, cross-country ski trails, tobogganing, croquet, horseshoes. Rates are MAP. AE, MC, V. Closed Apr. Expensive.

Bernerhof. This small, Old World hotel, built in the 1890s, is at home in its alpine setting, with a Finnish sauna on the third floor and a coal stove in the living room. Genteel touches include lace curtains in the bedrooms and champagne breakfast in bed for guests who stay three days. *Rte. 302, Glen 03838, tel. 603/383–4414 or 800/548–8007. 12 rooms with bath. Facilities: restaurant, playground, sauna. Rates include full breakfast. AE, MC, V. Moderate–Expensive.*

Hilltop Inn. It'd be easy to imagine staying for a week at this inn, with its front porch overlooking herb and flower gardens, and back deck shaded by a pair of massive black locust trees. In fact, the combination of thoughtfully placed antiques, abundant plump pillows and duvets, Victorian ceiling fans, and the innkeepers' warm hospitality might tempt you to move in altogether. This place is a real find. If you're in Room 3, don't forget to snoop in the bathroom medicine cabinet! *Rte. 117, Sugar Hill 03585, tel. 603/823–5695. 6 rooms with bath. Facilities: restaurant, 2 fireplaces. Rates include full breakfast. MC, V. Moderate.*

Wilderness Inn. This snug, warm inn features dark wooden beams, comfortable sofas dotted with embroidered pillows, and a glorious giant porch framed with plate-glass windows where a bountiful breakfast is served in the warmer months. The innkeepers offer a sincere, hearty welcome to their guests. Rooms are pretty and comfortable, decorated with exquisite antiques—there's a sleigh bed in one room and a cannonball bed in another—without being excessively fussy. *North Woodstock 03262, tel. 603/745–8890. 4 rooms with bath, 2 rooms share 1 bath. Facilities: fireplace. Rates include full breakfast. MC, V. Moderate.*

Crawford Notch Hostel. This clean, self-service accommodation is a comfortable option for those more interested in outdoor recreational activities than privacy and frills. There is a full kitchen with cooking facilities and utensils. Two bunk rooms sleep 24 and two adjacent cabins, heated by woodstoves, accommodate 8 people each. *Rte. 302, Crawford Notch 03812, tel. 603/466–2727 for reservations; sleeps 40. Facilities: kitchen. No credit cards. Closed late Oct.–early May. Inexpensive.*

CAMPING

BACKCOUNTRY Backcountry camping is permitted in almost all of the White Mountain National Forest, with the exception of certain fragile Restricted Use Areas (RUA). RUA rules prohibit camping and fires above timberline (where trees are less than 8 feet high), and require that visitors set up sites at least 200 feet from any trail, stream, pond, or road, except at specially designated camping sites. Hikers should contact the United States Forest Service (tel. 603/528–8721) or any ranger district office for current information regarding regulations. The forest service also expects visitors to abide by "no trace" camping procedures; pick up a copy of the "Backcountry Camping Rules" brochure for details. Although backcountry camping is permitted, and even encouraged in the national forest, hikers are urged to use existing shelters and established tent sites in popular, heavily used areas, especially along the Appalachian Trail.

NATIONAL FOREST CAMPGROUNDS The many roadside campgrounds that the national forest manages tend to provide less in the way of such facilities as hot water, showers, and electricity than private campgrounds; most can accommodate small trailers, but offer no hookups. The campgrounds listed below are among the most popular; reservations are taken for portions of Russell Pond, Basin, Campton, Blackberry Crossing, Covered Bridge, and Dolly Copp (tel. 800/280–CAMP) from March 1 through September 30. For a complete listing of the 22 national forest campgrounds in the White Mountains, contact the forest service (tel. 603/528–8721). Unless noted otherwise, the campgrounds described below are in New Hampshire.

Russell Pond (Tripoli Rd., Campton, 13 mi off I-93, Exit 31) is situated on a particularly scenic pond and offers interpretive nature programs Saturday evening at dusk during the summer; the boat launch and dock are designed for wheelchair access. It has 49 tent sites and 38 trailer sites. Fee: $10. **Basin** (Rte. 113, 15 mi north of Fryeburg, ME) has 21 sites, fishing, and a boat ramp. Fee: $8. **Hancock** (Kancamagus Hwy., 4 mi east of Lincoln) has 56 sites, 35 with trailer space, and was designed for easy access by trailers or RVs. An appealing swimming hole, Upper Lady's Bath, is a five-minute walk downstream from the campground. Fee: $10 (no reservations taken). **Campton** (2 mi east of the city of Campton on Rte. 49) has 58 sites in an area heavily wooded with towering white pines; it has a playing field and summer interpretive programs. Vacancies are usually available in the summer season, even on weekends and holidays. Fee: $10. **Blackberry Crossing** and **Covered Bridge** (Kancamagus Hwy., 6 mi west of Conway) are across the street from each other, and conveniently located for hiking and fishing; Blackberry has 26 sites (fee: $8), Covered Bridge has 49 sites (fee: $9). **Dolly Copp** (Rte. 16, 6 mi south of Gorham) is huge—as many as 1,000 people may be camped here at one time. It offers summer interpretive programs and is close to many of the popular hiking areas; there are 176 sites. Fee: $10.

STATE PARKS Several New Hampshire state parks have campgrounds in or near White Mountain National Forest, with fees ranging from $12 to $15 per night. No reservations are accepted: Sites are available on a first-come, first-served basis. Campgrounds are generally set up for tent camping; small trailers are welcome where they fit, but no hookups are provided. Campgrounds are open from mid-May through mid-October, with the exception of Lafayette Campground in Franconia Notch, which is open year-round, although there is no water in winter. Senior citizens get reduced rates Sunday through Thursday. A carry-in, carry-out policy has been established at the state parks: Trash barrels have been removed to provide visitors with a more pristine outdoor experience and to encourage wildlife to remain wild. Contact the New Hampshire Division of Parks and Recreation (172 Pembroke Rd., Box 856, Concord, NH 03302, tel. 603/271-3254) for more information about the campgrounds.

Crawford Notch State Park, on Route 302 and nestled in a stunning mountain pass, is a great base for hiking in the Whites, as well as fishing in nearby streams. The 6-square-mile park also offers nature trails to scenic waterfalls and picnic areas. The Dry River Campground has 30 tent sites, an information center, a gift shop, and a snack bar, but no showers or hot water.

Franconia Notch State Park, off I-93 between the looming peaks of the Franconia and Kinsman mountain ranges, abounds with dramatic natural wonders, including the Old Man of the Mountain (a great stone face) and the Flume (an 800-foot natural gorge). Lafayette Campground has 97 tent sites, showers, hot water, and a camp store, and offers interpretive activities in the summer. An ideal hiking and cycling base, the campground provides easy access to the Appalachian Trail and to a 9-mile paved recreation path.

Moose Brook State Park, off Route 2 near Gorham, is a beautiful, underutilized spot that has 42 tent sites, showers, and hot water. This park is an ideal base for hiking the Crescent and Presidential ranges, and for fishing in the heart of stream fishing country.

PRIVATE CAMPGROUNDS The only private campground in the national forest, **Crawford Notch Campground** (Rte. 302, Crawford Notch, NH, tel. 603/374-2779) has 75 wilderness sites, some with river frontage; there's easy access from here to hiking and fishing and swimming in the Saco River. It offers showers, a dishwashing station, chemical toilets, supplies, and gas, but no hookups. It's open May through October; reservations are accepted. Fees are $12 per night during the week, $15 per night on weekends.